CAROLINE FELLER BAUER'S

~ New ~
Handbook for
Storytellers

CAROLINE FELLER BAUER'S

～ New ～
Handbook for
Storytellers

With Stories, Poems, Magic, and More

Illustrations by

LYNN GATES BREDESON

American Library Association
Chicago and London 1993

Leading educator, author, and lecturer Caroline Feller Bauer travels around the United States and throughout the world, telling stories and giving seminars on her favorite subject—getting children and books together. She is the author of many books, including *Read for the Fun of It, Presenting Reader's Theater, Celebrations, This Way to Books,* and several collections of stories and poems, including *Rainy Day, Snowy Day, Windy Day,* and *Valentine's Day.*

The recipient of the Dorothy McKensie Award in 1986 for her contribution to children's literature, Bauer writes in her home overlooking the ocean on Miami Beach, where she lives with her husband, Peter, their pet ferret, and a collection of 10,000 children's books.

Composed by Publishing Services, Inc.
  in Aster and Melior
  on Xyvision/Cg8600
Printed on 50-pound Glatfelter,
  a pH-neutral stock, and bound in
  Kivar 9 Chrome by Edwards Brothers, Inc.

The paper used in this publication meets the minimum requirements of American National Standard for Information Sciences—Permanence of Paper for Printed Library Materials, ANSI Z39.48-1984. ∞

Library of Congress Cataloging-in-Publication Data

Bauer, Caroline Feller.
   [New handbook for storytellers]
   Caroline Feller Bauer's new handbook for storytellers : with stories, poems, magic, and more / by Caroline Feller Bauer : illustrations by Lynn Bredeson.
       p.   cm.
   Includes index.
   ISBN 0-8389-0613-3 (alk. paper)
   1. Storytelling—Handbooks, manuals, etc.   I. Title.
LB1042.B39   1993
372.64'2—dc20   93-14959

Printed in the United States of America.

97 96 95 94 93   5 4 3 2 1

For
P E T E R
who made
"... and they lived happily ever after"
a reality
(and that's a true story!)

Contents

Preface xiii
Acknowledgments xv

PART ONE

Getting Started 1

1 / Welcome to Storytelling 5
Age Groups 6
   Babies and Toddlers 6
   Preschool and Primary
    Programs 7
   The Middle Grades 7
   Young Adult Programming 8
   Adult Programming 8
   Family Storyhours 8
Program Techniques 9
   Single Programs or Series
    Planning 9
   Special Events 10
   Dial-A-Story 10
   Storytelling Festivals 11
   The Activity Program 11
Preplanning 12
   Physical Location 12
   Equipment Checklist 14
   Favors and Treats 14
Decorations and Exhibits 15
   Table Exhibit 16
   A Storytelling Symbol 17
   For Special Storyhours 18
   The Exhibit as Part of the
    Storyhour 18
   Bulletin Boards 18

   Picture Sources for Exhibits
    and Craft Projects 19
   Lettering Aids for Exhibits and
    Bulletin Boards 21

2 / The Storyteller 22
The Guest Storyteller 22
   Guestmanship 24
Volunteers 25
   A Storytelling Guild 25
   Student Storytellers 26
The Professional Storyteller
   28

3 / Promotion 29
Posters 30
Minisigns 32
Souvenirs and Bookmarks 32
Chalkboards 33
Chalkwalk 33
Sandwich Boards 34
Badges, Buttons, Balloons,
  and Bumper Stickers 34
Tickets 35
Special Invitations 35
Minispeeches 36
Telephoning 36
Mailers 36
The City Water Bill 36
Doorknob Hangers 36
The Fax Machine 37
Newspapers 37
Radio and Television 38
Paid Advertisements 38
Summing It Up 38

4 / Introducing and Closing
the Program   40
  Setting the Mood   41
    The Storyhour Symbol   41
  Introducing the Story or
    Program   41
  Artifacts and Crafts   42
    Things to Buy or Bring from
      Home   43
    Things to Make or Do   46
  Between Stories   49
  Closing the Program   49
    Something to Take Home   49
  Discipline or Holding Your
    Own   51

5 / Preparing and Telling
the Story   53
  Learning a Story   54
  Telling the Story   58
    Common Faults   60
  A Practice Story to Learn   62
  Booklist: Stories by Subject
    66
  Booklist: Illustrated Single
    Tales   78
  Booklist: Story Collections   85

6 / Reading Aloud   90
  Choosing Materials to Read
    Aloud   91
  How-To's   93
  Read Aloud Selections   94
  Booklist: Some Favorite Books
    for Reading Aloud   97

PART TWO

Sources for
Storytelling   105

7 / Narrative Sources   109
  And for Your Inspiration
    110
  Folktales   111
    Repetitive and Cumulative
      Tales   113
    Animal Tales   113
    How and Why Stories   114
    Adventure and Romantic
      Stories   114

Droll and Humorous Stories
  114
  Folk Characters   115
  Regions or Countries   115
Booklist: Folktales   120
Literary Tales   121
  Hans Christian Andersen   122
  Ruth Sawyer   122
  Eleanor Farjeon   123
  Howard Pyle   123
  Rudyard Kipling   124
  Carl Sandburg   124
  Laurence Housman   125
  Jane Yolen   125
  John Gardner   126
  Judith Grog   126
  Richard Kennedy   126
Booklist: Literary Tales and
  Short Story Collections   126
Fables   129
  Aesop's Fables   130
  Fables of La Fontaine   131
  Fables of Krylov   131
  Fables of India   131
Booklist: Fables   132
Myths   133
  Greek and Roman Myths   134
  Norse Myths   134
Booklist: Myths   135
Epics   136
  English Epics   136
  Greek Epics   137
  Epics of India   137
  Other National Epics   138
Booklist: Epics   138
Legends   139
Booklist: Legends   139
Religious Sources   140
Booklist: Religious Sources
  142
Other Literary Sources   143
  Whole Language Sources   145
  Children's Magazines   145
  Audio Tapes   145
Booklist: Other Literary
  Sources   145
Family Stories   146
  Creating a Family Story   148
Booklist: Family Storytelling
  149
Booklist: To Find Out More
  about Folklore   150

8 / Poetry   152
  Choosing a Poem   152
  Learning a Poem   155

Reading Poetry Aloud 155
Introducing a Poem 155
The Poetry Break 156
Visual Poetry 156
The Poetry Program 157
The Poetry Festival 157
Choral Speaking 158
Illustrations and Poetry 159
Creating a Poetry Tradition 159
Five Favorite Poems 160
Booklist: Poetry to Read or Recite 162
   Adult Sources 163
   For the Youngest 163
   Anthologies 164
   Poetry with Pictures to Share 165
   Some Favorite Poets 167
   Poetry by Theme 170

9 / Non-narrative Sources for Storytelling 173
Riddles 175
Booklist: More Riddles 176
Tongue Twisters 177
Booklist: More Tongue Twisters 178
Jokes 178
Booklist: More Jokes 180
Skip-Rope Rhymes 180
Booklist: More Skip-Rope Rhymes 182
Autograph Rhymes and Mottoes 183
Booklist: More Autograph Rhymes 183
Proverbs 184
   American Proverbs 184
   Jewish Proverbs 184
   Proverbs from Around the World 185
Booklist: More Proverbs 185
Word Games 186
Homonyms, Homographs, Antonyms 188
Booklist: More Word Games 189
Sign Language 190
Booklist: More Sign Language 190
Hieroglyphs 191
Booklist: More Hieroglyphs 191

Fan Language 191
Booklist: Fans 192
Folk Games 192
Booklist: More String Games 194
Booklist: More Folk Games 195
Folk Toys 196
Booklist: More Folk Toys 197
Paper Stories 197
Booklist: More Paper Stories 199

PART THREE

Multimedia Storytelling 201

10 / Pictures and Objects in Storytelling 205
Flip Cards 205
Big Books 206
Paperback Cut-ups 207
Roll Stories 207
The Copy Machine 208
Object Stories 208
A Story to Tell Using Objects 209
   Rosette Fan 210
   Hanging Paper Lantern 210
Stories about Color to Tell Using Objects 211
Booklist: Books about Color 212
Poems to Tell Using Objects 212
Booklist: Books for Object Story Use 213
Booklist: For Adults 214

11 / Board Stories 215
Hints for Using Boards 217
The Chalkboard 217
Books for Chalkboard Use 219
Flannel or Felt Boards 220
Magnetic Boards 221

Velcro or Hook 'n' Loop Boards 222
Using Paperbacks with Boards 223
Stories to Tell on a Board 224
Booklist: Books to Use on Felt, Magnetic, and Velcro Boards 232

12 / Slides 234
Equipment and Use 235
Copying 235
Handmade Slides 236
Photographic Slides 236
Screens 237

13 / The Overhead Projector 238
Uses 239
Light Show Magic 239
Trace a Transparency 240
Photocopy Transparency Machines 240
Overlays 240
Booklist: Books for Overhead Projector Use 241

14 / Video and Film 242
Commercial Videos and Films 242
Choosing a Video or Film 243
Showing a Video or Film 243
Making Videos or Films 244
With a Video Camera 244
Without a Camera 245
A Final Word 247
Booklist: Video Production 248
Booklist: Film and Video Reviews 248

15 / Television and Radio 249
Producing a Television Show 251
Booklist: Television 254
Radio 254

16 / Puppetry 256
The Puppet Tradition 258
Types of Puppets 258
Commercial Hand Puppets 259
Glove Puppets 259
Finger Puppets 260

Marionettes or String Puppets 260
Stick Puppets 260
Booklist: Animal Books to Use with Picture Puppets 262
Masks and Body Puppets 263
Shadow Puppets 263
Booklist: Shadow Puppets 264
Magnetic Puppets 264
Stages 264
Portable Doorway Puppet Theater 265
Chinese Hat Puppet Theater 265
Uses for Puppets 265
The Puppet as Host 266
Practice with Your Puppet 267
Exercise in Performance 267
Puppet Plays 267
Puppet Plays to Perform 268
Finger Puppets Can Ask Riddles 276
Booklist: Picture Books to Use with Puppets 277
Booklist: Adult Sources 277

17 / Magic 280
Types of Conjuring 282
Mechanical Magic and Sleight-of-Hand 283
Books about Magic 283
Organizations of Magicians 284
Using Magic 284
Patter and Presentation 285
Magic Tricks 285
Mixing Colors 285
Read to Your Dog 286
Booklist: Dog Books to Exhibit 287
Biography Prediction 287
Booklist: Biographies to Exhibit 288
The Change Bag 289
Spring Flowers and the Botanica 289
Book Telepathy 289
Riddle Trick 290
Booklist: Riddle Books to Exhibit 290
Prediction Pencil 291
A Word from Smokey the Bear 291
Booklist: Books about Forests to Exhibit 291
A Proverb Trick 291

The Four Thieves 292
Television versus Books 293
The Dove Pan 294
Booklist: Magic 294

18 / *Music*   297
Music in Multimedia
  Presentations 299
A Musical Theme 300
Choosing Music 300
Singing 300
Making up Songs 301
For the Nonmusical 301
Dance 301
Field Trips 302
Homemade Rhythm
  Instruments 302
Songs to Use with Rhythm
  Instruments 303
Booklist: Stories with
  Rhythmic Phrases 304
Using Picture Book Versions
  of Songs 304
Booklist: Picture Book Versions
  of Single Songs 305
Songs to Sing 306
Stories to Tell about Music
  and Dance 320
Booklist: Music in the
  Storyhour 323

PART FOUR

Programs   331

19 / *Preschool and Primary*
  Programs   335
Setting the Stage 337
Introducing the Program and
  Follow-up Activities 338
What's in a Program? 338
Picture Books 339
Booklist: Picture Books for
  Preschool and Primary
  Children 340
Some Classic Picture Books
  347
Booklist for Toddlers 348
Books to Share at Home 350
Stories to Tell 351
Participation Stories 355

Booklist: More Participation
  Stories 359
Multimedia Storytelling 360
Fingerplays and Action
  Rhymes 360
Booklist: More Fingerplays
  365
Fold-and-Cut Stories 365
Booklist: More Papercraft
  Ideas 369

20 / *Programs for the*
  Intermediate Grades   370
Storytelling for the
  Middle-Graders 370
Stories to Tell 371
Participation Programs 376
Night of 1,000 Stars 381
Celebrating the Work of
  Johanna Hurwitz 382
Booklist: Johanna Hurwitz
  Program 383
Media and the Intermediate
  Grades 383
Read for Fun 384
Picture Books for
  Intermediate Grades 386

21 / *The Young Adult*
  Program   389
Simply Supernatural 390
Ghost Stories 391
Booklist: Ghost Story Sources
  393
Jump Stories 394
Booklist: Jump Story Sources
  394
Short Stories to Tell to Young
  Adults 395
Booklist: Young Adult
  Favorites 406
Grandpa Read It Too 408
Guys and Gals You'd Like to
  Meet 410

22 / *Programs for Parents*
  and Other Adults   413
Where Can You Tell Stories to
  Adults? 414
A Word about Adult Audience
  Reactions 415
What to Tell 415
A Story to Tell 416

Reading Aloud 421
Reader's Theater 423
Planning Programs for
 Parents 425
  *Programs for Parents and Other
   Adults—A Few Ideas* 425
  Still More Ideas 428
Booklist: Adult Storytelling
 429

23 / *Booktalks*   431
Booktalks for All Occasions
 432
The Teaser 433
Introducing a Single Title
 434
Introducing Several Books
 434
  *Some Women I'd Be Delighted
   to Host at a Tea Party* 435
Booklist 437
Book Review Booktalks 437
Booklist 438
The Bodart Way 439

24 / *Activity and
   Theme Programs*   442
Booklist: Theme Program
 Resources 443
The Moon and the Stars 444
Books to Exhibit 446
Fashion 447
Books to Exhibit 451
Baseball 451
Books to Exhibit 457
Mini-Theme Programs 458
Multicultural Programs 463
Booklist 466

25 / *Book Parties*   468
Placecards and Placemats 468
Book Decorations to Look at
 or Eat 469
  Baker's Clay Decorations 469
  Ethel's Book Cookies 470
Book and Food Pairs 471
Fun Food Facts Bulletin
 Board 476
Activities 477
Poetry Suggests Food Too
 478

Booklist: Poetry Featuring
 Food 480
A Story to Tell 480
Booklist: Stories to Tell
 Featuring Food 481
Food Books Good Enough to
 Read 482

26 / *Creative Dramatics Plus*   486
Starting at the End 487
Acting Out a Story 487
Continue at the Beginning 488
  The Senses 488
  Taste 489
  Books featuring taste 489
  Smell 490
  Books featuring smell 490
  Touch 490
  Books about touch 491
  Sound 491
  Books exploring sound 492
  Sight 492
  Books featuring seeing 493
  Books featuring visual games
   493
Pantomime 494
Animal Bag 495
Charades 495
Improvisation 496
Stories to Dramatize 497
Storytelling with Masks 501
Reader's Theater 505
Audience 506
Evaluation 506
Prop Box and Costume Box
 507
Booklist: Creative Dramatics
 Plus 507
Booklist: Picture Books about
 Young Players 510
Booklist: Novels Featuring
 Child Performers 510
Booklist: Not for Children
 Only 511
Booklist: Adult References
 511

General Index 513
Title Index 527

Preface

Dear Caroline,

Do not revise, *repeat*, do not revise *Handbook for Storytellers.* It is truly one of the great books and deserves to be left as it is.

xxx to you, Joan

Dear Joan,

Don't panic. I love the *Handbook*, too. It's just that since I first wrote it in 1977, there have been so many wonderful children's books published that I want everyone to know about them. I've also had such lovely comments about the book through the years that I felt it was my responsibility to update it, add to it, and make it even more useful for you.

As you'll see, much of the information that was contained in the original version is still here. In my introduction to the book then, I said that the *Handbook* was intended "to help you learn how to present literature to children, young adults, and adults through storytelling." That still remains my objective. But now I've added new material (a whole section on family storytelling, for instance, which has become so popular), brand new booklists, and many, many stories, poems, songs, riddles, jokes, and patterns. This way, just in case you happen to be stranded on a desert island with a group of children and my book, it will be many years before anyone becomes bored!

I have also had many more personal successes and failures out "on the road" since *Handbook* was first published, some of which I've included here, in hopes that others can learn from my joys and foibles. In fact, see if you don't think the following is an example of a "True Story Designed to Show That Telling Stories Leaves a Lasting Impression."

After a storytelling presentation in Fort Riley, Kansas, a fourth-grader came up to me and said, "You came and told stories in my old school."

"I did?" I said. "Where was that?"

"In Dhaka, Bangladesh," he said.

Well, I thought that was a pretty good vignette, but last week in Germany a sixth grader came up to me and said, "You came to my old school, too."

"I did?" I said. "Where was that?"

"In Fort Riley, Kansas," she said.

Honest. It's a true story.

Hope you love the new edition even more than the old.

Love,
Caroline

P.S. And to anyone else who is reading this: My friend Joan McLemore tells stories out of Roxie, Mississippi. She's been a pen pal of mine since she read the first edition of *Handbook for Storytellers*, fifteen years ago. If you would like to be one, too, write me in care of the American Library Association, 50 E. Huron Street, Chicago, IL 60611. They will know where I am since we move so often.

Acknowledgments

Every effort has been made to trace the ownership of all copyrighted material and to secure the necessary permissions to reprint these selections. In the event of any question arising as to the use of any material, the editor and publisher, while expressing regret for any inadvertent error, will be happy to make the necessary correction in future printings.

Grateful acknowledgment is made to the following for permission to reprint the copyrighted material listed below:

"Tuning" from THE WINTER ROOM by Gary Paulsen. Copyright © 1989 by Gary Paulsen. Used with permission of the publisher Orchard Books, New York.

"The Frog on the Log" by Ilo Orleans from *The Zoo That Grew*, published by Henry Z. Walck, 1960. Reprinted by permission of Karen S. Solomon.

"Lines and Squares," from WHEN WE WERE VERY YOUNG by A. A. Milne. Copyright 1924 by E.P. Dutton, renewed 1952 by A. A. Milne. Used by permission of Dutton Children's Books, a division of Penguin Books USA Inc., and Methuen Children's Books, London, England.

"Running the Gauntlet" from STILTS, SOMERSAULTS AND HEADSTANDS by Kathleen Fraser. Copyright © 1968 by Kathleen Fraser. Used by permission of Marian Reiner for the author.

"Arithmetic" from THE COMPLETE POEMS OF CARL SANDBURG, copyright 1950 by Carl Sandburg and renewed 1978 by Margaret Sandburg, Helga Sandburg Crile and Janet Sandburg, reprinted by permission of Harcourt Brace Jovanovich, Inc.

"Some Favorite Words" by Richard Edwards from *The Word Party*, © 1986 by Richard Edwards. Used by permission of Delacorte Press and Lutterword Press.

"Jumping Rope Rhyme" is reprinted with the permission of Atheneum Publishers, an imprint of Macmillan Publishing Company from ALL THE DAY LONG by Nina Payne. Copyright © 1973 by Nina Payne.

The story of "The Three Billy Goats Gruff" from *Paper Cutting* by Eric Hawkesworth, published in 1984 by The Supreme Magic Company Limited, Supreme House, Bideford, Devon EX39 2AN, England is reproduced by kind permission of the Copyright owner, Barry Laymond, Copperfield House, 20 Spencer Walk, Chorleywood, WD3 4EE, England.

"In a great green room . . ." Text copyright © 1947 by Margaret Wise Brown from *Goodnight Moon*. Selection reprinted by permission of HarperCollins.

"Vancouver" from *Don't Eat Spiders*, poems copyright © Robert Heidbreder 1985. Reprinted by permission of Oxford University Press Canada.

"Pockets" from *Blackberry Ink* by Eve Merriam. Copyright © 1985 by Eve Merriam. Used by permission of Marian Reiner.

"Strange Events in the Life of the Delmonico Family" reprinted with the permission of Margaret K. McElderry Books, an imprint of Macmillan Publishing Company from NONSTOP NONSENSE by Margaret Mahy and J. M. Dent & Sons, Ltd. Publishers. Copyright © 1977 Margaret Mahy.

Foam ball puppets and animal puppets adapted from puppets by Lynne Jennings, 281 E. Millan Street, Chula Vista, California 91910.

"The China Spaniel" by Richard Hughes from *The Spider's Palace and Other Stories* reprinted by permission of Harold Ober Associates Incorporated and David Higham Associates Limited. Copyright 1932 by Harper & Brothers, Copyright renewed 1960 by Richard Hughes.

"Excerpt" from *Going the Moose Way Home* by Jim Latimer reprinted with the permission of Charles Scribner's Sons, an imprint of Macmillan Publishing Company and Ruth Cohen, Inc. from GOING THE MOOSE WAY HOME by Jim Latimer. Text copyright © 1988 James Latimer.

"I Love a Rainy Day," "Animal Salad," and "Ropes" © copyright 1993 Susan Birkenhead. Used with permission.

"The Goat Well" from THE FIRE ON THE MOUNTAIN, by Harold Courlander and Wolf Leslau. Copyright © 1950, 1978 by Harold Courlander, Wolf Leslau and Robert W. Kane. Reprinted by permission of Harold Courlander.

"Cheese, Peas and Chocolate Pudding" by Betty Van Witsen, from BELIEVE AND MAKE BELIEVE by Lucy Sprague Mitchell and Irma Simonton Black. Copyright © 1956 by Bank Street College of Education, renewed © 1984 by Bank Street College of Education. Used by permission of Dutton Children's Books, a division of Penguin Books USA Inc.

"The Story of Joshua Who Jumped" by Morris Lurie. Used with permission.

"Two of Everything" from THE TREASURE OF LI-PO by Alice Ritchie, copyright 1949 by Harcourt Brace Jovanovich, Inc. and renewed 1977 by M.T. Ritchie, reprinted by permission of the publisher and Random Century Group.

"The Calendar" is reprinted from the book *Jesse's Ghost and Other Stories* by Barbara Ann Porte, Greenwillow Books, 1983.

"All Summer in a Day" by Ray Bradbury. Reprinted by permission of Don Congdon Associates, Inc. Copyright © 1954, renewed 1982 by Ray Bradbury.

"Summer Nights" from ACT ONE by Moss Hart. Copyright © 1959 by Catherine Carlisle Hart and Joseph M. Hyman, Trustees. Reprinted by permission of Random House, Inc.

Diane P. Tuccillo and Joni Bodart, Booktalks from the May 1991 issue of *WLB Booktalker*. © Copyright 1991 by the H. W. Wilson Company. Reprinted by permission of the publisher.

"Stars" from THE COMPLETE POEMS OF CARL SANDBURG, copyright 1950 by Carl Sandburg and renewed 1978 by Margaret Sandburg, Helga Sandburg Crile and Janet Sandburg, reprinted by permission of Harcourt Brace Jovanovich, Inc.

"In a Starry Orchard" by Norma Farber reprinted by permission of Coward, McCann & Geoghegan from SMALL WONDERS, text copyright © 1964, 1968, 1975, 1976, 1978, 1979 by Norma Farber.

"Stars" from *Out in the Dark and Daylight* by Aileen Fisher. Text Copyright © 1980 by Aileen Fisher. Selection reprinted by permission of HarperCollins Publishers.

"Southpaw" by Judith Viorst, copyright © 1974 by Free to Be Foundation from FREE TO BE ... YOU AND ME by Marlo Thomas and Associates. Used by permission of Bantam Books, a division of Bantam Doubleday Dell Publishing Group, Inc.

Permission to model drawings for cookie shapes after illustrations in *Blueberries for Sal* and *Make Way for Ducklings* courtesy of Penguin USA.

"If the Moon Were Made of Cheese," from THE BUTTERFLY JAR by Jeff Moss. Copyright © 1989 by Jeff Moss. Used by permission of Bantam Books, a division of Bantam Doubleday Dell Publishing Group, Inc.

"I eat my gum drops" by Freya Littledale from *I Was Thinking*. Reprinted by permission of Curtis Brown, Ltd. Copyright © 1979 by Freya Littledale.

"Bananas and Cream" from ONE AT A TIME by David McCord. Copyright © 1961, 1962 by David McCord. By permission of Little, Brown and Company.

"Eighteen Flavors" from *Where the Sidewalk Ends* by Shel Silverstein. Copyright © 1974 by Evil Eye Music, Inc. Selection reprinted by permission of HarperCollins Publishers and Edite Kroll, Literary Agency.

"I Liked Growing" by Karla Kuskin from *Dogs & Dragons, Trees & Dreams*. Copyright © 1980 by Karla Kuskin. Selection reprinted by permission of HarperCollins Publishers.

"Peanut Butter" from ONE AT A TIME by David McCord. Copyright © 1974 by David McCord. First appeared in *Yankee*. By permission of Little, Brown and Company.

"John Wins a Bet" from THE ADVENTURES OF HIGH JOHN THE CONQUEROR by Steve Sanfield. Copyright © 1989 by Steve Sanfield. Used with permission of the publisher Orchard Books, New York.

"The Silly Farmer" from *Twenty-two Splendid Tales to Tell* by Pleasant de Spain. Merrill Court Press, POB 85785, Seattle, WA 98102. Used with permission.

"A Boy and His Dog" by Zaro Weil from "Mud, Moon and Me" first published in 1989 by Orchard Books, London and published in USA 1992 by Houghton Mifflin Co.

"To Catch a Fish" from *Under the Sunday Tree* by Eloise Greenfield. Text copyright © 1988 by Eloise Greenfield. Selection reprinted by permission of HarperCollins Publishers and Marie Brown Associates.

"Broom Balancing" by Kathleen Fraser. From *Stilts, Somersaults and Headstands* by Kathleen Fraser, Copyright © 1968 by Kathleen Fraser. Used by permission of Marion Reiner for the author.

"Clothe the Naked," from THE PORTABLE DOROTHY PARKER by Dorothy Parker. Introduction by Brendan Gill. Copyright 1928, renewed © 1956 by Dorothy Parker. Used by permission of Viking Penguin, a division of Penguin Books USA Inc.

84, Charing Cross Road. Copyright © 1970 by Helene Hanff. Used by permission of Flora Roberts, Inc.

Getting Started

PART ONE

You've just learned a new story and you can't wait
to tell it, but where will you find an audience?
You can't exactly run out into the street and call,
"Anyone want to hear a story?" You'll have to find
slightly more discreet methods of promotion.

Or you think you'd like to begin telling stories,
but you don't know how to start. What story
should you learn first? Something tried and true,
like "Little Red Riding Hood?" Or something contemporary, instead? And what's the best way to
begin learning it?

Then, once you've learned your new story, what
comes next: the audience, the publicity, or the site?
If you are a beginning storyteller, welcome! This
section is intended especially for you. It will help
you to answer these questions, start you off with
a wonderful selection of stories from which to
choose, and offer you some sure-fire ideas for successfully planning and holding your first book-
sharing program.

If you're a more experienced storyteller, planning your one hundredth storyhour, think of this
section as a refresher course. Browse though the
chapters, and see if you don't find a creative promotion tip you haven't tried, a new idea for a guest
storyteller, or, best of all, a brand new story to
learn and tell.

1 / Welcome to Storytelling

It was raining. No, it was pouring. The promised picnic was definitely out of the question. My daughter, Hilary, wasn't crying yet, and her friend, Holly, was being polite, but clearly they were disappointed and I felt badly. After all, I'd promised a picnic. So we had a picnic. On a make-believe beach, under our dining room table, with a blanket tent constructed over the table to provide privacy and a sense of mystery.

Marshmallows taste just as good when they fall onto the floor as they do when they fall onto the sand (maybe even better!). Our dog, Susie, enjoyed the leftovers, and with the rain drumming on the roof, our blanket tent turned out to be the perfect place to tell and listen to ghost stories. Even my husband, Peter, crawled into our tent and told us about a snowbound ski trip in Vermont. I didn't even know he could tell a story.

Since that winter picnic, I've told stories in many settings, but that memory remains special. You too will soon have memories to share as you embark upon the storytelling adventure. Where do you begin?

You could start your planning with the location of the program, remembering that a potential audience may range from preschool children to senior citizens. A book program can be held in many different locations and for a variety of different occasions, wherever people gather. Here are just a few possibilities:

Libraries	Police stations
Hospitals	Boy Scout, Girl Scout,
County fairs	Campfire Girl meetings
Classrooms	Opening of a new building
Little League practice	Christmas tree lighting
Neighborhood garage sales	ceremony
Playgrounds	Birthday parties
Moonlight sales	Firehouses
Detention centers	Art festivals
Senior citizens' clubs	Adult club meetings
Backyards	Book fairs
Shopping center malls	Saturday markets
Your own home	School buses during field trips
Churches and temples	A community outing:
Child-care centers	the 4th of July breakfast?
Craft fairs	the water carnival?

Sometimes it pays to use your imagination to find a location for a planned or spur-of-the-moment storytime. There you are at the ball field with your Little League team, waiting for last year's champions to arrive to play this season's Big Game. The members of your team are nervous and excited. What do you do? *Tell a story!*

Choosing the site and the occasion for your storyhour is only the beginning. You must also determine the age of your target audience, for you may want to divide the program by age groupings or combinations of groups. And finally, you must decide whether a single program or a series of programs aimed at a specific audience is your goal. As a classroom teacher, you may plan a single story session and find that it develops into a weekly or monthly event. As a Scout leader, you may find that a continuing series simply requires too much time (although it is always hard for me to imagine that someone would rather not hear a story at any time!). In any case, often the location itself will dictate the type of program to present.

Age Groups

Babies and Toddlers

Begin with the babies, who will enjoy storytimes planned just for them. They will usually be accompanied by adults, so keep in mind that the programs you present will be for the caregivers as much as for their children. Two-year-old toddlers may have their own book-sharing times, too. Short short stories, simple books,

fingerplays, and a rhyme or two introduce these youngsters to the treasures of the library.

Preschool and Primary Programs

The preschool storytime, for children aged three to five, will usually include simple stories, songs, and picture books. Many of these children, if they attend school at all, do not attend full time and are an eager audience for any organized entertainment. Programming for this age group is usually strongly supported by parents who are looking for activities outside the home— especially if they are book-oriented. If you are a teacher of preschool or primary children, storytime is undoubtedly a daily activity in your classroom. It is through stories, poems, and songs that children acquire information as well as appreciation for words and fine illustrations.

Children in the primary grades, the five- to eight-year-olds, are also active listeners. The classroom is a perfect place to hold storyhours for these youngsters. If you are a public librarian or church-group leader you may be tempted to include both preschool and primary children in one storyhour, especially if the groups can be kept small. Keep in mind, however, that many primary-grade children are able to listen longer and understand on a higher level than preschool children. One of the objectives of your program will be to teach your audience to listen to more complicated stories. This comes about as children become more accustomed to listening.

The Middle Grades

The children who are in grades four through six simply love book- and story-oriented programs and are old enough to appreciate longer folktales and myths. Members of this age group like to belong to organized clubs (Boy Scouts, Girl Scouts, Campfire Girls, etc.) and provide a ready-made audience. With good publicity, a loyal storytelling following can be built in your library or other location.

Programs for middle-graders may be of a traditional and formal nature, but they also offer the storyteller an opportunity to experiment with multimedia programs as well as group participation stories.

Young Adult Programming

Stories from classic literature, poetry, and excerpts from contemporary favorites will probably be the most popular program offerings for teenagers and young adult groups. Booktalks, which combine storytelling with reading aloud, are also popular, as many young people have begun to enjoy the language of good literature. Young adults may be reached in the classroom, in the library, or through special interest clubs: they are a challenging audience, but ultimately a satisfying one!

Adult Programming

Adult storytelling is back in vogue! A few generations ago stories were told almost exclusively for the enjoyment of adults; the presence of children, if allowed at all, was merely tolerated. Adults today enjoy stories just as much as they once did and just as much as children. Men's and women's clubs might welcome oral presentations of literature. Retirement homes will be delighted to hear the old familiar stories in a modern setting. Parents, as a group, present a particular challenge since they may want to attend adult storytelling festivals, but will also welcome special children's programs, because they are parents.

Family Storyhours

If you have a professional interest in storytelling because you are a teacher or librarian, or a volunteer in a hospital, club, or day-care center, use your art and perfect your skills with your own family. Start a family storytelling tradition. Choose a night to relax and enjoy stories or read aloud as a family affair. Don't limit these sessions to the preschoolers at home either. Your entire family can enjoy a good story well told. As your children grow up they can tell stories of their own or take turns at reading alternate chapters aloud. If one parent is home with the children most of the time, ask the other parent to read aloud. Don't reserve those multimedia storytelling projects for your work at the day-care center. Treat your own family to a special evening too.

Now think in terms of families where you work. Would it be feasible to plan some family programs at your school or library? When I lived in Oregon, our local public library held well-attended family evenings featuring a film, a guest artist, or a storyteller. The families came to enjoy the program, punch and cookies, and some casual get-together conversation. At the end of one program, I remember, there was even a flurry of activity at the reference desk when one of the businessmen present suddenly remembered that he had been meaning to get to the library to look up some facts. An entertaining program, some socializing and simple refreshments, and the availability of useful information and reference sources add up to an enthusiastic library patron and supporter.

Program Techniques

Single Programs or Series Planning

The division of groups by age is just one possibility for programming. If you are a public librarian, for instance, you may want to simply schedule an event and welcome whoever comes. Obviously, a program scheduled for 10 AM Wednesday morning during the school term will attract mainly preschoolers and their parents or caregivers. On the other hand, a 9 PM program will almost certainly exclude the preschoolers. Keep in mind that planning a young adult program on the eve of a championship basketball game is a sure way to reduce the attendance at your program, unless you advertise it as a "Down-with-Basketball" event for the anti-athletes!

In a way, it is easier to plan for a series of programs than a single program. Promotion for a single evening of poetry takes the same amount of time and effort as promotion for an entire series of guest artist appearances. If you decide on a series of after-school children's programs, I suggest that you plan a set session of storyhours for a limited period, perhaps once a week for six weeks. This will enable you to plan six outstanding programs without feeling the pressure of "putting on a show" every week forever. Series planning also enables you to begin with simple stories and poems at the outset of the series and advance to more sophisticated and longer stories at the end. Such planning also enables you to estimate the number of children that may attend each program in the series.

Should the demand and your energy seem to warrant another series, you can begin a new series almost immediately. Probably many of the same children will continue to come to the next series, but since your earlier series was a great success, the new one will attract some new faces. If too many children sign up for a given session or series, they can be placed on a waiting list for the next time. Don't be tempted to include too many children at once. It is far better to serve a small group well than a large group inadequately.

You will probably find that participation tends to be more constant with a series. Signing up for a series is rather like signing up for a course and implies a certain obligation on the part of those children and parents who come. If you are a classroom teacher or school librarian with a captive audience you might also consider scheduling in terms of a series. A series not only provides you with the opportunity for progressively teaching your audience to listen and participate, it also forces you to plan your material well in advance.

Before you schedule your program series, find out what other offerings there are in the community. Autumn, when school re-opens, may be a good time for beginning a new storyhour series, but children and their parents may be overwhelmed with choices then. Sometimes there is a restless period just after Christmas. That might be the perfect time for book programs. Spring could be a poor time for indoor activities as children may be eager to be out-of-doors. On the other hand, in some communities regularly organized activities come to an end in the spring, and this could be just the right time for a new storyhour series. Sometimes the summer months are among the library's busiest. Children are anxious for organized activities and attend summer library programs with great enthusiasm. In other places library attendance may slacken off in the summer because children are away at camp or vacationing with their parents. You may just need to plunge in and learn from your first experience for the future.

Special Events

Occasionally you will want to schedule a special program to honor a particular group, to celebrate a holiday, to commemorate an anniversary or some other event. Traditional holidays such as Christmas, Thanksgiving, Cinco de Mayo, or Independence Day often inspire such a storyhour. There are also minor holidays such as Arbor Day, birthdays of favorite authors or artists, as well as intriguing holidays of your own invention, perhaps Magic Day (when you may tell stories featuring magicians), Haiti Day (the day you will tell stories featuring Haiti or the Caribbean), or any other special "day" you decide to celebrate with stories.

Dial-a-Story

Preschoolers delight in playing with the telephone, but ordinarily have no one to call. One way to capitalize on this preoccupation and introduce children to stories at the same time might be a Dial-a-Story program. The San Francisco Public Library has sponsored a Dial-a-Story program for over 20 years. The stories are offered in Spanish, English, and Cantonese. In this program young children are encouraged to call a designated telephone number to hear a three-minute story that is changed each week.

To begin such a project contact the local telephone business office. A knowledgeable service representative will explain the various methods of providing this popular service. Careful planning is necessary. You also must have the storytelling personnel capable of recording the stories and sufficient phone lines to handle the incoming calls.

One small Oregon county library used county recreational funds to rent two recording playback machines to play into two telephone lines. The Dial-a-Story program seemed such a good idea that the plan was covered by the neighboring big city newspapers and television stations. The county library was thrilled, until the city children began calling in to hear stories, overloading and tying up the phones so that no one was properly served. The moral is if you have limited equipment, keep your audience small. It is better to serve a smaller population with quality service than a large metropolitan region with mediocre or poor service.

Storytelling Festivals

Another special event to consider is a storytelling festival planned for adults only, for children only, or for a mixed age group. The festival can feature stories from a particular country or region or stories centered around a single theme or subject. The program can be put on by a lone storyteller or by a group of storytellers. If you are fortunate enough to have several tellers, concurrent sessions may be held to keep your groups small.

A special springtime festival is held for the children's librarians at New York Public Library. Stories are told to the librarians by selected storytellers new to the system as well as by a few old-timers. In schools throughout the state of Oregon, an Arts Day held each spring features short sessions with talented local artists and storytellers. Plan a festival for your school, staff, or community.

NAPPS FESTIVAL

The National Association for the Preservation and Perpetuation of Storytelling (NAPPS) holds the biggest and best attended festival in the country. In 1992 NAPPS celebrated its twentieth National Storytelling Festival with more than 80 tellers. Everyone agrees that the annual event is well organized, and despite the attendance of thousands of people, a feeling of intimacy is somehow still achieved.

NAPPS also has information on other storytelling festivals around the United States. You can write to NAPPS at P.O. Box 309, Jonesborough, TN 37659.

The Activity Program

Yet another type of storytelling program features the formal telling of stories, followed by a period in which the audience participates by playing games or making things that are related to the stories. This kind of program with specific examples is more fully described in chapter 24.

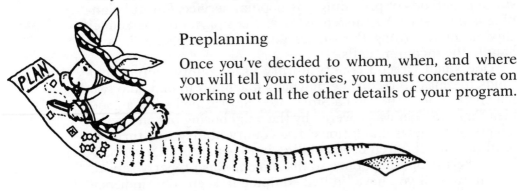

Preplanning

Once you've decided to whom, when, and where you will tell your stories, you must concentrate on working out all the other details of your program.

Physical Location

I attended a birthday party of a professional storyteller in a private room at a restaurant. Naturally, she was asked to tell a story when the ice cream and cake were served. I was awed at her insistence on having people move their chairs so that everyone could see. She even made sure that the waiter would not enter while she was telling her story.

I've thought of that evening often when I have insisted that people sit up front and move close together in an auditorium. Several times, knowing that I would be speaking in a large auditorium, I've brought yarn with me to close off the back rows. At a recent presentation I got everyone to sit up front by threatening not to give handouts to anyone seated beyond the first five rows.

The importance of the physical setup cannot be underestimated. It will determine whether your listeners truly feel a part of the presentation, or like observers, just looking in.

No matter where the venue is located, think about how your stories will be received. If your storyhour will take place in a park, try to select a shady area, or at least a quiet one. Obviously it is less desirable to try to compete with the noise of traffic or the cheers and whoops of the playground or a baseball game. This means that you should select a story site at the same time of day that the program will take place, not on a romantic moonlit night when the park is devoid of children.

A hospital storytime may present additional considerations. It might mean telling tales to a bedridden audience, which would eliminate some of the usually desirable eye contact, but would nevertheless be gratefully received.

In a library or school the program takes on an added dimension when it is given in a completely separate room from the classroom or the main room of the library. However, be adaptable. Sometimes, particularly as a visiting storyteller, your heart may drop as you enter a proposed storytelling site, but it could and often does turn out to be a good experience for you and your audience. Once I drove in a dreadful rainstorm to a campsite to put on a program. I was the first one to arrive. There I found only a bare bulb hanging from a ceiling in a leaking, chairless barn and I said to myself, "What a good place to tell a ghost story." Yet, when the campers arrived, the whole atmosphere changed. They were wet but attentive and receptive, and the gloom I had anticipated never materialized.

My first stories were told when the New York Public Library's Central Children's Room was located at 42nd Street. The storyhour was held in another room, two flights up. Led by an assistant, the children would slowly make their way up the stairs and down a long corridor to the storyhour room. There the story-teller was waiting behind closed doors for the magic signal. A child was chosen to knock three times on the door. The story-teller slowly opened the door, invited the children in, and the storyhour began. It must have been a real adventure, even for sophisticated New York children, to be led through marble halls up stairs to this special room, and added something to the story-hour, even though it seemed inconvenient to the library staff.

When I was a branch librarian in the same system, story-hours were held in a dusty attic piled high with broken, unused furniture. At first, from my adult point of view, it seemed an entirely unattractive place; but when I saw the children's reactions of awe and wonder, I realized what a splendid story room it really was. Not many of the apartment-dwelling children who came to my storyhour had ever seen a real attic, let alone spent time in one. I'm certain that those stories were long remembered in part because of the magical atmosphere in which they were told.

SCHOOL ASSEMBLIES

Although storytelling might seem best suited to a family gathering around a peat fire in Ireland or a casual group in a coffee house in Turkey, the most prevalent contemporary setting may be the school assembly.

For years, trained by the New York Public Library, I resisted presenting stories to groups as large as school assemblies. But eventually I gave in, simply because the average school population hovers around 800–1000 children, and most administrators would like all their students to hear a guest storyteller. You might typically greet 300 or 400 children at an assembly. These assemblies are often held in a combination cafeteria and auditorium, or in a gym, which can seem cavernous, but I often get around this by having everyone sit on the floor, where they seem closer to each other and to me. I enjoy telling participation stories and stories that bring overt responses (such as a good laugh!) when I'm telling to large groups, but of course you must tell whatever suits your particular style of telling.

BOOKSTORES

And then there is the bookstore. As children's bookstores proliferate around the country, they too are presenting book, activity, and author programs. As a consultant for a large bookstore chain, I was asked to give book programs around the United

States. It didn't help that I had to follow a chimpanzee who rode a bicycle (have *you* ever had to follow a performing monkey?), but even more difficult was the presence of the adults who accompanied their children. The children would wander up and pick up my puppets and other props not yet in use, throw temper tantrums, and generally misbehave. The storekeepers were loathe to offend their customers and, as a performer/storyteller, I felt that it was hardly my job to make a suggestion to the child or parent. If you decide that the shopping mall is a high traffic area that is perfect for a storyhour, or if the bookstore is your beat . . . good luck! Actually, a bookstore can be the perfect setting. After all, you are surrounded by books!

Equipment Checklist

If you plan to do any multimedia storytelling you will surely need equipment of some kind. After you decide on your program, be sure to arrange for the equipment you will need—an easel, a felt board, a slide projector and screen—to carry it out successfully. Although it seems obvious to suggest that you will have to use the proper projector to show a film, filmstrip, or slides, don't forget to check whether the room can be adequately darkened. Of course you also must know how to run the projector or find someone else who can before the program. Make sure you know where the electrical outlets are and whether an extension cord will be needed. Set up chairs, exhibits, and equipment well before your audience arrives.

Favors and Treats

A souvenir passed out to each member of the audience to take home will transform a storyhour program into a truly remarkable event. Obviously it is not feasible or even advisable to provide a memento at each program; however, I personally love to give gifts. When I find something appropriate and timely, I like to hand it out after the program.

Bookmarks make useful favors. They can be used to impart information about the books available in the library, announce a future story session, or serve as a written program. Almost any object, however simple or ordinary, can take on significance in association with a story. Once, after I had told the Japanese story "Momotaro" about the little boy who came out of a peach pit, I gave everyone a peach pit saved from summer and sprayed with gold. A local printer provided the small paper pads I handed out after telling "The Nuremburg Stove," a story about an aspiring artist. A suitable favor need not even cost anything more than some creative effort on your part. *Stone Soup* suggests that each child in the audience go home with a pretty stone you collected on your last trip to the beach.

Holidays naturally lend themselves to gift giving and also avail children an opportunity to make and give gifts. A birthday

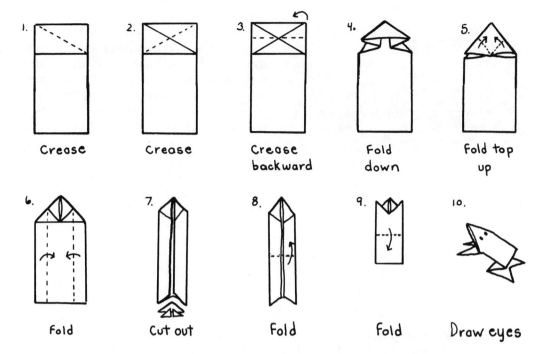

1. Crease
2. Crease
3. Crease backward
4. Fold down
5. Fold top up
6. Fold
7. Cut out
8. Fold
9. Fold
10. Draw eyes

candle to celebrate Hans Christian Andersen's birthday or dried pumpkin seeds to handcraft a Halloween necklace could be given as holiday favors. Origami, the age-old Japanese art of paper-folding, can be used in conjunction with storytelling to create a variety of animals and interesting objects that make lovely presents. Everyone can make a dog when you tell a favorite dog story. Why wait for a traditional holiday? Originate a special event of your own to celebrate. Teach the children step by step how to make a frog after you tell them "The Frog Prince" to observe Kindness Day, a holiday you invented to remind everyone how important it is to treat others as you would wish to be treated.

Sometimes something to eat is the magic ingredient needed to round out a program. Obviously you cannot feed a hundred or so children at an assembly, nor should you consider providing an edible treat for every program in a series, even if you could afford to do so. It just seems very appropriate, even irresistible, on occasion. How about fortune cookies to accompany a Chinese New Year celebration or slices of pizza to munch after you tell *Pizza for Breakfast* by Maryann Kovalski and share *Pizza Man* by Marjorie Pillars? Everyone can go home enjoying a lollipop when you read and show the enticing artwork for *Many Luscious Lollipops: A Book about Adjectives* by Ruth Heller.

Decorations and Exhibits

Recall a bygone era—the wind whistling around the eaves of a stone house built on the heath, light from a peat fire flickering on the storyteller, Granny in her rocking chair, and all the listeners crowded close. This nostalgic and picturesque scene

exists mostly in our imaginations. What we are really seeing or reacting to is the ambiance evoked by the storyhour, more often than not presented in the somewhat humdrum environment of a classroom or library. It is up to the storyteller to create a particular mood or feeling and convey it to an audience. Sometimes a change to a natural setting such as a backyard, the library steps, or even a different arrangement of the chairs will provide the right background or generate the feeling of anticipation we want for our stories. The use of exhibits and decoration is yet another way to conjure up a desired mood or produce a different frame of reference.

Table Exhibit

A table placed behind the storyteller makes a handy "shelf" for the storyhour exhibit. A solid colored tablecloth on the table will add a festive air and a welcome touch of color to the room. Now you have a place to display the storyhour "wishing candle" in its special candleholder, a vase of cut flowers or a plant, and the books that the stories you will tell come from. Use well-arranged fresh cut flowers whenever possible. They not only add a gracious tone to the program, but also provide an aesthetic experience for those children who rarely see fresh flower arrangements in their homes.

If you have just one object to represent a particular story (an old-fashioned iron cooking pot representing "The Wonderful Pot" or an hourglass as a symbol for the "Lost Half Hour"), it can be effectively displayed on the storytime table. This symbolic artifact should not, however, be so intriguing that everyone's attention is drawn to the table instead of the storyteller. This kind of exhibit is more decorative than informational, rather like the flower borders or illuminated letters in a book. There is no need to mention the fact that the object relates to the stories you are telling, for your listeners should make the connection on their own. A few may come up after the stories to examine the item at a closer range. If you do have a story-related object that you feel would be too distracting, share it with your group at the end of the session. At one time I kept a fully furnished doll house on permanent display in the storyhour room. One day as I was giving a booktalk on stories about dolls, eyes started turning to look at the doll house in the corner of the room. I suppose the children were looking to see if the doll family were walking around inside the house. Now I've learned to bring the doll house to the front of the room as a display, but only when I want it to be the focus of attention.

A Storytelling Symbol

Create an individual symbol that instantly pro-
claims "Storytime!" and use it to decorate the
corner or room in which you tell stories. Consider making a standing screen ornamented
with book covers or character cutouts to sym-
bolize the storyhour and also serve as a back-
drop to your stories. A wall hanging or felt
banner complete with your storytelling logo
that can be brought out from a closet and hung
on the wall or fastened to a stand is another
way to personalize your classroom or club
program. Encourage the children to design a
storyhour logo for the banner you or the
Friends of the Library will sew. A large black

spider on a field of red could represent Anansi, the African
spider that "owns all the stories"; a felt cutout of a candle
representing the storytime wishing candle might be another
program symbol.

An almost life-sized book character, a clown, or an animal cut
from plywood or constructed from papier mâché to stand at the
entrance to the storyhour area could become a permanent
storyhour symbol. This special figure might hold the book or
books you are going to use in your next story program or
it could be used to hold a sign announcing an upcoming
storyhour special.

Even a stuffed doll can serve as a storyhour symbol.
One of my students made a four-foot-high Laura Ingalls
Wilder doll to use in her storyhour. Raggedy Ann, Twee-
dledum and Tweedledee, Peter Rabbit, and Babar are
other student-made storybook character dolls that children will recognize and enjoy.

If you use cushions instead of chairs for storytelling
you may want to have a permanent collection of cushions (each individually decorated by the children in your
school or by the Friends of the Library group). These
could be embroidered, painted with textile paints, or ap-
pliqued with storybook characters and used exclusively
for storytime.

For Special Storyhours

It's Christmas! It's Kwanzaa! Valentine's Day! Or the day you've planned to tell stories from China or Spain, about dogs or the circus. It's a special storyhour. Why not make it even more special by decorating the room with student-made murals, artifacts, posters, or seasonal decorations? If you are lucky enough to have a separate room for your storyhours you can really be creative in your decorations. Make your room cozier by stringing figured or patterned bed sheets around the walls of the room, changing the room's character entirely. Caution! Don't attempt to use this total decoration idea too often, and try to steer away from those trite, commercially produced items available at card shops and party-goods counters.

The Exhibit as Part of the Storyhour

Occasionally you will find that you or a friend own a particular collection relevant to the story you are telling. Decide on the best way to display these artifacts. If they are to be displayed on a table, put them behind the children so that they are not tempted to look instead of listen. If the things are valuable, or fragile, and therefore not touchable, make sure that you can exhibit them in locked glass cases to protect them. Perhaps you may choose first to tell the story and then show an artifact or collection. For instance, I collect anything and everything that has to do with Little Red Riding Hood: antique mugs, lantern slides, dolls, miniatures, wall hangings, advertising cards, whatever. Naturally, if I tell Little Red Riding Hood or a variant of the story I like to show some of the things in my collection as part of the storyhour. Since the "story is the thing," I try not to let the exhibit overpower the telling of the story, but use it only to increase an awareness of the different ways that artists and artisans interpret a traditional tale.

Bulletin Boards

Don't overlook the potential of the permanent bulletin board that may be hanging in the story room. Often a permanent bulletin board is an unsightly mess covered with notices of events long since over. Use the bulletin board to your advantage. It can publicize your next story session or be used as a display area to decorate for the book program. Don't permit displays or announcements on the bulletin board to become a permanent part of the room's decoration. It should be changed periodically and completely or you are not using it effectively. Even if you are announcing the same event, use the same information with a different arrangement and vary your materials from one time to another—fabrics, tissue paper, construction paper, cut-out letters, small objects are all suitable and potentially eye-catching.

If you want your bulletin board display to be effective:

Keep it simple; the crowded configuration placed among the usual bulletin board clutter is asking to be ignored.

Keep it bright; happy colors catch the passerby's eye.

Use three-dimensional objects; the unexpected captures attention.

Be sure your lettering is neat and professional; don't ruin artwork and displays with amateurish lettering.

Don't keep the same display up too long; too long is when you no longer look at it admiringly.

Picture Sources for Exhibits and Craft Projects

Many of the exhibits and craft ideas mentioned in this handbook need pictures. Naturally you will want such pictures to be associated with the books you use in your storyhour programs. Either draw your own (if you are artistically inclined!) or look for what you need in one of the picture sources that follow.

It is important to start collecting potentially useful pictures and other things because you never know when a really exciting idea for a program will come to mind. Then when it does, you can go to your "goodies" drawer or cabinet and pull out what you need to make that idea a reality, rather than begin the long, tedious, and often fruitless search for the right items. Who knows, perhaps your collection, as it grows, will suggest what your next program will be. These collections are also useful for creating exhibits, favors, and treats.

Rule 1. Do *not* throw away any usable picture source, for you may find that you have just tossed out a potential program idea. Set aside a spare drawer or box to save pictures for later use; better still, keep an organized picture file by subject. Don't wait till you need a picture. You won't find it then.

Junk mail. Are you inundated with unwanted junk mail at your house? An advertisement for a forthcoming travel book or a land development corporation often yields some lovely color photographs. Mail-order catalogs also contain pictures of almost anything you might need.

Publishers' catalogs. Catalogs from publishers often contain small reproductions of their books and are an excellent source of book-oriented material.

Conference pickups. If you attend library or education conferences and walk around the exhibits, you will return home with an armful of handouts—bookmarks, prints, advertisements, and posters—materials often illustrated with pictures of and from your favorite books.

Discarded books. Are your picture books becoming tattered and torn? When you replace them, be sure to save any potentially useful pictures.

Stamps. Foreign and domestic stamps often have outstanding pictures on them. Ask your friends to save their stamps for you.

Greeting cards. Stationery is becoming so attractive that it's a shame to use it only once—to send a message. Save all the tasteful greeting cards you receive. Christmas cards, valentines, or friendly notes all are potential sources of colorful pictures.

Magazines. Browse through the special interest magazines on nature, boats, animals, etc. Before you throw away a magazine, clip and file interesting pictures.

Photographs. Did you take pictures of your last book week activities, summer book activities, book fair? Photographs are pictures, too, although we sometimes think of them as something to store separately.

Original drawings. Pictures drawn by you, by a talented staff member, or by children are the most personal illustrations of all and provide a magnificent contrast to the commercialism of some of today's advertising art.

Sale books. In your browsing around the sale tables of the local bookstore, take the opportunity to flip through a beautifully illustrated book of animals, art, travel, or a specialized subject. Even if you never actually read such a book, it could contain a wealth of pictorial source material. Don't let your upbringing (*never* destroy a book) keep you from cutting up a book for a good use.

Garage sale books. Your next-door neighbors may provide you with an excellent choice of titles in good condition. Look over the weekend ads listing garage sales and stop at the houses that are having garage and moving sales. You will often find available at nominal cost among the items for sale books that children feel they have outgrown. Those that you don't add to your collection can be cut up for crafts and exhibit projects.

Wrapping paper. If you received a beautifully wrapped gift for your birthday, save the paper. Don't throw it away or put it in your wrapping paper drawer. (Is anyone that organized?) Think of it as a potential picture source.

Stickers. These are usually imported and available at gift counters in animal, flower, and abstract designs. Stay away from the "cute" or the obvious. No use putting your energy into something that won't be artistically superior to the slap-dash, prosaic art of the commercial.

Postcards. When you receive a lovely postcard from a traveling friend, don't be envious, be thankful. Then save the card for future use in your storyhour program.

Wallpaper samples. Ask your local paint and wallpaper dealers to save their discontinued wallpaper samples for you. These discards are a valuable source of materials for storyhour projects.

Antique advertising cards. As you browse through thrift shops, antique shows, and garage sales in your area, keep your eyes open for old advertising cards. Some are considered collector's items and may be fairly expensive. Others are real bargains and make charming pictures for storytime projects.

Coloring books. Today there are a great variety of story-related coloring books that will provide you with quality outline drawings for your art projects.

Photocopied pictures. The copy machine can be used to reproduce your favorite storybook illustrations. Color these with felt pens or watercolors or splurge on a color photocopy.

Lettering Aids for Exhibits and Bulletin Boards

After you have expended a considerable amount of time and energy planning and assembling an exhibit, it really is a pity to spoil it with crude, amateurish lettering. Unless you are skilled at lettering, your posters, bulletin board displays, and exhibit signs will look better and more professional if you use a lettering device, precut letters and numbers, or transfer letters and numbers to get your message across. Ask your local art supply dealer, school supply dealer, or stationer for suggestions on how to make your lettering jobs easier and more professional-looking. If you have access to a Macintosh or other personal computer with an array of fonts, so much the better!

Almost everyone enjoys a story, whether it is told or read, but not every story will appeal equally to everyone who hears it. For that reason, keep in mind that there are going to be occasions when you will be unable to please or capture the attention of someone in the audience. Remember that tastes do vary and that no two children are or ever will be impressed with the same things at the same time. In fact, you may never know what has impressed a child. It could be your voice, the language of the story you've just told, its characters, its plot, your gestures or lack of them, the flowers on the table, the doll that represents the story's central character, or the special story-related activity you provided afterward.

Your enthusiasm for the stories you share, your evident enjoyment of the books from which you select those stories, and the rapport you establish with an audience and each of its members may stimulate some of the nonreaders among them to read a book or two themselves. And this could be habit-forming, which makes all the planning you do and all the effort you expend on your program worth every minute. Happy telling!

2 / The Storyteller

Who will actually tell the stories at your story program? You. Yes, you should be your first choice. Why shouldn't you be the person to get that wonderful feeling that comes with telling a good tale to an audience of enthralled listeners? After reading this book and telling your first story, I know you will be reluctant to let anyone else have the pleasure of the actual telling. From time to time, however, you may wish to include other storytellers in your program. Here are some ways to add variety to your storyhour.

The Guest Storyteller

A guest storyteller may make a storyhour special by providing a welcome change of pace as well as briefly relieving you of your storytelling responsibilities. Look for storytelling talent at your local college theater department and amateur theater group or among the retired teachers and librarians in your community.

Many professional people really enjoy participating in an ongoing program, and the busier they are, the better. Some may not have time to spare for your group and probably will tell you so when you ask. Still, if you establish contact but are turned down with a "maybe some other time," be sure to call again.

Of course, the "proper" way of approaching an outside speaker is to write a letter, but the most efficient and personal way is to visit or use the telephone. In my experience, it is more difficult to turn down a telephoned or person-to-person request than a letter. A letter is much too easily answered with a "no."

Incidentally, you should be aware that prominent professionals often charge for their services. If you don't have enough money for a fee or expenses, don't be discouraged. A speaker might want to reach your group for his or her own reasons—to become better known in your community, to publicize an event of his or her own, for public service, or the best reason of all, for enjoyment.

In your initial contact with a potential guest be specific about what you want. Give complete details of what is involved: where the program will take place, who the audience is, how much time is involved, and whether you expect the guest to attend a dinner or autograph party. Make certain that you are clear about any financial arrangements. Will you pay for transportation, arrange for a room, pay a speaker's fee or honorarium? All these facts will help the potential guest decide whether to accept or reject the invitation and to plan his or her involvement in the subsequent program.

Don't assume that all potential performers in a storyhour program must be professionals. You may find possible guests almost anywhere—the browser in the children's area at the bookstore or the person sitting next to you at a dinner party may provide you with a lead to just the program guest you have been looking for. If the banjo player, the radio announcer, or the amateur magician you meet casually has never before performed for children but finds the prospect intriguing, she or he may spend extra time and effort to prepare for your audience. How do you determine whether a guest will be a smash hit or a flop? Before you delegate the responsibility of an entire program to an untried performer, "audition" him or her first in a segment of one of your programs. However, it is really better to take a chance and risk being disappointed than to lose a volunteer talent by default.

An incidental benefit of having a guest storyteller is that he or she may invite you to do a return program. A reciprocal invitation enables both of you to tell stories you have learned to new audiences. If you have been meaning to take time to learn some new stories but just haven't gotten around to it, you may find that an invitation as a guest to another group is just the incentive you need to prepare a new story or finish that scratch film you started months ago.

Guestmanship

  Before the program. After your guest has agreed to come, make certain that you follow up with a written reminder of the date, time, and place well before the day of the event. By doing this you not only inform your guest when and where he or she is expected, you also avoid disappointing your audience and yourself because of a possible misunderstanding.

Some speakers appreciate being told exactly what you want them to do. Others want to be told only the time, the place, the size of the group, and its composition (ages, interests). Try as much as possible to cater to a guest's desires and needs. However, sometimes you, the program organizer, have more suitable ideas than the guest. Some time ago I was asked to take part in a week-long arts festival. The organizer wanted all the performers to meet together to plan how they would relate to each other. It was a very ambitious and probably valid idea, but I was simply too busy to take part in the planning. We never did get together, which may have been a mistake. The festival attracted many children and with more preplanning, could have been even better than it was. Another time I was asked to be a dinner speaker at a banquet. It seemed to me that a committee member called daily about my talk. I even had a visit from the banquet chairman inquiring if I had composed my speech yet. At first I was annoyed but in the end was delighted, for he had many ideas geared to make the evening a grand success. He encouraged me to duplicate a handout for the guests. We jointly decorated the tables with ceramic figures of characters from children's books. The door prize was the book I featured in my talk. Without continued communication we wouldn't have been able to coordinate our efforts.

If a guest comes from out of town and must stay overnight or for a meal, be hospitable and make sure he or she feels at home and at ease. Try to have someone meet the guest at the airport or bus station, and, if possible, arrange for meals at private homes. However, always check with the guest beforehand. He or she may prefer a quick meal at the hotel coffee shop and an early-to-bed evening.

Once, during a week's lecture tour far from home, I arrived at the airport of the first of my scheduled stops with three large trunks of exhibit materials. No one was on hand to meet me and there were no messages. Worrying and uncertain about whether I was in the right town on the right day, I took a taxi to the hotel. Eventually someone did contact me there, but with this unsettling experience my trip started off on the wrong note.

 After the program. Be sure to send a follow-up thank you to the guest. It may be appropriate to mention some of the favorable comments that you heard. You'll find that this is always appreciated! It also reestablishes contact in the event you want to invite your guest back another time.

Volunteers

A Storytelling Guild

A successful storytelling program doesn't just happen, as the Storytelling Guild of Medford, Oregon, could tell you. It takes organization and hard work. The Medford program began when Myra Getchell, the children's librarian at the public library in Medford, gathered together five interested women to help plan and contribute to the library storyhours. Originally the volunteers limited their efforts to the central county library and a school or two. When they discovered that there were lots of neighborhood children who were unaware of the library's storyhours, they recruited and trained other volunteers and organized mobile storytelling units.

Today, 26 years later, in addition to the library and school storyhours, mobile story units make scheduled stops in a once-a-week, ten-week spring storytelling program series that reaches thousands of children. Not only do the decorated storymobiles (privately owned cars, by the way) carry books and, occasionally, live animals, their programs include puppet shows and group singing in addition to traditional storytelling. Each week storytellers go to the Head Start Center, and at Christmastime every Head Start child receives a book of his or her own as a present. One or two storytellers also will go to local birthday parties in return for a small donation to the Storytelling Guild.

As if all this was not enough activity for one group, the guild also holds an annual children's festival. The first year the festival was financed as a joint project by the Jackson County Library System and the Medford American Association of University Women. The $50 it cost to put on that first festival was repaid from the 25¢ admission fee. Although the guild had planned for 50 to 100 children a day for the three days, a total of 1,500 actually came. Several years later the attendance had swelled to 11,000! A thousand volunteers helped put on a recent festival, which now includes ballet, mime, puppetry, storytelling, an animal fair, arts and crafts, Pageant Wagon Theater plays, and a poetry tree.

In the arts and crafts section of the festival there are separate booths where children can create do-it-yourself projects from materials donated by local merchants. My daughter came home with a batik hanging, a sandcasting, a carpentry project, a dried plant arrangement, macaroni jewelry, and a clay sculpture. She had danced Greek dances and eaten Greek food (each year another country is featured), seen a puppet show, participated in a creative dramatic presentation of *The Wizard of Oz,* and listened and listened to stories under a storytelling tree.

The Storytelling Guild of Medford is headed by a board of directors that includes the editor of its newsletter, *The Satchel* (donation, $2), a consultant from the public library, a director of party storytelling, a director of storymobiles, a director of school storytelling, Head Start storytelling, and the children's festival director. Every other year a storytelling forum featuring workshops and a guest speaker is held for the member-volunteers and potential guild members.

Obviously, the activities of such an ambitious group take an enormous amount of planning. Potential members of the guild are put through a training session in order to determine individual talents, and each member is encouraged to contribute in her own way: driving storymobiles, baking cookies, sewing costumes, making puppets, or telling stories. Why not try this in your own community? At least three other towns in Oregon have benefited from Medford's example with festivals of their own.

Remember that training is an essential element in any volunteer program. Take the time to properly educate your volunteers, to assure quality programming. Good leadership and the reactions of delighted children should attract volunteers who will take their job seriously. It is unnecessary to begin your volunteer program with something as ambitious as a storytelling guild. Start with a few friends or colleagues. Organizations such as Friends of the Library or the PTA could well be excellent sources of "storytelling power." Don't be discouraged if some of your recruits are not good storytellers. They may have other talents you need. Perhaps they can help with publicity, arrange for transportation, or make props. The National Story League, an organization dedicated to the art of storytelling, could be another source of volunteers. Write to Elizabeth Raabe, 52 Stephen F. Austin Dr., Conroe, TX 77302, to find out if there is a local chapter in your community.

Plan your volunteer program with care and creativity and you will be rewarded with popular, smoothly run storytimes.

Student Storytellers

You may discover that some of the older children and young adults who have been coming to your storyhours at the library, school, church, or club are as interested in learning and telling stories as you are. Since these young people are potential volunteers, consider organizing a storytelling class for them. Keep the class small. If you limit your learner's group to as few as three to no more than ten children, the members will be assured of your personal attention and guidance. It is important for members of the group to feel at ease with one another and this is best accomplished when the group is small.

Begin their training by letting them perform informally by telling jokes, describing their families, or relating school experiences. Tell them a story or anecdote yourself or perhaps invite a guest. You may want to begin with a discussion of what makes a good story or what makes a good storyteller (I don't do this myself; I go right to work). Explain that there are different types of stories, such as folktales, fables, myths, epics, and modern short stories. Show your students books that will provide story ideas and encourage them to browse and read through these, and decide which stories they would like to learn, beginning, as you did, with something short and simple. Make sure you have the time to devote to helping each child individually from the beginning. Give them each a chance to be heard and encourage them to practice on each other to develop their proficiency and gain self-confidence. To help your students select appropriate stories, provide them with a list of stories particularly suited to the beginner.

Permit the student who is ready to perform to tell his or her story all the way through. Don't interrupt to make suggestions. Take notes as you listen. Be responsive. Don't frighten a novice performer with a frozen or disdainful expression on your face. Be sure to say something positive about each performance when it is over. Point out any common faults, those shared by other student performers, but do not permit a situation to develop in which everyone acrimoniously criticizes everyone else. To pinpoint and correct particular faults, talk privately to each child.

If you have access to a video camera and VCR this is a good time to put them to use, for the students can each tell a story and see themselves as others see them. Although videotaping may be a frightening experience, it can also be a great deal of fun and makes performing in front of a live audience seem easy.

Working one story over and over again to perfection can be boring. Let each student try a variety of stories in the shelter of the group. When an individual seems comfortable in front of his or her friends, then you might begin work more seriously with the idea of performance. Try to work individually with each student to build confidence.

To whom can the students tell stories? Fifth graders can tell them to third graders, seventh graders to fourth graders, and second graders can entertain high school seniors. Wherever an adult can tell stories your student group should be welcome too: hospital wards, the public library, day-care centers, and playgrounds.

If administrators and teachers are reluctant to take time away from other activities to permit your group to tell stories, approach and convince them personally. After the initial storyhour success make plans for another, for by then the administrator will have heard that the program was enthusiastically received. Don't let success go to your head. Be cautious about performing in front of an assembly or other large group. Storytelling is really intended for small, intimate groups, not mobs. Even the most experienced storyteller finds it difficult to effectively show his or her art to a group of a hundred or more people.

Keep the program brief. Twenty minutes is more than enough. It is not necessary to coordinate the program around a theme, for each storyteller can tell his or her story in turn. However, opening and closing with a song might help to give cohesiveness to the program. Let your students travel together. They can take comfort in each other's presence, and half the fun is discussing the experience later. A storytelling class can be a useful elective in a junior high or high school curriculum. After all, the students actually are studying literature, folklore, theater, and child-care activities, all in one class!

The Professional Storyteller

Who would have thought in this age of electronic entertainment that there would be a resurgence of the professional bard? North America has become the leader in a virtual renaissance of interest in storytelling. There are clubs throughout Canada and the United States devoted to developing skills of adult storytellers. There are classes given in colleges and by independent storytelling teachers, and emerging from these organizations are men and women who are devoting their professional lives to storytelling.

It is interesting to note that while educators and media specialists think of storytelling as a children's activity, the majority of professional tellers are more interested in telling to adults. Coffeehouses and festivals are the major venues for these professionals. There are, of course, those who tell exclusively to children, working in libraries, day-care centers, and schools.

A note about fees: they should be discussed directly with the storyteller or his or her agent. If you are strapped for funds, don't be shy about asking if fees are negotiable. It is possible that your storytelling choice is anxious to come to your city because her mother-in-law lives there.

The best way to find a professional storyteller is to use the NAPPS National Directory of Storytelling (P.O. Box 309, Jonesborough, TN 37659). The directory lists people, places, and events involving storytelling throughout the United States. Listings are arranged both alphabetically and geographically. The listings are paid for by the storytellers themselves and are not "recommended" by NAPPS. Ask the storyteller for references or, better yet, try to observe the storyteller in action.

The National Story League, an organization of mostly amateur storytellers, could offer a source of storytellers as well. There are leagues throughout the United States. The League's quarterly magazine should help you locate the chapter nearest you: Story Art, 555 Tod Ave. N.W., Warren, OH 44485.

In Canada you can get in touch with the Alberta League of Storytellers, Wordworks, 10523–100 Ave., Edmonton, Alberta T5J OA8, Canada. Good luck!

3 / Promotion

In 1977 I wrote a book called *Handbook for Storytellers*. My publisher, the American Library Association, invited me to its annual conference where I was to give mini-storytelling sessions in the exhibit area. To promote these programs, I donned a flowing cape and a fabulous mask representing a fairytale castle, and walked through the exhibit hall giving out flyers announcing the time of my next storytelling session. It worked! Before long, a small crowd was waiting to hear me at the ALA booth. Unfortunately, I wasn't there. Because I couldn't wear my glasses under the mask, I became hopelessly lost in the maze of exhibit booths. Eventually a kind person led me back to the proper location. "And that's a true story," as Hans Christian Andersen would say.

What if you planned a storyhour and nobody came? If it was your first storyhour you might even feel relieved for a moment or two. But of course the real purpose of the book program, reaching the children, would have been lost. Part of planning and producing an event is thinking and doing something about publicity. How many children can your storyhour room comfortably accommodate? Is it better to have a small, interested group of the same age or a larger group of children of mixed ages in the audience? Is it better to publicize a single, special event or an entire series? What is the purpose of the publicity? Is it a public relations campaign for your organization or is it an invitation to the public to come and enjoy a particular event? These are all questions that deserve careful consideration.

Invited to speak at my first international conference in Geneva, I worried that no one would attend my sessions because no one had ever heard of me. Before I left for Europe I printed a number of bookmarks listing the subjects and times of my presentations. I also offered a certificate for attending all six lectures. A former student of mine was also attending the conference, so I enlisted her aid to hand out the bookmarks. We left them in the coffee shop and in the rest rooms at the conference hotel, we handed them to people in the elevator, and we left them on the chairs at the first general session. I watched as the conference delegates picked up the bookmarks and, just because they were there, read them! My first lecture was well attended, which left me feeling confident, for I knew if I could get people to the first lecture, I'd gather a following for the remainder of the conference. To be truthful, I don't know whether it was my personal publicity campaign or the subject of my first lecture that appealed to that audience. My first presentation was titled "Sex in Books."

Undeniably, publicity for an event is almost as important as planning the program itself, but keep in mind that whatever you choose to do will involve spending some money. Your expenditures need not be high, for there are many ways of achieving effective, low-cost publicity. Your promotional efforts can range from informal notices posted on bulletin boards to paid commercial advertising.

Here, I think I ought to make a distinction between teachers and other storytellers. Teachers are fortunate, of course, because they essentially have captive audiences. If you are a second grade teacher, for instance, you can simply declare that Tuesdays at 2:00 are reserved for storytelling, and you will have instantly created an audience of 25 or 30 six- and seven-year-olds for yourself. But even though you may not wish to draw additional listeners to your storyhour, you can still create a poster promoting the stories you will tell at your next session, and tickets to hand out to your children. Such promotional devices will help to build interest in your program, and your children will love them!

For all storytellers, planning and budgeting for publicity give you an opportunity to exercise your imagination and involve all of your staff (if you have one) or your friends and family. What works best? This chapter is filled with ideas for you.

Posters

It may seem obvious, but be sure that the posters you make clearly spell out the *name* of the event, the *time,* the *date,* and the

place! You may also want to include such information as names of performers, or a phone number for additional details.

Always keep in mind that posters are advertisements on which the information you want to disseminate should be clearly presented by means of eye-catching graphics. At the same time, beware of the prevailing trend to make poster art so clever, so unconventional, that the message it is supposed to convey becomes lost in the design. The challenge is to make your poster both different and clear. Try a new shape. Make it three-dimensional by attaching objects to it—boxes, fabric dolls, dried flowers, feathers. Look at signs around your town and take special note of any that you have been ignoring and ask yourself why. Have they been in the same spot too long? Do they contain too much information? Are their colors drab? Are they in the wrong place? Analyze each problem to avoid making a similar mistake.

The most important element in poster composition is good lettering. Your best friend (whom you may have cajoled into "creating" for you) may be a wonderful artist; but if he or she cannot letter well by hand, then you do it. Today a number of quick and easy ways are available to do a professional job of lettering—with stencils, cutout wood, plastic, or cardboard letters, stick-on letters, and transfers. If you have access to a Macintosh or other personal computer with an array of type fonts, your job is even easier. Many copy shops now have computers and printers that you can use for a small charge. There really is no excuse for crude or illegible lettering on your posters or displays.

After all the work you've put into creating your poster, you will want to find exactly the right place to hang it. If you are working in an institution—a school, church, or clubhouse—you should certainly place your posters around your building. But be sure to look beyond that conventional bulletin board where others usually tack their announcements. Discover a new place—perhaps a telephone booth, the ceiling of a classroom, the stairwell wall, the entrance door to the building—all are potential exhibit spaces for your eye-catching graphics.

Outside the building, ask shopkeepers for window space, but consider where you are most likely to attract the audience you are aiming for: the ice cream store, variety shop, toy shop, local bar, hardware store, or garden shop? No use wasting posters. And don't forget to go back and remove your signs after the event is over.

Minisigns

Even in our literate society there are numerous people who automatically ignore any printed matter that is put in front of them. To capture this otherwise oblivious audience, try placing tiny signs, 1 inch by 2 inches or smaller, in obvious places. Make your minisigns on some easily *removable* material, such as masking tape or small peel-off labels, and attach to doorknobs,

the top step, locker doors, milk cartons, toothpick holders, salt shakers, or on the library checkout counter. Use your imagination and these tiny advertisements for a blitz minicampaign.

Souvenirs and Bookmarks

Give something away. People wonder why you're doing it, which is why they read any attached advertising copy. A souvenir need not be expensive; it can be a cut flower, a peanut in a shell, a pine cone, or a seashell. Hanging on the "present" is a small announcement of the upcoming event. Be imaginative and make the giveaway appropriate to the program theme. Are you having a pet show or a storyhour featuring dogs? Give away a dog biscuit. Are animal stories on the program? Animal crackers make fine souvenirs. Native American stories today? A small colorful bead may well end up a cherished gift. Any small present, especially if unexpected, is endowed with a certain magic. Children especially enjoy getting something, no matter how trivial, and adults at least will be curious about why they are being handed a present. Keep in mind that because it is an adult who drives or brings a child to the storyhour, or reminds him or her that "today is the day," your efforts to reach adults are worthwhile.

Bookmarks are eminently suitable giveaways, especially so since your programs are book-oriented. Of course, bookmarks

Come and have fun!
what:
where:
when:

can be printed, but those you make yourself can be very effective. Save used greeting cards. All those Christmas cards, valentines, birthday cards, and pretty little everyday cards that your friends send can be of practical use. All you need to do to turn them into bookmarks is to cut off the greeting and print your message on the back, perhaps while you're watching the late movie on television. That way you can recycle and spread the word.

Don't just slip a bookmark, announcement or memo into a package or book. Hand it directly to the child or adult with a simple oral greeting and reminder such as "Don't forget our storyhour Wednesday." This implies a personal invitation, which is more effective than an inanimate notice, even one printed on the back of a pretty picture.

Chalkboards

A chalkboard hanging on the wall of your library or classroom or resting on a checkout counter or desk is a good place to write a "Daily Reminder." When you arrive at work each morning make it a habit to write a new message on the chalkboard. Changing the message daily will build up a chalkboard following who automatically look for each day's bulletin on your board. To publicize your storyhour that will be held a week from Wednesday, begin the week before with

reminders or quotes or illustrations (if you are artistic!) from the stories you'll be telling. Keep changing the message daily to alert your potential audience that the time for the program is at hand.

Although the chalkboard message is most often encountered in schools, there is no reason why this practical gimmick should not be utilized elsewhere. Instead of a poster, hang a blackboard in your clubhouse, church, or even the window of a much frequented grocery store. Drop in on your way about town and change the message on the board daily.

Chalkwalk

Chalk, particularly the colored kind, not only is fun to use, but it also washes away easily. The day before your event, make a drawing on the sidewalk outside your meeting hall to remind the public of your program, or perhaps enlist some of your regular storyhour children who enjoy drawing pictures to do so for advertising purposes. A drawing contest may even help bring newcomers to the storyhour. Do, however, be a good citizen and wash the sidewalk down to remove your artwork after it has served its purpose.

Sandwich Boards

The old-fashioned sandwich board still catches people's attention, especially if the person wearing it is attractively costumed. Use cardboard that is not too heavy and wear the sandwich board as you walk around a shopping center or through a grocery store.

Badges, Buttons, Balloons, and Bumper Stickers

Make your own button with your mininotice attractively printed on it—duplicate this one if you'd like. Simply photocopy the image, attach it to a round piece of cardboard, and affix a pin to the back. Stationery stores usually sell blank name tags and some stock blank buttons for you to transform. Inexpensive make-your-own button kits can also be purchased. Pin on your badge or button whenever you will be out in public.

Balloons, because of their great appeal, can also serve as publicity, especially if you are trying to reach children. Use

permanent ink felt markers to letter a notice or reminder on the inflated balloons. If you think you will be using this idea more than once, buy an inexpensive pump, for the idea begins to lose its charm after you've blown up the tenth balloon!

For a special event or to publicize your organization, you might want to buy some professionally printed balloons or bumper stickers. Look in the yellow pages under "Advertising Specialties" for names of merchants specializing in personalized souvenirs. Wouldn't it be grand to have the whole town driving around with bumper stickers advertising the library storytime?

Tickets

There is something about having a ticket to an event that makes the holder feel obliged to go. You may want to send out tickets on request, which provides you with a way to estimate how many children to expect. Also, you might encourage an audience by leaving tickets to be distributed in classrooms, Sunday schools, and other appropriate agencies. The tickets need not be printed. They can be photocopied or even handwritten. You can begin simply by enlarging and photocopying on colorful paper the ticket above; then giving the pertinent information on the back. Carnival tickets can also be purchased in any full-scale stationery or party supply store.

I like to use tickets in other ways. While the children are assembling for the storyhour, tickets are handed out. These are then collected as the children enter the room. Somehow this gives the storyhour a more festive feeling and heightens anticipation. Because I collect the tickets at the door, I can reuse them over and over again. This also enables me to count attendance without taking time from the session itself. Because I reuse my tickets, I've tried to make them attractive and durable. One way to do this is to silkscreen them on heavy paper stock. Once in a while, usually for a holiday storyhour, I create a special ticket that can also be used as a bookmark or souvenir. Of course, these special tickets are not collected. Some storytellers prefer to put each child's name on a ticket and give it to him or her before every storyhour. No doubt this welcomes and involves the child, but I personally find this awkward for a variety of reasons: my memory for names is atrocious, and it is not polite to ask a child his or her name for the fifteenth time. Furthermore, children often mumble their names which can complicate the distribution of the tickets. Yet, if you can remember names easily because the group is small enough and stable, try using personalized tickets. Children do like them. This method works especially well if you are a teacher or day-care provider who does not need to promote a storyhour (since you probably have a captive audience!), but rather wish simply to get the children excited about it.

Special Invitations

The best way to draw an audience is to invite people personally. It is generally impractical to address and send individual invitations to a large number of children, but you can invite particular groups such as Ms. Jensen's fourth grade class, Brownie troop 614, or the Little League team. Other children come, of course, but even so, make it a practice to invite a new group to each session.

Minispeeches

Attending a meeting? Ask for a few minutes to announce your project. Keep it short! Try to sound enthusiastic. If you know in advance that you will be given some time, you might arrange a "visual" to gain your audience's full attention. Use the overhead slide projector that might be set up already. Bring a poster or related artifact to hold up. If you don't have a captive audience, try to capture one by an announcement in a crowded place. However, if a gathering fails to present itself, go on a walking campaign, visiting classrooms or groups to make your announcement.

Telephoning

Telephoning is another way to make personal contact. Call the children in your area (you may be able to get current telephone numbers through class lists or registration materials). When you reach a child or his parents, suggest the child bring a friend along.

Mailers

A personal computer and printer or photocopy machine can help you produce announcements in quantity for mailing. Keep your message simple and print it on eye-catching, colored paper. Because we are all inundated with "throw away mail," design your flyer so that it will be opened and, more important, read.

Try to send mailers to people who you know might be interested. You don't want to waste time and money sending announcements of a preschool storyhour to a retirement home unless it happens to have a volunteer grandparent program.

The City Water Bill

Many libraries seek and receive permission for city water bills or other monthly mailers to give news of current or upcoming library events. Contact your city hall to see if this is a possibility in your town. Wouldn't you love to receive news of a storytelling festival along with your bill for your March water usage?

Doorknob Hangers

When you are attempting to introduce a new program in your community, don't hesitate to borrow ideas from the commercial advertisers. For example, give something away in a door-to-door canvass, perhaps a package of a few seeds for the garden along with a notice describing the forthcoming event; hang the surprise on the doorknobs in the neighborhood you would most like to reach. Even in the city where no one has a yard? All the more reason to cheer up the residents with seeds, but choose some that will grow and thrive indoors. Ask your local wholesale florist what seeds are available and suitable to your purpose. Would he be a prospective contributor to the project? Consult your local garden club or horticultural society—either may be intrigued with an idea that promotes their interests at the same time.

Come grow with me! Library Story hour Saturday 2:00

The Fax Machine

What an invention! My husband works for a Korean company and he communicates with his colleagues almost entirely by fax. I send faxes all over the United States and to many overseas locations. I still find it incredible that I can send a message to Shanghai, China, or Dhahran, Saudi Arabia, from Miami Beach and receive a response almost immediately. I predict that every public library and school will soon have these machines in place. In fact, I think they will proliferate like the telephone in private residences. At the moment, faxes are still new enough that people pay attention to them, so send your promo piece via fax, and be sure that it will be noticed.

Newspapers

Many adults are somewhat hesitant about approaching a newspaper for publicity, but announcements of upcoming events are news too. Editors need to be told what is being planned, or they can't possibly publish any news about it. Write a publicity release with all the names and places spelled correctly and drop it off at the newspaper office yourself. You may even be able to suggest a time for taking pictures. Is your announcement an item for the community calendar or local news section? Maybe even the sports page? Ask the receptionist to help you contact the appropriate editor or reporter.

A follow-up news story or picture after the event is over creates a good image for the future. However, if there is a superabundance of activity at the same time—Christmas, for instance, usually crowds the community calendar—you may want to consider whether publicity before or after the event would be most helpful to your program in the long run.

Don't forget to write a thank-you note to the paper if it did a good job of covering your event. Reporters are human, too, and appreciate a kind word. Many libraries establish contact with a particular reporter or editor on a newspaper so that they can always speak to the same person when they have news. Remember that your news about a program of stories about Spain might just possibly be the most exciting item in the paper for the reader who is planning a trip to that country.

Radio and Television

Radio and television stations are licensed by the Federal Communications Commission, and, as part of their obligation to the public, they are required to offer a certain amount of public affairs programming. This includes announcements for non-profit organizations which should encourage you to establish contact with your local radio and TV stations. Well in advance of your event, find your way to the right office and ask the receptionist whom to contact. Be prepared to supply written copy for the announcements, for the less work a station has to do, the more likely it will be inclined to help you.

Paid Advertisements

If you find it impossible to get an article in the newspaper or an announcement on the air, consider buying an ad. This may be much less expensive than you think. By all means, try to get someone to donate the price of the ad but if that fails, try for a discount at least.

Summing It Up

You're probably saying to yourself, "You mean I have to plan the storyhour, learn the stories, and do all this to publicize it?" The answer, of course, is that you may not need to do all of the foregoing to publicize your program, but you may have to do some. In many communities, if you whisper, a crowd appears. In others, the first few story sessions have to be advertised, and after that you may not need to do another thing.

Furthermore, no one says that you personally have to handle the promotion by yourself. Perhaps you have people on your staff who would enjoy doing the publicity. Allow on-the-job time to create materials or suggest that they go home early in order to make posters at home. If you are part of a school system, ask the graphic arts department to help you. Solicit help—a high school art class project to make posters for your event may be just what the art teacher was looking for.

There are always people who volunteer their time to worthwhile projects, if they are asked. Whether you enlist their aid formally through the Friends of the Library or informally by asking your own friends and contacts, be sure you tell your volunteers exactly what you would like done and when you expect it to be finished. Also, be sure that you send a thank-you note when the project is over, even if the volunteer is your sister.

One of my former students, now head of a library, reported to me that she had tried all of my publicity ideas except dressing up as a witch and walking through the community to advertise a Halloween program. I have, therefore, left that particular idea off this list. You may find some of these publicity ideas more useful or easier to use than others. Fine! Whatever works for you is best. The point is: *Spread the Word!*

4 / Introducing and Closing the Program

What a nightmare. We were called up to defend our tax returns by the IRS twice in one year. One case had been pending for several years as we moved three times, switched accountants, and appealed through several levels of the tax department.

Since my husband, Peter, and I both travel extensively it is difficult to get us together in the same place at the same time. At last, Peter, our accountant, and I were all going to be in town at once. I am not known for keeping terribly good records, so on the way to our appointment I was briefed by both the accountant and by my husband. "When she says This, you should say That," instructed the accountant. "And when she says That, you should say This," said Peter. "Yes, sir. Yes, dear," I replied as we walked to the IRS office.

"Dr. Bauer, please explain what it is you actually do on your travels," the IRS representative asked.

I opened my briefcase, took out my cheerleading pom poms, and began my explanation with the library cheer originated by Garrison Keillor. I use this cheer to begin many of my programs for both children and adults. Not long afterwards, we were told by the IRS that our case was closed.

A good opening can make your program. Did my silly introduction make a good impression on the Internal Revenue Service? I don't know, but it makes a great . . . and true story.

It's not enough to have developed good content for your presentation; you must also plan the introductions, the transitions between stories, poems, magic tricks and puppet plays, and your conclusion.

Setting the Mood

The introduction to a single story or to the program as a whole often sets the mood for the entire period. A question such as "How many of you like to laugh, raise your hands?" suggests that the story will be funny, and in effect, you have set the mood that will elicit a humorous response to whatever you tell. On the other hand, if you want to create an atmosphere of romance or suspense, you might use only a candle for lighting and introduce the story at a slower, more reserved tempo.

The Storyhour Symbol

A traditional opening is the lighting of a candle. When the candle is burning the children learn that the time has come to settle down and listen. After the last story is told, the storyteller or a child from the audience blows out the candle and everyone silently makes a wish. If you don't want to use the storyhour candle, substitute your own trademark. Perhaps you have a banner that you unfurl at the beginning of each program or a bell that rings to summon your audience. If you play the guitar, harmonica, or some other portable instrument, you may want to begin and end each program with your own theme song. Whatever you choose, it is pleasant in this era of sudden change to build and maintain a tradition in the storyhour, something that automatically means "It's time for stories."

Introducing the Story or Program

If you have planned the program around a theme, you may want to make some sort of general introduction before announcing each story. Suit the introduction to the group and to yourself, but keep it brief, taking care not to overwhelm the story itself.

One way to introduce the individual story is with a personal comment, perhaps to tell where you learned it, why you like it, or how it relates to a personal incident of your own.

For instance, you might tell about the time that you forgot to bring the salt on a camping trip. Everything tasted so flat that you were reminded of the English story "Cap O'Rushes," the story you are going to tell.

Another style of introduction is more academic. Look up some background information beforehand. Briefly discuss the author, country, or type of story you have chosen, but try not to make your introduction sound like a lecture. Choose information that is of interest to you so you will sound enthusiastic when you present it. Such material frequently is found in the preface or introduction to a collection. Mira Ginsburg prefaces her collections of Russian stories with factual information about the lands and the peoples from whom the stories were collected. Books such as Georgess McHargue's *The Impossible People* offer a wealth of speculations on the origins and characteristics of giants, dwarfs, dragons, and fairy folk. Don't overlook the encyclopedia as a source of pertinent information for a lively, informative introduction.

The book itself can provide yet another introductory approach. You are, after all, telling stories to children to make them aware of the fact that stories come from books and to encourage them to read stories on their own. A good introduction, then, might be simply to display the book and tell your listeners that in it is the story they are about to hear. Nearby, you might also exhibit several books containing similar stories, either variants of the one you are about to tell or with related themes.

Still another way of introducing material, related to the theater program, is to borrow a useful device from vaudeville: an

easel holding large cards, on each of which is printed the title of the story you will tell and the title of the book it comes from, if they differ. Display the appropriate title card immediately before you tell the story. The lettering on the cards must look professional and be large enough to be read easily. If you have access to a personal computer or to paste-on letters, this may be a useful idea for you.

Artifacts and Crafts

An artifact or exhibit, when you include it as part of the storyhour, may serve to focus attention, aid the listener to recall the story, or arouse curiosity and assuredly helps make the storyhour an exciting, special time. Experience will bear out that a variety of objects used in different ways really does make the program visually as well as aurally interesting. Besides, looking for, selecting, or making just the right item to introduce a story is a fascinating and often satisfying part of the storyteller's preparation.

If you do sometimes use an artifact in the storyhour, make sure it is an item of quality. Mass-produced gimmickry that passes for art abounds in our country and we need not make a special effort to show it to children. At the same time, before you go on to the sections with ideas for buying or making objects relating to storytelling, let me caution you about becoming too involved with the visual at the expense of the proper learning and telling of your story. For those who delight in "little things"—antiques and crafted objects—this can be a danger. On the other hand, if you think of yourself as all thumbs, incapable of making anything, I encourage you to try some of these projects, since most not only are simple to do but also are fun and otherwise rewarding. Then too, consider the possibility of trading your time. For example, if you can't sew and a friend or colleague is an excellent seamstress, trade her a freshly baked pie or some baby-sitting time for the storytelling apron you've been yearning to have. Have you ever noticed, though, that if a person can sew she can usually bake, too?

Many of the ideas I suggest may seem more appropriate for the preschool or primary program, and they are, but older children and even middle schoolers will enjoy seeing your treasured childhood stuffed animal. For older audiences, I suggest using advertising gimmicks as your visuals. Try giant dollar bills from a promotional bank brochure if your story is about money or greed. Or how about photographs of slick automobiles or boats from magazine ads, if they fit your subject matter? Too, many fine bookstores give out beautifully illustrated bookmarks that make nice gifts for older audiences.

Things to Buy or Bring from Home

Antique book and game replicas. These are interesting for children to see, but go in and out of print too quickly to list. Check during the Christmas shopping season and in country gift shops for these items. I have seen Alice in Wonderland, Babar, and Paddington Bear games, for instance.

A box. Find something pretty, perhaps antique silver or carved wood. When you open it, the magic of storyland flies out. Keep the lid open until the storyhour is finished. Let the children help you catch the magic and close the box for another day.

Coloring books. Browse through the trade coloring books in a bookstore or gift shop to find book character designs. This sort of book is not usually available in toy stores. Use the pictures in an exhibit or create souvenirs of your book program.

Doll house furniture. Children are always fascinated with miniature furniture and home furnishings. Check at hobby and gift shops. There are also shops devoted exclusively to miniatures.

Draw a shirt. You'd like to wear an illustration from your favorite book on a tee shirt? Or the wildly imaginative drawing made by a child in your storytelling program? Many tee shirt shops will reproduce any artwork or photograph on a tee shirt for you to wear at your next storyhour special. Other firms that do this often advertise in the shopper's sections of magazines and the Sunday newspapers.

Figurines. You may find book characters or nursery figures at your local bookstore or gift shop. Some favorites are Winnie the Pooh and his friends from the Hundred Acre Wood, Alice in Wonderland, and the characters from *The Wonderful Wizard of Oz.*

Finger puppets. Knitted finger puppets to use with nursery rhymes and other children's poetry are easily made, if you knit. If you don't, you can often buy such characters at craft fairs or hobby shows. Felt finger puppets are somewhat easier to make. Cut out characters in duplicate and use craft glue or sew together leaving the bottom open for your finger. Remember, you don't need to duplicate a character from a favorite illustration precisely. Use these patterns for Little Red Riding Hood as a guide.

Holiday decorations. You will want to have appropriate decorations and maybe even a special storyhour on the major holidays. A Halloween jack-o-lantern, a Christmas tree or gingerbread house, and so on. Chase's Annual Events Calendar, available from Contemporary Books, 180 North Michigan Ave., Chicago, IL 60601, is a must for alerting the program planner to real and imagined celebrations.

Interesting and unusual containers. Often something is packaged in such an imaginative way it seems as though there must be a storytelling use for it. The plastic "eggs" that contain pantyhose and other attractive packages can be decorated and filled with objects or book titles and opened before you tell each story.

Live animals. Bring a rabbit, a bird, a dog, or a cat from home to show the children, then read books or tell stories about that

animal. Caution: Be aware that this does not always work out and that a live animal can be incredibly distracting. One of my students once brought a real bear cub to the university for a storyhour. Although the cub was very young, the situation got completely out of hand when he began clawing, growling, and knocking over the furniture in the receptionist's office. The uproar attracted a crowd outside the library door before the animal finally calmed down. It was fortunate that our spectators were college students rather than impressionable three-year-olds.

Music box. You may have one with a tune that lends itself to a program theme, e.g., "Raindrops Keep Falling on My Head" (rain stories) or "Who's Afraid of the Big Bad Wolf?" (*The Three Little Pigs*). If you don't have a music box, perhaps you can borrow one that plays an appropriate tune for that special storyhour you've been wanting to present.

Postcards and greeting cards. Searching for book-oriented cards can be an all-consuming hobby . . . and an expensive one. They make excellent exhibits, however. Illustrators of juvenile literature, such as Sandra Boynton, Wallace Tripp, and Tomie de Paola, have drawn lovely cards for greeting card companies.

Puppets. A handmade or purchased monkey puppet for the *Curious George* stories or a favorite puppet, named by the children, who becomes your constant storyhour friend and assistant, may help identify your storyhour program (see also chapter 16, Puppetry).

Recordings or tapes. Music at the beginning or the end of the storyhour helps give the program a feeling of continuity. Choose something to fit the mood of your stories.

Stack boxes or nesting dolls. Although these articles are usually imported, they are not necessarily expensive. They come from Scandinavia, Russia, Poland, Germany, and Japan and are generally available at Christmas. Introduce the first story, tell it, then open the outer doll. Introduce a finger play and open the next doll. Tell a story and open the third, continuing in this manner until there is only one doll left to say good-bye to the children. Use the stacking boxes in the same way.

Storytelling apron. You can make a muslin apron with removable pockets in primary colors. I depend on mine! The storytell-

er's apron enables you to put objects representing each of the stories you plan to tell in the pockets. As a child calls out a color, you extract the object representing that story, and begin to tell it.

Stuffed animals or dolls. Use an old favorite such as a worn stuffed rabbit to represent Margery Bianco's *The Velveteen Rabbit* or a fuzzy teddy bear when you tell about Winnie the Pooh and Christopher Robin. Be aware that the Walt Disney Pooh characters are not modeled after the original illustrations by Ernest H. Shepard. However, you can find a *Cat in the Hat* doll that young children easily recognize as well as dolls representing the characters in *Wild Things* by Maurice Sendak and *Where's Waldo?* books. Try to find handmade, quality stuffed animals and dolls to use in your storyhours. The children already see too many shoddily made stuffed animals and dolls with fixed plastic smiles everywhere else.

Treasure trunk. Use a trunk, suitcase, or specially decorated cardboard box to hold the books of the day. If your trunk is pretty and small enough, it can become the permanent surprise box in your library or classroom.

Things to Make or Do

Following are some suggestions for things to make for introducing the books in a program or for exhibits. If you enjoy arts and crafts you won't mind the time it takes to complete these projects. Remember too, that once you make something it may be used many times in many different ways.

Book bracelets. Reproduce the bracelets illustrated here on heavy colored stock. Fasten with tape or Velcro and offer as a souvenir of your book program.

Clothespin dolls. Search through the stores in your town until you find some old-fashioned wooden clothespins. Dress these with felt and fabric to represent the characters in the stories you tell.

Giant books. Use poster board to make giant book covers. Such a "book" can serve as a permanent beginning to your storyhour. Inside the covers, on individual sheets of paper, you can list the program of today's storyhour, changing the listing for each storyhour.

Go Fish game. Cut several 2-inch fish from posterboard and attach a paper clip to the mouth of each. Then print the title of a story or program theme on the back of every fish. Removable labels (available at the stationery store as mailing labels) make the fish reusable. Next, make a fishing rod with a stick, a length of string, and a magnet for bait. (Small inexpensive magnets can be bought at toy shops and hardware stores.) The fish pond can be a sturdy corrugated box with high sides (hand-decorated, of course) so that the fisherman doesn't see what he or she is fishing for. Choose a child from the group to fish for the stories and as each fish is caught, be prepared to tell the story it represents. Change the titles for each session.

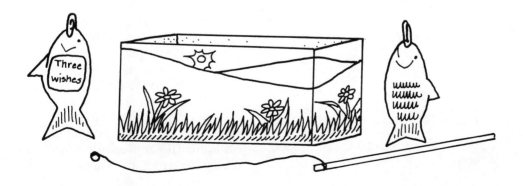

Handmade blocks. Cut a length of 4-inch by 4-inch lumber into equal sections to make 4-inch by 4-inch blocks. For smaller blocks cut 1-inch by 1-inch lumber in a similar manner. Sand the wood and apply a coat of shellac or polyurethane varnish

as a sealant. Paint the blocks if you prefer them to be more colorful. Cut out and paste pictures from discarded books on the sides of the blocks. Some illustrated examples are shown here. I think Beatrix Potter's pictures perfectly suit these storytime blocks. Cover the pictures with several coats (the more the better) of polyurethane varnish. Let each coat dry overnight for a smooth finish. If you hate cleanup jobs as much as I do, wrap your varnish brush in aluminum foil and store it in the freezer after each use.

Miniature books. Children like small things. Try making a miniature posterboard folder that looks like a book. Decorate it with a drawing representing a specific title and place inside a quote that will serve as an introduction. To finish your book, cover it with clear contact paper or laminate it if you have access to a laminating press.

Painted rocks. What do you do with those pretty rocks you brought home from your vacation? Paint them with a book title on one side, a picture representing the book on the other.

Puzzles. Make use of the illustrations from a discarded book or book jackets. Mount them on cardboard, laminate or cover them with clear contact paper, and cut out the pieces for a puzzle. Make sure you identify the pieces by a number or symbol on the back so that you can gather them back together. You may have enough puzzles for each child or two children working as a team; when all the puzzles are together, it's book time. You can make your own puzzles from scratch by drawing freehand or tracing a picture from a book and proceeding as above.

Story bag. Draw the figures of animals and characters, as well as other identifiable objects from your favorite picture books on stiff paper or tagboard. Cut out and place in a special large bag or envelope. Let a child reach into the bag and pick out a figure. Whichever one he or she chooses represents the book you read. Be sure you always have on hand the represented books, ready to read or show. Small animals, other book-related figurines, and objects carved of wood or made of other materials also are suitable for the story bag.

Story map. On a mounted map of the world mark with tacks or small flags the origin of the stories you will tell. Point out to the group where the story you are about to tell, or have told, comes from.

Between Stories

Some storytellers find the transition between two formal story presentations somewhat awkward. The atmosphere or mood you wish to maintain should dictate your handling of the time between stories. If your preference is for the more formal mood, such as that suggesting a theater presentation, you might simply pause briefly between stories, then launch into an introduction for the next story. Or, if time permits, you might give a brief booktalk to introduce a new addition to the library or to promote an old favorite. In this more formal, dignified atmosphere the children will remain seated and participate by listening only.

If you prefer a more relaxed atmosphere, you may want to use your transition period for participation activities: games, responsive songs, riddles, or creative dramatics. You will find in the chapters on Non-narrative sources, Music, and Creative Dramatics Plus, lots of lively suggestions for transitional material.

Closing the Program

Some storytellers sing a song or recite the same rhyme to begin and end the storyhour. Do what you find works for you. A simple "Thank you for listening" might be sufficient. If the storyhour opens with a ritual, perhaps you will want to close it with a similar ritual, such as blowing out the storyhour candle.

Is there something you'd like your listeners to do at the close of the storyhour? Instead of sending them straight home, perhaps you will invite them to look at, touch, or play with exhibit material. When the program is held in a library, you'll want to suggest that the audience might want to check out a book. Don't forget to remind the group about the next program.

Something to Take Home

The book you featured in the storyhour might just lend itself to inexpensive or virtually free souvenirs. Of course you can't give something away every time, but for that special occasion, keep your imagination open. Here are a few ideas about what to give after the story:

Apple seeds. (It won't take long to save enough to hand out.) To remember Charles Micucci's *The Life and Times of the Apple* (Orchard, 1992) or Betsy Maestro's *How Do Apples Grow*; art by Giulio Maestro (Harper, 1992).

Balloons. (Do not have to be blown up!) To remember "In which Eeyore has a birthday and gets two presents" in A. A. Milne's *Winnie the Pooh*; art by Ernest H. Shepard, colored by Hilda Scott (Dutton, 1974) or Bernie Zubrowski's *Balloons*; art by Roy Doty (Morrow, 1991).

Beads. (Available at craft or hobby shops.) To remember Byrd Baylor's *One Small Blue Bead*; art by Ronald Himler (Scribner, 1992).

Buttons. To remember Margarette S. Reid's *The Button Box*; art by Sarah Chamberlain (Dutton, 1990).

Cheerios. To remember the doughnuts in Robert McCloskey's *Homer Price* (Viking, 1943).

Chocolate chip cookies. To remember James Marshall's *George and Martha* (Houghton, 1972).

Fudge. To remember James Howe's *Harold and Chester in Hot Fudge*; art by Leslie Morrill (Morrow, 1990).

Muffins. To remember Laura Joffe Numeroff's *If You Give a Moose a Muffin*; art by Felicia Bond (Harper, 1991).

Paper-folded boats. To remember Rabindranath Tagore's *Paper Boats*; art by Grayce Bochak (Caroline House, 1992).

Peach pits. (Paint them gold.) To remember Nathan Zimelman's *I Will Tell You of Peach Stone*; art by Haru Wells (Lothrop, 1976).

Peanut butter cookies. To remember Sue Alexander's *World Famous Muriel and the Magic Mystery*; art by Marla Frazee (Crowell, 1990).

Pebbles. (Available free on the beach and purchased inexpensively at the aquarium or garden shop.) To remember William Steig's *Sylvester and the Magic Pebble* (Windmill, 1969).

Pizza. To remember Marjorie Pillar's *Pizza Man* (Crowell, 1991).

Play money. To remember Sarah Stewart's *The Money Tree*; art by David Small (Farrar, 1991) or David M. Schwartz' *If You Made a Million*; art by Steven Kellogg (Lothrop, 1989).

Pumpkin seeds. (Save them from the jack-o-lantern.) To remember Gloria Skurzynski's *The Magic Pumpkin*; art by Rocco Negri (Four Winds, 1971) or Lennart Hellsin's *The Wonderful Pumpkin*; art by Svend Otto (Atheneum, 1976).

Raisins. To remember Russel Hoban's *A Baby Sister for Frances*; art by Lillian Hoban (Harper, 1964).

Stones. To remember Susan Patron's *Burgoo Stew*; art by Mike Shenon (Orchard, 1991).

Vegetable seeds. (Buy at less than half price at the end of the growing season from seed wholesalers.) To remember Ruth Krauss's
The Carrot Seed; art by Crockett Johnson (Harper, 1945).

Walnut shells. (Save them till you have enough.) To remember
Jean B. Hardendorff's *A Bed Just So*; art by Lisl Weil (Four
Winds, 1975).

Discipline or Holding Your Own

I like to pretend that there is no such thing as having a discipline
problem in the storyhour. How could anyone not want to hear a
story, I think to myself. However, a former student of mine called
me up recently in great distress, complaining about the vandal-
ism in her inner-city library and the disruptions in her storyhour. Each person must react to these situations as he or she
sees best, but here are a few general thoughts:

Not every disruption is a destructive disruption. You should
not necessarily consider it to be a problem if children articulate
their reactions: "Look at that elephant!" "Oh, no, she better watch
out!" Such verbal reactions reflect interest and attention. You do
not always have a problem if one child hits another—that too is
also natural and can be taken care of by calmly and quietly sepa-
rating them. You may be able to minimize problems of discipline
if the storyhour is an elective activity. It may help if you are fortunate enough to have separate facilities for programs. If someone wants to come to the storyhour, which is a special treat, he
or she must behave or not be allowed to come the next time.

It is well to remember that not everyone is interested in books;
indeed, some may have had bad book experiences. Once during
my career as a high school librarian, I was reduced to tears when
the students refused to listen to a carefully chosen short story I
had prepared for them. My first reaction was to forget the whole
thing. Then I slowly realized that part of the problem was my
own shortsightedness. The school was attended by "difficult" students. They had very little interest in literature, but loved magazines and books with pictures. To them the library was a place to
play cards, to listen to music, and to exchange gossip with friends.
These young adults had never heard a story meant for adults or

a booktalk. I'd simply gone about the whole matter too fast, deciding suddenly one day, "Today I'm going to tell you something about a book you'd enjoy." No wonder they thought I'd lost my senses.

After I had swallowed my pride and reconsidered, I started over again. I had been writing little notes on a blackboard near my desk each day suggesting books or articles to read. Now I began writing "Next drop-out soon" or "Have you been invited to drop-out?" Since the students were always talking about leaving school I thought my programs should be times to "drop out." I asked, by written invitation, only five people to the first program, which I held in the book stacks, no other secluded place being available. The kids I chose I hoped were the leaders of the rebellion and one very pretty girl. They all came, out of curiosity I suppose, and I kept them less than ten minutes with a recording of two "in" songs and two books: the *Encyclopedia of Sports* (I also could have used the *Guinness Book of World Records*) and a new book on sports car racing.

The next time I invited three of the same boys back and invited four new ones. By the tenth week I was back in the library proper, talking to everyone. Many were still ignoring me, listening to the radio and playing cards while I talked, but at least they weren't throwing things, and I had reached a few.

5 / Preparing and Telling the Story

The plane is heading for Fairbanks, Alaska. I've listened to the second officer describe the scenery, eaten my little bag of peanuts, and finished my mystery. Now what? Easy. Take out the story I'd like to tell next and continue the learning process. For the purist, the ultimate in storytelling is to tell a story without props or pictures—just *you* and the story. However, whether you tell a story simply standing or sitting in front of an audience or with a stage full of production items, your storytelling techniques will be the same.

What is this mysterious art? Is there really a magical secret to learning and telling a story that only a few can discover? I don't think so. In my experience with several hundred storytelling students, I've found that nearly everyone can tell an acceptable story. As for being an outstanding storyteller, that is a different matter, for storytelling is like other arts: in order to be truly great, you almost have to be born with inner talent. How do you know whether or not you have it? Only by working on some stories and telling them to an audience. But, to repeat, almost everyone who takes the time to learn can become a competent storyteller. When I used to teach, for example, I noticed that many Asian students were much more advanced in drawing than my American students. I was curious about this phenomenon and when I visited Asia I inquired about art training in the schools. It turned out that my students' art talent did not spring from nothing. The simple fact is that instead of being a sometimes-taught elective, art is part of the curriculum. The moral that applies here is: what you are exposed to, you can learn. It holds true of storytelling. Please try. Those of us who are telling stories need you out there to carry on an age-old tradition.

Perhaps the most important element in good storytelling is finding the right story for you. Each of us has a distinct personality that should be capitalized upon. Are you someone who speaks softly and slowly? Or do you have a deep booming voice and a bawdy nature? Maybe you are "the life of the party," always the first with a new joke that you tell with vigorous, flamboyant movements. What is your taste in literature? Do you like to cuddle up with long philosophical treatises, or do you prefer gothic novels? You don't have to actually sit down and analyze yourself. As you read through story collections, myths, epics, short stories, and other materials suitable for storytelling use, you will find something that appeals to, and is usually suitable for, you.

We are always reading about professional actors and actresses who don't want to have a reputation for doing only one role. We hear of the comedian who would like to play serious roles or the character actor who wants to attempt a role as a musical comedy hero. You too may wish that you had a genuine Appalachian accent so you could tell a Jack Tale with authenticity. But for now, start at the beginning: choose something that suits you. I find, for instance, that I'm mostly attracted to humorous folktales, but I don't want to have a one-sided repertoire. As I learn new stories I try to add new types to my list so that I can end up with a Russian fable, a Greek myth, a story by Oscar Wilde, or any other kind of story a program requires.

Choosing the story to tell is important, so take it seriously. Read as much as you can and make sure that you like your final selection; you'll be spending a lot of time together!

Learning a Story

After you have chosen a story that you feel is worth your time, the actual learning begins. No one can tell you how to learn a story, for each of us has a method of his or her own. You will find, as with all endeavors, that the key lies in practice. Your first attempt may take a great deal of time, but after you learn how to learn, the whole process will become much easier. You will probably want to begin with a simple folktale. An authored story, one that relies heavily on the flavor of the language, has to be learned almost word for word. This is a more difficult project and can be tackled later.

You may want to adapt my way of learning a story to suit your needs. First, I find that I want to own the story that I'm going to learn; this usually means actually buying a copy of the book. My interest in storytelling has resulted in a large personal library (10,000 books at last count!). I bought the book that contained the first story I ever learned and I have been buying books ever since. Owning the book means that I can at any time go back to a story to refresh my memory, and I am always certain of having a copy of the book to exhibit on my storyhour table. If I don't want to carry a book around with me, I take along a copy of the story (three cheers for the invention of the copy machine!). Whenever I get the chance I read the story over. You'll be amazed at the number of spare moments you can find in your day: standing in line to get into a movie, the waiting room at the dentist, waiting for a bus, in the bathtub, waiting for a meal to cook, and coffee breaks at the office. How wonderful to put all that waiting time to real use! I read a new story all the way through at least three times. Then I begin telling it to myself. If I forget a section I stop for that session. The next time I start from the beginning again and try to learn a little more. Much of my learning process entails other people. I like to practice on people. Some storytellers look in a mirror to practice. I find this absolutely terrifying, but you should try it; it may be the right thing for you. Whom do I practice on? On everyone, the family first. Children are critical and appreciative, roommates are amused, spouses are sometimes bored. Friends are willing, at least the first time. But I find strangers the best listeners of all. They can be caught completely unaware. Try this: You're out for a day of skiing and find yourself on a ski lift with a man you don't know in the opposite chair, a 15-minute ride with no escape. Simply ask "Want to hear a story?" He has to say "yes," so tell your story. Imagine how he'll describe this experience when he returns from his ski trip. Or this: You are at a dinner party. Someone asks what you do, and you answer, "I'm a librarian," "I'm a teacher," or "I'm a volunteer storyteller at the local library." Of course, then someone else will say, "Tell a story." Do it. It's good practice. The more you actually tell the story the better storyteller you will be.

When you feel you really know the words of the story, you can begin working on what the words mean and how to express that meaning. Beginners often make the mistake of thinking they are ready for a group of children once they have learned the words of the story. You also must feel so comfortable with the words that you will not panic if you forget where you are in the story. You must be able to give thought to "feeling" the events of the story. It is helpful to keep a file of stories that you have learned or want to learn for easy availability.

Your next question will probably be, "Should I memorize the story?" The answer is that all-encompassing: "That depends."

Some storytellers feel that, except in the case of a literary tale or a story someone has written, memorization should be kept at a minimum or that it should not be a part of learning a story at all. They feel that you make a story more personally your own if you tell it in your own words. I do not agree. In nearly every instance, the stories you tell will have been selected from books. No matter that originally the story existed in the unwritten province of folklore. The source you are using was adapted by someone. If you choose your material carefully, your author will be competent as a collector and as a writer. Unless you feel that your phrasing is better, why not lean heavily upon the printed word? This does not mean that you will sit down and learn word for word what is in a book. It means that you will memorize some key phrases, or that you will memorize only the beginning and ending of a work, or that you will memorize a particularly enchanting passage or two.

One suggestion that I hope you will take is to list the events of each story in your mind. After all, you can't kill the dragon until the hero has met that fearsome beast. Think logically and you will learn logically. After you tell the story to an audience you will find yourself making subtle changes; you are making it your own. When I first began taping a children's television storytelling series, my director asked me for a script. I gave him a copy of a folktale taken from a book. Halfway through rehearsal, I could see him in the director's glass booth jumping around and literally tearing his hair. He stopped the show and started ranting through the loudspeaker, "What king? There's no king here!" Indeed, I had added a character without even realizing it and thought that I was telling the story exactly as printed. But I did not remove the king from the story; I liked him. Eventually the director and I decided not to use a script at all, since I changed the stories with each telling!

What needs to be emphasized is that there is no right or wrong way to go about learning a story. In my seminars and workshops I spend little time discussing the actual learning process. Anyone who has gone through an organized educational system in the United States or abroad has found his or her own way of learning material. The only encouragement I can really give is to those who have been out of a formal learning situation for some time. At first, learning a story will take some time, but after a short period it will be easier.

This is a good place to mention the art of relearning a story. Obviously, you are not going to all the trouble of learning a story to tell it only once. Or at least, I hope you're not. It would be a pity not to tell your stories on many different occasions. However, there are stories that are only used once a year, or on special holidays, such as Christmas stories. You may be actively engaged in storytelling activities one year, but then be away doing other things for a time. What do you do when you want to reuse a story that's been dormant in your mind? Take it out, dust it off, shine it up a bit, and you're ready to go. The second time around is much easier, especially if you learned the story well initially. It is now that your copy of the story comes in handy. Simply take it out, read it through a time or two, practice a little, and you're all set. Sometimes you will be astonished to discover that when you tell the story the next time you do it even better than before. Somewhere, somehow, the story has jelled and truly become your own. Don't take a chance, though, on dredging a story back up through your memory; always look at the story again before telling it.

At times you will find a story that is too long to learn, or one that has a good plot but is written in stilted or unsuitable language. It's tempting to try to cut or rewrite the story to suit your own purposes. My advice in this situation depends on your own storytelling experience. What I strongly suggest is that you look for another story to learn, because adapting a story can be a difficult procedure. If you are a late-night TV-movie viewer, you have seen that even professional editors often make mistakes, often sacrificing the more poignant and important scenes for spectacle. You might well find yourself doing something similar. This is not to say that you should never cut a story; it just means that you should be extra careful when you do it. You may be able to find another version of the story that better fits your needs. A popular picture-book version of a nonsense story is Arlene Mosel's *Tikki Tikki Tembo*. However, I prefer a much shorter, more compact version collected by Jeanette Perkins Brown in *The Storyteller in Religious Education* (Pilgrim, 1951).

If you work at an institution, school, library, church, or temple telling stories on a regular basis, or if you run a birthday party storytelling business, or if you plan to become a professional storyteller, you will want to keep records of your storytelling activities. Your records will include information on what stories were told, on what date, and to whom. You might even want to include comments on the proceedings and on the success or failure of the programs.

Wherever you tell stories, you will want to keep your own personal file. Even a simple list of the stories in your repertoire is better than nothing at all. At first it will seem silly to write down the one story that you know. How could you ever forget that you learned it? Doubtless you will learn many stories, and, as your general knowledge increases, your memory for details may decrease. The story file is somewhat like a recipe file. If you own the actual books you may not need to keep a copy of the story in another location, but at least make a notation of which book the story is from. I am merely trying to spare you some of the agonizing moments I've spent searching for a lost story. I've been known to run all around the library, school, and my own home screaming, "Thief! Thief!" only to find out that the robber is my own sloppiness. But I do have a list of stories I tell carefully tucked into my wallet. One never knows when one will be asked to tell a story. So, when I am asked, I just whip out my little list and decide what to tell. The list is especially useful as an indicator that you need to broaden your horizons. One glance will tell you that it's time to look for a suitable Greek myth because you already know so many stories about witches.

Telling the Story

Now you are ready to tell your story. The most important advice I can give you is this: Do not "act out" the story. You are not an actor, but a storyteller. Don't use your voice to convey characterization, unless you have had voice training. Portraying Father Bear with a big powerful voice, and a squeaky voice for Baby Bear turns out to be a disaster for most people. Characterization emerges through descriptive language: "a little wisp of a girl . . ." or "he was so thin he could only eat noodles." Let the language tell the story.

I once had a very competent acting student in my storytelling class who insisted on using dialects in her telling of Joseph Jacobs's *Tom Tit Tot,* an English variant of *Rumpelstiltskin.* Her plan was to have the girl speak with a cockney accent and the prince with an educated Oxford accent. She did it the first time so charmingly that I invited her to tell the story to another class. In the middle of the story, the characters switched roles. The girl became the Oxford graduate; the prince, the cockney. This experience heightened my resolve to caution novices on the use of dialects. On the other hand, a regional story is very much improved with an authentic dialect. A good Irish brogue improves an Irish story 100 percent. However, be aware that some dialects can be offensive to their respective ethnic groups if they are used incorrectly. I personally try to stay away from most accented stories, although I feel that I don't do a bad job with a French or a Jewish accent. If you come from an ethnic or national background and have heard a particular accent for a number of years, you might want to try a story using that accent.

Difficult or unpronounceable words are another problem. If you don't know what a word means, look it up. Don't guess. It is not only embarrassing, it's unprofessional to say a word sweetly and gently that turns out to be an insult that should be said harshly and with a certain amount of venom in the voice. You don't want to be caught without a correct answer when someone asks you what is a "calabash," a "billet" of wood, or a "dreidel." I don't think it is necessary to give another meaning to the word while you tell the story, either. Nor do I advise simply removing the word and substituting something easier. It ruins the original spirit of the story. I am appalled by the number of books in the library that have been mutilated by teachers, who, in rewriting a book to read aloud, have gone through it, deleting words, replacing them with simpler words. An edition of a children's biography of Abraham Lincoln is an extreme example of this. An unknown hand had gone through changing words, even in direct quotations from letters written by Lincoln. It may sometimes be advisable to explain, before you begin your telling, a word or phrase that is central to the understanding of the story. One of my favorite stories is Isaac Bashevis Singer's "The First Shlemiel" in his *Zlateh the Goat*. In New York I told the story many times and to everyone's great amusement. The first time that I told it in Oregon it didn't get the same reaction. Much to my dismay I discovered that many Oregonians didn't know the meaning of the word "shlemiel." I puzzled about how to introduce the story in the future. At last I found a way that involved teaching the audience two Yiddish terms instead of one. "The difference," I now explain, "between a shlemiel and a shlimazl is that a shlemiel is the kind of a guy who is always spilling his soup and a shlimazl is the guy he spills it on."

If you are wondering what to wear, wear whatever you feel comfortable in, but I suggest that you wear something a little special, not just the clothes you wear to rake leaves. However, keep in mind that no one is coming to look at you. They are coming to hear you tell a story. Don't wear anything that might be particularly distracting or that you might play with. Beware of the locket or chain around your neck that you unconsciously twist and untwist as you speak. I usually don't recommend a costume, a witch or whatever, unless the occasion is a dressing-up day and you are portraying a favorite character. Some people choose to wear the same distinctive article of clothing for each storyhour; this may be a storytelling apron or they may copy the African custom of wearing a story hat.

I like to stand while I'm telling a story for two reasons. The first is that I like to be able to express myself somewhat with body movements. The other reason is that I want to create a more formal atmosphere when I am telling a story in the traditional manner. Standing separates the storyteller from the audience and creates the more formal feeling of the theater.

A case for sitting can be made for exactly the opposite reasons. Sitting in a chair or on a stool confines your movements so that the audience must get most of the impact of the story aurally. If you and your audience are sitting, a more intimate atmosphere is established. Choose whichever suits *you* best.

It happens to the inexperienced and the experienced. It happens at the worst of times. You forget. You suddenly go quite blank. What should you do? Stop, and think. That is the only way out. A friend of mine was telling *Prince Sneeze* when she suddenly forgot what happened on the third sneeze, a very important part to the conclusion of the story. After a moment, she simply told her audience, "Remember that third sneeze and later I'll tell you what happened." When finally the phrase came to her, she stopped and said, "Remember that third sneeze? Now I'll tell you what happened," did just that, and continued her story.

You won't always possess such presence of mind. Sometimes you have to just quietly stand there until the story comes back to you. Maybe forgetting is one reason that we exhibit the book the story comes from. You can always pick up the book and glance at the story. Sometimes merely looking at the book will help you recover. Just don't panic.

Stage fright is a malady that strikes with various symptoms, including nausea, hot flashes, quavering voice, and frequent trips to the restroom! Some of us never have it, some of us always have it. I used to suffer dreadfully as a child from this peculiar sickness. Now it rarely strikes me. The reason for this is that I have much more self-confidence and feel sure of my material. One reaches this stage through experience. I do occasionally suffer various degrees of stage fright when I conjure up thoughts of an unseen audience. Suddenly my stomach will drop a foot or two at the thought of facing a possibly hostile group of colleagues at a conference. My fears have always been unjustified. Once I was asked to give a paper before the Philological Association of the West. Naturally, I pictured the association as being peopled with serious, grave gentlemen all contemplating the comma in Shakespeare. My subject was "Violence in Children's Folklore." I planned to show transparencies and sing (off-key) as part of my speech. After my introduction, I wobbled to my feet and croaked out the first sentence of two. When I recited the first bit of folklore,

> Mary had a little lamb
> Her father shot it dead
> And now it goes to school with her
> Between two chunks of bread

the audience of dark-suited men laughed—happily, joyously. They liked it! I had conjured up dire reactions for nothing. From this experience I learned the first rule to dispel stage fright: the audience is for you, they want you to succeed. They are so much on your side that they are afraid to react and sometimes you don't know what their reactions really are. This is, of course, one of the problems with adult groups. Children are easier to work with, and you probably will not suffer as much stage fright working with them (except at first) as you will with adults. Children react! They laugh and cry out loud.

My favorite story regarding stage fright is one purported to be a statement by Dwight D. Eisenhower: "I never feel stage fright anymore, I just imagine that the whole audience is naked, but I, the speaker, am fully clothed."

Common Faults

Ask your friends to tell you if you do any of these things:

Speak too fast. In an effort to "get it over with" we sometimes race through material. As a first-year storyteller at the New York Public Library, my storytelling supervisor came to observe me giving a storyhour. I told Harold Courlander's "The Goat Well." Afterwards she took me to lunch. Her remarks are stamped permanently into my memory. "Miss Feller, you have good expression. Someday you might be a good storyteller, but that story usually takes 15 minutes to tell and you told it in four minutes and 38 seconds."

Speak too slowly. Sometimes the whole pace of a story drops. We tend to talk too deliberately, almost caressing each word. This sometimes happens if you tell the story too often. You are actually a victim of boredom. I recall one school's Festival of Arts that a student and I were invited to attend. We went to at least 12 classes separately. My repertoire, at the time, was varied enough so that I could tell a different story to each class. The poor student only knew one story, which she told over and over. The pace of the story became slower and slower. She confessed afterward that near the end of the day she was no longer thinking about the story she was telling, but instead was planning an entire menu in her head for the guests who would be at her home that night!

Speak too softly. Remember that everyone has to hear you. Speak up and out. Don't be afraid to be heard. I was amused recently at a meeting in which the dean of a college had been asked to introduce a children's poet. He mumbled a few words, all the while looking at his feet. When the audience in the back complained of not being able to hear, he murmured that maybe a microphone was needed. "I don't think we'll need one," boomed the poet from the opposite side of the room. The dean shuffled off the platform and a tiny woman walked on to dominate the entire room with her resonant voice, without any mechanical aid.

You may find yourself in a situation where a microphone is needed. Be aware that using a microphone takes some experience. The most common pitfall is to stand too close to the microphone, thereby obstructing the audience's view of the speaker as well as distorting the sound. Because I often speak before large audiences, however, and since I like to move when I speak, I have purchased my own wireless microphone. It is small enough to carry with me and it plugs into audio systems at hotels, conference halls, and schools. As new equipment is purchased or replacements are made, I think the wireless microphone will be in more institutions. At a recent presentation in Japan at a rural junior high school, I was delighted to find that both the teacher who introduced me and I were provided with wireless microphones.

Speak with too high a voice. A common fault with many women is that their voices are naturally high. If you have this problem, and many women do, consciously practice dropping your voice when you speak publicly. It was interesting to me to hear tapes of the time I spent as a disc jockey. Between records, when I spoke extemporaneously, my voice was unpleasantly high; however, when I read the news my voice perceptibly dropped. That's when I made a conscious attempt to get my voice into a lower register.

Avoid eye contact. When you are talking to a group, you must make its members feel as though you are talking to each one individually. This is the great advantage of traditional storytelling. Freed from props and books, you are able to establish direct eye contact with every single member of your audience. Glance at a selected few in a random pattern. You will find yourself gratefully looking at someone who seems constantly nodding her or his head with approval and smiles. There is one of these in nearly every group. That person may be thinking about something else, but she or he seems to be hanging onto your every word. Contrasted to this person is the listener whose face is stone-blank. I sometimes find myself directing my entire presentation to what seems like a hostile face until that person reacts in some way. Try not to lose hope if someone in the audience actually falls asleep. Perhaps you've done it yourself when you were very tired and relaxed. Just remember that most of the audience is attentively listening.

Use distracting gestures. To gesture or not to gesture? I hope that I don't sound like a broken robot, but the answer is: it's up to you. My grandmother, who could recite poetry in nine different languages, had taken what she called "elocution." In elocution you were taught exactly when and which gesture to use. To a modern audience such mechanical gesturing may be comical, but I don't ever remember laughing at my Grandma, so all that arm waving, head hanging, and body turning must have been effective.

One of my students used to tell stories as if he were tied to a post and told not to move a muscle, not even to blink; yet his voice was mesmerizing and we fell completely under his spell. I know that I move around quite a bit when I tell a story, making particular use of hand gestures. If the question of what to do with your hands is at first a problem for you, my advice is to lightly clasp them behind you. When you feel that you must demonstrate the smallest or the tallest, show the size with your hands and again put them behind your back.

You may be unaware of aimless, distracting movements such as swaying or biting your lip; it helps to have a friend critique you to discover such faults. One of the torturous but effective devices I use in my storytelling classes is the videotape machine. If you have access to such a machine through the school system or library, use it to practice telling a story. It only takes a few minutes of watching a rerun of yourself to spot any outstanding shortcomings. Microphones are usually sensitive enough to pick up the sound of your voice, even if it is hoarse with fright. After an artificial situation such as this, you will find telling a story to a real live audience easy and enjoyable.

A Practice Story to Learn

No point in putting off your first storytelling attempt. Start today with this story. Try it now.

Start by reading the story, which begins on page 64. Obviously, if it doesn't appeal to you you'll have to use another story for this exercise.

Now read it again—this time paying special attention to the plot. Sound familiar? It's a variant of Hans Christian Andersen's "The Emperor's New Clothes." Recognizing that you already know the point of the story will make it easier to learn. Now list on paper, or in your head, the events in the story.

Tyll comes to town and represents himself as a portrait painter.

He is hired by the Duke and set up in comfortable quarters.

Various members of the Duke's family give Tyll suggestions for the portrait.

Tyll pretends to be painting but doesn't show his work.

The painting is shown and everyone pretends to see it.

The Duke's small son voices the message: "I see what I want to see."

The Duke recognizes that he has been duped, but takes it in good humor.

Tyll enjoys his new leisure with the Duke's son.

You see, eight sentences tell the whole story.

Now you add the touches that make it a story worth telling (and hearing). My version is told in the clicking cadence of the opening "clip, clop" of the donkey's hooves: *Tyll is ensconced comfortably at court.*

If you don't like the way I did it, add your own details. I chose several members of the court—the Grand Duchess, the Duke's daughter, the Duke, his steward, his advisor, and even the cook to make certain requests. Use my characters or make up your own.

I'm suggesting that you may change the story by adding or subtracting details. As I mentioned earlier, however, another way to learn the story is to essentially memorize the words as they are written.

Read the story over several times. Can you see the room where Tyll is "painting?" How about the Cook's puppy? What does it look like? It helps to visualize the setting and the characters and to hear the dialogue in your head.

Now tell it out loud to your mom, a good friend, or your cat. Don't worry that it is still a rough effort. After you know the words you can perfect the telling.

Once you are comfortable with the order of the story, you can play with voice intonation or gestures that may help your listeners visually see the characters you are representing. You may want to touch your "bald head" or show the girth of your stomach with your arms.

Now that you know the story, find someone else to tell it to. The story is not yours until you give it away.

TYLL PAINTS THE DUKE'S PORTRAIT

Clip, Clop. Clip, Clop. Here comes Tyll Ulenspiegel riding his old grey donkey into town.

And here comes the Duke riding on his sleek black horse.

"Good morning, your Honor," hails Tyll.

"Good morning to you," says the Duke. "What brings you to town?"

"I'm a portrait artist looking for work."

"Is that so?" says the Duke. "I just happen to be looking for someone to paint my family and the people of the court on the wall of my throne room. Let me see your work."

Tyll opens one of the saddle bags and takes out a painting of two older people and a dog.

"My parents and Ignatz, their dog," he introduces his relatives with a flourish.

"Nice work," says the Duke. "You're hired."

"Not so fast," says Tyll. "I have a few requests for my working conditions."

"Anything you want," says the Duke.

And that is how Tyll Ulenspiegel spent four months at court.

His donkey had a private stall and his own groom. He was brushed twice a day and ate heartily of the freshest green grass.

As for Tyll, he had requested three meals a day and a snack before bedtime. He was pampered by a servant who ran his bath and washed his painting smock.

Each day Tyll went to the chamber where the wall portrait was to be painted. He always carefully locked the door so that no one would enter while he was at work. "No one is to see the mural until I am ready to show it."

Every afternoon, Tyll entertained the Duke's family and their friends at tea, the tea provided by the Duke, of course. The guests were all curious to see their portraits and were constantly admonishing Tyll.

The Grand Duchess was so old that even she had forgotten how many years she had saluted the daily rising of the sun. She always wore

her best for tea with Tyll. "I know I am no longer beautiful," she would croak, "but in my day I was famous for the curl in my hair and the twinkle in my eye. I hope that you will paint me as I was in my twenties. Remember that my skin was as smooth and as rosy as the first apples of fall."

Tyll always smiled. "You are beautiful today, my lady."

The Duke's eldest daughter visited Tyll at teatime too. "Please, pretty please, may I see the portrait of me? I hope you didn't paint my bangs. I don't want to be remembered forever with this haircut. It was a mistake. Nurse cut it this way."

Tyll always smiled. "No, my lady, you can not see the portrait until it is done, but of course I painted you with the hairstyle of your dreams."

Even the Duke himself, who surely had other things to do, came by for tea one day. He was accompanied by his steward and his advisor. They all made requests for the mural.

"I hope you will represent me with a fuller beard."

"I can no longer fit into my purple pantaloons, but I'm sure you won't paint my stomach. It's here only temporarily."

"I had more hair when I was younger. I certainly hope the mural will depict me with a full head of hair."

Tyll always smiled. "I am listening to your requests."

Every day Tyll would disappear into the throne room where the mural was to be painted. He took his paints and his brushes and a good book to read. Hours later he emerged yawning with fatigue.

Court members and friends waited at the door until Tyll emerged. "Is it finished yet?" But Tyll was having too much fun. "No the mural isn't finished, but it would help to have venison for dinner, please, and a bit of chocolate cake."

At teatime the Duke's cook came by. "I hear that the entire household is being represented in your wall mural. I certainly hope that you will paint me holding my new puppy. She is a member of the family too."

The Duke's groom had a request too. "The mare is expecting her foal next month. I hope you will include it. Make it a stallion, please."

Tyll always smiled at all the requests. "I'm sure you will all be pleased."

The Duke's five-year-old son was Tyll's most devoted admirer. He never requested how he should be painted. He only wanted Tyll to read to him and share his tea. Together they ate cream puffs and marzipan. They shared picture books. Little Peter learned to smile just like his friend Tyll.

But what was Tyll doing in the throne room? Why wasn't the painting done?

The Duke was impatient. "My father-in-law will be visiting next week. I would like to show him the portraits. I insist that you finish the painting."

Tyll agreed. He demanded a bag of gold for more paint, and a horse and buggy to fetch it from the market. He needed money to buy red velvet curtains and he would also like the Duke to provide him with a cottage. "Just a humble house, your Lordship."

The Duke was anxious to see the finished painting. "Yes, yes, whatever you want," he wearily agreed.

The Duke's father-in-law arrived. There was a feast and dancing. "Now we shall see the painting," announced the Duke. The entire household gathered outside the throne room.

"Ladies and Gentlemen," intoned Tyll. "You are about to see my masterpiece. As you know, it has taken four months to paint it. I have had suggestions from each and every one of you and I have listened and satisfied your wishes. I think that you will be pleased with my interpretation of this lovely assemblage."

The Grand Duchess, the Duke, his children, the people of the court and the household all filed into the throne room.

The wall was completely covered with a red velvet curtain with gold tassels. The court musicians played a fanfare and Tyll pulled the curtain aside.

The people gasped. The wall was blank, completely white. There was nothing to see. No one said anything. They were all waiting for the Duke's reaction. The Duke and his father-in-law were too astonished to speak.

"Each of you asked me to paint you as you, yourself, saw yourself. Now you can gaze at your portraits and see exactly what you would like to see."

"But," sputtered the Duke, "there is nothing to see."

"Father," said small Peter. "You are wrong. I see what I want to see. There I am right in the middle of the picture eating cream puffs with Tyll."

The Duke laughed. "Yes, you are right. I see my whole family dressed for a party, perpetually young. Let us all have some cream puffs."

Clip, Clop. Clip, Clop. There is Tyll's donkey. He is being led by a groom who is switching flies off his back as they stroll through town.

There is Tyll with the Duke's son, small Peter, taking tea in front of Tyll's new house. He no longer paints portraits.

Booklist: Stories by Subject

After you have learned a story or two, you might find that the stories you know have common elements: the same theme, a similar background, or characters with the same desires. After you become aware of these categories you are ready to create a storyhour around a particular theme. Advertise your storyhour by announcing the subject: "Wishes" or "Tales from Japan." You might mix and match too. A story that fits into a wishes theme one week might be used in a storyhour featuring magic another time. The stories in the following list are among my personal favorites. While some are now out of print, they remain classics in the field, and are worth a little extra effort to find. If some intrigue you, look them up, read them through, and learn them to tell. The stories listed under a subject heading are not necessarily all to be used in the same storyhour. And of course, you don't need to have a theme to make a good storytelling program—just good stories.

Anansi

Anansi is a folk character who figures in African and Jamaican lore. A trickster, he is half man, half spider. Many stories about Anansi are included in *The Hat-Shaking Dance and Other Ashanti Tales from Ghana* by Harold Courlander with Albert Kofi Prempeh (Harcourt, 1957). *A Story, A Story* by Gail E. Haley (Atheneum, 1970) is a picture-book version of an Anansi story.

FROM AFRICA

"The Hat Shaking Dance," title story in Courlander's *The Hat-Shaking Dance*. This story explains why spiders are bald. The dance itself can be acted out. Start out slowly, building up to a zany movement in climax.

FROM JAMAICA

"Bandalee" in Philip M. Sherlock's *Anansi, the Spider Man* (Crowell, 1954). Land Turtle races Anansi and almost outwits him.

"Kisander," also in Sherlock's *Anansi, the Spider Man.* Anansi and Mouse steal from Cat in this tale.

Artists and Stories for Art Lovers

"The Boy Who Drew Cats" by Lafcadio Hearn in Bryna and Louis Untermeyer's *Unfamiliar Marvels* (Golden Press, 1962). A goblin rat is killed by the cats the boy draws. A scary Japanese story.

"A Chinese Fairy Tale" by Laurence Housman in Eileen Colwell's *A Storyteller's Choice* (Walck, 1964). A long and beautiful story in which an artist's apprentice becomes a great artist under unusual circumstances. To be told with quiet dignity. Also in Mary Davis's *A Baker's Dozen* (Harcourt, 1930).

"The Nuremberg Stove" by Louise de la Ramee in Margaret Hodges' *Tell It Again* (Dial, 1963). A young aspiring artist hides in a beautiful stove and meets a king.

"The Two Painters" in Louis Untermeyer's *The World's Greatest Stories* (Evans, 1964). The rivalry of two great artists, Zeuxis and Parrhasius.

Authors

"The Peterkins Try to Become Wise" in Lucretia Hale's *Peterkin Papers* (Osgood, 1880). The foolish Peterkins attempt to write a book.

"Rhyming Ink" by Margaret Baker in Sidonie M. Gruenberg's *Favorite Stories* (Doubleday, 1942). Simon Smug's wife buys ink that helps him become a poet. A nonsense story.

"A Scrap of Paper" in *Chance Luck and Destiny* by Peter Dickinson (Little, 1976). A judge discovers that a witch's incantation is in his own handwriting.

Birds

"The Bird's Wisdom" in *Jewish Stories One Generation Tells Another* (Jason Aronson, 1987). A bird teaches a prince the three rules of life.

The Canary Prince by Eric Jon Nones (Farrar, 1991). In this Italian tale, a prince turns into a bird to reach his love.

Jorinda and Joringel by the Grimm Brothers (World, 1964). A witch turns children into birds.

"The Seven Lazy Sisters" in Helen Olson's *Stupid Peter* (Random, 1970). The sisters are turned into crows for lying.

Camels

"Ali and the Camels" in Robert Gilstrap's *The Sultan's Fool* (Holt, 1958). Ali can't manage to count the correct number of camels.

The Dancing Camel by Betsy Byars (Viking, 1965). This modern story can be shortened for a lively storyhour.

"How the Camel Got His Hump" in Rudyard Kipling's *Just So Stories* (Doubleday, 1946). Kipling's stories should be told in *his* words. This one is short.

"How the Camel Got His Proud Look" in Eulalie Steinmetz Ross's *The Buried Treasure and Other Picture Tales* (Lippincott, 1958). This Chinese story is much kinder to the camel than Kipling's story.

Cats

"King of the Cats" by Paul Galdone in *Halloween*, ed. by Caroline Feller Bauer. Art by Peter Sis (Lippincott, 1989). A short, scary story.

"The Priceless Cats" in Edna Johnson's *Anthology of Children's Literature* (4th rev. ed.; Houghton, 1970). An Italian cat tale.

"Mr. Samson Cat" by Valerian Karrick in Johnson's *Anthology*. Also in Ross's *The Buried Treasure and Other Picture Tales*. A Russian story about a "dreadful animal."

The Clever Three

"Clever Elsie" in *Tales from Grimm*; tr. by Wanda Gág (Coward, 1936). Elsie isn't clever at all, but neither is her family.

"Clever Grethel" in Mary Bleecker's *Big Music* (Viking, 1946). Grethel wears red rosettes on her shoes and eats her master's chicken.

"Clever Manka" in Parker Fillmore's *The Shepherd's Nosegay* (Harcourt, 1958). Manka outwits her husband.

Clothes

The Emperor's New Clothes: A Fairy Tale by Hans Christian Andersen; retold by Anthea Bell. Art by Dorothée Duntze (North-south, 1986). One of the best loved of all stories, this is one of my favorite versions.

"A Guest for Halil" in Alice Kelsey's *Once the Hodja* (Longmans, 1943). A short story in which a suit of clothes is invited to a banquet. A variant appears as "King Clothes" by M. A. Jagendorf in *The Arbuthnot Anthology of Children's Literature* by May Hill Arbuthnot and others, 4th ed., revised by Zena Sutherland (Scott, Foresman, 1976).

New Patches for Old by Barbara Walker and A. E. Vysal (Parents, 1974). Hasan alters some trousers, but his wife, daughter, and mother-in-law work on the same trousers with hilarious results.

"The Obsession with Clothes" in I. L. Peretz's *The Case against the Wind* (Macmillan, 1975). The Devil tempts Basia Gittel into spending her money for finery.

The Wonderful Shrinking Shirt by Leone Castell Anderson. Art by Irene Trivas (Whitman, 1983). Each time a shirt is washed it shrinks and finds a new owner.

Cooks

"The Baker's Daughter" in Margery Bianco's *A Street of Little Shops* (Doubleday, 1932). Also in Bleecker's *Big Music* and in Phyllis Fenner's *Fools and Funny Fellows* (Knopf, 1961). The beautiful baker's daughter has her own ideas about which cake to bring to a friend's birthday party. A tongue-in-cheek satire.

The Funny Little Woman by Arlene Mosel (Dutton, 1972). A laughing woman is captured by underground monsters. A Japanese story.

"The Lady Who Put Salt in Her Coffee" in Hale's *Peterkin Papers*. The Peterkins try to change salt to sugar.

"The Woman Who Flummoxed the Fairies" in Leclaire Alger's *Heather and Broom* by Sorche Nic Leodhas, pseud. (Holt, 1960). The fairies are happy to send a master baker back to her own home in this Scottish story.

Dancing

These stories are for the storyteller who would like a little movement in storytelling.

"Cinderella" in Andrew Lang's *The Blue Fairy Book* (Longmans, 1948) or Arthur Rackham's *The Arthur Rackham Fairy Book* (Lippincott, 1950). The English version is "Cap O'Rushes," in Joseph Jacobs's *English Fairy Tales* (Dover, 1967). This traditional French tale also appears in a picture book by Marcia Brown (Scribner, 1954). Also in Charles Perrault's *Perrault's Fairy Tales* (Doubleday, 1972).

"Murdoch's Rath" by Juliana H. Ewing in Johnson's *Anthology of Children's Literature*. Pat dances with the fairies on the Rath and becomes a rich man.

"Nella's Dancing Shoes" by Eleanor Farjeon in Eulalie Steinmetz Ross's *Blue Rose* (Harcourt, 1966). Nella loses her dancing shoes and finds them in a jungle.

The Twelve Dancing Princesses by Andrew Lang (Holt, 1966). A soldier outwits twelve princesses who dance each night.

"Wee Meg Barnileg and the Fairies" in Ruth Sawyer's *The Way of the Storyteller* (Viking, 1962). This story should be told in Sawyer's words and, if possible, with a slight Irish brogue. Meg dances with the fairies after a year of penance for naughty manners.

Dogs

"Jean Labadie's Big Black Dog" in Natalie Carlson's *The Talking Cat* (Harper, 1952). Also in Eileen Colwell's *A Second Storyteller's Choice* (Walck, 1964). An imaginary dog is the main culprit in this amusing French-Canadian story.

"The Poor Old Dog" in Arnold Lobel's *Fables*. Art by author (Harper, 1980). A one-page story about a dog who gets his wish.

"The Tinderbox" in Hans Christian Andersen's *It's Perfectly True*; tr. by Paul Leyssac (Macmillan, 1937). Three huge dogs run errands for a young soldier. Tell this story with as many of Andersen's original words as possible.

Dolls

"The Magic Glass" in Richard Hughes's *The Spider's Palace* (Looking Glass Library, 1960). The real people become toys.

"The Steadfast Tin Soldier" in Andersen's *It's Perfectly True*. A tin soldier is in love with a ballet dancer.

The Velveteen Rabbit by Margery Bianco (Doubleday, 1926). A long sensitive story about a stuffed animal who is loved by a small boy.

Dragons

The Fourth Question by Rosalind C. Wang (Holiday, 1991). Yee-Lee helps an old man, an old woman, and a dragon and is rewarded.

The Loathsome Dragon by David Wiesner and Kim Kahng (Putnam, 1987). A daughter is turned into a dragon by a wicked queen.

Families

Some especially interesting families, that is.

Anansi the Spider by Gerald McDermott (Holt, 1972). Each of Anansi's six sons has a particular talent.

"Long, Broad and Sharpsight" in Ruth Manning-Saunders' *A Book of Wizards* (Dutton, 1967). Three comrades with unusual traits help a prince.

"The Three Brothers and the Giant" in Beatrice Schenk de Regniers' *The Giant Book* (Atheneum, 1966). Three French boys outwit a giant and marry the king's daughters.

Tuck Everlasting by Natalie Babbitt (Farrar, 1975). The Tucks live forever, but is that enviable? A thought-provoking fantasy.

Foolish Fellows Who Made Good

"Doctor Know It All" in Gág's translation of *Tales from Grimm*. Peasant Fish makes observations that turn out to be well-kept secrets and becomes a wealthy man. A variant is "Doctor and Detective Too" in Mary Hatch's *13 Danish Tales* (Harcourt, 1947).

"How Boots Befooled the King" in Howard Pyle's *The Wonder Clock* (Dover, 1965). A foolish boy is able to fool a king. A long story by a master storyteller.

"The Lost Half Hour" by Henry Beston in Eulalie Steinmetz Ross's *The Lost Half Hour* (Harcourt, 1963). Also in Child Study Association's *Castles and Dragons* (Crowell, 1958). Bobo appears to be quite stupid, but wins a Princess in this longer, imaginative story.

Forgetfulness

"Icarus and Daedalus" by Josephine Preston Peabody in Johnson's *Anthology of Children's Literature*. Also in Untermeyer's *The World's Greatest Stories*. Icarus forgets that his wings are made of wax in this Greek legend.

"Poor Mr. Fingle" in Bianco's *A Street of Little Shops*. Also in Sidonie M. Gruenberg's *More Favorite Stories* (Doubleday, 1948). Mr. Fingle spends years wandering about the hardware store, because he's forgotten what he came to buy.

"Soap, Soap, Soap" in Richard Chase's *Grandfather Tales* (Houghton, 1948). Another story about a boy who can't remember what he's shopping for.

Foxes

"El Enamo" in Charles Finger's *Tales of Silver Lands* (Doubleday, 1924). The terrible El Enamo is outwitted by the fox.

"The Fox and the Bear" in Yoshiko Uchida's *The Magic Listening Cap* (Harcourt, 1955). A Japanese story in which the bear finally outwits the fox.

"Mighty Mikko" in Fillmore's *The Shepherd's Nosegay*. A lovable fox finds a princess and a suitable castle for his master. Similar to *Puss in Boots*.

Gifts and Presents

"How the Good Gifts Were Used by Two" in Pyle's *The Wonder Clock*. Also in Fenner's *Fools and Funny Fellows*. A rich brother and a poor one encounter St. Nicholas.

The Swineherd by Hans Christian Andersen; tr. by Naomi Lewis. Art by Dorothe Duntzée (North-south, 1987). An ungrateful princess turns down a swineherd's thoughtful gifts.

The Third Gift by Jan Carew (Little, 1974). Work, beauty, and imagination are the three gifts.

Goats

The first two are for older children, the last three for preschoolers.

"The Goal Well" in Harold Courlander's *Fire on the Mountain* (Holt, 1950). An African trader is tricked into believing that a well produces goats.

"A Horned Goat" in Lucia Borski's *The Jolly Tailor* (Longmans, 1957). A Polish story about a fierce horned goat.

The Three Billy Goats Gruff by Peter C. Asbjørnsen and Jorgen E. Moe (Harcourt, 1957). "Who's that tripping over my bridge?"

"Ticky-Picky Boom-Boom" in Sherlock's *Anansi, the Spider Man*. The goat butts the ghostlike yams into many pieces.

The Wolf and the Seven Little Kids by the Grimm Brothers (Harcourt, 1959). "Never open the door to strangers" is the moral of this popular story.

Greed

"The Fisherman and His Wife" in Gág's translation of *Tales from Grimm*. The discontented wife of a fisherman finally wishes for too much. A similar story is "The Golden Fish" in Arthur Ransome's *Old Peter's Russian Tales* (Dover, 1969), and also "The Beautiful Birch" in Mirra Ginsburg's *How Wilka Went to Sea* (Crown, 1975).

Once a Mouse by Marcia Brown (Scribner, 1961). An Indian fable pictured in woodcuts by a distinguished artist.

"The Rat Catcher's Daughter" in Laurence Housman's *The Rat Catcher's Daughter* (Atheneum, 1974). A father insists that his daughter be turned into gold. A beautiful story that should be told in Housman's own words.

"Shrewd Todie and Lyzer the Miser" in Isaac Bashevis Singer's *When Shlemiel Went to Warsaw* (Farrar, 1969). Todie tricks Lyzer into believing that his silver spoons give birth to teaspoons.

Heroines

Famous folktale heroines who don't just sit back and wait to be rescued.

"The Barber's Clever Wife" by Flora A. Steel in Fenner's *Fools and Funny Fellows*. An "exceedingly clever person" sets her wits to work.

"Elsie Piddock Skips in Her Sleep" in Association for Childhood Education International's *Told under the Magic Umbrella* (Macmillan, 1962). Also in Colwell's *A Storyteller's Choice*. A long and beautiful story by Eleanor Farjeon featuring a skipping contest.

"Mólly Whuppie" in Joseph Jacobs's *English Fairy Tales*. A girl outwits a giant.

Holidays

BLACK HISTORY MONTH

Aunt Flossie's Hats (and Crab Cakes Later) by Elizabeth Fitzgerald Howard. Art by James Ransome (Clarion, 1991). Tell one or all of Aunt Flossie's hat stories.

Bicycle Rider by Mary Scioscia. Art by Ed Young (Harper, 1983). The story of Marshall Taylor's first race victory. Adapted from the longer book.

The Black Americans: A History in Their Own Words (Crowell, 1984). These short selections from primary sources can be read or told in several voices.

Let Freedom Ring: A Ballad of Martin Luther King, Jr. by Myra Cohn Livingston. Art by Samuel Byrd (Holiday, 1992). Combines biography and poetry in a picture book poem.

Martin Luther King, Jr. Free At Last by David A. Adler. Art by Robert Casilla (Holiday, 1986). Tell about King's childhood or about his involvement with the Montgomery bus boycott.

CHRISTMAS

A Child's Christmas in Wales by Dylan Thomas. Art by Trina Schart Hyman (Holiday, 1985). Parts or all of this boy's memories are worth sharing.

"The Christmas Apple" by Ruth Sawyer in Caroline Feller Bauer's *Celebrations*. Art by Lynn Gates Bredeson (H. W. Wilson, 1985). The story of a kind clockmaker and a miracle.

"The Christmas Roast" by Margret Rettich in Bauer's *Celebrations*. How can you eat a goose who has become a friend?

The Gift of the Magi by O Henry (Berkley, 1990). The story of love and Christmas sacrifice is best appreciated by young adults.

The Night before Christmas by Clement C. Moore. Art by James Marshall (Scholastic, 1991). This version of the classic Christmas poem is illustrated with a wry Santa and his reindeer.

"The Peterkin's Christmas Tree" by Lucretia Hale in Diane Goode's *American Christmas* (Dutton, 1990). How can the tree fit into the Peterkin's house?

HALLOWEEN

"The Jigsaw Puzzle" by J. B. Stamper in Bauer's *Halloween*. Art by Peter Sis (Harper, 1989). Lisa puts together a strange jigsaw puzzle.

Monster Soup and Other Spooky Poems, ed. by Dilys Evans. Art by Jacqueline Rogers (Scholastic, 1992). Spice up your Halloween with a scary poem or two.

"The Pumpkin Giant" by Mary E. Wilkins in Mary Gould Davis's *A Baker's Dozen* (Harcourt, 1930). This story about the origin of pumpkin pie can be told for Halloween or Thanksgiving. A long and amusing story.

JEWISH CELEBRATIONS

Cakes and Miracles: A Purim Tale by Barbara Diamond Goldin. Art by Erika Weihs (Viking, 1991). Blind Hershel finds a way to celebrate Purim with the baking of the traditional cookie, *Hamentaschen*.

"A Celebration" in Steve Sanfield's *The Feather Merchants and Other Tales of the Fools of Chelm*. Art by Mikhail Magaril (Orchard, 1991). A proud father ends up serving water to celebrate his daughter's birth. A similar story featuring a wedding celebration is *Simon Boom Gives a Wedding* by Yuri Suhl. Art by Margot Zemach (Four Winds Press, 1972).

The Chanukah Guest by Eric A. Kimmel. Art by Giora Carmi (Holiday, 1988). An old woman mistakes a hungry bear for the village Rabbi.

The World's Birthday: A Rosh Hashanah Story by Barbara Diamond Goldin. Art by Jeanette Winter (Harcourt, 1990). Daniel and his friends give a backyard birthday party for the world to celebrate Rosh Hashanah, the Jewish New Year.

KWANZAA

Kwanzaa by A. P. Porter. Art by Janice Lee Porter (Carolrhoda, 1991). Describes the origins and practices of Kwanzaa.

My First Kwanzaa Book by Deborah M. Newton-Chocolate. Art by Cal Massey. (Scholastic, 1992). This picture book shows a family celebrating the original African-American holiday first established in 1966.

VALENTINE'S DAY

"Ellie's Valentine" by Cynthia Rylant in Caroline Feller Bauer's *Valentine's Day: Stories and Poems*. Art by Blanche Sims (Harper, 1992). It turns out to be the perfect Valentine's Day after all. A good read-aloud choice.

One Zillion Valentines by Frank Modell. Art by author (Greenwillow, 1981). Marvin and Milton treat their neighbors to Valentines.

Valentine's Day by Gail Gibbons. Art by author (Holiday, 1986). A good source of background material.

Horses

"The Magical Horse" in *Tongues of Jade* by Laurence Yep. Art by David Wiesner (Harper, 1991). A father leaves a painting to his son that comes to life as a horse at night.

Rocking-Horse Land by Laurence Housman (Lothrop, 1990). Prince Freedling's rocking horse turns into a dashing steed who wishes to be set free.

"The Taming of Bucephalus" in *Herds of Thunder Manes of Gold*, ed. by Bruce Coville (Delacorte, 1991). The young Alexander uses his head and his heart to tame a feisty horse.

Laziness

"Ah Tcha the Sleeper" by Arthur Bowie Chrisman in Johnson's *Anthology of Children's Literature*. Ah Tcha can't seem to stay awake in this story of the origin of tea.

"Fool's Paradise" in Isaac Bashevis Singer's *Zlateh the Goat* (Harper, 1966). Atzel wishes to die because he hears that there is no work in Paradise.

"Lazy Heinz" in Gág's translation of *Tales from Grimm*. Lazy Heinz and his wife rationalize so that they never have to get out of bed.

Marriage

"Bluebeard" in Lang's *The Blue Fairy Book*. Or his Finnish counterpart of "The Three Chests" in Fillmore's *The Shepherd's Nosegay*. Curiosity gets a young wife into trouble.

Even the Devil Is Afraid of a Shrew by Valerie Stadler (Addison, 1972). A man married to a shrew outwits her and the Devil in a folktale from Lapland. Picture-book version.

"The First Shlemiel" in Singer's *Zlateh the Goat*. Shlemiel tries to end his life with a pot of poison that is really a pot of jam.

"Gone Is Gone" in Wanda Gág's *Gone Is Gone* (Coward, 1935) or in Fenner's *Fools and Funny Fellows*. A man changes places with his wife with disastrous results.

"Gudbrand-on-the Hillside" by Peter C. Asbjørnsen in Phyllis Fenner's *Time to Laugh* (Knopf, 1942). A Norwegian wife constantly forgives her foolish husband.

"Mary, Mary So Contrary" in Fillmore's *The Shepherd's Nosegay*. A farmer's wife is so contrary that she floats upstream.

Mosquitoes

"Brother Rabbit and the Mosquitoes" in Bleecker's *Big Music*. One of Joel Chandler Harris's Brer Rabbit stories. Use gestures to "act out" this dialect story.

"The Conceited Elephant and the Very Lively Mosquito" by Lobagola in Bleecker's *Big Music*. The small wins over the big. A short story.

Why Mosquitoes Buzz in People's Ears by Verna Aardema. Art by Leo and Diane Dillon (Dial, 1975). A cumulative story that ends with a good slap.

Multiplication

These stories all feature the multiplication of objects or people.

"The Doughnuts" in Robert McCloskey's *Homer Price* (Viking, 1943). This is a single chapter in a book of episodic small-town adventures. A doughnut machine continues to produce doughnuts until an entire luncheonette is crowded with them. A long story that is easily shortened and not difficult to learn.

"Millions of Cats" by Wanda Gág (Coward, 1928). The classic picture book in which a man finds "hundreds of cats, thousands of cats, millions and billions and trillons of cats."

"Palace on the Rock" by Richard Hughes in Fenner's *Time to Laugh*. A king has so many children they must be hung outside the palace on a rock.

"Sorcerer's Apprentice" in Roger L. Green's *A Cavalcade of Magicians* (Walck, 1973). A student of the greatest magician in all of ancient Egypt misuses his power and gets into trouble.

"Two of Everything," included in chapter 20. A magic pot produces two of everything, even people.

"Uncle Bouqui Rents a Horse" in Courlander's *Piece of Fire*. An action-packed story from Haiti. Ti Malice keeps adding imaginary people and animals to the back of a rented horse.

Music

The Bremen Town Musicians by Hans Wilhelm. Art by author (Scholastic, 1992). Four animal friends rout out a band of robbers.

"Mr. Benjamin Ram and His Wonderful Fiddle" in Julius Lester's *Further Adventures of Uncle Remus* (Dial, 1990). Mr. Benjamin Ram's old-time fiddle playing gets him out of trouble with Brer Wolf.

The Nightingale by Hans Christian Andersen. Art by Demi (Harcourt, 1985). The Emperor discovers that a real bird is superior to a mechanical one.

"Orpheus" by Padraic Colum in Johnson's *Anthology of Children's Literature*. In this Greek legend the music of Orpheus drowns out the voices of the sirens that beckon ships to disaster.

Names

The first three are variants of Rumpelstiltskin.

"It's a Good Honest Name" by Dick King-Smith in *The Read-to-Me Treasury*, ed. by Sally Grindley (Doubleday, 1990). Mr. and Mrs. Doddipoll name all their children "John."

"The Ogre Who Built a Bridge" in *The Sea of Gold and Other Tales from Japan* by Yoshiko Uchida (Gregg, 1980). The carpenter must guess the Ogre's name.

"Tom Tit Tot" in Jacobs's *English Fairy Tales*. Also a picture-book version by Evaline Ness (Scribner, 1965). "Nimmy nimmy not, My name's Tom Tit Tot."

"Yung-Kyung-Pyung" in Sherlock's *Anansi*. The names of the king's three daughters are discovered by Anansi and his friends.

Night

Hildilid's Night by Cheli Ryan (Macmillan, 1971). An old woman tries to destroy the night.

"Juan Bobo" by Rafael Ramírez de Arellano in Dorothy Carter's *Greedy Mariani* (Atheneum, 1974). Juan thinks a pot is lazy and challenges it to a race.

"The Milky Way" in Adet Lin's *The Milky Way and Other Chinese Tales* (Harcourt, 1961). A popular Chinese story about the origin of the Milky Way.

"A Pot of Gold" in Ellen Margolis's *Idy the Fox-chasing Cow and Other Stories* (World, 1962). To claim the gold, one must work in complete silence.

"The Sack of Diamonds" by Helen Kronberg Olson in Caroline Feller Bauer's *Read for the Fun of It* (H. W. Wilson, 1992). A little woman uses a slingshot to send diamonds up to the sky.

Nonsense Words

These stories feature silly nonsense words and phrases. Be prepared to have the children chant them back to you endlessly.

"Cheese, Peas and Chocolate Pudding," included in chapter 19. A little boy refuses to eat anything but . . .

"The China Spaniel" by Richard Hughes, included in chapter 18. A school, a town, and finally the world chant a nonsense sentence.

"Crab and the Jaguar" in Valerian Karrick's *Picture Folktales* by Valery Carrick, pseud. (Dover, 1967). "Eyes, little eyes of mine! Fly back to me from the blue sea, from the blue sea, quick, quick, quick, quick!"

"How Bozo the Button Buster Busted All His Buttons When a Mouse Came" in Carl Sandburg's *Sandburg Treasury* (Harcourt, 1970). One of Sandburg's *Rootabaga Stories*.

"Master of All Masters" in Jacobs's *English Fairy Tales*. A short funny story in which a master insists on calling things by names he has invented.

"Ticky-Picky Boom-Boom" in Sherlock's *Anansi*. The yams chant while chasing a tiger.

Rain

"The Jolly Tailor" by Lucia Mercka Borski and Kate B. Miller in *Rainy Day*, ed. by Caroline Feller Bauer (Lippincott, 1986). The tailor and his friend Scarecrow repair a hole in the sky.

"When the Rain Came Up from China" by Dell J. McCormick in Bauer's *Rainy Day*. "It's raining from China" in this Paul Bunyan story.

Riddles

These stories incorporate riddles in the stories. Use a few of the riddles you know between stories (see chapter 19, Non-narrative Sources).

"The Flea" in Ross's *The Buried Treasure*. Also in Bleecker's *Big Music*. An ant, a rat, and a beetle help a shepherd boy solve a riddle.

"How to Become a Witch" in Maria Leach's *Whistle in the Graveyard* (Viking, 1974). Just one of the short ghost stories in a good collection.

"Princess and Jose" in Anita Brenner's *The Boy Who Could Do Anything* (W. R. Scott, 1942). The riddle of the sphinx is featured in this Mexican story.

"Riddle in the Dark" in J. R. R. Tolkien's *The Hobbit* (Houghton, 1938). This section of *The Hobbit* makes a good introduction to Tolkien's writings.

"The Riddlemaster" by Catherine Storr in Kathleen Lines's *The Faber Storybook* (Faber, 1961). Polly solves riddles to keep from being eaten by a wolf.

"The Riddling Youngster" in Vivian Thompson's *Hawaiian Legends of Tricksters and Riddlers* (Holiday House, 1969). A young boy has a riddle contest with a high chief in old Hawaii.

Shoes

"The Golden Shoes" in *My Grandmother's Stories: A Collection of Jewish Folk Tales*. Art by Jael Jordan (Knopf, 1990). How do you show off your golden shoes when the streets are muddy?

"Smelly Sneakers" in *A Messy, Messy Room* by Judith Gorog (Philomel, 1990). Toad wins first prize for his smelly sneakers, but is it worth it?

"Sunday Boots and Working Boots" by Annette Penny in *The Read-to-Me Treasury*, ed. by Sally Grindley (Doubleday, 1990). The snobbish Sunday boots end up as plain old working boots.

The Old Woman and the Willy Nilly Man by Jill Wright. Art by Glen Rounds (Putnam, 1987). An old woman's shoes sing and dance all night.

Short, Short Stories

Sometimes you need a short story at the beginning or the end of a storyhour. These are perfect.

"The Gunniwolf" in Wilhelmina Harper's *The Gunniwolf* (Dutton, 1967). An amusing variant of Little Red Riding Hood with lots of action.

"The Princess on the Pea" in Andersen's *It's Perfectly True*. The Princess felt a pea under 35 mattresses and featherbeds.

"The Snooks Family" in Virginia Tashjian's *Juba This and Juba That* (Little, 1969). No one can blow out the candle.

"The Storyteller" in Courlander's *Fire on the Mountain*. Similar to the endless story in the Arabian Nights.

"The Tail" by Joseph Jacobs in Fenner's *Fools and Funny Fellows*. "If it had not been for that, this tale would have been a great deal longer." A really short story.

"The Three Fridays" in Kelsey's *Once the Hodja*. The Hodja can't decide what to preach on Friday. See also the other stories in this book.

Sneezes

"Ebenezer-Never-Could-Sneezer" by Gilbert Patillo in Fenner's *Time to Laugh*. "Ah-ah-ah-Choo!"

"Prince Sneeze" in Henry Beston's *Henry Beston's Fairy Tales* (Aladdin, 1958). "Everytime the Prince sneezes, something shall change." An original and amusing story.

"The Stolen Turnips, the Magic Tablecloth, the Sneezing Goat, and the Wooden Whistle" by Arthur Ransome in Effie L. Power's *Bag O' Tales* (Dover, 1969). "And as it sneezed, good gold pieces flew from it in all directions, till the ground was thick with them."

"The Three Sneezes" by Roger Duvoisin in Fenner's *Fools and Funny Fellows*. "You will die when your donkey has sneezed three times." A Swiss droll.

Snow

"New Year's Hats for Statues" by Yoshiko Uchida in *Snowy Day*, ed. by Caroline Feller Bauer (Harper, 1986). An old man gives his reed hats to some snow-covered statues and is rewarded for his kindness. Poems and two more snow stories in this book.

"The Silver Hen" by Mary E. Wilkins in Ross's *The Lost Half Hour*. The children spend a night at the snowman's house.

Tricksters Who Get Tricked

Come Again in the Spring by Richard Kennedy (Harper, 1976). Old Hark wins a wager with Death.

"How the Clever Doctor Tricked Death" by Manuel J. Andrade in Sharp's *Greedy Mariani*. The Doctor saves his own life and those of his patients through trickery. A story from the Dominican Republic to learn and tell.

"Nuts" in Natalie Babbitt's *The Devil's Storybook* (Farrar, 1974). A not-so-greedy farm wife tricks the Devil, giving him a stomach-ache as well.

The Parrot and the Thief by Richard Kennedy (Little, 1974). A caged parrot outwits a sly thief.

Turtles

"Anansi and His Visitor, Turtle" by Edna Mason Kaula in *The Laugh Book*, ed. by Joanna Cole and Stephanie Calmenson (Doubleday, 1983). "When you set out to outsmart another person to your own advantage, there is usually someone who can outsmart you."

"The Singing Tortoise" in *The Cow-tail Switch and Other West African Stories* by Harold Courlander and George Herzog (Holt, 1988). The tortoise can't keep a secret.

"The Singing Turtle" in *Look Back and See: Twenty Lively Tales for Gentle Tellers* by Margaret Read McDonald (H. W. Wilson, 1991). The turtle refuses to sing for the mean rich man.

Unwanted Guests

"Go Close the Door" in Solomon Simon's *More Wise Men of Helm* (Behrman House, 1965). Jewish version of the ballad story "Get Up and Bar the Door" in Johnson's *Anthology of Children's Literature*.

"Leave Well Enough Alone" in Rose Dobbs's *More Once-Upon-a-Time Stories* (Random, 1961). A young wife takes her husband's directions literally with unhappy results. A short funny story.

"The Old Woman and the Tramp" by G. Djurkla in Elizabeth Sechrist's *It's Time for Storyhour* (Macrae Smith, 1964). Also in May Hill Arbuthnot's *Time for Old Magic* (Scott, Foresman, 1970). A tramp makes soup from a 4-inch nail. Parallel stories appear as the Russian *Nail Soup* by Harve Zemach (Follett, 1964) and Marcia Brown's picture-book version of the French story *Stone Soup* (Scribner, 1947).

"Winnie the Pooh Goes Visiting" in A. A. Milne's *Winnie the Pooh* (Dutton, 1926). In one chapter Pooh gets stuck in Rabbit's hole and must stay for a week.

Wind

"Little Pieces of the West Wind" by Christian Garrison in *Windy Day*, ed. by Caroline Feller Bauer (Lippincott, 1988). A clever old man loses his socks and makes a bargain with the wild and reckless West Wind.

"When the Wind Changed" by Ruth Park in Bauer's *Windy Day*. Josh makes an ugly face and the wind changes.

Wishes

"Did the Tailor Have a Nightmare?" in Blanche Serwer's *Let's Steal the Moon* (Little, 1970). Napoleon grants a poor tailor three wishes.

"The Three Wishes" in Child Study Association's *Castles and Dragons*. All the wishes come true without making a single one. A longer story by Barbara Leonie Picard.

"The Three Wishes" in Joseph Jacobs's *More English Folk and Fairy Tales* (Putnam, 1922). A man gets his wishes, but with ridiculous results. A similar story in Dobbs's *Once Upon a Time* and Gruenberg's *Favorite Stories*. Also "If You Had a Wish" in Association for Childhood Education International's *Told under the Magic Umbrella*.

"Wishes" in Babbitt's *The Devil's Storybook*. A search for the perfect wish.

Booklist: Illustrated Single Tales

Artists often illustrate traditional and original folktales in single volumes. At first glance these picture books may seem suitable only for preschoolers but this is not always the case. Usually these picture books are excellent for use in telling stories to an older group. In some instances you will want to share the artist's interpretation of the story with the older children just as you do with those who are younger.

One way of using these often beautiful books is to display them after the story is told. Another way is not to show the pictures during the storyhour at all, but to have the book ready for children to take home and enjoy at their leisure. From time to time you will want to read and show the pictures to a group as you would during the primary book program, and sometimes you will want to use the text of one edition with the pictures of another. A particular story might be told on several occasions, the first time without showing the pictures so that your listeners "see" their own interpretation, the next time showing the artist's work. Whichever way the illustrated books are used, they promise a treat.

Aardema, Verna. *Borreguita and the Coyote.* Art by Petra Mathers. Knopf, 1991. A lamb outwits Coyote. (Mexico)

Afanasyev, Alexander Nikolayevich. *The Fool and the Fish*; retold by Lenny Hort. Art by Gennady Spirin. Dial, 1990. "Fish, fish, fish! Grant my wish." (Russia)

Alexander, Sue. *Nadia the Willful.* Art by Lloyd Bloom. Pantheon, 1983. Nadia shows her father how to come to terms with the death of his son. (Middle East)

Andersen, Hans Christian. *The Emperor's New Clothes*; retold by Anthea Bell. Art by Dorothée Duntze. North-south, 1986. Share the art of this version of the popular story of a vain emperor. (Denmark)

Asbjørnsen, Peter C. and Jorgen E. Moe. *The Three Billy Goats Gruff*; from the translation of G. W. Dasent. Art by Marcia Brown. Harcourt, 1957. Classic Norwegian folktale.

Belpré, Pura. *Oté: A Puerto Rican Folktale.* Art by Paul Galdone. Pantheon, 1969. The Devil is outwitted by a Puerto Rican family.

_____. *Perez and Martina.* Art by Carlos Sanchez. Warne, 1961. An old Puerto Rican folktale retold by a gifted storyteller.

Bernstein, Margery and Janet Kobrin, retellers. *The First Morning: An African Myth.* Art by Enid Warner Romanek. Scribner, 1976. The animals bring back from above the sky a box that is supposed to contain light. Vivid black-and-white silhouette drawings.

Bianco, Margery. *The Velveteen Rabbit.* Art by William Nicholson. Doran, 1926. A stuffed toy is loved with such intensity it comes to life.

Brett, Jan. *The Mitten.* Art by author. Putnam, 1989. Woodland animals take refuge in a lost mitten. (Ukraine)

Brown, Marcia. *Once a Mouse.* Art by author. Scribner, 1961. A mouse is given a chance to be a bigger, more powerful animal.

Butler, Stephen. *Henny Penny.* Art by author. Tambourine, 1991. Henny Penny and her friends think that the sky is falling.

Carrick, Carol. *Aladdin and the Wonderful Lamp.* Art by Donald Carrick. Scholastic, 1989. A genie helps Aladdin, who is imprisoned in an underground cave.

Cooper, Susan. *Tam Lin.* Art by Warwick Hutton. McElderry, 1991. Compare this version of the Scottish ballad to Jane Yolen's. (Scotland)

Croll, Carolyn. *The Three Brothers.* Art by author. Putnam, 1991. Three brothers vie for their father's inheritance. (Pennsylvania German)

De Beaumont, Marie LePrince. *Beauty and the Beast*; tr. by Richard Howard. Art by Hilary Knight. Simon, 1990. A kind girl releases a prince from his enchantment as an ugly beast.

Dee, Ruby. *Tower to Heaven.* Art by Jennifer Bent. Holt, 1991. The people build a tower to reach Onyankopon, the sky god. (Ghana)

dePaola, Tomie. *Fin M'Coul: The Giant of Knockmany Hill.* Art by author. Holiday, 1981. Oonagh, the giant's wife, outwits her husband's rival, Cucullin. (Ireland)

Fleischman, Sid. *McBroom Tells a Lie.* Art by Walter Lorraine. Little, 1976. An original tall tale in which a farm is saved by a popcorn mobile.

French, Fiona. *Anancy and Mr. Dry-Bone.* Art by author. Little, 1991. Two men try to win the hand of Miss Louise through laughter. (Caribbean)

Gág, Wanda. *Gone Is Gone.* Art by author. Coward, 1935. A man does the housework for a day. A single story for the advanced storyteller.

Galdone, Paul. *The Gingerbread Boy.* Art by author. Seabury, 1975. The lively pictures in color add to the enjoyment of this classic story.

———. *The Monkey and the Crocodile: A Jataka Tale from India.* Art by author. Seabury, 1969. A curious monkey uses his wits to trick a crocodile.

Ginsburg, Mirra. *Two Greedy Bears.* Art by Jose Aruego and Ariane Dewey. Macmillan, 1976. A Hungarian tale in which a sly fox gets the better of two bear cubs who insist on equal shares of everything.

Goble, Paul. *Dream Wolf.* Art by author. Bradbury, 1990. A wolf befriends two lost children. (Native American)

Guy, Rosa. *Mother Crocodile.* Art by John Steptoe. "Maman-Caïman" by Birago Diop. Delacorte, 1981. The little crocodiles don't believe the tales that Dia tells until they get in trouble.

Hadithi, Mwenye and Adrienne Kennaway. *Lazy Lion.* Little, 1990. Lion is too lazy to build his own house.

Haley, Gail E. *A Story, A Story: An African Tale.* Art by author. Atheneum, 1970. Explains the origin of the spider tale. A good introduction to African stories.

Hancock, Sibyl. *Esteban and the Ghost.* Art by Dirk Zimmer. Dial, 1983. A tinker spends all night in a haunted house. (Spain)

Harper, Wilhelmina. *The Gunniwolf.* Art by William Wiesner. Dutton, 1967. A funny variant of *Little Red Riding Hood.* Tell with or without the pictures.

Hodges, Margaret. *The Fire Bringer: A Paiute Indian Legend.* Art by Peter Parnall. Little, 1972. How the fire came to people. Beautifully illustrated.

Hogrogian, Nonny. *The Contest.* Art by author. Greenwillow, 1976. Two men are engaged to the same girl in this Armenian folktale.

Hutton, Warwick. *The Nose Tree.* Art by author. McElderry, 1981. Three soldiers are rewarded for their kindness to an ugly little man. (Germany)

Ishii, Momoko. *The Tongue-cut Sparrow*; tr. by Katherine Paterson. Art by Suekichi Akaba. Dutton, 1982. Classic Japanese tale of a couple who receive gifts from a tongue-cut sparrow. (Japan)

Jacobs, Joseph. *Master of All Masters.* Art by Marcia Sewall. Little, 1972. This short story from Joseph Jacobs' collections is more effective without pictures, but children might enjoy looking at the book after they've heard the story.

Johnston, Tony. *The Soup Bone.* Art by Margot Tomes. Harcourt, 1990. An old woman searches for a soup bone and finds a skeleton instead.

Keats, Ezra Jack. *John Henry: An American Legend.* Art by author. Pantheon, 1965. A simple retelling of the American folk hero's story.

Kennedy, Richard. *The Parrot and the Thief.* Art by Marcia Sewall. Little, 1974. An intelligent parrot tricks a thief and attains his freedom.

Kent, Jack. *The Fat Cat: A Danish Folktale.* Art by author. Parents, 1971. A variant of the gingerbread boy. Use with or without the pictures.

Kimmel, Eric. A. *Bearhead.* Art by Charles Mikolaycak. Holiday, 1991. A man with a bear's head takes directions literally when he becomes a servant to a witch.

_____. *Boots and His Brothers.* Art by Kimberly Bulckenroot. Holiday, 1992. A storyteller's adaptation of the Norwegian tale.

Kipling, Rudyard. *The Elephant's Child.* Art by Emily Bolam. Dutton, 1992. Bright bold art illustrates this classic Kipling tale of how the elephant got his trunk.

Kirstein, Lincoln. *Puss in Boots.* Art by Alain Vaës. Little, 1992. The art for this version of the Perrault story is a must to share.

Knutson, Barbara. *How the Guinea Fowl Got Her Spots.* Art by author. Carolrhoda, 1990. A pourquoi tale explaining how the guinea fowl got its color. (Africa)

Lobel, Anita. *The Dwarf Giant.* Art by author. Holiday, 1991. A dwarf visits a bored prince and learns a lesson from his wife. (Japan)

Lobel, Arnold. *Ming Lo Moves the Mountain.* Art by author. Greenwillow, 1982. Ming Lo and his wife ask a wise man how to move the mountain in front of their home. (China)

Louie, Ai-Ling. *Yeh-shen: A Cinderella Story from China.* Art by Ed Young. Philomel, 1982. This version of Cinderella was told during the T'ang dynasty (618–907 A.D.). (China)

Luttrell, Ida. *Three Good Blankets.* Art by Michael McDermott. Atheneum, 1990. An old woman's children try to help their mother keep warm, but she gives the blankets to her animals. (United States)

MacGill-Callahan, Sheila. *And Still the Turtle Watched.* Art by Barry Moser. Dial, 1991. A turtle carved in stone observes the gradual pollution of the countryside. (Native American)

McAllister, Angela. *Matepo.* Art by Jill Newton. Dial, 1991. A monkey finds the perfect present for his mother.

McCunn, Ruthanne Lum. *Pie-Biter.* Art by You-shan Tang. Design (Box 14695, San Francisco, CA 94112), 1983. Hoi emigrates from China to work on the railroads and uses his wits and his love of pies to become a legend. (Chinese-American)

McDermott, Beverly Brodsky. *The Golem: A Jewish Legend.* Art by author. Lippincott, 1976. Powerful paintings bring the ancient legend of a man fashioned from clay to all ages.

McDermott, Gerald. *Anansi the Spider: A Tale from the Ashanti*; adapted and illustrated by author. Holt, 1972. A picture book based on a film. Stylized illustrations.

———. *Arrow to the Sun*; adapted and illustrated by author. Viking, 1974. The solar fire as the source of life is presented in a stunning picture book.

McKissack, Patricia. *Flossie and the Fox.* Art by Rachel Isadora. Dial, 1986. Flossie outwits a wily fox in a lively tale to tell. (African-American)

Mahy, Margaret. *The Seven Chinese Brothers.* Art by Jean and Mou-sien Tseng. Scholastic, 1990. Seven brothers use their talents to escape execution. (China)

Marshak, Samuel. *The Month-Brothers*; tr. by Thomas P. Whitney. Art by Diane Stanley. Morrow, 1983. The month-brothers help a little girl fulfill impossible tasks.

Martin, Claire. *Boots and the Glass Mountain.* Art by Gennady Spirin. Dial, 1992. Boots wins the hand of a princess who lives in a glass mountain in this beautifully illustrated version of the Norwegian tale.

Mollel, Tolowa M. *The Orphan Boy.* Art by Paul Morin. Clarion, 1990. Why the planet Venus is known to the Maasai as Kileken, the orphan boy. (Maasi)

Morimoto, Junko. *The Inch Boy.* Art by author. Viking, 1986. The adventures of Issunbohi, the famous Japanese miniature warrior. (Japan)

Morris, Winifred. *The Magic Leaf.* Art by Ju-Hong Chen. Atheneum, 1987. Lee Foo is sure he has found a magic leaf that will make him invisible. (China)

Mosel, Arlene. *The Funny Little Woman.* Art by Blair Lent. Dutton, 1972. This Caldecott winner, based on a Japanese tale, is an exciting story to tell.

———. *Tikki Tikki Tembo.* Art by Blair Lent. Holt, 1968. Picture-book version of a popular nonsense story.

Ormerod, Jan. *The Frog Prince.* Art by author. Lothrop, 1990. The traditional Grimm's tale in a sprightly retelling.

Paterson, Katherine. *The Tale of the Manderin Ducks.* Art by Leo and Diane Dillon. Dutton, 1990. Yasuko and Shozo free a wild duck and are rewarded for their kindness. (Japan)

Perrault, Charles. *Cinderella.* Art by Marcia Brown. Scribner, 1954. The crayon drawings add much to this classic fairy tale of magic and romance.

_____. *Puss in Boots.* Art by Fred Marcellino. Farrar, 1990. Lush art for the famous Puss.

Rappaport, Doreen. *The Journey of Meng.* Art by Yang Ming-Yi. Dial, 1991. A young Chinese wife goes in search of her husband who has been kidnapped. (China)

Robbins, Ruth. *How the First Rainbow Was Made.* Art by author. Houghton, 1980. The Old-Man-Above sends the rainbow, or giant-colored foxtail, as a sign when the rain has cleared.

Saunders, Susan. *A Sniff in Time.* Art by Michael Mariano. Atheneum, 1982. James is granted the ability to smell into the future.

Say, Allen. *Once under the Cherry Blossom Tree: An Old Japanese Tale.* Art by author. Harper, 1974. A wicked landlord swallows a cherry pit and a tree sprouts from his head.

Shute, Linda. *Momotaro the Peach Boy.* Art by author. Lothrop, 1986. Born from a peach, a small warrior takes off to fight the evil oni.

Sloat, Teri. *The Eye of the Needle.* Art by author. Dutton, 1990. Amik devours a number of animals before returning to his grandmother. (Yupik Eskimo)

The Squire's Bride; originally collected and told by Peter C. Asbjørnsen. Art by Marcia Sewall. Atheneum, 1975. The bride is a horse in this picture-book version of an old favorite.

Stalder, Valerie. *Even the Devil Is Afraid of a Shrew*; adapted by Ray Broekel. Art by Richard Brown. Addison, 1972. A folktale of Lapland, in which a peasant husband outwits his shrewish wife and the devil, too.

Stamm, Claus. *Three Strong Women: A Tall Tale from Japan.* Art by Jean and Mou-sien Tseng. Viking, 1990. Forever-Mountain, a mighty wrestler, learns humility from three generations of women. (Japan)

Stevens, Janet. *Androcles and the Lion.* Art by author. Holiday, 1989. A young slave helps a lion and his kindness is not forgotten. (Greek fable)

Stevens, Kathleen. *Molly McCullough and Tom the Rogue.* Art by Margot Zemach. Crowell, 1982. Tom is an expert at duping the local farmers, but meets his match in Molly McCullough.

Suhl, Yuri. *Simon Boom Gives a Wedding.* Art by Margot Zemach. Four Winds, 1972. Wishing to provide the best for his daughter's wedding, Simon ends up serving the "best" water.

Tolhurst, Marilyn. *Somebody and the Three Blairs.* Art by Simone Abel. Orchard, 1990. A bear visits a family in a reversal of *The Three Bears.*

Tom Tit Tot. Art by Evaline Ness. Scribner, 1965. The English version of *Rumpelstiltskin.*

Towle, Faith M. *The Magic Cooking Pot.* Art by author. Houghton, 1975. This folktale from India is illustrated with batik prints that give the book a special traditional quality.

Travers, P. L. *Two Pairs of Shoes.* Art by Leo and Diane Dillon. Viking, 1980. Two Middle Eastern tales about the shoes of the rich and the poor.

Ungerer, Tomi. *Zeralda's Ogre.* Art by author. Harper, 1967. A little girl tames a hungry ogre with her gourmet cooking.

Wahl, Jan. *Tailypo!* Art by Wil Clay. Holt, 1991. "Jump story" in which a varmint's tail haunts a woodsman. (African-American)

Walker, Barbara K. and A. E. Uysal. *New Patches for Old.* Art by Harold Berson. Parents, 1974. Hasan alters some trousers, but his wife, daughter, and mother work on the same trousers with hilarious results.

Wildsmith, Brian. *The Hare and the Tortoise,* based on a fable by La Fontaine. Art by author. Watts, 1966. Vibrant full-color illustrations add to the meaning of this traditional fable. Also illustrated by Wildsmith in single picture-book versions: *The Lion and the Rat* (Watts, 1963), *The North Wind and the Sun* (Watts, 1964), and *The Rich Man and the Shoemaker* (Watts, 1965).

Williams, Jay. *One Big Wish.* Art by John O'Brien. Macmillan, 1980. In an original story, Fred is granted one wish that is too big to handle. (United States)

Winthrop, Elizabeth. *Vasilissa the Beautiful.* Art by Alexander Koshkin. Harper, 1991. Vasilissa uses a magic doll to escape from Baba Yaga, the witch. (Russia)

Wisniewski, David. *Rain Player.* Art by author. Clarion, 1991. Pik plays Pok-a-tok with the rain god to relieve the drought. An original Mayan tale. Share the paper-cut art.

Withers, Carl. *Painting the Moon.* Art by Adrienne Adams. Dutton, 1970. Gouache paintings illustrate an old folktale from Estonia.

Wolkstein, Diane. *Little Mouse's Painting.* Art by Maryjane Begin. Morrow, 1992. "What did little mouse paint?"

Yolen, Jane. *The Girl Who Loved the Wind.* Art by Ed Young. Crowell, 1972. The art for this book is a mixture of collage and watercolor and gives a Persian air to an original fairy tale.

_____. *Tam Lin.* Art by Charles Mikolaycak. Harcourt, 1990. Jennet challenges the Faery Queen to win back her home and the life of Tam Lin. (Scotland)

Young, Ed. *Lon Po Po: A Red-Riding Hood Story from China.* Art by author Philomel, 1989. A Chinese version of a classic tale.

Zelinsky, Paul O. *Rumpelstiltskin.* Art by author. Dutton, 1986. The Miller's daughter must guess the name of the little man who helps her spin straw into gold. (Germany)

Zemach, Harve. *Duggy and the Devil: A Cornish Tale.* Art by Margot Zemach. Farrar, 1973. A hilarious variant of *Rumpelstiltskin.* Use it with or without the wonderful illustrations.

Ziner, Feenie. *Cricket Boy.* Art by Ed Young. Doubleday, 1977. Is Scholar Hu's fighting cricket a match for the Emperor's? (China)

Booklist: Story Collections

The collections of good storytelling material could fill an entire library. Editors have gathered together stories with a theme, stories from a particular region or country, and popular or favorite stories. As you become more and more interested in storytelling, you will want to leaf through as many books as you can to find the stories most suited to you and your group. Here are some good collections to begin with. Happy browsing!

Barchers, Suzanne I. *Wise Women: Folk and Fairy Tales from Around the World.* Libraries Unlimited, 1990. Barchers has collected both popular and little-known tales featuring women from all over the world.

Bauer, Caroline Feller, ed. *Valentine's Day: Stories and Poems.* Art by Blanche Sims. Harper, 1993. Stories and poetry to celebrate Valentine's Day. Also see the author's *Windy Day,* 1988, *Snowy Day,* 1986, and *Rainy Day,* 1986.

Best-Loved Stories Told at the National Storytelling Festival. Selected by the National Association for the Preservation and Perpetuation of Storytelling. National Storytelling Press, 1991.

Bierhorst, John. *The Monkey's Haircut and Other Stories Told by the Maya.* Art by Robert Andrew Parker. Morrow, 1986. Animal and pourquoi stories, short and conversational.

———. *The Naked Bear: Folktales of the Iroquois.* Art by Dirk Zimmer. Morrow, 1987. Short and lively tales from the Native American tradition collected by a folklorist.

Booss, Claire, ed. *Scandinavian Folk and Fairy Tales: Tales from Norway, Sweden, Denmark, Finland, Iceland.* Illustrated. Avenel, 1984. Two hundred stories from Scandinavia.

Brenner, Anita. *The Boy Who Could Do Anything and Other Mexican Folktales.* Art by Jean Charlot. Shoe String, 1992. First published in 1942, these tales are easy to learn and still retain their original charm.

Bryan, Ashley. *Lion and the Ostrich Chicks and Other African Folk Tales.* Art by author. Atheneum, 1986. Animal trickster tales from Africa.

Climo, Shirley. *Someone Saw a Spider: Spider Facts and Folktales.* Art by Dirk Zimmer. Crowell, 1985. The subject is spiders, the venue is folktales, legends, facts, and poetry.

Coatsworth, Emerson and David Coatsworth. *The Adventures of Nanabush: Ojibway Indian Stories.* Art by Francis Kagige. Atheneum, 1980. Adventure and pourquoi stories, short enough to learn quickly.

Curry, Jane Louise. *Back in the Beforetime: Tales of the California Indians.* Art by James Watts. McElderry, 1987. Coyote and gopher feature in these regional tales.

De Spain, Pleasant. *Twenty-Two Splendid Tales To Tell.* 2v. Art by Kirk Lyttle. Merrill-Court Press (Box 85785, Seattle, WA 98145), 1990. Short, funny, and very easy to learn.

dePaola, Tomie. *Tomie dePaola's Favorite Nursery Tales.* Art by author. Putnam, 1986. Includes such favorites as "The Three Bears," "The Three Little Pigs" and other traditional fables and poems. Large format illustrated in dePaola's distinctive style.

Fowke, Edith. *Folklore of Canada.* Art by Laszlo Gal. McLelland & Stewart (481 University Ave., Toronto, Ontario M5G2E9), 1976. A survey of Canadian folklore.

Garner, Alan. *A Bag of Moonshine.* Art by Patrick James Lynch. Delacorte, 1986. Stories of Welsh and British origin.

Geras, Adèle. *My Grandmother's Stories: A Collection of Jewish Folk Tales.* Art by Jael Jordan. Knopf, 1990. Written in the first person, a young girl relates the stories her grandmother tells.

Gold, Sharya and Mishael Maswari Caspi. *The Answered Prayer and Other Yemenite Folktales.* Art by Marjory Wunch. The Jewish Publication Society, 1990. Little known folktales from Yemen are attractively illustrated.

Goss, Linda and Marian E. Barnes, eds. *Talk That Talk: An Anthology of African-American Storytelling.* Simon, 1989. An extensive collection of short stories and folktales by African-American storytellers. A good adult resource.

Greenwood, Marie. *Fifty Stories for 8 year olds.* Art by Alice Englander. Gallery (112 Madison Ave., New York, NY 10016), 1990. One of three collections with mostly traditional stories to read or tell. Also see *Fifty Stories for 7 year olds,* 1990 and *Fifty Stories for 6 year olds,* 1989.

Grinnell, George Bird, collector. *The Whistling Skeleton: American Indian Tales of the Supernatural.* Edited by John Bierhorst. Art by Robert Andrew Parker. Four Winds, 1982. Several tribes are represented in these mysterious Native American stories.

Hamilton, Virgina. *The Dark Way: Stories from the Spirit World.* Art by Lambert Davis. Harcourt, 1990. Hamilton has used her own literary style to present 25 "dark" tales.

_____. *The People Could Fly: American Black Folktales.* Art by Leo and Diane Dillon. Knopf, 1985. Trickster tales, ghost stories, and animal stories.

Jaffrey, Madhur. *Seasons of Splendour: Tales, Myths and Legends of India.* Atheneum, 1985. Each of these vivid tales is introduced by the collector. Large format with full-color art to share.

Joseph, Lynn. *A Wave in Her Pocket: Stories from Trinidad.* Art by Brian Pinkney. Clarion, 1991. Joseph uses stories told by Tantie as the framework for these short island tales.

Kawana, Kiri Te. *Land of the Long White Cloud: Maori Myths, Tales and Legends*. Art by Michael Foreman. Little, 1989. The author introduces each of these tales from New Zealand with a personal note.

Lester, Julius. *How Many Spots Does a Leopard Have? and Other Tales*. Art by David Shannon. Scholastic, 1989. Twelve stories from African-American and Jewish traditions.

Low, Alice. *The Family Read-Aloud Holiday Treasury*. Art by Marc Brown. Little, 1991. Full-color art enhances this collection of stories celebrating traditional holidays.

Lyon, Mary E. *Raw Head, Bloody Bones: African-American Tales of the Supernatural*. Scribner's, 1991. Stories from the African-American tradition and the Caribbean.

MacDonald, Margaret Read. *Look Back and See: Twenty Lively Tales for Gentle Tellers*. Art by Roxane Murphy. H. W. Wilson, 1991. A storyteller and folklorist has designed these stories for beginning tellers.

_____. *When the Lights Go Out: 20 Scary Tales to Tell*. Art by Roxane Murphy. H. W. Wilson, 1988. Twenty stories suitable for children.

_____. *Twenty Tellable Tales: Audience Participation Folktales for the Beginning Storyteller*. Art by Roxane Murphy. H. W. Wilson, 1986. Written for beginning storytellers, but perfect for any teller.

Martin, Eva. *Tales of the Far North*. Art by László Gál. Dial, 1986. Canadian tales from the French and English traditions.

McCarty, Toni. *The Skull in the Snow*. Art by Katherine Coville. Delacorte, 1981. Folktales featuring strong women characters from around the world.

O'Mara, Lesley, ed. *Classic Animal Stories*. Art by Angel Dominguez. Arcade, 1991. Kipling, Grimm, La Fontaine and folktales from here and there in an attractive layout.

Perrault, Charles. *Cinderella and Other Tales from Perrault*. Art by Michael Hague. Holt, 1989. "Little Red Riding Hood," "Sleeping Beauty" and other tales collected by Charles Perrault and illustrated with Hague's paintings.

Philip, Neil, ed. *The Spring of Butterflies and Other Folktales of China's Minority Peoples*; tr. by He Liyi. Art by Pan Aiqing and Li Zhao. Lothrop, 1985. A collection of little-known folktales.

Price, Rosalind and Walter McVitty. *The Viking Bedtime Treasury*. Art by Ron Brooks. Viking, 1987. An attractive collection of nursery stories from Australia.

Raychaudhuri, Upendrakishore. *The Stupid Tiger and Other Tales*; tr. from the Bengali by William Radice. Deutsch, 1981. Twenty tales star the jackal, the tiger, and the crocodile.

Retan, Walter. *Favorite Tales from Many Lands*. Art by Linda Medley. Grosset, 1989. Nursery tales told simply for younger children and beginning tellers.

Sanfield, Steve. *The Adventures of High John the Conqueror.* Art by John Ward. Orchard, 1989. A well-known storyteller tells stories about an African-American folk hero. Trickster tales.

_____. *The Feather Merchants and Other Tales of the Fools of Chelm.* Art by Mikhail Magaril. Orchard, 1991. Lively Jewish tales of the silly folk of Chelm.

Scholey, Arthur. *The Discontented Dervishes and Other Persian Tales from Sa'di.* Art by William Rushton. Deutsch, 1977. These are short jokes from the Middle Eastern tradition of the Hodja.

Schram, Peninnah. *Jewish Stories One Generation Tells Another.* Jason Aronson, 1987. Almost 500 pages of stories perfect for reading aloud, collected by a professional storyteller and professor.

Schwartz, Alvin. *Gold and Silver, Silver and Gold: Tales of Hidden Treasure.* Farrar, 1988. The source for each of these short tales is listed. Legends, true stories, and tall tales, all about treasure.

_____. *Scary Stories 3: More Tales to Chill Your Bones.* Art by Stephen Gammell. Harper, 1991. Easy to learn and tell, here are tales from the folk tradition as well as contemporary stories.

_____. *Tales of Trickery from the Land of Spoof.* Art by David Christiana. Farrar, 1985. Short, easy-to-tell, silly tales.

Schwartz, Howard and Barbara Rush. *The Diamond Tree: Jewish Tales from Around the World.* Art by Uri Shulevitz. Harper, 1991. These Jewish tales from around the world are perfect for younger children.

Scott, Bill. *Many Kinds of Magic: Tales of Mystery, Myth and Enchantment.* Viking, 1990. These stories from around the world have been collected by an Australian writer.

Shah, Idries, ed. *World Tales: The Extraordinary Coincidence of Stories Told in All Times in All Places.* Harcourt, 1979. These 65 tales include notes describing the appearance of similar stories found in other countries.

Smith, Jimmy Neil, ed. *Homespun: Tales from America's Favorite Storytellers.* Crown, 1988. This anthology features stories told by some of the best-known American storytellers, collected by the founder of NAPPS. Chapters on collecting and telling and a bibliography of sources are also included.

Timpanelli, Gioi. *Tales from the Roof of the World: Folktales of Tibet.* Art by Elizabeth Kelly Lockwood. Viking, 1984.

Tyler, Royall, ed. *Japanese Tales.* Pantheon, 1987. Just one example from an extensive series of collections of folklore by country. A good adult reference.

Vuong, Lynette Dyer. *The Brocaded Slipper and Other Vietnamese Tales.* Art by Vo-dinh Mai. Addison-Wesley, 1982. Nicely presented tales from Vietnam.

Walker, Barbara K. *A Treasury of Turkish Folktales for Children.* Shoe String, 1988. Quirky humor from the Middle East.

West, John O., ed. *Mexican-American Folklore: Legends, Songs, Festivals, Proverbs, Crafts, Tales of Saints, of Revolutionaries, and More.* August House, 1988. Good background material, part of the American Folklore Series.

Wolkstein, Diane, ed. *The Magic Orange Tree and Other Haitian Folktales.* Art by Elsa Henriquez. Knopf, 1978. Collected by an editor who is also a storyteller, these Haitian stories have humor and warmth.

Wood, Ruzena. *The Palace of the Moon and Other Tales from Czechoslovakia.* Art by Kryslyna Turska. Andre Deutsch, 1981. Familiar themes with a Czech background.

Yeats, W. B. *Fairy Tales of Ireland.* Selected by Neil Philip. Art by P. J. Lynch. Delacorte, 1990. Nineteen tales chosen from two volumes of fairy stories collected by the nineteenth-century poet.

Yee, Paul. *Tales from Gold Mountain: Stories of the Chinese in the New World.* Art by Simon Ng. Macmillan, 1989. Contemporary stories about Chinese immigrants to North America.

Yolan, Jane, ed. *Favorite Folktales from Around the World.* Pantheon, 1986. Almost 500 pages of folktales from many countries. Good for browsing.

Zaum, Marjorie. *Catlore: Tales from Around the World.* Art by author. Atheneum, 1985. Some poignant, some sad, these cat tales are collected from 23 countries.

6 / Reading Aloud

Sometimes I think we overdid reading aloud in my family. We eat out quite a bit together. Naturally, the whole family brings along something to read. Reading at the dinner table is not only allowed, but encouraged at the Bauers'. Last week, my husband, Peter, was browsing through the *Wall Street Journal*, my daughter, Hilary, was reading *War and Peace*, and I was finishing a rather silly book with well-written dialogue. Each of us kept calling, "Attention! Attention!" in order to read aloud to the others something especially wonderful. The result was a sort of "my book is more interesting than yours" competition. Actually, I suppose this offers a good example of a family reading aloud together, even though I have to admit that I lost the game!

I can't prove this, but I think that the books we read to Hilary when she was younger, and the reading aloud habit that we instilled in her, may be the reason that she is both a devoted reader and a comfortable speaker. When she was younger, we always read to her before bedtime and often found the time to squeeze in a book before she went off to school. If you haven't found the time to do this yourself as you frantically race around in the morning to get your family out of bed and everyone's lunches made, I'll share my secret with you. To gain 15 minutes more a day, simply set your alarm clock to ring 15 minutes earlier than usual—without telling anyone, of course. Now you have at least a quarter of an hour more to read a book each day. Shh . . . you must promise not to tell anyone in my family.

Reading aloud is the natural way to present literature that is too long or too difficult to memorize or learn to tell. This method of presentation was particularly popular in the Victorian era, when families would gather in the salon to read the latest Dickens or Bronte. But with the advent of television (or maybe it was Little League), the family and classroom tradition of reading aloud waned until the present renaissance, which has been encouraged by such read aloud advocates as Judy Freeman and Jim Trelease. Reading aloud promoters applaud the current trend in "whole language" that allows time for reading aloud in the classroom. Our current task seems to be to convince teachers of older students that reading aloud is a valid way to introduce and promote literature. My friend Kate Loggen, the librarian at the Oregon Episcopal School, has been reading aloud to her middle school and high school students for a decade with enviable results. "Please, please read another chapter!" is a frequent plea.

When I was a child my best friend's mother had a tea at four o'clock every afternoon, complete with a silver tea service and a tray of homebaked goodies for us. For an hour she read to us from the greats of children's literature. We met Walter de la Mare, C. S. Lewis, and Eleanor Farjeon during teatime at Helen's house. Helen now lives in England. She carries on the same tradition of teatime reading even though her children are of high school age. There is no reason why the oral sharing of books needs to stop just because everyone knows how to read to themselves. My former library school dean read aloud to his family after dinner long after his children were adults with children of their own.

If you are a busy classroom teacher, a reading aloud session can be a daily occurrence with a formal storyhour taking place as a special treat once a week. But please don't do what Mrs. Morrison did to us in the fourth grade. Halfway through one book she felt the class needed to be punished, so she never finished it. I'm still searching for that story (it's about this elephant . . .) so I can find out what happened.

If you are a public librarian you might find that school vacations are a good time to schedule daily read aloud sessions so that you may offer a chapter or two of a longer book to your patrons.

Choosing Materials to Read Aloud

Choose any materials of high literary quality that appeal to you. These may be short stories, plays, longer folktales, original fairy tales, poetry, picture books, even a longer book to read a chapter at a time. If the selection is too long to learn to tell comfortably, prepare it for reading aloud. If the language of a story or book could be spoiled unless read word for word, consider reading aloud instead of telling the story.

If you are reading this book, then you are probably interested in children and already familiar with many children's books. If you read children's books on a regular basis, you are bound to come across titles that you'll want to present. While you are reading, think of some of the elements that make a book a good one to read aloud. Children like action, suspense, and lots of conversation. This doesn't mean that a book that seems slow and contains long descriptive passages doesn't make an excellent read-aloud book. Hearing description gives children time to absorb the images presented by the author, imagine the scene, and feel the mood of the book.

Don't choose a book merely because a colleague says it's good. Be sure you have read and familiarized yourself with any recommended book. If you think you will be bored reading aloud a book you've just read to yourself, put it aside for a later reading. When you find a book that you like, you'll be surprised, however, that even the most familiar story will seem different when a new audience is hearing it for the first time, for each group reacts differently to the same book.

You might choose a book the children are unlikely to read on their own. For example, if they are reading Lynn Hall's dog books, there is little need to introduce them to more of her books. Try *Call of the Wild* by Jack London or William H. Armstrong's *Sounder*, books that are a little more sophisticated and that they might have difficulty reading on their own. This also applies to types of books. If a majority of children in your group are addicted to formula mystery stories, reading aloud might be the perfect opportunity to introduce something entirely different, such as poetry.

Try to vary the mood and type of material each time you read aloud. Don't always read funny books or animal books. Each story should fill a different need for your audience. Fantasy provides a departure from reality and takes the listeners on a voyage to a new and strange world. Humorous books are usually very popular and give your group a chance to share in laughter. On the other hand, sad books often bring an audience closer together. Most adults are reluctant to cry in public, although children are less embarrassed at showing a normal emotion. You might plan in advance for the sad parts of a book. If you are reading aloud *Charlotte's Web*, dim the lights so that the audience will have more of a feeling of privacy in their grief. Realistic animal stories will give listeners a chance to broaden their understanding about life in the wild. Books that emphasize human characters are also satisfying to read. These books might stimulate spontaneous discussion questions such as "What would you do in the same situation?" Nonfiction should not be ignored as a source for books to read aloud. A variety of subjects can be introduced in the informal atmosphere of group listening.

If the ages of your group are disparate, and you have time to read only one book, I suggest you choose a book more appropriate for the older children. The younger children will understand enough of what they hear to enjoy the more advanced title. Do not dismiss the picture-book format, however; it is often suitable for an older as well as younger group of children. Picture books are usually short enough so that they can be completed in one session. The fine illustrations should be shared with the children while you're reading, and introducing a worthwhile book in a format often considered "for babies" might overcome some of the prejudices these books face at the checkout desk.

How To's

If at all possible choose a gentle atmosphere for reading aloud. A warm fire and comfortable seating obviously add to your performance. But even if that's not possible, a little preparation and planning can make reading aloud a more enjoyable experience. An overstuffed chair purchased at a garage sale or a colorful quilt rescued from an attic trunk for your audience to sit on may make the difference between full attention and wandering minds. Make sure that both you and the children are comfortable. Read with expression. There is no point in reading aloud at all if you are going to rush through the reading, mumble, or skip passages. Remember, you are competing against television, the VCR, and video games! If you don't take your role seriously, your audience might choose mechanical over live entertainment. I still can't imagine a child who would really rather watch television than hear a good story read with feeling and enthusiasm by someone he or she loves!

I could repeat the old adage "Practice makes perfect" on every other page in this book, but the phrase truly does apply to the art of reading aloud. The more you read aloud, the more adept you'll become. When I first became a radio announcer, I panicked every hour just before news time for in the radio world, there was no time to prepare the hourly news bulletin. It was great experience, though.

Be sure you have looked up the pronunciation of any unfamiliar words before you begin reading. Don't be tempted to change or simplify words because you think your audience will not understand them. Not only is it unfair to an author, it is also unfair to the listeners too. The way we learn new words is to hear them repeated in different contexts. What better way to increase a child's vocabulary than to hear words properly used in an exciting story?

You may be tempted to do less preparation for reading aloud than for a memorized oral presentation. Just keep in mind this picture: a number of years ago a student and I were doing a series of story programs at a school arts festival. While we waited for our turn in one classroom we listened to a monitor who was struggling through a reading of Kipling's *The Elephant's Child*. I'm sure she was grateful to be relieved of her task; so were the children. She had obviously never read the story before. And if you meet such Kipling phrases as "... the Precession had preceded according to precedent ..." or "... the banks of the great grey-green, greasy Limpopo River, all set about with fever trees ..." for the first time in front of forty critical children, it has to be a harrowing experience. My companion turned to me and said, "Too bad we can't bring that lady back to class with us; she's the best example of not doing her homework I've ever seen."

Be aware of your phrasing. Do you tend to take a break after exactly the same syllables each time? Does your voice rise or drop at the end of a sentence? Don't bury your head in the print; look up from time to time. Don't always look at the same person; favor different members of the audience each time you glance up. Be careful not to always pick your head up at the same rhythm. It gets monotonous to see a head bobbing up and down after each comma. If you come to an illustration in the text, pause and show it to the group. The pictures are part of the book, after all, and part of the enjoyment of reading. If you are reading to a large group, you might explain at the beginning of the session that the children can come up after the session to examine the pictures. If you come to a spot in the text that contains extensive conversation it might be more effective to leave out the "he said," "she said" since this becomes clear as you read. When you pick up the book again the next evening or day, quickly summarize in a sentence or two the preceding events to refresh your memory and theirs too. At the close of the daily reading, a relaxed discussion of the events may seem in order. I don't think this should be a forced session. It is only worthwhile if questions and comments come out naturally. Some books need a little time to be digested.

If it is at all possible, duplicate copies of the book, and other books by the author or books with a similar theme should be available for take-home reading. As a school librarian I once had a call from a parent whose child wanted to leave the house with a bad case of scarlet fever because she didn't want to miss the daily episode of Esther Hautzig's *The Endless Steppe*. Luckily we had an extra copy to send to her.

A last word: Reading aloud is not to be substituted for traditional storytelling. It's just one other way to present literature orally.

Read Aloud Selections

Here are two stories for you to begin with right away. One is a funny, nonsense story; the other is a thoughtful, beautifully written introduction to a book. Share one, or both of them, with a group today.

TOO MANY APPLES

Even though I wrote "Too Many Apples," I still find it difficult to memorize because of the many apple variations. It doesn't really matter in which order the family eats what, but I offer it to you as a read aloud sample in case you have the same problem. After you have read it aloud a number of times you may find that you have learned it and can tell it instead of reading it. You might browse through a history of apples to introduce or follow "Too Many Apples." Charles Micucci's The Life and Times of the Apple *offers good material for this purpose.*

"Apples. I'm tired of apples."

All the Martin family were tired of apples. Their tree had yielded enough apples to feed them for a decade. No one ever asked, "What's for dinner?" Everyone knew, apples.

Mom tried to be creative. Apple fritters, apple tarts, apple pancakes, applesauce, apple ice cream, apple compote, apple puffs.

Dad tried to keep up the family's spirits, "An apple a day keeps the doctor away," he intoned every morning and every night.

"Dad, we'd rather have the doctor. We're tired of apples," said Eric.

"Motherhood and apple pie is patriotic," said Dad. "Let's move to Togo," said Martha. "Maybe they don't have apples there."

Mom continued to serve apples. For breakfast there were sliced apples. For lunch, apple compote, and for dinner—more apples.

There was apple pudding, apple crisp, and apple slaw. Apples, apples, apples.

One day Mom said, "I've run out of ideas. I can't think of another way to serve apples."

"Waste not, want not," said Dad. "How about apple salad, apple stuffing, baked apples."

The Martin family kept eating apples. They had Apple Betty, apple dumplings, and glazed apples.

Eric and Martha decided to rebel. "We refuse to eat any more apples."

"I have to admit that I'm getting bored, too," said Mom. "All apples and nothing else makes Jack a dull boy," intoned Dad.

"I have an idea," said Martha. "Let's invite our neighbors for an apple banquet and use up all the apples on them."

What a wonderful idea.

On Saturday night, the Bensons, the Levinsons, and the Kims came for dinner.

The whole family helped to prepare the apple banquet.

There were apple pancakes, apple dumplings, apple turnovers, dried apples, apple vinegar, apple cake, apple wedges, apple taffy, apple sauerkraut. There were grilled apples, baked apples, and fried apples. Boiled apples, apple flambé, apple souffle, and apple muffins.

Apples, apples, and more apples.

The Bensons smiled, the Levinsons cheered, and the Kims were delighted.

"Best meal I ever ate."

"What an incredible variety of apple dishes."

"I loved everything."

When the neighbors had left, Mom made an announcement. "They're gone. The apples are finished. We won't have to eat another apple all year.

"Hurrah," said Eric and Martha.

"Don't count your chickens before they hatch," said Dad.

"What does that mean," asked Mom.

"I don't know," said Dad. "I just felt I should say something serious."

The next morning Dad packed a picnic lunch. "How wonderful that we can have peanut butter sandwiches and no apples."

Just then the doorbell rang. Mom went to answer it.

"Oh, no. No. No," the family heard her sigh.

"What is it?"

"A present from the Bensons, the Levinsons, and the Kims."

"What is it?"

"Come see for yourself."

Dad, Eric, and Martha all stared at the present.

Three bushel baskets of apples and a note: "Thank you for dinner. We are so sorry that we ate all your apples. We thought we should re-place them."

TUNING

Gary Paulsen

"Tuning," the introduction to the Newbery Medal Honor book, The Winter Room, *is best read aloud rather than memorized and told, because each word is perfectly chosen by the author. I also think that the subject of reading books ought to be read . . . from a book. I have found that this selection makes a lovely introduction to a presentation on the value of reading for an adult group such as a PTA group or a Chamber of Commerce. Be sure to have the actual book ready for someone in the audience to take away and read independently.*

If books could be more, could show more, could own more, this book would have smells . . .

It would have the smells of old farms; the sweet smell of new-mown hay as it falls off the oiled sickle blade when the horses pull the mower through the field, and the sour smell of manure steaming in a winter barn. It would have the sticky-slick smell of birth when the calves come and they suck for the first time on the rich, new milk; the dusty smell of winter hay dried and stored in the loft waiting to be dropped down to the cattle; the pungent fermented smell of the chopped corn silage when it is brought into the manger on the silage fork. This book would have the smell of new potatoes sliced and frying in light pepper on a woodstove burning dry pine, the damp smell of leather mittens steaming on the back of the stovetop, and the acrid smell of the slop bucket when the lid is lifted and the potato peelings are dumped in—but it can't.

Books can't have smells.

If books could be more and own more and give more, this book would have sound . . .

It would have the high, keening sounds of the six-foot bucksaws as the men pull them back and forth through the trees to cut pine for paper pulp; the grunting-gassy sounds of the work teams snorting and slapping as they hit the harness to jerk the stumps out of the ground. It would have the chewing sounds of cows in the barn working at their cuds on a long winter's night; the solid thunking sound of the ax coming down to split stovewood, and the piercing scream of the pigs when the knife cuts their throats and they know death is at hand—but it can't.

Books can't have sound.

And finally if books could be more, give more, show more, this book would have light . . .

Oh, it would have the soft gold light—gold with bits of hay dust floating in it—that slips through the crack in the barn wall; the light of the Coleman lantern hissing flat-white in the kitchen; the silver-gray light of a middle winter day, the splattered, white-night light of a full moon on snow, the new light of dawn at the eastern edge of the pasture behind the cows coming in to be milked on a summer morning—but it can't.

Books can't have light.

If books could have more, give more, be more, show more, they would still need readers, who bring them sound and smell and light and all the rest that can't be in books.

The book needs you.

Booklist: Some Favorite Books for Reading Aloud

There are many books that make fine read-alouds, so many in fact that there are several books devoted exclusively to listing titles that work well when read aloud. The most practical book is Judy Freeman's *Books Children Will Sit Still For*. This 660-page text lists books by subject, author, title, genre, and grade level. It is also filled with ideas about how to use the suggested books in activities after they have been read aloud. The books are cross-referenced, too, for those who wish to collect a set of books on a similar subject or theme.

Jim Trelease self-published his first book on reading aloud and it was subsequently published by Viking. When it was mentioned in a "Dear Abby" column it became an instant bestseller. Trelease is popular as an inspirational speaker and has done much to further the read-aloud renaissance with parents and teachers. *The New Read-Aloud Handbook* lists books to read aloud as well as valuable tips for choosing and presenting books.

For Reading Out Loud, compiled by Margaret Kimmel, a well-known storyteller and professor, and her co-author, Elizabeth Segal, is another good collection of successful read-alouds.

I have reluctantly put some general grade categories on the books that follow. It is almost impossible to predict at what age or grade a particular child will enjoy listening to a particular book; however, for those who would like some guidance, the approximate grade level given should help. The listening level is usually somewhat higher than the independent reading level, which may add further confusion, I know. The members of your group may have different levels of emotional maturity as well. But since you will be familiar with your own group and will have read the books you are considering, you can probably make good choices for your particular listeners. I have selected the books listed here for children in the elementary and middle schools. They are categorized by subject so that you can vary the types of books you read; an animal story followed by a biography, perhaps. As you read new titles each year add to this list those few outstanding titles that might be worthy of reading aloud. If you are primarily interested in read-alouds for preschool and primary age children, please see the preschool and primary programs in chapter 19.

In revising this booklist for the second edition of this book, I noted that the books chosen for the first edition are all still good candidates for reading aloud. But there are wonderful new titles that need a chance to become read-aloud classics, so I have dropped some old titles and added some new favorites. Of course this is just a sampling of the titles available.

Animals

Adams, Richard G. *Watership Down*. Macmillan, 1972. Grades 5 and up. This is a long book, but each of the chapters (there are 50) is short enough to read in one sitting. Wild rabbits search for a better home in this intricate fantasy.

Byars, Betsy. *The Midnight Fox*. Art by Ann Grifalconi. Viking, 1968. Grades 4–6. Tommy reluctantly spends a summer on a farm and saves a fox that he learns to respect.

Cummings, Sue. *Turtle*. Art by Susan Dodge. Atheneum, 1981. Grades 4–8. Told by a turtle and an old woman, this short novel tells the story of a turtle's adventures in the world.

Eckert, Allan. *Incident at Hawk's Hill*. Art by John Schoenherr. Little, 1971. Grades 5–7. Based on a true frontier incident, this is the story of a boy who lives with a badger.

Howe, Deborah and James Howe. *Bunnicula: A Rabbit-Tale Mystery*. Art by Alan Daniel. Atheneum, 1979. Grades 2–5. Chester, the dog, tries to warn his family that their rabbit is a vampire. Silly and fun.

King-Smith, Dick. *Babe the Gallant Pig.* Art by Mary Rayner. Crown, 1983. Grades 3–6. Have you ever heard of a sheep pig? Farmer Hogget enters a clever pig in the Grand Challenge Sheepdog Trials and . . . wins.

Marshall, James. *Rats on the Roof and Other Stories.* Art by author. Dial, 1991. Grades 3–5. Seven amusing stories featuring some wacky animals. After you read them aloud, you may want to learn one or two to tell.

Naylor, Phyllis Reynolds. *Shiloh.* Atheneum, 1991. Grades 4–6. Can a 12-year-old boy save a dog from his cruel owner?

Rylant, Cynthia. *Every Living Thing.* Art by S. D. Schindler. Bradbury, 1985. Grades 4 and up. Every story in this book is a superb animal or people story. A personal favorite of mine.

Seidler, Tor. *A Rat's Tale.* Art by Fred Marcellino. Farrar, 1986. Grades 5–7. Montague Mad-Rat the Younger meets Isabel Moberly-Rat and falls in love, sort of. A good adventure tale.

Seligson, Susan and Howie Schneider. *Amos: The Story of an Old Dog and His Couch.* Art by Howie Schneider. Little, 1987. All ages. When Amos, an old dog, discovers that his couch is motorized, he begins zooming around town when his "folks" are out of the house. Hilariously funny, this is a picture book with small illustrations. Use it with a small group or pass the book around so that everyone can see a master cartoonist at work.

Taylor, William. *Agnes the Sheep.* Scholastic, 1990. Grades 5–8. Belinda and Joe are put in charge of a feisty sheep named Agnes. A romp by a New Zealand author.

Biography

Adler, David A. *Martin Luther King, Jr.* Art by Robert Casilla. Holiday, 1986. Grades 3–6. A short book that shows the spirit and determination of the minister who fought for an end to prejudice and discrimination.

Aliki. *The King's Day: Louis XIV of France.* Art by author. Harper, 1989. Grades 2–6. This lively picture book follows Louis XIV through a single day. Read the book's text and then let the children read the picture titles and enjoy the art independently.

Burleigh, Robert. *Flight.* Art by Mike Wimmer. Philomel, 1991. Grades 3–8. Captures the physical and emotional strain of Charles Lindbergh's flight across the Atlantic in 1927. Share the art as you read.

Fritz, Jean. *Homesick: My Own Story.* Art by Margot Tomes and photographs. Putnam, 1982. Grades 4–6. An author best known for her biographies of famous Americans writes about her own childhood in China.

Golenbock, Peter. *Teammates.* Art by Paul Bacon. Harcourt, 1990. Grades 3–6. The friendship between Pee Wee Reese and his teammate Jackie Robinson, the first African-American major league baseball player, is explored.

Hautzig, Esther. *The Endless Steppe: Growing Up in Siberia.* Crowell, 1968. Grades 5–7. The story of the author's five years in Siberia during World War II.

Hurwitz, Johanna. *Anne Frank: Life in Hiding.* Art by Vera Rosenberry. Jewish Publication Society, 1988. Grades 4–6. A short biography about the author of one of the world's most famous diaries.

Little, Jean. *Little by Little: A Writer's Education.* Viking, 1987. Grades 4–6. This children's book author writes about her childhood in China and Canada.

Schroder, Alan. *Ragtime Tumpie.* Art by Bernie Fuchs. Little, 1989. Grades 1–4. The childhood of Josephine Baker is explored in a beautifully illustrated picture book.

Stanley, Diane and Peter Vennema. *Good Queen Bess: The Story of Elizabeth I of England.* Art by Diane Stanley. Four Winds, 1990. Grades 4 and up. Perfect to share in just one sitting, the authors have captured the life of Queen Elizabeth I in a picture book.

Fantasy

Babbitt, Natalie. *Tuck Everlasting.* Farrar, 1975. Grades 4–6. If you could, would you choose to live forever?

Banks, Lynne Reid. *The Indian in the Cupboard.* Doubleday, 1980. Grades 4–6. A miniature toy Indian, Little Bear, comes to life for 9-year-old Omri.

Brittain, Bill. *Devil's Donkey.* Art by Andrew Glass. Harper, 1981. Grades 3–6. Dan'l Pitt is transformed into a flea-bitten donkey by Magda, the witch. Lots of fun.

Carroll, Lewis. *Alice's Adventures in Wonderland.* Art by Peter Weevers. Philomel, 1989. Grades 4 and up. It's a bit heretical not to recommend the Tenniel illustrations, but I like Weevers as an alternative in this classic story.

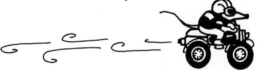

Cleary, Beverly. *The Mouse and the Motorcycle.* Art by Louis Darling. Morrow, 1965. Grades 1–5. Ralph, the mouse has the adventure of his life on Keith's toy motorcycle.

Cresswell, Helen. *Time Out.* Art by Peter Elwell. Macmillan, 1990. Grades 3–5. The family of a nineteenth-century butler and parlor maid is transported for a day to the twentieth century.

Fletcher, Susan. *Dragon's Milk.* Atheneum, 1989. Grades 4–8. Kaeldra, who can communicate with dragons, is asked to be a dragon babysitter for three young dragons in return for milk to cure her ailing sister. Over 200 pages, but well worth it.

Gormley, Beatrice. *Mail-Order Wings.* Art by Emily Arnold McCully. Dutton, 1981. Grades 2–5. Andrea orders a pair of Wonda-Wings and they really work!

Lofting, Hugh. *The Story of Doctor Dolittle.* Art by author. Delacorte, Centenary, 1988. Grades 3–6. The good Dr. Dolittle, who can understand animal talk, voyages to Africa to help cure the monkeys. First published in 1920, this revised edition leaves out the racist bits of the original.

Milne, A. A. *Winnie the Pooh.* Art by Ernest Shepard. Dutton, 1988. Grades 2–5. An assortment of animals cavort in the hundred-acre wood. A special classic, first published in 1926.

Roberts, Willo Davis. *The Girl with the Silver Eyes.* Atheneum, 1980. Grades 4–6. Katie meets three other people with the same telekenetic powers that she has.

Turner, Ann. *Rosemary's Witch*. Harper, 1991. Grades 5–8. Nine-year-old Rosemary meets a 50-year-old witch who is trying to reclaim her family's home.

Wrightson, Patricia. *A Little Fear*. Atheneum, 1983. Grades 5–7. Old Mrs. Tucker outwits a Njimbin all by herself.

Folklore (see also Story Collections in chapter 5)

Hastings, Selina. *Sir Gawain and the Loathly Lady*. Art by Juan Wijingaard. Lothrop, 1987. Grades 6–8. Can Sir Gawain survive marriage to the most repulsive woman on earth?

Haviland, Virginia. *The Talking Pot: A Danish Folktale*. Art by Melissa Sweet. Little, 1990. Grades 1–3. New illustrations update this Danish tale about a pot that helps a poor man.

Kimmel, Eric A. *Hershel of Ostropol*. Art by Arthur Friedman. Jewish Publication Society, 1981. Grades 2–5. Five amusing joke tales about a clever man in Central Europe to tell or read aloud.

Lester, Julius. *The Tales of Uncle Remus: The Adventures of Brer Rabbit*. Art by Jerry Pinkney. Dial, 1987. Grades 3–8. The first of three collections of traditional short tales from the American South.

Lister, Robin. *The Legend of King Arthur*. Art by Alan Baker. Doubleday, 1988. Grades 5–8. This large format works well for the retelling of the Arthurian legend. Fourteen chapters to share.

Osborne, Mary Pope. *American Tall Tales*. Art by Michael McCurdy. Knopf, 1991. All ages. Each chapter introduces a different American tall-tale character.

Patron, Susan. *Burgoo Stew*. Art by Mike Shenon. Orchard, 1991. Grades 2–5. In picture-book format, this varient of "Stone Soup" features five rowdy bad boys.

Sanfield, Steve. *The Adventures of High John the Conqueror*. Art by John Ward. Orchard, 1989. Grades 5–8. These stories are based on the legendary antics of an African American.

Historical Fiction

Fitzgerald, John D. *The Great Brain*. Art by Mercer Mayer. Dial, 1967. Grades 4–6. First in a series featuring a young boy growing up in Utah in the 1900s.

Lawson, Robert. *Ben and Me*. Art by author. Little, 1939. Grades 2–4. Ben Franklin as seen through the eyes of the mouse, Amos, who takes the credit for many of Franklin's inventions.

Levitin, Sonia. *The Return*. Atheneum, 1987. Grades 6–8. Desta and her family flee discrimination in Ethiopia and make their way to Israel as new immigrants. This fascinating adventure takes place during the secret airlift of 1984–85.

Lowry, Lois. *Number the Stars*. Houghton, 1989. Grades 5–7. Annemarie's family takes in a Jewish girl to protect her from the Nazis during World War II. A Newbery Award winner.

Moore, Yvette. *Freedom Songs*. Orchard, 1991. Grades 5–7. Fourteen-year-old Sheryl travels to the South from Brooklyn to take part in the Civil Rights freedom train in the 1960s.

Moskin, Marietta. *The Day of the Blizzard*. Art by Stephan Gammell. Coward, 1978. Grades 3–4. Katie must venture out into the blizzard of '88 in New York City.

Page, Michael. *The Great Bullocky Race.* Art by Robert Ingpen. Dodd, 1984. Grades 2–5. Two competitive bullock drivers and their children race to the port in Australia to sell their wool.

Paterson, Katherine. *Lyddie.* Dutton, 1991. Grades 6–8. Lyddie takes a job as a factory girl in Lowell, Massachusetts in the 1840s.

Stoltz, Mary. *Bartholomew Fair.* Art by Pamela Johnson. Greenwillow, 1990. Grades 4–7. The adventures of six people who meet each other at a fair in sixteenth-century England.

Westhall, Robert. *Blitzcat.* Scholastic, 1989. Grades 6–8. The reader follows Lord Gort, a black cat, through war-torn Europe during World War II.

Humor

Avi. *Romeo and Juliet, Together (and alive) at Last.* Orchard, 1987. Grades 5–7. Laugh out loud as Pete Saltz organizes a seventh-grade production of *Romeo and Juliet.*

Cresswell, Helen. *Ordinary Jack: Being the First Part of the Bagthorpe Saga.* Macmillan, 1977. Grades 5–7. First in a series about a hilarious and wacky family.

Davis, Edward E. *Bruno the Pretzel Man.* Art by Marc Simont. Harper, 1984. Grades 2–4. Bruno wonders of there is more to life than selling pretzels on the streets of New York City.

Heide, Florence Parry. *Tales for the . . . Perfect . . . Child.* Art by Victoria Chess. Orchard, 1985. Grades 3–5. Seven short tales featuring naughty, inventive children.

Hurwitz, Johanna. *Ali Baba Bernstein.* Art by Gail Owens. Morrow, 1985. Grades 2–4. Use this episodic novel as an introduction to Hurwitz's many gently amusing books for children.

Kirby, David and Allen Woodman. *The Cows Are Going to Paris.* Art by Chris L. Demarest. Caroline, 1991. All ages. A herd of cows visits Paris while people from a touring train enjoy the cow field. Silly fun in a picture book.

Lowry, Lois. *Anastasia at This Address.* Houghton, 1991. Grades 4–6. Anastasia writes a letter to a man in the personal column of her father's magazine in another warm, humorous adventure with this irrepressible girl.

Porte, Barbara Ann. *Fat Fanny, Beanpole Bertha, and the Boys.* Art by Maxie Chambliss. Orchard, 1991. Grades 3–5. Fanny teachers her friends, the triplets, to tap dance. Will her parents, who are theatrical agents, discover them . . . or her?

Sacher, Louis. *Sideways Stories from Wayside School.* Art by Dennis Hockerman. Follett, 1978. Grades 2–5. Wacky stories about the students and teachers in a mythical school.

Smith, Janice Lee. *The Kid next Door and Other Headaches: Stories about Adam Joshua.* Art by Dick Gackenbach. Harper, 1984. Grades 1–3. Short stories about the friendship between two boys who have opposite tastes in almost everything.

Information

Blumberg, Rhoda. *The Great American Gold Rush.* Illustrated with prints. Bradbury, 1989. Grades 5–8. Describes the scramble for gold during the California Gold Rush years from 1848 to 1852.

Canadian Childhoods. Tundra, 1989. Grades 4 and up. A Tundra anthology in words and art showing children of many backgrounds growing up in different parts of Canada.

Fraser, Mary Ann. *On Top of the World: The Conquest of Mount Everest.* Holt, 1991. Grades 4–7. Explores the early expeditions of Mount Everest with emphasis on the successful climb of Edmund Hillary and Tenzing Norgay.

Freedman, Russell. *Buffalo Hunt.* Illustrated with paintings. Holiday, 1988. Grades 5–8. Traces the history of the buffalo and the importance of this animal to the life of Native Americans.

Giblin, James Cross. *Chimney Sweeps.* Art by Margot Tomes. Crowell, 1982. Grades 3–6. A historical survey of the life and work of the chimney sweep.

Gilbert, Sara. *You Can Speak Up in Class.* Art by Roy Doty. Morrow, 1991. Grades 2–5. This is a self-help book for children. Try selected parts to read aloud.

Kendall, Russ. *Eskimo Boy: Life in an Inupiaq Eskimo Village.* Scholastic, 1992. All ages. This photo essay illustrates the life of a 7-year-old boy in an Alaskan village.

Kligsheim, Trygve. *Julius*; tr. by Linda Sivesind. Delacorte, 1986. Grades 2–4. A photo essay showing the life and talents of a Norwegian chimpanzee.

Pitkänen, Matti A. with Reijo Härkönen. *The Children of Egypt.* Photos by author. Carolrhoda, 1991. All ages. Glorious full-color photos concentrate on the life of children in Egypt. One in a series.

Ride, Sally and Susan Okie. *To Space and Back.* Photos. Lothrop, 1986. Grades 5–7. The first woman astronaut tells us about life in space.

Schwartz, David M. *If You Made a Million.* Art by Steven Kellogg. Lothrop, 1989. Grades 3–6. A lavishly illustrated picture book describes the monetary system.

Simon, Seymour. *Stars.* Morrow, 1986. Grades 4–6. An introduction to the stars. One of many wonderful books by a seasoned non-fiction writer.

Memorable People

Avi. *Nothing But the Truth: A Documentary Novel.* Orchard, 1991. Grades 6–8. Through memos, telephone calls, conversations, letters, and minutes of meetings, the reader sees all sides of a school controversy.

Bauer, Marion Dane. *On My Honor.* Houghton, 1986. Grades 4–6. Joel promises not to play by the river, but he does and a friend drowns. A story of the consequences of responsibility.

Cech, John. *My Grandmother's Journey.* Art by Sharon McGinley-Nally. Bradbury, 1991. Grades 3–5. Korie's grandmother relates the story of her journey through war and hunger to America. Picture-book format.

Crew, Linda. *Children of the River.* Delacorte, 1989. Grades 8 and up. A 17-year-old Cambodian girl adjusts to life in an Oregon farming community.

Gleitzman, Morris. *Two Weeks with the Queen.* Putnam, 1989. Grades 5–6. Colin is sent to London to stay with relatives while his younger brother is dying in Australia. This book has it all: humor, pathos, sibling rivalry, and love.

Howard, Ellen. *Circle of Giving.* Atheneum, 1984. Grades 4–6. Marguerite befriends Francie, a girl with cerebral palsy, and discovers a "circle of friendship."

Lord, Bette Bao. *In the Year of the Boar and Jackie Robinson.* Art by Marc Simont. Harper, 1984. Grades 4–6. Shirley Temple Wong finds a place for herself in her new life in Brooklyn when she discovers baseball.

Magorian, Michelle. *Good Night, Mr. Tom.* Harper, 1981. Grades 6–8. Willie, an abused child, is evacuated from London during World War II and makes friends with a crusty old man.

Paulsen, Gary. *The Monument.* Delacorte, 1991. Grades 5–8. An artist commissioned to create a war memorial in a small Kansas town influences 13-year-old Rocky to draw. A book that explores the meaning of art.

Schwartz, David M. *Supergrandpa.* Art by Bert Dodson. Lothrop, 1991. All ages. In Sweden, 66-year-old Gustav Håkansson is denied a place in the 1000-mile-long bicycle race, but enters anyway.

Shreve, Susan. *The Gift of the Girl Who Couldn't Hear.* Tambourine, 1991. Grades 6–7. Talented, but insecure Eliza learns a valuable lesson from her deaf friend Lucy.

Picture Books for Older Children and Adults

Browne, Anthony. *Piggybook.* Art by author. Knopf, 1986. Mr. Piggott and his two sons turn into pigs when Mom leaves.

DeFelice, Cynthia C. *The Dancing Skeleton.* Art by Robert Andrew Parker. Macmillan, 1989. Aaron gets up out of his grave and sits in his rocker and refuses to budge.

Griffith, Helen V. *Georgia Music.* Art by James Stevenson. Greenwillow, 1986. A little girl brings back the music her Grandfather misses.

Rankin, Laura. *The Handmade Alphabet.* Art by author. Dial, 1991. Objects illustrate each letter of the alphabet in American Sign Language.

Sara. *Across Town.* Art by author. Orchard, 1990. In black, tan, and white the artist shows a sinister man walking in the night and finding a cat.

Scheffler, Ursel. *Stop Your Crowing Kasimir!* Art by Silke Brix-Henker. Carolrhoda, 1988. An old woman and her rooster are brought to court for disturbing the new neighbors. Who wins?

Scieszka, Jon. *The True Story of the 3 Little Pigs, by A. Wolf.* Art by Lane Smith. Viking, 1989. The classic tale told from the point of view of the wolf.

Van Allsburg, Chris. *The Wretched Stone.* Art by author. Houghton, 1991. A glowing stone transforms a sailing ship's crew into monkeys.

Wisniewski, David. *The Warrior and the Wise Man.* Paper-cutting by author. Photography of paper-cutting by Lee Salsbery. Lothrop, 1989. The Emperor must decide which of his twin sons will rule the kingdom.

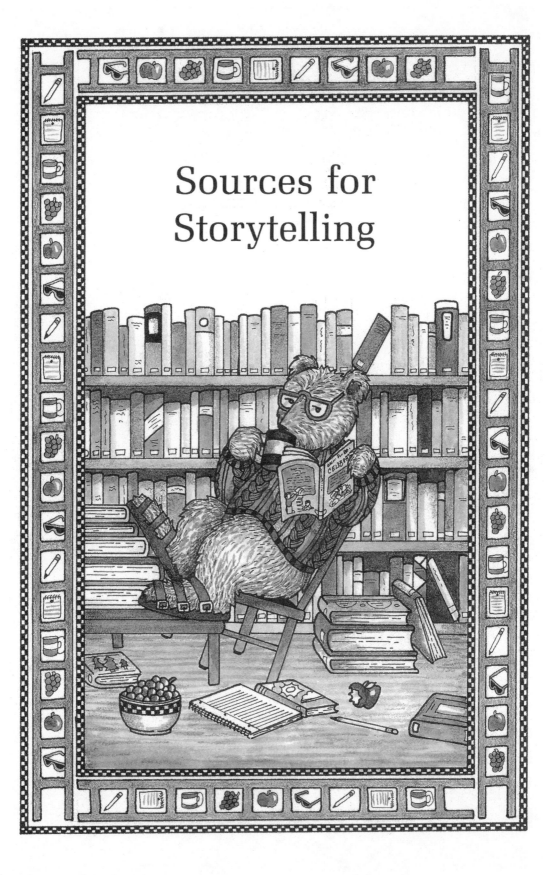

Sources for
Storytelling

Where will you find material for your storytime?
Start at the library, of course. There you will find
folklore, poetry, picture books, informational
books, short stories, and longer books—enough
material for a lifetime of storytelling. But don't forget your Uncle Ken, your neighbor Eddie, or your
Great Aunt Bess. They may have stories for you,
too.

Books of folktales, fables, myths, epics, and legends collected by professional folklorists offer a
good starting point. Short stories written by contemporary authors also provide a wealth of material for your storyhour.

Poetry, available both in useful anthologies and
in attractive single volumes, offers another good
source of storytelling material. Create an entire
program around poetry, or choose a few poems to
use as transitional material between longer stories.

Picture books, long considered the particular
province of small children, are now a primary
source of material for all storytelling programs. In
fact, I'll tell you a secret: I find many of my new
favorite stories in the beautifully illustrated picture books that are published each year.

Riddles, jokes, tongue twisters, and proverbs
are all part of a tradition of non-narrative folklore
that children especially enjoy. Browse through the
references listed here, but don't forget the jump
rope rhyme or riddle your third grader shared with
you yesterday.

Finally, mine the memories of your family and friends for anecdotes and remembrances that can add a special, personal touch to your storyhour. The tradition of family storytelling has reemerged in storytelling festivals all over the country, so why not make it part of your tradition, too?

Whatever you do, don't worry about what you can use for source material. There's a whole world of stories, poems, and riddles, whatever you want, just waiting for you to begin.

7 / Narrative Sources

Looking for a good story to tell? So am I. I've been looking for just one more dazzling story to learn for the next chance I have to tell a story. You can always ask me what I'm currently attempting to learn since I always have a story in my tote bag or purse.

The key to a successful program lies in the story or stories that you use. Planning, production, promotion, and attention to other details are important, but the story remains the single most important element.

Above all, choose a story that you like, one that fits your own individual personality. By finding stories to suit you, I simply mean that if you think of yourself as vivacious and sparkling, you might tend to enjoy telling some of the funny or silly folktales; if you have a quiet, shy personality you might capitalize on it and choose the more romantic or magical tales. You must read a number of stories until you find those that appeal to you.

Although you will begin by using stories familiar to you, you will want to continue your search for new stories. When local collections are exhausted, ask for an interlibrary loan of some of the other collections you've missed. Ask librarians, teachers, and friends who tell stories to name their favorites. When you attend an educational or library conference, ask your colleagues if they tell stories and find out their favorites. On vacations, visit the local library and ask if the librarians keep records of the stories they tell. You might get ideas of already tried and successful stories told. As you read, note selections that seem to you to have possibilities. Some stories might not be appropriate for your present audience, but write down their names for consideration at a later date. Now read some of your selections over again. One may fit into a particular holiday storyhour, a good Thanksgiving story perhaps. It may be from a country that interests you or fits into the school curriculum with which you are associated. The story may be similar to one you liked as a child. The best reason of all is that it seems attractive to you at the time. Some of the literature about storytelling attempts to list the components of a story that make it worthwhile. This may be of use to you; however, when you're just beginning, I suggest that you start with stories that have already been told and loved by hundreds of children through the generations.

After you have learned and told a folktale or two you can advance to the literary tale. When you think that you understand the structure of a story you may feel ready to try composing your own stories. You'll probably want to start with stories about your own family, or you may feel comfortable with a particular genre that you enjoy: fantasy, science fiction, or bedtime stories.

I still feel that a beginning teller should stick with the stories that have been successful with generations of children and young adults, but you must do what is right for you. If you prefer to try making up your own stories, then you will probably be successful!

As a teacher, librarian, or media specialist your primary aim may be to introduce your students or patrons to literature through storytelling. (This has been my own quest for nearly 30 years!) If this is the case you will want to use stories published in books so that you can actually hold up the book before or after the telling, encouraging your listeners to read the story, or others in the collection, for themselves.

In general, folklore will be the core of your booksharing, since so many stories have their basis in folklore. Let's explore some of the narrative sources that you will find in your school or public library.

And for Your Inspiration

Every serious storyteller in search of program materials should become familiar with the resources that follow.

Baker, Augusta and Ellin Greene. *Storytelling: Art and Technique.* rev. ed. Bowker, 1987. A survey of traditional storytelling techniques.

Bettelheim, Bruno. *The Uses of Enchantment: The Meaning and Importance of Fairy Tales.* Knopf, 1976. A scholarly defense of folk literature.

Colwell, Eileen. *Storytelling.* Bodley Head, 1980. A British storyteller and collector gives suggestions for learning and telling stories. The chapter on voice and speech is especially interesting.

de Vos, Gail. *Storytelling for Young Adults: Techniques and Treasury.* Libraries Unlimited, 1991. Techniques, an extensive booklist by tale type, and a selection of stories to present to a young adult audience.

Farrell, Catherine. *Storytelling: A Guide for Teachers.* Scholastic, 1991. Short and to the point, this guide includes sample stories and a seven-step process for learning stories.

Folklore: An Annotated Bibliography and Index to Single Editions; comp. by Elsie B. Ziegler. Faxon, 1973. Subject, motif, country of origin, type, and illustrator are listed. Companion volume to *Index to Fairy Tales 1949 to 1972.*

Hamilton, Martha and Mitch Weiss. *Children Tell Stories: A Teaching Guide.* Richard Owen, 1990. Offers exercises and sample stories to try when teaching children to tell stories.

Index to Fairy Tales 1949 to 1972, Including Folklore, Legends, and Myths in Collections; comp. by Norma Olin Ireland. Faxon, 1973. Analyzes over 400 collections of stories.

Kinghorn, Harriet R. and Mary Helen Pelton. *Every Child a Storyteller.* Art by Myke Knutson. Libraries Unlimited, 1991. Original stories and activities introduce children to storytelling.

Livo, Norma J. and Sandra A. Rietz. *Storytelling: Process and Practice.* Libraries Unlimited, 1986. An academic approach to collecting sources, practicing your technique, and telling a story. Over 400 pages.

Maguire, Jack. *Creative Storytelling: Choosing, Inventing, and Sharing Tales for Children.* Art by Dale Gottlieb. McGraw, 1985. A survey of traditional storytelling techniques with emphasis on preparation. Original story examples.

Painter, William M. *Musical Story Hours: Using Music with Storytelling and Puppetry.* Shoe String, 1989. Written with charm and clarity, this book concentrates on the inclusion of music in story presentations.

_____. *Story Hours with Puppets and Other Props.* Shoe String, 1990. Presenting children's books with easy-to-acquire props and puppets.

Pellowski, Anne. *The World of Storytelling.* H. W. Wilson, 1990. A classic text, expanded and revised.

Sawyer, Ruth. *The Way of the Storyteller.* rev. ed. Viking, 1962 (first published in 1942). A classic introduction to storytelling. The 11 stories in the appendix are a bonus for the advanced storyteller.

Shedlock, Marie L. *The Art of the Storyteller.* Dover, 1951 (first published in 1915). Shedlock is considered responsible for bringing traditional storytelling to American libraries. Good background reading and a collection of stories.

Stories: A List of Stories to Tell and Read Aloud; comp. by Marilyn Berg Iarusso. 8th ed. New York Public Library, 1990.

Folktales

Stith Thompson, the recognized authority of the folktale, defines the traditional prose tale as a story "which has been handed down from generation to generation either in writing or by word of mouth." As potential storytellers living in today's world, we

usually take our material from printed sources. Few working teachers or librarians will have access to oral story sources. Scholars engaged in the study of folklore might complain that most folktales that have been published no longer belong to the true tradition since they have been frozen in print and therefore can no longer develop and change. For our purposes this may actually be an advantage, for it is not just the plot of the story that we wish to convey but the spirit and style as well. We want to introduce the language of literature.

The audiences that listen to you tell these stories will benefit in a variety of ways too. Some individuals will be influenced by the ethical values inherent in most of the tales; others will be stimulated by the images and situations to create in artistic ways; whereas still others will view the storyhour as pure entertainment, unaware that they are learning about other lands and people. Ultimately you will receive requests for the books in which the stories appear, and this will lead to further reading and study. Familiar stories such as "Goldilocks and the Three Bears," "Little Red Riding Hood," and "Cinderella" are all examples of the folktale. The versions of these stories with which we are most familiar originate in three different countries: "The Three Bears" from England, "Little Red Riding Hood" from Germany, and "Cinderella" from France. All three stories exist in many versions. In fact, more than 400 versions of the Cinderella stories have been recorded around the world. The formula for virtually all folktales is the same: the characters and problem are introduced, an obstacle is set up, and a resolution ends the story. Usually folktales are devoid of long descriptive passages and concentrate almost entirely on plot. Even the characters are not developed to any great extent and tend to be stereotypes of good or evil, cleverness or stupidity. The shorter folktales rely on a single theme: the triumph of good over evil or of a poor man outwitting a rich man. If you wish to pursue a more academic study in this area, you will want to begin with some of the adult studies listed at the end of this chapter. You may also be interested in the notes at the end of the story collections that you read, for some authors and folklorists provide extensive notes regarding the source of the story, the circumstances under which it was collected, what parts were deleted, or what additions were made. Some of the material may be of particular interest to your audience and the background on collecting the story may, in some situations, provide useful introductory material.

Many modern authors have been much influenced by folktales and have attempted to write their own, some quite successfully. These original stories are sometimes referred to as "literary folktales." Some famous storytellers have written both kinds of folktales, those based directly on folklore and literary folktales. Hans Christian Andersen is a good example. His earlier work is based upon folklore, probably the stories he learned as a child. His later work is entirely original and no folk literature has been identified as its source. Usually, the original or literary folktale or fairy tale is more difficult to tell since you will want to retain the beauty of the author's language by virtually memorizing the story word for word. The stories of Hans Christian Andersen, Rudyard Kipling, Eleanor Farjeon, and Laurence Housman all fall into this category.

It is useful to be aware of some of the major types of folktales, for it is then possible to identify the particular types that suit your personality for telling. Identification of common themes can help you create thematic programs and broaden your repertoire to include particular types of tales or motifs that appeal to you or your audiences. Following are descriptions of some of the types of stories you will find in your search for program material.

Repetitive and Cumulative Tales

These tales are the easiest to learn since they have a minimum of plot and usually a repetitive rhythm occurs throughout. While some adults may find these stories boring to tell because of the constant repetition, they are particularly popular with young children. After you have actually told one of these tales to a group of preschoolers and have experienced their delighted reaction, you may be a fan too.

Typical of the repetitive story is the familiar, foolish Henny-Penny who meets Cocky-Locky, Ducky-Daddles, Goosey-Loosey, Turkey-Lurkey, and Foxy-Woxy on the way to tell the king that the sky is falling. In "The Gingerbread Boy" the proud gingerbread hero repeats, "Run! Run! as fast as you can! You can't catch me, I'm the Gingerbread Man!" to a host of would-be captors. A delightful variant to this story is a picture-book adaptation of a Danish tale by Jack Kent of *The Fat Cat* who devours with relish a number of objects, animals, and people until a crafty woodcutter puts an end to the greedy cat. Joseph Jacobs's "The Cat and the Mouse" delights youngsters with its rhythmic refrain:

Then the baker gave mouse bread, and mouse gave butcher bread, and butcher gave mouse meat, and mouse gave farmer meat, and farmer gave mouse hay, and mouse gave cow hay and cow gave mouse milk, and mouse gave cat milk, and cat gave mouse her own tail again!

A similar story in picture-book form is Nonny Hogrogian's *One Fine Day*, in which a fox loses his tail.

Animal Tales

Many of the folktales deal with talking animals who are often really humans in disguise, exhibiting very recognizable human faults and foibles. The simpler tales such as "The Three Bears," "The Three Pigs," or "The Three Billy Goats Gruff" are easily learned and are appropriate for use with small children. Longer and more sophisticated animal stories often involve animals in relationships with human beings. In the German "The Fisherman and His Wife," a fish can carry on a conversation as well as grant wishes. In the French "Puss in Boots," a cat takes care of his master, while in the Finnish variant, "Mighty Mikko," it is a gentle and clever fox that guides his master into marrying a princess.

Enchanted humans take on animal form in stories collected from around the world. In the well-known German story a prince lives his life as a frog until he is freed by a princess. In the Finnish tale, "The Forest Bride," it is an enchanted mouse that befriends a younger son and then becomes his bride.

How and Why Stories

Sometimes referred to as "pourquoi" stories, these tales explain how and why a physical or cultural phenomenon began. Some of these stories are closely related to myth since a god often intervenes in the climax. The African folktale retold by Elphinstone Dayrell in picture-book form with illustrations by Blair Lent explains *Why the Sun and the Moon Live in the Sky*. A story collected by Pura Belpré (in *Once in Puerto Rico*) from Puerto Rican folklore explains the origin of the royal palm tree, while Harold Courlander's story from El Salvador explains the origin of the balsam tree (in *Ride with the Sun*). A charming Chinese story tells "How the Camel Got his Proud Look." And a Norwegian story explains "Why the Sea Is Salt." Marcia Leach has collected a number of how and why stories in *How the People Sang the Mountains Up*.

You might be able to find Native American "pourquoi" stories that explain why mountains or rivers in your area exist.

Adventure and Romantic Stories

These two types often join together in one story. A foolish lad, or a clever prince in search of a wife might be led on fantastic adventures that take him deep inside a hill or to a glass mountain. The most famous of the romantic stories is probably "Cinderella." The version we know was collected in France in the seventeenth century, but there are so many known variants of the Cinderella story that a storyteller could specialize in telling just this one story. One of the characteristics of the folktale is the simplicity with which people, places, and actions are described. Usually the characterizations are scanty; heroes and heroines are kind and good, while their enemies are often portrayed as trolls, giants, or witches.

Droll and Humorous Stories

Stories that make your audience laugh are fun to tell. You know through their laughter if the story has been well received. Drolls are those silly stories that rely on ridiculous situations or witless characters to create their humor. In Jewish folklore there is a mythical town called Chelm in which all the inhabitants are incredibly stupid. The stories of the people of Chelm can be found in several collections: *Zlateh the Goat* by Isaac Bashevis Singer and *The Wise Men of Helm* by Solomon Simon. A typical story of the citizens of Chelm goes like this:

Once the people of Chelm thought they could make money by selling lumber from the mountain that overlooked their town. For weeks the men of Chelm chopped down the largest trees and cut off the branches until they had a fine pile of large logs. Then it took a month for the men to carry the great tree trunks down the mountain. At last the horrendous job was almost done. Two strangers arriving in town on the last day watched in amusement as the men carried the logs down the mountain. "Why didn't you just roll the logs down the hill instead of carrying them?" suggested one of the strangers. "What a good idea," exclaimed the men of Chelm. "Let's do it." And with that they began the long trek back up the mountain, each man hauling a log so that when they reached the top they could roll them back down again.

Folk Characters

In your reading of folktales you will find many collections that revolve around one folk character, animal or human, who seems to be wise and foolish at the same time. A majority of these folk characters trick their adversaries through their cleverness. Tyll Eulenspiegel, a German folk character and merry trickster who outwits a variety of established scholars and businessmen with his clever pranks, has had many stories written about him. I have included one of my favorites, "Tyll Paints the Duke's Portrait," in chapter 5 for you to learn and tell.

Baron Munchausen, another German tall-tale character, inevitably emerges triumphant from the conflicts in his humorous adventures. The popular Turkish folk character, the "Hodja," is a simple soul who is often taken advantage of and finds his revenge in ingenious trickery. The Haitian "Uncle Bouqui" is often bested by his friend "Ti Malice," just as the American "Br'er Rabbit" takes advantage of his "friends." Steve Sanfield, a popular professional storyteller, has collected and retold stories of the African-American trickster High John—stories that originated during the days of American slavery.

Supernatural characters such as the Scandinavian trolls and ogres, the Irish fairies, and the Slavic domovoi are just a few of the unusual inhabitants of the folktale. Some of these creatures are workers of evil; others may be a blessing for those who come in contact with them. If you become interested in one of these folk characters, you can gather a number of stories together to create an entire program.

Regions or Countries

One obvious grouping is to collect stories that are popular in a particular region or country. Well-written collections from every part of the world, ranging from the islands of the Caribbean to the mountains of Russia, are available to the interested story-teller. It is interesting to note that Americans are often more familiar with the folktales of France, Germany, England, and Norway than they are with the native American tales.

France. The first book of "fairy tales" published in France is still read and relished by children in Western Europe and America. The book, *Histoires ou contes du temps passe avec des moralités (Histories or tales of long ago with morals)* and subtitled *Contes de ma mère l'oye (Tales of Mother Goose)* was published in 1697. Charles Perrault (1628–1703), usually credited with their authorship, collected these folktales and rewrote them for the amusement of the adults at the French court, but the tales became popular with children as well. The eight tales in his collection (whose subtitle, incidentally, seems to be the first mention of the name "Mother Goose") were "The Sleeping Beauty," "Little Red Riding Hood," "Blue Beard," "Puss in Boots," "Diamonds and Toads," "Cinderella," "Riquet with the Tuft," and "Tom Thumb." Perrault added morals to the stories for the amusement of adults, although these are usually omitted for children.

Other French tales, some of which were written in the same period as Perrault's stories, are still enjoyed today. For example, Comtesse D'Aulnoy's "The White Cat" and Madame LePrince de Beaumont's "Beauty and the Beast" both appear in many story collections.

Germany. In Germany, Jacob and Wilhelm Grimm collected folktales as part of their study of philology in order to examine the roots of the German language. Their first volume of *Kinder und Hausmarchen (Children's and Household Tales)* was published 1812, and subsequent volumes followed in later years. The stories were recorded exactly as the Grimm brothers heard them, usually from country peasants. Although not all the Grimm tales are appropriate for children, many have been consistently popular: "Hansel and Gretel," "Rapunzel," "Rumpelstiltskin," "Snow White and the Seven Dwarfs," and "The Bremen Town Musicians" are just a few of the ever-popular stories they gathered.

The Grimm tales, originally collected in German over a hundred years ago, reach us in many different translations and versions. A large library can easily have a whole shelf of different books all devoted to these tales the Grimms collected. Which version should you use to learn and tell these tales? If you took the time to thoroughly study each version of Grimm, each version of the Arabian Nights, and each version of Perrault you would become an expert folklorist, but you might not ever have time to learn a story! As a beginner in the field you may wish to trust the judgment of experienced storytellers in choosing a good version for telling. Several libraries have published excellent storytelling bibliographies or you could begin by using the bibliographies at the end of this chapter. There is, of course, no one perfect version. For instance, even though several new, beautifully illustrated translations of the Grimm tales have been published, I still prefer the older retelling by Wanda Gág, who wrote the rhythmic *Millions of Cats*.

As a storyteller you do not need to be convinced that folktales should be introduced to children, but you might be amazed at the amount of violence in some of the tales. It is true that many of the stories are unsuitable for children for various reasons but, as for the concern about violence, the reader will discover, on closer examination, that what is being portrayed is simply symbolic of the struggle between good and evil. The triumph of good often comes out through some sort of sacrifice, but rarely with the graphic presentation of blood and gore so often emphasized in the media today. For example, "The Seven Ravens" is the story of a sister searching for her seven bewitched brothers. In the course of the story, the girl cuts off her finger to use as a key to open the door of the glass mountain. This act symbolizes a sacrifice in exchange for love and forgiveness. Even so, it is overshadowed by the brothers' return to their human form and their reunion with their sister. If a young child seems to be frightened by a story from Grimm then certainly he or she should not be further exposed to these stories until more mature and able to deal with their frightening aspects.

As a visiting storyteller with the New York Public Library, I was once invited to tell stories to a multi-ethnic group on the Lower East Side of New York. I told the librarian that I had recently learned Wanda Gág's version of *Rapunzel*, but that I felt the story was too familiar to tell. She advised me to tell it anyway. The experience really taught me why these stories have remained popular down through the generations, for the children listened with such eagerness and afterwards asked many questions. Did it hurt to have someone climbing up your hair like that? And what happened to the witch? I was too inexperienced to come up with any satisfactory answers but I promised to find out. The next week they were ready for me as I came through the door, but I had done my homework and was prepared to field their questions. I had found two perfect visual answers: Arthur Rackham, the distinguished British artist, had painted a clear illustration of Rapunzel's long tresses wrapped several times around a hook outside her tower window showing that having a prince or a witch climb up your braids might be almost a comfortable experience. As for what happened to the witch, Felix Hoffmann's picture book of *Rapunzel* showed a picture of the witch being carried off by a bird, which satisfied the most curious of the children. It was this experience that made me realize that there is a place for good visual material in a storyhour as well as for exciting words.

England. The name that stands out above all others in the collecting of English tales is that of Joseph Jacobs (1854–1916). His purpose was somewhat different from that of the Grimm brothers; he was deliberately trying to find stories that would be suitable for children. In his versions of the English tales, he left out incidents that he felt would be inappropriate, but each of his omissions is recorded in the notes at the end of his collections. Although he changed the language slightly where the heavy dialects would make reading difficult, the tales still retain their original folk flavor.

The stories that Jacobs collected range from the simple nursery favorites, such as "The Three Little Pigs," "The Three Bears," and "Teeny-Tiny" to the more sophisticated "Cap O'Rushes," a variant of Cinderella. Whereas the German folktales often have a somber mood, many of the English tales contain a measure of gentle humor. Giants and giant killers abound in these tales. One of my favorites features a brave girl, Molly Whuppie, who outwits a giant. Even though Jacobs's tales cannot be considered authentic folklore, since he attempted to give literary character to the stories, his versions have a distinction worth retaining. Think of the bowdlerized versions of "The Three Little Pigs" you've encountered. Now enjoy Jacobs's introduction to the popular story:

Once upon a time when pigs spoke rhyme
And monkeys chewed tobacco,
And hens took snuff to make them tough,
And ducks went quack, quack, quack, O!

There was an old sow with three little pigs, and as she had not enough to keep them, she sent them out to seek their fortune.

For years Joseph Jacobs's collections were the only source of English folktales readily available to children. However, well-known folklorist Andrew Lang included English tales with tales from all over the world in his famous "color" fairy books. More recently James Reeves, the English poet, published a collection of English tales, *English Fables and Fairy Stories*.

The popularity of these English stories has inspired some fine picture-book versions. Evaline Ness has illustrated an edition of *Tom Tit Tot* emphasizing the humor of this light-hearted variant of the German *Rumpelstiltskin*. Marcia Brown used two-color linoleum cuts to illustrate *Dick Whittington and His Cat*. Marcia Sewell's delightful black-and-white sketches adorn a picture-book version of *Master of All Masters*. In my opinion these illustrated versions should be used sparingly in the actual program and reserved, for the most part, for individual reading after the story has been told. An oral presentation of *Master of All Masters* has got to be funnier without pictures, no matter how skillfully they are drawn.

Norway and Sweden. When one thinks of Norwegian folktales, one inevitably comes up with two names. Just as the Grimm brothers collected tales from the German countryside, so two friends, Peter Christian Asbjørnsen (1812–1855) and Jorgen E. Moe (1813–1882), gathered stories they heard from peasant storytellers and published them in a still famous collection, *East O' the Sun and West O' the Moon*. Much of the popularity and success of this collection in English-speaking countries must be attributed to the excellent translation done by the English scholar, George Webbe Dasent (1817–1896). Here, as in the German and English collections, are simple stories for the very youngest like the rhythmic "The Three Billy Goats Gruff" and the short "Why the Bear Is Stumpy-tailed." A nonchalant humor prevails in some of the tales, such as "Gudbrand-on-the-Hillside," in which everything that the man does, no matter how foolish, is supported with good humor by his loving wife. A similar story to Wanda Gág's *Gone Is Gone* is "The Husband Who Was to Mind the House," whose housekeeping efforts end in humorous disaster. Trolls and giants appear in the stories with enough frequency for listeners to call out "Tell another scary one like the last story!"

If you are interested in older illustrated versions, you might want to locate Kay Nielsen's strong interpretations of these Norwegian stories to share with your group. Erik Werenskiold and Theodor Kittelsen's black-and-white traditional illustrations for the Asbjørnsen and Moe *Norwegian Folk Tales* are also worthwhile.

Although the Norwegian collection is by far the best known of the Scandinavian collections, an English translation of Swedish tales, illustrated by John Bauer in a style reminiscent of Nielsen, makes these Swedish tales come to life. Selected by Elsa Olenius and translated by Holger Lundbergh, *Great Swedish Fairy Tales* is filled with wonderful stories of terrifying trolls usually outwitted by clever simple folk.

The United States. Although it would take several volumes to just introduce folklore of the world and its storytelling editions, we mustn't forget to mention at least one more folk region.

While many folktales read in the United States are European in origin, distinct American folklore is found in Native-American tales, African-American folktales, folk songs, and tales of American folk heroes. Native American lore, in which animals figure so prominently, seems to hold a never-ending fascination for children. These legends of the origins of our lakes, rivers, and mountains may be difficult to understand, however, without some background explanation. African-American folktales have been gathered largely from the South. Many of these stories are written in a dialect that may be difficult for the average reader or storyteller. Folk songs are also a part of American folk tradition. You will find collections of songs, complete with music, and many attractive picture books based on individual songs listed in the music chapter.

Not all of the American tall-tale heroes are authentic derivations from folklore, but the tales of their deeds and their colorful characters have captured the hearts of school-age children who have been introduced to them. Many of these folk stories are based on the adventures of historical personages, such as Davy Crockett, Johnny Appleseed, and John Henry. Others, such as Mike Fink, the river boatman; Pecos Bill, the cowboy; and Paul Bunyan, the mighty logger, are probably not genuine folklore heroes, but stories about them are written in folktale form and are delightful to tell.

Some other American folktales are actually variants of European tales, imported and adapted to the American experience. For example, some of the tales collected by Richard Chase in the southern mountain regions of Appalachia for his *Grandfather Tales* and *The Jack Tales* are European stories transformed by American settings and dialects.

Other countries.   France, England, Germany, and the United States have provided familiar folktales for generations of storytellers. For those in search of lesser known folktales for presentation, a wealth of material awaits you. Luckily, talented folklorists have collected authentic tales in book form. Harold Courlander's African collections provide scholarly interpretations suitable for the storyteller. *The Hat-Shaking Dance and Other Ashanti Tales from Ghana* and *The Fire on the Mountain and Other Ethiopian Stories* are only two of the books providing material for oral presentation. Yoshiko Uchida's *The Dancing Kettle* and *The Sea of Gold* introduce the English-speaking storyteller to Japanese stories. Isaac Bashevis Singer has retold some of the stories of the Middle European Jews in *Zlateh the Goat* and *When Shlemiel Went to Warsaw*. Russian, Polish, and South American stories represent just a few of the regions in the story collections waiting for you in your local library or available through your favorite bookstore.

Booklist: Folktales

Asbjørnsen, Peter C. and Jorgen E. Moe. "Gudbrand-on-the Hillside," "The Husband Who Was to Mind the House," "The Three Billy Goats Gruff," "Why the Bear Is Stumpy-tailed," and "Why the Sea Is Salt" in *East O' the Sun and West O' the Moon*; tr. by George Webbe Dasent. Art by Erik Werenskiold. Dover, 1970.

_____. *Norwegian Folk Tales*; tr. by Pat Shaw Iversen and Carl Norman. Art by Erik Werenskiold and Theodor Kittelsen. Viking, 1961.

Belpré, Pura. "The Legend of the Royal Palm" in *Once in Puerto Rico*. Art by Christine Price. Warne, 1973.

Brown, Marcia. *Dick Whittington and His Cat*. Art by author. Scribner, 1950.

Chase, Richard. *Grandfather Tales*. Art by Berkeley Williams, Jr. Houghton, 1948.

_____. *The Jack Tales*. Art by Berkeley Williams, Jr. Houghton, 1943.

Courlander, Harold. "The Origin of the Balsam Tree" in *Ride with the Sun*. Art by Roger Duvoisin. McGraw-Hill, 1955.

Courlander, Harold and A.K. Prempeh. *The Hat-Shaking Dance and Other Ashanti Tales from Ghana*. Art by Enrico Arno. Harcourt, 1957.

Courlander, Harold and Wolf Leslau. *The Fire on the Mountain and Other Ethiopian Stories*. Art by Robert Kane. Holt, 1950.

Dayrell, Elphinstone. *Why the Sun and the Moon Live in the Sky*. Art by Blair Lent. Houghton, 1968.

Gág, Wanda. *Gone Is Gone*. Art by author. Coward, 1935.

Grimm Brothers. *Grimm's Fairy Tales*. Art by Arthur Rackham. Viking, 1973.

_____. *Rapunzel*. Art by Felix Hoffmann. Harcourt, 1961.

_____. *The Seven Ravens*. Art by Felix Hoffmann. Harcourt, 1963.

_____. "Rapunzel" in *Tales from Grimm*; tr. and illustrated by Wanda Gág. Coward, 1936.

Hogrogian, Nonny. *One Fine Day*. Art by author. Macmillan, 1971.

Jacobs, Joseph. "Cap O' Rushes," "The Cat and the Mouse," "Teeny-Tiny," "The Three Bears," "The Three Little Pigs" in *English Fairy Tales*. Art by John D. Batten. Dover, 1967.

Kent, Jack. *The Fat Cat: A Danish Folktale*. Art by author. Parents, 1971.

Leach, Maria. *How the People Sang the Mountains Up: How and Why Stories*. Art by Glen Rounds. Viking, 1967.

Master of All Masters. Art by Marcia Sewall. Atlantic-Little, 1972.

Olenius, Elsa. *Great Swedish Fairy Tales*; tr. by Holger Lundbergh. Art by John Bauer. Delacorte, 1973.

Reeves, James. *English Fables and Fairy Stories*. Art by Joan Kiddell-Monroe. Oxford, 1954.

Ross, Eulalie Steinmetz. "How the Camel Got His Proud Look" in *The Buried Treasure and Other Picture Tales*. Art by Josef Cellini. Lippincott, 1958.

Simon, Solomon. *The Wise Men of Helm and Their Merry Tales*; tr. by Ben Bengal and David Simon. Art by Lillian Fischel. Behrman House, 1945.

Singer, Isaac Bashevis. *When Shlemiel Went to Warsaw and Other Stories*; tr. by the author and Elizabeth Shub. Art by Margot Zemach. Farrar, 1969.

_____. *Zlateh the Goat*; tr. by the author and Elizabeth Shub. Art by Maurice Sendak. Harper, 1966.

_____. *Tom Tit Tot*. Art by Evaline Ness. Scribner, 1965.

Uchida, Yoshiko. *The Dancing Kettle and Other Japanese Folk Tales*. Art by Richard Jones, Harcourt, 1949.

_____. *The Sea of Gold and Other Tales from Japan*. Art by Marianne Yamaguchi. Scribner, 1965.

There are, of course, many more folktales for you to choose from in the bibliographies included in chapters 5 and 6. Find some that appeal to you and learn to tell them.

Literary Tales

After you feel comfortable telling the simple and then the more complex folktales, you may want to attempt to learn a literary tale, a short story written with elements reminiscent of folklore. These stories are more appropriate for the advanced storyteller because, to retain the beauty of the language, you will need to almost memorize the entire story, to know it so perfectly that you will be able to concentrate completely on an expressive presentation. It would be impossible to list all those authors who have contributed by writing original fairy tales, but a few should be mentioned. In the course of your storytelling career you may want to examine the work of each of these authors more closely. The booklist gives suggested titles by these featured authors, as well as other titles and collections that contain literary tales by a whole variety of contemporary authors.

Hans Christian Andersen

A favorite interview question is, "If you could meet a famous person from the past, who would you pick?" I think my choice would be the Danish author and storyteller Hans Christian Andersen, who published his first book of fairy tales in 1835. It is my opinion that he was the most talented of all writers, the father of modern storytelling. Although his greatest desire was to be well thought of as a playwright and serious author, his fairy tales were an instant success and are still read with great enjoyment today. Some of his first stories can be traced to folk sources, but his later work is entirely original. Since Andersen wrote in Danish, the work you will be reading will, of course, be a translation. For that reason it is necessary to find an edition that retains the original flavor of Andersen's work. A 1937 translation by Paul Leyssac, *It's Perfectly True*, is the one I still use. Erik Haugaard's *Hans Christian Andersen: The Complete Fairy Tales and Stories*, published in 1974, is also a good edition, with lots of stories but, unfortunately, no pictures.

The fantasy of Andersen's world is suitable for a wide age range. His satirical comments on human nature are universally understood and his stories are enjoyed by children and adults the world over. Although Andersen told his stories while performing intricate paper cuttings, telling an Andersen story usually requires a good bit of concentration. Therefore attempting to emulate his artistry with paper while telling a story may be difficult to do. But if you want an activity after your storyhour, some of the paper-cutting ideas in chapter 9 may be useful and entertaining or maybe you know an amusing and appropriate papercraft trick of your own to demonstrate. Andersen's birthday, April 2, is a good time to plan an Andersen storyhour. This date also happens to commemorate International Children's Book Day, so if you don't want to "tell an Andersen," feature stories from some foreign countries instead.

The Andersen museum in Odense, Denmark, is housed in the cottage where he was born. The collection contains memorabilia as well as Andersen books that have been translated and illustrated around the world. Should you want to send for the museum's catalog of books and souvenirs, the address is: Hans Christian Andersen Museum, Munkemøllestroede, Odense, Denmark.

Ruth Sawyer

Ruth Sawyer, an American storyteller and author of children's books, wrote a classic on traditional storytelling, *The Way of the*

Storyteller, which should be required background reading for every serious storyteller. The stories she has collected in the back of her book and those stories she wrote herself are as robust, humorous, and thoughtful as any you will find. "The Flea" in Eulalie Steinmetz Ross's *The Buried Treasure* is a tongue-in-cheek romp whose plot hinges on a shepherd boy guessing a cryptic riddle. There are a few Spanish words in the story that add to its enjoyment. "The Princess and the Vagabond" is an Irish version of *The Taming of the Shrew* and is suitable for both young adults and adults. The story I wish I could do justice to is "Wee Meg Barnileg and the Fairies," which appears in the appendix of Sawyer's book on storytelling. The phrases and wording in this story are so perfect that it would be a desecration to change any of it. For some reason I cannot seem to get it right and so have never been able to share it. However, some of my students have managed to tell it with the combination of verve and dreamlike quality it needs. Maybe you can do it justice, too. The Sawyer stories are long, so be prepared to take some time to learn them.

Eleanor Farjeon

I first discovered the English Eleanor Farjeon in a full-length novel of hers called *The Glass Slipper,* which is based on the Cinderella story. Naturally I had to read her other full-length novel, *The Silver Curlew,* based on the Tom Tit Tot story. The charm of Farjeon's novels is further enhanced by Ernest Shepard's drawings. Both of these books are good reading-aloud sources, but it is the sensitive charm of her short stories that makes her work a storyteller's dream. In the best fairy-tale tradition her stories transport one to a delicate world of poets and princesses. The theme of personal freedom is beautifully portrayed in "The Seventh Princess," while the quickly learned "The Lady's Room" is reminiscent of "The Fisherman and His Wife." Both stories are from *The Little Bookroom.* My favorite Farjeon, "Elsie Piddock Skips in Her Sleep," from *Martin Pippin in the Daisy-Field,* is perfect for a spring storyhour because the plot revolves around skipping rope. This story takes nearly half an hour to tell, so you can imagine the time and effort it takes to learn. It is worth it, though, since once you have learned it you will have it forever. Every story you learn can be told over and over again for years of good telling and listening. And with such a long story as this one, you needn't plan to tell another one for that session.

Howard Pyle

Howard Pyle's stories are funny. Many are lengthy, but they should be learned just as Pyle wrote them. *Pepper and Salt,* first published in 1885, and *The Wonder Clock,* published in 1887, provide humorous stories written in a folktale style that are suitable for storytellers and for those who feel Pyle's tales are best read aloud. "How the Good Gifts Were Used by Two" makes an excellent Christmas story. His Cinderella story is entitled, "The Apple of Contentment." The beginning of the latter story will give you an idea of Pyle's style: "There was a woman once, and she had three daughters. The first daughter squinted with both eyes, yet the woman loved her as she loved salt, for she herself squinted with both eyes." If you'd like to share pictures with your group, Pyle's own wry illustrations are most appropriate to his stories. For illustrations that are in a more modern style, Trina Schart Hyman has done a broad, colorful interpretation in *King Stork*, a story taken from Pyle's *The Wonder Clock*.

Rudyard Kipling

Rudyard Kipling's longer works are somewhat out of fashion these days, mainly because they seem wordy and decidedly racist to the modern reader. However, two of his works, *The Jungle Book* and the *Just So Stories*, are treasure troves for the storyteller. By learning parts of *The Jungle Book* you can introduce potential readers to this special book and the *Just So Stories* are original pourquoi stories that have great appeal. Kipling imaginatively explains "How the Leopard Got His Spots," "How the Camel Got His Hump," and, in "The Elephant's Child," he tells why elephants all have trunks instead of "a blackish, bulgy nose as big as a boot." The wonderfully imaginative language of these stories is what makes them so delightful.

Carl Sandburg

Carl Sandburg is well known for his works for adults, but he wrote successfully for children as well. His *Rootabaga Stories*, which abound in nonsense phrasing and bizarre situations, should be popular with any group. It takes a skilled storyteller, however, to offer these stories with just the right amount of tongue-in-cheek gravity. As with the tales of Andersen, many of Sandburg's *Rootabaga Stories* feature inanimate objects: umbrellas, rag dolls, and even skyscrapers. If you are fascinated by interesting names, Sandburg will supply them in abundance. His "How Bozo the Button Buster Busted All His Buttons When a Mouse Came" is told to three girls named Deep Red Roses, The Beans Are Burning, and Sweeter Than the Bees Humming. Not so elaborate but as delightfully descriptive is Shush Shush, the big buff banty hen who rings the doorbell when she lays an egg, also from the *Rootabaga Stories*. For a potpourri of Sandburg, try *The Sandburg Treasury*. A picture-book version of one of his stories, *The Wedding Procession of the Rag Doll and the Broom Handle and Who Was in It*, is illustrated with zany humor by Harriet Pincus.

Laurence Housman

Laurence Housman's stories have a completely different tone than Sandburg's. They grip the reader with a quiet intensity. To capture and transmit to an audience the full flavor of his words a slower, more deliberate telling is most successful. The settings of Housman's stories create vivid pictures in the mind. In "The Rat-Catcher's Daughter," much of the story takes place in the dwelling of a gnome deep underground where a greedy man's daughter must spend three years of her life. In "Rocking-Horse Land" a young prince dreams of his toy rocking horse's success. Although Housman's descriptions tend to be lengthy, they are essential to an understanding of the stories. A modern edition of many of Housman's tales has been issued by Atheneum under the title story *The Rat-Catcher's Daughter*. Housman also did an admirable job retelling some of the more familiar stories from the *Arabian Nights*.

Jane Yolen

One of the happy things about finding a good folk story to learn is that it doesn't become dated or go out of fashion. This does not mean, however, that we should rely solely on the old, the tried and true. We need to keep a lookout for new material as well. Jane Yolen's work is one such example. An editor, author and storyteller, she writes picture books, beginning-to-read stories, novels, and non-fiction, and she collects and edits folklore. Her original tales are truly "literary" tales. Her special way with language and her knowledge of myths and legends give her tales mystery and spirituality. In *The Girl Who Loved the Wind*, Danina, a lonely princess, joins the wind to explore the "ever-changing" world. The pictures in this book by Ed Young remind the reader of Persian miniatures and might be shared with a small group. The stories in *The Girl Who Cried Flowers and Other Tales* and *The Moon Ribbon and Other Tales* not only have the spirit and warmth of some of the older tales but also a special lyrical romantic quality that predict a long shelf life for this contemporary author. Yolen's longer story, *The Transfigured Hart*, is a timeless tale of two children of very different temperament who have an equally strong belief in the existence of the fabled unicorn. This book is probably too long to learn as a story, but should not be overlooked for reading aloud. In her *Writing Books for Children*, Jane Yolen reflects that "The writer lights many candles in a good fantasy novel. The shadows they cast in a child's soul will last for the rest of his life."

John Gardner

John Gardner, an author who has written mainly for adults, might be another source of literary fairy tales. Gardner has written two collections of magical and witty tales for children. His stories are reminiscent of well-known fairy tales, but in a contemporary mood. "The Tailor and the Giant" in *Dragon, Dragon and Other Tales* reminds the reader of the Grimm story, but in the Gardner version the tailor makes signs that say LOVE in big red letters and prepares to demonstrate in front of the king's palace.

The beginning of the title story in *Gudgekin the Thistle Girl and Other Tales* is representative of Gardner's humorous approach:

In a certain kingdom there lived a poor little thistle girl. What thistle girls did for a living—that is no longer known, but whatever the reason that people gathered thistles, she was one of those that did it.

Mature audiences familiar with the traditional tales will enjoy Gardner's wry, tongue-in-cheek humor.

Judith Gorog

Most of Judith Gorog's stories are more appropriate for young adult or adult audiences, but you can introduce younger audiences to her stories with *In a Messy, Messy Room*. The title story tells of Sam and his pet chameleon, Champ. Everyone tells Sam to clean his room, but Champ prefers it messy and commands Sam, "Never. Never. Never clean your room!" In "Smelly Sneakers," Toad is winner of the smelly sneaker contest, but where are his feet?

Gorog's young adult stories are rooted in urban folklore and each is a gem of the bizarre. One title, *Winning Scheherazade*, shows the reader what happens to the most famous storyteller of all time, after she is released from the Sultan's palace.

Richard Kennedy

Richard Kennedy's stories seem to be rooted in folklore, but they are entirely original. Published in some cases as picture books, Kennedy's stories are often hauntingly beautiful. "Come Again in the Spring" is a good example of his work. In it, Old Hark refuses to accept Death's invitation until he is ready. He wins a wager with Death and is allowed to live until the following spring. In the funny "The Parrot and the Thief," a bird cleverly outsmarts a thief. Kennedy's "love" stories are intriguing also, as each incorporates a bizarre twist.

Booklist: Literary Tales and Short Story Collections

Ahlberg, Janet and Allan Ahlberg. *The Clothes Horse and Other Stories*. Viking, 1987. These six stories take English expressions literally. Includes "The Jack Pot," "Life Savings," and "No Man's Land."

Aiken, Joan, *The Last Slice of Rainbow and Other Stories*. Art by Alix Berenzy. Harper, 1990. Fairies interact with children in these nine stories by a British author.

Andersen, Hans Christian. *The Complete Fairy Tales and Stories*; tr. by Erik Haugaard. Doubleday, 1974.

_____. *It's Perfectly True*; tr. by Paul Leyssac. Art by Vilhelm Pedersen. Macmillan, 1937.

_____. *Michael Hague's Favorite Hans Christian Andersen Fairy Tales*. Art by Michael Hague. Holt, 1981. "The Ugly Duckling" is a favorite among the nine selections in this illustrated edition.

Carlson, Lori M. and Cynthia L. Ventura, eds. *Where Angels Glide at Dawn: New Stories from Latin America*. Introd. by Isabel Allende. Lippincott, 1990. Contemporary short stories translated with zest.

Christian, Peggy. *The Old Coot*. Art by Eileen Christelow. Atheneum, 1991. A prospector tells stories he has heard from a coyote in the old west. Lively and amusing.

Corrin, Sara and Stephen Corrin. *The Faber Book of Modern Fairy Tales*. Art by Ann Strugnell. Faber, 1981. Excellent collection of contemporary stories from Ted Hughes, Joan Akin, Alison Uttley and others.

Coville, Bruce, ed. *Herds of Thunder, Manes of Gold: A Collection of Horse Stories and Poems*. Art by Ted Lewin. Doubleday, 1989. Short stories and excerpts from longer works by Mary O'Hara, Carl Sandburg, and Marguerite Henry.

_____. *The Unicorn Treasury: Stories, Poems and Unicorn Lore*. Art by Tim Hildebrandt. Doubleday, 1987. Jane Yolen, Madeleine L'Engle, C. S. Lewis and other favorite authors have all contributed to this collection of writings about the mythical unicorn.

Dickinson, Peter. *Merlin Dreams*. Art by Alan Lee. Delacorte, 1988. Dickinson uses Arthurian legends to create his stories. The large, attractive format showcases the art in this collection.

Farjeon, Eleanor. *The Glass Slipper*. Art by Ernest Shepard. Viking, 1956.

_____. "The Lady's Room," "The Seventh Princess" in *The Little Bookroom*. Art by Edward Ardizzone. Oxford, 1956.

_____. "Elsie Piddock Skips in Her Sleep" in *Martin Pippin in the Daisy-Field*. Art by Isobel and John Morton-Sale. Stokes, 1938.

_____. *The Silver Curlew*. Art by Ernest Shepard. Viking, 1954.

Gardner, John. *Dragon, Dragon and Other Tales*. Art by Charles Shields. Knopf, 1975.

_____. *Gudgekin the Thistle Girl and Other Tales*. Art by Michael Sporn. Knopf, 1976.

Gorog, Judith. *In a Messy, Messy Room and Other Strange Stories*. Art by Kimberly Bulcken Root. Philomel, 1990.

_____. *No Swimming in Dark Pond and Other Chilling Tales*. Philomel, 1987. This collection for young adults is representative of Gorog's slightly sinister tales featuring strong characters and twisting plots.

_____. *Winning Scheherazade*. Atheneum, 1991.

Haas, Jessie. *The Sixth Sense and Other Stories*. Greenwillow, 1988. Short stories that explore the relationship between humans and animals.

Hamilton, Virgina. *The All Jahdu Storybook*. Art by Barry Moser. Harcourt, 1991. Trickster stories by a Newbery Medal Award-winning author.

Housman, Laurence. "The Rat-Catcher's Daughter," Rocking-Horse Land" in *The Rat-Catcher's Daughter*, ed. by Ellin Greene. Art by Julia Noonan. Atheneum, 1974.

Hughes, Ted. *Tales of the Early World*. Art by Andrew Davidson. Farrar, 1991. A poet writes 10 creation myths.

Jennings, Paul. *Uncanny! Even More Surprising Stories*. Viking, 1988. This collection for young adults is representative of several short story collections by an Australian author with a distinctly weird imagination.

Johnston, Tony. *The Cowboy and the Black-eyed Pea*. Art by Warren Ludwig. Putnam, 1992. In this variant of "The Princess and the Pea," an heiress searches for a real cowboy.

Kennedy, Richard. *Richard Kennedy: Collected Stories*. Art by Marcia Sewall. Harper, 1987. Some of the stories in this wonderful collection appeared previously as single titles with illustrations.

Kipling, Rudyard. *The Elephant's Child*. Art by Ulla Kampmann. Follett, 1969.

_____. *The Jungle Book*. Art by Fritz Eichenberg. Grosset, 1950.

_____. "How the Camel Got His Hump," "How the Leopard Got His Spots" in *Just So Stories*. Art by Etienne Delessert. Doubleday, 1972.

_____. *Just So Stories*. Art by author. Doubleday, 1946.

_____. *Just So Stories*. Art by Michael Foreman. Viking, 1987. Brilliantly hued paintings and black-and-white drawings enhance this edition of Kipling favorites.

_____. *Just So Stories*. Art by Safaya Salter. Holt, 1987. The art for this classic animal collection is distinguished by an Eastern influence.

Peretz, I. L. *The Seven Good Years and Other Stories of I. L. Peretz*; tr. and adapted by Esther Hautzig. Art by Deborah Kogan Ray. Jewish Publication Society, 1984. Ten stories by the Yiddish writer. Appropriate for young adults and up.

Poe, Edgar Allan. *Tales of Edgar Allan Poe*. Art by Barry Moser. Morrow, 1991. The classic "The Tell-Tale Heart," "The Pit and the Pendulum," and "The Gold Bug" are among the macabre tales by the inventor of this genre.

Porte, Barbara Ann. *Jesse's Ghost and Other Stories*. Greenwillow, 1983. A story-teller relates these original tales, including a frightening "Cinderella."

Pyle, Howard. *King Stork*. Art by Trina Schart Hyman. Little, 1973.

_____. *Pepper and Salt, or Seasoning for Young Folk*. Art by author. Harper, 1885.

_____. *The Wonder Clock*. Art by author. Dover, 1965.

Rettich, Margret. *The Silver Touch and Other Family Christmas Stories*; tr. by Elizabeth D. Crawford. Art by Rolf Rettich. Morrow, 1978. Short stories featuring a family on vacation.

Rylant, Cynthia. *A Couple of Kooks and Other Stories about Love*. Orchard, 1990. Warm portraits of a variety of people in "love."

Sandburg, Carl. "How Bozo the Button Buster Busted All His Buttons When a Mouse Came" in *The Rootabaga Stories*. Art by Maud and Miska Petersham. Harcourt, 1974.

_____. *The Sandburg Treasury*. Art by Paul Bacon. Harcourt, 1970.

_____. *The Wedding Procession of the Rag Doll and the Broom Handle and Who Was in It*. Art by Harriet Pincus. Harcourt, 1967.

_____. *Rootabaga Stories: Part 1*. Art by Michael Hague. Harcourt, 1988. (See also Part 2, published in 1989.) First published in 1922, these original nonsense stories have retained their charm.

Sawyer, Ruth. "The Flea" in *The Buried Treasure*, ed. by Eulalie Steinmetz Ross. Art by Josef Cellini. Lippincott, 1958.

_____. "Wee Meg Barnileg and the Fairies," "The Princess and the Vagabond" in *The Way of the Storyteller*. Viking, 1962.

Soto, Gary. *Baseball in April and Other Stories*. Harcourt, 1990. Too long to learn to tell, these stories with a Hispanic background are perfect to read aloud.

Stories from the Arabian Nights; retold by Laurence Housman. Art by Girard Goddenow. Junior Deluxe Editions, 1955.

Wilde, Oscar. *Oscar Wilde: Stories for Children*. Art by P. J. Lynch. Macmillan, 1991. A lushly illustrated edition of Wilde's stories for children.

Yolen, Jane. *The Girl Who Loved the Wind*. Art by Ed Young. Crowell, 1972.

_____. *The Girl Who Cried Flowers and Other Tales*. Art by David Palladini. Crowell, 1972.

_____. *The Moon Ribbon and Other Tales*. Art by David Palladini. Crowell, 1972.

_____. *The Transfigured Hart*. Art by Donna Diamond. Crowell, 1975.

_____. *Dream Weaver*. Art by Michael Hague. Collins, 1978.

Yolen, Jane, Martin H. Greenberg and Charles G. Waugh, eds. *Dragons and Dreams: A Collection of New Fantasy and Science Fiction Stories*. Harper, 1986. These three editors have found intriguing stories for several theme collections.

Zipes, Jack, ed. *Spells of Enchantment: The Wondrous Fairy Tales of Western Culture*. Viking, 1991. Eight hundred pages of literary fairy tales collected for adults.

Fables

Fables are short, didactic tales that attempt to teach a lesson or convey a moral. The main characters are often animals who behave like humans. Some fables are so well known that expressions from them, such as "sour grapes," have become part of our everyday language. Although some of these didactic tales might provoke even young children into thinking about the "message," most will be enjoyed simply for the story. Of course, some fables present philosophical concepts that are too abstract for many children to understand; these are best left for telling to those who are mature enough to comprehend.

However, because so many fables feature animal characters that do appeal to children, there have been many editions of fables published especially for them. In particular, some attractively illustrated picture books by distinguished artists have become very popular. Two adaptations by Doris Dana in picture-book form offer fables in both English and Spanish text by the Chilean poet Lucilla Godoy-Alcayaga, who writes under the pseudonym Gabriela Mistral. Both books, *Crickets and Frogs* and *The Elephant and His Secret*, are illustrated with colorful woodcuts by Antonio Frasconi. More recently, two favorite children's book illustrators, Leo Lionni and Arnold Lobel, have given us beautifully illustrated fables.

Tell a fable at the beginning of a storyhour. They are easy to learn and may stimulate some serious thought in young listeners. Only one fable at a time, please; too many at one session tend to be tiresome.

Aesop's Fables

The best-known fables are those in the Greek collection commonly known as *Aesop's Fables*. It is believed that Aesop was a Greek slave who lived about 600 B.C. The earliest known written versions of these stories are the ones recorded in Latin by Phaedrus in the first century A.D. In the third century, Babrius wrote a collection of some 300 of the fables in Greek verse. Subsequent compilations were made by Aviares in the fourth century, and by Romulus in the tenth century. Later, these fables reached Northern Europe, and were among the stories printed by William Caxton. They have survived until the present in various versions. There is no one accepted version, nor is there any classic illustrator of these fables. The Metropolitan Museum of New York exhibited a number of pictures gathered from the last 500 years of illustrated versions of the Aesop fables. *Aesop: Five Centuries of Illustrated Fables* is a book based on this exhibit. It may be an inspiration to any potential illustrators in your folk program.

My favorite modern adaptation of an Aesop's fable is James Daugherty's picture book *Andy and the Lion*, which has the same theme as "Androcles and the Lion" and can also be compared with La Fontaine's "The Lion and the Mouse." A brand new interpretation to try is Tom Paxton's *Androcles and the Lion*. For older children there is the picture-book version of Chaucer's "Nun's Priest Tale" (which is adapted from Aesop's "The Cock and the Fox") with scratchboard drawings by Barbara Cooney and titled *Chanticleer and the Fox*. John Bierhorst's *Doctor Coyote: A Native American Aesop's Fables* offers a new twist on an old favorite. You can also take your choice of illustrators. For those who enjoy the traditional, there are Arthur Rackham's black-and-white silhouette drawings interspersed with full-color traditional paintings in the V. S. Vernon Jones translation of *Aesop's Fables*. The happy cartoon interpretation of Jack Kent's *Fables of Aesop* gives the old moralistic tales a fresh, new, humorous twist that will make you and your audiences laugh aloud.

Fables of La Fontaine

Jean de La Fontaine used various sources, including Aesop, for his verse fables which first appeared in 1688. French school children know the fables almost as well as American children know their Mother Goose. They hear them when they are young and study them in school, memorizing them for recitation contests. Although La Fontaine suffers somewhat in translation, his poems are still delightful versions of the traditional fables. One of the more exciting ways of presenting these works of La Fontaine to children is by using the single-fable picture books of Brian Wildsmith. Through his use of rich, glowing colors and strong, bold lines, he has added visual excitement to five of the fables.

Fables of Krylov

Just as French children are weaned on La Fontaine, Russian children grow up with Krylov. Ivan Andreevich Krylov worked as a librarian in the St. Petersburg Library. His first collections of fables consisted of translations of La Fontaine's tales; but later he wrote fables that expressed harsh political and social criticism, attacking hypocrisy in particular. The first complete collection of Krylov's fables appeared in 1843. While English editions are not plentiful, the *15 Fables of Krylov,* a fine translation by Guy Daniels, is suitable for older children.

Fables of India

The *Pañchatantra,* which contains the earliest recorded fables of India, originated somewhere between 275 B.C. and 275 A.D. In these fables the Vishnu Sarma attempts to teach the three sons of the king some principles of conduct that they are to follow. There are some 200 delightful versions of *The Pañchatantra,* recorded in more than 50 languages. These fables, which are much more complex than those of Aesop or La Fontaine, have stories within stories. The Arthur W. Ryder translation, *Gold's Gloom: Tales from the Pañchatantra,* tells 34 of the stories separately and in random order, thus making them easier for readers of other cultures to enjoy.

The *Hitopadeśa,* or *Book of Good Counsels,* is actually a rearrangement of *The Pañchatantra* with a few additional stories that date from the tenth century. One story from this collection has been made popular in this country, Marcia Brown's excellent picture-book version, *Once a Mouse,* which won the Caldecott Medal in 1962 with its bold woodcut illustrations. In this story a hermit befriends a mouse and turns him into various animal forms. When the mouse, now a proud tiger, expresses his ungratefulness to the hermit he is turned once more into a humble little mouse.

The *Jatakas* are a series of animal stories describing the lessons of life that Gautama Buddha preached in northeast India between 563 B.C. and 483 B.C. The stories, numbering some 500, remained in the oral tradition until several hundred years after Buddha's death, when they were written down in the Pali language. Although they were first translated into English in the nineteenth century, these fables have been told and enjoyed for over two thousand years in various parts of the world.

Two collections by Ellen C. Babbitt that were designed for children have brought these stories to American children. Her version of the fable of "The Turtle Who Couldn't Stop Talking" is my favorite. A turtle meets some geese who are flying back to their home. The turtle would like to join them and the geese suggest that he hold a stick between his teeth while they each take an end and fly into the air. When the village children see the odd sight they jeer and laugh at the turtle. Because he is unable to keep quiet, the foolish turtle lets go of the stick to answer the children and falls to his death. A book edited by Nancy DeRoin retells 30 of the 500 fables in a more detailed version than Babbitt's.

Booklist: Fables

Anno, Mitsumasa. *Anno's Aesop: A Book of Fables by Aesop and Mr. Fox*. Art by author. Orchard, 1987.

Bierhorst, John. *Doctor Coyote: A Native American Aesop's Fables*. Art by Wendy Watson. Macmillan, 1987.

Brown, Marcia. *Once a Mouse*. Art by author. Scribner, 1961.

Chaucer, Geoffrey. *Chanticleer and the Fox*; adapted and illustrated by Barbara Cooney. Crowell, 1958.

Clark, Margaret. *The Best of Aesop's Fables*. Art by Charlotte Voake. Little, 1990.

Daugherty, James. *Andy and the Lion*. Art by author. Viking, 1938.

DeRoin, Nancy. *Jataka Tales: Fables from the Buddha*. Art by Ellen Lanyon. Houghton, 1975.

Gold's Gloom: Tales from the Pañchatantra; tr. by Arthur W. Ryder. Univ. of Chicago Pr., 1925.

Jataka Tales; retold by Ellen C. Babbitt. Art by Ellsworth Young. Prentice-Hall, 1912. Also *More Jataka Tales* (Century/Prentice-Hall, 1922).

Jones, V. S. Vernon. *Aesop's Fables*. Art by Arthur Rackham. Watts, 1968.

Kent, Jack. *Jack Kent's Fables of Aesop*. Art by author. Parents, 1972.

Kherdian, David. *Feathers and Tails*. Art by Nonny Hogrogian. Philomel, 1992.

Krylov, Ivan A. *15 Fables*; tr. by Guy Daniels. Art by David Pascal. Macmillan, 1965.

Lionni, Leo. *Frederick's Fables*. Art by author. Random, 1985.

Lobel, Arnold. *Fables*. Art by author. Harper, 1981.

MacFarland. John. *The Exploding Frog and Other Fables*. Art by James Marshall. Little. 1981.

McKendry, John J., comp. *Aesop: Five Centuries of Illustrated Fables*. Metropolitan Museum of Art, 1964.

Mistral, Gabriela (pseud. for Lucilla Alcayaga-Godoy). *Crickets and Frogs*; adapted and tr. by Doris Dana. Art by Antonio Frasconi. Atheneum, 1972.

_____. *The Elephant and His Secret*; adapted and tr. by Doris Dana. Art by Antonio Frasconi. Atheneum, 1974.

Paxton, Tom. *Androcles and the Lion*. Art by Robert Rayevsky. Morrow, 1991.

Reed, A. W. *Aboriginal Fables and Legendary Tales*. Art by E. H. Papps. Reed (53 Myoora Road, Terrey Hills, Sydney, Australia), 1965.

Ross, Tony. *Foxy Fables*. Art by author. Dial, 1986.

Steptoe, John. *Mufaro's Beautiful Daughters: An African Tale*. Art by author. Lothrop, 1987.

Myths

Traditionally, myths have been regarded as stories that represent the attempts of early people to explain the nature of the world around them and human existence. Whether these tales were actually part of the religion of ancient cultures is not clear, but we generally define a myth as having something to do with religion. The Greek, Roman, and Norse cultures have been the major sources of our most familiar myths, but Native American mythology is also finding its way into many new and beautifully illustrated collections.

Myths are most suitable for the upper grades of elementary school, junior high, and beyond. Some writers have attempted to adapt them for younger children, but this often necessitates stripping away the beautiful language and more significant philosophical musings, leaving only the bare threads of the plot.

Myths are more difficult to introduce to children than folktales. While a folktale usually can be enjoyed without a knowledge of the culture of its origin, myths cannot so easily be removed from their cultural context. The relationships of the gods and the patterns of the culture are expressed in continuous relationships rather than in individual tales. However, these stories, like most folklore, were originally told orally; and, with some care, they may be read or told aloud. If they seem too long or complicated, some condensation may be desirable; but care must be taken not to shorten or simplify them so drastically that the majesty and power of these ancient tales are lost. Margery Bernstein and Janet Kobrin have successfully retold several myths for younger children. *The First Morning*, a myth told by the Sukuma people of East Africa, charmingly relates how the animals acquire light from the land above the sky. A group of Abo students have collected and illustrated Australian aboriginal myths, such as "How the Kangaroo Got His Tail," in *Djugurba: Tales from the Spirit Time*. (For storytellers, that's pronounced "jook-urr-pa.") Two new books by John Bierhorst celebrate the rich culture of South America: *The Mythology of Mexico and Central America* and *The Mythology of South America*.

It is important to note that the myths we read are not mere translations of the original. The literary styles of writers who do the retellings vary widely. While some versions are well suited for oral storytelling, others can best be enjoyed by individual readers. For instance, Lillian Smith points out in her book on children's literature, *The Unreluctant Years*, that the different literary styles of Charles Kingsley, Nathaniel Hawthorne, and Padraic Colum have produced three vastly different versions of the same Greek myths. Adults who wish to introduce mythology to children should take the time to sample several collections in order to know what styles are available and to become acquainted with them. Don't cross myths off your list of possible storytelling material, however; these are vital, exciting, and meaningful stories to share with an audience.

Greek and Roman Myths

The stories of the gods and heroes of ancient Greece and Rome are among many storytellers' favorite myths. With their fantastic events, abundant action, complex characters, and involved relationships among gods and mortals, these myths comment on human and divine foibles, explain natural phenomena, and describe the beginning of the world. While the capricious cruelty of the gods in those myths often causes painful tragedy for humans, the myths also exude a sunny optimism that celebrates the beauty and excitement in life.

Today, there is a wide choice of retellings, narrative styles, and styles of illustration available. Whichever you or a child chooses, these well-known myths are likely to stimulate the imagination. For a short introduction to Greek mythology, Robert Graves's *Greek Gods and Heroes* offers an entertaining look at the classics. Edith Hamilton's scholarly *Mythology* is a noted classicist's retelling that includes valuable background that you may wish to include in your introduction to a storytelling program. On the other hand, Ingri and Edgar Parin d'Aulaire's *Book of Greek Myths* has a humorous and earthy folktale quality that is reflected in both the text and illustrations. Pamela Oldfield's *Tales from Ancient Greece*, with beautiful full-color artwork by Nick Harris, includes retellings of two favorites: "King Midas and the Golden Touch" and "Persephone and the King of Darkness." Whether you enjoy stark or poetic prose, collections of stories or a single favorite tale, these books offer a rich array of stories to share with your listeners.

Norse Myths

The Norse myths of Iceland are contained in two collections, the *Elder* or *Poetic Edda* and *Younger* or *Prose Edda*. The *Poetic Edda* tells of the creation of the world and the evolution of the gods. It also contains the Norse epic story of Sigurd the Volsung. The *Prose Edda* is a collection of important Norse myths gathered in the thirteenth century. Incidentally, the word "edda" originally meant great-grandmother, which gives a rather folksy air to these sometimes difficult stories. To some readers the

Norse myths may seem considerably more somber and tragic in tone than those of the Greeks and Romans. For instance, unlike the immortal deities of classical Greek and Roman mythology, the Norse gods are mortal and prepare to perish in a tragic battle at the end of the world. If these stories appeal to you, you may choose from several versions. Padraic Colum and Olivia Coolidge relate both the myths and the hero or epic tales in their collections, while Dorothy Hosford devotes her *Sons of the Volsungs* to the Sigurd tales and her *Thunder of the Gods* to the myths about Odin, Thor, Baldur, Loki, and the other gods and goddesses. The d'Aulaires' version, *Norse Gods and Giants*, which is amply illustrated and manages to emphasize points of beauty and humor in these sometimes dark tales of the North, may even appeal to a somewhat younger age group. Margaret Hodges has also rewritten one of the Icelandic myths as a single tale, *Baldur and the Mistletoe*, which relates the story of Baldur's death and why the use of mistletoe stands for hope.

Booklist: Myths

Bernstein, Margery and Janet Kobrin, retellers. *The First Morning: An African Myth*. Art by Enid Warner Romanek. Scribner, 1976.

Bierhorst, John. *The Mythology of Mexico and Central America*. Illustrated. Morrow, 1990.

_____. *The Mythology of South America*. Illustrated. Morrow, 1988.

Billout, Guy. *Thunderbolt and Rainbow: A Look at Greek Mythology*. Art by author. Prentice-Hall, 1981.

Colum, Padraic. *The Children's Homer: Adventures of Odysseus and the Tale of Troy*. Art by Willy Pogány. Macmillan, 1962.

Coolidge, Olivia E. *Greek Myths*. Art by Edouard Sandoz. Houghton, 1949.

d'Aulaire, Ingri and Edgar P. d'Aulaire. *Ingri and Edgar Parin d'Aulaire's Book of Greek Myths*. Art by authors. Doubleday, 1962.

_____. *Norse Gods and Giants*. Art by authors. Doubleday, 1967.

Djugurba: Tales from the Spirit Time. Univ. of Indiana Pr., 1976.

Fisher, Leonard Everett. *Jason and the Golden Fleece*. Art by author. Holiday, 1990.

Graves, Robert. *Greek Gods and Heroes*. Art by Dimitri Davis. Doubleday, 1960.

Hamilton, Virginia. *In the Beginning: Creation Stories from Around the World*. Art by Barry Moser. Harcourt, 1988.

Hodges, Margaret. *Baldur and the Mistletoe*. Art by Gerry Hoover. Little, 1974.

_____. *Persephone and the Springtime*. Art by Arvis Stewart. Little, 1973.

_____. *The Other World: Myths of the Celts*. Art by Eros Keith. Farrar, 1973.

Hosford, Dorothy. *Sons of the Volsungs*. Art by Frank Dobias. Holt, 1949.

_____. *Thunder of the Gods*. Art by Claire and George Louden. Holt, 1952.

Hutton, Warwick. *Theseus and the Minotaur*. Art by author. McElderry/Macmillan, 1989.

Ions, Veronica. *Indian Mythology*. Illustrated with prints and paintings. Newnes, 1983.

Kingsley, Charles. *The Heroes.* Art by Joan Kiddell-Monroe. Dutton, 1963.

Leach, Maria. *The Lion Sneezed: Folktales and Myths of the Cat.* Art by Helen Siegl. Crowell, 1977.

Low, Alice. *The Macmillan Book of Greek Gods and Heroes.* Art by Arvis Stewart. Macmillan, 1985.

Monroe, Jean Guard and Ray A. Williamson. *They Dance in the Sky: Native American Star Myths.* Art by Edgar Stewart. Houghton, 1987.

Oldfield, Pamela. *Tales from Ancient Greece.* Art by Nick Harris. Doubleday, 1989.

Shetterly, Susan Hand. *Raven's Light: A Myth from the People of the Northwest Coast.* Art by Robert Shetterly. Atheneum, 1991.

Smith, Lillian. *The Unreluctant Years: A Critical Approach to Children's Literature.* American Library Assn., 1953.

Epics

Whereas the myth focuses on the gods, the epic centers on an earthly hero. Originally the epics were collections of individual songs or poems about a particular hero and his adventures, but modern authors have collected these stories in prose form, which makes them particularly useful to the storyteller. Usually the epic hero is one whose character and moral code express not only universal, but national ideals as well, and the tales, therefore, impart a very nationalistic flavor. While one adventure is sometimes extracted from an epic and presented to children as a single tale, the appeal of the epic form lies in following the complete adventures of the hero, often from birth to death. Most adults will recognize some of their old childhood favorites in the epic literature and present-day children continue to enjoy them.

Teachers especially might find that an entire program can be built around a popular epic; combining storytelling and reading aloud can make such a program series a memorable experience.

English Epics

The exploits of Robin Hood, one of the most popular children's heroes, appear in several forms of literature and film, including prose stories and numerous old English ballads. These stories,  abounding with amusing and fascinating characters such as Little John, Will Scarlet, Friar Tuck, and Maid Marian, are filled with wit, courage, and fellowship. Robin Hood is an outlaw, but one who embodies many exemplary traits. His robbing of the rich to give to the poor may be a questionable ethic, but it is heartily approved by his many followers who see it primarily as a brave attempt at justice. Howard Pyle's version, *The Merry Adventures of Robin Hood,* is a superb edition, good for reading aloud or for extracting incidents for a more traditional oral presentation. Actor and director Kevin Costner's production of *Robin Hood: Prince of Thieves* was an immensely popular movie; as a result, you may find that there is a renewed interest in this epic. By all means, take advantage of it!

King Arthur is the hero of a long series of medieval romances. Arthurian stories in the oral tradition were first written down in French, the language of the English court in Norman times. A progressive elaboration of the material culminated in Sir Thomas Malory's fifteenth-century version, *Le Morte d'Arthur.* Malory's tales of this romantic figure and his chivalrous knights have been the source for later versions, of which Lord Tennyson's *Idylls of the King* is typical. The concept of chivalry exemplified by Arthur and his knights reflects a more sophisticated ethic than that of the Robin Hood epic, but whether or not children understand chivalry as such, they find knights and their ladies particularly fascinating. Howard Pyle, who so aptly portrays Robin Hood, has also written an excellent version of this epic, *The Story of King Arthur and His Knights,* which still remains popular after so many years. I'm especially fond of a more recent telling, Margaret Hodges' *The Kitchen Knight: A Tale of King Arthur,* illustrated with Trina Schart Hyman's artwork.

The oldest epic in English is *Beowulf,* an Anglo-Saxon saga believed to have been written in the eighth century. It celebrates the sheer courage, strength, wit, and cunning by which the hero Beowulf destroys the man-eating monster, Grendel, Grendel's cruel mother, and a fiendish dragon. Robert Nye's *Beowulf: A New Telling* is a strongly dramatic prose version that renders the action with all the gory detail inherent in this tale.

Greek Epics

The Iliad and *The Odyssey* of Homer are the famous Greek epics. *The Iliad,* which relates the events of the Trojan war, is extremely complex and is probably too confusing to be told to very young children. The central figure is Achilles, but many other legendary heroes also take part, among them Agamemnon, Patrocles, Hector, and Priam. *The Odyssey,* which is much easier to understand, relates the strange and wonderful adventures that befall Odysseus on his return voyage to Ithaca after the capture of Troy. Adult versions of these Homeric epics are usually too difficult for children, but there are several adaptations or retellings designed for young readers that give the storyteller some material with which to work. Padraic Colum's *The Children's Homer* emphasizes action, while Barbara Leonie Picard's *The Odyssey of Homer* concentrates on character portrayal. The collaboration of author Jane Werner and illustrators Alice and Martin Provensen has produced yet another exciting version, *The Iliad and the Odyssey.*

Epics of India

The Ramayana, a collection of stories often told through dance, describes the earthly life of the god Vishnu in his human form as Prince Rama. It relates Prince Rama's marriage to Sita and the adventures they share before her death. A new telling is Lakshmi Lal's *The Ramayana,* with art by Badri Narayan.

Other National Epics

Program planners might also enjoy children's versions of the tales of other national heroes. The Irish heroes of Cuchulain and Finn MacCool, the ancient Babylonian hero Gilgamesh, the Cid of Spain, Roland of France, and Siegfried of Germany are examples of other epic heroes. Barbara Leonie Picard retells stories of three hero-kings, "Gilgamesh, King of Erech"; "Hrolf Kraki, King of Denmark"; and "Conary, High King of Ireland" in *Three Ancient Kings.* These can be adapted for storytelling but would probably be better for reading aloud. An epic poem from the Sudan of West Africa, *Gassire's Lute,* has been translated and adapted by Alto Jablow and is suitable for young adults.

Booklist: Epics

Bowen, Olwen. *Tales from the Mabinogion.* Art by Richard Kennedy. Vanguard, 1978.

Colum, Padraic. *The Children's Homer: Adventures of Odysseus and the Tale of Troy.* Art by Willy Pogány. Macmillan, 1962.

Evslin, Bernard. *Hercules.* Art by Joseph A. Smith. Morrow, 1984.

Gaer, Joseph. *The Adventures of Rama.* Art by Randy Monk. Little, 1954.

Gassire's Lute; tr. by Alta Jablow. Art by Leo and Diane Dillon. Dutton, 1971.

Hastings, Selina. *Sir Gawain and the Loathly Lady.* Art by Juan Wijingaard. Lothrop, 1985.

———. *Reynard the Fox.* Art by Graham Percy. Tambourine, 1990.

Hodges, Margaret. *The Kitchen Knight: A Tale of King Arthur.* Art by Trina Schart Hyman. Holiday, 1990.

Lal, Lakshmi. *The Ramayana.* Art by Badri Narayan. Orient Longman, 1988.

Lanier, Sidney, ed. *The Boy's King Arthur.* Art by N. C. Wyeth. Scribner, 1924.

Lister, Robin. *The Legend of King Arthur.* Art by Alan Baker. Doubleday, 1988.

Nye, Robert. *Beowulf: A New Telling.* Art by Alan E. Cober. Hill & Wang, 1968.

Picard, Barbara Leonie. *Iliad and Odyssey of Homer.* Simon & Schuster, 1991.

———. *Three Ancient Kings: Gilgamesh, Hrolf Kraki, Conary.* Art by Philip Gough. Warne, 1972.

Proud Knight, Fair Lady: The Twelve Lais of Marie de France; tr. by Naomi Lewis. Art by Angela Barrett. Viking, 1989.

Pyle, Howard. *The Merry Adventures of Robin Hood.* Art by author. Scribner, 1946.

———. *The Story of King Arthur and His Knights.* Art by author. Scribner, 1903.

Talbot, Hudson. *King Arthur: The Sword in the Stone.* Art by author. Morrow, 1991.

Seeger, Elizabeth. *The Ramayana.* Art by Gordon Laite. W. R. Scott, 1969.

Werner, Jane. *The Iliad and the Odyssey.* Art by Alice and Martin Provensen. Golden Pr., 1964.

Legends

As you read through various studies of folklore you will find many overlappings of types of stories; the words, "myth," "legend," "epic" sometimes are used interchangeably, too. A legend, however, usually refers to a story relating to the history of a culture. The story revolves around an incident that is believed to have taken place or a person who may actually have lived, but, in most instances, these tales have been retold so often and embellished to such an extent that it would be all but impossible to discover a factual account. Did Johnny Appleseed and John Henry really live? Was the Swiss William Tell a real person? Did he actually shoot an apple from his son's head? These, and other legends like them, provide a wealth of material for the storyteller.

Just as you will find similarities in folktales from one country to another, so you will find yourself being led from one book to another when you find an interesting legend. Hans Baumann collected 27 legends from the world of folklore in his book *The Stolen Fire*. In the title story Maui defies the gods to gain for mankind the gift of fire. If this story sparks your interest, you may be led to Westervelt's *Hawaiian Legends of Ghosts and Ghost-Gods*, many of whose stories deal with the same Maui and his exploits. On the other hand, it may be the fire of the story that interests you and you may be led to Margaret Hodges' Indian legend, *The Fire Bringer*, which gives another interpretation of how man acquired fire. Perhaps you are more fascinated by the origin of the legend than by the subject.

Written in a terse style, *The Travels of Atunga* by Theodore Clymer offers us an Eskimo legend of a visit to Moon in a starkly illustrated picture-book format. Louis Untermeyer introduces 55 legends in *The World's Great Stories* by reminding us that while most legends have their origins in history, they survive not because they may be based on facts but because "they touch on fundamental traits of human nature." This collection should give any storyteller a good start with some of the world's great legends.

Myths and epics are usually more difficult to learn and tell than folktales and legends. The language and background are often more sophisticated. They are very much appreciated by young adults, however, and should not be ignored in the storyteller's repertoire.

Booklist: Legends

Baumann, Hans. *The Stolen Fire: Legends of Heroes and Rebels from Around the World*; tr. by Stella Humphries. Art by Herbert Holzing. Pantheon, 1974.

Clymer, Theodore. *The Travels of Atunga*. Art by John Schoenherr. Little, 1973.

Erdoes, Richard and Alfonso Ortiz. *American Indian Myths and Legends*. Pantheon, 1984.

Esbensen, Barbara. *Ladder to the Sky*. Art by Helen K. Davie. Little, 1989.

Hodges, Margaret. *The Fire Bringer: A Paiute Indian Legend.* Art by Peter Parnell. Little, 1972.

Lee, Jeanne M. *Legend of the Milky Way.* Art by author. Holt, 1982.

Lee, Robin Korna. *Legends of the Hawaiian Forest.* Makapu'u Press (P.O. Box 26404, Honolulu, Hawaii 96825), 1985.

Quale, Eric. *The Shining Princess and Other Japanese Legends.* Art by Michael Forman. Little, 1989.

San Souci, Robert D. *Larger than Life: The Adventures of American Legendary Heroes.* Art by Andrew Glass. Doubleday, 1991.

Scribner, Charles Jr. *The Devil's Bridge.* Art by Evaline Ness. Scribner, 1978.

Untermeyer, Louis. *The World's Great Stories: Fifty-five Legends That Live Forever.* Art by Mae Gerhard. Evans, 1964.

Van Laan, Nancy. *Rainbow Crow: A Lenape Tale.* Art by Beatriz Vidal. Knopf, 1989.

Westervelt, W. D., comp. and tr. *Hawaiian Legends of Ghosts and Ghost-Gods.* Tuttle, 1964.

Religious Sources

Oral presentation has traditionally played an important part in the teaching of religion. The teacher or leader stands or sits in front of a group and tells a story based on the religious principles of the order. Today storytelling is still used as a way to teach, as well as a way to entertain.

Many of the stories that have been orally handed down or printed make direct reference to religious incidents or persons. "The Jolly Tailor Who Became King," a Polish folktale, is a humorous nonsense story about an exceptionally thin tailor who sews up a hole in the sky and wins a princess as his wife. In the story the tailor and a friend are entertained by the devil's representatives; the frightened tailor and a friend are entertained by the devil's representatives; the frightened tailor invokes the protection of the Holy Virgin by singing a song in her praise, and the devils disappear. Although this part of the story seems quite incongruous in context, it does illustrate the religious influence on a simple folktale. Oscar Wilde, the talented nineteenth-century playwright, contributed to children's literature by writing a book of original fairy tales. The most impressive of these tells of a selfish giant who lets no one visit his beautiful garden. Because he is so selfish, winter lingers within its walls while it is springtime outside. When the neighborhood children sneak into the garden and the trees burst into blossom, the giant befriends a little boy. Years later the boy, a Christ figure, turns up to accompany the giant to the garden of Paradise. This religious symbolism may not be understood by children, but the story is lovely and beautifully written. It is yet another example of the religious influence on written and oral sources.

For those seeking obviously religious stories, there is a wealth of material. Remember that nearly every story has some sort of worthwhile message to impart. Even a seemingly frivolous nonsense story can be telling us that "happiness is laughter." Just because a story doesn't specifically mention religion doesn't mean that it might not serve your purpose.

I was once at a religious camp meeting where my friend introduced me as a storyteller. Without warning, the camp PA system announced that a visiting storyteller would now entertain. While my friend cringed, wondering what stories I could use, I simply told two of my favorites. The audience could easily find appropriate morals in them, even though they were not truly religious stories.

Stories involving beliefs of many of the world's religions can easily be found on library shelves. A brief examination of the availability of books based on Judaic-Christian heritage gives an idea of the variety and types of stories within easy reach for the storyteller. Beginning with the Bible we can choose from many interpretations. In *Tomie dePaola's Book of Bible Stories: New International Version*, full-color art accompanies the retellings of stories from both the Old and New Testaments. For those who like a more chatty, informal Bible scattered throughout with British colloquialisms, there is the British Broadcasting Corporation's *Bible Stories*, written originally for television production, which explores the Old Testament. Of course, the Bible, with its many interpretations, is only one way of presenting religious stories. Meindert DeJong, the Newbery Medal Award winner, has written stories of the people in the Bible: Noah, Abraham, Isaac, Sarah, David, and many others as he remembered them told by his teacher and read to him by his grandfather. Each section of his *The Mighty Ones* begins with a quotation from the Bible and then in strong prose relates an incident from the lives of these Old Testament people. Another modern retelling of the Bible stories is Jan Wahl's *Runaway Jonah and Other Tales* in which

five of the more familiar Old Testament stories are given a new and slightly offbeat vitality. I also like a new collection by Alice Bach and J. Cheryl Exum, *Miriam's Well: Stories about Women in the Bible*. Legends based on religion can always be found too. Uri Shulevitz, in *The Magician*, writes of Elijah, a favorite figure of Jewish folklore who, on the eve of Passover, conjures up a feast for a needy couple. Another Jewish legend, gloriously illustrated as a picture book but suitable for a large age range, is Beverly Brodsky McDermott's *The Golom* in which a

lump of clay fashioned into a man becomes a monster with a power all its own.

Retellings of single Bible stories are popular. The story of Noah and the ark has inspired a number of picture books. *Noah and the Rainbow*, as retold by Max Bollinger and illustrated by Helga Aichinger, with stark simplicity, alternating warm with cool colors, is based on that familiar story. Another, *The Endless Party* by Etienne Delessert and Eleonore Schmid, departs from tradition and has Noah inviting all the animals aboard the ark for a party. Isaac Bashevis Singer's picture-book version *Why Noah Chose the Dove*, illustrated by Eric Carle's tissue paper collages, shows the animals arguing about who is the more worthy animal. It is the dove who says, "Each one of us has something the other doesn't have, given us by God who created us all." At that point Noah invites all the animals into the ark. Still another dimension is added to the story of the ark when Noah's grandson is lost before embarkation in Norma Farber's *Where's Gomer?* The illustrator, William Pène du Bois, pictures Noah and his family in trim yachting outfits eating chocolate layer cake and drinking milk. The old folksong *One Wide River to Cross* inspired still another picture-book version of the Noah story by Ed and Barbara Emberley, illustrated in decorative woodblock designs on brightly colored paper. For storytellers who are musically talented, the music is printed in the back of the book. *Will I Go to Heaven?* by Peter Mayle is an informally written picture book that explains various concepts of Heaven and Hell to those who have no direct affiliation with an organized religious group but who wish to impart some moral values to children. The lightly humorous cartoon drawings make it a good book to share with young children. Those interested in using their storytelling skills in their church or synagogue activities can find an endless supply of source materials for visual presentation, storytelling, and reading aloud.

Booklist: Religious Sources

Bach, Alice and J. Cheryl Exum. *Moses' Ark*. Art by Leo and Diane Dillon. Delacorte, 1989. Old Testament stories retold in narrative form.

_____. *Miriam's Well: Stories about Women in the Bible*. Art by Leo and Diane Dillon. Delacorte, 1991.

Baylor, Byrd. *A God on Every Mountain Top: Stories of Southwest Indian Sacred Mountains*. Art by Carol Brown. Scribner, 1981. Short, short myths that the Southwest Indians tell about their mountains.

Bleecker, Mary Noel, comp. "The Jolly Tailor Who Became King" in *Big Music; or Twenty Merry Tales to Tell*. Art by Louis S. Glanzman. Viking, 1946.

Bollinger, Max. *Noah and the Rainbow*; tr. by Clyde Robert Bulla. Art by Helga Aichinger. Crowell, 1972.

DeJong, Meindert. *The Mighty Ones: Great Men and Women of Early Bible Days*. Art by Harvey Schmidt. Harper, 1959.

Delessert, Etienne and Eleonore Schmid. *The Endless Party.* Harlin Quist, 1967.

dePaola, Tomie. *Tomie dePaola's Book of Bible Stories: New International Version.* Putnam, 1990.

Diamond, Barbara. *Cakes and Miracles: A Purim Tale.* Art by Erika Weihs. Viking, 1991. A blind boy finds a special way to celebrate Purim.

Dickinson, Peter. *City of Gold and Other Stories from the Old Testament.* Art by Michael Foreman. Houghton, 1992. A wonderful new collection.

_____. *The World's Birthday: A Rosh Hashanah Story.* Art by Jeanette Winter. Harcourt, 1990. Daniel organizes a birthday party for the world.

Eisler, Colin. *David's Psalms.* Art by Jerry Pinkney. Dial, 1992. The psalms are retold to reflect the life of David.

Farber, Norma. *Where's Gomer?* Art by Wiliam Pène du Bois. Dutton, 1974.

Gellman, Marc. *Does God Have a Big Toe? Stories about Stories in the Bible.* Art by Oscar de Mejo. Harper, 1989. A humorous interpretation of some of the better known stories from the Bible.

Kossoff, David, reteller. *Bible Stories.* Art by Gino D'Achille. Follett, 1969.

Langstaff, John, ed. *Climbing Jacob's Ladder: Heroes of the Bible in African-American Spirituals.* Art by Ashley Bryan. Piano arrangements by John Andrew Ross. McElderry, 1991. Each of these spirituals has a short introduction and full-color art.

McDermott, Beverly Brodsky. *The Golem.* Art by author. Lippincott, 1976.

Mayle, Peter. *Will I Go to Heaven?* Art by Jem Gray. Corwin, 1976.

Noah's Ark: Words from the Book of Genesis. Art by Jane Ray. Dutton, 1990. The double spreads in this picture book use folk motifs to illustrate the popular bible story.

One Wide River to Cross, adapted by Barbara Emberley. Art by Ed Emberley. Prentice-Hall, 1966.

Sherman, Ori. *The Four Questions.* Art by Lynne Sharon Schwartz. Dial, 1989. The Passover symbols are explained in a picture book.

Shulevitz, Uri. *The Magician;* an adaptation from the Yiddish of I. L. Peretz. Art by author. Macmillan, 1973.

Singer, Isaac Bashevis. *Why Noah Chose the Dove;* tr. by Elizabeth Shub. Art by Eric Carle. Farrar, 1973.

Titherington, Jeanne. *A Child's Prayer.* Greenwillow, 1989. A child is shown saying a prayer at bedtime.

Turner, Phillip. *Brian Wildsmith's Illustrated Bible Stories.* Art by Brian Wildsmith. Watts, 1969. Attractive pen-and-ink drawings are matched by a graceful commentary.

Wahl, Jan. *Runaway Jonah and Other Tales.* Art by Uri Shulevitz. Macmillan, 1968.

Wilde, Oscar. "The Selfish Giant" in *The Happy Prince and Other Stories.* Art by Lars Bo. Penguin, 1962.

Other Literary Sources

Don't confine your search for the perfect story to folklore; remember that you have the rest of the library to help you also.

Start with picture books. The pictures may even help you to visualize the story as you practice telling it. Even if you are working with high school students or adults, don't let the picture-book format deter you, for many of these books contain stories that are also appropriate for older children. And keep in mind, of course, that you will find more folklore shelved in this section of the library. You will find many picture books listed in chapters 19 and 20.

The I Can Read books, or Beginning to Read books can also be good sources for storytelling. Barbara Ann Porte's Read-alone books reflect familiar children's problems. In *Harry's Dog*, a little boy finally gets the dog of his dreams, only to discover that his father is allergic to dogs. In *Harry's Mom*, the family remembers happy times with Harry's mother. *Stan the Hot Dog Man* offers more wonderful storytelling material. In this story, Stan retires from his job at the bakery and starts a new career as the driver of a hot dog truck. Throughout the course of the story, Stan meets everyone in the neighborhood and even saves a group of children during a snowstorm. In another early reader, *In a Dark, Dark Room*, the folklore collector Alvin Schwartz retells short scary stories.

Anthologies are another excellent source of material. Often an anthology will feature one subject, country, or theme. *The Canadian Children's Treasury*, a collection of excerpts from longer books by Canadian authors, is one good example. In my own work, I found that I was constantly trying to gather material for theme programs and wondered if others might be doing the same. My attempts to collect stories, poems, and activities for programs about Halloween, Spring, Grandparents' Day, and many other special occasions resulted in *Celebrations*, a book of holiday and theme book programs. In *Windy Day, Rainy Day* and *Snowy Day*, I gathered poems especially for children to read, but I know that adults who work with children also enjoy using these books when the weather matches the subject.

Don't rule out novels as a source for material. Pick a favorite young adult novel and select a chapter that lends itself easily to storytelling. After all, what better way to promote a title than to give your audience just a hint of what it offers? "2,147 Beer and Pop Cans" in Betsy Byars' *The Not-Just-Anybody Family* would be a delight to present. Pap, Junior's grandfather, is arrested when the cans he has collected for deposit fall out of his pickup and bystanders think he is brandishing a shotgun at them. The "baby-sitting" chapter in Johanna Hurwitz's *Tough-Luck Karen* would be another good choice. In it, Karen takes a job as a baby-sitter, but ends up at a surprise party.

Biography and informational books also offer interesting material. "The Grand Banquet," in Rhoda Blumberg's *Commodore Perry in the Land of the Shogun*, would make a wonderful story, filled with details about the feast given by Perry for the Japanese dignitaries and their retainers. "Growing Up Rich," from *Franklin Delano Roosevelt* by Russell Friedman, tells about the childhood of the man who grew up to be president of the United States. Here is an example of a biography that could be turned into a perfect storytime presentation.

Short stories are listed under literary tales, but they deserve their own mention here as well. Just browsing through the table of contents of Margaret Mahy's *Nonstop Nonsense* should pique your interest. Chapter titles include such intriguing titles as "Green Marmalade to You" and "Frightening the Monster in Wizard's Hole."

Whole Language Sources

Have you overlooked the textbook you are using with your class as a source of oral literature? The new literature series are chock full of excerpted chapters from children's books and folklore ready to learn and tell. Your students will be delighted to hear one of the selections they have studied told orally.

Children's Magazines

Cricket magazine (P.O. Box 51145, Boulder, CO 80323–1145) is the perfect example of a children's periodical filled with carefully chosen stories and poetry that you might find useful for your story presentations. This magazine uses contemporary authors as well as older literature suitable for 7–12 year-olds. *Ladybug* (P.O. Box 50284, Boulder, CO 80323–0284) for younger children is also a treasure trove of literature waiting to be told.

Audio Tapes

Many professional storytellers have produced their own story-telling tapes. These are useful because they give you an opportunity to hear different styles of telling. They can also be a good source of stories. A current listing can be found in the NAPPS resource catalog, P.O. Box 309, Jonesborough, TN, 37659.

Booklist: Other Literary Sources

Bauer, Caroline Feller. *Celebrations: Read-aloud Holiday and Theme Book Programs.* H. W. Wilson, 1985.

_____. *Windy Day.* Harper, 1988. (See also *Rainy Day* and *Snowy Day.*)

Blumberg, Rhoda. *Commodore Perry in the Land of the Shogun.* Illustrated. Lothrop, 1985.

Byars, Betsy. *The Not-Just-Anybody Family.* Art by Jacqueline Rogers. Delacorte, 1986.

The Canadian Children's Treasury. Illustrated. Key Porter (70 The Esplanade, Toronto, Ontario M5E 1R2, Canada), 1988.

Friedman, Russell. *Franklin Delano Roosevelt.* Clarion, 1990.

Hurwitz, Johanna. *Tough-Luck Karen,* Art by Diane De Groat. Morrow, 1982.

Kessler, Ethel and Leonard Kessler. *Stan the Hot Dog Man.* An I Can Read Book. Art by Leonard Kessler. Harper, 1990.

Mahy, Margaret. *Nonstop Nonsense.* Art by Quentin Blake. McElderry, 1977.

Porte, Barbara Ann. *Harry's Dog.* Greenwillow Read Alone. Art by Yossi Abolafia. Greenwillow, 1984.

_____. *Harry's Mom.* Greenwillow Read Alone. Art by Yossi Abolafia. Greenwillow, 1985.

Schwartz, Alvin. *In a Dark, Dark Room.* Art by Dirk Zimmer. Harper, 1984.

Family Stories

At every storytelling festival there is sure to be at least one session devoted to family storytelling. Telling stories that feature an incident from personal experience or that describe an eccentric relative have become popular with both amateur and professional storytellers. At first I was reluctant to participate in this movement. I had been so indoctrinated by the traditions of the New York Public Library and Columbia University that I didn't see how this sort of storytelling could possibly help further my interests in promoting reading. I had made a private rule for myself that if the story wasn't published somewhere, I shouldn't tell it. After all, how could I recommend reading something that didn't exist?

Still I was intrigued. It seemed as though anyone could tell this sort of story. I heard one woman tell a funny story about how her best dress was ruined while she hastily polished her nails, and another storyteller relate her first experience in splunking. Too bad, I thought. I have dozens of wonderful travel stories, but they are not found in books, of course. At a story session in Louisiana I heard Donald Davis tell some of his famous family stories. He really was wonderful. Again, I thought, too bad I can't tell my own family stories. I certainly have some good ones! And then, one day, I had a revelation. I could tell my own family stories, and then recommend books on the same theme that my audience might enjoy reading. In fact, I could create entire book programs around Feller Bauer family stories!

"Grandma and the Birds" is one such story. It is about my own grandmother and it really happened. Now I can tell an unpublished story and exhibit books on a variety of subjects: city birds, older people, nursing homes. I can even print it here and say, "It's in a book!"

GRANDMA AND THE BIRDS

My Grandma is a very friendly person. She speaks to everyone: the clerk at the post office, the butcher, the bus driver, and the little girls who jump rope in front of her apartment. We are always told not to talk to strangers, but I guess Grandma doesn't think that at 87 anyone is going to spirit her away.

Grandma loves animals and always had an assortment of dogs, cats, birds, and an occasional rabbit in her apartment. Naturally, we were always excited to visit Grandma and play with her creatures.

When Grandma broke her hip she could no longer manage the three flights of stairs to her apartment. So she gave her current dog to me, her two cats to her next door neighbor, and her rabbit to my cousin Stevie. Then she moved into the Towers Nursing Home in Manhatten.

Since she was no longer as mobile as she had once been, my mother and I were constantly running errands for Grandma. I hated chores like buying shoes for her. They rarely fit, which meant a trip back to the store to return or exchange them. But I never minded bringing the birdseed. Grandma missed her own animals, but she said that

New York City provided free birds to anyone who cared to have them.

"All you do," she said, "is put out a handful of birdseed on the windowsill and you'll have all the pigeons you could want flying around your window."

For three months I brought a bag of birdseed every Friday. "They sure do eat a lot," I exclaimed. "They can have as much as they want," said Grandma. "If they fly all the way up to the fourth floor, the least I can do is make it worth their effort!"

One Friday I was met at the door of the nursing home by the director, Mr. Crufts. He was furious. "Have you seen the front of our building? There is no way we can keep it clean when your grandmother attracts hundreds of pigeons every day. Please don't bring her any more birdseed or she will have to leave the facility."

When I entered my grandmother's room with the news she was writing to her friends. She had friends and acquaintances all over town. Many of them she had met at church, or temple, or mosque. Grandma went to services and . . . potlucks all weekend. "I like the music at St. Mary's, I like the sermons at the Cathedral, and I like the women's group at the Synagogue," she'd say.

"Who are you writing to?" I asked. "I got a lot done today," she answered. "Remember that lovely man who owns that car company? And I know you liked that actress I met. They've both read the new Jon Hassler. We're comparing notes." My Grandma is far more impressed if people have read the same book than if they own "that car company."

"I have some bad news for you, Grandma. Mr. Crufts says that I can't bring you birdseed anymore. He says that you can no longer feed the birds."

"That young man will never own a car company," my Grandma said indignantly. "He thinks small."

I thought that was the end of the birds, but I should have realized that my Grandma would find another way to feed her birds. "I'm so happy," she said one day. "The birds really love it here now. It turns out that they don't like birdseed all that much. I've been feeding them gourmet meals instead, just like the brochure for this place advertises.

"What do you mean?" I asked?

"They give you much too much food here. There's really plenty for the pigeons. For breakfast they get a little leftover egg and toast. For lunch they seem to like sandwich bread and lettuce. For dinner I give them chocolate cake or sometimes a bit of potato."

When I left after my visit, Mr. Crufts was standing in the entry way. "I am sorry. I am going to have to ask you to find another facility for your grandmother. I have repeatedly asked her not to feed the birds. The situation is really quite intolerable. Now, in addition to bird droppings, the building front is spotted with leftover food!"

I argued, of course, but Mr. Crufts was adamant. I returned to Grandma's room and explained the situation. She was already writing to "that man who has the theatrical agency who helped me get tickets to *M. Butterfly.*"

"That silly man" was her reaction. "I guess I'll have to do something. I'll call one of my friends. I met Mr. Restow that time they had the father/daughter dinner at Temple Emanuel. I'll call him."

Mr. Restow is a reporter for the *New York Times*. I won't tell you that there were headlines in the paper the next day. It was just a little article that appeared in section C, all about the little old lady in the nursing home who isn't allowed to feed the birds. Mr. Crufts received many phone calls and letters.

If you are driving past the Towers Nursing Home on Central Park West in New York City around noon, look up at the fourth floor, at the window in the center. You'll see a flock of birds flying in the vicinity and sitting on the window ledge. Be sure to wave. I'm sure Grandma will wave back. She is very friendly.

Creating a Family Story

Perhaps you would like to try telling your own family stories. Some people like to start by writing down their ideas, but because I feel that the print medium is different from the oral, I prefer to begin by telling my story. If you must, write a simple outline that you can refer to as you tell your story. The best personal stories are those that you may have told already—perhaps at a dinner party, a family gathering, or in the staff lounge. After you have told the story informally the first time, try to find another place to tell it. At each subsequent telling you will find yourself perfecting the story. For instance, a common fault of personal telling is the inclusion of too many details. If you are telling about the time that you got lost in a department store, it isn't necessary, and probably doesn't add to the story, to tell how you got to the store, why you went, and what you had purchased the day before. As you tell the story, notice where your listeners laugh, where they seem touched, and, most importantly, where they seem bored.

Another fault of the beginning teller is to drag the story out until it becomes too lengthy. If you are describing your first attempt at wind surfing, for example, it's not necessary to describe each and every time that you and your boat capsized!

Although I encourage teachers to use the skills of storytelling as a way to teach and encourage good writing skills, I caution storytellers not to transfer their personal stories into print too soon. The charm of everyday speech often seems stilted or awkward on the printed page.

What will be the subject of your story? There are certainly some universal experiences that many people seem to have shared. A popular subject for personal stories, often used as an exercise to teach storytelling, is to tell "how I got my scar." Amazingly, nearly everyone does have a childhood scar, along with crystal clear memories of how it happened. You might use this suggested title list to jog your own memory.

Suggested titles for family storytelling:

How I got my childhood scar
A memorable birthday party
The first day of school
The first day on my new job
The piano recital
My eccentric relative
The high school prom
The wedding
The new brother
My step mom
My dad is getting married
The prize I didn't win
How I decided what to wear
   this morning

My favorite place
The day I got lost
The county fair
My favorite place to read
The flood
The snowfall
My college roommate
My first job
My first girl friend
The argument
How I got my name
How I got my nickname

Booklist: Family Storytelling

Akeret, Robert U. with Daniel Klein. *Family Tales, Family Wisdom: How to Gather the Stories of a Lifetime and Share Them with Your Family.* Morrow, 1991.

Alessi, Jean and Jan Miller. *Once upon a Memory: Your Family Tales and Treasures.* Butterfly (Box 76, White Hall, VA 22987), 1987.

Davis, Donald. *Listening for the Crack of Dawn.* August House, 1990.

Fletcher, William. *Recording Your Family History.* Dodd, 1986.

Geras, Adele. *My Grandmother's Stories: A Collection of Jewish Folktales.* Art by Jael Jordan. Knopf, 1990.

Pellowski, Anne. *The Family Storytelling Handbook.* Art by Lynn Sweat. Macmillan, 1987.

Perl, Lila. *The Great Ancestor Hunt.* Clarion, 1989.

Stock, Gregory. *The Kid's Book of Questions.* Workman, 1988.

Weitzman, David. *My Backyard History Book.* Little, 1973.

Wigginton, Eliot. *Foxfire.* v. 1–9. Anchor, 1972–1986.

Zeitlin, Steven J., Amy J. Kotkin and Holly Cutting Baker. *A Celebration of American Family Folklore: Tales and Traditions from the Smithsonian Collection.* Pantheon, 1982.

Game

Lifestories. A board game that asks players to explore their lives. Available from Storylines, P.O. Box 7416, Saint Paul, MN, 55107.

Picture Books with Family Reminiscences

Childhood memories are featured in these picture books.

Allen, Thomas B. *On Granddaddy's Farm*. Art by author. Knopf, 1989.

Brusca, Maria Cristina. *On the Pampas*. Art by the author. Holt, 1991.

Cech, John. *My Grandmother's Journey*. Art by Sharon McGinley-Naly. Bradbury, 1991.

Dionetti, Michelle. *Coal Mine Peaches*. Art by Anita Riggio. Orchard, 1991.

Houston, Gloria. *My Great-Aunt Arizona*. Art by Susan Conde Lamb. Harper, 1992.

Levinson, Riki. *Watch the Stars Come Out*. Art by Diane Goode. Dutton, 1985.

Montaufier, Poupa. *One Summer at Grandmother's House*; tr. from the French by Tobi Tobias. Art by author. Carolrhoda, 1985.

Rylant, Cynthia. *When I Was Young in the Mountains*. Art by Diane Goode. Dutton, 1982.

Smucker, Anna Egan. *No Stars Tonight*. Art by Steve Johnson. Knopf, 1989.

Stevenson, James. *When I Was Nine*. Art by author. Greenwillow, 1986.

Booklist: To Find Out More about Folklore

And finally, some of the classic (and a few new) references on folklore.

American Folklore Society, Folklore Center, Social Work 306, Univ. of Texas, Austin, TX 78712.

Bronner, Simon J. *American Children's Folklore*. August House, 1988. One volume in the American Folklore Series. Includes song parodies, autograph rhymes, non-singing games, and more.

Brunvand, Jan Harold. *The Study of American Folklore: An Introduction*. Norton, 1968. Essays on verbal and nonverbal folklore.

Children's Folklore Review. Department of English, East Carolina University. Greenville, NC 27858–4353. Articles relating to children's folklore. Published twice a year by the Children's Folklore Section of the American Folklore Society.

Dorson, Richard M. *American Folklore*. Univ. of Chicago Pr., 1959. A survey of American folklore.

Dundes, Alan. *The Study of Folklore*. Prentice-Hall, 1965. An anthology of 34 essays that "surveys the discipline of folklore."

Epstein, Perle. *Monsters: Their Histories, Homes, and Habits*. Art by author. Doubleday, 1973. Mythical creatures are surveyed for children. Useful for background information.

The Foxfire Book, ed. by Eliot Wigginton. Doubleday, 1972. Articles on folk activities including hunting tales, mountain crafts, and foods. A second volume, *Foxfire 2* (Doubleday, 1973), contains ghost stories, spinning, and weaving. A third, *Foxfire 3* (Doubleday, 1975), features animal care, banjoes and dulcimers, hide tanning, summer and fall wild plant foods, butter churns, and ginseng.

Frazer, Sir James G. *The New Golden Bough*, ed. by Theodor H. Gaster. Criterion, 1959. An abridged, but still lengthy version, of Frazer's 1890 work. Studies the history of civilization from the point of view of primitive magic, taboos, and superstition.

Funk and Wagnalls Standard Dictionary of Folklore, Mythology and Legend, ed. by Maria Leach and Jerome Fried, 2 v. Funk, 1949–1950. A reference work that encompasses folklore around the world.

Krappe, Alexander H. *The Science of Folklore*. Norton, 1964. "A classic introduction to the origins, forms, and characteristics of folklore."

Opie, Ione and Peter Opie. *The Lore and Language of School Children*. Art by authors. Clarendon Pr., 1959.

_____. *I Saw Esau: The School Child's Pocket Book*. Art by Maurice Sendak. Candlewick, 1992. Rhymes, riddles, insults, and jump rope rhymes collected from children.

Raglan, FitzRoy Richard Somerset, Baron. *The Hero: A Study in Tradition, Myth and Drama*. Vintage, 1956. The myths as fictional narrative.

Thompson, Stith. *The Folktale*. Dryden Pr., 1946. The classic study of the folktale including motif and tale type index.

On the book cover:
For Laughing
Out Loud:
Poems to Tickle
Your Funnybone.

by
Jack Prelutsky

8 / Poetry

Sound the trumpets! Bang the drums! Children's poetry has come of age. True, we had a wealth of poetry appropriate for children from which to choose when this book was first published, but recently there has been a virtual avalanche of fresh new voices to add to the old favorites.

What a happy event for those who wish to present literature to children. By adding poetry to your storytelling presentation, you give the program a special, magical touch. Begin by presenting a single poem. Once you have become more familiar with the collections, you may wish to devote an entire program to poetry, or plan a poetry festival in which poetry is featured during a series of storyhours. Poems are meant to be read aloud, and a storyhour presents the perfect opportunity.

Choosing a Poem

As I travel around the country, visiting schools and public libraries, often the first thing I do is to check the poetry section on the library shelves to see if the collection can support a poetry program. I do find more and more poetry books on the shelves each year. It may be due to the Whole Language movement, or the fact that both children and adults increasingly recognize the delights of poetry, or perhaps because there is simply more poetry from which to choose. At the end of this chapter, you will find an extensive booklist that offers you a wide variety of books from which to choose your poetry selections.

If you are planning a program for younger children, preschool through third grade, you might begin by looking through some of the many editions of Mother Goose. Traditionally, Mother Goose is a child's first experience with formal rhyme. The sounds and rhythms of the language appeal to the ear, and for this reason, adults needn't worry about questions of "relevancy" or about unfamiliar language (such as Miss Muffet's "curds and whey," or Jack's broken "crown"). These verses, along with other childhood rhymes such as jump-rope jingles, are further distinguished by being perhaps the only widespread oral tradition still alive in our society.

Even though you may remember the more familiar Mother Goose rhymes, you will probably want a book not only to refresh your memory but also to show the attractive pictures that accompany the wonderfully rhythmic language. There are many beautiful editions currently in print. Some books contain collections of rhymes (e.g., Michael Foreman's collection), while in others a single rhyme is profusely illustrated (e.g., Peter Spier's books). There is, in addition, a wide choice in style of illustration ranging from the traditional (Kate Greenway) to the ultramodern (Beni Montresor). It is only a matter of exploring to discover which version will please you and your audience.

Once a child hears the music of Mother Goose, he or she will be open to hearing other poetry too. Nonsense verse is popular with small children, who love to repeat the sounds. Leslie Brooke's *Johnny Crow's Garden*, written in 1904, is still delighting today's children with its humorous animals and nonsensical verse. In *MA nDA LA*, Arnold Adoff uses nonsense syllables to make music for the child's ear, while at the same time telling a story through pictures. According to the jacket cover, "Ma" is mother, "Da" is father, "La" is singing, "Ha" is laughing, "Ra" is cheering. "Na" is sighing, and "Ah" is feeling good. The child, however, doesn't need this translation in order to joyfully join in the song, "Ma nDa La Ma nDa Ha / Ma nDa LaLaLa Ma nDa HaHaHa / Ma La Da La . . ."

There are also formal poems written expressly for very young children. Usually these poems are about children and their everyday experiences. Two classic poets of early childhood, A. A. Milne and Robert Louis Stevenson, both celebrated the daily events in a child's life. For example, in *A Child's Garden of Verses*, Stevenson wrote of going to bed, the passing of seasons, and the shadow that follows a child on a sunny day. These poets have succeeded in writing of childhood from the point of view of the child. Contemporary children's poets follow this tradition. Marchette Chute's *Rhymes about Us* includes short verses about a younger brother, drawing with crayons, and losing mittens.

Your storyhour can include one of the numerous picture books whose stories are told in rhymed verse. For example, Ludwig Bemelman's *Madeline* is a rhymed story about 12 little French girls. Robert Charles's humorous verse tale, *A Roundabout Turn*, relates the adventures of a toad who sets off to discover whether the world really is round, but ends up riding round and round on the merry-go-round, 72 times in one day!

It is often said that poetry should be read aloud to be fully enjoyed. Perhaps younger children, those who do not read yet, are fortunate in that their entire experience with poetry is aural; it is necessary to read aloud to them. Happily, children today have a rich treasury of books whose poetry is music to the ear, just as the pictures are delights to the eye.

You will also want to search through the poetry collection for poems that appeal to older groups. Obviously, the more familiar you are with poetry the easier it will be to present poems with enthusiasm and to choose subjects or themes that interest a specific audience. You might start by exploring the poetry of Eloise Greenfield, Myra Cohn Livingston, and Valerie Worth. A popular trend in poetry publishing is the publishing of poems by children or young adults. You might want to further your knowledge about poetry in general by reading one or two adult references about poetry for children, but the best way to begin is to simply start browsing.

If you have had little exposure to the world of poetry you may find that cuddling up with a poetry book for any length of time is confusing and even tedious. But none of us can say that we don't have time to read poetry. We all have odd snatches of time: between making the bed and fixing breakfast, while waiting for a friend to arrive for dinner, or even during television commercials.

You may decide to begin a personal poetry project. Find a number of poems that particularly please you to use with children. Or examine the work of one poet with the view of presenting it to a group of children. Keep a file of poems that you enjoy and, as your file gets larger, divide it by theme (circus poems, dog poems) or type (funny poems, story poems). If you also have a story file, you may want to integrate the two, matching poems with stories. A story about a clever son and a poem about a not-so-clever boy make a good storyhour.

When planning a program I find one type of poetry book especially useful. This is the poetry book that revolves around a particular theme, for in some instances the subject of the book will inspire an entire storyhour. Richard Shaw has edited several collections, each short volume emphasizing one animal; *The Cat Book*, *The Owl Book*, *The Fox Book*, *The Frog Book*, and *The Bird Book*. Think of the possibilities of planning a storyhour with such a resource available to you. You might tell a fox story such as "Mighty Mikko" from Parker Fillmore's *A Shepherd's Nosegay*, learn a poem or two from *The Fox Book*, and use that same book to show some of the artists' interpretations of foxes.

Lee Bennett Hopkins has many collections suited to theme programs. Use his *Dinosaurs* for a dinosaur program, *Good Books, Good Times!* to feature poems about reading and books, or *On the Farm*, illustrated with large color photographs, to design a program around animals.

However, don't feel that the theme of your poems must be related to your stories. A poem might appeal to you simply because it sets a special mood or tone, or because it makes you laugh. Use it at the appropriate point in your story session—at the beginning, perhaps, or in moving from one story to another.

Learning a Poem

Some adults find it difficult to memorize poetry. They may be able to learn a long folktale but freeze at the thought of a poem. This is not unusual. You can take liberties with the text of a folktale, whereas you must memorize a poem word for word. One way to go about it is to copy the poem on a card and carry it with you in your pocket or purse. Take it out several times a day, read it over, put it out of sight, and try to repeat it to yourself line by line. Memorizing the words is only the first step. Once you are comfortable with the words, begin to think of the meaning and you will find that expression will come more easily. After you've learned the first poem, I think you'll find that the next one is easier to learn. Soon you will have acquired an entire repertoire of poems!

Reading Poetry Aloud

May I tell you a secret? I have trouble memorizing poetry myself, so I often rely on visuals that I can hide behind as I read poems. For instance, I often put poems written on colorful greeting cards into the pocket of a special storytelling apron, basket, or bag. When it is time to present a poem, I simply take the card out of the pocket and read the poem aloud. This makes for a more formal presentation and, perhaps more importantly, masks the fact that I haven't quite memorized the poem! Sometimes I choose to read a poem directly from the book I have found it in, as a way of reminding my listeners where they can find poetry on their own. However, even if you haven't memorized a poem (and here I give you permission not to!), make sure that you have practiced reading the poem so that you can look at your audience as you speak, rather than down at your prop.

Introducing a Poem

A short introduction to the theme of the poem adds to the enjoyment of it. Usually a simple sentence or question is sufficient: "Have you ever wondered what it feels like to be a turtle?" or "Do you ever feel lonely?"

With some groups you may even want to avoid the actual word "poetry." There are those unfortunates who have been introduced to the wonderful world of poetry in a negative way and find it fashionable among their peers to fervently and volubly dislike it. For them, try introducing your poems as "stories" or "thoughts."

The Poetry Break

For the last six or seven years I have introduced the "Poetry Break" to my workshop audiences around the world. I've been pleased with the responses I have received from teachers and media specialists who have adopted this idea themselves. A Poetry Break is simply an easy way to add a dose of poetry to your daily diet. Here's how it works in a school. Assign a student, a volunteer, or a teacher's aide the job of traveling Poetry Break salesperson. He or she goes from classroom to classroom with a poem to present. The poem is usually read directly from a book, so once you have a good poetry collection, or even a single serviceable anthology, you're ready to begin. You do need one prop: a sign that announces "Poetry Break." The sign is important because you or your designated Poetry Break person will be walking around your school and popping into classrooms virtually unannounced. The sign provides you with an introduction and tells people immediately that "it's time for our daily poem." You don't want them wondering whether you are a visiting fireman who has come to explain the fire code! A Poetry Break takes only a few seconds, usually not even a full minute, so it barely disrupts regular classroom work, particularly if it is a regular event. If someone in your school prefers not to participate, or is giving a standardized test on a particular day and does not wish to be interrupted, he or she can always post a sign on the door that says "No poetry today, please."

Librarians take note: I have found that library patrons also enjoy Poetry Breaks, as they often provide a welcome change from more serious study. Simply walk up to a table or group of people and announce "Poetry Break!" You will be an instant success, I promise!

Don't worry that the daily selection may not be age appropriate for your entire school or library. Since you will be presenting a poem every day, you are sure to catch nearly everyone's interests eventually.

Visual Poetry

Occasionally you may want to introduce a poem visually, with a puppet, poster, or artifact. Such visuals should be used sparingly, however. You want your audience to feel the mood of the poem you have chosen, rather than become caught up in the picture or puppet. Also, you don't want to turn the easy, simple preparation of a poetry presentation into a production that takes up too much of your time. Today you may bring in a picture of an elephant to accompany a poem about elephants; tomorrow you may be tempted to bring a live elephant! Soon, your poetry breaks may seem like just too much trouble.

There are some simple visuals that you can use occasionally—once a week or even once a month—without detracting from the poems themselves or adding a lot of work to your busy schedule. For instance, sometimes I like to have a puppet or stuffed animal "read" a poem. This is a particularly good prop for a beginner who is unsure about reciting poetry. After all, if your puppet makes a mistake, you can correct him. Or, you can take a quick peek at the copy, if your puppet appears to need some coaching. A poem can also be acted out or read aloud by two volunteers who trade lines. Or try extracting a poem from an unusual box or bag before you read it. If you have a little extra time to prepare, you can hand out a special souvenir to go with your poem. See chapter 3, Promotion, for lots of souvenir ideas.

The Poetry Program

After you have used an occasional poem in your storyhour successfully, you may want to attempt something more ambitious. Do a session entirely devoted to poetry, perhaps featuring the poems of one writer. Introduce the session with a *short* discussion of the poet's life and a few brief remarks on the major characteristics of his or her poetry. Give this type of introduction only if you can keep it short, lively, and to the point. By all means, avoid lecturing! Be sure you have books available featuring the poet's poems. Show the children how a poem first published in an individual book of poetry is later used in an anthology. You might also exhibit a number of different illustrated versions of the poetry of one favorite poet.

Poetry on a single theme makes a lovely program, too. Take any subject (dogs, snow, loneliness, baseball, or the city) and search through your poetry collection for poems worthy of inclusion. Decorate your story room with large cutouts representing the theme. Serve a special treat, such as simple cutout cookies, to emphasize the subject. Create bookmarks listing the authors of the poems you will recite. Now let your audience sit back comfortably, listen, and enjoy.

The Poetry Festival

A still more ambitious project is a poetry festival to which you invite talented adults or children to perform. This can be a very informal session in which the children perform for each other or it can be a more formal festival, perhaps lasting for several sessions. A poetry festival might feature the works of an individual poet (maybe you can invite the poet as a guest), a particular theme, or just poetry in general.

A festival is a good time for children to present their own creations. If you do have children writing poetry, you may find that the writer does not necessarily want to be the performer. In this situation you might encourage some cooperation between two children with different talents—one who enjoys writing and one who enjoys performing. You might even open the secret doors of the storyhour to interested adults. Let them hear what your talented youngsters have written.

Choral Speaking

As a result of the Whole Language movement, choral speaking is back in vogue. Essentially, the idea is for a group to present poetry together. A poem may be read in unison, or as dialogue (as in Reader's Theater), or with a solo and a group refrain.

When I was a child, choral speaking was treated as a rigidly orchestrated activity. Although I usually enjoyed any kind of performance, I was often bored with the repetition and desire of the leader to perfect our rendition of the poem. So I prefer to treat choral speaking much more informally.

"The Frog on the Log" by Ilo Orleans is a lively, easy poem to try scripting for choral speaking. This poem could be spoken in unison—that is, the entire group could recite the poem together. Or six groups or individuals could each recite one verse. Or a leader could speak the first two lines of each verse and the group could recite the last line. Still another way might be to ask the audience to echo the last line of every verse. Pick one of these choices and try it with your group.

THE FROG ON THE LOG
Ilo Orleans

There once
Was a green
    Little frog, frog, frog—

Who played
In the wood
    On a log, log, log!

A screech owl
Sitting
    In a tree, tree, tree—

Came after
The frog
    With a scree, scree, scree!

When the frog
Heard the owl—
    In a flash, flash, flash—

He leaped
In the pond
    With a splash, splash, splash!

Illustrations and Poetry

Many children's books of poetry are beautifully and appropriately illustrated. A. A. Milne's *Now We Are Six* and *When We Were Very Young*, for example, would seem empty and incomplete without the charming illustrations by Ernest Shepard, and yet the Walt Disney Studios drew their own cartoons to replace the classic Shepard art. And some stories written in verse, such as Ludwig Bemelmans' *Madeline* or Dr. Seuss's *And to Think That I Saw It on Mulberry Street*, depend upon the illustrations to help tell the story. With other books, you might show the illustrations after you have recited the poetry.

Kathleen Fraser's *Stilts, Somersaults and Headstands* gives you an opportunity to introduce art while enjoying excellent poetry. The poet has written a delightful poem for each game or activity represented in the sixteenth-century painting "Children's Games" by the Flemish artist Peter Brueghel.

Several lavishly illustrated poetry anthologies have been designed around lovely collections of art. *Talking to the Sun*, sponsored by the Metropolitan Museum of Art, includes poems selected by Kenneth Koch and Kate Farrell. Charles Sullivan chose American paintings to accompany poetry for children in his *Imaginary Gardens*. Poems and fine paintings go hand in hand in *A Child's Treasury of Seaside Verse*, compiled by Mark Daniel. All three of these books introduce young people to poetry and art at the same time.

Often modern books of poetry are beautifully illustrated. Share an appropriate illustration with your group after you have recited or read one or more poems. However, keep in mind that although pictures do add much to the presentation, it is the sound of the words you are reciting or reading that makes poetry truly exciting.

Think of the many ways of using poetry while projecting visuals. Try taking 35mm color pictures (to make slides) of children acting out a poem. Or, put acetate (available in your art supply store) in 2 x 2 slide mounts and draw abstract images on them with permanent color felt pens. Recite poetry as you project the images.

Consider projecting a scratch film of your own making. To do this, ask your photo store for 16mm film leader. With a stylus or any sharp point—a nail or a knife—scrape away the emulsion on the leader to form abstract designs. Play music and recite poems while you project your film. The process is more fully explained in chapter 14.

Creating a Poetry Tradition

Why not decide that you are always going to begin or end your story sessions with a poem? The children will begin to eagerly expect your poem and this will compel you to build up your poetry repertoire. After you have learned ten poems for ten sessions, you will have an entire poetry program ready for the next poetry festival.

Five Favorite Poems

There are so many, many wonderful poems for children that I've had a difficult time choosing those to actually include in this chapter. But I've managed to select five of my very favorites for you. I hope you enjoy presenting them as much as I do.

Of the poets who write poems for younger children, A. A. Milne still remains at the top of my list of favorites. The poem that follows, from *When We Were Very Young*, captures the imagination of a child and remains in his memory as he grows up. Any adult that you see on a city street walking carefully in the squares and avoiding the lines has probably heard this poem.

LINES AND SQUARES
A. A. Milne

Whenever I walk in a London street,
I'm ever so careful to watch my feet;
And I keep in the squares,
And the masses of bears,
Who wait at the corners all ready to eat
The sillies who tread on the lines of the street,
Go back to their lairs,
And I say to them, "Bears,
Just look how I'm walking in all of the squares!"
And the little bears growl to each other, "He's mine,
As soon as he's silly and steps on a line."
And some of the bigger bears try to pretend
That they came round the corner to look for a friend;
And they try to pretend that nobody cares
Whether you walk on the lines or squares.
But only the sillies believe their talk;
It's ever so portant how you walk.
And it's ever so jolly to call out, "Bears,
Just watch me walking in all the squares!"

I like to use folk rhymes and sometimes children will contribute rhymes that they have heard out on the playground. The bad grammar in "The Frog" adds to its charm and gives it a colloquial air.

THE FROG

What a wonderful bird the frog are—
When he sit, he stand almost;
When he hop, he fly almost.
He ain't got no sense hardly;
He ain't got no tail hardly either.
When he sit, he sit on what he ain't got—almost.

The two voices in the next poem make it almost like a play. The uncertainty of the new boy is a common emotion, but his solution is unique and funny. Ask a friend to help you with the presentation of this poem, but don't fight over who gets which part!

RUNNING THE GAUNTLET
Kathleen Fraser

Big Neighborhood Boy:
    Want to run the gauntlet?
New Little Boy:
    How do you play?
Big Neighborhood Boy:
    Well, *we* all sit in a row on the grass, across from each other, and *you* have to run through our feet from one end of the row to the other.
New Little Boy:
    Through all your knees and all your boots?
Big Neighborhood Boy:
    Yep.
New Little Boy:
    Will you kick and bump? Will you trip me?
Big Neighborhood Boy:
    Well, sort of . . .
New Little Boy:
    Will it hurt?
Big Neighborhood Boy:
    Not if you cross your eyes and wiggle your ears and run as fast as a lizard.
New Little Boy:
    I think I'll just watch for a while.

Children are introduced to a fine poet in the following poem. A school-age child will easily relate to its subject. The conversational style makes it easier to memorize than lyrical poetry.

ARITHMETIC
Carl Sandburg

Arithmetic is where numbers fly like pigeons in and out of your head.
Arithmetic tells you how many you lose or win if you know how many you had before you lost or won.
Arithmetic is seven eleven all good children go to heaven—or five six bundle of sticks.
Arithmetic is numbers you squeeze from your head to your hand to your pencil to your paper till you get the answer.
Arithmetic is where the answer is right and everything is nice and you can look out of the window and see the blue sky—or the answer is wrong and you have to start all over again and try again and see how it comes out this time.

$= 8$

$2 \times 2 = 4$

$4 - 6$ $48 \div 2$

$3 \times 4 = 12$

um

$6 \overline{\smash{)}12}$ 2

If you take a number and double it and double it again and then double it a few more times, the number gets bigger and bigger and goes higher and higher and only arithmetic can tell you what the number is when you decide to quit doubling.

Arithmetic is where you have to multiply—and you carry the multiplication table in your head and hope you won't lose it.

If you have two animal crackers, one good and one bad, and you eat one and a striped zebra with streaks all over him eats the other, how many animal crackers will you have if somebody offers you five six seven and you say No no no and you say Nay nay nay and you say Nix nix nix?

If you ask your mother for one fried egg for breakfast and she gives you two fried eggs and you eat both of them, who is better in arithmetic, you or your mother?

The idea that a list of words can be poetry is intriguing. Try this delightful list.

SOME FAVORITE WORDS
Richard Edwards

Mugwump, chubby, dunk and whoa,
Swizzle, doom and snoop,
Flummox, lilt and afterglow,
Gruff, bamboozle, whoop
And nincompoop.

Wallow, jungle, lumber, sigh,
Ooze and zodiac,
Innuendo, lullaby,
Ramp and mope and quack
And paddywhack.

Moony, undone, lush and bole,
Inkling, tusk, guffaw,
Waspish, croon and cubbyhole,
Fern, fawn, dumbledor
And many more . . .

Worm.

Booklist: Poetry to Read or Recite

Choosing poetry to read or recite is an even more personal experience than choosing a story. Certainly no one can really preselect a poem or a poet for you. Simply explore the library's collection until the message, the mood, or the language of a particular poem inspires in you a wish to share it. This bibliography is highly selective. Its purpose is to remind you of some of the delightful books waiting to be enjoyed.

Adult Sources

Browse through some of these titles to give yourself an overview of how some scholars and educators view poetry for children.

Anderson, Douglas. *My Sister Looks like a Pear: Awakening the Poetry in Young People*. Hart, 1974. Relates the author's experiences as a poet in a school program.

Arnstein, Flora J. *Poetry and the Child*. Dover, 1962. Children as poets. An exploration of the relationship between teacher and child.

Booth, David and Bill Moore. *Poems Please! Sharing Poetry with Children*. Pembroke, 1988. Two Canadian educators discuss how to bring children and poetry together.

Hopkins, Lee Bennett. *Pass the Poetry, Please!* rev. ed. Harper, 1987. This practical, lively look at children's poetry includes ideas for introducing poetry to children.

Hughes, Ted. *Poetry Is*. Doubleday, 1970. A British poet shows how poets such as D. H. Lawrence, T. S. Eliot, and Theodore Roethke present nature and people through poetry.

Israel, Peter and Peg Streep. *The Kids' World Almanac Rhyming Dictionary: A Guide for Young Poets and Songwriters*. Art by Heidi Stetson. World/ Pharos Books, 1991. Organized by phonetic word endings, this is intended for children, but useful for adults as well.

Koch, Kenneth. *Wishes, Lies and Dreams: Teaching Children to Write Poetry*. Vintage, 1970. Discusses a method of teaching the writing of poetry. A companion volume is *Rose, Where Did You Get That Red?* (Vintage, 1973).

Koch, Kenneth and Kate Farrell. *Sleeping on the Wing: An Anthology of Modern Poetry with Essays on Reading and Writing*. Random, 1981. Emily Dickinson, Ezra Pound, and William Carlos Williams are among those writers examined.

Larrick, Nancy. *Let's Do a Poem: Introducing Poetry to Children*. Delacorte, 1991. An overview of methods to introduce poetry to children.

Livingston, Myra Cohn. *Climb into the Bell Tower: Essays on Poetry*. Harper, 1990. An articulate exploration of poets and poetry for children. Livingston is both a poet and anthologist.

_____. *Poem-Making: Ways to Begin Writing Poetry*. Harper, 1991. A sophisticated look at methods for writing poetry, particularly designed for young people.

Padgett, Ron, ed. *The Teachers and Writers Handbook of Poetic Forms*. Teachers' and Writers' Collaborative, 1987. A dictionary of the different forms of poetry.

For the Youngest

You will find more poetry books for young children listed in the Preschool and Primary Programs chapter, but for now take a look at some of these to see the wealth of material available for babies, toddlers, and preschoolers.

Bennett, Jill. *A Cup of Sunshine: Poems and Pictures for Young Children*. Art by Graham Percy. Harcourt, 1991. Charming art and gentle poems for young children.

Brooke, Leonard Leslie. *Johnny Crow's Garden*. Art by author. Warne, 1903. All the animals visit Johnny's garden in this nonsense rhyme.

Chute, Marchette. *Rhymes about Us*. Art by author. Dutton, 1974. Kittens, teddy bears, dinnertime, and other pleasures of childhood.

Cole, Joanna and Stephanie Calmenson. *The Eentsy, Weentsy Spider: Fingerplays and Action Rhymes*. Art by Alan Tiegreen. Morrow, 1991. These fingerplays are illustrated with black-and-white cartoons.

Corbett, Pie. *The Playtime Treasury: A Collection of Playground Rhymes, Games, and Action Songs*. Art by Moira and Colin Maclean. Doubleday, 1989. Truly a treasury.

Cousins, Lucy. *The Little Dog Laughed and Other Nursery Rhymes*. Art by collector. Dutton, 1989. Familiar nursery rhymes illustrated with bold, primary colors.

Foreman, Michael. *Michael Foreman's Mother Goose*. Art by author. Harcourt, 1991. An extensive collection for Foreman fans.

Lamont, Priscilla. *Ring-a-Round-a-Rosy: Nursery Rhymes, Action Rhymes and Lullabies*. Art by collector. Little, 1990. Expressive children romp through this nursery collection.

Langley, Jonathan. *Rain, Rain, Go Away!* Art by collector. Dial, 1991. Lots and lots of sprightly drawings adorn the pages of this nursery rhyme book.

Larrick, Nancy, ed. *The Merry-Go-Round Poetry Book*. Art by Karen Fundersheimer. Delacorte, 1989. Myra Cohn Livingston, John Ciardi, and Eve Merriam are among the poets represented in this endearing book for younger children.

Most, Bernard. *Four and Twenty Dinosaurs*. Art by author. Harper, 1990. Most rewrites nursery rhymes with a dinosaur theme.

Anthologies

You can't go wrong in choosing any one of these to take with you to a remote jungle or desert island. But how to choose which one to take? I think you'll love them all.

Booth, David. *Til All the Stars Have Fallen: A Collection of Poems for Children*. Art by Kady MacDonald Denton. Viking, 1989. Canadian poets are featured in this collection.

Cole, William. *Poem Stew*. Art by Karen Ann Weinhaus. Lippincott, 1981. Humorous poetry for children. Take a look at Cole's *Oh, Such Foolishness* (Harper, 1978), as well.

Daniel, Mark. *A Child's Treasury of Seaside Verse*. Dial, 1991. Poems and fine paintings go hand in hand in this collection.

dePaola, Tomie. *Tomie dePaola's Book of Poems*. Art by collector. Putnam, 1988. Holidays, seasons, animals, and people, all enhanced by dePaola's distinctive art.

Dunning, Stephen, Edward Lueders, and Hugh Smith. *Reflections on a Gift of Watermelon Pickle . . . and Other Modern Verse*. Photos. Lothrop, 1967. An exciting collection of contemporary poetry for young adults.

Elledge, Scott. *Wider than the Sky: Poems to Grow Up With*. Harper, 1990. Two hundred poems by a wonderful variety of poets. This collection is not illustrated.

Foster, John. *A First Poetry Book*. Art by Chris Orr, Martin White, and Joseph Wright. Oxford, 1979. The first in a series of several anthologies from Britain, this book is somewhat uneven in quality, but there are treasures here to find. The second book in this series is *Another First Poetry Book* (Oxford, 1988).

Harrison, Michael and Christopher Stuart-Clark. *The Oxford Treasury of Children's Poems*. Illustrated. Oxford, 1988. Humorous and serious poetry for children of all ages.

Heylen, Jill and Celia Jellett. *Someone Is Flying Balloons: Australian Poems for Children*. Art by Kerry Argent. Mad Hatter (c/o Slawson Communications, San Diego, CA 92103–4316), 1983. Traditional and contemporary poets are represented.

Hopkins, Lee Bennett. *Surprises*. Art by Megan Lloyd. Harper, 1984. A selection of poems especially chosen for beginning readers.

Kennedy, X. J. and Dorothy M. Kennedy. *Talking like the Rain: A First Book of Poems*. Art by Jane Dyer. Little, 1992. A substantial anthology compiled by a respected poet. Lovely.

_____. *Knock at a Star: A Children's Introduction to Poetry*. Art by Karen Ann Weinhaus. Little, 1982. An introductory anthology with notes on form and feelings.

Larrick, Nancy. *On City Streets*. Photos by David Sagain. Evans, 1986. Just one of Larrick's fine collections. This one features city poems.

Lobel, Arnold. *The Random House Book of Mother Goose: A Treasury of 306 Timeless Nursery Rhymes*. Random, 1986. You get both the 306 rhymes and Lobel's color art.

Prelutsky, Jack. *For Laughing Out Loud: Poems to Tickle Your Funnybone*. Art by Marjorie Priceman. Knopf, 1991. An attractive collection of 132 humorous poems.

_____. *The Random House Book of Poetry for Children*. Art by Arnold Lobel. Random, 1983. The favorite, with 572 poems, a subject index, and Arnold Lobel's art, too.

_____. *Read-Aloud Rhymes for the Very Young*. Art by Marc Brown. Knopf, 1986. Especially chosen for younger children, this outstanding anthology will be enjoyed by adults, too. Brown's art is a perfect complement to the selections.

Rosen, Michael. *The Kingfisher Book of Children's Poetry*. Illustrated. Kingfisher, 1985. Eve Merriam, Dorothy Aldis, and Mary Ann Hoberman are among the American poets represented in this British collection. There is also a subject index in this volume.

Schwartz, Alvin. *And the Green Grass Grew All Around: Folk Poetry from Everyone*. Art by Sue Truesdell. Harper, 1992. Autograph rhymes, street rhymes, love and work poems—all together 250 selections collected by a folklorist.

Sullivan, Charles, ed. *Imaginary Gardens: American Poetry and Art for Young People*. Abrams, 1989. Poetry illustrated with American art.

Poetry with Pictures to Share

Many children's poetry books have carefully chosen art work that enhances the language of the poems. Read or recite the poems and enjoy sharing the art with your audience.

Adoff, Arnold. *MA nDA LA*. Art by Emily McCully. Harper, 1971. A chant using nonsense words, with pictures that show planting and harvesting of crops.

Baylor, Byrd. *The Best Town in the World*. Art by Ronald Himler. Scribner, 1983. ". . . that town where everything was perfect."

Bemelmans, Ludwig. *Madeline*. Art by author. Simon & Schuster, 1939. Rhymed text tells the story of a vivacious little girl.

Bruchac, Joseph and Jonathan London. *Thirteen Moons on Turtle's Back: A Native American Year of Moons*. Art by Thomas Locker. Philomel, 1992. Imposing full-color paintings help illuminate these Native American poems.

Carroll, Lewis. *Jabberwocky*. Art by Graeme Base. Abrams, 1989. A lush interpretation of the poem from *Through the Looking Glass* with double-spread paintings.

Charles, Robert H. *A Roundabout Turn*. Art by L. Leslie Brooke. Warne, 1930. A toad sets out to see if the world is really round.

Degan, Bruce. *Jamberry*. Art by author. Harper, 1983. With each line rhyming with the word berry, this is an exuberant nonsense poem accompanied by happy pictures.

de Regniers, Beatrice Schenk et al. *Sing a Song of Popcorn: Every Child's Book of Poems*. Illustrated by nine artists. Scholastic, 1988. Nine Caldecott Medal winners take turns illustrating poems especially for children.

Farber, Norma. *How Does It Feel to Be Old?* Art by Trina Schart Hyman. Dutton, 1979. The advantages and disadvantages of old age are described in words and pictures.

Frost, Robert. *Birches*. Art by Ed Young. Holt, 1988. Muted art gives room for your own imagination. Compare this with Susan Jeffers' artistic interpretation of the same poem (Dutton, 1978).

Greenfield, Eloise. *Daydreamers*. Art by Tom Feelings. Dial, 1981. Tom Feelings' portraits of black children are accompanied by a poetic text.

_____. *Under the Sunday Tree*. Art by Amos Ferguson. Harper, 1988. Life in the Bahamas. The vibrant art works perfectly with Greenfield's poems.

Grimes, Nikki. *Something on My Mind*. Art by Tom Feelings. Dial, 1978. Each full-page portrait is accompanied by a short poem featuring families and feelings.

Highwater, Jamake. *Moonsong Lullaby*. Photos by Marcia Keegan. Lothrop, 1981. An original Native American lullaby with full-color photographs of people and scenery.

Koch, Kenneth and Kate Farrell, eds. *Talking to the Sun: An Illustrated Anthology of Poems for Young People*. Holt, 1985. This anthology includes many poems by traditional American and British poets, accompanied by reproductions of fine art prints from the Metropolitan Museum of Art.

Lenski, Lois. *Sing a Song of People*. Art by Giles Laroche. Little, 1987. A celebration of city people.

Lewis, Richard. *In a Spring Garden*. Art by Ezra Jack Keats. Dial, 1989. Japanese haiku from morning to night.

The Little Dog Laughed and Other Nursery Rhymes. Art by Lucy Cousins. Dutton, 1990. Mother Goose offerings with big, bold, brightly colored art.

Livingston, Myra Cohn. *Light and Shadow*. Photographs by Barbara Rogasky. Holiday, 1992. Color photographs, large enough to share, enhance these nature poems.

_____. *Space Songs*. Art by Leonard Everett Fisher. Holiday, 1988. Outer space is explored by a distinguished artist and poet. This winning combination has also teamed to give us *Sky Songs* (Holiday, 1984), *Earth Songs* (Holiday, 1986), *Sea Songs* (Holiday, 1986).

Longfellow, Henry Wadsworth. *Paul Revere's Ride*. Art by Nancy Winslow Parker. Greenwillow, 1985. Parker's clearly defined art illuminates this famous story poem.

Pomerantz, Charlotte. *If I Had a Paka: Poems in Eleven Languages*. Art by Nancy Tafuri. Greenwillow, 1982. Each of these poems uses a few foreign words.

Prelutsky, Jack. *Beneath a Blue Umbrella*. Art by Garth Williams. Greenwillow, 1990. Short poems and full-page art, this is a companion volume to *Ride a Purple Pelican* (Greenwillow, 1986), which features nonsense verse about place names.

Shaw, Nancy. *Sheep in a Jeep*. Art by Margot Apple. Houghton, 1986. Hilarious art matched to a funny read-aloud book.

Sing a Song of Sixpence. Art by Tracy Campbell Pearson. Dial, 1985. Delightfully illustrated, a pleasure to view.

Singer, Marilyn. *Turtle in July*. Art by Jerry Pinkney. Macmillan, 1989. Domestic and wild animal poems and full-page art for each poem.

Sullivan, Charles. ed. *Imaginary Gardens: American Poetry and Art for Young People*. Abrams, 1989. Contemporary and classic prints illustrate American poetry chosen for children.

Thompson, Pat, comp. *Rhymes around the Day*. Art by Jan Ormerod. Lothrop, 1983. Ormerod uses three preschoolers as background figures to illustrate this collection of nursery rhymes.

Westcott, Nadine Bernard. *Skip to My Lou*. Art by adapter. Little, 1989. The traditional folksong gaily illustrated.

Whipple, Laura, ed. *Eric Carle's Animals Animals*. Art by Eric Carle. Philomel, 1989. Each of the animal poems is illustrated with Carle's double-spread art.

Willard, Nancy. *A Visit to William Blake's Inn: Poems for Innocent and Experienced Travelers*. Art by Alice and Martin Provensen. Harcourt, 1981. Visitors to the Inn range from the Cat of Cats to a wise cow.

Some Favorite Poets

It seems as though a new poetry book arrives almost daily with a newly published poet, yet there are many old favorites that I cannot give up. Here you will find just a few of the many children's poets particularly worth exploring.

Ahlberg, Allan. *Please Mrs. Butler*. Puffin, 1983. Best known as a picture book author, Ahlberg writes about school and playtime.

Bodecker, N. M. *Water Pennies and Other Poems*. Art by Erik Blegvad. Macmillan, 1991. Slugs, moths, and other water subjects.

Cassedy, Sylvia. *Roomrimes*. Art by Michele Chessare. Crowell, 1987. Places, each beginning with a letter of the alphabet.

Chandra, Deborah. *Balloons and Other Poems*. Art by Leslie Bowman. Farrar, 1988. Thoughts about nature and self, illustrated with soft black-and-white pencil drawings.

Ciardi, John. *The Hopeful Trout and Other Limericks.* Art by Susan Meddaugh. Houghton, 1989. Humorous limericks by a popular children's poet.

Cummings, E. E. *Hist Whist and Other Poems for Children.* Art by David Calsada. Liveright, 1983. This American poet is better known for his adult poetry, but these selections have been especially chosen for their appeal to children.

de la Mare, Walter. *Peacock Pie.* Art by Louise Brierley. rev. ed. Holt, 1989. Enduring poems from a master poet.

de Regniers, Beatrice Schenk. *The Way I Feel . . . Sometimes.* Art by Susan Meddaugh. Clarion, 1988. Children's ups and downs are offered in short, upbeat poems.

Edwards, Richard. *A Mouse in My Roof.* Art by Venice. Delacorte, 1988. An appealing upbeat collection worth presenting.

Esbensen, Barbara. *Who Shrank My Grandmother's House? Poems of Discovery.* Art by Eric Beddows. Harper, 1992. Pencils, doors, and homework are among the subjects of these taut poems.

Fisher, Aileen. *Always Wondering: Some Favorite Poems of Aileen Fisher.* Art by Joan Sandin. Harper, 1991. A collection of some of the more popular of Fisher's work.

Giovanni, Nikki. *Vacation Time.* Art by Marisabina Russo. Morrow, 1980. From "Tommy's Mommy" to "Rainbows," these are poems with lilting rhythms.

Glenn, Mel. *Back to Class.* Photos by Michael J. Bernstein. Clarion, 1988. Outstanding poems illuminate the inner thoughts of high school students and teachers.

Greenfield, Eloise. *Honey, I Love and Other Poems.* Art by Diane and Leo Dillon. Crowell, 1978. Poems to make you feel and remember.

Janeczko, Paul B. *The Place My Words Are Looking for: What Poets Say about and through Their Work.* Bradbury, 1990. Contemporary poets discuss their poetry and give examples of their work.

Joseph, Lynn. *Coconut Kind of Day: Island Poems.* Art by Sandra Speidel. Lothrop, 1990. Rhythmic poems following a young girl's day in Trinidad.

Kuskin, Karla. *Near the Window Tree.* Harper, 1975. Notes precede each of these poems, which are about a wide range of subjects (from bugs to friends).

Lear, Edward. *Of Pelicans and Pussycats: Poems and Limericks.* Art by Jill Newton. Dial, 1990. This would be a good book to introduce your audience to the master of nonsense.

Lee, Dennis. *Alligator Pie.* Art by Frank Newveld. Houghton, 1975. Lee is known for his nonsense rhyme.

_____. *The Ice Cream Store.* Art by David McPhail. Harper, 1991. More nonsense verse from this Canadian poet.

Levy, Constance. *I'm Going to Pet a Worm Today and Other Poems.* Art by Ronald Himler. McElderry, 1991. Child-centered subjects from a first-time poet.

Lewis, J. Patrick. *Two-Legged, Four-Legged, No-Legged Rhymes.* Art by Pamela Paparone. Knopf, 1991. Astonishing animals in a collection by the author of the acclaimed *A Hippopotamusn't and Other Animal Poems* (Dial, 1990).

Little, Jean. *Hey World, Here I Am!* Art by Sue Truesdell. Harper, 1989. Thoughts of school, family, and friends.

Livingston, Myra Cohn. *There Was a Place and Other Poems*. McElderry, 1988. The thoughts and feelings of children with family problems, such as living with divorced parents, meeting fathers' girl friends, and dealing with lonely moms.

Merriam, Eve. *Chortles*. Art by Sheila Hamanaka. Morrow, 1989. Just one of Merriam's superb collections. Her trademark: a remarkable use of language.

McCord, David. *One at a Time: His Collected Poems for the Very Young*. Art by Henry B. Kane. Little, 1980. McCord's work is the quintessence of children's poetry. A subject index is included.

McNaughton, Colin. *Who's Been Sleeping in My Porridge? A Book of Silly Poems and Pictures*. Ideals, 1990. This collection is uneven, but it includes some very funny poetry that children will love.

Milne, A. A. *When We Were Very Young*. Art by Ernest H. Shepard. Dutton, 1924, 1961, 1988. It is still a pleasure to introduce a child to Milne. Also delightful is *Now We Are Six* (Dutton, 1927, 1961, 1988).

Moore, Lillian. *Think of Shadows*. Art by Deborah Robinson. Atheneum, 1980. Shadows on the playground, in a tunnel, on Ground Hog Day.

Moss, Jeff. *The Butterfly Jar*. Art by Chris Demarest. Bantam, 1989. Funny and poignant, this gives Shel Silverstein some competition.

Nash, Ogden. *Custard and Company*. Art by Quentin Blake. Little, 1980. From Nash, the supreme humorist, here are selections for children—and everyone else too.

Pomerantz, Charlotte. *The Tamarind Puppy and Other Poems*. Art by Byron Barton. Greenwillow, 1980. Poems in English with a few Spanish words.

Prelutsky, Jack. *The New Kid on the Block*. Art by James Stevenson. Greenwillow, 1984. Prelutsky's poems are humorous, bouncy, and happy; they have great appeal for children.

Rylant, Cynthia. *Waiting to Waltz: A Childhood*. Art by Stephen Gammell. Bradbury, 1984. Portraits in poetry of a spelling bee, swearing, and people from the poet's childhood. More of this author's haunting poems from a youthful perspective are found in *Soda Jerk*, for which Peter Calanotto did the artwork (Orchard, 1990).

Seuss, Dr. (pseud. for Theodor Seuss Geisel) *And to Think That I Saw It on Mulberry Street*. Art by author. Vanguard, 1937. Marco's imagination turns an ordinary horse and wagon into a mammoth extravaganza.

Silverstein, Shel. *Where the Sidewalk Ends*. Art by author. Harper, 1974. The A-1 humorous collection.

Simmie, Lois. *Auntie's Knitting a Baby*. Art by Anne Simmie. Orchard, 1984. Lots of fun and some serious thoughts, too.

Stevenson, Robert Louis. *A Child's Garden of Verses*. Art by Michael Foreman. Delacorte, 1985. Numerous artists have illustrated this classic collection. This is a sophisticated interpretation of the well-known poems.

Viorst, Judith. *If I Were in Charge of the World and Other Worries*. Art by Lynne Cherry. Atheneum, 1981. The joys and worries of childhood. Some spoofs of fairy stories are also included.

Worth, Valerie. *All the Small Poems*. Art by Natalie Babbitt. Farrar, 1987. Every poem is a gem of simplicity. Featured are animals and objects such as magnet, kitten, fence, and pie.

Poetry by Theme

Poetry arranged by theme is useful when you wish to present one subject or theme to a group, but don't forget to browse through these also when you are just looking for excellent poetry. If you purchase these books for your own library, think how valuable they will be any time you are looking for a single poem on a particular subject. You'll always have a variety to choose from within easy reaching distance.

Adoff, Arnold. *All the Colors of the Race*. Art by John Steptoe. Lothrop, 1982. Thoughts and feelings of a child with a black mom and a white dad.

———. *Chocolate Dreams*. Art by Turi MacCombie. Lothrop, 1989. For chocolate lovers everywhere.

———. *Sports Pages*. Art by Steven Kuzma. Lippincott, 1986. Training, injuries, playing, winning and losing, individual and team sports are all covered.

Bauer, Caroline Feller. *Windy Day: Stories and Poems*. Art by Dirk Zimmer. Harper, 1988. Poems and stories on weather themes. Similar themed anthologies include *Rainy Day* (Harper, 1986), *Snowy Day* (Harper, 1986), and *Halloween* (Harper, 1989), and *Valentine's Day* (Harper, 1993).

Baynes, Pauline. *Thanks Be to God: Prayers from Around the World*. Art by author. Macmillan, 1990. An interesting collection of multi-national prayers.

Bennett, Jill. *Spooky Poems*. Art by Mary Rees. Little, 1989. These are humorous poems featuring a Halloween theme.

Booth, David. *Voices of the Wind: Poems for All Seasons*. Art by Michele Lemieux. Morrow, 1990. An upbeat collection of seasonal poems.

Brewton, Sara, John E. Brewton, and John Brewton Blackburn. *Of Quarks, Quasars and Other Quirks: Quizzical Poems for the Supersonic Age*. Art by Quentin Blake. Crowell, 1977. The Brewtons have edited many collections. This one features poems about television, think tanks, and IBM.

Clark, Emma Chichester. *I Never Saw a Purple Cow and Other Nonsense Verse*. Art by collector. Little, 1991. Short nursery rhymes and nonsense verses in an attractive collection.

Cole, Joanna and Stephanie Calmenson. *Miss Mary Mack and Other Children's Street Rhymes*. Art by Alan Tiegreen. Morrow, 1990. Rhymes for hand-clapping, ball-bouncing, counting-out.

Dahl, Roald. *Rhyme Stew*. Art by Quentin Blake. Viking, 1990. An irreverent look at some old folktales in rhyme.

Daniel, Mark. *A Child's Treasury of Seaside Verse*. Dial, 1991. Traditional British and some American poems featuring the sea.

Day, David. *Aska's Animals*. Art by Warabe Aska. Doubleday, 1991. Lush paintings accompany poems about wild animals.

Demi. *In the Eyes of the Cat: Japanese Poetry for All Seasons*; tr. by Tze-si Huang. Holt, 1992. Short, pithy expressions of nature.

Duncan, Beverly K. *Christmas in the Stable*. Art by collector. Harcourt, 1990. Christmas poems from the animals' point of view.

Esbensen, Barbara. *Who Shrank My Grandmother's House? Poems of Discovery*. Art by Eric Beddows. Harper, 1992. Pencils, friends, and clouds are revealed in unique interpretations.

_____. *Words with Wrinkled Knees: Animal Poems*. Art by John Stadler. Crowell, 1986. When the name or word for the animal becomes as important as the animal.

Fleischman, Paul. *Joyful Noise: Poems for Two Voices*. Art by Eric Beddows. Harper, 1988. Poems about insects, to be presented with two voices.

Foster, John. *Let's Celebrate: Festival Poems*. Oxford, 1989. Holiday poems from around the world.

Frazer, Kathleen. *Stilts, Somersaults, and Headstands: Game Poems Based on a Painting by Peter Breughel*. Atheneum, 1968. Poems related to the games shown on a sixteenth-century painting by the famed Flemish painter.

Goldstein, Bobbye S. *Bear in Mind: A Book of Bear Poems*. Art by William Pène duBois. Viking, 1989. The theme is bears, the art is by the bear expert.

Gordon, Ruth. *Under All Silences: Shades of Love*. Harper, 1987. Kenneth Patchen, Paul Verlaine, Rainer Maria Rilke. Love poems for young adults.

Greenberg, David. *Slugs*. Art by Victoria Chess. Little, 1983. Not all adults will like this slightly gross, funny look at slugs, but children love it.

Hoberman, May Ann. *Fathers, Mothers, Sisters, Brothers: A Collection of Family Poems*. Art by Marilyn Hafner. Little, 1991. A picture book collection featuring family poems.

Hopkins, Lee Bennett. *Ring Out, Wild Bells: Poems about Holidays and Seasons*. Art by Karen Baumann. Harcourt, 1992. Hopkins is a master collector of theme poetry. Other favorites are *Dinosaurs*, *Good Books, Good Times!* and *On the Farm*.

Hubbell, Patricia. *A Grass Green Gallup*. Art by Ronald Himler. Atheneum, 1990. Ponies, horses, and horseshows.

Janeczko, Paul B., ed. *The Music of What Happens: Poems That Tell Stories*. Orchard, 1988. Story poems for young adults.

Jones, Tim. *Wild Critters*. Photos by Tom Walker. Epicenter Press (18821 64th Ave. NE, Seattle, WA 98155), 1992. Excellent color photographs accompany each poem about Alaskan animals.

Kennedy, X. J. *Brats*. Art by James Watts. Atheneum, 1986. One verse poems describing a variety of brats.

Knudson, R. R. and Mary Swenson. *American Sports Poems*. Orchard, 1988. Baseball, football, soccer, volleyball and more represented by poems.

Larrick, Nancy. *Cats Are Cats*. Art by Ed Young. Philomel, 1988. A lovely package of art and poetry—all about cats.

_____. *Mice Are Nice*. Art by Ed Young. Philomel, 1990. Mice are the subject of this illustrated volume.

Livingston, Myra Cohn. *Poems for Brothers and Poems for Sisters*. Art by Jean Zallinger. Holiday, 1991. These are selected by a premier poet whose other collections feature mothers, fathers, and grandmothers.

Marzollo, Jean. *Pretend You're a Cat*. Art by Jerry Pinkney. Dial, 1990. Poems about pretending, accompanied by pictures showing various animals and children imitating them.

Mathis, Sharon Bell. *Red Dog, Blue Fly: Football Poems*. Viking, 1991. Touchdown, coach, and quarterback are some of the subjects covered in this picture-book–format collection.

McMillan, Bruce. *One Sun: A Book of Terse Verse*. Holiday, 1990. A great introduction to two-word poems illustrated with colorful photographs.

Merriam, Eve. *Halloween ABC*. Art by Lane Smith. Macmillan, 1987. Sophisticated Halloween poetry for older children and young adults.

O'Neill, Mary. *Hailstones and Halibut Bones*. Art by John Wallner. Doubleday, 1989. The classic poems about colors reissued with new color art.

Prelutsky, Jack. *It's Halloween*. Art by Marilyn Hafner. Greenwillow, 1977. Prelutsky has written several holiday books, all published by Greenwillow, featuring easy-to-read poems, including *It's Christmas* (1981), *It's Thanksgiving* (1982), *It's Valentine's Day* (1983).

Radley, Gail. *Rainy Day Rhymes*. Art by Ellen Kandoian. Houghton, 1992. The gentle art adds to the enjoyment of these rain poems.

Shaw, Richard, ed. *The Bird Book*. Warne, 1974. Poems and short stories about birds. Nineteen different artists contributed illustrations. Also see *The Cat Book* (Warne, 1973), *The Fox Book* (Warne, 1971); *The Frog Book* (Warne, 1972); *The Mouse Book* (Warne, 1975); and *The Owl Book* (Warne, 1970).

Sneve, Virginia Driving Hawk. *Dancing Teepees: Poems of American Youth*. Art by Stephen Gammell. Holiday, 1989. Short poems collected from the oral tradition of Native Americans.

Steig, Jeanne. *Consider the Lemming*. Art by William Steig. Farrar, 1988. Excellent use of language and wit to describe a variety of animals, from the beaver to the penguin.

Streich, Corrine, ed. *Grandparents' Houses*. Art by Lillian Hoban. Greenwillow, 1984. Grandmothers and grandfathers from around the world.

Turner, Ann. *Street Talk*. Art by Catherine Stock. Houghton, 1986. City poems: people and places (the museum), street painting.

Whipple, Laura. *Eric Carle's Dragons and Other Creatures That Never Were*. Art by Eric Carle. Philomel, 1991. Dragons illustrated with Carle's trademark colorful collages.

Yolen, Jane. *Best Witches: Poems for Halloween*. Art by Elise Primavera. Putnam, 1989. A prolific author gives us her views on Halloween.

9 / Non-narrative Sources for Storytelling

A chicken walked into the library looking for something to read. The librarian offered her a book, which she accepted, but she returned almost immediately. The librarian offered her another book; again she accepted the book and left the library, but returned almost immediately. This time, after selecting a third book for the chicken, the librarian followed her outside, and watched as she held up the book for her friend, the frog, to see.

"Red-it," said the frog. "Red-it!"

Silly isn't it? But it may be perfect to use as transitional material between stories or poems in your storyhour. I'm always amazed at how successful riddles and jokes are with children. Even adults laugh (as they groan!) at the mostly oldies. You will find that the riddles and jokes collected in the unending supply of children's books are almost always recycled from your own childhood. These are examples of true folklore passed on from generation to generation. In fact, most of the material you will use in your programs has its origins in folk literature, and, if you have been telling stories to a group, its members may already be aware of the various sources—folktales, myths, fables, and the like—from which you have chosen your material. Some of your listeners may even be ready to explore with you the world of folklore in more personal terms. Inasmuch as a folk group is comprised of people who have one thing in common, explain that all of us are members of more than one folk group at any given time. For example, the students in a school belong to a large folk group and within this group there are smaller folk groups—the sophomore class, the track team, the cheerleaders, the science club, among others. Each of these groups may have its own customs and sayings that can be collected. Explain that proverbs, riddle jokes, and tongue twisters are folk sayings and that the games, crafts, food preparation, and graffiti of a group are also considered part of its folklore. Point out too that folklore is transmitted by word of mouth or by means other than books, schools, churches, and other formal institutions.

Apparently the word "folklore" gives some people the impression that to collect "lore" one has to know peasants or grandmothers. Emphasize that everyone is part of a group. Start collecting for yourself, from your family and friends. One need not take a trip to some faraway place, for folklore is all around us.

The interest in some forms of folklore has led to collections of riddles, handicrafts, recipes, and the like. Lately there have been books published about such traditional crafts as soapmaking, sheep shearing, and graffiti. Encourage your groups to make collections of their own.

One way to begin a collection of riddles or other folklore of your own is to recite a few folk sayings in a storyhour and hope this will remind your listeners of sayings that they know. To formally collect folklore you should encourage students to write down what they hear exactly as it is related. The person who gives you the material is the "informant," whose name, address, age, background, and education also should be recorded for inclusion in an organized collection. The group might be interested in the notes of origin appearing in some of the books in the library's collection: Richard Chase and Maria Leach, for instance, give notes at the back of their collections. Joseph Jacobs, in his notes, explained how he changed the original stories to make them more appropriate to tell to children.

A haphazard but uninhibited way of collection is to simply put a box in the library or classroom and request jokes and riddles or whatever you are collecting; in some ways this is the best method of all. You will receive completely authentic, but unsigned responses. I have included several examples of some of the more popular types of folklore here. If some of the examples seem familiar to you, don't be surprised. It always amazes people to see how folklore is transmitted over large geographic areas and over several generations with so few changes.

This non-narrative folklore can be used to create a whole session in your programming or you may find it perfect to use between stories as a change of mood.

Riddles

Riddles have been used as tests in literature and folk stories, but generally they are considered word games to be used just for fun and may be used as such to introduce the reluctant reader to the world of books. It is a pity that today's children often need a manufactured toy to play with, when the realm of words is free, doesn't break, and never becomes outdated! Since riddles are popular you will be able to find a number of collections in your library. You should find, as you search for riddles to use in your storyhour program, that some in your storyhour group already know the riddle and shout out the answer. It's amusing to find a riddle that they cannot guess, but the ones they do know will stimulate the children into contributing riddles of their own. If you become interested in riddles, you might want to identify the country of origin or to mention that a particular riddle was recorded in the Tennessee mountains in 1911, for example.

Ask that each member of your group find a riddle and bring it to the next folk session to present to the group. There may be many duplicates, but you'll also have a lively session. Children participating in extemporaneous storytelling sometimes tend to wander away from the subject, but a riddle gives them a chance to "perform" briefly before a group.

A *riddle* is a question with an unexpected answer that is supposed to demonstrate the brilliance of the questioner and test the wit and intelligence of the respondent. A *conundrum* is a riddle based on punning or a play on words.

What does a pig use for a sore throat?
Oinkment.

What do you call a general's assistant at the North Pole?
A Kool Aid.

What did the walls say to each other?
Meet you at the corner.

What goes Ho Ho Thump?
Santa Claus laughing his head off.

What did the judge say when the skunk came into the court?
Odor in the court.

What does a tuba call his father?
Um pa pa.

What is black and white and red all over?
A blushing zebra or a hot fudge sundae with catsup on it.
(New variations on an oldie.)

What gets wetter and wetter the more it dries?
 A towel.

Why does a school yard get bigger when school starts?
 It has more feet in it. (A nonmetric riddle.)

Who is bigger, Mrs. Bigger or Mrs. Bigger's baby?
 The baby is just a little Bigger.

When is a turkey like a ghost?
 When he's goblin.

How do you keep a tiger from charging?
 Take away his credit card.

Where were the first doughnuts fried?
 In Greece.

What walks on four legs in the morning, two legs in the afternoon,
and three legs at night?
 Man.
 As a baby he crawls on all fours.
 As a young man he walks on two legs.
 As an old man he walks with a cane.
 (Riddle of the Sphinx)

Why won't you ever see a full moon again?
 Because the astronauts brought back pieces of it.

What gets bigger the more you take away?
 A hole.

What is the difference between an elephant and peanut butter?
 An elephant doesn't stick to the roof of your mouth.

What do you get when you cross a dummy with a flower seed?
 A blooming idiot (with an English accent).

What would you call a country where all the cars were pink?
 A pink carnation.

What's the difference between a donkey and a postage stamp?
 You lick a donkey with a stick and stick a stamp with a lick.

Booklist: More Riddles

Riddles collected for children tend to be illustrated with cartoons and are often recycled over and over, so that the riddles that you asked *your* best friend in second grade are the same riddles your students are asking each other today. To give old riddles a new look, publishers often thematically package them. Here are some examples:

Adler, David A. *Wild Pill Hickok and Other Riddles of the Old West*. Art by Glen Rounds. Holiday, 1988. "Why weren't there any horse doctors in the old west?" Horses couldn't get into medical school.

Bierhorst, John, ed. *Lightning inside You and Other Native American Riddles*. Art by Louise Brierley. Morrow, 1992. A lovely and unusual collection.

Hall, Katy and Lisa Eisenberg. *Spacey Riddles*. Art by Simms Taback. Dial, 1992. "What kind of light goes around the earth?" A satel-lite!

Koontz, Robin Michal. *I See Something You Don't See*. Art by author. Cobble-hill/Dutton, 1992. Guess the answer to the riddle in each picture.

Maestro, Giulio. *Razzle-Dazzle Riddles*. Art by author. Clarion, 1985. "How does an evergreen tree keep its hair neat?" It uses a pinecomb.

Smith, William Jay and Carol Ra, eds. *Behind the King's Kitchen: A Roster of Rhyming Riddles*. Art by Jacques Hnizdovdky. Wordsong, 1992. A catchy collection.

Terban, Marvin. *Hey, Hay! A Wagonful of Funny Homonym Riddles*. Art by Kevin Hawkes. Clarion, 1991. "How do you say, "Get away, footwear!" Shoo, shoe.

Walton, Rick and Ann Walton. *Ho Ho Ho! Riddles about Santa Claus*. Art by Susan Slattery Burke. Lerner, 1991. Just one of a collection of theme books featuring children's riddles. Others include *Out on a Limb* (riddles about trees and plants), *Here's to Ewe* (riddles about sheep), and *Hide and Shriek* (riddles about ghosts and goblins).

Tongue Twisters

The tongue twister is a game in which you pronounce a combination of difficult sounds fast but clearly. A few speech teachers use them for the practice of clarity in speech, but usually the tongue twister exists for the simple purpose of playing with words. As with any other folk material, most tongue twisters have been passed orally among children or adults. The most popular have been collected and can be found in books. A tongue twister contest can be great fun. Announce the contest in advance so that the contestants have time to practice. Tongue twisters also make a good ending for a program. The audience leaves the room practicing loudly and reciting as fast as they can such sentences and rhymes as:

Unique New York

Lemon liniment

Fruit float, fruit float, fruit float

Double bubble gum gives double bubble trouble

Six, slick, slim saplings

Sallow Sally

The sixth sick sheik's sixth sheep's sick.

Strange strategic statistics

Three new blue beans in a new blown bladder

I saw Esau kissing Kate
I saw Esau, he saw me
And she saw I saw Esau

A FLY

A fly and a flea flew up a flue.
Said the flea, "What shall we do?"
Said the fly, "Let us flee!"
Said the flea, "Let us fly!"
So they flew through a flaw in the flue.

A CANNER

A canner, exceedingly canny,
One morning remarked to his granny,
"A canner can can
Anything that he can;
But a canner can't can a can, can he?"

SEASHELLS

She sells seashells by the seashore.
The shells she sells are sure seashells.
So if she sells shells on the seashore
I'm sure she sells seashore shells.

Booklist: More Tongue Twisters

Arnold, Arnold. *The Big Book of Tongue Twisters and Double Talk*. Art by author. Random, 1964. A good source for tongue twisters.

Rosenbloom, Joseph. *World's Toughest Tongue Twisters*. Art by Dennis Kendrick. Sterling, 1986. An A-Z listing of tongue twisters.

Schwartz, Alvin, comp. *A Twister of Twists, A Tangler of Tongues*. Art by Glen Rounds. Lippincott, 1972. A good collection arranged by subject.

Wiseman, Bernard. "The Tongue Twister" in Caroline Feller Bauer's *Read for the Fun of It*. Art by Lynn Bredesen. H. W. Wilson, 1992. A Reader's Theater script that offers a tongue twister.

Jokes

In some instances the stories you will tell are really extended jokes; the Turkish Hodja stories are a series of jokes, for instance. Children's jokes do differ from adult jokes; the latter tend to be political or ethnic, and of course there is the "dirty" joke, which has a sexual connotation, whereas children's jokes are usually quite simple and often involve a play on words. To adults these jokes often seem silly and inconsequential. Perhaps this is true, but a sophisticated sense of humor is something that must be developed; it doesn't just happen, and nonsense is

a good place to begin. Jokes ought to play only a very minor role in the storyhour; they should be used sparingly but are effective to relax a tense group or to set a happier mood after you have told a sad or touching story. Many children's jokes are in the form of riddles, as the following examples indicate:

My sister and I together know everything in the whole world.
    Really? What's the capital of France?
That's one my sister knows.

What is the similarity between a hippopotamus and an elephant?
    Neither one plays golf.

Get up, I heard a mouse squeak.
    What do you want me to do? Oil it?

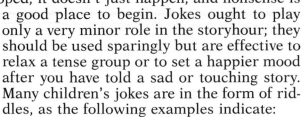

I can tell the score of this football game before it even begins.
    Nothing to nothing.

Finish your alphabet soup, dear.
    I can't eat another word.

Where was the Declaration of Independence signed?
    At the bottom.

What is a small joke called?
    A mini ha ha.

My cat is lost.
    Why don't you put an ad in the newspaper?
She can't read.

Why did the elephant stand
on the marshmallow?
    So he wouldn't fall into
    the cocoa.

I'm glad that I'm not a bird.
    Why?
I can't fly.

What is history's
favorite fruit?
    Dates.

What do elephants have
that no other animals
have?
    Baby elephants.

Knock, knock.
    Who's there?
Honeydew and cantaloupe.
    Honeydew and cantaloupe who?
Honeydew you love me? We cantaloupe now.

Knock, knock.
    Who's there?
Boo.
    Boo who (hoo)?
Well, you don't have to cry about it.

You know that you've gained too much weight when you step on a scale and a sign flashes on saying "Only one person at a time please."

They used to call the Middle Ages the Dark Ages because there were so many knights.

A man asked the horse trainer why the racehorse was traveling by train rather than plane. "Oh, he's already seen the movie this week."

A friend was amazed at a dog's obvious attention at a drive-in theater's showing of *The Little Prince*. "I'm amazed too," said the owner. "He didn't enjoy the book at all."

Shopper: I'd like some alligator shoes, please.
Shoe Salesman: What size is your alligator?

What nut is like a sneeze?
A cashew (ca-shoo).

What happened when the hippie put dynamite in the refrigerator?
He blew his cool.

What kind of dog is that?
A police dog.
He doesn't look like one.
Of course not. He's in the Secret Service.

Booklist: More Jokes

Hall, Katy and Lisa Eisenberg. *101 Rock 'n Roll Jokes and Riddles*. Art by Don Orehek. Scholastic, 1991.
> Knock, knock!
>> Who's there?
> Lou Reed!
>> Lou Reed who?
> Lou Reed books instead of watching TV!

Hartman, Victoria. *Westward Ho Ho Ho! Jokes from the Wild West*. Art by G. Brian Karas. Viking, 1992.
> "What do you call twin boys in California?" Son-sets in the West.

Johnstone, Michael. *1,000 Crazy Jokes for Kids*. Ballantine, 1987.
> Patient: Doctor, people always ignore me. What can I do about it?
> Doctor: Next.

Kessler, Leonard. *Old Turtle's 90 Knock-Knocks, Jokes, and Riddles*. Art by author. Greenwillow, 1991.
> Doctor, Doctor, Little Pig has a bad rash.
> Let's give him some *oink-ment!*

Perret, Gene. *The Laugh a Minute Joke Book*. Art by Sanford Hoffman. Sterling, 1991.
> "Boy, do I have a tough instructor. She has a black belt in teaching."

Phillips, Louis. *Wackysaurus: Dinosaur Jokes*. Art by Ron Barrett. Viking, 1991.
> Adam: What do you get when you cross a wooly mammoth with a parrot?
> Rachel: What?
> Adam: I don't know what to call it, but when it asks for a cracker, you better give it one.

Skip-Rope Rhymes

School-age children will have no trouble telling you—or showing you—their favorite jump-rope rhymes. If you haven't recently participated in a jump-rope game, you may have forgotten the words of these jingles, but they'll soon come back. You may even be amazed that the rhymes and rhythms you jumped to as a child in Washington, D.C. are the same that the children are using in a small town in Nebraska today. If your community has super special playground equipment and organized play the children may have forgotten how to jump rope. Reintroduce this traditional spring activity by bringing a length of clothesline rope to school.

Skipping rope and the accompanying jingles are a part of folklore too. To refresh your own memory, a few perennials follow:

House for rent
Inquire within
When I move out, let
Hilary move in.
    (Jumper moves out and
    next in line moves in.)

When you fall down
And hurt your knee
Just jump up quick,
And think of me.

Fudge, fudge tell the judge
Mama's going to have a baby.
Wrap it up in tissue paper
Send it on the elevator.
How many floors did it go?
1, 2, 3 (Until the jumper misses.)

Sheep in the meadow
Cows in the corn
Tell me the month that you were born.
January, February, March
(Jump out on the month of your birthday.)

Las' night, night before
Twenty-four robbers came to my door.
I got up, let 'em in
Hit 'em on the head with a rollin' pin.
One, two, three, four . . .

HILARY'S CHANT

Miss Mary Mack, Mack, Mack
All dressed in black, black, black
With silver buttons, buttons, buttons
All down her back, back, back
She asked her mother, mother, mother
For fifty cents, cents, cents
to see the elephants, elephants, elephants
Jump the fence, fence, fence
They jumped so high, high, high
They reached the sky, sky, sky
And they never came back, back, back
Till the Fourth of July, lie, lie
"It's not good to lie!" (spoken)

SALT, MUSTARD

Salt, mustard, vinegar, pepper,
French almond rock,
Bread and butter for your supper
That's all mother's got.
Fish and chips and coca cola,
Put them in a pan,
Irish stew and ice cream soda,
We'll eat all we can.

Salt, mustard, vinegar, pepper,
French almond rock,
Bread and butter for your supper
That's all mother's got.
Eggs and bacon, salted herring,
Put them in a pot,
Pickled onions, apple pudding,
We will eat the lot.

Salt, mustard, vinegar, pepper,
Pig's head and trout
Bread and butter for your supper
O-U-T spells out.

Order in the court
The Judge is eating beans
His wife is in the bathtub
Shooting submarines

Fireman! Fireman!
False alarm
There goes Hilary (jump out)
in the fireman's arms.

LITTLE BROTHER

I had a little brother
His name was Tiny Tim
I put him in the bathtub
To teach him how to swim
He drank up all the water
He ate up all the soap
He died last night
With a bubble in his throat
In came the doctor
In came the lady
With the alligator purse
Dead said the doctor
Dead said the nurse
Dead said the lady
With the alligator purse
Out went the doctor
Out went the nurse
Out went the lady
With the alligator purse.

As I was in the kitchen
Doing a bit of stitchen
In came a bogey man
And pushed me OUT

Hold 'em up
Stick 'em up
Drop your gun
And pick 'em up
And OUT you go

JUMP ROPE RHYME
Nina Payne

Orange marginella
Crackers in a pan
I am going to marry
A Minnesota man

He'll be sweet and green-eyed
And just a little stout
Any time we want to
We'll eat our dinner OUT

Booklist: More Skip-Rope Rhymes

Cole, Joanna. *Anna Banana: 101 Jump-Rope Rhymes.* Art by Alan Tiegreen. Morrow, 1991. Rhymes are accompanied by directions for jumping.

Farjeon, Eleanor. "Elsie Piddock Skips in Her Sleep" in *Eleanor Farjeon's Book.* Art by Edward Ardizzone. Penguin, 1960. Also in her *Martin Pippin in the Daisy-Field*;

art by Isobel and John Morton-Sale. Lippincott, 1963. And in Colwell, Eileen, ed. *A Storyteller's Choice*; art by Carol Barker. Walck, 1964. Tell this delightful story for the skip-rope season. It is quite long but well worth the trouble to learn.

Skolnik, Peter L. *Jump Rope!* Photos by Jerry Darvin; art by Marty Norman. Workman, 1974. Rhymes, tricks, and the physical fitness of jumping rope.

Autograph Rhymes and Mottoes

Autograph books, yearbooks, and autograph dolls appear as summer vacations shine on the horizon. The sayings that are written in memory books are often the same ones your grandmother wrote in her best friend's book way back in the old days. You may enjoy using these in a storyhour if you are discussing different types of folk sayings.

Yours till banana splits

Yours till ice screams

Yours till dogwood barks

U, R, 2 young, and
    2 pretty 4 boys

When you're in the kitchen
Learning how to cook
Remember it was Joni
Who wrote this in your book

Roses are red
Violets are blue
The sidewalk is cracked
And so are you

I saw you on the mountain
I saw you in the sea
I saw you in the bathtub
Oops! Pardon me

U R 2 good
2 B 4 gotten

Happiness is having a friend like you

As you slide down the banister of life
May you always be one of the splinters.

May the bird of paradise never peck a hole in your water-bed.

We're in a hammock, ready to kiss
In less than a second
We'll look like this.

Booklist: More Autograph Rhymes

Geringer, Laura. *Yours 'til the Ice Cracks: A Book of Valentines*. Art by Andrea Baruffi. Harper, 1992. Autograph verses as valentines.

Morrison, Lillian, comp. *Remember Me When This You See!* Art by Marjorie Bauernschmidt. Crowell, 1961. A collection of autograph verses. And also *Yours till Niagara Falls*; art by Marjorie Bauernschmidt. Crowell, 1950. And *Best Wishes, Amen: A New Collection of Autograph Verses*; art by Loretta Lustig. Crowell, 1974.

Proverbs

Proverbs are folk sayings that contain popular advice, state a moral, or confirm a judgment. Different folk groups have their own proverbs, but often they can be recognized as different ways of expressing similar thoughts. You can find proverbs listed in adult folklore collections. Use them in between stories if you wish to begin a discussion. Children might like to remind you of some they are familiar with. Think of the possibilities of these selected proverbs as they relate to today's society.

American Proverbs

Don't count your chickens before they hatch.

You can't make a silk purse out of a sow's ear.

Never criticize a man until you've walked a mile in his moccasins.

Live and let live.

Penny wise and pound foolish.

Out of sight, out of mind.

A new broom sweeps clean.

A watched pot never boils.

A rolling stone gathers no moss.

The love of money is the root of all evil.

Don't kill the goose that lays the golden egg.

He couldn't be elected dog catcher in a ward full of cats.

Look before you leap.

Absence makes the heart grow fonder.

Haste makes waste.

An apple a day keeps the doctor away.

No news is good news.

Two wrongs don't make a right.

All work and no play makes Jack a dull boy.

Old soldiers never die; they just fade away.

You can lead a horse to water, but you can't make him drink.

Lie down with cats, get up with fleas. (My mother, a dog lover, substituted the cat in this familiar saying.)

Jewish Proverbs

The worst informer is the face.

Charge nothing and you'll get a lot of customers.

Do not worry about tomorrow, because you do not even know what may happen to you today.

The sun will set without your assistance.

Your friend has a friend, and your friend's friend has a friend: Be discreet.

The luck of an ignoramus is that he doesn't know that he doesn't know.

An insincere peace is better than a sincere war.

Poverty is no disgrace, but it's no great honor, either.

Everywhere it's good, and at home it's even better.

What is cheap is dear.   At the baths, all are equal.

What three know is no secret.

What good can a lamp and spectacles be when a man just doesn't want to see?

Proverbs from Around the World

You can't make an owl out of a falcon.—Russia

A hungry cat likes a well-fed mouse best.—Russia

When the cat's away, the mice do play.—Germany

An old fox is hard to catch.—Germany

Even a rooster lays an egg for one who is lucky.—Russia

Whoever plays with cats must not fear their claws.—Egypt

He who lives without folly is not so wise as he thinks.—Hungary

Booklist: More Proverbs

The Bible (Old Testament). *The Proverbs: A Selection* by Elvajean Hall. Art by Charles Mozley. Watts, 1970.

Fraser, Betty. *First Things First: An Illustrated Collection of Useful and Familiar for Children*. Art by author. Harper, 1990.

Kelen, Emery, comp. *Proverbs of Many Nations*. Art by author. Lothrop, 1966.

Mason, Bernard S. and Elmer D. Mitchell. *Party Games for All*. Barnes & Noble, 1946.

Opoku, Kofi Asare, comp. *Speak to the Winds: Proverbs from Africa*. Art by Dindga McCannon. Lothrop, 1975.

Word Games

Words make books, so why not have fun with words? Your group might enjoy playing traditional games that use words as their materials and tools.

I Packed My Trunk (at least two players)

Players sit in a circle. First player says, "I packed my trunk to visit my aunt and in it I put an apple." Then the next player repeats the first player's statement and adds an object beginning with the letter "B." Each player repeats that which went before and adds an object beginning with the next letter in the alphabet. If a player makes a mistake, he or she is out until the next game. If the alphabet is completed, begin again and pick two things beginning with each letter of the alphabet.

Ghost (at least three players)

This spelling game begins when one player calls out a letter. The next one thinks of a word beginning with the letter and calls out a second letter and so on around the group. The object of the game is to keep the word going without saying a letter that will end it. The first time a player loses a round he or she gets a "G," the next time an "H," and so on until he or she is a GHOST. If one player thinks the player before used a letter that cannot be a part of a word, he or she can challenge that player. If the preceding player does have a word in mind, the challenger loses the round and earns a letter; if not, the challenged player loses the round and earns a letter instead.

Hangman (for two players or teams)

This game, a favorite in our family, is similar to Ghost, but in it you "kill" your opponent. First think of a word and draw dashes on paper to indicate the number of letters in the word. The players call out a letter. If it belongs in the word the leader writes it in the appropriate space. If the letter is not in the word draw a part at a time to the hanged man. The player that needs the fewest guesses to guess the word wins. Hints: Start by guessing the vowels. If you're feeling really generous, give your opponent more chances by making the drawing of the hanged man more and more elaborate (add hair, shoes, facial features).

Continuous Story (for two or more players)

The leader begins with the first sentence of a story such as "Once upon a time I went into the woods." Each player in turn, adds another sentence to the story, such as "It was very cold and dark. Suddenly. . . ." The next player might say "I saw a bear" and so on, around the group.

This can also be done as a paper-and-pencil game. Write a sentence of a story on a sheet of paper. Fold the paper over and pass it to the next person all the way around the group, folding each sentence down. Let the last person read the story aloud.

The Newspaper Game (one or more players)

Each player is given a newspaper, scissors, paste, and blank paper. Each player cuts words from a newspaper and pastes them together to make a story. Put a time limit on this game so that no one attempts to write the great American novel.

Telegram (two or more players)

Each player in turn calls out one letter of the alphabet. The other players write down a word beginning with each letter called and then each tries to write a telegram using the words.

Alphabet Salesperson (two or more players)

Each player in turn must make up a sentence, the main words of which must begin with the letter of the alphabet in turn; e.g., "My name is Allen and I sell ants in Africa." The next player begins with "B," saying something like "My name is Betty and I sell bananas in Boston," and so on.

Dog to Cat

Change dog to cat in three moves by changing one letter at each move.

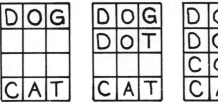

Picto Puzzle

First, select the name of a famous person, perhaps a noted president or a well-known author. Then gather together pictures of objects, the first letter of which, when arranged in the proper order, one below the other, will spell out the name of that person.

L	Lollipop	P	Pie
I	Ice cream	O	Onion
N	Nails	E	Egg
C	Car		
O	Octopus		
L	Lion		
N	Necktie		

Homonyms, Homographs, Antonyms

The English language has some weird, yet wonderful, confusions. Some words sound the same, but mean different things; some sound different, but are spelled the same. Instead of sighing at the difficulties these words present, enjoy them. Show your group one of the picture books by Fred Gwynne—*The King Who Rained* (Windmill, 1970) or *A Chocolate Moose for Dinner* (Windmill, 1976). How many others can your group add to the collection? Keep a list of favorites.

Homonyms

Homonyms are words that sound the same but are differently spelled: Hare/hair; flee/flea; bear/bare; flower/flour.

Homographs

Homographs are words that are spelled the same but sound different: tear/tear; dove/dove; wind/wind.

Antonyms

Antonyms are words that are opposite in meaning: hot/cold; high/low; open/closed; hard/soft; rough/smooth.

Word-Game Riddles

What three words contain a silent B?
    Doubt, subtle, debt.

What keys are too large to carry in your pocket?
    A mon*key*; a tur*key*, a don*key*.

Which word in the English language has the most letters?
    Antidisestablishmentarianism (28 letters).

What letters in the alphabet are the opposite of stupid?
    Ys (wise).

What two letters in the alphabet spell a word meaning jealousy?
    NV (envy).

Play with Metaphors

In case you have forgotton the definition of a metaphor, it is a word or phrase used to denote comparison. Try these food metaphors with your children. Fill in the blank with a word from the list below.

1. A couch _____
2. Packed like _____
3. Cool as a _____

4. The _____ train

5. Bringing home the _____

6. A fine kettle of _____

7. Flat as a _____

8. The _____ of his eye

9. Like taking _____ from a baby

10. He can't cut the _____

11. The world is his _____

12. Not her cup of _____

13. The proof is in the _____

14. Slow as _____

15. A tough _____ to crack

apple	gravy	pancake
bacon	molasses	potato
candy	mustard	pudding
cucumber	nut	sardines
fish	oyster	tea

Booklist: More Word Games

Ammer, Christine. *It's Raining Cats and Dogs and Other Beastly Expressions.* Paragon, 1989. The origins of common expressions.

Bryson, Bill. *Mother Tongue: English and How It Got That Way.* Avon, 1990. The history and eccentricities of the English language.

Ernst, Margaret. *In a Word.* Art by James Thurber. Harper/Perennial, 1989. Word derivations first published in 1939.

Espy, Willard R. *A Children's Almanac of Words at Play.* Art by Bruce Cayard. Potter, 1982. Arranged by days of the year, this is a collecton of riddles, jokes, puns, and word games.

Feldman, David. *Who Put the Butter in the Butterfly? . . . And Other Fearless Investigations into Our Illogical Language.* Harper, 1989. An explanation of some of the more bizarre word origins.

Gardner, Martin. *Aha! Gotcha: Paradoxes to Puzzle and Delight.* Freeman, 1982. Puzzles from logic, probability, numbers, geometry, time, and statistics.

Gwynne, Fred. *The King Who Rained.* Art by author. Windmill, 1970. From "Daddy says there are forks in the road" to ". . . the Foot Prince in the snow." Also *A Chocolate Moose for Dinner* (Windmill, 1976). Hilarious romps with semantics in picture-book format.

Hanlon, Emily. *How a Horse Grew Hoarse on the Site Where He Sighted a Bare Bear: A Tale of Homonyms.* Art by Lorna Tomei. Delacorte, 1976. A clever, funny poem full of homonyms that are listed on the book's last page.

Hanson, Joan. *Homonyms.* Art by author. Lerner, 1972. Also, *Homographs* (Lerner, 1972) and *Antonyms* (Lerner, 1972). Cartoon drawings show the differences in these words.

The Hodgepodge Book: An Almanac of American Folklore; collected by Duncan Emrich. Art by Ib Ohlsson. Four Winds, 1972. Rhymes, riddles, jokes, cumulative stories.

Lederer, Richard. *The Play of Words: Fun and Games for Language Lovers*. Art by Bernie Cootner. Pocket, 1990. A must for anyone interested in the vagaries of the English language. Logic puzzles, games, word origins, and more.

Manchester, Richard B. *The Mammoth Book of Word Games*. Hart, 1976. Five hundred pages of anagrams, crossword puzzles, and other word games.

Phillips, Louis. *263 Brain Busters: Just How Smart Are You, Anyway?* Art by James Stevenson. Viking, 1985. Questions and word games.

Schwartz, Alvin. *Tomfoolery: Trickery and Foolery with Words*. Art by Glen Rounds. Lippincott, 1973. Word tricks collected from folklore. Also *Kickle Snifters and Other Fearsome Critters*. Art by Glen Rounds. Lippincott, 1976.

Sign Language

The idea of communicating nonverbally is not a new one. Try these Native American hand motions to see if you can make yourself understood:

You (point) come (beckon) with me (point to yourself) to hunt (pull imaginary bow):
> Deer (fingers at side of head represent antlers)
> Buffalo (thumbs for ears, index fingers for horns)
> Bear (hands cupped around ears).

We all (point to each person and then indicate entire group) dance (move both hands up and down, palms open vertically to group).

Booklist: More Sign Language

Ancona, George and Mary Beth Miller. *Handtalk Zoo*. Photos by George Ancona. Four Winds, 1989. Color photos show children signing at a visit to the zoo.

Axtell, Roger E. *Gestures: The Do's and Taboos of Body Language around the World*. John Wiley, 1991. Not about sign language in the traditional sense, but an interesting discussion of both accepted and rude gestures from around the world.

Greene, Laura and Eva Barash Dicker. *Sign Language Talk*. Art by Caren Caraway. Watts, 1989. A survey of the development of sign language and practice examples.

Gross, Ruth Belov. *You Don't Need Words! A Book about Ways People Talk without Words*. Art by Susannah Ryan. Scholastic, 1992. Describes sign language and other nonverbal ways of communicating.

Liptak, Karen. *North American Indian Sign Language*. Art by Don Berry. Watts, 1990. Black-and-white drawings and narrative explanations describe words in Indian sign language.

Rankin, Laura. *The Handmade Alphabet*. Art by author. Dial, 1991. Each full-page drawing shows the sign for a letter of the alphabet with a picture of that object. Lovely.

Sesame Street Sign Language Fun with Linda Bove. Featuring Jim Henson's Sesame Street Muppets. Random, 1980. The Sesame Street puppets and an actress demonstrate hand positions for signed words.

Hieroglyphs

The ancient Egyptians used picture language. Several books created for children allow them to re-create this beautiful form of writing.

Booklist: More Hieroglyphs

Katan, Norma Jean with Barbara Mintz. *Hieroglyphs: The Writing of Ancient Egypt*. Photos. Atheneum, 1981. A brief history with photos of ancient writing instruments and symbols and their meanings.

Roehrig, Catharine. *Fun with Hieroglyphs*. Metropolitan Museum of Art/ Viking, 1990. This kit contains a hieroglyph alphabet chart, 24 rubber stamps, an ink pad, and a booklet. Great fun.

Scott, Joseph and Lenore Scott. *Egyptian Hieroglyphs for Everyone: An Introduction to the Writing of Ancient Egypt*. Crowell, 1968. The alphabet, pronunciation, and history.

Fan Language

In Fairbanks, Alaska, recently I was talking with Ron Martin, director of Media Services for the schools. We were discussing antiques or, rather, I was trying to sound somewhat knowledgeable, since Ron was obviously a true expert. We discovered some common ground when I said that when I lived in France I began collecting ladies' fans. I had become intrigued by fans and fan language when I learned that fans were traditionally used by women to communicate nonverbally with young men. Ron shared with me his list of fan language, and I have compared it to the one I found in France.

Fans were formally as much a part of a lady's outfit as hats and gloves were just a few decades ago. In Europe, in the American South, and in many other places, it was considered rude to appear in public without a fan. In Spain, where young ladies were not allowed to communicate without a chaperone, the fan became an important instrument of communication. This whole idea seems romantic to me. I have especially enjoyed using it with middle school students, who like to make up their own nonverbal skits.

Of the two lists that I have in my possession, there seems to be some difference in what some of the actions mean, but since it is unlikely that your students or patrons will actually use fan language to communicate, I think it is safe to offer you this list to begin with. Give your group a chance to experiment with fan language; then share a story about fans.

The Language of the Fan

With handle to lips	Kiss me
Carrying in the right hand front of face	Follow me
Placing it on left ear	You have changed
Twirling in left hand	I wish to get rid of you
Carrying in right hand	Desirous of acquaintance

Drawing across forehead	We are watched
Carrying in right hand	You are too willing
Drawing across cheek	I love you
Drawing through hand	I hate you
Twirling in right hand	I love another
Closing it	I wish to speak to you
Drawing across eyes	I am sorry
Letting it rest on right cheek	Yes
Letting it rest on left cheek	No
Opening and shutting	You are cruel
Dropping	We are friends
Fanning slowly	I am married
Fanning fast	I am engaged
Opening wide	Wait for me

Booklist: Fans

Baker, Keith. *The Magic Fan*. Art by author. Harcourt, 1989. Yoshi uses a magic fan to guide him to adventure and self-worth.

Johnson, Tony. *The Badger and the Magic Fan*. Art by Tomie dePaola. Putnam, 1990. Adapted from a Japanese folktale, a badger steals a goblin's magic fan in this story.

Folk Games

Games can be considered folklore too. You may not want to turn your storyhour into a gym period, but games that travel from one generation to the other and from region to region by the private oral route of children can make a fascinating study. Many adults see the passing of street games in favor of Little League and traffic jams as sad. Some of these people have recalled the games of their childhood and compiled books; others have collected the games currently played on the streets and playgrounds of the country. As you browse through these books you will be reminded of games that you played, some quiet, some active.

Archimedes' Puzzle

Archimedes was a mathematician who invented the "stoma-chion" or "the thing that drives one wild." It is simply a rectangle cut into 14 pieces, which can be moved around to create figures or pictures. Enlarge and reproduce the pieces cut from poster board for each member of your audience to "play with" at the story session or to take home.

Tangrams

The Chinese invented a seven-piece jigsaw puzzle that is used to make hundreds of different shapes. The seven pieces form a square and can be rearranged to make geometric animals and people.

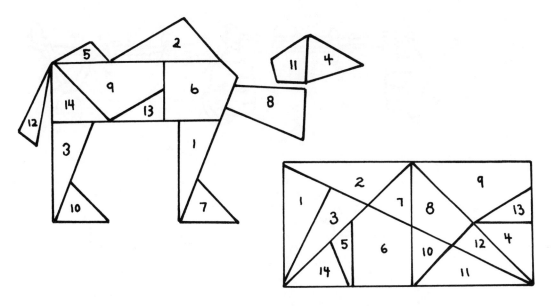

Many puzzle and game books include a selection of these shapes. These titles are particularly good:

Brandreth, Gyles. *The Book of Solo Games*. Bonanza, 1983.

Elffers, Joost. *Tangram: The Ancient Chinese Shapes Games*; tr. by R. J. Hollingdale. Penguin, 1973.

Tompert, Ann. *Grandfather Tang's Story: A Tale Told with Tangrams*. Art by Robert Parker. Crown, 1990. Incorporates the Chinese puzzles into a story.

String Games

You might not have thought of cat's cradle as folklore, but it is a game that is passed on from person to person. If you are familiar with any of the string games of your childhood, why not show them to your storyhour group? No doubt they will in turn show you some you don't know.

Ring in the String. To play this game you need a ring, a length of string whose ends are knotted together to form a loop, and a volunteer from the audience.

First draw the string loop through the ring. Then stand facing the volunteer, loop the string around his or her thumbs, and reach across the loop with your right forefinger to catch the far side of the string at X, pulling it downward across the top of the near strand and holding it there. Next, with your left hand reach under the strand you are holding with your right hand and hook the other strand with the left forefinger at Y, pulling it under the strand held by the right hand and *up* over the volunteer's left thumb. Still holding the strand with your right forefinger, reach with left forefinger across the strand, catching it *back* of the volunteer's right thumb at Z, bringing it up and toward you, and looping it over his or her left thumb. Now grasp the ring with the thumb and forefinger of your left hand, at the same time releasing the strand held by the right forefinger. The string will

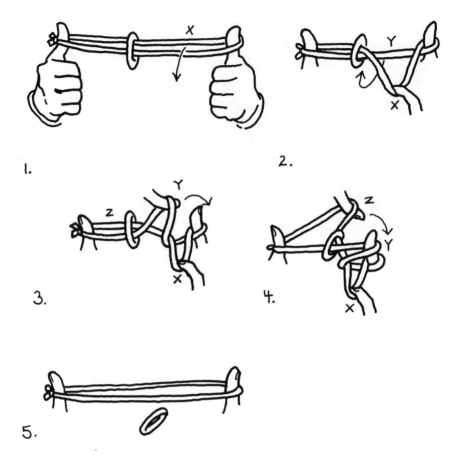

1.

2.

3.

4.

5.

snap free from the ring, leaving the ring free in your hand and the looped string still encircling the volunteer's two thumbs.

Booklist: More String Games

Adkins, Jan. *String: Tying It Up, Tying It Down.* Art by author. Scribner, 1992. Directions for making lots of knots.

Gryski, Camilla. *Super String Games.* Art by Tom Sankey. Morrow, 1987. Directions for making a turtle, a dog, a butterfly are given in narrative and line drawings. Another collection by Gryski is *Many Stars and More String Games* (Morrow, 1985).

Hindley, Judy. *A Piece of String Is a Wonderful Thing.* Art by Margaret Chamberlain. Candlewick, 1993. Explores the origins and uses of string in verse.

Jayne, Caroline Furness. *String Figures and How to Make Them: A Study of Cat's-Cradle in Many Lands.* Dover, 1962. This book gives directions for hundreds of string games, but it takes patience and practice to master many of them.

Active Games

If you are holding your storyhour outside on a lovely day you might want to play an active "folk" game before settling down to hear a story. Jacks and marble contests can be held indoors for those rainy days.

Kick the Can: a city game. To play Kick the Can as we did when I was growing up, you will need an empty can, a big paint can or coffee can, and a group of friends.

This is the way you play: The can is placed about 10 feet from "Home Base." One person is "IT." IT faces away from the players, counts to 50 while they run away and hide, and then turns around. The object of the game is to get to Home Base without being tagged. Even though IT has tagged nearly all the players, if anyone succeeds in kicking the can before being tagged, all the players revert to "Free" unless IT retrieves the can and reaches Home Base before the player who has kicked the can.

Pump Pump Pull Away: a country game. This is the way this game was played in Owatonna, Minnesota, by my friend Arvid when he was a boy. You will need lots of room and a group of friends. IT stands in the middle of a playing field. All the players stand on one end of the field. IT yells, "Pump, Pump, Pull Away" and all the players try to run past IT to the other end of the field. Those players that IT manages to tag as they run by then join hands with IT in the center of the field for the next run-through. The winner is the player who has not been tagged after all the remaining players have been tagged and are forming a wall by holding hands.

Booklist: More Folk Games

Arnold, Arnold. *The World Book of Children's Games.* Art by author. World, 1972. A large collection of informal games.

Brandreth, Gyles. *The Book of Solo Games.* Bonanza, 1983. Paper, pencil, and children's games.

Carlo (pseud.). *The Juggling Book.* Art by author. Vintage, 1974. Directions for juggling, but you still have to practice!

Fowler, Edith. *Red Rover, Red Rover: Children's Games Played in Canada.* Doubleday, 1988. A survey of games played by English-speaking children in Canada.

Frey, Richard L., Geoffrey Mott-Smith and Albert H. Moorhead. *The New Complete Hoyle: The Authoritative Guide to the Official Rules of All Popular Games of Skill and Chance.* Revised. Doubleday, 1991. This book describes how to play nearly every type of game played by children or adults.

Gregson, Bob. *The Incredible Indoor Games Book: 160 Group Projects, Games, and Activities.* Fearon (Belmont, Calif.), 1982. Games appropriate for large and small groups.

Koch, Karl-Heinz. *Pencil and Paper Games.* Sterling, 1992. Strategic games, action games, and games with letters and numbers.

Langford, Mary D. *Hopscotch around the World.* Art by Karen Milone. Morrow, 1992. Directions for playing this popular game from 16 countries, in a picture-book format.

Lappe, Frances Moore and family. *What to Do After You Turn Off the TV? Fresh Ideas for Enjoying Family Time.* Art by Kevin Bartlett and Anthony Lappe. Ballantine, 1985. Silly fun, make-believe games, and storytelling.

Maguire, Jack. *Hopscotch, Hangman, Hot Potato, and Ha,Ha,Ha: A Rulebook of Children's Games.* Prentice, 1990. Cootie catcher, shadow buff, hide and seek, and others are detailed.

Newell, William Wells. *Games and Songs of American Children*; introduction by Carl Withers. First published in 1883. Dover, 1963.

Pentagames. Compiled by Pentagram. Simon, 1990. A lavishly printed collection of string, hand, and paper games.

Ravielli, Anthony. *What Are Street Games?* Art by author. Atheneum, 1981. History and directions for playing stickball, tag, and hide and seek.

Sloane, Paul. *Lateral Thinking Puzzlers.* Art by Myron Miller. Sterling, 1992. Story puzzles useful as participation stories or critical thinking exercises.

Weigle, Marta. *Jacks and Jack Games: Follow My Fancy*; ed. by Jessica Hoffman Davis. Dover, 1970. Directions for all the games of jacks you ever played.

Wiswell, Phil. *Kids' Games: Traditional Indoor and Outdoor Activities for All Ages.* Doubleday, 1987. Instructions for 130 traditional games. An excellent resource.

Wood, Clement and Gloria Goddard. *The Complete Book of Games.* Art by author. Halcyon House, 1940. Rules for every imaginable game and sport.

Yolen, Jane. *Street Rhymes around the World.* Art by 17 international artists. Boyds Mills, 1992. Rhymes and art depicting games and chants from around the world.

Folk Toys

Toys too can be part of folklore just as jokes, riddles, myths, and folktales are. Folk toys are playthings made by one generation and passed on to the next as a form of entertainment. Collecting some of these old toys, making them yourself or with your group can be part of the story program, especially if you find stories that relate to a particular toy. For instance, displaying or making a hobbyhorse fits in with any horse story. Apples, nuts, cornhusks and cobs, twigs, spools, string—all kinds of materials go into the making of folk toys that you and your group can make and enjoy.

Hobbyhorse

You need: A large cotton sock
Cotton or polyester batt
Felt scraps
Yarn
3-foot length of ½-inch cotton tubular trim
3-foot length of 1-inch dowel or broomstick

How-to: Make head by stuffing sock with cotton or polyester batt. Make eyes, ears, and nose from felt scraps and sew on or glue to head. Use looped yarn to make mane and forelock. Sew tubular trim to head to make bridle. Attach dowel or broomstick to head with staples or craft glue.

Booklist: More Folk Toys

Burns, Elizabeth. *Hanky-Panky: Traditional Hankerchief Toys* (available from Elizabeth Burns, 7351 Mesa Dr., Aptos, CA 95003). Directions for making a doll, horse, and mouse with a handkerchief.

Joseph, Joan, comp. *Folk Toys around the World.* Art by Mel Furukawa; working drawings and instructions by Glenn Wagner. Parents, 1972. Instructions and background material for a toy from each of several selected countries.

Schnacke, Dick. *American Folk Toys and How to Make Them.* Art by author. Putnam, 1973. A practical collection of toy-making crafts.

Paper Stories

Last night I hosted a party for seven Japanese junior high students. It was their first night in America after a long, long flight. Even so, after our classic American barbeque, they took origami paper from their suitcases and showed the American teens how to fold intricate birds, animals, and flowers. Then the Americans folded an airplane and flew it to a crash landing in the living room!

Remember that paper, especially waste paper, is an inexpensive and readily available source of material for your book program. Try telling this story using paper cutouts.

Billy Goats Gruff and the Troll

This is a fun story to tell using paper props. The three Billy Goats Gruff go trip-trapping over the bridge until they are stopped by the Troll. Each goat sends his bigger brother in turn to face the Troll and it is the eldest goat that finally butts the Troll into the river to clear the way to the greener fields on the other bank. A shortened paper strip is used to produce the three goats, and the Troll is an example of combining a symmetrical design with a folded vertical strip. At the end of the story the Troll figure falls open to demonstrate his tumbling action into the river.

Preparing the paper folds. Cut a large double news sheet in half in the usual way to form a pair of long paper strips. These are used to make both the folds in the story. Both strips need cutting to a modified size as described.

Three Billy Goats Gruff. Trim off an 8-inch section from one of the strips to give you a paper piece measuring 12 inches high by 24 inches long. Make two folds—one from each end of the strip—so that the folded-down pieces overlap each other exactly as shown in the sketch. If you mark these folding lines at 8-inch intervals you can be sure the widths will all be the same. Make a further fold from right to left to give you a center line; then the goats can be marked out. No holding strip is needed across the top of the packet because the goats' horns are adequate to support the figures; the chain link pattern at the base ties the three heads firmly together.

The Troll. Use the second long strip for this figure but first cut a piece from one of the long edges to bring the sheet size

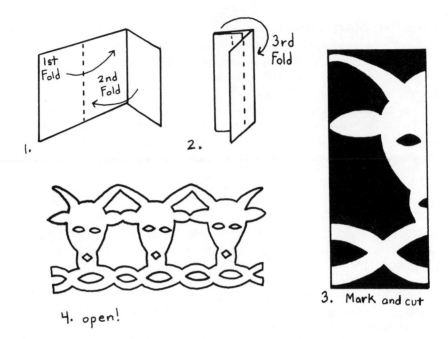

1.

2.

3. Mark and cut

4. open!

down to 32 inches long by 9 inches wide. Fold this strip up from the bottom twice and then make a third fold across the packet as shown. Now make a fourth fold from bottom to top for marking out a design of a symmetrical pattern. The sketch shows how the Troll is pencilled to the *lower* fold-edge so that his eyes are cut to this line. Ears, mouth, nose, and feet are all very simple shapes that are easily cut out during the story to give you a surprisingly intricate design from a small amount of cutting when the figure is opened.

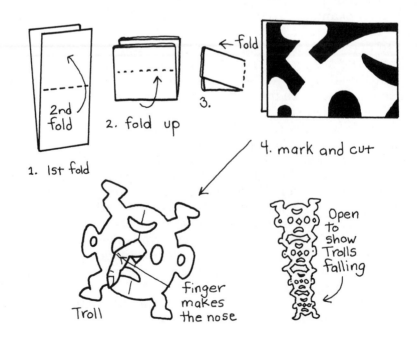

1. 1st fold

2. fold up

3.

4. mark and cut

Troll

finger makes the nose

Open to show Trolls falling

Presenting the story: what to say and do. "The three Billy Goats Gruff were feeling very hungry and they decided to go across the river to where the fields were lush and green. The journey was but a short distance . . . just over the narrow river bridge . . . and they little realized the difficulties they would encounter along the way!"

By cutting the first strip while you make this introduction—there are no special problems since all the cuts, except the eyes, are made from either side of the folded packet. Press open the center fold when the cutting is complete and show just one goat as you say: "The little Billy Goat Gruff was the first to go over the bridge . . . here he is . . . trip-trapping over the shaky wooden timbers to get to the other side. But halfway over the rickety bridge he was stopped by a strange creature! Let me cut this other folded paper packet and show you how it looked!"

Place the goat figure—still only opened to show one goat—on the table while you trim away the surplus areas to make the Troll. Open the cut figure one fold to show the full face of the Troll and then poke your first finger through the central cut-out to form a long nose for the figure. The sketch shows how this appears to the audience. Lay the Troll down on the table as you continue the tale.

"The Troll had great staring eyes . . . and a nose like a carrot! At first, he wanted to eat up the little goat . . . but the goat told him to wait till his bigger brother came along. Here is the second goat trip-trapping over the rickety bridge!"

Open the goat strip one fold and show a pair of Billy Goats Gruff. Explain how the second goat told the Troll to wait for their elder brother to come over the bridge and then open the strip wide to display all three goats.

"The greedy Troll had a great shock when he saw the size of the big Billy Goat Gruff! . . . he had bitten off more than he could chew! . . . because the eldest goat put down his head and charged with his horns! The Troll was butted into the river . . . and this is how he looked as he tumbled off the bridge and fell into the water with a mighty splash!"

Pick up the Troll and hold him by his heels, then release the strip so that the chain of Trolls falls down. Because of the symmetrical design of the figures, their faces appear the right way up down the length of the paper strip. Conclude the story: "With the Troll vanquished, the three Billy Goats Gruff were able to walk across the rickety bridge and eat their fill of the green, green grass!"

Booklist: More Paper Stories

Anderson, Gene and Frances Marshall. *Newspaper Magic.* Magic, Inc. (5082 N. Lincoln Ave., Chicago, IL 60625), 1975. The standard work on using newspaper to create magical effects.

Feller, Ron and Marsha Feller. *Paper Masks and Puppets for Stories, Songs and Plays.* Art by Kathryn Kusche Hastings. Arts Factory (P.O. Box 55547,

Seattle, WA 98155), 1985. Directions for making paper masks to use with stories and songs.

Hawkesworth, Eric. *Pleated Paper Folding*. Art by Margaret and Eric Hawkesworth. Supreme Magic (64 High St., Bideford, Devon, England EX39 2AN), 1984. The all-time classic introduction to beautiful cut-out shapes plus stories complete with patterns; hardback book—95 pages—excellent entertainment. One of eight books in a series covering paper cutting, origami, puppets, magic, and related titles.

_____. *Paper Cutting*. Art by Margaret and Eric Hawkesworth. Supreme Magic, 1984. "Jack and the Beanstalk," "Jason and the Golden Fleece" and other favorites are told using papercutting techniques.

Kallevig, Christine Petrell. *Folding Stories: Storytelling and Origami Together as One*. Storytime Ink International (Box 813, Newburgh, Indiana 47629), 1991. Nine original stories illustrated with directions for folding the origami to go with them.

McGill, Ormond. *Paper Magic: Creating Fantasies and Performing Tricks with Paper*. Art by Anne Canevari Green. Millbrook, 1992. Some of the more popular paper tricks are explained.

Severn, Bill. *Magic with Paper*. Art by Katharine Wood. McKay, 1962. Magic with paper bags, tissue paper, and newspaper.

Multimedia Storytelling

Turn a flower into a book. It's magic. Sing a song. Transform yourself into a velcro board. Have a conversation with a puppet.

Now that you've begun to master the art and science of pure storytelling, it's time to explore the world of puppetry, magic, music, and film—all of which add another layer of enjoyment to your storytelling program. This section offers you a wealth of new ways to offer stories and poems using visual props and pictures. Not every storyteller will be captivated by these techniques, of course, but I encourage you to try at least a few of the ideas presented here. That way, you'll know whether multimedia storytelling is right for you!

Do keep in mind that throughout this section there are many ideas that require props, patterns, and mechanical devices. In some cases I have provided detailed instructions for making a particular prop or storytelling aid. In other cases, I've simply tried to present enough of an idea of how things work so that you can start experimenting on your own. Should you find yourself intrigued by multimedia storytelling, the booklists offer more detailed references.

As my husband can tell you (and the piles of multimedia props in our garage proves!), I love extending my own storytelling programs in this way. But beware: a prop should never outshine the material itself. After all, the story's the thing!

10 / Pictures and Objects in Storytelling

Warning! Before you read this chapter you should know that your author loves visuals. I'd like to see almost everything illustrated. I know that we are supposed to use our imaginations to "picture" characters and events for ourselves when we read, but wouldn't it be nice to have an illustration to break up the tax code, for instance?

Think of ways that you might use pictures and objects in your storytelling programs.

Flip Cards

One way to share illustrations with a group is to enlarge pictures and attach them to cards. By cards I really mean large sheets of tagboard or heavy paper. "Large" can range from 8 inches by 10 inches to 2 feet by 3 feet. Anything much bigger really becomes physically difficult to handle. Rest the cards on an easel or a table or hold each one up as your story progresses.

Flip cards can be made in a variety of ways. If you enjoy drawing, you may want to illustrate stories yourself. Folktales illustrated by flip cards decorated with your own drawings or with children's art can make the story more personal and meaningful. Remember that you want to show your story to a group. Keep your pictures simple and uncluttered so that the sense of each will immediately be clear to your audience. Not every scene in the story needs to be illustrated, for you don't want your flip cards to be distracting to the story. Review the story in your mind and pick out the main points for illustration. For example, to tell *Little Red Riding Hood* with flip cards, draw her with her mother as she sets out for Grandma's house; then show the first encounter with the wolf; next illustrate the wolf in bed, pretending to be Grandma; and finally present the scene when the hunter frees Grandma and Little Red Riding Hood. You can also illustrate a chapter from one of your favorite books with flip cards, or even create a picture book of your own for a favorite story that has no suitable illustrations.

You can become an instant artist by using the opaque projector. This bulky, heavy machine is used to project books, pictures, or objects on a wall or screen. Many of these machines are gathering dust, unused in schools and libraries, replaced by the overhead projector or other equipment. Resurrect this machine and use it as a copying aid. Insert a picture in the machine so that the page you want to reproduce is projected onto a wall. Now attach a posterboard or paper onto the wall with masking tape. Trace around the outlines of the picture with felt pen, crayon, pencil, or whatever you wish. You can fill in the colors later.

Now that you know how to use the opaque projector to reproduce a picture or draw your own, do something with your pictures that is usually too expensive for a publisher to do with a book. Use fabric, tissue paper, string, and whatever else you can think of to actually dress the characters in the story, thereby creating a three-dimensional effect on your flip cards. The pictures then become tactile, too, so that the children can touch and feel the story after they have seen and heard it.

Big Books

Big Books are oversized books that were developed in New Zealand to help children to learn to read and think. They are useful to the program planner who would like to use picture books with large groups of children but wants to make sure that all the pictures can be seen. The first Big Books published in the United States were simply reprints of successful picture books. Not all of these early attempts worked as Big Books, since the art was originally planned for a much smaller page. However publishers soon realized this and chose more wisely. *Hattie and the Fox* by Mem Fox, with art by Patricia Mullins, is even better as a Big Book than it was as a standard picture book where the art almost spilled off the pages. Lois Ehlert's bright bold art for Gene Baer's *Thump, Thump, Rat-a-Tat-Tat* is exciting as a poster size offering.

Big Books are often used in classrooms—the teacher reads the text aloud and the children repeat it, thus showing the relationship between a word as it sounds and as it is written. Big Books are also used as group thinking skills exercises; the teacher breaks up the story by posing such questions as "What do you think happened next?" or "Can you identify words that use the same sound?" As a visiting storyteller, however, I prefer to share these books for their entertainment value. The Big Book becomes a treat for the audience just because it offers a new way to hear a story.

I did visit a K–1 class once that had an impressive library of Big Books with specially built racks to hold them. However, there weren't any plain old ordinary books in the room. Apparently the children were never given time for individual reading, but were always read to in a group. I have written one book designed for use as a Big Book, but the book is distributed with a set of smaller books for individual reading. I do think it's important for us to remember that Big Books shared with a group shouldn't replace independent reading.

Paperback Cut-ups

Sometimes you will have two copies of a juvenile paperback. You can cut them apart and mount the characters or scenes on posterboard. Then display them on an easel or stand them up with cardboard stands, use them like stick puppets, or mount them on a roll of paper. Books that have repetitive action or sequential characters work well for such use.

Although we are taught never to mutilate a book, some may be put to better use by cutting them up. Take, as an example, the remaindered art books you frequently find on sale at the bookstore. You're tempted to purchase them after which they sit unused on your library shelf or coffee table. Instead, why not put such books to use? Consider cutting up an art book to use for exhibit purposes, bookmarks, posters, or on a magnetic board. Perhaps you own a book whose text is outdated. Why give the book away to an organization that will find the book equally outdated? Perhaps the pictures in it can be used to good advantage in your storytelling programs.

Roll Stories

On a roll of adding machine paper, which is available from your stationery store, draw an appropriate story, scene by scene, so

that when it is unrolled the scenes and characters of the story will appear in sequence. After the story has been told, the long length of paper can be used on a bulletin board or as a wall decoration. The roll can also be installed in a box cut out to look like a television set. A sturdy shoe box is ideal. Cut a square hole the size of the width of the paper in the bottom of the shoe box. Cut slits above and below the viewing window for the paper to pass through. The paper roll can be pulled through as the story is told or you can use wooden doweling, available at the lumber yard or hardware store, to make a neater roll.

Paper such as newsprint and wrapping paper is also sold in bulk rolls and can be used for this same storytelling technique. The larger the roll, the greater the number of children who will be able to see the story. A handcrafted box can be made to file an oversized roll of paper.

This is a good technique for children to try themselves. After you tell a story, have each child draw a picture. Paste all the pictures onto the roll in a sequence. Now each child will be able to say to himself or herself or more often aloud to the group, "That's my picture." To avoid having too many pictures of the same scene (12 Rapunzels in the tower, for instance, and no witches), you might go over the story, characters, and scenes, reminding the children that other things happen besides the main thing that they remember.

The Copy Machine

The versatile copy machine can help you with visuals in many ways. Use the enlarging mode to make graphics larger and easier to see by big groups. The reducer can make pictures smaller for use on bookmarks or tickets. The color copier can be useful to duplicate art work. Since fancy machines like these can be found in many quick print shops, now you can use the same art in a variety of ways. Use the pictures on a magnetic board or velcro apron. Mount them on posterboard to be used as flip cards in a presentation. Or use them to make stick or picture puppets.

Object Stories

Another way of presenting a story with visuals is to show objects as you tell the story. For example, if you want to tell Ezra Jack Keats' *Jennie's Hat*, you can actually act it out by asking a little girl in the audience to be Jennie. As you tell the story, try on the different objects that Jennie tries on: a TV antenna, a basket, a flowerpot, a saucepan. When the birds bring objects to decorate Jennie's hat, you decorate a hat with the eggs, flowers, and greeting cards.

One of my favorite books is Margaret Wise Brown's *Goodnight Moon*. The book is traditionally used as a bedtime story, but as an object story, it becomes a perfect story to share during a storyhour. The book begins:

> In a great green room
> There was a telephone
> A red balloon
> And a picture of the cow
>   jumping over the moon.

I use a dollhouse, and as each object is named, I place it in a room. As the narrator says goodnight to each object in the room, I remove that object. It doesn't take long for the children to want to participate by placing and removing the objects as the story is told.

One of my students told *Stone Soup* by Marcia Brown to a fourth-grade class. Before the story he passed out vegetables: turnips, onions, carrots, beets, and potatoes. As the soldiers in the story asked the town's citizens to contribute to the soup pot, the children contributed their vegetables to a large pot also. That night the storyteller went home and cooked up a big pot of soup to serve at snack time the next day!

A Story to Tell Using Objects

WIND AND FIRE

Here is one of my favorite stories to tell using visuals. The two objects can be produced with a flourish at the end of the story. Import shops will have fans and paper lanterns, since both objects are still used in China. Or you can make your own, and demonstrate to your audience how to make their own fans and lanterns, just in case they are ever asked for an impossible present!

Qwan and Ming Li were both young and silly girls. Young brides married to brothers, they lived in their husbands' home with their mother-in-law. Their own mother lived in a village a day's walk from their new homes. So after some time they became homesick for their own family.

"We want to go home and visit our mother," the girls said to their husbands. "Ask my mother," the husbands said. "If she says 'yes' then it is all right with us."

Ming Li and Qwan pleaded with their mother-in-law to let them leave for a visit. At last she said that they could go, so long as they brought back a present. "Of course," agreed the girls. "What would you like?"

"Bring me the wind in paper and fire in paper." The girls were appalled. How could they leave if they had to bring back something so impossible? They decided to go on their trip anyway. Laughing and giggling all the way to their own village the girls arrived home.

Their mother was overjoyed to see them. When she heard about the strange request from their mother-in-law she told the girls to enjoy their visit. "I will see to it that you have wind in paper and fire in paper to bring back with you."

After several days Qwan and Ming Li were homesick for their husbands and even their mother-in-law. "We are ready to return to our husbands, but what shall we do about the present for our mother-in-law?"

"Have no fear," said their own mother. "I have prepared the gift. Have a safe journey."

Giggling and laughing all the way back, the two young brides enjoyed happy reunions with their husbands, and even their mother-in-law treated them with new respect when they returned with wind in paper—a fan—and fire in paper—a paper lantern!

Rosette Fan

You will need: Newspaper or wrapping paper.

How to: Pleat the paper in alternate folds of 2 inches each. Open the fan by holding one end.

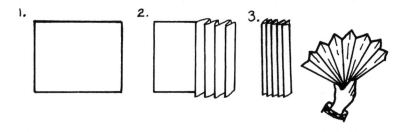

Hanging Paper Lantern

You will need: a square of colored paper (12″ × 12″)
scissors
tape or glue

How to: Take a square sheet of paper and fold it in half diagonally. See figure 1. Then, fold the triangular shape in half two more times, as shown in figures 2 and 3.

Now, take this folded triangle of paper and cut into the two folded edges of the paper, first from one size and then from the other, as shown in figure 5. Do not cut all the way across the triangle! Leave about half an inch of fold paper intact. After you've made your cuts, unfold the paper, as in figure 6.

Bring the four outer corners of the paper together and tape or glue them in place. Then, gently pull the center of the paper down.

Optional: Use a string or ribbon as a handle for your lantern. Shine a flashlight from the bottom to show how the "fire" would look.

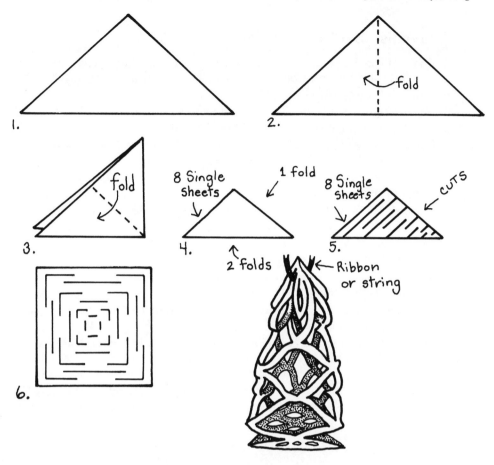

Stories about Color to Tell Using Objects

Stories about color lend themselves especially well to telling with objects or pictures, so I include two of my favorite titles here and a list of books for you to explore.

In Valrie M. Selkowe's *Spring Green*, Danny, a duck, is looking for the perfect object to bring to the spring green contest at Woody's party. His friends show what they are bringing to the party: a leaf, a green apple, a green crayon, a banana that is not ripe yet, and a green balloon. Finally Danny gives up his search and simply goes to the party with his friend Ricket. Lo and behold! He wins first prize in the contest anyway, because his friend Ricket is—a green frog!

This story was reprinted in the March 1987 issue of *Cricket* magazine. Collect green objects around your house or classroom to accompany this story. Older children will enjoy hearing this story told to younger children if they help to gather the green objects.

If you have an abundance of red objects, try telling "Pog Painted" in *Pog* by Peter Haswell. In this story, Pog paints the wall, the floor, the fireplace, and even his feet red. When everything has been painted red, Pog says, "I don't know why I did all that . . . I don't like red."

Booklist: Books about Color

Bond, Michael. *Paddington's Colors*. Art by John Lobban. Viking, 1990. Paddington is shown decorating a room. Color mixing is clearly demonstrated with Paddington's bear paws.

Burningham, John. *John Burningham's Colors*. Crown, 1985. Introduces 11 colors through attractive drawings for each color.

Dodds, Dayle Ann. *The Color Box*. Art by Giles Laroche. Little, 1992. A monkey follows the colors through a die-cut hole.

Ehlert, Lois. *Planting a Rainbow*. Art by author. Harcourt, 1988. Primary colors grow in a flower garden.

Goennel, Heidi. *Colors*. Art by author. Little, 1990. Simple shapes, delicately shaded, compare colors in nature.

Jonas, Ann. *Color Dance*. Art by author. Greenwillow, 1989. Young dancers cavort through the book with colored scarves.

McMillan, Bruce. *Growing Colors*. Photos by author. Lothrop, 1988. Each fruit or vegetable photograph shows a color.

"Pog Painted" in *Pog* by Peter Haswell. Art by author. Orchard, 1989. Pog paints everything red.

Remkiewicz, Frank. *The Last Time I Saw Harris*. Art by author. Lothrop, 1991. Luckily Edmund has taught Harris, his parrot, the colors, because that is the way they find one another when they become separated.

Selkowe, Valrie M. *Spring Green*. Art by Jeri Crisler Bassett. Lothrop, 1985. A spring green contest party—the perfect story to welcome spring!

Poems to Tell Using Objects

VANCOUVER
Robert Heidbreder

Poetry often lends itself well to the use of visuals. Open an umbrella on the last line of the poem "Vancouver" (in *Don't Eat Spiders*) by Robert Heidbreder.

In Spring it sprinkles
In Summer too

In Fall it pours
Buckets on you.

In Winter it rains
Cats and dogs

From heavy clouds
Through soupy fogs.

All year long
Rain drops and drops

In Vancouver
It never stops.

POCKETS
Eve Merriam

After you have recited or read Eve Merriam's poem from *Black-berry Ink* several times, you might wish to present it visually. On the last line pull out your pocket and show a hole, or exhibit the pile of objects mentioned in the poem.

Something's in my pocket,
What do you think?
It's nothing that goes down
The kitchen sink.

It isn't a penny,
It isn't a nail,
It isn't a cookie
That's nice and stale.

It isn't a whistle,
It isn't a stamp,
It isn't a toad
That's nice and damp.

It isn't an eraser
Or a ticket stub,
It isn't a piece
Of pocket flub.

It isn't a ring
Or string
Or a stone,
It isn't a bead
Or a weed
Or a bone.

I won't give it to you—
Get a hole of your own.

Booklist: Books for Object Story Use

Any ABC book: Use objects to represent each letter.

Baylor, Byrd. *Everybody Needs a Rock.* Art by Peter Parnall. Scribner, 1974.

Brown, Marcia. *Stone Soup.* Art by author. Scribner, 1947.

Brown, Margaret Wise. *Goodnight Moon.* Art by Clement Hurd. Harper, 1947.

Hilton, Nettie. *The Long Red Scarf.* Art by Margaret Power. Carolrhoda, 1987.

Keats, Ezra Jack. *Jennie's Hat.* Art by the author. Harper, 1966.

Lionni, Leo. *Let's Make Rabbits.* Art by the author. Pantheon, 1982.

Marshall, James. *Yummers!* Art by the author. Houghton, 1973.

Patron, Susan. *Burgoo Stew.* Art by Mike Shenon. Orchard, 1991.

Robbins, Ken. *Tools*. Art by author. Four Winds, 1983.

Sawicki, Norma Jean. *The Little Red House*. Art by Toni Goffe. Lothrop, 1989.

"The Tail Who Wagged the Dog" by Robert Krauss in Caroline Feller Bauer's *Read for the Fun of It*. H. W. Wilson, 1992.

Tusa, Tricia. *Maebelle's Suitcase*. Art by author. Macmillan, 1987.

Zolotow, Charlotte. *Mr. Rabbit and the Lovely Present*. Art by Maurice Sendak. Harper, 1962.

Booklist: For Adults

Pellowski, Anne. *Hidden Stories in Plants*. Art by Lynn Sweat. Macmillan, 1990. "Unusual and Easy-to-Tell Stories from Around the World Together with Creative Things to Do While Telling Them."

_____. *The Story Vine*. Art by Lynn Sweat. Macmillan, 1984. Shows how to use dolls, string, and pictures to present stories.

11 / Board Stories

Why were 60 ten-year-olds laughing so loudly? The principal wanted to know. He was even more puzzled when he looked at the chalkboard at the front of the classroom. It was covered with a most peculiar symbol.

The principal was looking at a drawing for Frank Asch's *Monkey Face*, a story that I had just told in tandem with my friend Sunjin to a fifth grade class in Seoul, Korea. I told the story in English and Sunjin told it in Korean.

I told the same story using the back of a wall calendar to the youngest class in a boarding school in the mountains of northwest India. One of the boys was celebrating his birthday, so after I had finished the story I gave him the picture as a present.

Even the most primitive classrooms have some form of a chalkboard that can be used to draw a story. Sand on the beach or a clearing in the dirt in a field or around a campfire works well as a drawing surface. The southwest American Indians told stories in the desert sand. In Alaska I was given a little booklet of stories prepared by children in Kipnuk, complete with a wooden storyknife. The girls clear a place in the mud and tell original stories or stories they have heard from their families, while drawing with an ivory or wooden knife.

If you have never used props to tell a story and are a bit wary of the whole idea, experimenting with one of the various types of boards is a good way to begin. Using a felt board to tell a story is as much of a tradition in some classrooms and libraries as telling a story without props. Years ago I visited a children's room in a public library in St. Louis. The librarian and I began discussing storytelling and she showed me her felt-board file in which each story was carefully stored in a labeled manila envelope. I was intrigued, yet at the same time alienated, for my first thought was, "But why do you need all that paraphernalia? Why not just tell the story?" Later, returning home to tell stories at the local schools, and thinking of the librarian in St. Louis, I decided to try my own board story. I cut out paper figures and while telling the story, attached the pictures to a window screen using pins. This was, admittedly, a rather crude and unwieldy attempt, yet it was instantly successful. I now had two stories in place of one, for although the children had heard the story many times, they delighted in this new presentation. I now wish I knew the name of that librarian in St. Louis, for I would like to thank her for moving me out of the traditional past into another realm where I can make use of new media and different techniques, all while retaining the spirit and heritage of the old stories.

With the story board the idea is to tell a story while illustrating it with cut-out figures that are placed on the board. As in any storytelling, the most important part is to choose a good story, but you have the added challenge of choosing one that is suitable for storyboard presentation. To do this you want a story that has only a few simple, large characters or objects. You won't want to be putting up a lot of tiny objects that crowd the board. Nor do you want to be constantly changing the pictures. This can be distracting unless you become adept at talking and doing at the same time and can concentrate on telling the story to the audience. Particularly successful is the story that begins with one character and builds up to many. The storyteller simply adds to the cutouts on the board rather than adding and removing. Some stories are just not suitable for board use. I keep wanting to try Polly Goldberg's *Oh Lord, I Wish I Was a Buzzard* as a felt-board presentation. I keep thinking what fun it would be to start with a board filled with cotton balls and as I removed them, the animals that the little girl wishes to be could be seen. Yet I know that making a trick out of this particular book would cheapen the message. But there are other books and many stories that are suitable for storyboard use. Try a board story with a group of eager and receptive preschoolers or middle grade students and you'll soon find that you have a drawer of your own full of carefully labeled envelopes containing stories for board use.

Hints for Using Boards

Boards can be used most effectively on an easel, although you may want to sit on the floor and simply lean the board against a wall. You might have your most often used board permanently fastened to the wall. You will also need a table, or a floor area on which to arrange the cutouts that will go on the board. Number these on the back for easy identification. I like to put my pieces behind the board, or in a box or basket so that the audience doesn't see what is coming next.

Care should be observed in using these boards. There is a tendency to talk to the board rather than to the audience. Be sure that you face the audience after you have put the object or picture on the board. If something falls off, simply pick it up and put it back. If you don't, the children will remind you and disrupt the presentation. Try to choose a story in which the placement of the object on the board is not crucial. Otherwise, you will take excessive amounts of time carefully arranging your board. The pictures should merely supplement your story. They should not be too detailed. Outline silhouettes may be all you really want because you want to leave room for a child's imagination to work.

Occasionally you may want to use a bird or rabbit from one story in another story. Try to resist the temptation, for you may later find yourself in the middle of a story and discover that you forgot to replace the character. Try to keep all the pictures belonging to one story in a manila envelope that is clearly marked for identification. A copy of the story should also be included in this envelope so that you can easily relearn it for telling without searching for the book. If you do have a copy of the book, it should be shown to the children before or after you tell the story so that they know that the story came from print.

Once you have told the story you might ask for some help in taking down the pictures, for you will discover that the children who handle the figures may be better able to recall the story. You will also find that children enjoy telling the story to each other and making their own cutouts.

Background music, on a record, cassette, or compact disc, serves to make your presentation truly professional and is particularly useful during the interlude when you have a lot of pictures to put up or take off a board.

The Chalkboard

Most classrooms, lecture halls, and clubhouses have a chalkboard. Make use of this permanent fixture by illustrating your story as you tell it. Although the same thing may be accomplished with a drawing pad, the chalkboard has the advantage of being reusable and there also is something magical about a story disappearing under an eraser. Choose a story that will require a few simple clues. The audience will become restless if you turn your back and painstakingly complete a master drawing. Although this book emphasizes do-it-yourself projects for people who are not artists, if you are skilled the possibilities of the chalkboard are extensive. Draw your own illustrations while you tell a folktale or relate an author's story. If you don't consider yourself artistic there are some stories and rhymes that require only simple drawings. Among these are the "drawing stories" collected by folklorists which, by their nature, require only minimal drawing ability. Mother Goose rhymes are adaptable to the chalkboard too. Drawing to music is another possibility for using the chalkboard for storytelling. Be sure that you stand to the side as you draw so that everyone can see. Colored chalks may be used to identify or highlight figures. Always practice before presenting a story, so that you feel at ease with the combined drawing-telling activity. The following suggestions should start you on your way to creating with chalk.

Drawing Stories

"T" IS FOR TOMMY

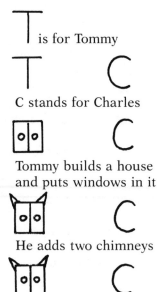

T is for Tommy

C stands for Charles

Tommy builds a house
and puts windows in it

He adds two chimneys

Tommy visits Charles' house

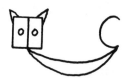

He comes back by way of
another route

He's been bewitched because he
kicks, and kicks, and kicks,
and kicks

And turns into a cat.

Chalkboard Rhymes

April showers
Bring May flowers.

Rain, rain go away
Come again another day.

Jack, be nimble,
Jack be quick,
And, Jack, jump over
The candlestick.

Familiar Folk Songs

(The children sing while leader draws)

Oh where, oh where has my little dog gone?
Oh where, oh where can he be?
With his ears so short
And his tail so long
Oh where, oh where can he be?

Leave the drawing of the dog on the chalkboard, and because it could be a fox as well, direct the children to sing the next song. When they "catch" the fox, draw a box around the animal, erasing it as they sing the last line.

Oh, a-hunting we will go
A-hunting we will go
We'll catch a fox
And put him in a box
And then we'll let him go.

Books for Chalkboard Use

Asch, Frank. *Bread and Honey.* Parents, 1981. Bear draws a picture for his mother. (*Monkey Face* is now out of print, but you may still be able to find a copy in your library.)

Carle, Eric. The *Mixed-Up Chameleon.* Art by author. Crowell, 1975. A chameleon not only changes colors, but shapes.

Christelow, Eileen. *Henry and the Red Stripes.* Art by author. Clarion, 1982. Draw Henry and add his red stripes as you tell the story.

Ctvrtek, Václav. *The Little Chalk Man*; tr. from the Czech. Art by Muriel Batherman. Knopf, 1970. Episodic chapters of a magical chalk world.

Dodgson, Charles L. *The Diaries of Lewis Carroll* (pseud.); ed. by Roger Lancelyn Green. Oxford Univ. Pr., 1954, v. 2, pp. 572–73. "Mr. C and Mr. T," a variant of the black cat drawing story.

Du Bois, William Pène. *Lion.* Art by author. Viking, 1956. Lion is created in heaven after a number of false starts.

Duffy, Dee Dee. *Barnyard Tracks.* Art by Janet Marshall. Bell/Boyd's Mill, 1992. The book is beautiful and worth sharing, but you may want to use it as a board story, drawing the tracks on the chalkboard.

Freeman, Don. *The Chalk Box Story.* Lippincott, 1976. Eight pieces of colored chalk change a blank piece of paper into a story.

Hutchins, Pat. *The Doorbell Rang.* Art by author. Greenwillow, 1986. Draw a plate of cookies on the chalkboard and erase them as they are eaten.

Johnson, Crockett (pseud. for David Johnson Leisk). *Harold and the Purple Crayon.* Art by author. Harper, 1958. A little boy draws simple pictures.

Koontz, Robin M. *I See Something You Don't See.* Art by author. Cobblehill, 1992. Draw the answers to these rhymed riddles on the chalkboard.

Langstaff, John. *Oh, A-Hunting We Will Go.* Art by Nancy Winslow Parker. Atheneum, 1974. The familiar folk song with enchanting illustrations.

Lehan, Daniel. *This Is Not a Book about Dodos*. Art by author. Dutton, 1991. Draw a board full of dodos as you introduce or tell the story.

Lionni, Leo. *Little Blue and Little Yellow*. Art by author. McDowell, 1959. Use colored chalk in this adventure of two blobs of color that join to create green.

Olsen, Margaret J. *Tell and Draw Stories*. Arts and Crafts (Box 572, Minneapolis, MN 55440), 1963. Gives step-by-step drawings for short original stories.

Pinkwater, Daniel. *Bear's Picture*. Art by author. Dutton, 1972. Draw bear's picture or your own.

Silverstein, Shel. *The Missing Piece*. Art by author. Harper, 1976. A circle searches for a missing part, only to discover that life loses its fascination when everything is too perfect. Simple, easy-to-reproduce drawings.

Thompson, Richard. *Frog's Riddle*. Art by author. Annick, 1990. Original draw and tell stories by a talented Canadian. Also *Draw and Tell*, 1988.

Wilder, Laura Ingalls. *On the Banks of Plum Creek*. Art by Helen Sewell and Mildred Boyle. Harper, 1937, pp. 318–19. A drawing of a duck is the final picture in this drawing story.

Withers, Carl. *The Tale of a Black Cat*. Art by Alan Cober. Holt, 1966. A picture-book version of a well-known drawing tale.

_____. *The Wild Ducks and the Goose*. Art by Alan Cober. Holt, 1968. A goose emerges during the telling of this story.

Flannel or Felt Boards

When I first wrote this book, the most popular boards for story-time use were the flannel and felt boards. While they are being replaced in many libraries and classrooms by the Velcro board, I find that they are still used extensively in many places. I think their popularity stems from the fact that they are inexpensive to produce and easily stored. Although the felt board is a little more costly to make than the flannel, its versatility more than justifies the extra expense.

A variety of different materials will stick to felt. Felt itself is probably the most popular choice for figure cutouts. It comes in vibrant colors and is readily available, already cut into squares, at craft and fabric shops. Pellon, a material that is used to stiffen fabrics, makes perfect felt board cutouts. It easily adheres to the felt or flannel board and can be colored with paint or crayon. Pellon also makes a product called Wonder Under Web, which is essentially a glue used to fasten fabric to fabric or to poster board surfaces. Tagboard or any art paper may also be used to make cutouts. Simply paste sandpaper to the back of the cutout picture and it will stick to the board. The hook side of Velcro can be glued or sewn to the figures; this way they will adhere to felt as well as to the loop side of the Velcro. Velcro strips or squares are available in fabric shops, electrical departments of hardware stores, and in hobby shops. Finally, pattern spray, available in fabric stores, sprayed on the back of cutouts will also adhere them to felt. If you use this technique, place paper between the figures when storing them. The felt board is wonderfully useful to tell simple stories and to illustrate riddles and poems, but it may not be the most practical for your particular needs. Larger figures have a tendency to droop or fall off the board, disrupting the story and the viewer's attention. Felt boards may be purchased commercially, but they are also easy to make.

To make a felt board you will need:

An artist's cardboard portfolio. These come in various sizes and can be purchased wherever art supplies are sold. The most versatile for classroom use is 17″ × 22″ folded. A larger size, for stage use in the auditorium, is 34″ × 42″.

Rubber cement

Felt cut to the size of the board. The color of the felt depends on your personal preference. White does show soil more quickly, but a less neutral color has its problems too. My portable felt board is red. I found to my chagrin that one of my favorite stories, Robert Bright's *My Red Umbrella*, didn't work on my board. The leading character, the umbrella, which is red, doesn't show up on a red background and would have to become "My Blue Umbrella" to be seen on my board.

Plastic tape for binding. Simply glue the felt to the portfolio, trim with tape (it covers the edge for neatness), and you have a portable, easily stored felt board.

These directions can also be followed to make a Velcro board; simply substitute the loop part of the Velcro for the felt.

Magnetic Boards

A magnetic board utilizes magnets to attach pictures or artifacts to its surface. One of the advantages of the magnetic board is that pictures adhere quickly and securely, almost like magic. Even adults are impressed by the way pictures can be almost thrown onto the surface of the magnetic board, where they really stay put. If you have had problems with objects falling from felt boards, I think you will welcome the use of this more secure method!

The board itself can be any metal surface to which a magnet will cling. For a small board to use with groups of three or four children, the steel cookie sheet from your kitchen will work. In fact, the kitchen abounds in useful "magnetic boards." The refrigerator is the largest surface, but even your toaster will work. The side of a steel filing cabinet also makes a useful board if it happens to be well placed in your classroom or library. A magnetic board also can be cut to size by your local roofing supplier. Sheet metal shops will sell you sheet metal that can be framed in plywood. Sheet metal comes in different weights. The thinnest is, of course, lighter and more transportable, but it will flex unless mounted on plywood. A metal automobile drip pan, available in auto supply stores, can be used too. Magnetic boards are also available commercially. Look for these in toy departments and stationery stores.

To make the board more useful, buy a can of chalkboard paint, which is available in a variety of colors. Paint the surface of the board; you now have a combination chalkboard and magnetic board to use with an easel. If you glue Velcro or felt on the reverse side of your combination board you will have created a three-in-one board: magnetic, chalk, and Velcro or felt.

Several types of magnets are now available for use with your magnetic board. The crafts or sewing department of the local variety store or the art department of the stationery store usually sells rubberized strip magnets. These magnetic strips, about ¾-inch wide and 12 inches long, are easily cut to length with scissors. These have an adhesive on one side that readily sticks to fabric, tagboard, or paper. Although the strip magnets might seem expensive, they can be reused again and again; and only a small piece is necessary to hold most cutouts to the board.

The small magnets that are used to stick potholders to a stove are available in the housewares department of your local hardware store, and although these are a little more cumbersome to use since you must affix the glue to them yourself, they are less expensive than the strips. Besides, if you plan to use heavier objects on your board, these small individual magnets are more serviceable since they can hold more weight. If you don't find magnets in your local stationery or department store, order them from a mail order craft and hobby supplier such as Kirchen Bros., Box C1016, Skokie, IL 60076. Write for a catalog. The Highsmith Co., Inc., Fort Atkinson, WI 53538, and Dick Blick, Galesburg, IL 61401, are other sources.

Velcro or Hook 'n' Loop Boards

A man walking in a field was annoyed to find his flannel trousers covered with burrs afterward. However, his experience inspired him to develop the two-part nylon fabric closure we all know by the trade name Velcro, which works on the same principle as the burr: the tiny hooks on the one fabric catch the tiny loops of the second fabric.

You can hang almost anything on Velcro—from a sheet of paper to a heavy book. As you tell a story, each object that you name can be hung on a board or a strip fastened to the wall. Commercial boards are available from Charles Mayer, 140 E. Market St., Akron, OH 44308, or if you want to make your own board, order the fabric from him by the yard. Another possibility, if you feel that your use of it would not justify the expense of an entire board, is to buy a strip of Velcro (available by the yard where sewing notions are sold). Remember, it comes in two parts and you need both the hook side and the loop side. Small pieces of the loop side may be fixed to the other side of a felt or magnetic board, or, if you always tell stories in the same location, you may want to attach a strip to the wall and use it with stories involving three-dimensional objects.

Be sure to use strong glue to affix the hook part to the selected object so that it doesn't pull away. It rarely, if ever, will pull away from the loops by itself. Once you have used Velcro you will find many other uses for it, perhaps holding puppet theaters together, and so on. One caution: Don't try to use the hooked side of Velcro on a felt board. It does not hold well to the felt. However, the loop side of a Velcro-covered board does function very well as a substitute felt board and sandpaper-backed objects will adhere to it well.

The Velcro Apron and Vest

I take my apron with me wherever I go. Those of you who know me know that I rarely cook, so that statement may sound strange! It is not an apron for cooking, however; it is my storytelling apron. Throughout the years I have experimented with all kinds of boards: chalk, magnetic, felt, and Velcro. Now I almost exclusivly use a Velcro apron or a vest made of the hook 'n' loop fabric.

Originally I carted an auto drip pan with me on my storytelling trips. On one side it was a magnetic board; on the other side it was a Velcro board. One night I flew home from a trip and went to the baggage pickup to look for my bags. There was a disgruntled crowd around the baggage carousel. Apparently a large board had been caught in the mechanism of the carousel and all the bags were backed up. I knew just whose board it was, but I joined the disgruntled crowd anyway. I didn't want to get lynched!

I did try to travel with a suitcase-sized board, but it was quite heavy. When I decided to be the board myself, life became much easier. I had both an apron and a vest made. The vest uses more fabric and is therefore more expensive, but it allows you to put objects on your back and turn around for another scene in your story.

I think there are several advantages of the apron besides the easy storage and transport. As storyteller, you are more mobile and can walk up to your audience to show the pictures at close hand. If two children are misbehaving, you can walk up to them and quickly separate them without stopping the story. You have full view of your "board," and need never turn your back to affix the next object.

Using Paperbacks with Boards

Many delightful picture books are now in paperback form. You may wish to cut some of these up to use with your board. Purchasing two copies of a book to destroy may seem extreme, but if you want to introduce the real book in an interesting fashion it may be worth it. Simply cut the figures from the book and mount each on thin cardboard. Glue sandpaper on the backs for use with a felt board, rubberized magnets for a magnetic board, or

Velcro for a Velcro board or apron. In many instances you will need two copies of the book if you like to use every picture. Telling a favorite story with one of these boards will provide you and your audiences with a new and interesting change of pace.

Stories to Tell on a Board

THE OSSOPIT TREE

Reproduce and enlarge, as needed, the animals and place them on your board or apron as you tell this lively story. Be prepared for laughter as you repeat and mispronounce ossopit.

One terribly hot summer in the forests of Africa there was a great shortage of anything to eat. The animals had been hunting around here, there and everywhere and had finally eaten up the very last twig and root. They were very hungry indeed.

Suddenly they came upon a wonderful-looking tree, hung with the most tempting, juicy-looking fruit. But, of course, they didn't know whether the fruit was safe to eat or not because they had no idea what its name was. And they simply had to know its name.

Luckily they did know that the tree belonged to an old lady called Jemma. So they decided to send the hare, their fastest runner, to ask her what the name of the tree was.

Off went the hare as fast as his legs could carry him and he found old Jemma in front of her hut.

"Oh, Mrs. Jemma," he said. "We animals are dying of hunger. If you could only tell us the name of that wonderful tree of yours you could save us all from starving."

"Gladly I will do that," answered Jemma. "It's perfectly safe to eat the fruit. Its name is Ossopit."

"Oh," said the hare. "That's a very difficult name. I shall forget it by the time I get back."

"No, it's really quite easy," said Jemma. "Just think of 'opposite' and then sort of say it backwards, like this: opposite—Ossopit."

"Oh, thanks very much," said the hare, and off he scampered.

As he ran he kept muttering, "Opposite, ottipis, ossipit" and he got all mixed up. So that when he got back to the other animals all he could say was:

"Well, Jemma did tell me the name but I can't remember whether it's ossipit, ottipis, or ossupit. I do know it's got something to do with 'opposite'."

"Oh dear," they all sighed. "We had better send someone with a better memory."

"I'll go," said the goat. "I never forget anything." So he headed straight for Jemma's hut, grunting and snorting all the way.

"I'm sorry to bother you again, Mrs. Jemma," he panted, "but that stupid hare couldn't remember the name of the tree. Do you mind telling it me once more?"

"Gladly I will," replied the old woman. "It's Ossopit. Just think of 'opposite' and then sort of say it backwards: opposite—Ossopit."

"Rightee-oh," said the goat, "and thank you very much, I'm sure."

And off he galloped, fast as he could, kicking up clouds of dust, and all the way he kept saying:

"Ottopis, oppossit, possitto, otto . . ." until he got back to the other animals.

"I know the name of that tree," he said. "It's oppitis, n . . . no . . . ossipit, n . . . no . . . otup . . . oh dear . . . I just can't get it right."

"Well, who can we send this time?" they all asked. They didn't want to bother old Jemma again.

"I'm perfectly willing to have a go," piped up a young sparrow. "I'll be back in no time," and with a whisk of his tail he had flown off before anyone could stop him.

"Good morrow, gentle Jemma," he said. "Could you please tell me the name of that tree just once more. Hare and goat could not get it right."

"Right gladly I will," said old Jemma patiently. "It's Ossopit, Oss-o-pit. It's a wee bit difficult but just think of 'opposite' and then sort of say it backwards: opposite—Ossopit."

"I'm most grateful, madam," said the sparrow and flew off twittering to himself: "Opposite, ossitup, ottupus, oissopit," until he finally got back to his famishing friends.

"Do tell us, sparrow," they all cried.

"Yes," chirped the sparrow, "It's definitely 'ossitup', n . . . no . . . oittuisip, n . . . no . . . oippisuit . . . Oh dear, I give up. So very sorry."

By now the animals were desperate. Just imagine them all sitting round the gorgeous tree and unable to pick any of its mouth-watering fruits.

Suddenly up spoke the tortoise. "I shall go," he said. "I know it will take a bit of time but I will not forget the name once I've been told. My family has the finest reputation in the world for good memories."

"No," they moaned. "You are too slow. We shall all be dead by the time you get back."

"Why not let me take tortoise on my back?" asked the zebra. "I'm hopeless at remembering things but my speed is second to none. I'll have him back here in no time at all." They all thought this was a splendid idea and so off raced the zebra with the tortoise clinging to his back.

"Good morning, Madam Jemma," said the tortoise. "I'm sorry I have no time to alight. But if we don't get the name of that tree most of

us will be dead by tonight. That's why I've come on zebra's back. He's a bit faster than I am, you know."

"Yes, I rather think he is," smiled old Jemma benignly.

"Well, it's Ossopit. Just think of 'opposite' and then sort of say it backwards, like this: opposite—Oss-o-pit."

"Just let me repeat it three times before I go," said the tortoise, "just to see if I get it right." And then he said it very, very slowly, deliberately and loudly, and nodding his tiny head at each syllable:

"Oss-o-pit, oss-o-pit, oss-o-pit."

"Bravo!" said Jemma, "you'll never forget it now."

And she was right.

The zebra thudded back hot foot and the tortoise was never in any doubt that he had the name right at last.

"It's Oss-o-pit," he announced to his ravenous friends.

"Ossopit, ossopit, ossopit," they all cried. "It's an ossopit tree, and it's perfectly safe to eat." And they all helped themselves to the wonderful fruit. You just can't imagine how delicious it tasted.

And to show how grateful they were, they appointed the tortoise Chief Adviser on Important Matters (he has C.A.I.M. after his name). And he still is Chief Adviser to this very day.

You might also enjoy seeing a picture book version of this story: *The Name of the Tree* by Celia Barker Lottridge. Art by Ian Wallace. Macmillan, 1989.

STRANGE EVENTS IN THE LIFE OF THE DELMONICO FAMILY:
THE BIRTHDAY PRESENT

Margaret Mahy

This story also works well as a traditional story without props. Each person in the audience can see his or her own version of the wizard and Mr. Delmonico and the birthday present, but what fun it is to show each animal, and then the monster at the end.

One morning a word-wizard was walking home from a successful all-night wizards' party given to open the Monster Sale at the Wizards' Bargain Stores. He heard voices coming through an open window. Mr. and Mrs. Delmonico were having breakfast and discussing important business. The word-wizard, who liked to know about other people's business, stopped and listened carefully.

"Our dear twins are growing up," sighed Mrs. Delmonico. "Sarah is so dashing with her beautiful black curls and shining eyes, and Francis is every bit her equal. He says he wants to be an astronomer and study comets. Do you think that is a good career for a boy?"

"I would rather he went into real estate," Mr. Delmonico replied. "There is a lot of money in land."

"And what shall we give the twins for their birthday?" Mrs. Delmonico went on. "What about a pet of some kind? Children love a pet."

Mr. Delmonico did not want his twins, Sarah and Francis, to have pets, but he did not like to argue with his wife. He decided to get his own way by cunning.

"What a good idea!" he exclaimed. "I wish I could have ideas like yours, my dear. What sort of pet do you have in mind?"

"A pony perhaps," Mrs. Delmonico said doubtfully, but her husband replied:

"What a pity! You know I can't stand creatures with eight legs."

"But, Mr. Delmonico, my love, horses don't have eight legs. You're thinking of spiders."

"Oh!" said Mr. Delmonico rather crossly, "How many legs do they have then?"

"Four each," Mrs. Delmonico told him.

Mr. Delmonico smiled. "But we'd have to get two ponies—one for Sarah and one for Francis. Two horses with four legs each. That makes eight I'm sure you'll agree, my dear."

"Oh goodness me, yes, so it does," sighed Mrs. Delmonico.

("This man is a very tricky customer!" thought the word-wizard, listening carefully.)

"Well then, what about a dog?" asked Mrs. Delmonico.

"A dog!" muttered Mr. Delmonico, pretending to consider. "The trouble with dogs is their barking."

"Oh, Mr. Delmonico, a dog's bark is harmless."

"No," Mr. Delmonico replied quickly, "I understand a dog's bark can be worse than his bite, and not only that—dogs are well known for barking up the wrong tree. I don't think a dog would suit this family. We've got so many trees in the garden the poor dog would wear himself out trying to find the right tree to bark up. No. I don't think a dog would do."

"Well, what about a kitten?" asked Mrs. Delmonico, crunching toast daintily. "Kittens are pretty and, besides, they're a good investment. Cats have nine lives, you know."

"True! True!" answered Mr. Delmonico, supping his hot coffee. "But they have their disadvantages. You know how any music on the violin brings on my hay fever."

"But dear, what does a violin have to do with a kitten for the twins?"

"Don't you remember, 'Hey diddle diddle, the cat and the fiddle'?" Mr. Delmonico cried.

"But, dear Mr. Delmonico, that was only one cat," his wife protested.

"If one can play the fiddle, they all can," Mr. Delmonico declared. "I don't fancy taking the risk. Besides, they're so everyday and all over the place, cats. How about something more unusual?"

"What do you say to a lion, then?" Mrs. Delmonico asked. "Lions are very beautiful and very brave. There is a well-known saying, 'As bold as a lion.'"

"Oh my dear," Mr. Delmonico exclaimed, laughing, "the real saying is, 'Bald as a lion.' Lions are only beautiful to begin with. On their

second birthdays they suddenly go instantaneously bald, and the chairs and the carpets are covered in lion hair."

Mrs. Delmonico supped a cup of tea in a disappointed fashion. "I should hate that," she said. "Perhaps we'd better get the twins a pet next year."

"Goodness me, what a woman you are for good ideas," cried Mr. Delmonico. "You are very wise, my dear. Leave the twins' birthday presents to me."

("Well," thought the wizard, "here's a man who uses words for the purposes of confustication. Here's a man who chops words and changes meanings. A word-wizard can't stand for that. I'll teach him a lesson. Let me see now—what can I contrive?")

The wizard tossed an idea into the air. It buzzed off like a mosquito, over the lawn, straight to Mr. Delmonico and stung him on the end of his nose.

Mr. Delmonico brought his twins, Sarah and Francis, presents beginning with C, like camera and crayons, clarinets and comics, and a great big fire-engine-red Christmas cracker. It had a black label on it, saying: "Beware. Monster Cracker."

"I bought it at the Wizards' Bargain Store Monster Sale," Mr. Delmonico said. "I can't wait to see what's inside it."

Francis took one end, and Sarah took the other. They pulled and they pulled and they pulled and they pulled, and then, suddenly, the cracker burst with a snap and a roar like a cannon let off in a cave full of echoes. The room filled with smoke and the smell of gunpowder.

But when the smoke cleared away, there, sitting in the middle of the floor, was a monster.

It had eight legs and carried a violin tucked under its chin. It wore a collar and tie and had a hundred teeth, all sharp. It had horns and hairy ears, but the top of its head was quite bald. It smiled at Sarah and Francis and barked.

"A monster! A monster!" cried the twins. "At last we've got a pet. Thank you, thank you, darling Father."

Mr. Delmonico had to let them keep it, of course, but he couldn't help feeling that someone had got the better of him after all.

THE COWS

Place Paul on his rock and the animals on the board as they appear in the story. Encourage your audience to join in and make the animal sounds. This story is particularly appropriate for preschoolers, or for older children who are learning English or wish to tell their own stories to younger children.

Paul called to the cows in the meadow. "Come home, cows."

The cows continued to graze.

Paul sat on a rock in front of the barn and cried "Boo Hoo."

A cat walked up to Paul and asked, "Why are you crying?"

"I'm crying because the cows won't come home."

"I'll help you," said the cat. She ran to the field and "Meoowed."

The cows continued to graze.

Paul sat on a rock and cried. The cat cried too.

A dog walked up to Paul and asked, "Why are you crying?"

"I'm crying because the cows will not come home."

"I'll help you," said the dog. He ran to the field and barked "Bow Wow."

The cows continued to graze.

Paul sat on a rock in front of the barn and cried. The cat cried. The dog cried.

A duck waddled up to Paul and asked, "Why are you crying?"

"I'm crying because the cows won't come home."

"I'll help you," said the duck. She ran to the field and "Quacked."

The cows continued to graze.

Paul sat on a rock in front of the barn and cried. The cat cried. The dog cried. The duck cried.

A bee flew up to Paul and asked, "Why are you crying?"

"I'm crying because the cows will not come home."

"I'll help you," said the bee.

She flew to the field where the cows were grazing. She buzzed and buzzed and sat down on the rump of one of the cows.

"Buzz. Sting!"

The cow lumbered to the barn. The other two ran after her.

Paul stopped crying and laughed. "Thank you, Bee," he said.

The cat meowed, the dog barked, the duck quacked, and the cows mooed.

Booklist: Books to Use on Felt, Magnetic, and Velcro Boards

Bozylinsky, Hannah Heritage. *LaLa Salama: An African Lullaby in Swahili and English*. Art by author. Philomel, 1993. Add the animals as they appear in the lullaby.

Bright, Robert. *My Red Umbrella*. Art by author. Morrow, 1959. A small book to enlarge with board cutouts.

Carle, Eric. *The Very Hungry Caterpillar*. Art by author. World, 1970. An engaging story perfect for board telling.

Flack, Marjorie. *Ask Mr. Bear*. Art by author. Macmillan, 1958. Use gifts offered the animal as objects for the board.

Gibbons, Gail. *Tool Book*. Art by author. Holiday, 1982. Attach tools to the Velcro board as identified.

Ginsburg, Mirra. *Which Is the Best Place?* Art by Roger Duvoisin. Macmillan, 1976. Each animal chooses a location to rest that is best suited to it.

Godds, Siobhan. *Grandpa Bud*. Art by author. Candlewick, 1993. Banana sandwiches, Jell-o, ice cream, hot dogs, and chocolate cake can be put on your board.

Gunthorp, Karen. *Adam and the Wolf*. Art by Attilio Cassinelli. Doubleday, 1968. Adam tells stories to a wolf to keep from being eaten.

Hutchins, Pat. *Good-Night, Owl!* Art by author. Macmillan, 1972. Keep adding new birds to a tree as you tell the story.

Kroll, Steven. *The Biggest Pumpkin Ever.* Art by Jeni Bassett. Holiday, 1984. A felt pumpkin can be shown getting bigger and bigger.

Kulman, Andrew. *Red Light, Stop: Green Light Go.* Art by author. Simon & Schuster, 1993. Show the different vehicles that wait at the traffic light.

Kundhart, Dorothy. *Pudding Is Nice.* Art by author. Bookstore Press, 1975. Pictures of what the old man is thinking of can be used on the board. Originally published in 1933 (Harcourt) as *Junket Is Nice.*

Lacome, Julie. *Walking through the Jungle.* Art by author. Candlewick, 1993. Wild animals are the stars of this story.

Lewis, Richard. *In a Spring Garden.* Art by Ezra Jack Keats. Dial, 1989. Japanese haiku to show and recite.

The Little Red Hen/La Pequeña Gallina Roja, by Letty Williams; tr. by Doris Chávez and Ed Allen. Art by Herb Williams. Prentice, 1969. An old favorite retold in Spanish and English.

Mollel, Tololwa M. *The King and the Tortoise.* Art by Kathy Blankley. Clarion, 1993. The hare, the fox, the leopard, the elephant, and the tortoise all enter a contest. Who will win?

Rikys, Bodel. *Red Bear.* Art by author. Dial, 1992. Add colored objects to the bear.

Seuss, Dr. (pseud. for Theodor Seuss Geisel). *And to Think That I Saw It on Mulberry Street.* Art by author. Vanguard, 1937. Figures are added until the entire board is a grand parade.

Sharratt, Nick. *The Green Queen.* Art by author. Candlewick, 1992. Dress the queen for her walk.

Shaw, Charles G. *It Looked like Spilt Milk.* Art by author. Harper, 1947. A cloud can look like many things.

Slobodkina, Esphyr. *Caps for Sale.* Art by author. W. R. Scott, 1947. Caps and monkeys are the cutouts for this story of imitation.

Westcott, Nadine Bernard. *I Know an Old Lady Who Swallowed a Fly.* Art by author. Little, 1980. Add animals to this folksong.

Williams, Linda. *The Little Old Lady Who Was Not Afraid of Anything.* Art by Megan Lloyd. Crowell, 1986. A variant of "The Strange Visitor."

Wood, A. J. *Egg!* Art by Stella Stilwell. Little, 1993. Show the variety of eggs and the animals that hatch from them.

12 / Slides

The slide projector—what an ingenious invention! It's easy to operate and its flexibility enables you to mix and match slides at your convenience. Since you operate the machine, you control the speed of your presentation. The slide projector also enables a large group of children to see a small book or intricate illustration with great clarity. You can use your own slides: pictures taken to illustrate a poem or folktale, hand-drawn slides to create realistic or abstract pictures, or slides from your own collection to illustrate a booktalk. Commercially produced slides are available, too. The possibilities are endless. In fact, once you have become fascinated with slides, you might tend to overdo it! Many years ago, when I was just beginning in this field, I thought that using slides in the classroom was such a wonderful way to teach that I taught practically the whole quarter in the dark! Before too long I had to reevaluate my methods or be content never to see the faces of my students.

Equipment and Use

Start with a good piece of equipment. I've found that the carousel type of projector is one of the most versatile. Carousels hold a large number of slides and are easy to load and operate. A good machine enables you to go forward or reverse, to focus, or to voluntarily put a slide out of focus for effect. The machine is also relatively quiet. Some people like to combine their slides with a recorded sound track. I prefer to use slides and narrate them myself. This gives a certain intimacy and sense of sharing that is lost if both the visual and the audio are done mechanically. (It also lessens the chance of equipment failure, since two machines are twice as likely to break down as one!) If you do have a projector jam, or any other catastrophe, during a presentation, try to fix it, but if the machine is obviously out of commission move on to another subject that doesn't need slides. Familiarity with the operation of a slide projector will lessen the chances of failure. Be sure that you know, for instance, how to remove a jammed slide. A dime inserted into the center screw of the carousel tray loosens the tray for easy removal. Don't panic—this does not happen often.

For an effective presentation, I strongly recommend a remote control extension cord. Set the machine in the back of the room and stand in front of the room next to the screen. Don't worry about lighting; the audience will see enough of you from the light spilling over from the screen. Seeing you gives the group a further visual interpretation of the story. Your listeners can look at the pictures and at the same time see your animated expressions. As you tell the story, press the button that automatically advances the slide. It's like turning the page in a picture book. Do make sure the image is properly focused before beginning your presentation.

Copying

Although this generation has been exposed to many machines, there is still something fascinating about turning out the lights and turning on a magic projector. To produce your own slides you will need a 35mm camera, a copy lens, and high speed film. To ensure quality pictures use a tripod or copy stand to make certain the camera does not move during shooting. These copying kits are available commercially, or you can convert your own equipment. If you work for a school system, you might have access to a media center that owns copying equipment, or has personnel who will take the pictures for you. A photographic workshop may also be available in your community.

What to copy? You can copy pictures from books. You can copy art pictures, or pictures drawn by your own students, but whatever you choose, be cautious and avoid violating the author's or artist's copyright.

Handmade Slides

To realize the full potential of the projector, experiment with making your own slides by hand. Cardboard or plastic slide mounts can be purchased for a few pennies each. Three common sizes are: half frame, regular 35 mm, and 2 × 2 super slide size. The larger slide is easier to work with, of course, but different sizes add variety. Acetate cut to size can be mounted in the slide holders to produce a drawing surface. The holder is then sealed by using a low heat clothes iron around the edges. Use permanent ink felt pens to draw on your slides and let your imagination and creative instincts run wild.

For a variation on hand-drawn slides, you can draw pictures on a sheet of paper. Use a slide mount as a stencil to show the exact size of the opening. Press the paper with a sheet of transparent film through a thermofax machine that reproduces your pictures as transparencies. Now you can mount the pictures into the slide mounts. One of my students used this method by making tiny drawings to illustrate animal poems. Using the thermofax enables the artist to achieve finer lines and subtleties.

Glass slides, available at your camera store, offer a creative challenge. Between two pieces of thin glass you mount actual objects: moss, leaves, string, or paper cutouts. You can also make use of the fact that glass slides warm up when projected. This adds a dimension of texture and movement. Use a few drops of cooking oil between the slides, colored with food coloring. The heat of the slide projector will cause the oil to expand and move, giving a colorful, shifting illusion. To prevent the liquid from running into the machine, tape the glass together. Using glass or acetate, experiment with string, sequins, tissue paper, construction paper, gelatins, and any other interesting material you can think of. Remember that if the material is not transparent or translucent, it will appear as a silhouette on the screen. That's all right, of course. I'm just trying to spare you my experience of laboriously pasting strings of different colors to 2 × 2 mounts to give the appearance of a string web growing and contracting in multi-colored shapes. The string appeared solid and all the color turned out to be a black silhouette, but it was an intriguing effect anyway.

Photographic Slides

Take pictures of children acting out a poem or a story. Show them for your next storyhour. Sort through your private collection of slides. Will any of them fit naturally into a story you have already learned or would like to learn? Could the pictures you took on your trip to Germany introduce a Grimm's tale? Maybe your pictures of New York City would set the scene for a program featuring urban stories or books centered in and around New York. Have you been collecting pictures of rain, bridges, sunsets? They might fit into the mood of the stories you are telling at your next session. Always remember, however, that too few are better than too many. If your pictures are of poor quality—out of focus or overexposed—it's better to try again. Show only pictures you can be proud of, and don't tire your audience with too many. Whatever you do, don't subject your audience to the "home movie syndrome!"

Screens

Experiment with screens as well as slides. The rear projection screen will give an unusual effect in your presentations and eliminate the beam of light thrown from the back of the room. The screen is translucent; a piece of matte acetate or a white sheet will do. The slide projector is placed behind, instead of in front of, the screen. This way the storyteller can stand in front of the screen without fear of having the slide project directly on her or him. The rear projection screen is most useful to create unobstructive backgrounds. A single slide of a busy street, a quiet mountain, or a ship at sea can be projected throughout the story to set the scene.

If you feel ambitious, consider using two projectors and two screens or even three of each. Choose slides that complement each other to show at the same time, or actually plan a three-screen performance. Take a scene in three picture sections, with the idea of multiple projection. You may decide to use more than one screen simply to give continuity to your program. As one picture fades out, fade the next picture in. You will need an electronic switching device to control both projectors. Ask your local camera store or media department for information.

Another idea for projection is to hang a curved screen around your room—a white sheet hung on a rope will provide a reasonable substitute for a continuous screen. Or simply give a show on a wall, shifting the position of the projector for variety. Try showing your slides, handmade or photographed, on something other than a flat screen. You can experiment with tubes or cylinders made from construction paper taped to the wall. Or use the floor on which you have placed irregular shapes as a screen. You can even use your hands or body. Once you have made the decision to use slides, creative variety in using them may add a new element to the magic of storytelling.

13 / The Overhead Projector

The overhead projector is so versatile that in many instances it is actually replacing that age-old traditional teacher's helper, the chalkboard, probably because the overhead projector, unlike the slide projector, can be used effectively with the lights on. The storyteller may face the audience while writing or drawing on acetate and can also produce transparencies in advance, thereby saving time and allowing preparation of slides of greater clarity. I used the overhead as a teaching device in my children's literature classes for several years before it occurred to me to use it for storytelling; it opened a whole new world of possibilities. Some aspects of using the overhead may not occur to you while you're in the process of telling a story, so consider them in advance. Be sure that your transparencies are in order—they may have become mixed up after your last performance. Make certain that you stand to the side of the projector so that you don't block the screen from the audience. Make sure that the projector lens is in focus. It always amazes me that adults are often so polite that they will let you go through an entire session with your transparencies out of focus or with your arm blocking their view and never say a word. If you are working with children, you needn't worry about these problems. Children will always tell you if they can't see properly! Also make sure that you don't leave the overhead on without a transparency, so that all the audience sees as you talk is a distracting, glaring light. The same transparency should not be left on indefinitely. When your audience has received the information from the transparency, change it or turn off the machine. Most overheads have a fan that automatically turns itself on and off to cool the machine, so remember to speak loudly enough to be heard over the whir of the motor. Practice with your story and the transparencies so that you will give a smooth delivery. If you find yourself with a pile of transparencies but without an overhead, in a pinch you can always hold them up to a window for illumination—so long as your group is small enough. You can also mount them accordion fashion with a light behind them. As you tell your story, move the transparencies past the light.

Experiment with your overhead. The light reflector can be moved in many directions, enabling you to project up, down, and around. You can place acetate on the surface and write or draw on it while you talk. Some machines come equipped with a roll of acetate that rolls out of sight when not in use. You can place an opaque object on the overhead and its shape will project, thereby creating a shadow show. You can even use it to project liquid color, for a light show effect. And, of course, transparencies of all descriptions may be used.

I didn't want to tell this story in the chapter on slides, so I've saved this experience to relate in this chapter on transparencies. Several times in the last year I've wished that I was working with transparencies instead of slides. I've been giving a slide lecture on recent children's books, both around the United States and in various overseas locations. The slides show book jackets and selected pages from the books I am discussing. I also offer a printed list of the books in the order that they appear on the screen. Once the slides are arranged in the tray for projecting, it is quite time-consuming to change the order or eliminate any of the slides. Why does this matter? Well . . . I was invited to Saudi Arabia to lecture to the staff at the international schools. I brought with me my children's literature lecture, forgetting that this presentation includes pages from a children's book on the differences between males and females. As a consequence, I soon found myself in one of the most conservative countries in the world, projecting the naked bodies of men and women, 12 feet high, to my audience! If I had been using transparencies, I could have quickly shuffled through the pile until I found something more appropriate.

Uses

Light Show Magic

Take a clear glass pie dish and fill it with water. Float a few drops of food coloring and cooking oil on the water. Put the dish and its contents on an overhead and gently turn the dish. Magic shapes will appear on your screen or wall. Tell your story with the moving colors as a background, or simply play music as an accompaniment to the rhythmic designs.

Trace a Transparency

Use either prepared transparencies (these are cut to fit the overhead and mounted with a cardboard frame) or be more economical and buy a roll of acetate and some frames, separately. Materials are available in most art supply shops. You will also need felt pens. Oil-base pens are permanent; water-base pens are for temporary use, made to easily wipe off with a damp cloth. Choose a book that has simple line drawings. Place the acetate over the book and trace some of the pictures. Now you have reproduced pictures to be shown on an overhead projector. Color can be applied to the acetate with felt pens or even paint. The color should be even and translucent so that the light shows through. Make sure that you have a copy of the book available to hold up and show to the group before you show your transparencies and tell the story.

Photocopy Transparency Machines

Many school systems, libraries, and offices have access to machines that can produce transparencies from an original drawing or from photocopied portions of a book. The original sheet, together with a piece of transparency film, is run through the machine, producing a black-and-white image that you can later color with theatrical gelatins (available in stationery and theatrical supply stores) glued to the surface.

Again, be careful not to violate copyright restrictions when copying.

Another way to color your transparencies is to photocopy the art using a color copy machine. You will get a perfect copy from the original, which can then be made into a transparency. This is not an inexpensive process, but perhaps you can find a time when the print shop is running a sale, or maybe by the time you read this book, the color copier will be priced for the masses . . . us.

Overlays

It's possible to create an interesting effect by using one transparency on top of another. Using "Little Red Riding Hood" as an example, you could begin with a transparency of a little girl. The next layer could be her cloak. The next one the basket she carries. Leaving these three slides on the overhead you could add the wolf and so on. Remember too that you can use prepared transparencies and draw on an acetate overlay with a felt pen. You can create movement by having a single character or animal on one transparency and the background on another transparency. By moving one or the other, you can actually simulate animation.

Booklist: Books for Overhead Projector Use

Carle, Eric. *Draw Me a Star.* Art by author. Philomel, 1992. An artist draws a star and creates a universe. You and your children may draw stars on the overhead.

Crews, Donald. *Parade.* Art by author. Greenwillow, 1983. Use overlays to add the band, people, and floats of your own to create a parade.

Demarest, Chris L. *My Little Red Car.* Art by author. Boyds, 1992. A boy imagines driving with his little red car. Add your own background and use a silhouette of a car.

Gardner, Beau. *The Turn About, Think About, Look About Book.* Art by author. Lothrop, 1980. Turn the pages of the book around to create four different drawings. Can your children create their own?

Hoban, Tana. *Look! Look! Look!* Photos by author. Greenwillow, 1988. Peek-a-boo holes invite you to guess the object on the next page. Make your own "part to whole" pictures.

Johnson, Ryerson. *Kenji and the Magic Geese.* Art by Jean and Mou-sien Tseng. Simon, 1992. A goose flies off a picture. You can use an overlay to make a goose disappear and fly, or children can draw their own interpretations of this story for projection.

Pirotta, Saviour and Nancy Hellen. *Hey Riddle Riddle!* Art by Nancy Hellen. Bedrick/Blackie, 1989. Guess the animal in the riddle. Children can also make up their own riddles and draw pictures to go with them.

Ray, Mary Lyn. *Pumpkins.* Art by Barry Root. Harcourt, 1992. A man saves a field from development by planting pumpkins. You add pumpkins to the field and draw jack o'lanterns.

Rounds, Glen. *Old MacDonald Had a Farm.* Art by author. Holiday, 1989. Add your own animals to this classic folksong.

14 / Video and Film

Once when I was visiting my cousin in Brooklyn, the girl up the street invited us to her basement to see a film. I was awed that a plain ordinary person could show a film in her own home! Today, of course, almost everyone can view a film in their own home. Television and the videocassette recorder (VCR) have given us this privilege.

Still, it is thrilling to go someplace to view a movie with others. Children especially consider a film a special treat. A storytelling film program is likely to attract a large number of children to your library, and is always a favorite classroom treat.

Commercial Videos and Films

There are many good production companies, small and large, producing good and not-so-good films and videos. It takes time and much critical viewing to choose a film or video for a particular group. Since the objective of a book program is to introduce or enrich a child's experience with books, an obvious choice for your program is a film or video based on a children's book or story.

Choosing a Video or Film

Some excellent films based on children's books have been made. Some use animation; some have actors; and some are iconographic, actually filming the book, but moving the camera in and around the illustrations to give the illusion of movement. The length of a film or video may be important if you have a scheduling problem such as a school class period. Film lengths range from three and four minutes to two hours. If you decide to use several short picture-book films, you may want to use both iconographic and animated films (real actors are used primarily in longer stories). You may want to keep a particular theme for your film and video program, perhaps animal stories, fairy tales, adventure stories. If you decide to combine films and storytelling, tell your stories first, then show the film. It may be that the story you tell will remain in the children's memory, but a film or video, particularly if it is of high quality, is momentarily more exciting.

Films and videos are not as easy to evaluate as books; you can't usually cuddle up with one on the beach or on a camping trip, but previewing all films before you use them is an absolute necessity. Unhappy surprises can await you if you depend on the brief description in a dealer's catalog. Films with live actors become quickly dated as hairstyles and fashions change. No matter how good the story or message, if the people are supposed to be in a present-day setting and look dated and old-fashioned, children will become distracted. Even a film with a historical fiction setting can become dated. Today's dialogue moves faster, audiences are trained to assume the passage of time, instead of being shown the pages of a calendar flipping. Films that have a lecturer sitting immobile behind a desk will rarely hold the attention of a group. Even the films or videos you used two years ago should be reviewed again to make sure they are still appropriate. Many books and professionals give a long checklist to be used when previewing a film, and while these may be useful, my personal advice is that if you actually watch a film or video, you will know best if it fits your group's needs and interests. Do you like it? Show it.

Showing a Video or Film

Showing a Video

Although many libraries and classrooms are equipped with television monitors, the television media is not always effective unless each and every spectator can see the screen easily. The usual formula given is one monitor for every 25 viewers, but this depends on the size of the screen and the arrangement of the room. It sounds obvious to say that if you use video you should be able to see the screen, but you've probably been at presentations where you couldn't see the screen. When you're in charge this shouldn't happen.

The statistics tell us that 80 percent of U.S. households have a VCR. This means that most of your audience will be able to help you when there is a problem with a videotape. On the other hand, because so many people have access to videos, they may not seem as magical and different as the large screen used for showing a film.

Showing a Film

There are several different formats of film, but the most popular for theater, classroom, or library viewing is the largest size, the 16mm.

Remember that to show a film you will need the film, the proper projector, a screen, and often an extension cord. I usually bring a cord and an adapter (for three prong plugs), even if I've been promised the proper equipment. It's frustrating to arrive at a location and find that the cord doesn't reach to the plug outlet.

Now you are ready to show the film. No one wants to hear a long lecture before a film, but some sort of introduction is in order. You might mention why you chose the film, or explain that it is similar in theme to the rest of the program. Perhaps it has won a prize, or uses an interesting technique. If the book is based on a film, point out that the library has a copy or even several copies of the book to circulate. Other books by the author, or books on the same theme, may also be exhibited.

If there is more than one film on the program, introduce each film just before the showing. Don't try to make announcements or speeches after the program, unless it is to remind the audience of the next program, since people are usually ready to leave after the last film.

Be prepared for the worst. Although films and film projectors seem to be magic, something can go awry. The film can break, the sound can blur. If some disaster of this sort should happen, try to repair the damage, keeping the audience posted of your valiant efforts. People are more patient if they know the cause of the delay. If the damage is irreparable it is better to abandon the film than show one that is impossible to understand. You will now be happy that you are a storyteller, since you can always tell a story in place of the film. However, having the proper equipment and knowing how to run it is still the best insurance against technical problems.

Making Videos or Films
With a Video Camera

I live in a resort area that attracts tourists from all over the world. It's difficult to tell what they look like, though, since every third person is holding a camcorder up to his eyes. I get the impression that the world is observing us through a camera lens.

Everyone can now produce his own videos. It is as simple as pointing the camera. In addition, the cameras are getting smaller and lighter, so they are easy to tote along for "on location" shots.

After you have filmed the baby's first steps and the new puppy, perhaps you will want to think about uses for your new toy that relate to storytelling and book promotion.

Consider filming your students giving their own booktalks, reciting poems, or telling stories. Videos or films can help with storytelling training too. Tell a story to the camera and critique yourself. Record over your efforts and no one will know that you were once an amateur! Or save your first story on tape and watch it from time to time to remind yourself how far you've come. If you run for president of the United States or prime minister of Canada, someone may want to show your story tape on national television during your campaign!

Filmmaking or videotaping can be divided into technical and creative activities. The person who enjoys fiddling with equipment may not be the same person who enjoys the creative aspect of filmmaking. Most of us, however, can't afford to sit in a chair marked "Producer" or "Director" thinking creative thoughts. You'll have to learn a little about both operations in order to begin. This is the important part: if you think you might be interested in filmmaking, begin with an inexpensive or secondhand camera, and, if you enjoy the process and are pleased with the effort, you can take filmmaking more seriously.

Start small. Don't try for too much action at first. If possible, film outdoors in sunlight—it's simply easier than trying to learn about indoor lighting. Hold your camera steady or use a tripod. You must plan what to shoot. Nursery rhymes or simple familiar fairy tales, such as "The Three Bears," make good subjects to begin with. Use your own storytelling group as the actors or make your film the culmination of a project in creative dramatics. You might choose one of the creative drama activities given in chapter 26 to begin.

Without a Camera

Fiddle-de-dee, a short film put out by the National Film Board of Canada, provided me with my first glimpse into the fascinating world of making films without a camera. The filmmaker, Norman McLaren, pioneered work in animation and drawing directly onto the film to produce fascinating effects. Lines of color drawn directly on the film surface seem to dance to the sound of music. Some adults who are accustomed to a story line have difficulty relating to this abstract art; most children, however, appreciate that not all of life needs to have an understandable theme. They let their imaginations go and simply enjoy what they see on the screen.

I thought it might be fun to try one of these films. As a student with a limited budget, I naturally wanted to experiment as cheaply as possible. I used discarded, overexposed film from the university film department and spliced bits and pieces together. If you do splice, be sure to keep the sprocket holes matched. I tried to time my film to music, laboriously counting the frames per second. My first effort was terribly time-consuming and resulted in only three minutes worth of film, but it was really fun to do. There are several techniques that may be used.

SCRATCH FILMS

If you have access to discarded 16mm film that is underexposed or black, you can try the scratch film technique. A good source of film is a motion picture processing laboratory, so use the yellow pages of your phone book to find the one nearest you. If underexposed 16mm film is not available, the motion picture processing laboratory may sell black leader for sound films (single or double perforation) in rolls of 150 or more feet. The cost for scrap film or black leader should be a few cents per foot.

Take a knife, stylus, or scissors blade and scratch away the exposed emulsion at random. One way to determine the film's emulsion side is to wet your finger and touch it to the film. The surface that sticks to your finger is the emulsion side. Strips, blotches, and spots all create interesting designs that project shapes onto the screen. You may want to experiment a bit, attempting to put film to music. Keep in mind that 24 frames (or seven inches of film) equal one second. If you want to set your scratch film to music, theoretically you time sections of the music, then measure off the amount of film, and start scratching, but my own experience is that almost any fast music will fit your handmade film since the abstract blobs and blotches seem to follow any jazzy beat. My advice, therefore, is to experiment with your first film. Find out if you enjoy working with the medium. And, after you have produced a few minutes of film, you can move on to a more sophisticated method.

HAND-DRAWN FILMS

Now that you have tried the scratch-film technique and found out how much fun it is, you are ready for a more advanced method. Buy clear 16mm film from the motion picture laboratory or film processor, or, if you have access to discarded film, you can always bleach it yourself. Dip the unrolled film into a strong solution of household bleach. Wait several seconds, then rinse it under water, and hang it up to dry.

Any water-soluble coloring—felt pens, colored inks, watercolors, food coloring—will work on the film. Again, draw on the emulsion side. I prefer working with felt pens, since these dry faster than the other media.

Felt pens and film, now what? You can continue with the idea of setting your work to music or try illustrating a story, perhaps "Little Red Riding Hood," for example. A red circle can represent the heroine, and a somewhat larger blue circle can be mother. Don't forget Little Red Riding Hood's basket—a small orange circle. Now you need the forest, represented by green lines and multicolored dots for the flowers. Depict the wolf as a large black circle and grandmother as a purple oblong shape. When the wolf eats the grandmother, put the purple shape inside the black circle. The woodcutter who saves the girl and her grandmother can be a brown circle. A good way to represent the conflict between the wolf and the woodcutter is a series of frames with black fragments flying all about in each.

How to begin. Measure 14 inches of masking tape and affix it to your worktable. This represents two seconds of film time, and enables you to instantly calculate, or guesstimate, film time. The blank film will probably be rolled up on a metal reel. As you work on the film, just let it drop off the edge of your worktable and spill onto the floor. (If you find that this has become a hobby, not just an experiment, you can rent a hand-operated film viewer, which will also have a take-up reel, to examine your work in progress.)

Now time the text of the story. This does not need to be completely accurate but more time allowed, rather than less, for each scene is advised. To say, "This is Little Red Riding Hood," takes about five seconds, which is approximately 2½ feet of film, or 120 frames. Using your masking tape guide of 14 inches, or two seconds, you will have to draw 2½ feet of red circles, one inside each frame.

I strongly advise that if you go beyond the abstract stage and get into a text, that you find a corner where you can set up a permanent worktable. When I used to create films more frequently, I would find an odd 10 minutes here and there, just before dinner, just before going to bed, and so forth. I would go into my workshop (the utility room), draw on a foot or so of film, then leave everything as I found it and go on with my life. Eventually the film is finished.

The ultimate in handmade films is the laborious process of actually drawing a story. Each action must be repeated countless times for it to appear as a smooth action to the eye. For this kind of film, you will need, besides the proper equipment, infinite patience and a steady hand.

Your children's book group may be inspired to try this non-camera kind of filmmaking, too. You can give each child a length of film to work with or you can let a child work on the film and when he or she finishes, give it to the next child. This eliminates splicing together several short lengths of film. However, if it is more convenient to give each child a separate length of film to work on, the children can learn how to splice the film themselves.

A Final Word

Obviously it would take an entire book to explore the intricacies of making a video or film with camera or without. The basic rule here, as elsewhere, is that you must jump in and try it. Start simply and you may find yourself fascinated and ready to devote some extra time to a new technique. While I have found few recent books on making films, Jacques Bourgeois' *Simple Film Animation with or without a Camera* (Sterling, 1979) offers a complete guide to drawing on film. An extensive list of books on making videos, plus a list of film and video reviews, is given below.

Booklist: Video Production

Fuller, John. *Prescription for Better Home Video Movies: How to Avoid the Most Common Mistakes.* Art by Erv Zackman. HP Books, 1988. A news cameraman gives practical and easy-to-follow advice for home video producers.

Levine, Pamela, Jeffrey Glasser and Stephan Gach. *The Complete Guide to Home Video Production.* Holt, 1984. "A ten-step plan for making your own movies."

Make Your Own . . . Videos, Commercials, Radio Shows, Special Effects and More by the Fun Group. Art by Ellen Saski. Grosset, 1992. Sample scripts and hints for creating home videos.

Schwartz, Perry. *How to Make Your Own Videos.* Lerner, 1991. Designed for the home video enthusiast, this book gives some technical information as well as practical advice.

Staples, Terry. *Film and Video.* Warwick, 1986. A technical survey and short history of the film/video industry.

Thomas, Erwin Kenneth. *Make Better Videos with Your Camcorder.* Art by Geralyn Yost. TAB Books, 1991. Picture composition, lighting, and audio problems are surveyed.

Booklist: Film and Video Reviews

ALSC Notable Films/Videos, Filmstrips, Recordings, and Software 1992 and YALSA Selected Films for Young Adults. ALA. Yearly selection by American Library Association Committees.

AV Marketplace. *The Complete Business Directory of Audio, Audio Visual, Film, Video Programming.* Bowker, 1989. Services and products.

Educational Film and Video Locator. 4th ed. Bowker, 1990. Lists 3,361 videos and films.

Gallant, Jennifer Jung. *Best Videos for Children and Young Adults: A Core Collection for Libraries.* ABC-Clio, 1990. Annotates the author's selection of 350 best videos.

Green, Diana Huss, ed. *Parent's Choice Magazine Guide to Video Cassettes for Children.* Consumer Reports Books, 1989. Lists videos by genre.

Hunt, Mary Alice. *A Multimedia Approach to Children's Literature: A Selective List of Films (and Videocassettes), Filmstrips, and Recordings Based on Children's Books.* 3rd ed. American Library Assn., 1983. Still a useful tool for the multimedia storyhour program.

School Library Journal. Bowker (Box 1426, Riverton, NJ 08077). Reviews film, videocassettes and multimedia kits 10 times a year.

15 / Television and Radio

On any given day, winter or summer, you will find the restaurants and bars of Miami Beach overflowing with people. So where is everyone today? Home, watching the World Series!

No matter where you go in the world, if there is electricity there is bound to be a television set and someone watching. In fact, statistics tell us that children spend more time watching television than any other activity. So instead of fighting it, let's think of ways to use television to our advantage.

There are, from time to time, really excellent children's specials on commercial television, carefully produced films that are based on children's books. Although television viewing is usually considered a home activity, many schools, libraries and other institutions own television sets. Since virtually every child in the United States has access to a television set, it is probably unnecessary and even intrusive to have a television set in the reading room of the library. My branch library in California was given a giant screen television by a local company. It was constantly playing the same cartoon that children could view in their own homes. I personally was insulted by its presence. It reminded me of George Orwell's "Big Brother Is Watching You." However, there were always children sprawled on the floor in front of it, cheering the hapless cartoon characters on. Keeping informed of good programs can sometimes be a problem if you are not in the habit of reading the television section of your newspaper or *TV Guide*, but you might make it a practice to check the listings from time to time. After all, if a television show is based on a children's book, wouldn't it be nice to have the book available for your children?

Occasionally watch some of the more popular programs yourself; then think of books that might have the same appeal or a theme that is similar to a particular series. A family series might suggest the Laura Ingalls Wilder Little House books (of course there was an actual television series based on the Little House books too). An adventure series might suggest an adventure book display. Exhibit such books with a sign that draws a comparison to a favorite TV series. And if a children's show or any other program host features a book on the show, why not prominently display a copy of that book, as well as other titles by the same author?

You might remember, too, that if you like or dislike something on television, a letter to the local station and network will usually be appreciated and noticed.

Public television was in the past sometimes referred to as "educational television," but that seemed to mean that its programs were not entertaining; now we say "public television" and more viewers tune in as a result. Surprisingly, it was children's television that finally made public television come alive for many people. After years of mediocre children's offerings on commercial television, the Children's Television Workshop produced *Sesame Street*, a series designed to provide an educational opportunity for culturally deprived preschool children. The program was an instant success, and six months into the first season the Nielsen rating survey indicated that it was watched by over half of America's 12 million three- to five-year-olds. This daily program has inspired similar ones for the primary grades. *Reading Rainbow* (P.O. Box 80669, Lincoln, NE 68501) is a series entirely based on children's books. Hosted by actor LeVar Burton, each program focuses on a special theme. It was exciting to watch one of the books I edited, *Snowy Day: Stories and Poems*, "live" on *Reading Rainbow*. The strength of the program is that the viewers are allowed to bring their own reactions. There are no play-by-play descriptions of the action, as there is with sports competitions. A scene showing children enjoying the snow has no extraneous commentary. Viewing the show and then reading the books makes a complete package.

Locally produced programs for children are increasing. For instance, in Oregon the Oregon Educational Public Broadcasting System offered a series designed for in-school viewing developed as a traditional storytelling program. In its first season the

Oregon Library Association donated funds to help make the series available after school as well. The program, *Caroline's Corner*, was simply conceived. The storyteller told a traditional folktale in a rather stark setting, relying on the words of the stories and facial expressions to carry the show.

In this age of advanced technology the producer of the show (I'll confess, it was me) was a bit worried that without any films, slides, puppets, or other paraphernalia the show would not be well received. Instead it turned out to be quite a success. A viewer's guide for *Caroline's Corner* was also offered, suggesting further reading and related individual and group activities for each of the shows.

The public library in Portland (Multnomah County Library), Oregon, successfully produced its own storytelling series for Sunday morning viewing. Using its own children's librarians as talent, the show's format included reading and showing picture books, riddles, and simple songs. Perhaps your community has interesting storytelling programs too. If not, why not start one yourself?

Producing a Television Show

If you should have the opportunity to do a single show or a series of shows for an educational or commerical television station, be prepared for a new and challenging experience!

The storyteller (or talent) is only one of the many people who make a television program possible. There are camera operators, a floorperson (who gives time cues and directs the performer from camera to camera), audio engineers (who control the sound), switchers (who put the picture on the air), the director (who is responsible for the entire production), and the engineer (who ultimately puts the show on tape and into homes). There may be a producer and even an executive producer (the program's idea people).

As the talent you may find the experience frustrating as well as exciting. You will be performing for an unseen audience and will be expected to be your most expressive for a red light on the lens of a television camera. At first I found it difficult to relate to machines. Even the people in the studio seemed mechanical. When I finished a program I'd say to the camera operator, "Did you like that story?" He would apologize and explain that he didn't hear the story, but only saw it. The same was true of the audio engineer. He heard the story, but didn't see it, and anyway he didn't actually listen. Sometimes I would invite a friend or two to the studio and I'd play to them. Afterwards I found they didn't listen either. They were much too interested in the complicated process of filming a show. Finally, after several years of television experience, I reached the right attitude. The lens of the camera is a "person," the one individual to whom you are talking. The lens may represent hundreds or even thousands of viewers, but you must feel that you are talking to just one person. Look directly into the camera, not at the floorperson or the monitor. If it is your first time on television, you'll probably be better off not having a monitor in view. People get so fascinated seeing themselves on TV that they start watching themselves, instead of performing.

In today's television studios a hectic pace is kept at all times. If you are invited to appear on someone's show you may not even meet the host until it is time to appear. As a consultant for a large bookstore chain, I was asked to tour the live daytime talk shows. I hadn't realized what a big business television was until they flew me to New York for "media message training." This tutoring showed me how to get my message in as quickly as possible since the segments on these shows are only two to three minutes in duration. I was told that I must give "my message" as quickly as I could lest an earthquake, typhoon, or war pre-empt my time. Usually I was escorted onto the set during the commercial break and was hurriedly introduced to the host of the show who had only a cue card to alert her to my purpose. Typically I was sandwiched in between the "pet of the month" and the "diet tip of the week!"

When a show is taped, however, there is usually more time allotted, so the show has a better chance of achieving perfection. This will mean a rehearsal, and often many delays while lights are arranged and the sound adjusted. It's possible that you might make a mistake, but there is a chance to re-do your mistake with tape. There may be a makeup person to help you with your make-up. If not, I suggest that women use their street makeup. If you are accustomed to wearing eyeshadow, be sparing, as it can make your eyes look cavernous. Larger television stations often have newer, sophisticated equipment that can tape almost anything, but the local station may own older cameras so don't wear clothing that is shiny or terribly bright.

If you are thinking of using children on the show, you should be aware that they probably will be awed by the equipment and may not perform as they usually do. Don't try to get too carried away with props and special effects unless you have many people to help you. Because television is a visual medium there is a great temptation for amateurs to over-visualize a show. A single narrator articulately explaining a process or describing an event can be more effective than a poorly filmed or amateurishly drawn picture. Remember that the screen on which people will see your show is very small.

Studio television requires an entire production staff to produce the simplest of programs. In my storytelling series I told stories without the aid of props on a simple set, and yet many people were involved in the taping of each program. If you are involved in even the simplest professional production you will need the following personnel:

Executive producer: Responsible for executive decisions that initiate a series or program.

Producer: Responsible for getting together the people, the content, and the props for a series or program.

Director: Coordinates the activities of all the people involved in production. Makes the artistic selection of images and sound for program airing.

Camera operators: Operate the studio cameras on the director's command.

Talent: The person or persons who perform in front of the cameras.

Floorperson: Gives hand signals to the talent that indicate when and in which direction to move or look and how much time remains in the program. The floorperson is the communication link between the director and the talent.

Audio engineer: Responsible for the audio portion of the program. This includes musical backgrounds and sound levels for the talent.

Boom operator: Operates an overhead microphone in the studio.

Video engineer: Responsible for the technical quality of television images.

Lighting technician: Responsible for studio lighting.

Switcher: Switches and mixes images on director's command.

Videotape operator: Operates and maintains videotape machine. Controls the electronic side of editing.

Chain engineer: Responsible for feeding film clips and slides onto videotape.

Graphic designers: Create the visuals, including slide titles.

Set designer: Responsible for designing the studio set.

Don't be awed by this mob of people. They are there to help you put on a fine production. Think of the small family group that used to hear a storyteller's voice. With the aid of television you can tell stories in thousands of homes at once. Keep your part in the performance simple and, above all, have fun.

Booklist: Television

Blumenthal, Howard J. *Careers in Television.* Little, 1992. Survey of the many jobs in the television industry.

Brown, Marc. *The Bionic Bunny Show.* Art by Krasny Brown. Little, 1984. This story follows a rabbit who is an actor on a television series.

Calabro, Marian. *Zap! A Brief History of Television.* Four Winds, 1992. Discusses the origins of television and explores different kinds of programming.

Gibbons, Gail. *Lights! Camera! Action! How a Movie Is Made.* Art by author. Crowell, 1985.

Hautzig, Esther. *On the Air: Behind the Scenes at a Television Newscast.* Photos by David Hautzig. Macmillan, 1991. Photo essay showing a day in the life of a TV newscaster.

Radio

Radio is no longer the glamour child of the communications industry, but what would we do without it? Storytelling is particularly well suited to this medium.

Those of us who grew up in the days of the radio soap operas, *Jack Armstrong,* and *Let's Pretend* know that we didn't need television to stimulate our imaginations. In fact, no television show or film could possibly reproduce the worlds we imagined when listening to a radio story. Storytelling is still a success on radio, as Garrison Keillor's immensely popular radio programs on National Public Radio prove.

There are great advantages for you, the storyteller, on radio. Since there is no viewing audience you can read the story aloud, although I still think there is no substitution for the spontaneity of storytelling without a script. If you are interested in radio work, I think the best way to get started is by visiting the program manager of a local radio station and suggesting that your library or school would like to have a storytelling show. Keep in mind, of course, that your ideas may receive better reception if you are willing to volunteer your own time and energy.

The Federal Communications Commission (FCC) encourages broadcasters to sponsor local programming, and many stations look for qualified individuals to appear on their stations. My first job on radio was doing a free weekly children's storytelling program. When a vacancy came up for a general announcer, I got that job, and the experience I gained was invaluable training for teaching and later for television work.

One of the more difficult things to learn is the matter of timing. Everything is blocked out into segments and your show has to fit into a prescribed slot. At first you may find it difficult to time yourself exactly. This becomes easy with practice and after a few tries you will find yourself speaking in fifteen-minute intervals, even at parties or on the job.

Almost any of your favorite stories will work on radio. Remember that you can't show illustrations on radio, so choose a story that does not rely on visuals. Be sure you give credit to the authors, publishers, and books that you use, and ask for copyright permission if necessary.

16 / Puppetry

And now, ladies and gentlemen, our featured speaker!

Heads turn to the back of the room where a black shrouded figure makes her way down the aisle and steps up on stage.

Two puppets pop out from under the cloth and lament the fact that children don't read enough anymore.

This odd entrance is greeted either with puzzled expressions or applause—depending on the audience. It's an arresting use of puppets, however, guaranteed to make an impression. Anyone who has used a puppet to introduce a story, present a booktalk, or give a puppet show knows that children (and adults) are fascinated with the way a seemingly inanimate object is suddenly imbued with life.

One of my best puppet memories of all is from a presentation I made to a special education class in a preschool in Alaska. I was to tell stories to a group of children, but one of them was not quite ready to listen, for she was having a tantrum. My first instinct was to let the teacher handle the situation, but since I was holding a cat puppet, I began to meow instead. The little girl was fascinated, and she became quiet immediately. It made me (and my cat!) feel good to make such an impression on a child.

Another time, my husband, Peter, and I became the awed audience. We were traveling on the island of Bali in Indonesia. I had made friends with a Swiss traveler, who invited us to visit a village in the mountains where he was staying the night. At dinner I asked our host, the headman of the village, if he knew of any *wayang kulit* (shadow puppet) performances in the area. He very helpfully wrote down the name of a puppeteer and his village several kilometers away. The next day, Peter and I rented a motor scooter and, with the aid of some creative sign language, found our way to the village. We didn't find anyone who spoke English, but we did find the *dalang*, or puppet master. When he read the note from our host in the mountains, he immediately clapped his hands and two men went sprinting off into the jungle. They returned minutes later with a banana tree. With machete-type knives they stripped the leaves from the trunk and brought it to a little outdoor stage. Word of our arrival and the start of a play brought the villagers, old and young, to the theater. We were seated on the stage itself, while others sat cross-legged on the ground below or on the bank above the stage. Although it was broad daylight and these kinds of puppet shows are usually given at night, we were seated in such a way that we could see both the shadow side and the working side of the puppets. The puppeteer put two pieces that looked much like chessmen between his toes, using them to create a drumlike sound on the horizontal tree trunk. Two other men played cymbals and a fourth the xylophone. The puppeteer sang a chant and then began to tell a story and manipulate the puppets. Although we didn't understand the language, it was easy to follow the action. The puppets swayed slowly during romantic scenes, and fought in what must have been a fierce battle. It was a thrilling performance, and both Peter and I found ourselves caught up in the drama of the story.

Before we mounted our scooter to return to our hotel, we were treated to a demonstration of puppet making by our host. These shadow puppets are made from flat pieces of dried buffalo hide. Tiny holes are hammered into the hide so that light will come through the figures. The characters represented are stock figures that have been used for centuries.

We now have two of these puppets on the wall of our living room. As I walk through the room I remember the soft hollow sound of the banana trunk, and the consummate skill of the *dalang*.

You may not have the training, talent, or skill of an Indonsesian puppet master, but I promise you that your children will long remember the show you put on in your library or classroom, just as I remember the power of a play in a language I couldn't even begin to understand.

As storyteller—teacher, librarian, parent, or helpful volunteer—you may enjoy learning to make and use puppets; incorporating puppetry into your storytelling presentations. You may also wish to involve your students or perhaps a group of library patrons, by holding a puppet-making session and then helping your group to put on a puppet show. You'll find lots of useful tips, puppet patterns, and puppet show suggestions here.

Give puppetry a try.

The Puppet Tradition

Puppetry has been performed for education and entertainment for thousands of years. It thrived in the society of ancient Egypt and in the religious rituals of Greece and Rome. In all corners of the earth, puppets have survived as a major art form and theatrical institution. In Europe, famous puppet troupes entertain adults as well as children. In Austria's Salzburg, a permanent puppet theater offers entire operas performed by marionettes. The Japanese Bunraku puppets perform serious classical drama, while the Turkish shadow shows feature the comic characters Hachivat and Karaghioz. The Japanese puppets also perform as shadow shows in Java and Bali, as Peter and I discovered. The traditional puppets perform in long shows depicting good and evil characters: princes, gods, or kings at war with evil villains, witches, giants, and demons. In Thailand intricately costumed rod puppets perform in temple courtyards. Indian marionettes are manipulated by street performers from Delhi to Calcutta.

The United States has borrowed from other traditions and has, as well, created its own tradition. Early TV favorites included puppets Kukla and Ollie, with live hostess Fran Allison, as created by Burr Tillstrom. Fred Rogers, host of *Mr. Rogers' Neighborhood*, offered an entire make-believe-land population in the form of hand puppets. And the Muppets of *Sesame Street*'s Jim Henson were an instant success. Many educational films feature puppets in starring roles. Join some of these famous puppeteers and begin your apprenticeship.

Types of Puppets

All puppets take thought, time, and effort to create and use. Although there are many varieties from which to choose, puppets fall basically into two major groups: the hand puppet that fits on the puppeteer's hand, and the marionette that is manipulated by strings.

Puppet aficionados will argue vigorously in favor of one type of puppet over the other. The hand puppet proponents will tell you that because the hand puppet is actually part of the puppeteer, the puppet is more realistic, and the manipulator feels at one with the puppet. Those who favor marionettes say that these puppets, because they are separated from the manipulator, have a life of their own and are therefore better. If this were the time for true confessions, I'd have to tell you that while I argue fairly effectively for the superiority of hand puppets, the real reason

I'm a hand puppet person is that marionettes take a lot more skill and patience to manipulate. The differences between the two groups will obviously determine your choice of one over the other. Hand puppets seem most useful in speaking dialogue since the head of the hand puppet is where the listeners will be most likely to rivet their attention. The marionettes are better suited to plays with a great deal of physical action. The most sophisticated marionettes have jointed arms, legs, and heads and can dance, pick up objects, and move with ease. They can even fly. If you are a beginning puppeteer there is no need to make a commitment to either major type. Experiment with a variety of puppets until you find the one that gives you the most pleasure and satisfies your needs.

Commercial Hand Puppets

Ordinarily I try to avoid using commercial products other than books in the storyhour. There is enough plastic, mass-produced cuteness on television, in advertising, and in shops. The traditional and handmade seem more suitable. If you feel, however, that you cannot make a good puppet, it is possible to find handmade puppets in shops. Try your senior citizens' shop. They often have knitted or sewn puppets for sale. The renaissance of handicrafts has revived the art of handmade puppets. Your town might have a crafts shop or street fair where puppets are sold. If you don't see what you want, special order it from one of these local artisans. They are usually delighted to respond to specific orders. You might even be able to cajole them into donating a puppet: "It's for the library, you know."

If you live in or visit a large city, you might have access to an import store. In the toy department you may find commercially produced puppets that have a handmade look. Spain, Germany, and Poland export quality puppets. And if you visit a resort town, ski or beach, or even a large airport, be sure to wander through the gift shops. Once in a while you'll find exactly what you've been looking for.

Glove Puppets

Most of the puppets that are available commercially or in kits are glove puppets because they are the easiest for beginners to make and manipulate. This puppet, which may be created from a variety of materials, fits onto the hand and is operated either by using the palm and thumb or by putting the index finger into the head, while the thumb operates one hand of the puppet and the remaining fingers operate the other.

It's fun to use an entire glove with each finger representing a different character. If you can, knit a pair of mittens with three fingers and sew a face in front. Another technique is to use a lunch-size paper bag as a hand puppet. Or take an odd sock, attach three buttons (two eyes and a mouth) with safety pins or needle and thread. Another idea is to split the back of a stuffed animal. Remove the stuffing and you have a hand puppet. Can you sew a tiny bit? Sew together two pieces of muslin or cotton. Turn it inside out and paint a character on it. This can be a hand puppet; if you don't paint anything on it, open it at the top and you have a costume for a hand puppet with a styrofoam ball as a head.

Finger Puppets

Little puppets that fit onto one or more fingers have the advantage of being extremely portable. They fit into a pocket or purse for those odd times when you might find yourself with a group of children. If I meet a child on the bus, or at a friend's house, I take out the finger puppet and shyness on both sides disappears.

Experiment with anything that fits over your finger: a cut-off glove makes a good beginning. Since finger puppets cannot be seen from far away, they should be reserved for storytelling with a small group. You will probably want to let them do the talking while you act as narrator simply introducing the characters as they appear.

Use your hand as a puppet. Washable felt tip pens are available if you choose to draw right on your fingers. Or use rubber cement to glue construction paper or felt to the hand to make faces and costumes.

Marionettes or String Puppets

There are puppeteers who feel that only the marionette can effectively create the illusion of life and an experienced marionetteer is a special treat to see. Marionettes vary in complexity, but since their strings tend to tangle easily they are probably not the best starting point for the beginning puppeteer.

The simplest marionette of all is a handkerchief tied onto a string. Make the handkerchief twist, dance, and go to sleep. Tie two inanimate objects on strings: for example, a comb and brush. Have them talk about their owner. Attach two strings to anything pliable: a chain, a bead necklace. Make your abstract puppet dance to music. Can you give it, him, or her a personality? Is she shy? tired? happy? Move your puppet to show the emotions and personality of your marionette.

Stick Puppets

My favorite puppet is the picture stick puppet. These puppets store easily and can be articulated by anyone, even toddlers. At a bilingual school in Istanbul, Turkey, recently, I used these puppets with city-wise seventh graders. I then used the same puppets and nursery stories with junior high school students in a rural school in Japan. Anyone who has worked with middle school or junior high school students in the United States is aware that these young teens can be unpredictable. Let me assure you that it is the same the world over! Do you work with this age group? Why not try stick puppets during your next storyhour?

A traditional stick puppet is made by attaching a solid rod or stick to the back of the puppet, and is held by the performer. It is one of the simplest of all for beginners to use. Puppet characters can be cut from cardboard or plywood. Sticks are then attached and you have a puppet that is quick and easy to use. A more sophisticated rod puppet uses several long rods to manipulate the arms, legs, or head of a jointed puppet.

Puppets can be made with popsicle sticks or with tongue depressors purchased at a drugstore. Seat the children around big tables. In the center put cloth scraps, yarn, sequins, other findings, scissors, and glue for them to share. Then, just let them create. I've done this with many adult groups as well, letting them make up skits after the puppets are completed. Try using the improvisational skit idea that appears later in this chapter.

Use a wooden spoon. Paint or paste a face on it, and you have a simple rod puppet. Cut out figurines of plywood or poster-board. Tape, staple, or glue the cutout characters and scenery to ¼-inch doweling, available at the hardware store or lumber yard. These will work as shadow-show characters as well as on-stage puppets.

There are scores of books featuring animal sounds that are perfect to use with animal puppets. To give you a chance to try this method, a set of animals is included on the preceding page for you to copy and enlarge on poster board. Decorate with crayons, poster paint, or felt tip pens. Using an index card, create a pocket on the back of the puppet by taping three sides with strapping tape (leaving the bottom open). Insert a paint stirrer, available from any paint or hardware store, into the pocket and tape closed, to make a handle.

Tell the story and, as each animal appears, hand the appropriate puppet to a child to hold. In this way you involve several members of the audience.

Booklist: Animal Books to Use with Picture Puppets

Brandenberg, Franz. *Cock-a-Doodle-Doo.* Art by Aliki. Greenwillow, 1986. Join in and make these animal sounds.

Brown, Craig. *My Barn.* Art by author. Greenwillow, 1991. A farmer enjoys all the sounds his farm animals make.

Caroll, Kathleen. *One Red Rooster.* Art by Suzette Barbier. Houghton, 1992. A counting book of animal sounds.

Demuth, Patricia Brennan. *The Ornery Morning.* Art by Craig McFarland Brown. Dutton, 1991. Rooster won't crow morning, so morning on the farm can't begin.

Kent, Jack. *Little Peep.* Art by author. Prentice, 1981. Little Peep would like to wake up the sun like the cock.

Lewison, Wendy Cheyette. *Going to Sleep on the Farm.* Art by Juan Wijingaard. Dial, 1992. Each of the farm animals in this Good Night book is illustrated in a double spread.

Lillie, Patricia. *When the Rooster Crowed.* Art by Nancy Winslow Parker. Greenwillow, 1991. The farmer is the last animal to get up on the farm.

Most, Bernard. *The Cow That Went Oink.* Art by author. Harcourt, 1990. A cow that says "oink" meets a cow that says "moo."

Peet, Bill. *Cock-a-Doodle Dudley.* Art by author. Houghton, 1990. The rivalry between Dudley the Rooster and Gunther the Goose is finally resolved.

Rockwell, Anne. *Root-a-Toot-Toot.* Art by author. Macmillan, 1991. A little boy toots his horn and all the farm animals follow him.

Runcie, Jill. *Cock-a-Doodle-Doo!* Art by Lee Lorenz. Simon, 1991. Each animal wakes the next animal until the farmer wakes up.

Shone, Venice. *Cock-a-Doodle-Doo! A Day on the Farm.* Art by author. Scholastic, 1991. The farm animals wake up.

Wilhelm, Hans. *The Bremen Town Musicians.* Art by author. Scholastic, 1992. This version of the Grimm's tale has lively art to share.

Masks and Body Puppets

Most of the puppet types already mentioned are manipulated with your hands. There are puppets that can be operated with other parts of the body. Masks carved from wood and fitting over the head were used by many American Indian tribes in the performance of stories and plays. The whole body is used in the body puppet in which the performer sticks his head and hands through openings in an immobile costume. Draw a figure without a face or arms on a large 2-foot by 3-foot posterboard. Cut a hole for the face and arm holes. Preschoolers can wear these costumes to act out a play. You will find two wonderful mask stories, "Dirt for Sale" and "Lazy as an Ox," in chapter 26.

You can use a large paper bag to make masks for your group, or, better yet, let your students or patrons create their own. Plan a show based on Maurice Sendak's *Where the Wild Things Are*, Pat Hutchin's *Good Night, Owl*, or Grimm's *Snow White and the Seven Dwarfs*.

Shadow Puppets

When you watch a shadow show, you see only the silhouette or shadow of the puppet rather than the puppet itself. Shadow shows usually are performed behind a screen, with the light source coming from behind the puppet and with the performer below the level of the screen. You can use hand puppets or cutouts or even human beings to create shadow shows. Any translucent material, such as thin paper or a sheet, will serve as a screen, and small spot reflector lights may be purchased at the

supermarket. The art of shadowgraphy is an ancient one. Most children have used their hands to create figures on the wall; as a storyteller you can manipulate your hands to tell an entire story. The overhead projector makes an instant shadow puppet stage. Experiment with both solid and translucent shapes.

Some books that can help you with the basic hand movements are listed below.

Booklist: Shadow Puppets

Joyce, Hope. *Me and My Shadows.* Joy-co Press (2636 Burgener Blvd., San Diego, CA 92110), 1981. Plays and patterns to use with the overhead projector.

Shadow Pictures Children Love to Make. Merrimack, 1984. Each page gives directions for making Victorian hand shadow puppets.

Zimmerman, Erika. *Shadow Puppets for Children.* Floris (15 Harrison Gardens, Edinburgh EH11 1SH, Scotland), 1983. Instructions for making simple puppets and a theater for shadow puppets.

Magnetic Puppets

Magnetized rubber strips can be fastened on the backs of small dolls or posterboard cutouts. Make a screen from posterboard and use a piece of iron or steel to manipulate the puppets from behind the screen.

Stages

Stage construction can range from a curtain hung over a door to complex permanent theaters. Start simply. Remember, you'll want to store and maybe transport your stage. Any number of items will serve as a stage for your performance.

You can use an empty refrigerator box as a stage, but since it is bulky to store, plan to use it also as a playstore or individual reading corner. Curtains over a doorway or strung on a rope across a corner make an instant stage. If you can't find a willing volunteer to construct a three-part screen puppet theater for you, check toy store catalogs. Tables will serve as an instant puppet stage too; kneel behind one that has been tipped on its side. An empty picture frame also can serve as a quick substitute for a more complicated stage. If you have nothing else suitable around, cover your head with black cloth and cut two openings for your eyes and one for your mouth and simply stand or sit behind your puppets. Actually, it often adds to the puppet performance for the puppeteer to be entirely visible. Just hold the puppet up and start talking. The audience will immediately transfer your voice to the puppet.

Make sure that there is adequate light on your puppets. You may need to use auxiliary lighting since your puppets will usually be small and may be hidden by side curtains.

Following are directions for making a simple theater for hand puppets.

Portable Doorway Puppet Theater

This puppet theater can be easily stored. It works in most doorways, is portable, and, best of all, it can be raised or lowered depending on the height of the puppeteer, child, or adult.

You will need:

A spring curtain rod 2½ feet long
A half-inch wood dowel 2½ feet long
3½ yards of heavyweight fabric, such as denim or duck, cut and hemmed to make a screen approximately 26″ × 54″.

How to: Sew a two-inch open hem across one width of the fabric for inserting the spring rod. This is the top of the screen. Then cut a 12″ × 17″ opening a foot (12″) from the top and hem around it to give it body. Sew a one-inch open hem across the other (bottom) width of the fabric for the half-inch wood dowel you will insert to give weight to the screen and keep it hanging evenly.

Chinese Hat Puppet Theater

Totally contained, one-person puppet theaters have been used for centuries in China. One idea for making your own requires the adaptation of a Chinese straw hat, or even a Mexican sombrero, either of which may be bought at import or gift shops. Attach to the hat's brim solid-color fabric that is long enough to reach to the floor and wide enough to encircle you and the hat. Sew a zipper in the front, leaving a two-foot opening for the puppets to perform. You, the puppeteer, wear the puppet theater on your head. At the end of the story and performance, the entire production— puppets, puppeteer, and stage—walks off.

Uses for Puppets

Puppets may be used as incidental visitors to your book program or as the basis for an entire story session as performers in a puppet show. Begin simply. Exaggerate your puppet's actions, but don't feel compelled to have your puppet moving continuously without a purpose. Haphazard movements distract from a finished looking show. Rather, plan each action so that it is meaningful. Be sure to speak up and out because the stage will muffle your voice. You might experiment with using a taped soundtrack so that the puppeteers can concentrate on moving the puppets. Don't try to use elaborate scenery or involve yourself in complicated scene changes. Music between acts or scenes helps the continuity of your performance. Lighting need not be complex, but it must be sufficient to light the action. Try using clip-on spot lights for flat bright lighting. Don't try to do everything yourself. Enlist the aid of friends, colleagues, and children. If you decide to perform for an invited audience, which after all is the point of puppetry, be sure you have rehearsed your show. If you think you would be proud to have your mother-in-law see your puppet show, then you are ready for an audience!

The Puppet as Host

When I am working with a preschool group, I often use a puppet to greet the children and introduce each story. If you have just one puppet (named Arnold, perhaps, by the children?) that you reserve for use for your preschool storyhour, you will find your children asking for "Arnold the Elephant" and they will come to associate Arnold with books, poems, and stories.

If you have a puppet—a dog, for example—that you feel comfortable with, take a few minutes to think about your dog's personality. Is it a girl or a boy? Shy, aggressive, knowledgeable, or naive? Introduce the puppet to your children as soon as they are settled. A simple "Boys and girls, this is my friend Arnold" will do. "Hello everybody," says your puppet. "What is your name?" "Would you like to pat me?" Surprisingly, you needn't change your voice when the puppet is speaking. In fact, I caution against a voice change unless you feel fairly confident that you can remember to use it consistently when the puppet is speaking. It can be embarrassing if you start speaking in a high puppet voice, and later your puppet's voice changes tone because you forgot! Children will respond to your puppet just as they will talk to a pet or stuffed animal. Most children understand make-believe much better than most adults. You can have a dialogue with your puppet introducing the stories:

You: "This morning we are going to read a story all about a boy's very first experience in the snow."

Puppet: "Oh good. What's it called?"

You: *The Snowy Day* by Ezra Jack Keats."

Puppet: "Hurry and read it!"

Now just put your puppet out of sight and read the story. At the end of the storyhour you might use the puppet again to say goodbye, and remind the children of the date of the next storyhour. If you use your puppet enough you will begin to think that it is alive, so don't lose it. You'll worry that it may have run into foul play!

Practice with Your Puppet

Here is a list of common emotions to practice with your puppet:

Happiness	Fright	Sleepiness	Curiosity
Loneliness	Sadness	Excitement	Thankfulness
Bravery	Anger	Repentance	Thoughtfulness

First practice with your puppet using actions alone to express emotions, then act out these feelings using simple phrases or sentences. Add to this list other feelings that might characterize your puppet. Each movement should be planned and fulfill a purpose, but movements usually need to be simplified and exaggerated to be interpreted by an audience. Puppets are too small for subtleties and yet they can be graceful as dancers. Puppets should perform to each other, but as producer you should be aware of the audience as well. The puppets should not be facing the puppeteer or constantly be seen in side view.

Exercise in Performance

If your middle grade students or young adults have made puppets and you are searching for an easy play to produce without any advance preparation, divide them into groups of five. Let each group pick three pieces of paper from a box: one indicating a character, one a setting, and one an object. The group must decide on a skit involving the character, setting, and object chosen. Suggest a time limit for the preparation and performance. Caution your students to speak up and out, so that they can be heard as they perform. The greatest failing for amateur puppeteers is their inaudibility. (This program may be too complicated for very young groups, but older groups will enjoy it. Of course a younger group would make the perfect audience!)

Here are some ideas for the big three:

Characters	*Setting*	*Object*
Teacher	Jungle	Diamond bracelet
Musician	New York City	Book
Explorer	Desert island	Treasure chest
Witch	Sailing ship	Telephone
Librarian	Haunted house	Magic wand
Monster	Department store	Roast turkey
Storekeeper	Cave	Baby elephant
Rock singer	Art museum	Flashlight
Pirate	Theater	Uncle Jonathan's will
King	Spaceship	Secret message
Ghost	Hotel	New shoes

Puppet Plays

One way to begin your work with puppetry is to find a story or play that appeals to you and then make the puppets to suit the play. If you are working alone, you will want to find a story with only two characters, three at the most. Only two puppets can be on the stage at once, but a third character can appear when one of the main characters is offstage. Remember that you will have to remove one puppet and exchange it for another. This may take time and fumbling while the audience waits.

You may want to have one of your puppets tell the story, or you, as narrator, can give the descriptive passages while the conversational parts are acted by the puppets. Another way to use a puppet is simply to hold each character up while you, the narrator, tell the story. In this way the puppet acts as a three-dimensional illustration of the story.

Some puppeteers script their plays. Each character has a set speech to deliver at a particular time. This has advantages and disadvantages. For one thing, if you're planning on using a published script your search may be a long and hard one, for many of them tend to be overly simplistic. A script also means that parts must be memorized, and if one person forgets his lines, there is liable to be an upset in the entire operation. If adults are presenting a skit or play to children, I think its best to begin with folklore sources. Since there are many variables to putting on a play, it is sometimes worthwhile to use something that your audience and cast are already familiar with. Start with "The Three Bears" or another of the nursery fairy tales. As you become more proficient, you can graduate to a more intricately plotted story. If students are presenting your play, let them write their own script. After you have decided on a story, cast the characters and improvise the story without the puppets. Tape the action or write it down. Now read it over and edit your script. This may be easier to memorize than a script from a book.

Scripting a play seems to make your project more formal and static. Improvising dialogue sometimes works better. Decide on the story you are going to present. Read it aloud. Discuss with your group the different characters and their personalities. Outline the plot so that everyone is sure what happens when. Decide who will take which parts. Try rehearsing your show, criticizing the dialogue and puppets' movements as you go. When the play is refined enough for presentation you will find that some of the speeches have become set while others vary. This often gives more spontaneity to a show. Of course, you must do what works best for you and your group.

Puppet Plays to Perform

Finding a Friend

If you are shuddering at the thought of making puppets and costuming them, constructing a stage, writing a script, and rehearsing a show, perform this instant play. It needs only two props: the hands. Use a piece of black fabric that covers your face and body as a stage or simply stand in front of your audience and manipulate your hands.

There was once a hand. (Show your hand to the audience.) He was very proud because he could do so many things. He could point (point); he could count one, two, three, four, five (show each finger); he could say "stop" (hold up hand palm outward); he could scratch himself (little finger scratches next finger); he could say "come here" (beckon); he could wave good-bye (wave); he could shake himself (shake your hand, fingers relaxed); he could chastise (shake a finger); he could be tough (make a fist); but he was very sad (fold fingers down in a droop) because he couldn't make any noise. Then the ring finger told the thumb about a noise the first three fingers could make. The hand tried it (snap your fingers); but the hand was dissatisfied. Then one day the hand met another hand (bring other hand up to audience). They discovered that they could make a noise together (clap hands). The moral of this story is (stand up and look at audience), it takes two hands to clap.

This play makes an excellent ending to your program. It can also be used to thank the organizers of a festival or to give any other appreciative message.

Pedro Courts Maria

Use the instructions for the picture puppets that are provided or fashion your own puppets. This play works well with hand or finger puppets.

Cast: A storyteller
        Pedro
        Mother
        Maria

Sets: Pedro's house
        Maria's garden
        The road between the two houses

Mother: Pedro, you need to get married.

Pedro: Who would marry me?

Mother: How about Maria? She is often sitting at home.

Storyteller: On Sunday Pedro went looking for Maria. She was on her way to church.

Pedro: Maria. Maria. How do you do? Why are you always sitting at home?

Maria: Pedro. Pedro. What are you saying? As you see I am not sitting at home. I'm on my way to church.

Storyteller: Pedro went home.

Mother: How did you get along with Maria?

Pedro: Badly. Very badly. She was on her way to church and I asked her why she was always sitting at home.

Mother: Oh Pedro. You should have said, "Would you like to go dancing?"

Storyteller: On Sunday Pedro went looking for Maria. Her father had died and she was sitting by his coffin.

Pedro: Maria, Maria. How do you do? Would you like to go dancing?

Maria: Pedro, Pedro. What are you saying? Can't you see my father has just died?

Storyteller: Pedro went home.

Mother: How did you get along with Maria?

Pedro: Badly. Very badly. She was sitting by her father's coffin and I asked her to go dancing.

Mother: Oh Pedro. You should have said, "May he go to heaven."

Storyteller: On Sunday Pedro went looking for Maria. She had just killed a pig.

Pedro: Maria, Maria. How are you? Ah, you have killed a pig. May he go to heaven.

Maria: Pedro. Pedro. What are you saying? You want my pig to go to heaven?

Storyteller: Pedro went home.

Mother: How did you get along with Maria?

Pedro: Badly. Very badly. She had just killed a pig and I said, "May it go to heaven."

Mother: Oh Pedro. You should have said, "May you have many more and may they grow fat."

Storyteller: On Sunday Pedro went looking for Maria. She was sitting in the sun touching a pimple on her chin.

Pedro: Maria, Maria. How are you? I see you have a pimple on your chin. May it grow fat and may you have many more.

Maria: Pedro. Pedro. What are you saying? You want me to have more pimples?

Storyteller: Pedro went home.

Mother: How did you get along with Maria?

Pedro: Badly. Very badly. I wished that her pimple would grow big and fat.

Mother: Oh Pedro, you should have said, "May it dry up and die."

Maria

Simple Foam Ball Puppets

Elementary People:

Basic Supplies:

> a foam ball
> one 3/8″ dowel at least 12″ long
> 2 wooden BBQ skewers
> a bandana
> 2 shank eyes
> fur, yarn, or boa for hair.

Directions:

1. Glue one end of 3/8″ dowel to inside center of bandana
2. Cut slit in ball, and glue firmly in place over center of dowel
3. Cut 2 small eye socket slits in ball, and glue shanked eyes in place
4. Glue hair in place
5. Knot scarf in 2 opposite corners for hands. Carefully insert BBQ skewers under knots and glue in place.

Note: You can make the puppet more elaborate by shaping the foam for detailed features. Sharp, curved fingernail scissors work well for this. You can use extra foam balls to carve features like noses, eyebrows, and ears. These can be glued on. You can cut out hands and attach them over the BBQ skewer rod controls as well. Glue helps hold them in place. You can make the puppet's costume as elaborate and detailed as your imagination dictates.

Storyteller: On Sunday Pedro went looking for Maria. She was in the yard watering a rosebush.

Pedro: Maria. Maria. How are you? I see you have a rosebush. May it dry up and die.

Maria: Pedro. Pedro. What are you saying? You want my rosebush to die?

Storyteller: Pedro went home.

Mother: How did you get along with Maria?

Pedro: Badly. Very badly. I wished that her rosebush would dry up and die.

Mother: Oh Pedro, you should have said, "May it grow roots and live 1,000 years."

Storyteller: On Sunday Pedro went to visit Maria. She was in the yard with a thorn stuck in the palm of her hand.

Pedro: Maria. Maria. How are you? I see you have a thorn stuck in your palm. May it grow roots and may you have a thousand more.

Maria: Pedro. Pedro, what are you saying? You want this thorn to grow roots. You want my rosebush to dry up and die. You want my pimple to grow fat. You want my pig to go to heaven. You want to go dancing when my father has died. You ask me why I am at home when I am on my way to church. What do you really want?

Pedro: Maria. Maria. Will you marry me?

Storyteller: What did Maria say?

The Dog and the Cat Go to Market

A simple nonsense play that will delight preschoolers. Make the puppets provided on pages 274–75, or use your own cat and dog puppets.

Puppets: The Cat
        The Dog

Sets: The meadow
        The fair

Props: Box of doughnuts
        Bushel basket of baked potatoes
        (The doughnuts and potatoes could easily be pretend, since they do not speak!)

Scene 1: The Meadow

Dog: Good morning, Cat.

Cat: Good morning, Dog.

Dog: Saturday is the Village Fair. Let's sell something. We can make enough money to go on a trip.

Cat: Good idea. I can sell doughnuts.

Dog: I can sell my famous baked potatoes.

Scene 2: The Fair

Dog: Good morning, Cat.

Cat: Good morning, Dog.

Dog: Look, I have brought a bushel basket of hot baked potatoes.

Cat: I have fried this box of doughnuts.

Dog: We should make a lot of money. Everything smells delicious.

Cat: Let's set up our stalls next to each other.

Dog: Good idea. I want to buy a doughnut from you right now.

Cat: That will be five cents, please.

Dog: Here you are. (Takes and eats doughnut.) Very good, Cat.

Cat: Thank you. Now that I have a nickel I can buy one of your potatoes. Here's a nickel. (Takes potato and eats it.)

Dog: Thank you. Now that I have a nickel I can buy another doughnut. Here you are. (Takes doughnut and eats it.)

Cat: Thank you. Now that I have a nickel I can buy another potato. Here you are. (Takes potato and eats it.)

Scene 3: The Meadow

Cat: What a day. I'm exhausted.

Dog: Me, too. We had so much business.

Cat: Yes. I sold a lot of doughnuts. I have none left.

Dog. I sold a lot of potatoes. I haven't got any left, either.

Cat: I bet we made a lot of money.

Dog: I'm sure we did.

Cat: Let's count it.

Dog: How much do you have?

Cat: I have the nickel you gave me.

Dog: I don't have anything.

Cat: How can that be? We have no food left to sell and business was brisk all day.

Dog: I think we were our only customers.

Cat: Yes. But still why aren't we rich?

Dog: Oh well, at least we aren't hungry anymore.

Cat: Good night, Dog.

Dog: Good night, Cat.

Exchangable Animal Head Puppets

Designed for flexibility, these puppets give you a basic body, a basic costume, and two heads. Included here are designs for a cat, dog, rabbit, and fox. Using these as examples, you can develop a whole menagerie of puppet players, for a wide variety of shows. The heads slip snuggly on and off the neck of the body pattern. If you care to add a tail, it can be attached by a safety pin, in the proper place. You can stick with just the basic costume, or make it as elaborate as you want.

Directions for Body and Costume:
(Use material with a lot of body for the body, and a soft, and/or flowing material for the costume.)
  1. Patterns given are on a ¼″ grid. Trace them onto a 1″ grid, and cut out. Laying patterns on fold of material, cut out two of each.
  2. Right sides together, sew along dotted lines as indicated. Hem around bottom. Turn right side out. On costume, sew around neck and sleeve edges. Neck of costume is made to be turned down in a turtleneck, to hide the body underneath.
  3. Attach curtain ring to back of bottom edge of body for hanging behind stage.
  4. Put the costume on over the body.

Directions for Head:
  1. Cut 1 head out of fur with the nap going in the direction of arrows, 4 ears (2 of fur with the nap toward the point of the ear, and 2 of cloth or felt for insides). In the case of the cat, cut out 2 circles with the nap pointing down from the dart, and cut out 1 nose from felt.
  2. Right sides together, sew darts together. Sew around head, leaving neck edge open.
  3. Turn right side out.
  4. To sew ears: while matching edges, place 1 piece of felt next to 1 of fur (with fur side inside), and sew together. Repeat for other ear. Sew ears and nose (pompom or store-bought plastic one) to head. In the case of the cat, the circular cheek pieces get sewed on carefully by hand to each side of the mouth, just under and touching the nose, with nap of fur going down.
  5. Attach eyes.
  6. Sew finger tube, and insert firmly into neck of puppet after stuffing head. A little glue on the end helps secure it in place. Sew by hand around neck edge.

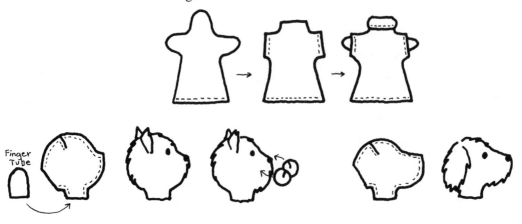

Finger Tube

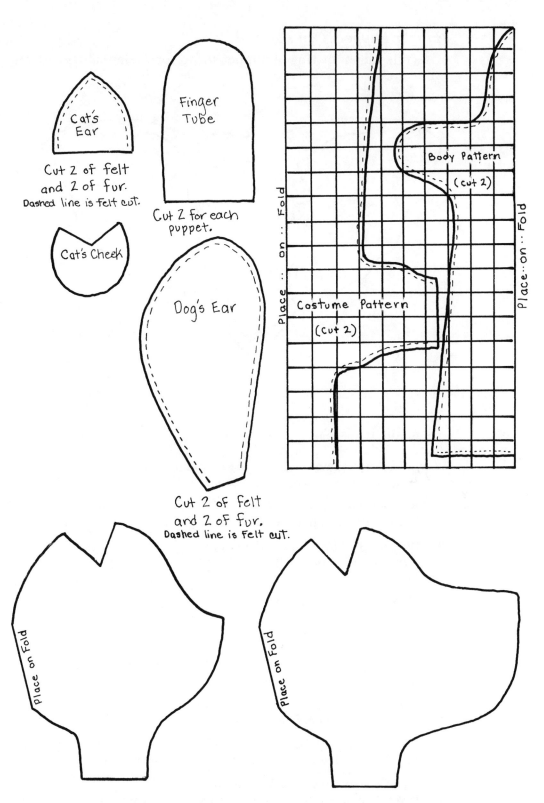

Cat's Ear

Cut 2 of felt and 2 of fur. Dashed line is felt cut.

Cat's Cheek

Finger Tube

Cut 2 for each puppet.

Dog's Ear

Cut 2 of felt and 2 of fur. Dashed line is felt cut.

Place ·· on ·· Fold

Place ·· on ·· Fold

Body Pattern (cut 2)

Costume Pattern (cut 2)

Place on Fold

Place on Fold

Finger Puppets Can Ask Riddles

Use this elephant finger puppet to perform elephant jokes for your group.

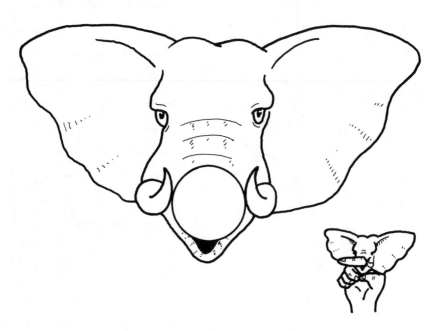

Elephant Jokes

Why did the elephant stand on the marshmallow?
    So he wouldn't fall into the cocoa.

In what way are an elephant and a hippopotamus similar?
    Neither one can play tennis.

What's grey, has four legs and a trunk?
    A mouse going on a trip.

How do you know that peanuts are fattening?
    Have you ever seen a skinny elephant?

Why does an elephant have cracks between his toes?
    To carry his library card.

How can you tell if an elephant has been in your refrigerator?
    By his footprints in the butter.

What time is it when an elephant sits on a fence?
    Time to buy a new fence.

What's the difference between an elephant and a jar of peanut butter?
    An elephant doesn't stick to the roof or your mouth.

Why do elephants wear dark glasses?
    If you had all those jokes told about you, you wouldn't want to be recognized, either.

Booklist: Picture Books to Use with Puppets

These picture books turn into puppet shows nicely. You need only have the appropriate puppets.

Allen, Jonathan. *Mucky Moose*. Art by author. Macmillan, 1990. A moose is so smelly that even the wolf is repelled. Use with stuffed animals for puppets.

Aylesworth, Jim. *Two Terrible Frights*. Art by Eileen Christelow. Atheneum, 1987. Two shows in one: both a little girl and a mouse have parallel night fears.

Demuth, Patricia Brennan. *Max, The Bad-Talking Parrot*. Art by Bo Zaunders. Dodd, 1986. Mrs. Goosebump is angry when Max insults her friend, but redeems himself by foiling a robbery.

Ginsburg, Mirra. *The Chinese Mirror*. Art by Margot Zemach. Harcourt, 1988. Each person sees a new stranger in the mirror.

Krauss, Robert. *Phil the Ventriloquist*. Art by author. Greenwillow, 1989. Phil, a ventriloquist rabbit, annoys his parents with his talent.

Lobel, Arnold. *A Treeful of Pigs*. Art by Anita Lobel. Greenwillow, 1979. How a farmer's wife gets her husband to help with the pigs.

Mathers, Petra. *Theodor and Mr. Balbini*. Art by author. Harper, 1988. A talking dog complains about his life.

Mueller, Virginia. *A Halloween Mask for Monster*. Art by Lynn Munsinger. Whitman, 1986. After trying on a number of frightening masks, monster goes to the party as himself.

Pilkey, Dav. *Dragon's Fat Cat*. Art by author. Orchard, 1992. Dragon and his cat are the main characters in these five stories.

Roberts, Bethany. *Waiting-for-Spring Stories*. Art by William Joyce. Harper, 1984. Seven short short stories that make charming skits.

Rose, Gerald. *The Tiger-Skin Rug*. Art by author. Faber, 1979. An old tiger finds a home in the Rajah's palace. Use with a tiger stuffed animal.

Ross, Tony. *Stone Soup*. Art by author. Dial, 1990. This version of the old tale uses animal characters.

Sharmat, Andrew. *Smedge*. Art by Chris L. Searest. Macmillan, 1989. A family dog leads a double life as a diplomat.

Waber, Bernard. *An Anteater Named Arthur*. Houghton, 1967. Each chapter makes a funny two-character puppet play.

Watson, N. Cameron. *The Little Pig's Puppet Book*. Art by author. Little, 1990. Pigs put on a puppet play.

Booklist: Adult Sources

This is a selected listing to inspire amateur puppeteers and guide them through their steps in making puppets and deciding which stories to produce. If you become particularly interested in puppetry I suggest that you join one of the puppetry organizations where you will find kindred souls willing to share their knowledge and talents with you.

Adachi, Barbara C. *Backstage at Bunraku: A Behind-the-Scenes Look at Japan's Traditional Puppet Theatre*. Photos by Joel Sachett. Weatherhill, 1985. An overview of the body-size Japanese puppets.

Baird, Bill. *The Art of the Puppet.* Photos. Macmillan, 1965. Puppets and puppetry around the world with a wealth of full color photographs.

Beaton, Mabel and Les Beaton. *Marionettes: A Hobby for Everyone.* Dallas Puppet Theater Press, 1948, 1989. Full treatment for the marionette.

Champlin, Connie. *Puppetry and Creative Dramatics.* Art by Nancy Renfro. Renfro Studios, 1980. A good introduction to using puppets in unscripted drama.

Currell, David. *The Complete Book of Puppetry.* Plays, 1974. History, puppet types, the show.

Feller, Ron and Marsha Feller. *Paper Masks and Puppets for Stories, Songs and Plays.* The Arts Factory (P.O. Box 55547, Seattle, WA 98155), 1985. Drawings and photographs make this book useful.

Fijan, Carol and Frank Ballard. *Directing Puppet Theater.* Resource Publications, San Jose, Calif., 1989. Step-by-step guide to production.

Hawkesworth, Eric. *Puppet Show to Make: How to Entertain with All Kinds of Puppets.* Supreme Magic (64 High St., Bideford, Devon, England EX39 2AN). Detailed instructions on how to make puppets and theaters with sample shows for each kind of puppet.

Hunt, Tamara and Nancy Renfro. *Pocketful of Puppets: Mother Goose Rhymes.* Renfro Studios, 1982. Mother Goose puppets made from cups, boxes, and paper bags.

Kominz, Laurence R. and Mark Levenson, eds. *The Language of the Puppet.* Pacific Puppetry Center, Tears of Joy Theater, Vancouver, Wash. Advanced presentations at the UNIMA conference on the nature of puppetry.

Magon, Jero. *Staging the Puppet Show.* 2nd ed. Art by author. Charlemagne Press (1384 Hope Road, No. Vancouver, BC V7P 1W7, Canada), 1989. Professional descriptions of lighting and staging.

Mahlmann, Lewis and David Cadwalader Jones. *Folk Tale Plays for Puppets.* Plays, 1980. Folktales scripted for puppets.

Marks, Burton and Rita Burton. *Puppets and Puppet Making: The Plays, the Puppets, the Production.* Plays, 1982. Short original scripts and simple puppet directions.

Masson, Anne. *The Magic of Marionettes.* Art by author. Annick, 1989. Marionettes are considered more difficult than hand or finger puppets. This is a beginner's book of marionettes.

Painter, William M. *Story Hours with Puppets and Other Props.* Shoe String, 1990. Ideas for presenting children's literature with easy-to-find and -make puppets. Another good resource by the same author is *Musical Story Hours: Using Music with Storytelling and Puppetry* (Shoe String, 1989).

Pittman, Jeanne W. *Fanciful Finger Friends from Sea and Shore.* Art by Lynne W. Jennings. Pittman (3821 Voltaire St., San Diego, CA 92107), 1989. Felt puppet patterns for creatures from the sea. Another by this author is *Fanciful Felt Finger Friends* (Pittman, 1989).

Robson, Denny and Vanessa Bailey. *Rainy Day Puppets.* Photos by Roger Vlitos. Gloucester, 1990. Photographs and easy directions for a variety of puppets.

Ross, Laura. *Holiday Puppets.* Art by Frank and Laura Ross. Lothrop, 1979. Directions for making holiday characters using rod puppets, hand puppets, and marionettes.

Sierra, Judy. *Fantastic Theater: Puppets and Plays for Young Performers and Young Audiences.* H. W. Wilson, 1991. Directions for making and manipulating shadow and rod puppets and scripts for puppet plays adapted from rhymes, folksongs, myths, and folktales.

Sullivan, Debbie. *Pocketful of Puppets: Activities for the Special Child with Mental, Physical and Multiple Handicaps.* Art by Nancy Renfro. Renfro Studios, 1982. Emphasis on puppets for the special child.

Tichenor, Tom. *Tom Tichenor's Puppets.* Art by author. Abington, 1971. Hand puppet plays and marionettes plus the author's personal philosophy.

Wright, Denise Anton. *One-Person Puppet Plays.* Art by John Wright. Libraries Unlimited, 1990. Short scripts and simple patterns to produce one-person puppet shows.

Wright, John. *Rod, Shadow, and Glove: Puppets from the Little Angel Theater.* Photos. Robert Hale, 1986. Puppet construction, costumes, scenery, production. An advanced book.

17 / Magic

"And now for some magic!" Whether you are speaking to elementary school children or senior citizens, such an invitation is sure to capture your audience's attention. In the fall of 1992, while I was lecturing in Saudi Arabia, I spent one leisurely Friday afternoon exchanging news with several storytelling friends. I had brought some easy magic tricks that I thought they might enjoy performing for their own storytelling group in Yanbu. Four adult Westerners playing with rope soon intrigued members of the staff at the residence hall where I was staying, and before long they joined us. Magic has such universal appeal. I like picturing my "students" showing rope tricks to their friends on several continents.

How did I ever have the confidence to teach magic? It all began over 20 years ago. I had volunteered to help a friend of mine, a law school professor, move his belongings from one apartment to another. I noticed that one of the boxes that I transferred from the hall closet to the borrowed pick-up was labeled "magic." "What's this?" I asked. "Those are my magic tricks," Don answered. It seemed that his interest in magic was sparked when he was given a magic kit for his eighth birthday. He became increasingly intrigued with magic, and his skills improved until soon he was performing at parties and service club meetings in his hometown. When I met Don he was no longer actively involved with magic, but he couldn't bring himself to part with his collection of effects.

It took much longer to move his belongings that day, because I insisted that he entertain me with the materials in his magic box. After all, it seemed like a fair trade for my efforts! Now, years later, I am a member of several magic clubs, a magician member of the Magic Castle in Los Angeles, and I've even been known to fly all the way to Las Vegas to see a magic show.

The performing of magic tricks is a natural addition to any book program. Many traditional tales deal with magic or magicians, and the art of conjuring is as old as the tales themselves.

You can use conjuring, or the performing of magic tricks, to introduce a story, or as transitional material from one story to another. Start with a simple trick that has probably been used by magicians for a hundred years, and gradually begin creating your own choreographed routine. Once you have performed a magic trick or two and have seen your audience's excited reaction, you will become hopelessly addicted to the world of magic. Then give me a call. We can go to a magic convention together.

Conjuring—magic for entertainment—may have originated in Greece. In the second century a Greek author, Alciphron, described a still-popular sleight-of-hand trick known as the "cups and balls." Conjuring as performed by a conjurer or magician—but not to be confused with witches, sorcerers, or demons—was a major form of entertainment in many different parts of the world. Today, even with the magic of fax machines, space travel, and other marvels, a good magician or conjurer can entertain and delight an audience with tricks that were invented centuries ago.

Children are particularly fascinated with magic tricks. Just like their parents, they want to figure out how the trick was done. Interestingly enough, very young children do not make good audiences for conjurers. Perhaps they simply take miraculous events for granted. Some magical tricks depend on *misdirection*. For example, the conjurer hides a ball in one hand while the other hand is moving in an eye-catching manner. The adult eye usually follows the larger action automatically and misses the smaller, more important action. Young children, however, are more likely to follow the smaller action, frustrating the magician. Children in the middle and upper grades, however, react in the same way as most adults and are excited by the simplest of tricks.

Magic shows are really suitable for all ages. At a recent show in Las Vegas, the adults were as awed as the children by the magician's ability to make a live white tiger appear and disappear. Siegfried and Roy, David Copperfield, and Blackstone are familiar names to audiences all over the world.

The mixture of awe and skepticism that accompanies the performance of magic will make the effort to learn the tricks worthwhile.

Types of Conjuring

At a magic show recently I was seated next to a 14-year-old boy and his 9-year-old brother. Every time a trick was performed on stage, the older boy kept up a running commentary on what would happen next and how he thought the effect was accomplished. I was sure that the older boy couldn't have been very knowledgeable about magic. No magician would willingly give away a secret.

You may be interested to know that it is possible to categorize magical effects. There is close-up magic, table or platform magic, and stage magic. Close-up magic requires that the audience is close enough to the conjurer to see small objects such as coins or cards being manipulated. In platform magic the audience can be a little farther away, and in stage magic the effects are often larger than life. Stage magic often uses big apparatus such as water tanks for spectacular escapes, large boxes to saw a lady in half, or cages in which people disappear and animals appear in their place.

Some magicians like to specialize in one form of magic. Card and coin magic performed in a close-up situation might be one specialty suitable for teachers and librarians. Stage magic, on the other hand, is usually performed by professional magicians on a theater stage before hundreds of people. While librarians and teachers may often perform before many children at once, they may not want to purchase large apparatus or be responsible for a live tiger or bear!

Magic effects usually come under one of seven categories. The more successful magic tricks include two or more of the following effects:

A *production or creation*. The magician produces something out of nothing, such as a rabbit from a seemingly empty hat.

A *disappearance*. The opposite of production, the rabbit will vanish.

A *transformation*. An object changes from one thing to another. For instance, a rabbit might seem to change into a duck.

A *transposition*. Two objects exchange places with each other. A red handkerchief seems to change places with a blue handkerchief in another location.

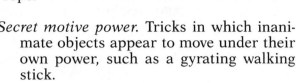

Defiance of natural laws. Tricks that seem physically impossible, such as cutting off someone's head or climbing an unsupported rope.

Secret motive power. Tricks in which inanimate objects appear to move under their own power, such as a gyrating walking stick.

Mental tricks. The performer apparently reads the thoughts of those in his audience.

Mechanical Magic and Sleight-of-Hand

If you are more than just casually interested in the art of conjuring, you will probably want to get involved with some sleight-of-hand. These are magical effects that rely mainly on manual dexterity. A typical sleight-of-hand maneuver is to show a single ball to an audience and with a series of hand movements seemingly make the ball disappear or multiply. Undoubtedly, because I've not taken the time to perfect any sleight-of-hand movements, I am in awe of this type of magic. There are books to teach you the basics of sleight-of-hand, but after you know the moves you will still have to spend hours practicing to become proficient. Another way of discovering the mysteries of this art is to find a willing magician to show you the moves. This really isn't as difficult as it appears. It's true that magicians don't like to give away secrets, but giving magic lessons is different. Those merchants in the business of selling tricks or books on magic will be happy to demonstrate techniques after a purchase. But, as with many ideas and techniques in this book, practice makes perfect.

We've finally arrived at my kind of magic, a trick whose secret you can buy. There are many magic suppliers in the country today. You can buy a trick through the mail from a catalog (instructions included) or you can shop in a retail store that sells novelties and magic. In most cases, the clerks are magicians themselves. They will be happy to demonstrate the secret of a trick after you purchase it. What sort of things can you buy? A cane that appears from thin air, a teapot that pours a variety of colored liquids, a milk pitcher that never empties, or a pan that produces endless silks or even a rabbit. Try not to buy on impulse; instead, plan how you can use a magic trick in your book programs.

Books about Magic

There are many, many books that give magic tricks with clear directions. In fact, you can still buy an entire at-home course (*Tarbell Course in Magic*, published by Louis Tannen and the *Chavez Course in Magic*, available from Dale Salwak, P.O. Box 8054, La Verne, CA 91750) and once you've seen a trick or two performed, you will find it much easier to understand written directions. It's rather like reading a cookbook. You may wonder that the secrets of magicians are so freely revealed. A famous magician once said that to publish a secret was the best way to keep it, meaning that no one will bother to read and learn it. This really isn't true, as attested by the number of magicians who write and collect books, but there are few secrets.

Organizations of Magicians

There are two nationally active magicians' clubs for adults and one for young people. Both the Society of American Magicians and the International Brotherhood of Magicians publish magazines complete with ideas for magic tricks and presentations, book reviews, and news of local clubs. To join either group you usually have to be sponsored by a member. Most local affiliates require an initiation magic performance by you. Don't panic, it's fun. You'll find that the experienced magicians will be delighted with whatever you attempt and will be kind and helpful. The society of American Magicians has a young members division, which publishes its own newsletter and offers member clubs for children and young adults. Addresses for these organizations are listed below.

The Society of American Magicians
    P.O. Box 290068
    St. Louis, MO 63129

The International Brotherhood of Magicians
    P.O. Box 19090
    St. Louis, MO 63126

The Society of Young Magicians
    c/o John Apperson
    2812 Idaho
    Granite City, IL 62040

Using Magic

Magic ties in well with any book presentation. Use it when you are reading aloud, telling stories, giving a booktalk, or presenting a poem. I think that one of my very favorite stories to read before presenting a magic trick is Leo Lionni's *Little Blue and Little Yellow*, which works perfectly with the "Mixing Colors" effect described below. Lots of other story and magic trick pairs are included in this chapter as well, but if you become as intrigued by matching magic with books as I am, you'll soon have your own favorite combinations.

    You may feel that you can do a whole program featuring magic. On the other hand, you may want to do one trick this week and another next week. Most beginners don't have a wide enough repertoire to sustain 40 minutes of magic. Instead, there are many stories with magical elements that lead nicely into a magic trick or two after the story presentation. I suggest that you perform your actual tricks after you tell a story rather than before. No matter how well you *tell* a story, it will be hard to follow a trick that your audience can actually *see*.

Remember that it is important to learn a trick thoroughly so that you feel comfortable performing it. Every magician occasionally fails, but it is embarrassing, and best to guard against mistakes by practicing well. One rule is to never repeat a trick in the same show, for if your audience knows what to expect, people will be much more alert the second time around. Another is to never reveal the secret of the trick—no matter how charming the request! If you are using misdirection as a magical element, remember that the audience looks where you look, will look at anything that moves, and will look in the direction of a light or sound. Practice, then perform.

Patter and Presentation

Patter refers to what the magician says while performing. It is not enough to simply follow the directions enclosed with a trick, for it is often what you say that actually makes the trick believable. On the other hand, some magicians don't say anything, but perform wordlessly to music. As you become more proficient as a conjurer, you will find yourself developing good general presentation skills that will serve you well even in book programs that do not include magic. The trick is to develop a good performer-audience relationship, whatever the subject of your presentation.

Magic Tricks

These tricks are easy to learn and require only a minimum of preparation—perfect for busy teachers and librarians. They are classic effects that have been specially adapted to fit into book or storytelling programs.

Mixing Colors

This trick can be used anytime you are reading a book that involves color or perhaps during a program in which you are describing the color printing process. The obvious choices are picture books about color, which can be exhibited for groups of all ages. Lois Ehlert's *Color Farm* and *Color Zoo* are perfect examples. Using die-cut pages and brilliant clear colors, these books are magical themselves, as they transform common shapes into animals. Ann Jonas' *Color Dance* is another good choice; children dance through the pages with colored scarves, illustrating the magic of color mixing. *The Color Box* by Dayle Ann Dodds and illustrated by Giles Laroche also uses the die-cut page to show a monkey crawling from one color to another through a hole in the page. Finally, a special favorite of mine is Michael Rosen's *How the Animals Got Their Colors*, illustrated by John Clementson. These are short folktales collected from around the world that tell why the tiger is striped, why frogs are green, and so on.

The trick: Plain clear water turns red, yellow, and blue, and then by combining the yellow and blue, you create green.

You will need:
Three small glasses and one large glass (I use plastic glasses so that I don't have to worry about breakage).
A box of food coloring

Pre-performance preparation:
Put a drop of red food coloring in one of the small glasses, a drop of blue in another and a drop of yellow in the remaining glass. Fill the larger glass with water.

Patter and presentation:
As you know, the primary colors are red, yellow, and blue. I have some glasses here (sweep your hand over the empty glasses) that I will fill with green water. First I fill this glass with water. (Pick up the glass with the red color in it and pour some water from the large glass into it. The water will turn red.) Whoops. Sorry. This is red. I'll try it with this glass. (Pick up the glass with the color blue.) Ladies and gentlemen, the color green! (Pour some water into the glass.) Whoops. Sorry again. This is blue. I'll try this one. (Pick up the glass with yellow color and add the remainder of the water.) Whoops. It's yellow. What do yellow and blue make? Right. Let's try the two together. (Pour the yellow water and the blue water into the larger glass.) I did it! (Triumphantly display the green water.)

Hint: You can offer the drinks to your audience once you're finished. Try using ginger ale or Seven-up. Children will love it!

Read to Your Dog

Try this trick with your favorite dog stories. I like to tell "The Poor Old Dog" from Arnold Lobel's *Fables*. This original fable should be told just as it is written. Fortunately, it is only one page long, so it is not difficult to memorize. A longer story that gives you a chance to use a foreign accent (unless you are French Canadian, of course!) is the story about an imaginary dog that terrorizes the neighborhood: "Jean Labadie's Big Black Dog" in Natalie Carlson's *The Talking Cat and Other Stories of French Canada*, illustrated by Roger Duvoisin.

The trick: The magician shows an empty envelope, representing a dog house. She puts a picture of a barking dog into the house. When the house is opened, out comes a sleeping dog.

You will need:
Two envelopes of the same size
A picture of a barking dog
A picture of a sleeping dog

Pre-performance preparation:
You will need to prepare a special envelope, which can be used for a variety of tricks. First, glue the front of two envelopes together. Then reproduce the pictures of the two dogs or draw your own.

Patter and performance:
My dog couldn't sleep. (Show the picture of the barking dog.) He was barking and keeping my Mom and Dad awake. Shh, I whispered, but he kept on barking. Go back to bed, I said. Here, I'll put you into your dog house. (Slip the picture into one side of the envelope, showing that there is nothing else inside.) I read him a story about a dog. (Mention your favorite dog title.) It seemed very quiet in the house. (Turn the envelope to the other side without being obvious.) I looked inside his house. At last he was

fast asleep. (Reach inside the envelope and take out the picture of the sleeping dog.) Oh, good, he's asleep. I better let the "sleeping dog lie."

Hint: On another occasion you can use the two-sided envelope to exchange one card for another, or you can show one side empty and magically make something appear.

Booklist: Dog Books to Exhibit

NOVELS

Byars, Betsy. *Wanted . . . Mud Blossom.* Art by Jacqueline Rogers. Delacorte, 1991. Has Mud, Pap's beloved dog, eaten Junior, the school hamster?

Cleary, Beverly. *Strider.* Art by Paul O. Zelinsky. Morrow, 1991. Leigh finds a dog on the beach and coaxes him home.

Cresswell, Helen. *Absolute Zero: Being the Second Part of the Bagthorpe Saga.* Macmillan. 1978. Jack's dog is a television star.

King-Smith, Dick. *Babe, the Gallant Pig.* Art by Mary Rayner. Crown, 1983. Stop. This is not a book about a dog, but about a charming pig who acts like a dog.

PICTURE BOOKS

Goennel, Heidi. *My Dog.* Art by author. Orchard/Watts, 1989. A little girl catalogs what she likes about dogs.

Muir, Frank. *What-a-Mess the Good.* Art by Joseph Wright, Doubleday, 1978. A charming puppy tries and fails to be good.

Seligson, Susan and Howie Schneider. *Amos: The Story of an Old Dog and His Coach.* Art by Howie Schneider. Little, 1987. A laugh-out-loud account of a dog and his motorized coach.

Biography Prediction

This is the perfect magic trick to accompany a booktalk about biographies.

The trick: You "magically" show a picture that you have drawn of the subject of a biography that a volunteer has secretly selected.

You will need:
A pad of drawing paper
A pencil
A selection of biographies

Patter and presentation:
Booktalk several of your favorite biographies. Then select a volunteer and tell him that you will draw a picture of the person in the biography of his choice. Take out your drawing pad and draw a picture while the volunteer chooses a biography. The volunteer then points to the biography of his choice as you show your picture, saying, "That's the picture I drew—a picture of Abraham Lincoln [or whoever he has chosen] as a baby!"

Hint: If you feel that you can't draw a baby, try drawing the baby's crib.

Booklist: Biographies to Exhibit

Fortunately there has been a renaissance in the writing of biographies for children and young adults. You will find biographies for all interests and reading levels on the shelves of your library. I think that the most welcome trend in biographical writing may be the picture book biography. In many cases, these picture books depict famous people as children, making their stories easily accessible even to preschoolers.

Adler, David. A. *Benjamin Franklin: Printer, Inventor, Statesman.* Art by Lyle Miller. Holiday, 1992. One of Adler's "first biography" series.

Blumberg, Rhoda. *Commodore Perry in the Land of the Shogun.* Lothrop, 1985. Details the story of Commodore Mathew Perry's excursion to Japan in the 1850s.

Brooks, Polly Schoyer. *Beyond the Myth: The Story of Joan of Arc.* Lippincott, 1990. The story of the popular French heroine who led an army to victory, but was eventually burned as a witch.

Byars, Betsy. *Betsy Byars: The Moon and I.* Messner, 1991. A lively autobiography of the author of *Bingo Brown* and *Cracker Jackson.* Look for other author biographies from Messner as well.

Downing, Julie. *Mozart Tonight.* Art by author. Bradbury, 1991. Mozart looks back on his musical successes and failures on the eve of the opening of *Don Giovanni.*

Fisher, Leonard Everett. *Galileo.* Art by author. Macmillan, 1992. Black-and-white paintings illustrate this picture book biography of the man who invented the telescope and the microscope.

Fritz, Jean. *The Great Little Madison.* Putnam, 1989. This is just one of Fritz's fine biographies of American historical figures.

Houston, Gloria. *My Great-Aunt Arizona.* Art by Susan Conde Lamb. Harper, 1992. A fictionalized picture book biography of a young girl who grows up to be a teacher.

Hoyt-Goldsmith, Diane. *Hoang Anh: A Vietnamese-American Boy*. Photos by Lawrence Migdale. Holiday, 1992. A photo essay showing the life of a Vietnamese-American living in California.

Levinson, Nancy Smiler. *Christopher Columbus: Voyager to the Unknown*. Dutton, 1990. The 500th anniversary of Columbus's "discovery" of the new world was celebrated in the publishing world by a plethora of Columbus biographies. This is a good choice.

Peet, Bill. *Bill Peet: An Autobiography*. Art by author. Houghton, 1989. Peet writes and draws his life from boyhood to successful picture book author/ artist.

Simon, Sheridan. *Stephen Hawking: Unlocking the Universe*. Dillon, 1991. This is the story of the theoretical physicist and his fight against Lou Gehrig's disease.

Stanley, Diane and Peter Vennema. *Good Queen Bess: The Story of Elizabeth I of England*. Art by Diane Stanley. Four Winds, 1990. A portrait of the Queen who ushered in the "Elizabethan" age.

Turner, Robyn Montana. *Georgia O'Keeffe*. Little, 1987. This picture book biography is one of a series, Portraits of Women Artists for Children.

Ventura, Piero. *Great Composers*. Art by author. Putnam, 1988. An attractive collective biography featuring composers from around the world.

The Change Bag

A commercial trick you can buy that has multiple uses is the change bag. You can show the bag empty and then produce an object. You can change an object into something else. I like to use it when I tell practically any story featuring American history or American heros. *Flight* by Robert Burleigh, the story of Charles Lindberg's flight across the Atlantic in 1927, is a fun choice. After showing the book or telling your own version of the historic flight, show the change bag empty. Then place in the bag a white silk, a red silk, and a blue silk. Reach in and pull out an American flag (or a French flag, since the colors are the same). Then show the bag empty once again.

Spring Flowers and the Botania

Other commercial tricks to consider purchasing are either spring flowers or the more advanced Botania. Spring flowers can be put into a dove pan, change bag, or even placed in a book. When triggered they expand into a bouquet of colorful blooms. The Botania is a more expensive version using lovely feather flowers. Any book about gardening or spring works perfectly with a flower trick. Or tell Robert Krauss's *Leo The Late Bloomer* before performing your magic.

Book Telepathy

Use three books you've planned to use in your book program. You will need three books (or their covers), a library card, two pieces of paper, and an envelope.

Suppose the books are *Tar Beach* by Faith Ringgold, *Oh, What Nonsense!*, edited by William Cole, and *Flight* by Robert Burleigh.

Pre-performance preparation:
On a piece of paper write "You will choose *Tar Beach*." Put the paper into an envelope. On the underside of the library card print "You will choose *Oh, What Nonsense!* On the underside of *Flight* attach a sign that says "You will choose *Flight*."

Patter and presentation:
Line up the three books in a row. Ask a child from the group to think of one of the three books. Now ask her to place the library card on her choice of one of the three books.

If *Tar Beach* is chosen, have her look inside the envelope.
If *Oh, What Nonsense!* is chosen, have her turn over the library card.
If *Flight* is chosen, turn the book over and let her read what is written there.
Now you can read or tell a story from the book the volunteer selected, but don't repeat this trick with the same group.

Riddle Trick

Use this at the end of a storyhour featuring stories about riddles. One of my favorite riddle stories is "The Princess and Jose" in Anita Brenner's *The Boy Who Could Do Anything and Other Mexican Folk Tales*, illustrated by Jean Charlot. This story uses a version of the riddle of the Sphinx: "What is it that goes first on four legs, then on two legs, and then on three legs?"

 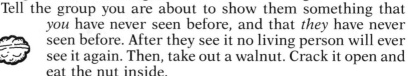 Tell the group you are about to show them something that *you* have never seen before, and that *they* have never seen before. After they see it no living person will ever see it again. Then, take out a walnut. Crack it open and eat the nut inside.

Booklist: Riddle Books to Exhibit

Adler, David A. *A Teacher on Roller Skates and Other School Riddles*. Art by John Wallner. Holiday, 1989.

Bierhorst, John. *Lightning inside You and Other Native American Riddles*. Art by Louise Brierley. Morrow, 1992.

Keller, Charles and Richard Baker. *The Star-Spangled Banana and Other Revolutionary Riddles*. Art by Tomie dePaola. Prentice, 1974.

Most, Bernard. *Pets in Trumpets and Other Word-play Riddles*. Art by author. Harcourt, 1991.

Nims, Bonnie Larkin. *Just beyond Reach and Other Riddle Poems*. Photos by George Ancona. Scholastic, 1992.

See the Riddles section in chapter 9, Non-narrative Sources, for even more suggestions.

Prediction Pencil

In this trick a rising pencil can answer yes and no questions such as "Did Harve Zemach write *Duffy and the Devil*?" or "Was Hans Christian Andersen a Dane?"

Preparation: Take a pencil and cut a slit in the eraser. Fasten a piece of dark thread about eight inches long to a button on your jacket or shirt. Slip the other end into the slit on the eraser. Drop the pencil eraser side down into an empty soda bottle. As you slowly draw the bottle away from you the pencil will rise in the glass. (The thread can be fastened with beeswax, sometimes called magician's wax, available from magic supply stores.)

   If you make the pencil rise, the answer to the magician's question is "yes"; if you let it drop back into the bottle the answer is "no."

A Word from Smokey the Bear

This trick can be used after telling stories with forest settings. Tell your listeners that they must be careful to always put out fires and be careful of matches. Remind them that matches should be broken in two to make sure that they are out. Show the group a wooden match that you then place under a scarf. Ask a child to break the match with the scarf still wrapped around it in two. When you take hold of the scarf, the match drops out unharmed. "You can never be too careful," you exclaim.

Preparation: Sew a match inside the hem of a scarf. When the child breaks the match he is really breaking the one sewn into the scarf. Meanwhile you take the match that you displayed into your hand. When you open the scarf, let the match in your hand fall out.

Booklist: Books about Forests to Exhibit

Anderson, C. W. *Blaze and the Forest Fire*. Art by author. Macmillan, 1938.

Anholt, Laurence. *The Forgotten Forest*. Art by author. Sierra Club Books, 1992.

Gackenbach, Dick. *Mighty Tree*. Art by author. Harcourt, 1992.

Goodman, Billy. *The Rain Forest*. Illustrated with photos. Tern (15 West 26th St., New York, NY 10010), 1991.

Jaspersohn, Willima. *How the Forest Grew*. Art by Chuck Eckart. Greenwillow, 1980.

Ryder, Joanne. *When the Woods Hum*. Art by Catherine Stock. Morrow, 1991.

A Proverb Trick

Tell the La Fontaine fable about the milkmaid who, coming home from work with a jug of milk on her head, thinks about all the things she will buy when she sells the milk. "With the money I'll buy some chickens. The chickens will

lay eggs. Chicks will hatch from the eggs; I'll sell them, then I'll buy a new dress and go to a dance. I'll dance with all the young men."

As the milkmaid danced in anticipation, the jug fell off her head and broke. There went milk, money, chickens, chicks, and party dress. *Moral*: Don't count your chickens before they hatch.

One version of this story appears in picture-book form in Ingri and Edgar Parin d'Aulaire's *Don't Count Your Chicks*; yet another version is Hans Christian Andersen's *The Woman with the Eggs*. A Mexican version, *Josefina*, can be found in Catharine Farrell's *Storytelling: A Guide for Teachers*.

Preparation: Blow out an egg by putting a pinhole in both ends of an egg and literally blowing the egg out. (Scrambled eggs for breakfast!) Let the eggshell dry for a few days or dry it out in a warm oven. Fill the egg with confetti through one of the holes. Seal the egg with tape or beeswax. After you've told the story crack the egg and let the confetti scatter. Make sure you have a broom and dustpan handy. This is a spectacular trick, but very messy.

The Four Thieves

Do this trick after you've told *The Traveling Musicians of Bremen*, a Grimm's tale retold by P. K. Page. To do so you will need a pack of playing cards. Hold up the four Jacks which, you tell your audience, represent the four robbers. Remind the audience that to spend the night the robbers each went into the house, which is represented by the rest of the deck of cards. Tell them you are going to put the robbers into different rooms in the house but they will all end up at the door ready to run away.

Patter and presentation:

Place any three cards behind the Jacks before you fan them out to show them. Show only the Jacks and keep the three extra cards behind the last Jack. Then explain:

"Here are the four robbers ready to enter the house. The deck of cards can represent the house." (Show the Jacks, then place them face downward on top of the deck. The three extra cards are now on the top of the deck.)

"The first robber went in and made himself comfortable in the basement." (Place one of the extra cards on the bottom of the deck.)

"The second robber went into the house and sat in the kitchen." (Place the second card anywhere in the deck.)

"The third robber went into the bedroom and lay down." (Place the third extra card anywhere in the deck.)

"The fourth robber stood guard at the door." (You can show this last card, the first Jack on the top of the pile.)

"The cock, the cat, the dog and the donkey began their concert. The robbers all ran out the door" (show all the Jacks—one, two, three, four, which seem to have risen to the surface) "and were never seen again."

Television versus Books

This is a fun way to illustrate the benefits of reading over watching television! For story suggestions, you could browse through the chapter on television in my book, *Celebrations: Read-aloud Holiday and Theme Book Programs.*

Preparation: You need a manila envelope just large enough to hold and easily permit removal of an 8″ × 10″ card. Draw differing TV call letters on each side so that the audience can tell when you have turned the envelope over.

Then you need an 8″ × 10″ card with a screen and wavy lines drawn on one side and a screen with stars and stripes drawn on the other. Carefully trim about ⅛″ from each side of this card. The reason for this soon will become clear.

You also need to make a "sheath" card. To do this, tape two 8″ × 10″ cards together, on the inside. On one side of the sheath card, draw the screen with the wavy lines again; on the other side, draw the screen with the words: NEXT TIME READ A BOOK.

Patter and presentation:

Tell your audience that books are better than television. Every time you sit down to look at television you get poor reception. (Show the side of the card with the wavy lines drawn on it.) So you usually switch to another channel. (Place the card inside the envelope. Turn the envelope around and pull out the card, showing the side painted with stars and stripes.) The reception is just as bad on that side. (The audience knows that you are just showing the other side of the card.) So I switch to another channel. (You put the card inside the envelope again and take out the card with the wavy lines on it. The audience expects to see stars and stripes on the other side, but instead when you turn the card around a notice is printed on the other side that says, "Next time read a book.") Now open the manila envelope, tearing it in pieces so that the audience knows there is nothing inside.

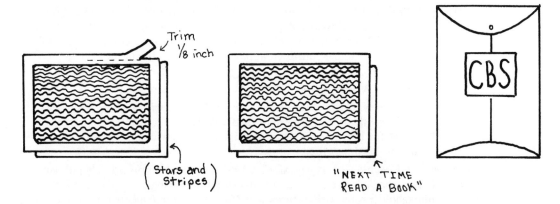

Trim ⅛ inch

(Stars and Stripes)

"NEXT TIME READ A BOOK"

CBS

The trick is that the second time you place the card inside the envelope you insert the first card in the "sheath" card and hold it up. The audience will never notice that it is slightly larger.

The Dove Pan

My favorite magic trick to buy for a book program is the Dove or Chick Pan. Show an empty pan to your audience. Fill it with "what makes a book"; cut up words and pictures. Light a match and it flames up instantly into a blaze that you cover with a pan top. When you remove the top the fire has been replaced with "spring" flowers, streamers, and a book or books that you proceed to read. A spectacular trick that you can use over and over again.

Almost any magic supplier will demonstrate the Dove Pan for you. Flash paper that burns so spectacularly, leaving no ash, and tissue paper flowers that spring to life are also readily available.

Booklist: Magic

For Adults

Adair, Ian. *Encyclopaedia of Children's Magic*. Art by Steve and Mavis Newby. Photos by Tim Cox. Supreme, 1991. Routines, promotion, patter, and business advice for the children's magician.

Behnke, Ed. Magic City Library of Magic. Magic City (Paramount, CA 90723), 1983–1990. Nineteen magic pamphlets on subjects including dove pans, change bags, cups and balls, and much more.

Eldin, Peter. *The Magic Handbook*. Simon, 1985. An excellent collection of magic tricks accompanied by color illustrations.

Fulves, Karl. *Self-working Paper Magic*. Dover, 1985. Magic tricks using money, cardboard, construction paper.

Ginn, David. *Kidbiz*. 4387 St. Michaels Drive, Lilburn, GA 30247. Ginn is also the author of *Professional Magic for Children, Comedy Warmups*, and more of the very best magic books for adults interested in magic for children.

Hawkesworth, Eric. *Practical Lessons in Magic*. Supreme, 1984. Hawkesworth also wrote *Conjuring* (Supreme, 1984), *A Magic Variety Show* (Supreme, 1984), and others. All are excellent short books with clear diagrams for close-up and stage magic.

Hooper, Edwin. *A Host of Surprises*. Art by Shawn Yee and Vanni Pulé. Photos by David Pusey. Edwin's Magic Arts (Bideford, Devon, England), 1990. The founder of Supreme Magic gives a clear explanation of commercial tricks as well as you-make-your-own apparatus and the effects they create.

Roper, David. *The Comedy Magic Textbook*. Snowflake (5687 Williams Road, Norcross, GA 30093), 1986. Routines using commercial effects.

Seabrooke, Terry. *Seabrooke's Book: Around the World with a Baking Tin*. Magical Publications (572 Prospect Blvd., Pasadena, CA 91103). Seabrooke is known for his fast-paced patter. This book has tricks, and also anecdotes on his professional life.

Severn, Bill. *Magic with Paper*. McKay, 1962. This book (appropriately published in paperback) is one of several by this author featuring easy-to-do magic using household props. Other titles are *Magic in Your Pockets* (McKay, 1968), *Magic Comedy* (McKay, 1968), and *Magic across the Table* (McKay, 1972).

Smith, Samuel Patrick. *Big Laughs for Little People: How to Entertain Children with Comedy and Magic*. SPS Publications (Tavares, FL 32778), 1990. Emphasis on children's comedy magic using commercial tricks.

For Children

NONFICTION

Bailey, Vanessa. *Rainy Days Card Tricks*. Watts, 1990. Clear, easy-to-follow photographs show exactly how to perform simple card tricks.

Baker, James W. *New Year's Magic*. Art by George Overlie. Lerner, 1989. One of the Holiday Magic Book series from Lerner, which also includes *Valentine Magic/Presidents' Day Magic* (1989), *April Fool's Magic* (1989), *Birthday Magic* (1988), and others. Excellent small-size books full of easy-to-do theme magic.

Barry, Sheila Anne. *Tricks and Stunts to Fool Your Friends*. Art by Doug Anderson. Sterling, 1984. Tricks to do with a calculator, cards, and numbers.

Broekel, Roy and Laurence B. White, Jr. *Now You See It: Easy Magic for Beginers*. Art by Bill Morrison. Little, 1979. Instructions for forty tricks.

Sheridan, Jeff. *Nothing's Impossible! Stunts to Entertain and Amaze*. Photos by Jim Moore. Lothrop, 1982. Clear photographs and easy-to-follow text teach tricks and stunts in a picture-book format.

White, Laurence B. Jr. and Ray Broekel. *Math-a-Magic: Number Tricks for Magicians*. Whitman, 1990. Magic with numbers.

_____. *Shazam! Simple Science Magic*. Art by Meyer Seltzer. Whitman, 1991. Directions for simple effects based on scientific principles.

Wyler, Rose and Gerald Amers. *Magic Secrets*. Art by Arthur Dorros. rev. ed. Harper, 1990. An I Can Read book featuring easy-to-do magic.

FICTION: PICTURE BOOKS

Alexander, Sue. *World Famous Muriel and the Magic Mystery*. Art by Marla Frazee. Crowell, 1990. World Famous Muriel solves the mystery of the Great Hokus Pokus . . . at the library. The perfect example of magic keyed to books.

Baker, Keith. *The Magic Fan*. Art by author. Harcourt, 1989. Yoshi finds a magic fan, but discovers that there is magic in himself.

Dubowski, Cathy East and Mark Dubowski. *Pretty Good Magic*. Art by authors. Random, 1987. Presto shows the town of Forty Winks a pretty good magic trick.

Eliot, T. S. *Mr. Mistoffelees with Mungojerrie and Rumpelteaszer*. Art by Errol LeCain. Harcourt, 1991. Mr. Mistoffelees uses his magical skills to confound his drawing room audiences.

Gauch, Patricia Lee. *Uncle Magic*. Art by Deborah Kogan Ray. Holiday, 1992. A young girl discovers where true magic is.

Houghton, Eric. *Walter's Magic Wand*. Art by Denise Teasdale. Orchard, 1990. Walter's magic wand works when he says the magic words.

Johnston, Tony. *The Badger and the Magic Fan*. Art by Tomie dePaola. Putnam, 1990. A badger steals a magic fan from three *tengu*, the goblin children of Japan.

Kraus, Robert. *Phil the Ventriloquist*. Art by author. Greenwillow, 1989. Phil, a rabbit, can throw his voice into objects or people.

Lagercrantz, Rose and Samuel Lagercrantz. *Is It Magic?* tr. by Paul Norlen. Art by Eva Eriksson. Farrar, 1990. Pete gets a magic wand, an old hat, and a special book that finally proves that "magic's something you must try your whole life through."

FICTION: LONGER BOOKS

Cresswell, Helen. *Time Out*. Art by Peter Elwell. Macmillan, 1990. The use of a book of spells makes it possible for a family from 1887 to vacation in 1987.

Edmunds, I. G. *The Magic Dog*. Dutton, 1982. Beauty, a dog, works with the Great Lafayette. She can make people appear and disappear with a wave of her wand.

Fleischman, Sid. *Mr. Mysterious and Company*. Art by Eric von Schmidt. Little, 1962. A family of traveling magicians encounters adventure in the 1880s.

McGowan, Tom. *The Magician's Apprentice*. Dutton, 1987. Tigg, a pickpocket, is apprenticed to an enchanter.

Morrison, Dorothy Nafus. *Vanishing Act*. Atheneum, 1989. Joanna is looking for the perfect trick to perform for the talent show.

Roberts, Willo Davis. *The Magic Book*. Atheneum, 1986. Alex uses a book of magic spells to try and outwit the class bully.

Schwartz, Alvin. *Tales of Trickery*. Art by David Christina. Farrar, 1985. Short trickster stories.

York, Carol Beach. *Rabbit Magic*. Art by Irene Trivas. Scholastic, 1991. Ms. Lavender finally finds a trick she can perform at The Good Day Orphanage for Girls.

Magic Videos

Be a Magician. Imagination Tree (Evansville, Ind.), 1985. 60-minute video. Featuring Martin Preston, this includes magic presentations and a box of materials.

Flora, Brian. *The Balloon Video*. Flora & Company, 1988. 55-minute video. Fifteen basic balloon sculptures are demonstrated.

Ginn, David. *It's About Time*. 4387 St. Michaels Drive, Lilburn, GA 39247, 1990. 55-minute video. David Ginn's magic and comedy performances for schools are featured. A book is included with the video.

Hickman, B. J. *The Magic of Reading*. B. J. Hickman Magic Show (623 6th Ave., Dover, NH 03820), 1992. 55-minute video. Audience participation and comedy magic for children.

Starring the Universal Nut Bev Bergeron, v. 3. The Magic Division of U.S. Toy Co., 1988. Masters of Excellence series. Birthday party magic.

18 / Music

Carmel, Indiana: "Pink and green silver-paper toffee-paper!
Pink and green silver-paper toffee-paper!"
chanted 300 children from the elementary school as they
marched down Palmer Street. Some of the children were playing
homemade instruments: clanging pot tops, strumming rubber-
band/boxes, drumming on cans.

Adding music to storytelling can help make your presentation lively and colorful, while encouraging your audience to join
in. Using Richard Hughes's nonsense story and pick-up instruments, our parade woke up all of the neighbors! Everyone had a
great time marching around town. I suspect a few of those children may even tell their grandchildren about the time "this
storyteller came to town and the whole school went outside and
caused a ruckus."

There are lots of different ways to include music in your
storytelling programs. Use a musical theme to begin and end the
program. Tell a story that includes singing or use a song to encourage audience participation. Even if you are not particularly

musical, don't skip this chapter! There are ideas for you here, too.

Here is Richard Hughes's story, "The China Spaniel," for you to tell today. Your audience will help you as they join in on the chant:

"Pink and green silver-paper toffee-paper!"

THE CHINA SPANIEL

Richard Hughes

There was once a school that was rather cross and dull, and it was run by one old woman.

Now it so happened that one of the children at this school was a china spaniel, the kind that has a gold chain round its neck, and doesn't look as if it had much sense. As a matter of fact, this one had practically no sense at all: he was easily the stupidest pupil in the whole school, and could never learn his lessons properly.

One day they were all given some poetry to learn for homework; and the china spaniel really did try his hardest: but when he came into school the next day he couldn't remember a single line of it.

In fact, the only thing that came into his head to say was:

> Pink and green silver-paper toffee-paper!
> Pink and green silver-paper toffee-paper!
> Pink and green . . .

"What!" screamed the old woman: "*That* isn't what I gave you to learn!"

But there must have been some sort of magic in the words, for immediately all the other children in the school, the good ones and the clever ones and everybody, rose up from the desks, and all began chanting together at the tops of their voices:

> Pink and green silver-paper toffee-paper!
> Pink and green silver-paper toffee-paper!

—and out into the street they all rushed, dancing and singing at the tops of their voices.

"What's this? What's this" said a policeman. "What's all the row about?"

"Pink and green silver-paper toffee-paper!" shouted the children.

And thereupon the policeman began to dance too, and chanted it with the children.

"What's this? What's this?" cried the Chief of Police, who happened to be passing: "One of my policemen dancing? What does this mean, sir!"

"Pink and green silver-paper toffee-paper!" replied the policeman: and no sooner did he hear it that the Chief of Police started chanting it too, with all the rest, for by now there were quite a lot of other people of the town who had joined the procession and went along chanting

> Pink and green silver-paper toffee-paper!

with the china spaniel, who had started it all, marching proudly at their head.

At last they came to the Royal Palace, whereupon the King came out on his balcony ready to make a speech.

"My loyal subjects, I see you gathered together before my palace in great numbers. Well, as you know, I am a kind king and always anxious to give you what you want, so what is it?"

"Pink and green silver-paper toffee-paper!" cried the people; "pink and green silver-paper toffee-paper!"

"*What* did they say they wanted?" whispered the Prime Minister, who was a little deaf, at the King's elbow.

"Pink and green silver-paper toffee-paper?" asked the Prime Minister's secretary in polite surprise.

And then, in a twinkling, they were all dancing and chanting and shouting in the palace as well as outside it:

> Pink and green silver-paper toffee-paper,
> Pink and green silver-paper toffee-paper,
> Pink and green silver-paper toffee-paper,
> Pink and green silver-paper toffee-paper,
> Pink and green silver-paper toffee-paper,
> Pink and green silver-paper toffee-paper!

Nor was it long before the whole nation was singing it: and some enemies who were besieging the town at the time, hearing it, thought it must be some sort of national anthem, till they found themselves starting to sing it too; and, in short, it wasn't long before the whole world was singing it—the whole world, that is to say, except the old woman who kept the school.

"It would take more than the whole world going mad," she said very firmly, "to make me start dancing and playing the goat!"

And she went on trying to run her school just as before it happened, the silly old thing.

Music in Multimedia Presentations

There may be times during the presentation of a multimedia story when nothing is actually happening, perhaps a scene change in a puppet show or while changing transparencies on an overhead projector. Then it is a good idea to plan for a musical interlude. Use a record, tape deck, or compact disc player; if you have a pianist, all the better. One time when music is especially useful is when you are showing a book without words on film slides or transparencies. Choose your music carefully to suit the mood of your story. Ask a friend or the local music store for suggestions if you are unfamiliar with the world of recorded music. Many libraries have extensive collections and the librarian is often well versed in what is contained in the collection. A local radio station may have a disc jockey delighted to share his or her knowledge of music and help you. Sometimes you may even prefer to tape your own background music and sound effects. This is worth experimenting with, but it may be more difficult than it appears. Extraneous noises (the dog barking, the baby crying) may make your recordings less than perfect.

A Musical Theme

Just as some disc jockeys have a musical theme to announce their program segments, you may want to choose a theme for your storyhour. Choose a recorded piece of music that suits you and play it throughout your library or classroom for a few minutes before the storytime is scheduled to begin.

Choosing Music

If you are knowledgeable about music, or have a friend or colleague who is, you can choose a different piece of music for every story session. This works well even if you have a theme for your storyhour. For example, you can use circus music for a circus program, quiet music for thoughtful books, folk songs or dances originating from the source country of the stories. Play the music as the children enter the room, find their seats, remove their coats, and place their toys or books on the floor. You might even leave the music on softly as you introduce the stories. When you open the first book, or light your wishing candle, turn the music down. You can turn it up again at the end of the storyhour when the children are leaving. This works rather like the overture of a musical comedy that is played as the audience enters and leaves the theater. If you or a friend can play a musical instrument with proficiency, you can accomplish the same purpose with "live" music.

Singing

Lucky you if you are blessed with a good singing voice. You can find folk songs to fit the stories you tell and incorporate the singing of songs in your storytime. Open the session with a song. Use music as a change of pace between stories and as an ending to your program.

Some storytellers greet their group with the same greeting song at each session and the children sing along. Depending on the sophistication of the song, the idea may not be suitable for all ages. If your storyhours tend to attract a majority of new children each time, singing a group song will be impractical since it will take too much time to learn it each session. If you are a classroom teacher, however, with a consistent group of children, you may enjoy trying this idea.

There are times when you may want to make singing the focal point of your storyhour. Celebrate the winter holiday season with group singing. Most children know the words of a variety of Christmas carols and Hanukkah songs. In fact, they'll remind you of the words you've forgotten and contribute an idea for a song or two.

Making up Songs

Encourage children to make up songs about their daily life. They may sing off key, but it's a delight to hear a preschooler singing happily about getting up or going to bed.

For the Nonmusical

Some stories from folklore contain a song to sing. If the character singing is meant to have a sweet, lilting young voice and you croak like a frog, you might consider another story. However, many songs may be spoken like poetry if the audience is first told that the character sang the song.

Do you have a friend who plays an instrument? Invite him or her to perform as a guest at your storyhour. After the performance, he or she may enjoy showing the instrument to the children and explaining a little about it. Books about music and instruments also can be exhibited.

You don't have to have any musical ability to pretend that you're in a band, as this excerpt from Jim Latimer's *Going the Moose Way Home* illustrates:

> Moose sometimes makes things up.
> Once along the country road, he saw a parade—a marching band. The air was filled with the sound of bells and crackling brass, and there were animal players in the band. There was a frog carrying the flag and a bear playing bells. There was a skunk on spoons and a hare on harp and a porcupine playing pianolin. Moose felt a tingling along his spine. The music was wild and beautiful. It made him want to move in rhythm. It made him want to play a musical instrument. A clarinet. Or maybe maracas.
> Along the country road Moose imagines he is a player in a marching band, going His Moose Way Home.

Dance

Of course you don't want to turn your storyhour into a dance class, but you might want your audience to respond to a story rhythmically. Let the children tap out the rhythm of a tongue twister, or the repeated rhyme in a story. Encourage them to respond with dance movements to the mood of a story or record.

If there is a ballet or modern dance studio in your community, invite these special students to your storyhour. Make absolutely certain that you provide a workable compact disc player, record player, tape deck or whatever they need. A good dance program may be hopelessly marred by a faulty musical background. Also don't forget that they will need enough floor space on which to perform.

Field Trips

Some adults have never attended an opera, ballet, or concert. You can insure that this doesn't happen to any of the future adults who come in contact with you in your storyhour. Plan a field trip for your class or library storytelling group to a dance festival or musical event in your town. If the nearest such event is some miles away, enlist the aid of parents or a local business to provide funds to rent a bus and purchase tickets. Let those families that can afford to help with the costs pay their way. Those children who cannot afford such a trip can be subsidized with donations or you might try putting the field trip idea into your next budget. (Don't forget to build in the cost of insurance as well.) Of course, to transport a group of any size you will need the help of volunteers, but the event, including the getting there and the sack lunches in the park, will be long remembered by the children. At the next session, appropriate stories and books can be presented and discussed.

Homemade Rhythm Instruments

Fill cottage cheese containers, jewelry boxes, hosiery "eggs," and match boxes with buttons, rice, macaroni, marbles, pebbles, or anything else that will rattle.

Use a large nail to thump a rhythm on a cake rack, pot top, tin can.

Put rubber bands across an open box, sugar scoop, or plastic cup to make a homemade stringed instrument you or a child can strum.

Use two of a kind to bump together: a variety of sizes of large bolts, jar lids, pot tops, tin cans. Drill a hole in the center of the tin can or lid so you can tie a string on the instrument which then can hang around your neck, leaving your hands free to tap, pound, or strum.

Make a glass piano by filling several water glasses to different levels, tune them, then tap them with a spoon to produce a melody.

Make a comb kazoo by wrapping tissue paper around a comb. Hum a tune through the paper. Use these instruments for children to participate in your storyhour. They can tap out a rhythm while singing. After you've told a suitable story let the audience chant a nonsense sentence and "play" the instruments in time to the chant.

Songs with familiar choruses make good material for rhythm instruments. Good and familiar folksongs appear in *The Fireside Book of Folk Songs*. Try "Clementine," "Sweet Betsy from Pike," "Funiculi, Funicula," "The Bluetail Fly," "Turkey in the Straw," "Oh Susanna," "The Erie Canal." Or begin with the two given right here.

Songs to Use with Rhythm Instruments

IF YOU'RE HAPPY

Sing this as a group or divide your group so that some are singing and some are playing their instruments. Many verses can be sung by adding actions such as: stamp your feet, turn around, touch the ground, raise your hands, or whatever you can think up.

If you're happy and you know it, clap your hands;

If you're happy and you know it, clap your hands;

If you're happy and you know it, then the whole world will know it;

If you're happy and you know it, clap your hands.

TIN FORD

collected by Robert Rubenstein

Sing the chorus of this jingle three times in a row, using actions for each word. Sing the chorus faster each time.

I've got a little pile of tin.
Nobody knows what shape it's in.
It's got four wheels and a running board.
It's a Ford. Oh! It's a Ford.

Chorus: Honk, Honk
Rattle, Rattle
CRASH
Screech, Screech
Beep, Beep.

Booklist: Stories with Rhythmic Phrases

Here are some stories and poems to use as rhythm activities.

Birdseye, Tom. *Soap! Soap! Don't Forget the Soap! An Appalachian Folktale.* Art by Andrew Glass. Holiday, 1993. This sprightly version of the Grandfather tale offers several repeating phrases to chant.

Brown, Jeanette Perkins. "Ticki, Ticki, Tembo" in *The Storyteller in Religious Education.* Pilgrim Pr., 1951. A spare telling of a popular nonsense story.

Carlstrom, Nancy White. *What Does the Rain Play?* Art by Henri Sorensen. Macmillan, 1993. A quiet book about a little boy and the rhythm of rain.

Chase, Richard. "Soap, Soap, Soap!" in *Grandfather Tales.* Art by Berkeley Williams, Jr. Houghton, 1948. "So he headed for the store, arunnin' along and sayin,' Soap! Soap! Soap!—so he wouldn't forget."

"Jack and Old Ragedy Bones" in Gail E. Haley's *Mountain Jack Tales.* Art by author. Dutton, 1992. "Whickety whack, get into my sack!"

Using Picture Book Versions of Songs

Even if you can neither sing nor play a musical instrument, you can introduce children to music through picture books. There are many fine books that use as their subject a folk song or opera. Use these books with or without the music. The book can be read aloud like poetry, showing the pictures, before, during, or after the music is heard. If the music is unavailable don't attempt to sing the song if you are really unmusical—just chant or read the words as you would any picture book. Simply tell the children the story is really a song. When my own daughter was young she objected to me singing a picture book. At first I was a bit hurt because I thought she was commenting on my tuneless croak. Now I understand; she feels books are to be read while music is to be played on the piano. With a storyhour group I am not so cowed and plunge into my singing if the children know the song and I think they will join me. Here is a special booklist devoted especially to picture book versions of songs. Start with these.

Booklist: Picture Book Versions of Single Songs

Bangs, Edward. *Yankee Doodle.* Art by Steven Kellogg. Four Winds, 1980. Kellogg's art adds to this American song. Music included.

Buffalo Girls. Art by Bobette McCarthy. Crown, 1987. Buffaloes dance to the light of the moon.

Child, Lydia. *Over the River and Through the Woods.* Art by Brinton Turkle. Scholastic, 1975. A family is on their way on Thanksgiving Day. Music included.

The Erie Canal. Art by Peter Spier. Doubleday, 1970. Pictures from the American past.

Fiddle-I-Fee: A Farmyard Song for the Very Young. Art by Melissa Sweet. Little, 1992. Cumulative folk song ends in a parade around the farm. Music included.

The Fox Went Out on a Chilly Night. Art by Peter Spier. Doubleday, 1961. Spier gives a New England setting to this folk song.

Go Tell Aunt Rhody. Art by Aliki. Macmillan, 1974. This story song is illustrated with full page art. Music included.

Hammerstein, Oscar II. *A Real Nice Clambake.* Music by Richard Rodgers. Art by Nadine Bernard Westcott. Little, 1992. A New England clambake with family and friends. Music included.

Hush Little Baby. Art by Aliki. Prentice-Hall, 1968. A colonial setting for this lullaby.

Hush, Little Baby; adapted and illustrated by Margot Zemach. Dutton, 1976. A Victorian setting to compare with that of Aliki's. Music included.

I Know an Old Lady Who Swallowed a Fly. Art by Glen Rounds. Holiday, 1990. The cumulative folk song with Round's distinctive art. Suitable for older children and adults.

Jingle Bells. Art by Maryann Kovalski. Little, 1988. Grandma and two little girls sing their way through Central Park. Music included.

Keats, Ezra Jack. *Over in the Meadow*; text based on the original version by Olive A. Wadsworth. Art by author. Four Winds, 1972. The art rather overpowers the simple counting rhyme, but choose for yourself. This version has no music.

King, Bob. *Sitting on the Farm.* Art by Bill Slavin. Orchard, 1991. The chorus: Munch, Munch, Munch of this song is fun to sing. Music included.

Knick Knack Paddywack. Art by Marissa Moss. Houghton, 1992. An old man builds a space ship from garbage cans and other junk and flies off to the moon to the text of the traditional song.

Langstaff, John. *Oh, A-Hunting We Will Go.* Art by Nancy Winslow Parker. Macmillan, 1974. Join the happy group as it tries to catch a fox.

London Bridge Is Falling Down! Art by Peter Spier. Doubleday, 1967. The panoramic drawings show the history of the building of the London Bridge.

Manson, Christopher. *The Tree in the Wood: An Old Nursery Song.* Art by author. North-South, 1993. Full-color woodcuts illustrate this traditional song.

O'Donnell, Elizabeth Lee. *Sing Me a Window.* Art by Melissa Sweet. Morrow, 1993. No music, but you'll want to "sing it" to your own tune.

Compare these illustrated versions of the traditional song:

Old MacDonald Had a Farm. Art by Lorinda Bryan Cauley. Putnam, 1989. Music included.

_____. Art by Nancy Hellen. Orchard, 1990. Music included.

_____. Art by Carol Jones. Houghton, 1989.

_____. Art by Tracey Campbell Pearson. Dutton, 1984. Music included.

_____. Art by Glen Rounds. Holiday, 1989. Music included.

Paterson, Andrew B. *Waltzing Matilda.* Art by Desmond Digby. Collins, 1970. Winner of the Australian award for children's illustrated books, this is a lovely version of the song, but with no music.

Prokofieff, Serge. *Peter and the Wolf;* foreword by Serge Koussevitzky. Art by Warren Chappell. Knopf, 1940. Music and pictures for the famous children's orchestral narrative.

Raffi. *Shake My Sillies Out.* Art by David Allender. Crown, 1987. Animals and campers jump, clap and shake. Music included.

Skip to My Lou. Art by Nadine Bernard Westcott. Little, 1989. Animals take over the house when a young boy is left alone. Music included.

There's a Hole in the Bucket. Art by Nadine Bernard Westcott. Harper, 1990. Henry does all the work . . . until the surprise ending in this version of the traditional song. Music included.

This Old Man. Art by Carol Jones. Houghton, 1990. Die-cut holes allow the reader to glimpse the next scene. Music included.

   *Three Blind Mice.* Art by Lorinda Bryan Cauley. Putnam, 1991. This sad song is illustrated with happy art. Music included.

The Wheels on the Bus. Art by Paul Zelinsky. Dutton, 1990. Pop-up, pull-out book with sophisticated art. Music included.

Zemach, Harve, *Mommy, Buy Me a China Doll;* adapted from an Ozark children's song. Art by Margot Zemach. Follett, 1966. Eliza Lou wants to "trade out daddy's feather bed" for a china doll.

Songs to Sing

If you can sing or play, no doubt you have your own favorites to perform. Following is a short selection of folksongs to introduce to your groups. Three of these selections ("Large Boots," "Old Joe Finly," and "Dunderbeck's Machine") are funny songs. You'll notice, however, that each of them has an element of violence or sadness. But children seem to accept this part as inevitable and ask for the songs, again and again.

"The Little Birds' Ball" and "Hush Little Children" are quieter songs for a change of pace. "Rocking Horse" is a short song to sing with very young children. Appropriate hand motions can be used with the participation song "Cows and Horses Walk on Four Feet." "Thanksgiving Song" is perfect—well, for your Thanksgiving storyhour, of course!

And last, my cousin, Susan Birkenhead-Couture, writes music and lyrics for Broadway shows in New York City. When her four children were younger she wrote for the children's television show *Captain Kangaroo*. Three of her songs are included here for you to try with your group.

HUSH, LITTLE CHILDREN

Traditional Southern lullaby;
collected by Edmund F. Soule

Hush, little children, don't say a word;
I'll give you a mockingbird.

If that mockingbird don't sing;
I'll give you a golden ring.

If that ring should turn to brass;
I'll give you a looking glass.

If that looking glass gets broke;
I'll give you a billy-goat.

If that billy-goat won't pull,
I'll give you a cart and bull.

If that cart and bull fall over,
I'll give you a dog named Rover.

If that dog named Rover won't bark,
I'll give you a horse and cart.

If that horse and cart fall down,
You're still the prettiest little children
  in town.

LARGE BOOTS

Australian marching song;
collected by Edmund F. Soule

Now there was a man named Anthony Dare,
And he was famous everywhere,
As a conjurer and a man of repute,
Because he could play with his boots!

Chorus:

For they were LARGE BOOTS, LARGE BOOTS,
Boots as heavy as lead,
With a circular twist of his muscular wrist
He could swing 'em right over his head!
Dee-dle-dee Um pum pum,
Dee-dle-dee Um pum pum!

As he was walking down the street,
He met a young lady so charming and sweet,
Who thought it would be such a wonderful treat
To see the man play with his boots . . .

As he was swinging them round and round,
One came down with a deuce of a bound
On the hairy head of her faithful hound
Who was watching him play with his boots.

She saw two policemen passing by
And loudly cried "Hi-Hi, Hi-Hi,
My faithful dog has been hit in the eye
By a man who has played with his boots!"

They took him to a magistrate
And lodged him in a cell of state
And there he had time to cogitate
And play with his wonderful boots.

Now the trial was held for straight away,
In fact it was held the very next day,
And the magistrate was heard to say:
"Why shouldn't he play with his boots?"

Now Anthony Dare has gone to rest;
As a swinger of boots he was the best;
He swung with a zoom and he swung with
    a zest,
That wonderful pair of boots!

OLD JOE FINLY

from Mrs. E. F. Gaines, Pullman, Washington, 1963;
collected by Edmund F. Soule

Old Joe Finly had a pig . . . Unh-huh!
Old Joe Finly had a pig,
It was so little it never got big . . . Unh-huh!

He went and put it in a sty . . . Unh-huh!
He went and put it in a sty,
And fed it on a sheaf of rye . . . Unh-huh!

The old woman went out to feed the pig . . .
  Unh-huh!
The old woman went out to feed the pig,
But when she got there the piggy was dead . . .
  Unh-huh!

The old woman she nearly grieved to death . . .
  Unh-huh!
The old woman she nearly grieved to death,
To think the piggy had lost its breath . . .
  Unh-huh!

The old woman she died soon after . . . Unh-huh!
The old woman she died soon after,
The old man he hung himself from a rafter . . .
  Unh-huh!

And that was the end of one, two, three . . .
  Unh-huh!
And that was the end of one, two, three,
The old man, the old woman, the little pig-ee . . .
  Unh-huh!

The lamp and book lie on the shelf . . .
  Unh-huh!
The lamp and book lie on the shelf,
If you want any more you can sing it your-
  self . . . Unh-huh!

DUNDERBECK'S MACHINE

Traditional text. Tune: A Rambling Wreck from Georgia Tech;
collected by Edmund F. Soule

There was a little Dutchy, and his name was Dunderbeck;
He kept cold meat and sauerkraut and sausage by the peck.
He had a little butcher shop, the finest ever seen
And one day he invented a sausage-meat machine.

Chorus:

O Dunderbeck, O Dunderbeck, how could you be so mean;
I'm sorry you invented that terrible* old machine;
The longtailed cats and billy-go-ats# will never more be seen,
For they'll all be ground to sausage-meat in Dunderbeck's
  machine!

One day a very little boy came walking into the store;
He wanted to buy a sausage that was lying on the floor.
While he waited for it, it whistled a merry tune
And all the sausages got up and danced around the room.

Now something was the matter, the machine it would not go,
And Dunderbeck he crawled inside the trouble for to know.
His wife was having nightmares and waking in her sleep;
She gave the crank a terrible yank and Dunderbeck was meat!

*horrible
#Variants can be invented: The short-haired cats and pussy-rats, etc.

THE LITTLE BIRDS' BALL

Anglo-American folk song as heard in Lewistown, Montana;
collected by Beverly Soule

Said the springbird to the nightingale
I mean to give the birds a ball;
Birdies great and birdies small
All will fly to the little birds' ball.

Chorus:

Tra-la-la-la-la, Tra-la-la-la-la
Tra-la-la-la-la . . . (Repeat)

O the woodpecker flew from his hole
    in the tree
And brought his bill to the companee;
Berries ripe and berries red,
A very large bill the little birds said.

O the awkward owl and the bashful
    jay
Bade each other a very good day;
The lark and the linnet danced for life
And the blackbird danced with the
    yellowhammer's wife.

They danced and sang till the sun was
    low
And the mother birds prepared to go;
Birdies great and birdies small
All flew home from the little birds'
    ball!

ROCKING HORSE

collected by Norma Borba

Rocking horse, rocking horse
Give me a ride to Spain.
Don't forget, don't forget
To bring me back home again.

COWS AND HORSES WALK ON FOUR FEET

collected by Alfred Bates

Cows and hoses walk on four
    feet
Little children walk on two
    feet
Birdies fly high in the air
Fishes swim in water clear
One, two, three, four, five
Catching fishes all alive
Heads and shoulders, knees
    and toes
Knees and toes, knees and
    toes
Head and shoulders, knees
    and toes
We'll all clap hands together.

THANKSGIVING SONG

This song will get your group in the mood for a celebration. Sing it to the tune of Brother John (Frère Jacque).

collected by Nell Givler

Turkey dinner, turkey dinner
Gather round, gather round
Who will get the drumstick?
Yummy, yummy drumstick
All sit down, all sit down.

Cornbread muffins, chestnut stuffing
Puddin' pie, one foot high
All of us were thinner
Until we came to dinner
Me-o-my, me-o-my.

Three by Susan Birkenhead-Couture

I LOVE A RAINY DAY

The more it pours
the more I like
to splishy-splash around

To paddle through
the little pools
and puddles on the ground

The slippy-slidey sidewalk
is the nicest place to play
Who cares if I am ever dry
I love a rainy day

Oh the plippety-plop
of each drippety-drop
is like music that comes
    from the sky

So I skip and I hop
And I hope it won't stop
till the last little raindrop
    goes by

I like the sun like everyone
But every now and then
I like to get a little wet
and splishy-splash again

So I get out my rubber boots
and hope the sky is grey
Who cares if I am ever dry
I love a rainy day!

ANIMAL SALAD

Nature's full of big surprises
Different colors
Different sizes
Floppy ears,
Trunks and tails,
Lumps and bumps and scrabbly scales . . .

Different legs
And different faces,
Ears and eyes
In different places
Just plain cute,
Or oddly made
Mother nature on parade

Chorus:

That's animal salad
The world is an animal salad
Animal salad
Spots and snorts and feathers and fur
Yessir!
A little of this,
A little of that,
Add paws and claws and stir . . . (Repeat)

Second Chorus:

That's animal salad
Yes animal salad
Oh my animal salad
Yessir!!!

ROPES

Jumping rope is lots of fun
But let me tell you, everyone
There are just about a ton of
things you can do with a rope

You can tie yourself in knots
You can be a horse that trots
Now you see that there are lots of
things you can do with a rope

Step, skip and jump around
Stretch it out along the ground
Tie your legs up, try to hop
Whoops-a-daisy down you flop!

Make the rope into a nest
Crawl inside and take a rest
I think ropes are just the best, don't you?

For tying,
wrapping,
skipping,
jumping,
pulling,
napping,
just galumping . . .

There's so much a rope can do
There's so much a rope can do!

Stories to Tell about Music and Dance

THE GOAT WELL

Harold Courlander

Harold Courlander collected many tellable tales. This one, from Ethiopia, contains lots of action. The teller gets a chance to call into the well, "Goats, are you there? Are you there, goats?" and, to the clapping of the audience, can dance at the end of the story.

A man named Woharia was once traveling across the plateau when he came to an abandoned house. He was tired and hungry, so he rested in the house and ate some of his bread, called injera. When he was about to leave he heard the baa-ing of a goat. He looked in all directions, but he saw nothing except the dry brown landscape. He heard the goat again, and finally he went to the old well and looked down into it. There, standing on the dry bottom, was the animal, which had somehow fallen in while searching for water to drink.

"What luck!" Woharia said. He climbed down and tied a rope around the goat, and then he came up and began to pull her out of the well.

Just at this moment a Cunama trader, with three camels loaded with sacks of grain, approached him. He greeted Woharia and asked if he might have water there for his thirsty camels.

"Naturally, if there were water here you would be welcome to it," Woharia said. "But unfortunately this is only a goat well."

"What is a goat well?" the Cunama asked.

"What do you think? It's a well that produces goats," Woharia said, and he pulled on his rope again until he got the goat to the top.

"This is really extraordinary!" the Cunama said. "I've never before heard of a goat well!"

"Why, I suppose you're right," Woharia said. "They aren't very common."

"How does it work?" the Cunama trader asked.

"Oh, it's simple enough," Woharia said. "Every night you throw a pair of goat's horns into the well, and in the morning you find a goat. Then all you have to do is draw her out."

"Unbelievable!" the Cunama said. "Man, how I'd like to own such a well!"

"So would everyone else," Woharia said, untying the goat and letting her run loose. "But few people can afford to buy such an unusual thing."

"Well, I'll tell you," the Cunama said, thinking very hard. "I'm not a rich man, but I'll pay you six bags of durra grain for it."

Woharia laughed.

"That wouldn't pay for many goats," he said.

"I'll give you twelve bags of durra, all that my camels are carrying!" the Cunama said anxiously.

Woharia smiled and shook his head.

"Seven goats a week," he said as though he were talking to himself. "Thirty goats a month. Three hundred sixty-five goats a year..."

But the Cunama had set his heart on owning the well.

"Look at my young sleek camels! I have just bought them in Keren! Where will you ever find better camels than these? I'll give you my twelve bags of grain and my three camels also. I'd give you more, but I own nothing else in the whole world, I swear it to you!"

Woharia thought silently for a moment.

"Since you want it so much, I'll sell it to you," he said finally.

The Cunama leaped down from his camel and embraced Woharia.

"For this goodness may you live long!" he said. "May Allah bring you many good things to give you joy!"

"Ah," Woharia said, looking at camels, "he has already done so."

He took the three camels loaded with grain, his goat, and his few other possessions, and prepared to leave.

"Before you go, tell me your name?" the Cunama asked.

"People call me Where-I-Shall-Dance," Woharia replied. And then he went away to the south, leaving the Cunama with the well.

The Cunama was very impatient to begin getting goats from the well. When evening came, he dropped two goat's horns into it and lay down in the house to sleep. The next morning, when it was barely light, he rushed out again to draw up his first goat, but when he peered into the well, he saw nothing except the old horns he had thrown in.

He became very anxious.

"There must be some mistake!" he said to himself.

That evening he threw down two more horns, and again in the morning he rushed out to get his first goat, but once more he saw only the old goat's horns there. This time he was very worried. He scoured the country to find old goat's horns, and he threw armful after armful into the well. And all night long he sat by the well shouting into it:

"Goats, are you there? Goats, are you there?"

But nothing at all happened. When morning came at last the Cunama was angry and unhappy. He realized that he had been duped by his own anxiousness to get the well. There was nothing left to do but to go out and find the man who had taken his camels and his precious grain.

The trader traveled southward, as Woharia had done. At last, when night had fallen, he came to a village. When he arrived in the village square, where many people were gathered, he went up to them and asked:

"Do you know Where-I-Shall-Dance?"

"Why, it doesn't matter, dance anywhere you like," the people answered. "Dance right here if you wish!" And they began to sing and make music for him.

"No, no, you don't understand," he said. "What I want to know is, do you know Where-I-Shall-Dance?"

"Yes, dance here!" they said again.

The Cunama was very angry because he thought the people were making fun of him, so he went out of the village and continued his journey southward, stopping only to sleep at the edge of the road.

The next day, he came to another village, and he went to the market place and said in a loud voice:

"Does anybody know Where-I-Shall-Dance?"

The people gathered around him instantly and shouted:

"Dance here! Dance here!"

They clapped their hands and a drummer came and beat his drum, and everyone waited for the Cunama to dance.

He turned and fled from the village, believing that the people were ridiculing him. Again, he came to a village, and again he asked:

"Do you know Where-I-Shall-Dance?"

And once more the people began clapping their hands and answered: "Yes, dance here!"

The same thing happened in every village the man entered. He began to feel very hopeless, and sometimes thought he might even be losing his mind. He began to be afraid to ask his question. Finally, one day, he came to the village of the chief of the district. When he asked his question here and the people gave him the usual answer, the news was carried to the chief, who immediately sent for him.

"Now, what sort of nonsense is this?" the chief asked. "You ask the people where you should dance and then you refuse to dance."

The unhappy man told how he had bought the dry well in exchange for his three young camels and his grain. The chief listened sympathetically. He remembered that a man named Woharia had recently settled in a nearby village, and that he had come with three camels and twelve bags of grain.

"Sit down and rest," the chief said. "I will handle this matter now."

He sent a messenger to Woharia, and when the messenger found him he said, as he had been instructed:

"There is a man waiting to see you at the house of the chief. His name is "What-I-Shall-Do. The chief wishes you to come at once."

Woharia went immediately to the house of the chief, and the servants let him in.

"What can I do for you?" the chief asked.

"Why, do you know What-I-Shall-Do?" Woharia asked.

"Yes, I know what you shall do," the chief said. "You shall give back the Cunama trader his three camels and his twelve bags of grain." Woharia was crestfallen and ashamed. He gave the Cunama back the camels and the grain. The Cunama took them and went out. As he passed through the market place the people shouted:

"Dance here! Dance here!"

And the trader was so happy that this time he danced in the market place.

MARLO

I've always wondered what happens to a child in a musical family who may not be as musically talented as everyone else! Here's one possibility.

When Marlo was a baby the family came from all over the world to celebrate her first birthday. Uncle Ken came from London, Aunt Sylvia arrived from India, and the Solovei sisters arrived with the cousins from Fort Wayne, Indiana. There was quite a crowd around the birthday cake. Everyone helped Marlo blow out the single candle. Marlo smiled and then she cried. She wailed. She snuffled.

The family smiled. "I knew she was a Solovie" beamed her father. "She will be a great violinist, just like me."

"I don't think so," said Uncle Ken. With those lungs she will be an opera singer, just like me."

"It's clear that she will be a country western singer, just like me," said Theresa from Fort Wayne.

The family argued about which musical instrument Marlo would play, or what kind of music she would sing. Marlo cried.

As the years went on Marlo had many birthday parties. The family always gathered to celebrate. While the children ate the cake, the grownups continued to predict Marlo's musical future.

Marlo tried to please everyone. She took lessons on the flute. She danced ballet and took voice lessons with Madame Tartare. At music camp she sang in a musical comedy and was mentioned in the local newspaper as "a fine talent."

She won a scholarship to music school in Vienna. She studied the viola, the French horn, and Italian opera.

When the family gathered for her sixteenth birthday, the uncles and aunts were beaming with certainty. Aunt Astrid announced, "It's obvious now that Marlo will be entering the ballet school where I have taught for 22 years."

"I don't think so," said Cousin Sue. "She will be continuing her studies with me in London at the conservatory."

While they discussed Marlo's future, Marlo wrote in her journal. She wrote and wrote and ignored her family. She knew that she wasn't quite good enough to be a professional dancer, singer, or musician.

However, Marlo was now quite competent in many fields of music. And when the time came for her to be a real adult, Marlo's career took her to London, India, New York, and even Fort Wayne, Indiana—for Marlo had become a music critic!

The family still gathers for Marlo's birthday each year, and they are pleased that she is so articulate about their talents.

Booklist: Music in the Storyhour

General Collections

Boni, Margaret, ed. *Fireside Book of Folk Songs*; arr. for piano by Norman Lloyd. Art by Alice and Martin Provensen. Simon and Schuster, 1947. A favorite collection of traditional American and foreign folk songs.

Bryan, Ashley. *I'm Going to Sing: Black American Spirituals*. 2v. Art by the compiler. Atheneum, 1982. "Joshua Fit the Battle," "Study War No More," and "Old Time Religion" are among the songs. Illustrated with block prints.

Colgin, Mary Lou. *One Potato, Two Potato, Three Potato, Four*. Gryphon (P.O. Box 275, Mt. Rainier, MD 20712), 1988. An old favorite that remains popular.

Delacre, Lulu, ed. *Arroz Con Leche: Popular Songs and Rhymes from Latin America*. English lyrics by Elena Paz; musical arr. by Ana-María Rosado. Art by editor. Scholastic, 1989. Illustrated folk songs accompanied by lyrics in both Spanish and English.

_____. *Las Navidades: Popular Christmas Songs from Latin America*. English lyrics by Elena Paz; musical arr. by Ana-María Rosado. Art by editor. Scholastic, 1990. Bilingual collection of Spanish Christmas songs.

Glazer, Tom. *Tom Glazer's Treasury of Songs for Children*. Art by John O'Brien. Doubleday, 1988. 131 songs. Western, nursery and folk songs arranged for piano and guitar.

Go in and out the Window: An Illustrated Songbook for Young People. Metropolitan Museum of Art/Holt, 1987. Sixty childhood songs illustrated with fine art paintings.

Guthrie, Woody with Marjorie Mazia Guthrie. *Woody's 20 Grow Big Songs*. Art by Woody Guthrie. Harper, 1992. Sing along with a famous folksinger.

Hart, Jane. *Singing Bee! A Collection of Favorite Children's Songs*. Art by Anita Lobel. Lothrop, 1982. Over 100 traditional children's nursery songs.

If You're Happy and You Know It: Eighteen Story Songs Set to Pictures; musical arr. by John Krumich. Art by Nicki Weiss. Greenwillow, 1987. These eighteen traditional songs are illustrated with lush, full-color art.

An Illustrated Treasury of Songs. National Gallery of Art, Washington. Rizzoli, 1991. Fifty-five songs for voice and piano illustrated with fine art paintings.

John, Timothy. *The Great Song Book*. Music edited by Peter Hankey. Art by Tomi Ungerer. Doubleday, 1978. A collection of game songs, folk songs, and lullabys.

Krull, Kathleen. *Gonna Sing My Head Off! American Folk Songs for Children*. Art by Allen Garns. Knopf, 1992. An attractive picture-book size collection of familiar and lesser known songs.

Langstaff, John, comp. *Hi! Ho! The Rattlin' Bog, and Other Folk Songs for Group Singing*; piano settings by John Edmunds and others; guitar chords by Happy Traum. Art by Robin Jacques. Harcourt, 1969. Less familiar folk songs for children.

Poston, Elizabeth, comp. *The Baby's Song Book*. Art by William Stobbs. Crowell, 1972. Songs from America, England, France, Italy, and Spain for young children to enjoy.

Raffi. *The Raffi Singable Songbook*. Art by Joyce Yamamoto. Crown, 1987. A collection of the Canadian songwriter's songs. Also *The Raffi Christmas Treasury*. Art by Nadine Bernard Westcott. Crown, 1988.

Sharon, Lois and Bram's Mother Goose: Songs, Finger Rhymes, Tickling Verses, Games and More. Art by Maryann Kovalski. Little, 1986. Words and music collected by a singing trio.

Usborne Children's Songbook. Art by Stephen Cartwright. Usborne, 1988. Music and words for over 50 traditional songs.

Winn, Marie, ed. *The Fireside Book of Children's Songs*; musical arr. by Allan Miller. Art by John Alcorn. Simon and Schuster, 1966. Singing games, nonsense and nursery songs with simple piano and guitar chord notations.

Yolen, Jane. ed. *The Lap-Time Song and Play Book*; musical arr. by Adam Stemple. Art by Margot Tomes. Harcourt, 1989. Words, music, and directions for playing the singing games.

Collections with a Theme

Boy Scout Songbook. Boy Scouts of America, 1974. Particularly useful for camps and children's groups.

Chase, Richard. *Singing Games and Play-party Games*; six piano settings by Hilton Rufty. Art by Joshua Tolford; Dover, 1967. A collection of traditional English and American folk games and dances with music and directions.

Engvick, William, ed. *Lullabies and Night Songs*; music by Alex Wilder; piano arr. by Seymour Barab; guitar chords by Happy Traum. Art by Maurice Sendak. Harper, 1965. A Caldecott winner has illustrated this book for use at home.

Fraser-Simson, Harold. *The Pooh Song Book*; words by A. A. Milne. Art by E. H. Shepard. Dutton, 1961. Containing the "Hums of Pooh," "The King's Breakfast" and 14 songs from *When We Were Very Young*. Difficult but beautiful musical arrangements from the Winnie the Pooh stories.

Free to Be . . . You and Me; conceived by Marlo Thomas; developed and edited by Carole Hart and others; ed. by Francine Klagsbrun. McGraw-Hill, 1974. Songs, poems, and stories to free children from sexism.

Garson, Eugenia, comp. *The Laura Ingalls Wilder Songbook*; musical arr. for piano and guitar by Herbert Haufrecht. Art by Garth Williams. Harper, 1968. Music from the *Little House* books for piano or guitar.

Glass, Dudley. *The Songs of Peter Rabbit*. Warne, 1951. Words and music based on Beatrix Potter's much-loved tale.

Ritchie, Jean. *The Swapping Song Book*; piano arr. by A. K. Fossner and Edward Tripp. Photos by George Pickow. Oxford, 1952. Appalachian folk songs by a distinguished folk singer.

Robinson, Adjai. *Singing Tales of Africa*. Art by Christine Price. Scribner, 1974. Stories that revolve around singing retold from African sources.

Sendak, Maurice. *Maurice Sendak's Really Rosie*; music by Carole King; design by Jane Byers Bierhorst. Harper, 1975. The words and music of the successful show.

Yolen, Jane, comp. *Jane Yolen's Songs of Summer*; musical arr. by Adam Stemple. Art by Cyd Moore. Boyd's Mill, 1993. Traditional summer tunes.

_____. *Jane Yolen's Mother Goose Songbook*; musical arr. by Adam Stemple. Art by Rosekrans Hoffman. Boyd's Mill, 1992. Familiar nursery rhymes set to music.

Picture Books about Music

Ackerman, Karen. *Song and Dance Man*. Art by Stephen Gammell. Knopf, 1988. Grandpa sings and dances for his grandchildren, remembering his vaudeville days.

Andersen, Hans Christian. *The Nightingale*. Art by Demi. Harcourt, 1985. An artificial bird replaces the nightingale's song in Andersen's classic.

Baer, Gene. *Thump, Thump, Rat-a-Tat-Tat*. Art by Lois Ehlert. Harper, 1989. Bright bold shapes march into view as marching band.

Barboza, Steven. *I Feel Like Dancing: A Year with Jacques d'Amboise and the National Dance Institute*. Photos by Carolyn George d'Amboise. Crown, 1992. Photo essay follows the children at the National Dance Institute, from auditions through polished performance.

Baylor, Byrd. *Sometimes I Dance Mountains*. Photos by Bill Sears. Art by Ken Longtemps. Scribner, 1973. A young girl tells how she feels while dancing.

Brett, Jan. *Berlioz the Bear*. Art by author. Putnam, 1991. A lavishly illustrated book shows Berlioz and his bear band as they travel to play at the village dance.

Catalano, Dominic. *Wolf Plays Alone*. Philomel, 1992. Wolf wants to play his horn alone but many animals join in with their own instruments.

Downing, Julie. *Mozart Tonight*. Art by author. Bradbury, 1991. Mozart looks back to the creation of *Don Giovanni* on opening night.

Ernst, Lisa Campbell. *When Bluebell Sang*. Art by author. Bradbury, 1989. A cow is a fantastic hit as a singer, but Bluebell is homesick for the farm.

Fleischman, Paul. *Rondo in C*. Art by Janet Wentworth. Harper, 1988. Each person is shown with their thoughts at a piano recital.

Gauch, Patricia. *Bravo, Tanya*. Art by Satomi Ichikawa. Philomel, 1992. A little girl dances to the music she hears in her head.

Griffith, Helen V. *Georgia Music*. Art by James Stevenson. Greenwillow, 1986. A little girl brings back the memory of music to an old man.

Hayes, Ann. *Meet the Orchestra*. Art by Karmen Thompson. Harcourt, 1991. Describes the instruments of the orchestra, illustrated with animal musicians.

Helprin, Mark. *Swan Lake*. Art by Chris Van Allsburg. Houghton, 1989. Illustrated version of the story of the famous ballet.

Hurd, Thatcher. *Mama Don't Allow*. Art by author. Harper, 1984. Possum Miles and his swamp band find that alligators don't make a good audience after all.

Isadora, Rachel. *Lili at Ballet*. Art by author. Putnam, 1993. Ballet steps and a performance through the eyes of a young ballet student. Also *Max* (Macmillan, 1976). When Max takes a ballet class his baseball skills improve.

Jabar, Cynthia, ed. *Shimmy Shake Earthquake*. Art by compiler. Little, 1992. Poetry reflecting the rhythm and rhyme of dance.

Joyce, William. *Bently and Egg*. Art by author. Harper, 1992. A musical frog is charged with guarding a duck's egg.

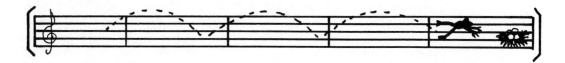

Kuskin, Karla. *The Philharmonic Gets Dressed*. Art by Marc Simont. Harper, 1982. The members of the orchestra are shown getting ready for their appearance on stage.

Lasker, David. *The Boy Who Loved Music*. Art by Joe Lasker. Viking, 1979. The story of the creation of Joseph Hayden's *Farewell Symphony*.

Lionni, Leo. Geraldine. *The Music Mouse*. Art by author. Pantheon, 1979. Geraldine whistles and plays for her friends.

Martin, Bill Jr. and John Archambault. *Barn Dance*. Art by Ted Rand. Holt, 1986. A little boy joins the farm animals and a scarecrow in a nighttime dance.

McAllister, Angela. *The Enchanted Flute*. Art by Margaret Chamberlain. Delacorte, 1991. A fussy queen learns a lesson with a magic flute.

McCloskey, Robert. *Lentil*. Art by author. Viking, 1940. Lentil saves the day with his harmonica. Still a great story!

McKissack, Patricia C. *Mirandy and Brother Wind*. Art by Jerry Pinkney. Knopf, 1988. Mirandy tries to capture the wind as her partner for the cakewalk.

Medearis, Angela Shelf. *Dancing with the Indians*. Art by Samuel Byrd. Holiday, 1991. An African-American family joins a Seminole Indian celebration.

Page, P. K. *The Traveling Musicians of Bremen*. Art by Kady MacDonald. Denton. Little, 1991. The Grimm brothers' story retold. Compare with Wilhelm's version.

Price, Leontyne. *Aïda*. Art by Leo and Diane Dillon. Harcourt, 1990. Picturebook version of the Verdi opera.

Sage, James. *The Little Band*. Art by Keiko Narahashi. Macmillan, 1991. A multicultural band walks through town playing for the town's people and animals.

Seeger, Pete. *Abiyoyo*. Art by Michael Hays. Macmillan, 1985. A story song featuring a giant and a boy who conquers him with music.

Simon, Carly. *Amy the Dancing Bear*. Art by Margot Datz. Doubleday, 1989. Amy uses dance to keep from going to bed.

Ventura, Piero. *Great Composers*. Art by author. Putnam, 1988. Read just one of these portraits at a time to spark the music program.

Verdy, Violette. *Of Swans, Sugarplums, and Satin Slippers: Ballet Stories for Children*. Art by Marcia Brown. Scholastic, 1991. The stories of six ballets including "Swan Lake" and "The Nutcracker."

Walter, Mildred Pitts. *Ty's One-Man Band*. Art by Margot Tomes. Four Winds, 1980. Ty enjoys the music of a one-legged man who plays a washboard, comb, and spoons.

Wilhelm, Hans. *The Bremen Town Musicians*. Art by author. Scholastic, 1992. This version of the Grimm's tale is illustrated with lively animals.

Williams, Vera B. *Music, Music for Everyone*. Art by author. Greenwillow, 1984. Four girls form a band to play in the neighborhood.

Ziefert, Harriet. *Andy Toots His Horn*. Art by Sanford Hoffman. Viking, 1988. Andy toots his horn in the house and is asked to toot somewhere else by family members!

Longer Books about Music

Berger, Melvin. *The Science of Music*. Art by Yvonne Buchanan. Crowell, 1989. Explains how instruments make their sounds.

Foley, Patricia. *John and the Fiddler*. Art by Marcia Sewell. Harper, 1990. A young boy is befriended by an old violin-maker.

Hill, Elizabeth Starr. *The Street Dancers*. Viking, 1991. Fitzi tries to juggle her family's life as street performers with her school life.

Hooper, Maureen Brett. *The Violin Man*. Art by Gary Undercuffler. Caroline House, 1991. Antonia searches for a treaured Stradivarius violin in his little Italian village.

McLachlan, Patricia. *The Facts and Fictions of Minna Pratt*. Harper, 1988. Minna is in love with her cello, music, and a young musician in her chamber music group.

Porte, Barbara Ann. *Fat Fanny, Beanpole Bertha, and the Boys*. Art by Maxie Chambliss. Orchard, 1991. Tap dance with Fanny and the triplets.

Streatfield, Noel. *Ballet Shoes*. Art by Diane Goode. Random, 1991. First published in 1937, this is the classic ballet story.

Thompson, Wendy. *Ludwig von Beethoven*. Viking, 1991. Illustrated with prints. Beethoven's life is shown in relationship to his world. See *Mozart* from the same series.

Wolff, Virginia Euwer. *The Mozart Season*. Holt, 1991. The reader follows 12-year-old Allegra Shapiro as she practices Mozart's Fourth Violin Concerto for a concert.

Making Music

Arnold, Caroline. *Music Lessons for Alex*. Photos by Richard Hewett. Clarion, 1985. The reader follows in text and photos the steps to playing the violin.

Beirne, Barbara. *A Pianist's Debut: Preparing for the Concert Stage*. Carolrhoda, 1990. A photo essay showing an 11-year-old's demanding musical schedule.

Hayes, Phyllis. *Musical Instruments You Can Make*. Art by Dennis Kendrick. Watts, 1981. Directions for making your own instruments.

McLean, Margaret. *Make Your Own Musical Instruments*. Lerner, 1988. Directions for making castanets, drums, and other simple instruments.

Palmer, Hap. *Homemade Band*. Art by author. Tape included. Crown, 1991. Directions for making instruments to play along with the tape.

Pillar, Marjorie. *Join the Band!* Photos by author. Harper, 1992. Photo essay shows a young girl choosing an instrument, practicing, and rehearsing for the school band.

Stecher, Miriam B. and Alice S. Kandell. *Max, the Music-Maker*. Photos by Alice S. Kandell. Lothrop, 1980. A little boy is shown finding music all around the house.

Adult Source

Painter, William M. *Musical Story Hours: Using Music with Storytelling and Puppetry*. Library Professional Publications, 1989. Excellent source book for the programmer looking for ways to use music.

Programs

Now it's time to put it all together. Gather your resources of stories, personal memories, favorite read-alouds, magic tricks, puppets, and songs, and plan a special program.

If you are a classroom teacher or day-care provider, you probably work with the same age group on a consistent basis. In that case, if you scanned the table of contents before beginning, you may have jumped in here immediately, for the first four chapters are designed for specific audiences. If you are a public or school librarian, you are probably accustomed to juggling diverse audiences, perhaps preschoolers one moment and young adults the next. So this section is for you, too, since you may find yourself moving from nursery rhymes to autobiographies to picture books in a single morning!

The last four chapters in this section each address a special kind of program, giving loads of my favorite examples, stories, and booklists designed to help you promote the joy of reading through a variety of activities.

19 / Preschool and Primary Programs

"Tell me, please, what is the curriculum for the 9–12-month-old children at your day-care center?" No need to read that again. You understood it correctly the first time. A mother, searching for the right day-care for her baby, was interviewing a day-care center director. The Oklahoma day-care center director who related this story to me told me that her parents are truly concerned about the education of even very young children, and that many parents actually keep a chart for each child, detailing the child's progress in various categories. "It gives the parents something to show to the grandparents, anyway. In actuality, we just try to give them love . . . and books." (Of course her comment endeared me to her immediately!)

There have been changes in the audience for the preschool program since I wrote the first edition of this book. When we say "preschool" now, we generally mean anyone who is six months to five years. Toddler storytimes are popular in many parts of the country and many programs are even organized for babies.

My first toddler storytime was given over 20 years ago in my own home. The occasion was my daughter's birthday. It's actually a rather painful memory. As I recall there was a lot of crawling, biting, crying, and slapping going on, and not much listening. I don't remember what story I told, but I do know I decided that for Hilary's next birthday we would plan an excursion to our local ice cream parlor! You know, I do remember Wendi's mom remarking, "That was a cute book, Caroline; could you write down the title for me?" Maybe I should be content with that memory instead. I like to think of Joni borrowing the book from her library and reading the story to Wendi again.

We do need to begin introducing children to literature before they begin their formal schooling. And we need to reach the adults who care for them with the message that nursery schools, day-care centers, and libraries are chockful of good materials to help.

Whether you are planning lap times for babies, programs for toddlers, or storytimes for nursery school age children, you will always face the same challenges: who, where, when, and what.

Start with who. Among infants, babies, toddlers, and older nursery age children (three to five years old), you will find that the level of understanding and attention span is dramatically different from one group to the next. So, while you can mix these age groups, your storyhour will generally be much more successful if you can limit your audience to a narrowly defined age group.

A program for these youngsters may be held in a public library, church or temple, playground, day-care center, or nursery school. The time will vary, of course, but the important thing is to choose a time when the children are not likely to be particularly hungry (before snack or lunch time) or tired (before nap or quitting time). If you are a nursery school teacher, librarian, or day-care provider, you will be able to select the best time for your group. If you are a visiting storyteller, you may wish to find out from your host when a story program would be most enthusiastically received.

The younger your children, the shorter your program will be. In fact, the reading of one book or the reciting of one fingerplay or the singing of one song—what I generally call a literature interlude—may be as much of a program as you'll need. Fingerplays, simple songs, big books, short picture books, a board story, the introduction of a puppet, and short traditional stories all make perfect literature interludes.

Slightly older children—first, second, and third graders (what we generally call the primary grades)—are especially fun. Overtly enthusiastic and appreciative, their enjoyment always makes me feel that all of my preparation was worthwhile. If a story has a repeating phrase, these children will join in immediately. And they love it when the storyteller makes exaggerated movements or uses a variety of different voices. These children will appreciate longer programs, perhaps half an hour to forty-five minutes in length. A funny story or two followed by a set of riddles, a picture book, and a poem to finish makes the perfect combination.

These primary grade children will enjoy picture books intended for preschoolers, in addition to more sophisticated material. In fact, one of my former students has volunteered to present to her son's second grade class on a daily basis. She comes to the elementary school 15 minutes before the end of the day, with her toddler and baby in tow. The presence of the baby and younger child gives her the perfect excuse to read what might otherwise be considered baby books by the older children. "Let's see how Sally likes this one," Lynette might say as she introduces a favorite picture-book title.

Setting the Stage

To begin, make sure that your children can all see you or the book you are presenting. Lately there seems to be some sort of contest to see how many children attend these programs—particularly at libraries. I understand that these statistics look good on an annual report and may impress the budget committee, but you diminish the enjoyment of the story if there are too many people.

If you are going to be presenting to children sitting on adult laps, you should even limit the number of listeners to a handful. When you are presenting to the three- to five-year-old group, make sure that everyone can see the pictures in the books that you are showing. This may sound obvious, but it is quite disruptive when children begin complaining, "I can't see, I can't see!" I used to be quite firm about not letting adults into the room at all when I was presenting to the preschoolers. Children act so differently when their parents are present. Now I come as a guest and often there are adults who have come just because they want to observe the techniques I use and the children's reaction to the stories.

A colleague of mine was giving a lecture-demonstration of book programs for young children. The children were accompanied by their teacher and one mother. The mother's three-year-old son was in the class, and she was also carrying his baby sister. The toddler was utterly impossible. He stood while his peers sat, ran around, and screamed as loud as he could. But when the baby began to cry, his mother left the room. Her little "Dennis the Menace" changed almost instantly. He stopped running, quietly walked over to the group, sat down, and began listening attentively. I'm sure that everyone in that workshop audience carries a vivid memory of the behavior of that child in the presence of his mother!

A final consideration is to decide whether you want your children seated on the floor, on cushions, or on chairs. Remember that these children are little as well as young. If they are sitting on the floor and you are standing, it may be too far for them to see. On the other hand, you can be seen by a larger group if you are standing or sitting above them. If you are a beginning storyteller, you should try different arrangements until you decide what works for you. Remember that if the children are sitting in adult-size chairs their feet will not touch the ground and they may be uncomfortable, swinging their legs and shifting around. But they often start wiggling soon after you begin—no matter where they are sitting! Don't worry; they *are* listening. Weeks later, one of your small patrons will return saying, "Do the bear book again, please."

If possible, I recommend that you enlist the help of an aide or volunteer with this age group. Sometimes a child "forgets" to go to the restroom and will need help. Often a young child really resents being separated from his father or mother, and an assistant can reunite a child with a parent without disrupting the other children. If you are short of staff and need help, one of the visiting adults can act as a substitute helper. If possible, recruit a volunteer who is not a parent of a group member.

Introducing the Program and Follow-up Activities

Opening the storyhour is discussed at length in chapter 4. This is only to remind you that you should specifically plan what you are going to do to begin the storytime. The settling down period is a time to get acquainted with the audience. I often use a puppet or an interesting artifact to introduce myself and the stories I am going to tell. I may encourage the children to talk to the puppet or comment on the artifact before the stories actually begin. This get-acquainted period should be kept brief, or the children might begin to chatter, becoming more interested in themselves than in the stories. During the actual telling of stories or books I usually ignore comments or questions until the presentation is finished. Between stories I encourage the children to relax and rearrange themselves for the next book. Often I invite them to participate in a group activity such as a fingerplay or song, which offers a good intermission. At the close of the session, you should allow enough time for the children to look at the books, touch the display if there is one, and articulate any thoughts they might have about the story they just heard, or one presented on another day.

What's in a Program?

The majority of time spent in preschool and primary sessions is usually devoted to reading and showing picture books. Folktales with simple plots and repetitive action are always popular. You may also enjoy introducing rhymes, short poems, and fingerplays, as well as singing and games, all of which make good transitional material.

Picture Books

Since picture books are to be the focal point of your program, you will naturally want to choose books of the highest literary and artistic quality.
You may already have your own favorites, but there are also many lists to help you select books to read. The Association for Library Service to Children, a division of the American Library Association (50 E. Huron St., Chicago, IL 60611), puts out annual lists (*Caldecott Medal Books*, *Newbery Medal Books*, and *Notable Children's Books*) as do organizations like the Association for Childhood Education International (3615 Wisconsin Ave. NW, Washington, DC 20016). Reviews of books in professional journals, and the annual lists can keep you up-to-date and aware of the latest books. Nothing, however, can take the place of your own reading to determine which books will best suit your interests and the needs and interests of your particular group. Many good editions of children's paperbacks have recently been published. Although paperbacks are useful, I highly recommend the use of hardcover editions, whenever possible, in storytelling situations. It is not only the story and beauty of the pictures you want to communicate, but the very essence of the book itself: fine paper, binding, and design. Beware of using the very small sized picture books for a large group; these are better reserved for taking home or for "individual reading."

Always give the title and name the author of the book. Books are by people, after all. And, if you like, you can give a one-sentence introduction to the book so that children know what to expect. "This is the story of a badger that didn't like to go to bed" (*Bedtime for Frances*) or "In this book an old lady receives a boa constrictor as a pet" (*Crictor*).

Despite the fact that you will be holding the book as you tell the story, you should be familiar enough with the text that you need only to glance at it now and then. It's even better if you've actually memorized the text or know it so thoroughly that you can use the book only as a display for the group's benefit. Hold the book in any way that seems comfortable for you and still enables your audience to see the pictures. Move the book slowly around the semicircle so that each child gets a chance to clearly see each and every picture. You might want to point out details in the pictures, "Does everyone see the mouse?", but keep interjections of this kind to a minimum. Children often see more detail than adults anyway. My own daughter had to show me the mouse on every page in Margaret Wise Brown's *Goodnight Moon*; I'd never noticed it before. Give the children time to discover that the pictures tell the story as well as the words.

For a new group unfamiliar with picture books, you will want to begin with shorter, simpler books. After the children have attended several sessions, they will be ready for longer, more complicated stories. It is not necessary to have the two or three books you use in each storyhour relate to each other.

However, books that complement each other do make a more cohesive session.

You will probably want to present the new and unusual, but don't feel that you have to present something different at each session. Remember that to children all the books are new, even those published when Mommy was a little girl. Moreover, it doesn't bore a child to hear a story again and again. Each telling is slightly different, and children seem to learn something new each time. At the end of the story session encourage the children to look at books on their own.

Booklist: Picture Books for Preschool and Primary Children

The following bibliography lists only a few of the hundreds of books that can be successfully used in preschool and primary storyhours. They are grouped by subject or theme to suggest possible "go together" books, but books listed under a heading are not necessarily to be used at the same time. More than one book about death, for instance, at one sitting would probably be too much. The same is true of birthday books, and yet if you are a classroom teacher, you probably would like a collection of books to read on these special days. The books that are too small to be seen by a group larger than four should be taken home and enjoyed or lovingly looked at before and after the program on an individual basis. Books that are completely unrelated by a theme are fine too. Choose books you personally enjoy and would like to share with children. Try to keep current through reviews and lists of new books published, but at the same time, don't forget all those books that you and others have enjoyed and loved through the years. In fact, I have included my own list of classic picture books for you at the end of this section.

Two reference books are invaluable for the program planner: *A to Z Subject Access to Children's Picture Books* by Carolyn W. Lima and John A. Lima (3rd ed., Bowker, 1989) lists 12,000 picture books by subject that will help if you are preparing a theme or subject program. *Books Kids Will Sit Still For* by Judy Freeman (2nd ed., Bowker, 1990) contains a superb annotated picture book list by age group and also by subject.

Apples

Maestro, Betsy. *How Do Apples Grow?* Art by Giulio Maestro. Harper, 1992.

Micucci, Charles. *The Life and Times of the Apple.* Art by author. Orchard, 1992.

Parnall, Peter. *Apple Tree.* Art by author. Macmillan, 1987.

Scheffler, Ursel. *The Giant Apple.* Art by Silke Brix-Henker. Carolrhoda, 1991.

Balloons

Baker, Alan. *Benjamin's Balloon.* Art by author. Lothrop, 1990.

Deacre, Lulu. *Nathan's Balloon Adventure.* Art by author. Scholastic, 1991.

Inkpen, Mick. *The Blue Balloon*. Art by author. Little, 1989.

Wilson, Sarah. *Three in a Balloon*. Art by author. Scholastic, 1990.

Baths

Cole, Brock. *No More Baths*. Art by author. Doubleday, 1980.

Conrad, Pam. *The Tub People*. Art by Richard Egielski. Harper, 1989.

White, Diana. *No Bath for Boris*. Art by author. Dutton, 1990.

Wood, Audrey. *King Bidgood's in the Bathtub*. Art by Don Wood. Harcourt, 1985.

Bears

de Beer, Hans. *Little Polar Bear*. Art by author. North-south, 1987.

Graham, Thomas. *Mr. Bear's Chair*. Art by author. Dutton, 1987.

Polushkin, Maria. *Bubba and Babba*. Art by Diane de Groat. Crown, 1986.

Yolen, Jane. *The Three Bears Rhyme Book*. Art by Jane Dyer. Harcourt, 1987.

Birthdays

Brown, Marc. *Arthur's Birthday*. Art by author. Little, 1989.

Carle, Eric. *The Secret Birthday Message*. Art by author. Crowell, 1972.

Noble, Trinka Hakes. *Jimmy's Boa and the Big Splash Birthday Bash*. Art by Steven Kellogg. Dial, 1989.

Books and Reading

Bauer, Caroline Feller. *Too Many Books!* Art by Diane Paterson. Warne, 1984.

Brillhart, Julie. *Story Hour—Starring Megan!* Art by author. Whitman, 1992.

Bunting, Eve. The *Wednesday Surprise*. Art by Donald Carrick. Clarion, 1989.

Edwards, Michelle. *Dora's Book*. Art by author. Carolrhoda, 1990.

Pinkwater, Daniel. *Aunt Lulu*. Art by author. Macmillan, 1988.

Caring

James, Simon. *Sally and the Limpet*. Art by author. Macmillan, 1991.

Patz, Nancy. *Sarah Bear and Sweet Sidney*. Art by author. Four Winds, 1989.

Chairs

Nordquist, Sven. *Porker Finds a Chair*. Art by author. Carolrhoda, 1988.

Root, Phyllis. *The Old Rocking Chair*. Art by John Sandford. Arcade, 1992.

Tennyson, Noel. *The Lady's Chair and the Ottoman*. Art by author. Lothrop, 1987.

Williams, Vera B. *A Chair for My Mother*. Art by author. Greenwillow, 1982.

Chickens

Bourgeois, Paulette. *Too Many Chickens!* Art by Bill Slavin. Little, 1990.

Edwards, Michelle. *Chicken Man*. Art by author. Lothrop, 1991.

Myers, Bernice. *The Millionth Egg*. Art by author. Lothrop, 1991.

Voake, Charlotte. *Mrs. Goose's Baby*. Art by author. Little, 1989.

Christmas

Aliki. *Christmas Tree Memories*. Art by author. Harper, 1991.

Bunting, Eve. *Night Tree*. Art by Ted Rand. Harcourt, 1991.

Edens, Cooper. *Santa Cows*. Art by Daniel Lane. Simon, 1991.

Say, Allen. *Tree of Cranes*. Art by author. Houghton, 1991.

Circus

De Regniers, Beatrice Schenk. *Circus*. Photos by Al Geise. Viking, 1966.

Ehlert, Lois. *Circus*. Art by author. Harper, 1992.

Spier, Peter. *Circus!* Art by author. Doubleday, 1992.

Vincent, Gabrielle. *Ernest and Celestine at the Circus*. Art by author. Greenwillow, 1988.

Wildsmith, Brian. *Brian Wildsmith's Circus*. Art by author. Watts, 1970.

Coats

Bunting, Eve. *Clancey's Coat*. Art by Lorinda Bryan Cauley. Warne, 1984.

Hest, Amy. *The Purple Coat*. Art by Amy Schwartz. Macmillan, 1986.

Ziefert, Harriet. *A New Coat for Anna*. Art by Anita Lobel. Knopf, 1986.

Color

Dodds, Dayle Ann. *The Color Box*. Art by Giles Laroche. Little, 1992.

Ehlert, Lois. *Color Zoo*. Art by author. Lippincott, 1989.

Hoban, Tana. *Is It Red? Is It Yellow? Is It Blue?* Photos by author. Greenwillow, 1978.

McMillan, Bruce. *Growing Colors*. Photos by author. Lothrop, 1988.

Cowboys

Gerrard, Roy. *Rosie and the Rustlers*. Art by author. Farrar, 1989.

Rounds, Glen. *Cowboys*. Art by the author. Holiday, 1991.

Scott, Ann Herbert. *Someday Rider*. Art by Ronald Himler. Clarion, 1989.

Cows

Grossman, Bill. *Donna O'Neeshuck Was Chased by Some Cows*. Art by Sue Truesdell. Harper, 1988.

Krasilovsky, Phyllis. *The Cow Who Fell in the Canal*. Art by Peter Spier. Doubleday, 1953.

Dance

Brighton, Catherine. *Nijinsky*. Art by author. Doubleday, 1989.

Gauch, Patricia. *Bravo, Tanya*. Art by Satomi Ichikawa. Philomel, 1992.

Martin, Bill Jr. and John Archambault. *Barn Dance!* Art by Ted Rand. Holt, 1986.

Dinosaurs

Carrick, Carol. *Patrick's Dinosaurs*. Art by Donald Carrick. Houghton, 1983.

Mosley, Francis. *The Dinosaur Eggs*. Art by author. Barrons, 1988.

Schwartz, David. *How I Captured a Dinosaur*. Art by Amy Schwartz. Watts, 1989.

Divorce

Caines, Jeannette. *Daddy*. Art by Ronald Himler. Harper, 1977.

Christiansen, C. B. *My Mother's House, My Father's House*. Art by Irene Trivas. Atheneum, 1989.

Girard, Linda W. *At Daddy's on Saturday*. Art by Judith Friedman. Whitman, 1987.

Dogs

Ernst, Lisa Campbell. *Walter's Tail*. Art by author. Bradbury, 1992.

Evans, Katie. *Hunky Dory Ate It*. Art by Janet Morgan Stoeke. Dutton, 1992.

Pearson, Tracey Campbell. *The Howling Dog*. Art by author. Farrar, 1991.

Seligson, Susan and Howie Schneider. *Amos: The Story of an Old Dog and His Couch*. Art by Howie Schneider. Little, 1987.

Ducks

Ellis, Anne Leo. *Dabble Duck*. Art by Sue Truesdell. Harper, 1984.

Gerstein, Mordicai. *Follow Me!* Art by author. Morrow, 1983.

Gibson, Betty. *The Story of Little Quack*. Art by Kady MacDonald Denton. Little, 1991.

Gordon, Gaelyn. *Duckat*. Art by Chris Gaskin. Scholastic, 1992.

Saunders, Dave and Julie Saunders. *Dibble and Dabble in Showtime*. Art by Dave Saunders. Bradbury, 1991.

Fairy Tales

Craig, Helen. *The Town Mouse and the Country Mouse*. Art by author. Candlewick, 1992.

Marshall, James. *Goldilocks and the Three Bears*. Art by author. Dial, 1988.

Zemach, Margot. *The Little Red Hen*. Art by author. Farrar, 1983.

Fathers

Collins, Judy. *My Father*. Art by Jane Dyer. Little, 1989.

Greenspun, Adele Aron. *Daddies*. Photos by author. Philomel, 1991.

Wood, Jakki. *Dads Are Such Fun*. Art by Rog Bonner. Simon, 1992.

Feelings

Everitt, Betsy. *Mean Soup*. Art by author. Harcourt, 1992.

Kachenmeister, Cheryl. *On Monday When It Rained*. Photos by Tom Berthiaume. Houghton, 1989.

Modesitt, Jeanne. *Sometimes I Feel like a Mouse: A Book about Feelings*. Art by Robin Spowart. Scholastic, 1992.

Friends

Dumbleton, Mike. *Dial-A-Croc*. Art by Ann James. Orchard, 1991.

Russo, Marisabina. *Alex Is My Friend*. Art by author. Greenwillow, 1992.

Waber, Bernard. *Ira Sleeps Over*. Art by author. Houghton, 1973.

Frogs

Parker, Nancy Winslow. *Working Frog*. Art by author. Greenwillow, 1992.

Velthuijs, Max. *Frog and the Birdsong*. Art by author. Farrar, 1991.

Weisner, William. *Tuesday*. Art by author. Clarion, 1991.

Wynne-Jones, Tim. *The Hour of the Frog*. Art by Catharine O'Neill. Little, 1989.

Gardens

Ernst, Lisa Campbell. *Miss Penny and Mr. Grubbs*. Art by author. Bradbury, 1991.

Lobel, Anita. *Alison's Zinnia*. Art by author. Greenwillow, 1990.

Houses

Barton, Byron. *Building a House*. Art by author. Greenwillow, 1981.

Emberley, Rebecca. *My House Mi Casa*. Art by author. Little, 1990.

Gibbons, Gail. *How a House Is Built*. Art by author. Holiday, 1990.

Mothers

Hazen, Barbara Shook. *Mommy's Office*. Art by David Soman. Atheneum, 1992.

Kasza, Keiko. *A Mother for Choco*. Art by author. Putnam, 1992.

Monfried, Lucia. *The Daddies Boat*. Art by Michele Chessare. Dutton, 1990.

Scott, Ann Herbert. *On Mother's Lap*. Art by Glo Coalson. Clarion, 1992.

Zolotow, Charlotte. *This Quiet Lady*. Art by Anita Lobel. Greenwillow, 1992.

Night Workers

Grossman, Patricia. *The Night Ones*. Art by Lydia Dacovich. Harcourt, 1991.

Henderson, Kathy. *In the Middle of the Night*. Art by Jennifer Eachus. Macmillan, 1992.

Opposites

Anholt, Catherine. *Good Days Bad Days*. Art by author. Putnam, 1990.

Bond, Michael. *Paddington's Opposites*. Art by John Lobban. Viking, 1990.

Cuyler, Margery. *That's Good! That's Bad!* Art by David Catrow. Holt, 1991.

Hoban, Tana. *Exactly the Opposite*. Photos by author. Greenwillow, 1990.

Koch, Michelle. *By the Sea*. Art by author. Greenwillow, 1991.

Picture Puzzlers

Martin, Jerome. *Carrot/Parrot*. Art by author. Simon, 1991.

Roennfeldt, Mary. *What's That Noise?* Art by Robert Roennfeldt. Orchard, 1992.

Young, Ed. *Seven Blind Mice*. Art by author. Philomel, 1992.

Puss in Boots

(Choose your favorite or share several versions.)

Goodall, John S. *Puss in Boots*. Art by reteller. McElderry, 1990.

Kirstein, Lincoln. *Puss in Boots*. Art by Alain Vaës. Little, 1992.

Perrault, Charles. *Puss in Boots*; tr. by Malcolm Arthur. Art by Fred Marcellino. Farrar, 1990.

Relatives

Rylant, Cynthia. *The Relatives Came*. Art by Stephen Gammell. Bradbury, 1985

Thomson, Pat. *Beware of the Aunts!* Art by Emma Chichester Clark. Macmillan, 1991.

Riddles

Calmenson, Stephanie. *What Am I? Very First Riddles*. Art by Karen Gundersheimer. Harper, 1989.

De Regniers, Beatrice Schenk. *It Does Not Say Meow!* Art by Paul Galdone. Seabury, 1972.

Shops

Field, Rachel. *General Store*. Art by Nancy Winslow Parker. Greenwillow, 1988.

Grossman, Bill. *Tommy at the Grocery Store*. Art by Victoria Chess. Harper, 1989.

Shelby, Anne. *We Keep a Store*. Art by John Ward. Orchard, 1990.

Sound

Cole, Joanna. *It's Too Noisy!* Art by Kate Duke. Crowell, 1989.

Fox, Mem. *Night Noises*. Art by Terry Denton. Harcourt, 1989.

Koch, Michelle. *Hoot Howl Hiss*. Art by author. Greenwillow, 1991.

Most, Bernard. *The Cow That Went Oink*. Art by author. Harcourt, 1990.

Peet, Bill. *Cock-a-Doodle Dudley*. Art by author. Houghton, 1990.

Snow, Alan. *The Monster Book of Sounds*. Art by author. Dial, 1991.

Whybrow, Ian. *Quack-Quack!* Art by Russell Ayto. Four Winds, 1991.

Snow

Bauer, Caroline Feller. *Midnight Snowman*. Art by Catherine Stock. Atheneum, 1987.

Mayper, Monica. *Oh Snow*. Art by June Otani. Harper, 1991.

Miller, Ned. *Emma's Snowball*. Art by Susan Guevara. Holt, 1990.

Teeth

Kaye, Marilyn. *The Real Tooth Fairy*. Art by Helen Cogancherry. Harcourt, 1990.

Macdonald, Maryann. *Rosie's Baby Tooth*. Art by Melissa Sweet. Atheneum, 1991.

Time

Grossman, Bill. *The Guy Who Was Five Minutes Late*. Art by Judy Glasser. Harper, 1990.

Krasilovsky. *The Man Who Tried to Save Time*. Art by Marcia Sewall. Doubleday, 1979.

Singer, Marilyn. *Nine O'clock Lullaby*. Art by Frané Lassac. Harper, 1991.

Trees

Behn, Harry. *Trees*. Art by James Endicott. Holt, 1992.

Ehlert, Lois. *Red Leaf, Yellow Leaf*. Art by author. Harcourt, 1991.

Gackenbach, Dick. *Mighty Tree*. Art by author. Gulliver/Harcourt, 1992.

Ryder, Joanne. *Hello, Tree!* Art by Michael Hays. Lodestar, 1991.

Trucks

Crews, Donald. *Truck*. Art by author. Greenwillow, 1980.

Pringle, Laurence. *Jesse Builds a Road*. Art by Leslie Holt Morrill. Macmillan, 1989.

Wake-up

James, Betsy. *He Wakes Me*. Art by Helen K. Davie. Orchard, 1991.

Morris, Linda Lowe. *Morning Milking*. Art by David Deran. Simon, 1991.

Tresselt, Alvin. *Sun Up*. Art by Henri Sorensen. Lothrop, 1991.

_____. *Wake Up, Farm!* Art by Carolyn Ewing. Lothrop, 1991.

Weddings

Drescher, Joan. *My Mother's Getting Married*. Art by author. Dial, 1986.

Samuels, Vyanne. *Carry Go Bring Come*. Art by Jennifer Northway. Macmillan, 1989.

Word Play

Hartman, Gail. *For Strawberry Jam or Fireflies*. Art by Ellen Weiss. Bradbury, 1989.

Shaw, Nancy. *Sheep in a Shop*. Art by Margot Apple. Houghton, 1991.

Some Classic Picture Books

We pass stories from one generation to another. Why not do the same with picture books? Here is my own favorite list of true classics.

Bemelmans, Ludwig. *Madeline*. Art by author. Viking, 1939. Madeline has her appendix out in a lovely, rhymed text.

Big Bear's Treasury. v. 1. Candlewick, 1992. Thirty-five stories by some of the best preschool authors and illustrators, including Helen Oxenbury, Shirley Hughes, Jill Murphy, and others.

Burton, Virginia Lee. *The Little House*. Art by author. Houghton, 1978. A small house survives as a city slowly forms around it.

Carle, Eric. *The Very Hungry Caterpillar*. Art by author. Putnam, 1981. The caterpillar eats through the numbers, the days of the week, and a variety of food on the way to becoming a butterfly.

Daugherty, James. *Andy and the Lion*. Art by author. Viking, 1938. A modern Androcles and the lion. Lots of action.

de Brunhoff, Jean. *The Story of Babar the Little Elephant*. Art by author. Random, 1937. Babar's adventures in an old lady's house in the city is still a favorite.

dePaola, Tomie. *Strega Nona*. Art by author. Prentice, 1975. In this variant of the sorcerer's apprentice, a pasta pot overflows.

Flack, Marjorie. *Angus and the Ducks*. Art by author. Doubleday, 1930. The irrepressible scotty is bested by some hissing ducks.

Freeman, Don. *Corduroy*. Art by the author. Viking, 1968. A stuffed bear searches for his missing button.

Gág, Wanda. *Millions of Cats*. Art by author. Coward, 1928. How can you choose one cat from hundreds and thousands of cats?

Heyward, DuBose. *The Country Bunny and the Little Gold Shoes*. Art by Marjorie Flack. Houghton, 1939. The story of a rabbit Mom chosen to be one of the five Easter bunnies. A bit saccharine, but always remembered with fondness.

Hutchins, Pat. *Goodnight Owl*. Art by author. Macmillan, 1972. The birds keep Owl awake with their racket.

Keats, Ezra Jack. *Whistle for Willie*. Art by author. Viking, 1964. Willie finally learns to whistle.

Krauss, Robert. *Leo the Late Bloomer*. Art by Jose Aruego. Windmill, 1987. A tiger can't do anything right, until in his own good time . . . he blooms.

Krauss, Ruth. *The Carrot Seed*. Art by Crockett Johnson. Harper, 1945. A little boy insists that his carrot will grow.

Leaf, Munro. *The Story of Ferdinand*. Art by Robert Lawson. Viking, 1936. A bull would rather sit and smell the flowers than fight.

Lionni, Leo. *Frederick*. Art by author. Pantheon, 1967. A mouse poet sustains his friends through the winter with words and color.

Lobel, Arnold. *Frog and Toad Are Friends*. Art by author. Harper, 1970. Originally published for the early reader, this is a charming collection of short stories. First in a series.

McCloskey, Robert. *Make Way for Ducklings*. Art by author. Viking, 1941. Mr. and Mrs. Mallard find the perfect home for their family in Boston.

Marshall, James. *George and Martha*. Art by author. Houghton, 1972. The five stories are laugh-aloud jokes featuring two hippos.

Martin, Bill Jr. *Brown Bear, Brown Bear, What Do You See?* Art by Eric Carle. Holt, 1983. A popular call and response chant.

Noble, Trinka Hakes. *The Day Jimmy's Boa Ate the Wash*. Art by Steven Kellogg. Dial, 1980. Jimmy's boa makes a class field trip hilarious fun.

Numeroff, Laura Joffe. *If You Give a Mouse a Cookie*. Art by Felicia Bond. Harper, 1985. Too new to be a classic? Call me in 20 years and tell me I was right.

Potter, Beatrix. *The Tale of Peter Rabbit*. Art by author. Warne, 1987. 1902 was the original publication date for this classic about a naughty bunny. Its small size makes it most appropriate to share with two or three children.

Prelutsky, Jack, ed. *Read Aloud Rhymes for the Very Young*. Art by Marc Brown. Knopf, 1986. A joyful collection of share-aloud poetry.

Sendak, Maurice. *Nutshell Library*. Art by author. Harper, 1962. Four tiny books: counting, alphabet, almanac, story.

Seuss, Dr. (pseud. for Theodor Seuss Geisel) *And to Think That I Saw It on Mulberry Street*. Art by author. Vanguard, 1937. Marco imagines a parade on Main Street.

Steig, William. *Sylvester and the Magic Pebble*. Art by author. Simon, 1988. A donkey finds a special pebble and finds himself turned into a rock.

Wright, Blanche. *The Real Mother Goose*. Art by compiler. Macmillan, 1987. Large-size drawings go with the traditional rhymes.

Zion, Gene. *Harry the Dirty Dog*. Art by Margaret Bloy Graham. Harper, 1956. Harry gets so dirty that even his family doesn't recognize him.

Booklist for Toddlers

This is a special list of books for your toddler book program. A toddler is generally characterized as a child who is just beginning to walk, anywhere from one to three years old. "Toddler Times" usually begin at age two. Books that are appropriate for this age group usually have a very simple text and pictures. They are often cumulative or rhythmic so that children can start to imitate sounds. Experiment with books that might be appealing to your particular group.

Allen, Pamela. *Who Sank the Boat?* Art by author. Coward, 1982. Many animals pile into the boat, but who sank it?

Baer, Gene. *Thump, Thump, Rat-a-Tat-Tat*. Art by Lois Ehlert. Harper, 1989. A bright bold band marches down the street.

Benjamin, Alan. *Rat-a-Tat, Pitter Pat.* Photos by Margaret Miller. Crowell, 1987. Black-and-white photos accompany familiar sounds that children can imitate.

Brown, Margaret Wise. *Big Red Barn.* Art by Felicia Bond. Harper, 1989. First published in 1956, the new art spruces the simple story up for a new generation.

Christelow, Eileen. *Five Little Monkeys Jumping on the Bed.* Art by author. Clarion, 1989. Join in this version of a traditional rhyme.

Cousins, Lucy. *What Can Rabbit Hear?* Art by author. Tambourine, 1991. A board pop-up about sound. Also *What Can Rabbit See?* (1991).

Crew, Donald. *Freight Train.* Art by author. Greenwillow, 1978. See the colors moving by in a freight train.

Dabcovich, Lydia. *Ducks Fly.* Art by author. Dutton, 1990. Watch the ducks fly.

Degen, Bruce. *Jamberry.* Art by author. Harper, 1983. Bouncing berry rhyming with happy art to match.

Ehlert, Lois. *Color Farm.* Art by author. Lippincott, 1990. Bright bold colors and shapes using die cuts show farm animals.

Flack, Marjorie. *Angus and the Cat.* Art by author. Doubleday, 1931. Angus, a curious scotty, chases the new cat around the house.

Fox, Mem. *Hattie and the Fox.* Art by Patricia Mullins. Bradbury, 1987. A chicken sees a fox, but the other animals ignore her warning.

Galdone, Paul. *Over in the Meadow: An Old Nursery Counting Rhyme.* Art by author. Prentice, 1986. A counting rhyme that's easy to memorize—even for the youngest.

Goennel, Heidi. *My Dog.* Art by author. Orchard, 1989. A little girl tells about the different kinds of dogs she likes.

Guarino, Deborah. *Is Your Mama a Llama?* Art by Stephen Kelloff. Scholastic, 1989. Who is your Mama? I like this because I own llamas, but everyone else does too.

Henley, Claire. *Farm Day.* Art by author. Dial, 1991. Farm animals enjoy a day on the farm.

Hoffman, Phyllis. *We Play.* Art by Sarah Wilson. Harper, 1990. Toddlers hug, play, hide, dance, and wave at a nursery school.

Hutchins, Pat. *Good-Night Owl!* Art by author. Macmillan, 1972. Imitate bird sounds as owl tries to sleep.

Keats, Ezra Jack. *The Snowy Day.* Art by the author. Viking, 1962. A child's enjoyment in the first snow.

Kovalski, Maryann. *The Wheels on the Bus.* Art by author. Little, 1987. Sing this nursery song as Grandma and the two girls miss the bus.

Lawson, Carol. *Teddy Bear, Teddy Bear.* Art by author. Dial, 1991. The traditional nursery rhyme illustrated with an expressive bear.

Lemieux, Michele. *What's That Noise?* Art by author. Morrow, 1985. The noise bear hears is his own heart thumping.

McCloskey, Robert. *Blueberries for Sal.* Art by author. Viking, 1948. A bear cub and a little girl reverse Moms as they search for berries.

Miller, Margaret. *Who Uses This?* Photos by author. Greenwillow, 1990. Shows children and adults using the tools of various careers.

Murphy, Jill. *Peace at Last.* Art by author. Dial, 1980. Papa bear can't sleep because of all the noises in the house.

Paterson, Bettina. *My First Animals.* Art by author. Crowell, 1990. Paper cutouts illustrate both domestic and wild animals. Also *My First Wild Animals* (Harper, 1989).

Peterson, Tracey Campbell. *Old MacDonald Had a Farm.* Art by author. Dial, 1984. Just one example of this easy-to-sing song.

Polushkin, Maria. *Mother, Mother, I Want Another.* Art by Diane Dawson. Crown, 1978. Mother thinks that baby bear wants a new mother when all he really wants is a good-night kiss.

Rikys, Bodel. *Red Bear.* Art by author. Dial, 1991. Names of the colors and art on each page showing a simple bear shape.

Roth, Susan L. *We'll Ride Elephants through Brooklyn.* Art by author. Farrar, 1989. Rhythmic poem accompanied by exuberant art.

Serfozo, Mary. *Who Said Red?* Art by Keiko Narahashi. Macmillan, 1988. A color rhyme is accompanied by lively art.

Shannon, George. *The Surprise.* Art by Jose Aruego and Ariane Dewey. Greenwillow, 1983. Squirrel gives his mother a present wrapped in one box inside another in another . . . until out pops . . . squirrel.

Sis, Peter. *Waving: A Counting Book.* Art by author. Greenwillow, 1988. Everyone gets a chance to wave from 1 to 15.

Slobodkina, Esphyr. *Caps for Sale.* Art by author. Scott, 1947. A favorite for storytime. Children can imitate the monkeys who imitate a peddler.

Stinson, Kathy. *Red Is Best.* Art by Robin Baird Lewis. Annick, 1982. A little girl celebrates the color red.

Tafuri, Nancy. *Have You Seen My Duckling?* Art by author. Greenwillow, 1984. Children will be able to see the duckling in the pictures as Mama looks for her.

Williams, Sue. *I Went Walking.* Art by Julie Vivas. Harcourt, 1989. Animals follow a child as she/he takes a walk. Refrain for participation.

Wishinsky, Frieda. *Oonga Boonga.* Art by Suçie Stevenson. Little, 1990. Big brother Daniel is the only one who can communicate with the baby.

Wood, Audrey. *The Napping House.* Art by Don Wood. Harcourt, 1984. A cumulative tale shows animals and a granny trying to take a nap until a flea starts a chain reaction and they all wake up.

Zolotow, Charlotte. *Mr. Rabbit and the Lovely Present.* Art by Maurice Sendak. Harper, 1962. Searching for the perfect present for her mother, a little girl ends up with a lovely fruit basket.

Books to Share at Home

Baby's World: A First Picture Catalog. Photos by Stephen Shott. Dutton, 1990. A star quality photo identification book.

Brown, Laurie Krasny. *Toddler Time*. Art by Marc Brown. Little, 1990. Bath time, toilet training, saying "no" and song and dance are shown for both adults and toddlers.

Brown, Margaret Wise. *Goodnight Moon*. Art by Clement Hurd. Harper, 1947. The very best goodnight book of all time.

Kunhardt, Dorothy. *Pat the Bunny*. Art by author. Western, 1942. A child's first book. Pat the bunny, feel Daddy's beard, and wave goodbye.

Strickland, Paul. *A Child's Book of Things*. Art by author. Orchard, 1990. Objects in and outside the house are labeled for toddlers and English learners.

Stories to Tell

Along with picture books you will enjoy presenting simple stories without books. Freed from using the actual book, you can concentrate on telling the story with expression and will be able to occasionally use your hands and even your body to help convey the message.

Start with the old familiar tales such as "The Old Woman and Her Pig" or "The Three Wishes." As the children learn to listen you can attempt slightly longer and less well-known stories such as *Oté*, a Puerto Rican folktale retold by Pura Belpré in which a devil is outwitted by a family shouting "Tam ni pu—tam ni be."

Authored stories such as the short and amusing "Cheese, Peas and Chocolate Pudding" have been enthusiastically received by my preschool audiences. It can also be exciting to tell rather than show a picture book. Try Wanda Gág's *Millions of Cats* as a picture book one time, but as a story the next time. Here are two stories for you to learn and tell to your preschool and primary groups.

HOW TO MAKE A SMALL HOUSE INTO A LARGE ONE

The following is a story that my Grandpa used to tell when I was a child. I've found variants in several collections, but of course I like the way my Grandpa told it best. Make sure that you imitate the sounds made by all the animals. Add as many animals to the house as you wish for as long as you have the children's attention. This is an old Yiddish story, so don't have a pig move into the house. That wouldn't be authentic.

There was once a man and a woman who lived in a small one-room cottage. It was very tiny. A table, some chairs, a bed, and a stove were the only furniture. It was really crowded, even for the old couple. One day the man received a letter from his daughter. She and her husband and their baby wished to come and live with their parents. The man was outraged. How could two more people and a baby possibly fit into their small house? The old woman suggested that her husband visit the Rabbi, the wisest man in town, and ask his advice.

The man explained his problem to the Rabbi. "Of course you must write immediately and tell your daughter's family to come. Your house

may not be as small as you think." In no time at all the daughter, her husband, and the baby arrived. Now the house was very crowded. The baby woke up every morning at six o'clock and cried "Wah, wah, wah."

The man returned to the Rabbi and asked his help.

"Ah, ha. I see you do have a problem. Indeed, I'm sure that I can help. Do you own a cow?"

Yes, of course, the man owned a cow. Her name was Yasha.

"Go home. Bring Yasha the cow into the house to live with you."

The man was astonished, but no one argued with the Rabbi. He went home and put Yasha the cow into the house. The baby cried "Wah wah," the cow mooed "Moo, moo," and indeed it was very cramped in the house. Yasha kept swishing her tail back and forth into the man's face. The baby crawled between the cow's legs.

The man returned once more to the Rabbi and pleaded for his help. This time the Rabbi ordered the man to let his rooster, the five hens, and the twelve baby chicks live in the house with the man and his family. What a ruckus this caused.

The baby cried, "Wah, wah, wah."

The cow mooed, "Moo, moo, moo."

The rooster woke up at four o'clock every morning: "Cock-a-doodle-doo."

"Cluck, cluck," screamed the hens.

"Wah, wah, wah," cried the baby.

"Moo, moo, moo," lowed the cow.

The hens had no place to lay their eggs. One lay an egg right on top of the man's head. The chicks darted in and out of the woman's path. "Here, chick, chick, chick" called the woman.

The man, in desperation, called on the Rabbi again. The Rabbi stroked his long white beard and suggested that still more animals be brought to live in the house.

Now the house was cramped and noisy.

Wah, wah, wah.

Moo, moo, moo.

Cock-a-doodle-doo.

Cluck, cluck.

Here chick, chick.
And now the sheep baaed "Baa, baa."
The ducks quacked "Quack, quack."
The geese honked "Honk, honk."
The horse neighed "Neigh, neigh."
There was no place for anyone to sleep, work, play or eat.

The man trudged back to the Rabbi's house haggard with lack of sleep. All the animals he owned were now living in the house with him and his wife, their daughter, her husband, and their baby.

"Help us, Rabbi. Our house is bursting and the noise is unbearable."
Moo, moo.
Quack, quack.
Cock-a-doodle-doo.
Baa, baa.
Neigh, neigh.
Honk, honk.
Cluck, cluck.
Here chick, chick, chick.
Wah, wah, wah.

"Go home," said the Rabbi, "and take the animals out of the house. Take the cow, the sheep, the ducks, the horse, the geese, the rooster, the hens and chicks all out of the house." The man was relieved. He went home and took all the animals out of the house. It seemed so large without the animals. With only four people and one small baby, the house felt empty. The only noise was the baby making a satisfying crying sound.

So, if you want to make a small house into a big house, just buy a few animals.

CHEESE, PEAS AND CHOCOLATE PUDDING

Betty Van Witsen

An effective introduction to this story is to ask your listeners what their favorite foods are. It is interesting that younger children often list healthy vegetables and fruit or chicken, while older children usually say pizza or ice cream! It's probably not cricket to change the ending, but I always say "he ate everything but chili and asparagus," two foods I dislike. If you invite me to dinner, though, I'll eat them happily!

There was once a little boy who ate cheese, peas, and chocolate pudding. Cheese, peas, and chocolate pudding. Cheese, peas, and chocolate pudding. Every day the same old things: cheese, peas, and chocolate pudding.

For breakfast he would have some cheese. Any kind. Cream cheese, American cheese, Swiss cheese, Dutch cheese, Italian cheese, blue cheese, green cheese, yellow cheese, brick cheese. Even Liederkranz. Just cheese for breakfast.

For lunch he ate peas. Green or yellow peas. Frozen peas, canned peas, dried peas, split peas, black-eyed peas. No potatoes, though—just peas for lunch.

And for supper he would have cheese and peas. And chocolate pudding. Cheese, peas, and chocolate pudding. Cheese, peas, and chocolate pudding. Every day the same old things: cheese, peas, and chocolate pudding.

Once his mother bought a lamb chop for him. She cooked it in a little frying pan on the stove, and she put some salt on it, and gave it to the little boy on a little blue dish. The boy looked at it. He smelled it. (It did smell delicious!) He even touched it. But . . .

"Is this cheese?" he asked.

"It's a lamb chop, darling," said his mother.

The boy shook his head. "Cheese!" he said. So his mother ate the lamb chop herself, and the boy had some cottage cheese.

One day his brother was chewing a raw carrot. It sounded so good, the little boy reached his hand out for a bite.

"Sure!" said his brother. "Here!" The little boy almost put the carrot into his mouth, but at the last minute he remembered, and he said, "Is this peas?"

"No fella, it's a carrot," said his brother.

"Peas," said the little boy firmly, handing the carrot back.

Once his daddy was eating a big dish of raspberry Jell-O. It looked so shiny and red and cool, the little boy came over and held his mouth open.

"Want a taste?" asked his daddy. The little boy looked and looked at the Jell-O. He almost looked it off the dish. But: "Is it chocolate pudding?" he asked.

"No, son, it's Jell-O," said his daddy.

So the little boy frowned and backed away. "Chocolate pudding!" he said.

His grandma baked cookies for him. "Nope!" said the boy.

His grandpa bought him an ice cream cone. The little boy just shook his head.

His aunt and uncle invited him for a fried-chicken dinner. Everybody ate fried chicken and fried chicken and more fried chicken. Except the little boy. And you know what he ate.

Cheese, peas, and chocolate pudding. Cheese, peas, and chocolate pudding. Every day the same old thing: cheese, peas, and chocolate pudding.

But one day—ah, one day, a very funny thing happened. The little boy was playing puppy. He lay on the floor and growled and barked and rolled over. He crept to the table where his big brother was having lunch.

"Arf-arf!" he barked.

"Good doggie!" said his brother, patting his head. The little boy lay down on his back on the floor and barked again.

But at that minute, his big brother dropped a piece of something from his plate. And the little boy's mouth was just ready to say "Arf!" And what do you think happened?

Something dropped into the little boy's mouth. He sat up in surprise. Because *something* was on his tongue. And *something* was warm and juicy and delicious!

And it didn't taste like cheese. And it did *not* taste like peas. And it certainly wasn't chocolate pudding.

The little boy chewed slowly. Each chew tasted better than the last. He swallowed *something* and opened his mouth again. Wide. As wide as he could.

"Want some more?" asked his brother.

The little boy closed his mouth and thought. "That's not cheese," he said.

"No, it's not," said his brother.

"And it isn't peas."

"No, not peas," said his brother.

"And it couldn't be chocolate pudding."

"No, it certainly is not chocolate pudding," smiled his brother. "It's hamburger."

The little boy thought hard. "I like hamburger," he said.

So his big brother shared the rest of his hamburger with the little boy, and ever after that, guess what!

Ever after that, the little boy ate cheese, peas, and chocolate pudding and hamburger.

Until he was your age, of course. When he was your age, he ate everything.

Participation Stories

Given the opportunity, young children in the United States and Canada will happily participate in any story. Their participation makes storytelling a group affair, exciting for both the presentor and the listeners. I have found, however, that this is not true in many other cultures, where students are expected to absorb information silently.

Not every story lends itself to interaction, of course. But when you tell a story with a refrain that can be repeated, or an action that can be imitated, you'll find that your whole group will want to join you. For the storyteller, such participation offers visual proof that the story is being enthusiastically received. You wouldn't want to feel that you must always find a story that invites everyone to respond or join in, but occasionally such a story will be the perfect choice.

I should add here that some storytellers feel that too much of an oral response may distract from the story, while others, particularly those engaged in the Whole Language movement, believe that stories that fall into the "call and response" category are the very best kind. I love them myself!

Participation stories are most often told to preschool and primary-age children, and to middle grade children; consequently I have included special sections on participation in both of these chapters. But other groups will enjoy this genre too. Adults are sometimes reluctant to join in, but are among the most enthusiastic once their reserve is broken. Even older elementary and junior high school students who are usually reticent about calling out when there are strangers present can be convinced to "help" tell the story.

Here I have included one of my favorite participation stories, as well as a booklist filled with other titles for you to try.

THE STORY OF JOSHUA WHO JUMPED

Morris Lurie

This story is a delight to tell. Unlike many participation stories, it does not contain a rhyme or refrain to echo; instead, it offers children a more active way to join in. The first time I tried it, I was speaking to 600 children (from kindergarten through sixth grade) in an outdoor auditorium. Toward the end of the story, I asked them all to join hands, stand up, and jump. It worked! Six hundred children and teachers all jumped and, miraculously, sat down again so that I could finish the story.

This is the story of Joshua, who jumped.
  Jumped like a rabbit. Jumped like a jack-in-the-box.
  Jumped like a jumping kangaroo.
  "Goodness me," said his father. "What a bouncy little fellow."
  This was when Joshua was still very small. He was still just a baby, in fact, only about six months old. But there he was, standing up in his cot, holding on to the rails with his tiny hands as firmly as he could.
  His blue eyes bright and his cheeks rosy red.
  And not only standing, but jumping.
  Over and over.
  Again and again.
  "Isn't he strong?" said Joshua's father proudly.
  "Doesn't he look wonderful?" said Joshua's mother, beaming.
Jump, jump, jump, went Joshua in his cot.
  And his parents stood there together, hand in hand, smiling down at their jumping son.
  Joshua learnt to crawl, of course, the way all babies do.
  And then he learnt to walk, holding on to things very carefully, the way all babies do.
  But the minute he learnt to walk without holding on to things, Joshua did something different.
  Quite different.

Joshua stopped walking.

He forgot all about walking.

He jumped instead.

Joshua jumped everywhere.

He jumped along the passage.

He jumped into the kitchen.

He jumped around the garden, under the fruit trees, round and round the lawn.

"You don't think he's swallowed a frog?" Joshua's father smiled.

"Or a bouncy rubber ball?" Joshua's mother laughed.

Jump, jump, jump, went Joshua in the garden.

Around the lemon tree.

Under the plum tree.

Past the flowers and the bushes and the next-door hedge.

And his parents stood there together, hand in hand, laughing to see their jumping son.

Joshua jumped everywhere.

He jumped around the supermarket, when his mother took him shopping.

He jumped at the dry-cleaner's.

He jumped at the butcher's.

"Hmm, there's a jumpy lad," said the butcher. "Been feeding him lots of spring lamb, have you?"

Joshua's mother laughed.

"No, he's always been a jumper," she said. "It's just the way he is. A dozen sausages, please."

When Joshua turned four, his mother took him to kindergarten. The teacher's name there was Miss Prime.

Joshua jumped up and down while he was being introduced.

"Oh, how nice!" said Miss Prime. "I like having a chap in the class who jumps. Keeps us all on our toes! Come along Joshua. Let's jump into some finger-painting first. And then we'll jump outside and play."

Joshua had a wonderful time at kindergarten.

Jumping in and out of the sandpit.

On and off the swings.

He even jumped when he did his finger-paintings, and what lovely jumping pictures they were.

And then Joshua turned five and started school. That's when the trouble began.

Joshua jumped into the classroom.

It was his very first day.

His teacher's name there was Miss Stern.

And when she saw Joshua jumping in, her eyes practically jumped right out of her head.

"What?" she cried, "'Jumping? Jumping is no way to come into a class!"

Joshua looked puzzled.

"But I've always jumped," he said. "I've always been a jumper, from the earliest I remember."

"Oh, how outrageous!" cried Miss Stern. "How dare you! I've never heard such preposterous nonsense! Well, I'll show you what jumping is! You can jump into that corner over there straight away!" She pointed with a long, mean, bony finger. "And when you get there, don't you dare move a single centimetre!"

"Yes, Miss Stern," said Joshua.

So Joshua stood in the corner as still as still could be.

Slowly a minute dragged past.

The second minute seemed even slower.

The third was worse.

Joshua felt miserable.

He had never felt so awful in his whole life.

It was absolutely terrible to have to stand like this.

It was torture.

And before he knew what he was doing, Joshua began to bounce up and down.

Little bounces at first.

Then bigger ones.

Bigger.

Big, springy jumps.

And then Miss Stern saw him.

"Joshua!" she shrieked. "Stop that at once!"

But Joshua could only shake his head.

"I'm terribly sorry," he said, "but I can't. I just can't. I have to keep jumping. It's how I am."

Miss Stern was almost beside herself with rage.

"Mary!" she shouted at a girl in the class. "Seize his left hand! Roger!" she shouted at a boy. "Seize his right! We'll stop this foolish jumping!"

Mary did as she was told, and so did Roger.

But Joshua's jumps were so springy now that, every time he jumped, Mary and Roger rose into the air with him.

"Oh, this is ridiculous!" shrieked Miss Stern. "Broderick! Take Mary's hand! Davinia! Take Roger's! We'll put an end to this!"

But still Joshua's jumps were too springy. And now each time he jumped all five children rose into the air.

"Harold!" shrieked Miss Stern. "Mavis!"

But they weren't enough either.

Miss Stern shrieked and shrieked.

And now the whole class, all holding hands in a long line with Joshua in the midle, rose into the air each time Joshua jumped.

Miss Stern ran shrieking outside.

She shrieked at this class.

That class.

The Juniors.

The Seniors.

And before long the whole school was joined in one long line with Joshua in the middle, all rising into the air each time Joshua jumped.

And Miss Stern shrieked and shrieked and didn't know what to do.

And no one cared.

Because the whole school had discovered what Joshua had always known.

Jumping makes you feel wonderful.

Absolutely wonderful.

And that's what they all did, until it was time to jump home.

Booklist: More Participation Stories

Anderson, Leone Castell. *The Wonderful Shrinking Shirt*. Art by Irene Trivas. Whitman, 1983. "She soused it and doused it and rinsed it clean and hung it in the sun to dry."

Asch, Frank. *Just like Daddy*. Art by author. Prentice, 1981. Follow little bear as he does "just like Daddy."

Fleming, Denise. *In the Tall, Tall Grass*. Art by author. Holt, 1992. Children will enjoy echoing the rhymed text.

Gross, Ruth Belov. *You Don't Need Words! A Book about Ways People Talk without Words*. Art by Susannah Ryan. Scholastic, 1991. Children can imitate the actions in this informational book.

Harper, Wilhelmina. *The Gunniwolf*. Art by William Weisner. Dutton, 1978. Echo the nonsense words or act them out.

"Hug Me" by Patti Stern in Caroline Feller Bauer's *Valentine's Day*. Art by Blanche L. Sims. Harper, 1993. Hug your partner slowly, carefully, gently.

Hutchins, Pat. *Don't Forget the Bacon!* Art by author. Greenwillow, 1976. A boy sent shopping mixes up the list.

Kaska, Keiko. *The Pig's Picnic*. Art by author. Putnam, 1988. Act out this story.

Massie, Diane Redfield. *The Baby Beebee Bird*. Art by author. Harper, 1963. Children can echo the nonsense refrain.

Murphy, Jill. *Peace at Last*. Art by author. Dial, 1980. Imitate the sounds that keep Papa Bear awake.

Patz, Nancy. *Pumpernickel Tickle and Mean Green Cheese*. Art by author. Watts, 1978. Children will learn the name faster than you will!

Polushkin, Maria. *Mother, Mother I Want Another!* Art by Diane Sawson. Crown, 1978. Chant the refrain as Little Mouse tries to get another kiss good-night.

Stern, Simon. *The Hobyahs: An Old Story*. Art by author. Prentice, 1977. Join in on the refrain.

Tolstoi, Alexei. *The Great Big Enormous Turnip*. Art by Helen Oxenbury. Heineman, 1968. Help pull up the turnip.

Watanabe, Shigeo. *How Do I Put It On?* Art by Yasuo Ohtomo. Collins, 1979. Show how you put on the clothes.

Wood, Audrey. *King Bidgood's in the Bathtub*. Art by Don Wood. Harcourt, 1985. Chant the page's lament.

Multimedia Storytelling

It is well known that small children have a short attention span. But this doesn't mean that they can't sit and listen to stories for half an hour to forty-five minutes. It does mean that the book activities during that time should be varied. Try letting the children participate in the storytelling between the more formal presentations of stories and poetry. If you are interested in trying any of the multimedia ideas suggested in other parts of this book you will find a most receptive audience in preschool and primary children. They will be delighted with the use of boards: felt, magnetic, or Velcro. Attaching and removing the objects will create a new center of attention, and they may even want to help you. The overhead projector and the slide projector will be particularly useful if you'd like to show and tell stories to larger groups. And don't forget puppetry!

Fingerplays and Action Rhymes

Fingerplays should be repeated several times so that the children can copy your actions. There is no need to stop and explain each action. Those children who couldn't follow you the first or second time will catch on at a later recitation. Although these rhymes do help with reading readiness through finger coordination, they also give the children a chance to stretch a bit between stories. Primarily, they are meant to be fun. This short collection of fingerplays and action rhymes are all traditional rhymes. You may know them, but not remember them. In any case, it will take only a minute or so for you to learn or relearn one or two for your preschool and primary story sessions.

THE ANT HILL

Here's the ant hill, with no ants about;	(Make a fist)
And I say, "Little ants, won't you please come out?"	(Look at fist)
Out they come trooping in answer to my call	(Lift each finger from fist and have the ants crawl
One, two, three, four, five, and that's all.	about)

JAPANESE RHYME

Hana, hana, hana, kuchi	(Nose, nose, nose, mouth)
Kuchi, Kuchi, Kuchi, Mimi	(Mouth, mouth, mouth, ear)
Mimi, mimi, mimi, me	(Ear, ear, ear, eye)

THE FROGS

Five little froggies sitting on a well   (Cup hands)
One peeped in and down he fell   (Raise one finger)
Froggies jumped high   (Raise hands and wave
Froggies jumped low   above head)
Froggies jumped everywhere to and fro   (Lower hands to the floor)
    Continue rhyme: Four little   (Wave arms in all
    froggies, etc.   directions)

TOUCH YOUR NOSE

(suit action to words)

Touch your nose
Touch your chin
That's the way this game begins.
Touch your eyes
Touch your knees
Now pretend you're going to sneeze.
Touch your hair
Touch one ear
Touch your two red lips right here.
Touch your elbows
Where they bend
That's the way this touch game ends.

FINGERPLAY

(suit action to words)

Draw a *little* circle in the air, in the air,
Draw a little circle in the air.
Draw with all your might,
Keep it up all night.
Draw a little circle in the air.

Draw a *bigger* circle in the air, in the air,
Draw a bigger circle in the air.
Going 'round in the breeze,
Keep it going, if you please!
Draw a bigger circle in the air.

Draw a *great* big circle in the air, in the air,
Draw a great big circle in the air.
Draw it higher, draw it lower,
Draw it slower, slower, slower. . . .
And now there's no more circle in the air!

A BUNNY

I'm a little bunny	(Make a fist)
With nose so funny.	(Wiggle thumb)
This is my home in the ground.	(Opposite hand on hip)
When a noise I hear	
I perk up my ears	(Put two fingers of fist up)
And jump into the ground	(Put fist into "hole" of arm)

THE DUCKS

Five little ducks
Over the hills and far away
Mother duck said "Quack, quack, quack"
But only four little ducks came back.

(Ducks are fingers of right hand. The head is the hill they go over; the left hand makes the mother duck's bill.)

Repeat rhyme with four little ducks until the mother duck is all alone. She quacks loudly and all five ducks come back.

THE LADY

Here are lady's knives and forks	(Intertwine your fingers, palms up)
Here is lady's table	(Turn hands over to make table)
Here is lady's looking glass	(Make a triangle)
Here is baby's cradle	(Clasp hands and rock)

THE ELEPHANT

An elephant goes like this and that.	(Stamp feet)
He's terrible big,	(Raise arms)
And he's terrible fat.	(Spread arms)
He has no fingers,	(Wiggle fingers)
He has no toes,	(Touch toes)
But goodness gracious, what a nose!	(Draw hands out indicating long curly trunk)

THE MOUSE

There is such a little tiny mouse	(Show how small he is with thumb and forefinger—walk fingers across table)
Living safely in my house	
Out at night he'll quietly creep	
When everyone is fast asleep	(Fold hands next to head)
But always by the light of day	(Open arms wide to show sun)
He'll quietly, quietly creep away.	(Walk fingers across table)

GRANDMA AND GRANDPA

(suit actions to words)

Here are Grandma's glasses
Here is Grandma's hat
Grandma claps her hands
  like this
And folds them in her lap.

Here are Grandpa's glasses
Here is Grandpa's hat
This is the way he folds
  his arms
And takes a little nap.

TEN LITTLE GYPSIES

(your fingers are the gypsies)

Ten little gypsies stand up straight — (Raise both hands, fingers rigid)

Ten little gypsies make a gate — (Fingers of both hands interlaced)

Ten little gypsies make a ring — (Make a circle with thumbs and forefingers)

Ten little gypsies bow to the queen — (Fold fingers of both hands forward)

Ten little gypsies dance all day — (Bend wrists, wiggle fingers downward)

Ten little gypsies run away — (Both hands behind back)

THE CHOCOLATE CAKE

This can also be done as a poster rhyme. Using Velcro, attach candles to a picture of a cake. Remove them as the children chant. (Start with your hands facing you. Each time you blow Wh! Wh!, put down a finger.)

Ten little candles on a chocolate cake
Wh! Wh! Now there are eight.
Eight little candles on candlesticks
Wh! Wh! Now there are six.
Six little candles and not one more
Wh! Wh! Now there are four.
Four little candles, red, white and blue
Wh! Wh! Now there are two
Two little candles standing in the sun
Wh! Wh! Now there are none.

LION HUNT

(Storyteller stands in front; children follow with voice and actions)

Everyone get ready
We're going on a lion hunt
Ready?
Ready!
Get set, go

I see
I see
I see a road
Let's walk down the road   (Tap hands on thighs)
Tramp, tramp, tramp

I see
I see
I see a field
Let's walk through the field   (Make wide swinging
Swish, swish, swish   motions with arms)

I see
I see
I see a swamp
Let's walk through the muck   (Lift legs up high)
Squish, squish, squish

I see
I see
I see a tree
Let's climb up it   (Climbing hand over
Climb, climb, climb   hand)

I see
I see
I see a bridge   (Running motion)
Let's run over the bridge   (Click tongue to roof of
Tap, tap, tap   mouth)

I see
I see
I see a cave
Let's go into the cave   (Drag feet slowly)
Slowly, slowly, slowly

I see
I see   (Make running motions
I see. . . . . a lion   in place)

(Repeat all actions in reverse quickly, then say, "Wow, we made it!"

An oversize picture book version of this action story is Michael Rosen's *We're Going on a Bear Hunt*. Art by Helen Oxenbury. Macmillan, 1989.

THE FARM

Start rhyme with closed fists facing towards you. Raise thumb of one hand first and then each finger up to ten. On the last line, put your hands under your arms and move your elbows up and down to create flapping wings.

> One is a cat that says meow!
> Two is a dog that says bow-wow!
> Three is a crow that says caw-caw!
> Four is a donkey that says hee-haw!
> Five is a lamb that says baa-baa!
> Six is a sheep that says maa-maa!
> Seven is a chick that says chuck-chuck!
> Eight is a hen that says cluck-cluck!
> Nine is a cow that says moo-moo!
> Ten is a rooster crowing cock-a-doodle do!

Booklist: More Fingerplays

Brown, Marc. *Finger Rhymes*. Art by author. Dutton, 1980. Fourteen finger rhymes with pictoral instructions.

Defty, Jeff. *Creative Fingerplays and Action Rhymes: An Index and Guide to Their Use*. Oryx, 1992.

Glazer, Tom. *Eye Winker, Tom Tinker, Chin Chopper*. Art by Ron Himler. Doubleday, 1973. Fifty musical fingerplays.

Hays, Sarah. *Stamp Your Feet*. Art by Toni Goffe. Lothrop, 1988. Action rhymes and songs in a picture-book format.

Leighton, Audrey Olson. *Fingerplay Friends*. Art by author. Judson (P.O. Box 877235, Wasilla, AK 99687), 1984. Excellent collection of contemporary and traditional fingerplays.

Matterson, Elizabeth. *Games for the Very Young: A Treasury of Nursery Songs and Finger Plays*. Art by author. McGraw-Hill, 1969.

Montgomerie, Norah, comp. *This Little Pig Went to Market*. Art by Margery Gill. Watts, 1966. 150 rhymes arranged by category, from hand clapping to tickling.

Poulsson, Emilie. *Finger Plays for Nursery and Kingergarten*; music by Cornelia C. Roeske. Art by L. J. Bridgman. Dover, 1971. This book was first published in 1893; we're still using the fingerplays.

Fold-and-Cut Stories

Paper and scissors will provide the tools for still another way of presenting stories or reciting nursery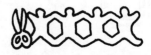

rhymes. This is the paper-cutting idea that Hans Christian Andersen used somewhat more ambitiously while he told stories. Try colored origami paper, which is thin and easy to cut; as you become more adept, construction paper can be used. The rhymes are very short and should be repeated several times, the children joining the leader. During the second and third recitation fold and cut the shape. Until you have done this several times, prefold the paper and draw the appropriate outline on the fold so that you need not think, only cut, while you are reciting. The grand finale is when you open up your cutout to reveal a shape or object relevant to the rhyme. All the children will want to have a shape, so choose the lucky one carefully each time. Like finger-plays, fold-and-cut stories and rhymes are fun for listener and leader alike, and are good fillers between stories or as the finale to your storytelling program.

Create each of the following fold-and-cut stories by making accordion folds in a wide sheet of paper and drawing the illustration as shown:

Rain on the green grass
And on the tree.
Rain on the house-top
But not on me.
Why not?
Because I have an umbrella.

Mary, Mary, quite contrary.
How does your garden grow?
With silver bells and cockle shells
And pretty maids all in a row.

Peter, Peter pumpkin eater,
Had a wife and couldn't keep her.
He put her in a pumpkin shell
And there he kept her very well.

Little Miss Muffet
Sat on a tuffet
Eating her curds and whey.
Along came a spider
And sat down beside her
And frightened Miss Muffet away.

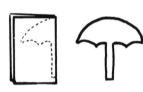

Hickety, pickety, my black hen,
She lays eggs for gentlemen.
Sometimes nine and sometimes ten,
Hickety, pickety, my black hen.

Fold five sheets of thin paper in fourths lengthwise and you will have ten eggs to give away.

HENRY AND MARY

Henry was a worthy king,
Mary was his queen.
He gave to her a lily
Upon a stalk of green.

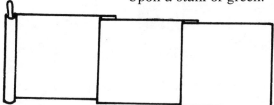

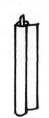

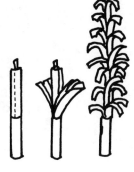

Make a roll of paper (painted green beforehand, if you like). A rubber band around the middle will keep it rolled. If you don't want to invest in wrapping or shelf paper, use three double-spread sheets of newspaper. To facilitate the rolling, fold down a few inches along the outer edge of the first sheet (a bit of masking tape at the top of the fold will be of help later) and start rolling. Lap each succeeding sheet several inches as you proceed. Hold the roll together with a rubber band and use a heavy-duty shears, sharp knife, or single-edged razor blade to make three or four vertical cuts into the roll. Fold back the "leaves" and pull upward gently at the center of the roll to form the lily stalk. If you used a piece of tape at the top of the fold when you started, the center will be very easy to find. Of course, the more paper you use, the leafier the stalk.

No rhyme, but the perfect fold-and-cut story for Earth Day. Say, as you cut:

Trees really are a renewable resource. If you plant a seed and maybe another and if you wait (while I make a few cuts), in a few years you will have. . . a forest of trees!

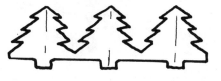

(The longer the paper, of course, the more trees you will have in your forest.)

Old Betty Blue
Lost a holiday shoe
What can old Betty do?
Give her another
To match the other,
And then she may swagger in two.

Fold lengthwise. Show single shoe, then open to show the pair of shoes.

Wee Willie Winkie runs
   through the town,
Upstairs and downstairs
   in his nightgown
Rapping at the windows,
   crying through the lock,
"Are the children in their
   beds, for now it's
   eight o'clock?"

Fold and cut to make the figure "8."

See-saw sacradown
Which is the way to London town?
One foot up and the other down,
And that is the way to
   London town.

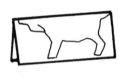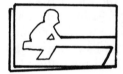

Little Bo-Peep has lost
   her sheep
And can't tell where
   to find them;
Leave them alone, and
   they'll come home,
And bring their tails
   behind them.

Fold lengthwise. Use triple thickness to make three sheep that will stand up.

Roses are red
Violets are blue
Sugar is sweet
And so are you.

And here's a heart for you.

RING AROUND THE ROSIE

Ring around the rosie
Pocket full of posies
Ashes, ashes
We all fall down.

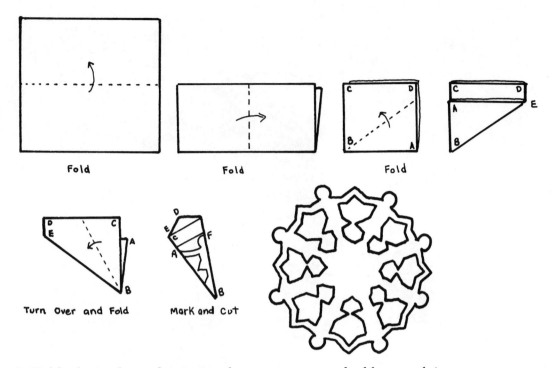

Fold

Fold

Fold

Turn Over and Fold

Mark and Cut

1. Fold a large sheet of paper, such as a newspaper double-spread, in half.
2. Fold in half again.
3. Fold corner A diagonally to bring folded edges AB and BC together.
4. Turn over and fold diagonally in half again, bringing edges BE and BAC together.
5. Draw figure on surface AFB and cut to make ring.
6. To make strip of paper dolls, recut as shown below.

Booklist: More Papercraft Ideas

Aytüre-Scheele, Zülal. *Paperfolding Fun: Origami in Color;* tr. by Linda Sonntag. Gallery, 1986. Full-color photos show the origami folds in full color.

Irvine, Joan. *How to Make Super Pop-ups.* Art by Linda Hendry. Morrow, 1992. Children will love to try these pop-up ideas.

Miyawaki, Tatsuo. *Happy Origami: Whale Book.* Art by author. Japan Publications, n.d. The Japanese art of paperfolding to make a whale, a penguin, a frog and several other animals and objects. One of a series. See also by the same author: *Happy Origami: Butterfly Book; Happy Origami: Swallow Book; Happy Origami: Tortoise Book.*

Stangl, Jean. *Paper Stories.* David S. Lake (19 Davis Drive, Belmont, CA 94002), 1984. Original stories and poems with directions for using paper cutouts.

Takahama, Toshie. *Quick and Easy Origami.* Shufunotomo (Kodansha Intl., 114 5th Ave., New York, NY 10011), 1988. Easy folding for animals, star, box, and basket.

20 / Programs for the Intermediate Grades

The children who attend the third through sixth grades are my choice for the perfect audience for book programs. They are the most receptive listeners, their interests are the most varied, their curiosity boundless. There is probably not a single idea in this book that would not be appreciated by a group of these children. They are ready not only to listen to longer and more mature selections from folklore and literature, but they are fascinated by multimedia presentations as well.

Storytelling for the Middle-Graders

In your traditional storyhours when you will be telling stories without the help of film or other media, the selection of what to tell becomes even more important. The children are now ready for longer, more sophisticated stories and will particularly appreciate the folktales of Hans Christian Andersen, Eleanor Far-jeon, and Oscar Wilde. Some of the short stories by present-day writers also might be enjoyed. Try those by Jane Yolen and Cynthia Rylant for a start.

Poetry is also popular with this age group. Story poems are particular favorites, as are the nonsense poetry of Shel Silverstein and the humorous collections of William Cole. If you are meeting on a regular basis with the same children, you might try a series of myths from the folk history of a particular country. This eliminates the need for overlong introductions to provide the necessary background material before each story. This age group listens with great enjoyment for a longer period of time than do preschoolers and you can schedule these pure storyhours for about an hour.

In presenting a preschool story session many storytellers prefer to remain seated. In the storyhour for older boys and girls I suggest that you consider standing. It can be argued that the story program is meant to create the close family gathering feeling reminiscent of sitting around a campfire or in a log cabin. I agree that this is also a good mood to capture. It's just that I prefer to appeal to the instinctive sense of the dramatic inherent in this age group and feel that it can be better expressed by standing. Moreover, with television the resident storyteller in the majority of homes, it is preferable for the child to be presented with "live" theater when attending a program in person. In this type of book program, when you will not be encouraging actual participation, it seems to me that by creating a theatrical atmosphere, with the storyteller separated from the audience and with the lights lowered, the listener will be encouraged to "see" the scene as the storyteller narrates.

Program your session in any way that is comfortable for you. A theme is not necessary, although I find that it helps to pull a program together. The longest story should be presented first while the audience is still fresh. A transitional poem might bridge the gap to a second long story. Save the short nonsense story for the end. I think you'll find that the story jokes and think stories included here serve perfectly as transitional material or at the conclusion of your storyhour. Finally, don't forget picture books! You might use some of the favorite picture-book stories in your preschool repertoire, or choose from the special list I have compiled for this chapter—picture books intended for older audiences. A picture-book story might offer the perfect way to close your program, as your audience calls out "just one more story, please!"

Stories to Tell

THE SMUGGLER

I first heard this story, which takes place just after World War II, when I was living in Europe at the time of the construction of the Berlin Wall. Now, of course, that the Wall is gone and Germany has been reunified, the context for this story has changed entirely. Still, it's an old favorite of mine, and I like to introduce it by saying: "Once upon a time, the city of Berlin was divided into two sections: East Berlin and West Berlin..."

After the Second World War Berlin was divided into sectors. To pass from Western Berlin to Eastern Berlin one had to go through control gates. Guards at the gates inspected identity cards and packages to guard against smuggling goods from one area to the other.

Each day Peter arrived at "Checkpoint Charlie" riding his bicycle on the way to work. Resting on the handlebars each morning was a large muslin bag filled with sand. Every morning Eric, the American guard, stopped Peter. "May I see your identity card, please?" he would ask. "Have you anything to declare?"

Peter always answered no, but still Eric was suspicious. Every morning he would eye the large bag of sand. And nearly every morning, but not every morning, he would dump the sand out onto a piece of burlap and run it through his fingers looking for something illegal. Eric was certain Peter was a smuggler, but he never found anything in the bag of sand no matter how carefully he searched.

For three months, five days a week, Peter crossed through "Checkpoint Charlie" on his bicycle carrying a muslin bag of sand on the handlebars.

The search became a morning ritual.

"Guten Tag, Herr Peter."

"Grüss Gott, Herr Eric."

"May I see your identity card, please."

"Certainly."

"Anything to declare?"

"No, sir."

"What's in the bag?"

"Nothing, sir, only sand."

"Sand? Empty it here and I will see for myself. Everything seems in order. You may pass. Have a good day."

"Thank you. Auf wiedersehen."

The months passed. One day Peter arrived on his bicycle carrying a large muslin bag on the handlebar. This time Eric talked to him in a low whisper. Eric was to leave that day to return to his home in the United States. He was to return to civilian life.

"Please," begged Eric, "Before I leave tell me what you have been smuggling all these months. I promise to tell no one."

"Certainly," answered Peter. "BICYCLES!"

TWO OF EVERYTHING

Alice Ritchie

This story has all the ingredients to be an instant hit with this age group: magic, humor, even suspense. I've lost count of the number of times I've told it since I first learned it on the way to a library meeting with Johanna Hurwitz. We were both first-year librarians at the New York Public Library. Once we heard "Two of Everything," we decided to learn it immediately. We told it back and forth to each other as we drove along the turnpike. It might seem like a long story to learn, but the events are all quite logical and once you've mastered it, it will become one of your favorites, too.

Mr. and Mrs. Hak-Tak were rather old and rather poor. They had a small house in a village among the mountains and a tiny patch of green land on the mountainside. Here they grew the vegetables which were all they had to live on, and when it was a good season and they did not need to eat up everything as soon as it was grown, Mr. Hak-Tak took what they could spare in a basket to the next village which was a little larger than theirs and sold it for as much as he could get and bought some oil for their lamp, and fresh seeds, and every now and then, but not often, a piece of cotton stuff to make new coats and trousers for himself and his wife. You can imagine they did not often get the chance to eat meat.

Now, one day it happened that when Mr. Hak-Tak was digging in his previous patch, he unearthed a big brass pot. He thought it strange that it should have been there for so long without his having come across it before, and he was disappointed to find that it was empty; still, he thought they would find some use for it, so when he was ready to go back to the house in the evening he decided to take it with him. It was very big and heavy, and in his struggles to get his arms round it and raise it to a good position for carrying, his purse, which he always took with him in his belt, fell to the ground, and, to be quite sure he had it safe, he put it inside the pot and so staggered home with his load.

As soon as he got into the house Mrs. Hak-Tak hurried from the inner room to meet him.

"My dear husband," she said, "whatever have you got there?"

"For a cooking pot it is too big; for a bath a little too small," said Mr. Hak-Tak. "I found it buried in our vegetable patch and so far it has been useful in carrying my purse home for me."

"Alas," said Mrs. Hak-Tak, "something smaller would have done as well to hold any money we have or are likely to have," and she stooped over the pot and looked into its dark inside.

As she stooped, her hairpin—for poor Mrs. Hak-Tak had only one hairpin for all her hair and it was made of carved bone—fell into the pot. She put in her hand to get it out again, and then she gave a loud cry which brought her husband running to her side.

"What is it?" he asked. "Is there a viper in the pot?"

"Oh, my dear husband," she cried. "What can be the meaning of this? I put my hand into the pot to fetch out my hairpin and your purse, and look, I have brought out two hairpins and two purses, both exactly alike."

"Open the purse. Open both purses," said Mr. Hak-Tak. "One of them will certainly be empty."

But not a bit of it. The new purse contained exactly the same number of coins as the old one—for that matter, no one could have said which was the new and which the old—and it meant, of course, that the Hak-Taks had exactly twice as much money in the evening as they had had in the morning.

"And two hairpins instead of one!" cried Mrs. Hak-Tak, forgetting in her excitement to do up her hair which was streaming over her shoulders. "There is something quite unusual about this pot."

"Let us put in the sack of lentils and see what happens," said Mr. Hak-Tak, also becoming excited.

They heaved in the bag of lentils and when they pulled it out again—it was so big it almost filled the pot—they saw another bag of exactly the same size waiting to be pulled out in its turn. So now they had two bags of lentils instead of one.

"Put in the blanket," said Mr. Hak-Tak, "and then when the cold weather comes there will be one for you as well as for me. Let us put in everything we have in turn. What a pity we have no meat or tobacco, for it seems that the pot cannot make anything without a pattern."

Then Mrs. Hak-Tak, who was a woman of great intelligence, said, "My dear husband, let us put the purse in again and again and again. If we take two purses out each time we put one in, we shall have enough money by tomorrow evening to buy everything we lack."

"I am afraid we may lose it this time," said Mr. Hak-Tak, but in the end he agreed, and they dropped in the purse and pulled out two, then they added the new money to the old and dropped it again and pulled out the larger amount twice over. After a while the floor was covered with old leather purses and they decided just to throw the money in by itself. It worked quite as well and saved trouble; every time, twice as much money came out as went in, and every time they added the new coins to the old and threw them all in together. It took them some hours to tire of this game, but at last Mrs. Hak-Tak said, "My dear husband, there is no need for us to work so hard. We shall see to it that the pot does not run away, and we can always make more money as we want it. Let us tie up what we have."

It made a huge bundle in the extra blanket and the Hak-Taks lay and looked at it for a long time before they slept, and talked of all the things they would buy and the improvements they would make in the cottage.

The next morning they rose early and Mr. Hak-Tak filled a wallet with money from the bundle and set off for the big village to buy more things in one morning than he had bought in a whole fifty years.

Mrs. Hak-Tak saw him off and then she tidied up the cottage and put the rice on to boil and had another look at the bundle of money, and made herself a whole set of new hairpins from the pot, and about twenty candles instead of the one which was all they had possessed up to now. After that she slept for a while, having been up so late the night before, but just before the time when her husband should be back, she awoke and went over to the pot. She dropped in a cabbage leaf to make sure it was still working properly, and when she took two leaves out she sat down on the floor and put her arms round it.

"I do not know how you came to us, my dear pot," she said, "but you are the best friend we ever had."

Then she knelt up to look inside it, and at that moment her husband came to the door, and, turning quickly to see all the wonderful things he had bought, she overbalanced and fell into the pot.

Mr. Hak-Tak put down his bundles and ran across and caught her by the ankles and pulled her out, but, oh, mercy, no sooner had he set her carefully on the floor than he saw the kicking legs of another Mrs. Hak-Tak in the pot! What was he to do? Well, he could not leave her there, so he caught her ankles and pulled, and another Mrs. Hak-Tak so exactly like the first that no one would have told one from the other, stood beside them.

"Here's an extraordinary thing," said Mr. Hak-Tak, looking helplessly from one to the other.

"I will not have a second Mrs. Hak-Tak in the house!" screamed the old Mrs. Hak-Tak.

All was confusion. The old Mrs. Hak-Tak shouted and wrung her hands and wept, Mr. Hak-Tak was scarcely calmer, and the new Mrs. Hak-Tak sat down on the floor as if she knew no more than they did what was to happen next.

"One wife is all I want," said Mr. Hak-Tak, "but how could I have left her in the pot?"

"Put her back in it again!" cried Mrs. Hak-Tak.

"What? And draw out two more?" said her husband. "If two wives are too many for me, what should I do with three? No! No!" He stepped back quickly as if he was stepping away from the three wives and, missing his footing, lo and behold, he fell into the pot!

Both Mrs. Hak-Taks ran and each caught an ankle and pulled him out and set him on the floor, and there, oh, mercy, was another pair of kicking legs in the pot! Again each caught hold of an ankle and pulled, and soon another Mr. Hak-Tak, so exactly like the first that no one could have told one from the other, stood beside them.

Now the old Mr. Hak-Tak liked the idea of his double no more than Mrs. Hak-Tak had liked the idea of hers. He stormed and raged and scolded his wife for pulling him out of the pot, while the new Mr. Hak-Tak sat down on the floor beside the new Mrs. Hak-Tak and looked as if, like her, he did not know what was going to happen next.

Then the old Mrs. Hak-Tak had a very good idea. "Listen, my dear husband," she said, "now, do stop scolding and listen, for it is really a good thing that there is a new one of you as well as a new one of me. It means that you and I can go on in our usual way, and these new people, who are ourselves and yet not ourselves, can set up house together next door to us."

And that is what they did. The old Hak-Taks built themselves a fine new house with money from the pot, and they built one just like it next door for the new couple, and they lived together in the greatest friendliness, because, as Mrs. Hak-Tak said, "The new Mrs. Hak-Tak is really more than a sister to me, and the new Mr. Hak-Tak is really more than a brother to you."

The neighbors were very much surprised, both at the sudden wealth of the Hak-Taks and at the new couple who resembled them so strongly that they must, they thought, be very close relations of whom they had never heard before. They said: "It looks as though the Hak-Taks, when they so unexpectedly became rich, decided to have two of everything, even of themselves, in order to enjoy their money more."

Participation Programs

A participation or interaction program can be anything from group singing to the more complicated activity programs suggested at the end of this book. I have separated the pure storytelling program from the participation program because I think there is a danger in too much participation. It is primarily the story, the word that we are trying to promote. I personally love and encourage activities and crafts in conjunction with book programs! I sometimes have to remind myself that they should never overwhelm the story.

Begin your participation programs in a small way. After you have presented a story or two, explain how folklore is passed from one person to another. You might say that riddles and tongue twisters are a part of folklore. Recite a few yourself and then encourage the children to offer riddles or tongue twisters they have heard. Try a story joke or a pair of think stories. A guitar and a folksinger might be another simple participation program encouraging a sing-along atmosphere. A simple dramatization of a folktale could be the focus of a special storyhour.

The following play is adapted from a West African folktale, and is most effective when simply performed. The characters may sit on the floor or on the edge of a desk while the narrator stands. As each character speaks he or she should perform the same mechanical action that his character dictates.

DOWN WITH PRESIDENT STOMACH

The cast of ten and the exaggerated actions they perform:
Narrator: Stands and narrates action
Feet: Lifts feet up and down
Hands: Moves hands up and down and sideways mechanically

Nose: Wrinkles nose
Teeth: Opens and closes mouth, clicking teeth
Eyes: Circles eyes with hands and opens wide
Stomach: Sits up straight and pats stomach with both hands
Throat: Strokes throat
God: Speaks without moving; arms folded in front of chest
Mouth: Circles hands around mouth

Narrator: God created man with feet, hands, eyes, nose, teeth, throat, and a stomach. God made the heart the Secretary and the stomach the President. Each part of the body had a particular job to perform.

Eyes: We see.

Nose: We smell.

Teeth: We chew.

Hands: We hold, cut, and grab.

Stomach: I keep all the things that come into the body.

Narrator: Once the parts of the body began to feel jealous. They seemed to be working for Stomach and getting nothing in return.

Throat: Listen, all the food that goes through me is gone in a minute. I think Stomach ties a rope around it and pulls it down for himself. Let's elect a new president and do away with Stomach.

Teeth: You're right. We chew the food, but Stomach is the one who takes it in and enjoys it by himself. You better vote against this president or I will leave and go to live in a foreign country.

Eyes: You're in a better situation than we are. After all, at least friend Throat, the food does pass through you; all we do is get to look.

Narrator: Now Feet wished to be heard.

Feet: We are also unhappy. We only walk to the food, but never get anything to eat.

Hands: Let's go and talk to God. We will tell him that Stomach is greedy and makes a poor president.

All: Yes! Yes! Let's go.

Narrator: The body parts all agreed. A delegation was sent to God.

All (Except Stomach): We are against President Stomach.

Narrator: God asked them if they knew what they were talking about.

God: Do you know what you are talking about?

Nose: You made us. Yes, we know what we are talking about. We do not want Stomach for President. Look, he even looks like an overstuffed lady's handbag.

God: Say nothing that you will be sorry for in the future.

Narrator: God suggested that they return to their home to decide who they wanted for President. He cautioned them not to eat anything lest President Stomach keep using their work. They were happy.

Mouth: Stomach thinks he is the only one created by God. We'll show him we don't need him.

Throat: I'm glad God said we shouldn't feed him.

Narrator: God had promised to meet them in two days' time.

All (except Stomach), chanting: No! No! Down with President Stomach!

Narrator: On the morning of the third day the opposition had not eaten for two long days. Each part of the body was mighty hungry. They asked Left Eye to be President, but Left Eye said:

Eye: I cannot see very well today, I cannot be President.

Narrator: Then they asked Left Foot.

Foot: Sorry, I cannot be President. I can hardly stand up today.

Teeth: I couldn't chew anything even if there was something to chew. I cannot be President.

Nose: I haven't smelled anything for at least a day. I cannot be President.

Hands: It is hard for me to hold, cut, or grab. I must decline any suggestion that I be President.

Narrator: They returned to God and explained that they had reconsidered. They wanted Stomach to be their leader since he could hold so much. Now they could see that Stomach had been fair dividing the food equally among them.

Hands: Lord, we want Stomach to be our leader.

Teeth: Yes, we would like him for our king.

God: Hands, cook dinner and feed it to the Stomach. He shall be your king.

Narrator: Hands made supper and the body ate it. A short time later everyone was feeling better.

Eyes: I can see again.

Feet: I can walk again.

Throat: I feel better.

Teeth: I feel better.

Nose: I can smell again.

Mouth: Let us sing to our new leader.

All (except Stomach): Long Live King Stomach! Long Live King Stomach!

Stomach: (Stomach smiles and pats his stomach).

Story Jokes

These short, short stories are fun fillers—perfect participation opportunities between longer stories or more serious fare.

THE GRASS IS ALWAYS GREENER

There was once a cow who lived by the river. She longed to cross the river where a field of green grass was growing. But she couldn't swim.

She had no boat. There was no bridge across the river. She couldn't fly. So how did she get across the river to the nice green grass?

Give up? Don't feel badly, so did the cow!

TIME FOR SCHOOL

Ramon's mother called upstairs: "Ramon, get up. You'll be late for school."

"I don't want to go to school. I don't like it there. The kids are mean to me. The teachers shout at me. I don't want to go to school."

"But darling, you have to go to school."

"WHY?"

"Because you are 50 years old and you are the principal of the school!"

FOLK CHARACTERS FROM THE MIDDLE EAST

Whenever I journey to the Middle East I'm always treated to the joke stories of the Hodja of Turkey, the Goha of Lebanon and Saudi Arabia, and the Mullah of Iran. I was even told one once at a hotel newsstand in Baghdad, Iraq.

THE BEAUTIFUL DREAM

The Goha was sleeping in bed. Suddenly he sat up and called to his wife.

"Quick, wife, hand me my glasses!"

"Here they are," she said. "Why do you want your glasses in the middle of the night?"

"I was having a very exciting dream," said the Goha, "but I couldn't see anything clearly."

The Goha put on his glasses and went back to sleep. He smiled and laughed as he slept.

THE LETTER

A farmer brought the Hodja a letter. "Please read this for me," he said.

"I can't understand this letter," said the Hodja.

"Why not? You are wearing a turban of a wise and learned man."

"Here is the turban," said the Hodja. "If a turban makes a person wise, maybe now you'll be able to read the letter yourself."

THE FALL

The Goha's next door neighbors met him at the market.

"What was the noise we heard in your house last night?" they asked.

"My cloak fell down the stairs," answered the Goha.

"A cloak doesn't make any noise."

"True," said the Goha, "but I was wearing it at the time."

THE LOST RING

The Hodja lost his gold ring in the house. His next door neighbor saw him looking for it in the garden.

"Why are you looking for your ring out here in the garden if you lost it inside the house?"

"I am looking out here," said the Hodja, "because it is such a nice day, I thought I would enjoy the sunshine."

HOUSE FOR SALE

The Goha wanted to sell half of his house.

"Why do you want to sell only half a house?" asked his next door neighbor?

"I need the money to buy the other half."

WHERE'S THE FISH?

The Hodja bought a kilo of fish at the market and brought it home. The next day his wife cooked it and served it to her friends. When the Hodja came home for the evening meal, he asked his wife why she wasn't serving the fish.

"Very sad," said his wife. "The cat found it and ate it."

The Hodja went outside and found the cat looking his usual skinny self. He brought the cat inside and weighed it.

"The cat weighs exactly one kilo. If this is the cat, where's the fish? If this is the fish, where's the cat?"

Think Stories

Each "Think Story" offers an intriguing dilemma. Ask your children to think first; then raise their hands when they have the answer.

THE WINTER HIKER

A woman was hiking in the woods on a very cold night. She thought that she was lost until she saw an empty cabin through the trees and the snow drifts. She knocked on the door. No one answered but the door was open. She went inside the cabin. She saw a candle, a kerosene lamp, and a wood stove. She reached inside her knapsack and discovered that she had only one match. What did she light first?

(Think before you answer: The hiker would light the match first.)

JOHN AND MARY

Mary and John are found lying dead on the floor in a country house. A broken bowl is found near their bodies. There are no marks on the bodies and they have not been poisoned. No one was in the house when they died. How did they die?

(Think before you answer: John and Mary are goldfish. Their bowl was broken when it was knocked to the floor by the family dog.)

Can your students answer these three queries about family relationships? "The Accident" seemed awfully old-fashioned to my editor, a product of the 1960s, but to me, from the 1950s, it's "right on" (as they said in the 1970s!).

THE PHOTO

Mr. Smith was showing his friends a photo of a man. He said to them, "Brothers and sisters have I none. But this man's father is my father's son." How is Mr. Smith related to the man in the photo?

(Think before you answer: The man in the photo is Mr. Smith's son.)

THE DINNER

Mom, Dad, Daughter, Son, Aunt, Uncle, Sister, Brother, Niece, Nephew, and Cousin were all having dinner. But there were only four people at the table. Why?

(Think before you answer: The son of the brother and the daughter of the sister are having dinner. The son and daughter are cousins. Now you can figure out the rest!)

THE ACCIDENT

A boy and his father were in an automobile accident. Both are brought into the hospital unconscious. The boy had to have surgery right away. In the operating room, the surgeon looked at the boy and said, "I can't operate on this child. He is my son!" How can this be?

(Think before you answer: The surgeon is the boy's mother.)

Night of 1,000 Stars: A Reading Aloud Program

"Night of 1,000 Stars" is a program begun by the American Library Association to introduce children to books through reading aloud. On chosen nights, libraries invite their local celebrities to read selections from their favorite books. The Great Neck (New York) Public Library, for instance, celebrated the work of just one of their famous residents by honoring children's book author Johanna Hurwitz. Children of staff members chose their favorite passages from Hurwitz's books, and both they and Johanna took turns reading aloud.

This sort of round-robin reading can work beautifully with the books of a single author or with a theme program. Children who volunteer to read aloud at the program may already have a favorite passage to share, or they may need your help to find a selection. Remind them that many people in the audience will not have read the book, so the passage they choose needs to stand well on its own.

These are the passages that were read aloud at the Hurwitz program. I have included them here so that you can duplicate this program at your own library or in your classroom without any further planning. You don't have an author living in your town? The words of the author will feel just like a visit!

Celebrating the Work of Johanna Hurwitz

Cake, as well as pickles (to go with the passage from *Teacher's Pet*), were served after the program. Believe it or not, the pickles disappeared as quickly as the cake! The jacket from each book featured was illuminated by an overhead projector as the passage was read aloud.

from *The Law of Gravity*, pp. 78–82: a picnic on the George Washington bridge, halfway between New York and New Jersey.

from *Class Clown*, pp. 63–69: Lucas Cott gets his head caught in a chair in the middle of a mime performance.

from *Teacher's Pet*, pp. 8–13: Sharing a pickle in the lunchroom.

from *Baseball Fever*, pp. 50–55: Ezra tries to listen to a baseball game and his father at the same time.

from *Aldo Ice Cream*, pp. 91–97: Aldo concentrates on wearing out his sneakers for the grubby sneaker contest.

from *Yellow Blue Jay*, pp. 100–105: Mickey and Jay build an elf house.

from *Tough-Luck Karen*, pp. 104–106: Aldo's cat "murders" a bird.

from *Funny You Should Ask*, "Rabbits," pp. 178–188. Lucas' silent mischief results in the birth of five rabbits. (This selection was read by the author.)

Consider including these ideas in your Hurwitz program also:

The David Game
    Bill Painter of the North Miami, Florida Public Library uses this activity with "Too Many Daves" from Dr. Seuss's *The Sneetches and Other Stories*. To make it part of your Johanna Hurwitz Program, you might try it after reading a portion of *Ali Baba Bernstein*. When young David Bernstein finds that the New York City telephone book is filled with dozens of other David Bernsteins, he decides to change his name from David to Ali Baba. To play the David Game, ask your audience to pretend that they are all named David. Now ask them a series of questions and let them all answer at the same time to show how confusing it would be if everyone had the same name. For instance, "David, what is your favorite color?" "David, what is your favorite ice cream?" "David, what is your favorite sport?"

Reader's Theater
    There are parts for five players to read aloud "Ali Baba and Princess Farrah" in *Presenting Reader's Theater*, pp. 78–82.

Booklist: Johanna Hurwitz Program

"Ali Baba and Princess Farrah" in *Presenting Reader's Theater* by Caroline Feller Bauer. H. W. Wilson, 1987.

Hurwitz, Johanna. *Aldo Ice Cream*. Art by John Wallner. Morrow, 1981.

_____. *Baseball Fever*. Art by Ray Cruz. Morrow, 1981.

_____. *Class Clown*. Art by Sheila Hamanaka. Morrow, 1987.

_____. *The Law of Gravity*. Art by Ingrid Fetz. Morrow, 1978.

_____. *Teacher's Pet*. Art by Sheila Hamanaka. Morrow, 1988.

_____. *Tough-Luck Karen*. Art by Diane De Groat. Morrow, 1982.

_____. *Yellow Blue Jay*. Art by Donald Carrick. Morrow, 1986.

"Rabbits" by Johanna Hurwitz in *Funny You Should Ask*, ed. by David Gale. Delacorte, 1992.

Media and the Intermediate Grades

If you have any interest at all in any of the multimedia techniques, I think you will enjoy presenting them to this responsive age group. Devote entire programs to multimedia or use sparingly in your storyhour or folklore program. Film programs, puppet shows, overhead light shows will all appeal to these children. Most board stories, with the exception of poetry presentations, are less satisfactory, for they are really designed for younger children. But talks about magic accompanied by demonstrations, music, and dance programs will all be popular. Once you've piqued their interest in these kinds of activities, you'll find that your children will be excited to participate in more advanced programs. You can devote an entire series to working with slides, producing a hand-drawn or moving picture film, making and performing with puppets, learning Indian sign language or dance steps. You will be limited only by time and your own resources, never by the enthusiasm of your listeners.

Again, since there is the danger of placing the story itself in the background, you may want to separate the media from the pure storytelling programs. After you have gained experience, however, the two will fuse and you will arrive at a successful combination of media and traditional storytelling that will delight your audience.

Read for Fun: A Classic Booklist for the Middle Grades

One of my primary objectives in this book is to help you present literature through storytelling—so enthusiastically that your audience will run to the library to borrow books after every presentation! As you know by now, I always suggest exhibiting a collection of books during any storyhour.

Now I know that printing a "best books" list for middle-graders is fraught with pitfalls (I can already hear the cries of "where's my favorite?"). But we need to begin somewhere. Eric Donald Hirsch's *Cultural Literacy* suggested that there was a body of knowledge with which everyone should be familiar to satisfactorily operate in the United States. Of course books play an important role in any definition of cultural literacy. Toward this end, here is my own list of books that I'd like every child to read by the time he or she enters junior high school.

Atwater, Richard and Florence Atwater. *Mr. Popper's Penguins.* Art by Robert Lawson. Little, 1938. A mild-mannered housepainter and his wife live with 12 penguins.

Avi. *Romeo and Juliet Together (and alive) at Last!* Orchard, 1987. The seventh grade puts on a production of "Romeo and Juliet" with hilarious results.

Babbitt, Natalie. *Tuck Everlasting.* Art by author. Farrar, 1975. If you had the chance, would you choose to live forever?

Bauer, Marion Dane. *On My Honor.* Clarion, 1986. Joel promises not to play by the river, but he does and his friend drowns.

Blume, Judy. *Are You There God? It's Me, Margaret.* Bradbury, 1970. Margaret is trying to come to terms with God, her family, and puberty.

Byars, Betsy. *The Midnight Fox.* Art by Ann Grifalconi. Viking, 1968. Tom hates the country until he sees the fox.

Cleary, Beverly. *Ramona Forever.* Art by Alan Tiegreen. Morrow, 1984. This is just one of Cleary's books about an engaging little girl and her family.

Cohen, Barbara. *Thank You, Jackie Robinson*. Lothrop, 1974. Sam and an elderly black man share a love for the Brooklyn Dodgers.

Cresswell, Helen. *Ordinary Jack: Being the First Part of the Bagthorpe Saga*. Macmillan, 1977. This first book in the series introduces you to a wacky but charming family.

Dahl, Roald. *Matilda*. Art by Quentin Blake. Viking, 1988. Matilda, a clever five-year-old, leads an insurrection against her evil parents and the equally evil headmistress. Children will laugh, adults will cringe.

George, Jean. *Julie of the Wolves*. Art by John Schoenherr. Harper, 1972. Miyax, an Eskimo girl, tries to adjust to the old and new ways of her people. A survival story.

Hautzig, Esther. *The Endless Steppe: Growing up in Siberia*. Crowell, 1968. Esther and her parents are sent to Siberia in a cattle car, and must learn to survive.

Hurwitz, Johanna. *Class Clown*. Art by Shelia Hamanaka. Morrow, 1987. Lucas is the third grader everyone remembers.

Juster, Norton. *The Phantom Tollbooth*. Art by Jules Ffeiffer. Knopf, 1988. Milo adventures in Dictionopolis and Digitopolis. First published in 1961.

King-Smith, Dick. *Babe, the Gallant Pig*. Art by Mary Rayner. Viking, 1982. A farmer is surprised and pleased that the runt pig has turned into an intelligent sheep herder.

Lawson, Robert. *Ben and Me*. Art by author. Little, 1939. A mouse claims to be the real inventor of Ben Franklin's inventions.

Lester, Julius. *The Knee-High Man and Other Stories*. Art by Ralph Pinto. Dial, 1972. Short trickster tales from the African-American tradition.

Lindgren, Astrid. *Pippi Longstocking*. Art by Louis S. Glanzman. Viking, 1950. Pippi lives all by herself with her pet monkey in a small Swedish town.

Little, Jean. *Little by Little: A Writer's Education*. Viking, 1988. A children's book author tells about her childhood.

Lofting, Hugh. *The Story of Doctor Dolittle*. Art by author. Delacorte, 1988. A doctor who can speak with animals journeys to Africa to cure the monkeys. First published in 1920.

Lowry, Lois. *Anastasia Again!* Art by Diane De Groat. Houghton, 1981. The irrepressible Anastasia and her family move to the suburbs.

MacLachlan, Patricia. *Sarah, Plain and Tall*. Harper, 1985. A mail order bride turns out to be an interesting woman.

O'Brien, Robert C. *Mrs. Frisby and the Rats of NIMH*. Art by Zena Bernstein. Atheneum, 1971. A group of intelligent rats leads its mice friends to safety.

O'Dell, Scott. *Island of the Blue Dolphin*. Houghton, 1960. Karana learns to survive on her own when she is left alone on an island off the California coast in the 1800s.

Paterson, Katherine. *Bridge to Terabithia*. Art by Donna Diamond. Crowell, 1977. Leslie and Joss are best friends until tragedy strikes.

Paulsen, Gary. *Hatchet*. Bradbury, 1987. Brian survives alone in the wilderness after a plane crash.

Porte, Barbara Ann. *Fat Fanny, Beanpole Bertha, and the Boys*. Art by Maxie Chambliss. Orchard, 1991. Tap dance with the triplets and Fanny and laugh.

Robinson, Barbara. *The Best Christmas Pageant Ever*. Art by Judith Gwyn Brown. Harper, 1972. The Herdman kids are the worst in the school, but they want to be in the pageant.

Rylant, Cynthia. *Every Living Thing*. Art by S. D. Schindler. Bradbury, 1985. Short stories featuring animals and children.

Soto, Gary. *Baseball in April and Other Stories*. Harper, 1990. Short stories about school, friends, and family in a Mexican-American setting.

Streatfield, Noel. *Ballet Shoes*. Art by Diane Goode. Random, 1991. First published in 1937, this story is about three orphans who attend a ballet school.

Ullman, James Ramsey. *Banner in the Sky*. Lippincott, 1988. Rudi insists on conquering the mountain that claimed his father's life.

White, E. B. *Charlotte's Web*. Art by Garth Williams. Harper, 1952. The classic friendship between a pig and a spider.

Wilder, Laura Ingalls. *Little House in the Big Woods*. Art by Garth Williams. Harper, 1953. The first book in a series about the Wilder family pioneering in America.

Picture Books for Intermediate Grades

As I said earlier, please don't forget the picture book collections in your program planning for your intermediate grades! Each year there are more and more carefully edited and beautifully illustrated picture books published. Some of us tend to discount these when planning for older children, but many picture books, particularly those in the 32-page format, are actually too long and much too sophisticated for three- and four-year-olds. You'll find that they're perfect for this age group, however. Here, I've listed some favorites. I suggest interspersing them with more traditional storytelling and reading aloud.

Brown, Marc. *Arthur Meets the President*. Art by author. Little, 1991. Arthur writes a winning essay, and he and his classmates are invited to meet the President in Washington, D.C.

Bunting, Eve. *Fly Away Home*. Art by Ronald Himler. Clarion, 1991. Andrew and his Dad use a busy airport as their home.

_____. *The Wall*. Art by Ronald Himler. Clarion, 1990. A boy and his father locate the boy's grandfather's name on the Vietnam Memorial in Washington, D.C.

Burleigh, Robert. *Flight: The Journey of Charles Lindbergh*. Art by Mike Wimmer. Philomel, 1991. A brilliant art and narrative combination relates the agonies and ecstasies of the first solo flight across the Atlantic.

Cowcher, Helen. *Antarctica*. Art by author. Farrar, 1990. A lovely glimpse into the lives of the wildlife in Antarctica and a subtle warning to the humans who arrive by helicopter, disturbing the ecology of the area.

Day, David. *The Walking Catfish*. Art by Mark Entwistle. Macmillan, 1992. Perfect read-aloud, share-the-art book about a three-day liars' contest.

Edwards, Patricia Kier. *Chester and Uncle Willoughby*. Art by Diane Worfolk Allison. Little, 1987. The child looks young, but the musings he exchanges with his uncle are worth sharing.

Fisher, Leonard Everett. *The ABC Exhibit*. Macmillan, 1991. This alphabet book of paintings is a museum in a book.

_____. *The Great Wall of China*. Art by author. Macmillan, 1986. Chronicles the building of the Great Wall.

Fox, Mem. *Wilfrid Gordon McDonald Partridge*. Art by Julie Vivas. Kane/Miller, 1985. A young boy searches for the meaning of "memory" at an old people's home.

Gerstein, Mordicai. *The New Creatures*. Art by author. Harper, 1991. An old sheepdog tells how the first humans were discovered, when dogs and cats ruled the world.

Gray, Nigel. *A Country Far Away*. Art by Philippe Dupasquier. Orchard, 1988. The lives of a boy in rural Africa and a boy in a western town are explored in pictures.

Heller, Ruth. *Many Luscious Lollipops: A Book about Adjectives*. Art by author. Grosset, 1989. One of a series of picture books that explores the parts of speech.

Hepworth, Cathi. *Antics!* Art by author. Putnam, 1992. In how many words can you find "art"?

Hong, Lily Toy. *How the Ox Star Fell from Heaven*. Art by author. Whitman, 1991. Why we eat three times a day and why the ox is a beast of burden is told in this ancient Chinese story.

Kirby, David and Allen Woodman. *The Cows Are Going to Paris*. Art by Chris L. Deamrest. Boyds Mill, 1991. The cows in a field exchange places with people on a train, and visit Paris.

Lyon, George Ella. *Come a Tide*. Art by Stephen Gammell. Orchard, 1990. Grandma and her kinfolk cope with a flood.

MacCarthy, Patricia. *Herds of Words*. Art by author. Dial, 1991. Explores pictorially the words used for collections of animals in the English language.

MacDonald, Amy. *Rachel Fister's Blister*. Art by Marjorie Priceman. Houghton, 1990. A rollicking silly rhyme tells how Rachel's blister was removed.

Maugham, W. S. *Appointment*. Art by Roger Essley. Simon & Schuster, 1993. The haunting art and surprise ending of this short story make it a perfect "Show and Tell" selection.

Miller, Edward. *Frederick Ferdinand Fox*. Art by author. Crown, 1987. A fox is entrusted with the fate of a nation. An amusing, subtly serious adventure.

Murphy, Jim. *The Last Dinosaur*. Art by Mark Alan Weatherby. Scholastic, 1988. How the last dinosaur might have spent her last days on earth.

Olson, Arielle. *Noah's Cats and the Devil's Fire*. Art by Barry Moser. Orchard, 1992. In a retelling of a Romanian tale, the Devil boards Noah's Ark, but is outwitted by the cats aboard.

Parnall, Peter. *Stuffer*. Art by author. Macmillan, 1992. The saga of a horse's life in several homes, some in which he is mistreated.

Pochocki, Ethel. *Rosebud and Red Flannel*. Art by Mary Beth Owens. Holt, 1989. An uppity nightgown is rescued by a besotted pair of longjohns. Inanimate objects fall in love.

Polacco, Patricia. *Just Plain Fancy*. Art by author. Bantam, 1990. Two Amish girls hide a peacock because they are afraid it is too fancy for their simple ways.

Scheffler, Ursel. *Stop Your Crowing Kasimir!* Art by Silke Brix-Henker. Carolrhoda, 1988. A rooster is tried for disturbing the peace. The annoyed neighbors win the case, but lose in the end.

Schwartz, David M. *Supergrandpa*. Art by Bert Dodson. Lothrop, 1991. Sixty-six-year-old Gustav was not allowed to enter the long distance bicycle race, but enters anyway and finishes the 1000 mile race, plus an additional 600 miles!

Scieszka, Jon. *The True Story of the 3 Little Pigs! by A. Wolf*. Art by Lane Smith. Viking, 1989. The traditional nursery story told from the wolf's point of view.

Tsuchiya, Yukio. *Faithful Elephants: A True Story of Animals, People and War*. Art by Ted Lewin. Houghton, 1988. In this true, but devastating story, the elephants in the Tokyo Zoo starve to death during World War II.

Williams, Karen. *Galimoto*. Art by Catherine Stock. Lothrop, 1990. An African boy searches through his village to find the parts for a special toy.

Williams, Vera B. *A Chair for My Mother*. Art by author. Greenwillow, 1982. A family saves to replace a chair.

Wisniewski, David. *The Warrior and the Wise Man*. Art by the author. Lothrop, 1989. The quest of twins—one a wise man, the other a warrior—is complemented by intricate paper cut art.

Yorinks, Arthur. *Louis the Fish*. Art by Richard Egielski. Farrar, 1980. Louis used to be a butcher, but now he is a salmon.

Zhitkov, Boris. *How I Hunted the Little Fellows*; tr. by Djemma Bider. Art by Paul O. Zelinsky. Dodd, 1979. Boris is entranced, then obsessed with his Grandmother's model ship.

21 / The Young Adult Program

Americans love to play around with terminology, so it is amazing to me that the library profession has been using the term "young adult" for so many years. Whatever does it mean? I'm sure people have attempted a definition—ages 12–15, perhaps, or middle school students, or why not include high school students too? My personal definition of the young adult or adolescent is "any audience whose response is completely unpredictable!" As a lecturer I can imagine fairly accurately how preschoolers will react to a story. I can almost bet someone that I will know the point in a story when fourth through sixth graders will laugh. I can even tell you how an adult midwestern audience's reactions will differ from an eastern audience's response! But when you ask me how ninth graders will receive me, I am completely at a loss. It usually depends on what they had for breakfast, what grades they got on their history test, and how their best friends greeted them that morning. They are, worldwide, the most interesting audience of all.

In Guam this year I presented a program of stories, booktalks, and poetry to 300 high school students in a technical school. In theory they should have been an impossible audience. First of all, my host was not at all sure that someone who speaks to children could possibly have anything to say to his students. Secondly, the audience was mostly comprised of boys who planned careers in construction or were trying to gain a place in the police academy. And finally, it was the last period of the day: an impossible situation in any case. This is a success story, though, so of course I had a wonderful time. The students laughed at every story I told, and the next day my host said, "They loved you! Al, the guy with the tattoos, even said, 'that was cool ass.' You can't do better than that."

What books work best with this age group? Stephen King and Dean Koontz are guaranteed winners for high school boys, while middle school girls are addicted to the series books. The success of Ann Martin's Babysitters Club series and the Sweet Valley High books is phenomenal. So what do you end up with—romantic horror? It seems that Charlotte and Emily Bronte may have gotten it right in the nineteenth century!

Seriously though, I usually include in this age group middle school and high school students—essentially 13- through 17-year-olds. By this time, I hope, they will have been "hooked" by good books, and your job—whether you are a teacher or a librarian—is simply the pleasant task of recommending new titles and perhaps encouraging them to explore new authors. This isn't always the case, of course. But there is a rich variety of subjects that appeal to this age group—ghost and horror stories, science fiction, classic "coming of age" stories, humor, biographies, and love stories are among the most popular. You don't necessarily need to plan an entire program of stories for this age group. You may find that it works best to tell a single story at the end of a class or after a library booktalk—this is often all it takes to encourage young adults to pick up a title for themselves.

In this chapter I have included a special section on the supernatural, a wonderful variety of short stories to tell or read aloud, a selection of new favorites for young adults, and a list of young adult classics, all of which I've found to be especially good choices. I have also designed a program I call "Guys and Gals You'd Like to Meet," which integrates storytelling with booktalking—a particularly successful combination for young adults. The art and science of booktalking is discussed in great detail later in this section, so you may wish to skip ahead and read more about it once you've digested this chapter.

Simply Supernatural

To begin then, I've capitalized on a favorite interest of many young adults—the supernatural. Here are suggestions for telling ghost stories and jump stories, along with two sample stories that I've enjoyed telling to this age group. Halloween is an obvious time to tell ghost stories, of course. But it's just as much fun to listen to a scary story by the light of a May or August moon as it is when the harvest moon is glowing. Too, some communities around the country have begun objecting to full blown Halloween celebrations that may get out of control. Moving these stories around the calendar gives them a chance to stand on their own, apart from a specific holiday.

Whatever your role—junior high school teacher, or perhaps middle school librarian—I think you will find that your students will love this genre. Make sure that you exhibit lots of good selections that they can take with them to read.

Ghost Stories

I didn't approve of the horror film my daughter rented for her sleep-over party. I would have preferred that she request something uplifting or something intellectual, something that would impress the other girls' mothers. But they were obviously enjoying it. We could hear the squeals of imagined terror all the way into the backyard, where my husband Peter and I had been banished for the evening. There are groups in the United States that object to young people reading and listening to any story that involves the supernatural, but now I might even go so far as to support a request for one of these films another time. They certainly stimulate the imagination. It's not always easy for adults to see the appeal of this genre. My daughter read the V. C. Andrews' *Flowers in the Attic* series in the sixth grade and she adored all of the fantasy blood and gore. Very grown up and in graduate school now, she pretends that she doesn't even remember reading "that trash!"

TELLING A GHOST STORY

The best ghost stories are those that are believable. Tell the story as though the experience you describe actually happened to you or to someone you know. A slower pace in telling is usually more effective than the snappy fast pace you might use to tell a humorous story. You'll know if you are telling well when you say something like "and here IT comes now . . ." as you point behind the audience and your listeners turn around to see IT coming!

My best advice for telling these stories is to act as though you believe every word that you are saying.

THE GHOST CATCHER

I've enjoyed telling this story. The heroine is a girl who seems concerned only with her appearance (a trait many teenagers will readily identify with!), yet she successfully routs a ghost.

Tilly paid great attention to her appearance. She was always combing her hair and checking her looks in the mirror. Her clothes were always

freshly pressed. She was chosen "best dressed" in her high school two years in a row. Her hobby was fashion; her avocation was cosmetology. She carried her cosmetics case with her wherever she went, even to the aerobics class that she attended twice a week at Gagny's gym. When she left the exercise session she always changed, showered, and primped.

One night as she left Gagny's, absorbed in the business of gracefully waving goodbye to the owner, she couldn't help but notice the glorious full moon, a harvest moon. "Bye Til. Watch out for ghosts. It's almost Halloween," Jim Gagny warned. "I don't believe in ghosts, Mr. Gagny," said Tilly as she glided out the door. She hadn't walked more than five yards when she took out her mirror to check her makeup. "Not bad," she thought to herself. "Here's hoping I meet the man of my dreams tonight."

Tilly's fantasy was that her pre-destined "knight in shining armor" would emerge one night from the shadows on Main Street and sweep her off her feet, marry her, and take her to live in a villa in southern France. So far she had met only old man Bundy and his dog, and once Ms. Pritkin, her math teacher, on her way home.

Ghosts do exist, whether you believe in them or not, and two swooped down from the roof of MacArthur's hardware store and barred Tilly's way.

"Woooooo. Hooooooo," they wailed as they floated around Tilly's head. "Woooooo. Hooooo. Prepare for a voyage. We're taking you to the boss in the dungeon."

"Don't be ridiculous," said Tilly. "I'm not dressed for an audience with a ghost, even if he is your leader."

"Wooooooooo. Hoooooooo. Now we will seize you."

"Don't come any closer," screamed Tilly. "I have my ghost catcher here in my bag. I've caught two ghosts already tonight. Here they are." Tilly reached into her cosmetic case and pulled out her mirror. The ghosts looked in the mirror and saw themselves.

"Woooooooooo. Hooooooooooo," screamed the ghosts. "Let's get out of here."

Tilly sat down on the curb in front of MacArthur's Hardware. She recombed her hair. She reapplied her lipstick. Then she put away her ghost catcher and went home to take a nice hot bath and to wash and blow dry her hair for tomorrow.

Booklist: Ghost Story Sources

For young adults:

Aiken, Joan. *Give Yourself a Fright: Thirteen Stories of the Supernatural*. Delacorte, 1989. Original stories by a British author known for the macabre.

Clarke, J. *The Torment of Mr. Gully: Stories of the Supernatural*. Holt, 1989. Original stories from an Australian author.

Cohen, Daniel. *Phantom Animals*. Putnam, 1991. Ghost stories featuring animals. This is just one of Cohen's collections. Also see: *Great Ghosts*. Art by David Linn. Cobblehill, 1990. And *Railway Ghosts and Highway Horrors*. Art by Stephen Marchesi. Cobblehill, 1991.

A Ghoul at Your Fingertips: Supernatural Fiction for Teens. Libraries Unlimited, 1992. 1500 titles are listed in this bibliography!

Gorog, Judith. *No Swimming in Dark Pond and Other Chilling Tales*. Philomel, 1987. Stories based on folklore and urban tales to tell or read aloud. Also see Gorog's *A Taste for Quiet and Other Disquieting Tales*. Philomel, 1982. And *Three Dreams and a Nightmare and Other Tales of the Dark*. Philomel, 1988.

Hill, Susan, ed. *The Random House Book of Ghost Stories*. Art by Angela Barrett. Random House, 1991. Seven stories, mostly British. Some are original for this collection; others are from previously published collections.

Hodges, Margaret. *Hauntings: Ghosts and Ghouls around the World*. Art by David Wenzel. Little, 1991. Sixteen stories featuring the supernatural from Japan, England, India, and Sweden.

Lyons, Mary E., ed. *Raw Head, Bloody Bones: African-American Tales of the Supernatural*. Scribner, 1991. Fifteen tales by Zora Neale Hurston and others.

McDonald, Collin. *Nightwaves Scary Tales for After Dark*. Cobblehill, 1990. Contemporary ghost stories.

Westall, Robert. *The Hunting of Chas McGill and Other Stories*. Greenwillow, 1983. Known for his novels, here Westall tries his hand at frightening fare.

For children (though young adults might like these also, especially if they are interested in telling their own stories):

Cecil, Laura. *Boo! Stories to Make You Jump*. Art by Emma Chichester Clark. Greenwillow, 1990. A lavishly illustrated collection of scary stories appropriate for children.

Cole, Johanna and Stephanie Calmenson. *The Scary Book*. Art by Chris Demarest, Marilyn Hirsh, Arnold Lobel, and Dirk Zimmer. Morrow, 1991. Stories and poems for young children. Also perfect for young adults who wish to tell stories. "Bony-Legs," "Taily-po," and "Wait Till Martin Comes" are favorites.

Schwartz, Alvin. *Scary Stories 3: More Tales to Chill Your Bones*. Art by Stephen Gammell. Harper, 1991. Collected from folklore. These short fragments work beautifully as transitional material between longer selections.

Young, Richard and Judy Dockrey. *Favorite Scary Stories of American Children*. August House, 1990. Twenty-three short and easy-to-tell stories.

Jump Stories

Stories that surprise and make an audience "jump" are also popular with young adults. They often rely on repetitive phrases that help to lull the listeners into a trance, until the surprising conclusion makes them . . . JUMP! A classic story of this genre is "The Golden Arm" found in Joseph Jacobs's *English Fairy Tales*. I first heard this story, told by a sixth grader, at a New York Public Library storyhour in the 1950s. Here is my own version.

THE GOLDEN ARM

There was this man. He had a wife. The wife had a golden arm. It was really gold from the fingers of her hand right up to her shoulder. Pure gold.

Only she died. The wife died. There was a funeral and they buried the wife, golden arm and all, right there in the graveyard.

The man he went on home. He went to bed. In the middle of the night he got to thinking about the golden arm.

"Sure would be nice to have that golden arm. Must be worth a pack of money."

So along about midnight he gets up out of bed and goes to the graveyard with a shovel. He digs up his wife and he gets that golden arm. He comes on home.

By now it's about one o'clock in the morning and the man is in bed, but not asleep. He keeps thinking that he hears noises, and then he does hear a voice, all mixed up in the wind, saying real slow and creepy like:

"Who's got my golden arm?"

"Who's got my golden arm?"

The man he pulls the covers up over his head, but he can still hear the voice:

"Who's got my golden arm?"

"Who's got my golden arm?"

The voice is inside the house now and coming up the stairs:

"Who's got my golden arm?"

"Who's got my golden arm?"

The man puts the pillow over his head, but he can still hear the voice and something coming up the narrow stairs of his house:

"Who's got my golden arm?"

"Who's got my golden arm?"

The man is lying still now, but he hears the voice and the something right in his room wailing:

"Who's got my golden arm?"

"Who's got my golden arm?"

"Who's got my golden arm?"

I GOT IT!

Booklist: Jump Story Sources

"The Big Toe" in Alvin Schwartz's *Scary Stories to Tell in the Dark*. Lippincott, 1981. Who has my big toe? Suitable for young children.

Carter, David A. *In a Dark, Dark, Dark Wood: An Old Tale with a New Twist*. Art by author. Simon, 1991. At the end of this picture book version of the chant is a pop-up ghost.

"Chunk o' Meat," in Richard Chase's *Grandfather Tales*. Houghton, 1973. Similar to "The Golden Arm." "Where's my chunk of me-e-eat?"

Jumping Jack, audiocassette. Jackie Torrance tells five of her favorite jump tales. Available from NAPPS, P.O. Box 309, Jonesborough, TN 37659.

"Teeny-Tiny" in Joseph Jacobs's *English Fairy Tales*. Dover, 1967. The teeny-tiny woman finds a teeny-tiny bone. Often a child's first jump story.

Wahl, Jan. *Tailypo!* Art by Wil Clay. Holt, 1991. Picture book version in graphic detail of the traditional fright tale. A gentler version is Johanna Galdone's *The Tailypo, a Ghost Story*. Art by Paul Galdone. Clarion, 1984. Still another version is "Tailybone" as told by storyteller David Holt in Jimmy Neil Smith, ed. *Homespun: Tales from America's Favorite Storytellers*. Crown, 1988.

Short Stories to Tell to Young Adults

I've chosen the following stories to show you the great variety that can be offered to this interesting age group. The first two are very thoughtful, serious stories; the next two are delightfully funny tales; and the last is a short excerpt from a classic coming-of-age story that young adults have enjoyed for more than 80 years.

CLOTHE THE NAKED

Dorothy Parker

I have found that young adults especially appreciate stories with great emotional impact. One of my favorites is Dorothy Parker's "Clothe the Naked," which I first read when I was 13 years old. After all these years, I still think of Big Lannie and Raymond. Read it aloud or tell it quietly, but with strength. I think you will find that it will leave an impression, even on those tough kids who seem not to show any compassion.

Big Lannie went out by the day to the houses of secure and leisured ladies, to wash their silks and their linens. She did her work perfectly; some of the ladies even told her so. She was a great, slow mass of a woman, colored a sound brown-black save for her palms and the flat of her fingers that were like gutta-percha from steam and hot suds. She was slow because of her size, and because the big veins in her legs hurt her, and her back ached much of the time. She neither cursed her ills nor sought remedies for them. They had happened to her; there they were.

Many things had happened to her. She had had children, and the children had died. So had her husband, who was a kind man, cheerful with the little luck he found. None of their children had died at birth. They had lived to be four or seven or ten, so that they had their ways and their traits and their means of causing love; and Big Lannie's heart was always wide for love. One child had been killed in a street accident and two others had died of illnesses that might have been no more than tedious, had there been fresh food and clear spaces and clean air behind them. Only Arlene, the youngest, lived to grow up.

Arlene was a tall girl, not so dark as her mother but with the same firm flatness of color. She was so thin that her bones seemed to march in advance of her body. Her little pipes of legs and her broad feet with jutting heels were like things a child draws with crayons. She carried her head low, her shoulders scooped around her chest, and her stomach slanted forward.

Big Lannie did not know it, when Arlene was going to have a baby. Arlene had not been home in nearly half a year; Big Lannie told the time in days. There was no news at all of the girl until the people at the hospital sent for Big Lannie to come to her daughter and grandson. She was there to hear Arlene say the baby must be named Raymond, and to see the girl die.

He was a long, light-colored baby, with big, milky eyes that looked right back at his grandmother. It was several days before the people at the hospital told her he was blind.

Big Lannie went to each of the ladies who employed her and explained that she could not work for some while; she must take care of her grandson. The ladies were sharply discommoded, after her steady years, but they dressed their outrage in shrugs and cool tones. Each arrived, separately, at the conclusion that she had been too good to Big Lannie, and had been imposed upon, therefore. "Honestly, those people!" each said to her friends. "They're all alike."

Big Lannie sold most of the things she lived with, and took one room with a stove in it. There, as soon as the people at the hospital would let her, she brought Raymond and tended him. He was all her children to her.

She had always been a saving woman, with few needs and no cravings, and she had been long alone. Even after Arlene's burial, there was enough left for Raymond and Big Lannie to go on for a time. Big Lannie was slow to be afraid of what must come; fear did not visit her at all, at first, and then it slid in only when she waked, when night hung motionless before another day.

Raymond was a good baby, a quiet, patient baby, lying in his wooden box and stretching out his delicate hands to the sounds that were light and color to him. It seemed but a little while, so short to Big Lannie, before he was walking about the room, his hands held out, his feet quick and sure. Those of Big Lannie's friends who saw him for the first time had to be told that he could not see.

Then, and it seemed again such a little while, he could dress himself, and open the door for his granny, and unlace the shoes from her tired feet, and talk to her in his soft voice. She had occasional employment—now and then a neighbor would hear of a day's scrubbing she could do, or sometimes she might work in the stead of a friend who was sick—infrequent, and not to be planned on. She went to the ladies for whom she had worked, to ask if they might not want her back again; but there was little hope in her, after she had visited the first one. Well, now, really, said the ladies; well really, now.

The neighbors across the hall watched over Raymond while Big Lannie looked for work. He was no trouble to them, nor to himself. He sat and crooned at his chosen task. He had been given a wooden spool around the top of which were driven little brads, and over these with a straightened hairpin he looped bright worsted, working faster than sight until a long tube of woven wool fell through the hole in the spool. The neighbors threaded big, blunt needles for him, and he coiled the woolen tubes and sewed them into mats. Big Lannie called them beautiful, and it made Raymond proud to have her tell him how readily she sold them. It was hard for her, when he was asleep at night, to unravel the mats and wash the worsted and stretch it so straight that even Raymond's shrewd fingers could not tell, when he worked with it next day, that it was not new.

Fear stormed in Big Lannie and took her days and nights. She might not go to any organization dispensing relief for fear that Raymond would be taken from her and put in—she would not say the word to herself, and she and her neighbors lowered their voices when they said it to one another—an institution. The neighbors wove lingering tales of what happened inside certain neat, square buildings on the cindery skirts of town, and, if they must go near them, hurried as if passing graveyards, and came home heroes. When they got you in one of those places, whispered the neighbors, they laid your spine open with whips, and then when you dropped, they kicked your head in. Had anyone come into Big Lannie's room to take Raymond away to an asylum for the blind, the neighbors would have fought for him with stones and rails and boiling water.

Raymond did not know about anything but good. When he grew big enough to go alone down the stairs into the street, he was certain of delight each day. He held his head high, as he came out into the little yard in front of the flimsy wooden house, and slowly turned his face from side to side, as if the air were soft liquid in which he bathed it. Trucks and wagons did not visit the street, which ended in a dump for rusted bedsprings and broken boilers and staved-in kettles; children played over its cobbles, and men and women sat talking in open windows and called across to one another in gay, rich voices. There was always laughter for Raymond to hear, and he would laugh back, and hold out his hands to it.

At first, the children stopped their play when he came out, and gathered quietly about him, and watched him, fascinated. They had been told of his affliction, and they had a sort of sickened pity for him. Some of them spoke to him, in soft, careful tones. Raymond would laugh with pleasure, and stretch his hands, the curious smooth, flat hands of the blind, to their voices. They would draw sharply back, afraid that his strange hands might touch them. Then, somehow ashamed because they had shrunk from him and he could not see that they had done so, they said gentle good-bys to him, and backed away into the street again, watching him steadily.

When they were gone, Raymond would start on his walk to the end of the street. He guided himself lightly touching the broken fences along the dirt sidewalk, and as he walked he crooned little songs with no words to them. Some of the men and women at the windows would call hello to him, and he would call back and wave and smile. When the children, forgetting him, laughed again at their games, he stopped and turned to the sound as if it were the sun.

In the evening, he would tell Big Lannie about his walk, slapping his knee and chuckling at the memory of the laughter he had heard. When the weather was too hard for him to go out in the street, he would sit at his worsted work, and talk all day of going out the next day.

The neighbors did what they could for Raymond and Big Lannie. They gave Raymond clothes their own children had not yet worn out, and they brought food, when they had enough to spare and other times. Big Lannie would get through a week, and would pray to get through the next one; and so the months went. Then the days on which she could find work fell farther and farther apart, and she could not pray about the time to come because she did not dare to think of it.

It was Mrs. Ewing who saved Raymond's and Big Lannie's lives, and let them continue together. Big Lannie said that then and ever after; daily she blessed Mrs. Ewing, and nightly she would have prayed for her, had she not known, in some dimmed way, that any intercession for Mrs. Delabarre Ewing must be impudence.

Mrs. Ewing was a personage in the town. When she went to Richmond for a visit, or when she returned from viewing the azalea gardens in Charleston, the newspaper always printed the fact. She was a woman rigorously conscious of her noble obligation; she was prominent on the Community Chest committee, and it was she who planned and engineered the annual Bridge Drive to raise funds for planting salvia around the cannon in front of the D.A.R. headquarters. These and many others were her public activities, and she was no less exacting of herself in her private life. She kept a model, though childless, house for her husband and herself, relegating the supervision of details to no domestic lieutenant, no matter how seemingly trustworthy.

Back before Raymond was born, Big Lannie had worked as laundress for Mrs. Ewing. Since those days, the Ewing wash tubs had witnessed many changes, none for the better. Mrs. Ewing took Big Lannie back into her employment. She apologized for this step to her friends by the always winning method of self-deprecation. She knew she was a fool, she said, after all that time, and after the way that Big Lannie had treated her. But still, she said, and she laughed a little at her own ways. Anyone she felt kind of sorry for could always get around her, she said. She knew it was awful foolish, but that, she said, was the way she was. Mr. Ewing, she said outside her husband's hearing, always called her just a regular little old easy mark.

Two days' work in the week meant money for rent and stovewood and almost enough food for Raymond and Big Lannie. She must depend, for anything further, on whatever odd jobs she could find, and she must not stop seeking them. Pressed on by fear and gratitude, she worked so well for Mrs. Ewing that there was sometimes expressed satisfaction at the condition of the lady's household linen and her own and her husband's clothing. Big Lannie had a glimpse of Mr. Ewing occasionally, leaving the house as she came, or entering it as she was leaving. He was a bit of a man, not much bigger than Raymond.

Raymond grew so fast that he seemed to be taller each morning. Every day he had his walk in the street to look forward to and experience and tell Big Lannie about at night. He had ceased to be a sight of the street; the children were so used to him that they did not even look at him, and the men and women at the windows no longer noticed him enough to hail him. He did not know. He would wave to any gay cry he heard, and go on his way, singing his little songs and turning toward the sound of laughter.

Then his lovely list of days ended as sharply as if ripped from some bright calendar. A winter came, so sudden and savage as to find no comparison in the town's memories, and Raymond had no clothes to wear out in the street. Big Lannie mended his outgrown garments as long as she could, but the stuff had so rotted with wear that it split in new places when she tried to sew together the ragged edges of rents.

The neighbors could give no longer; all they had they must keep for their own. A demented colored man in a nearby town had killed the woman who employed him, and terror had spread like brush fire. There was a sort of panic in reprisal; colored employees were dismissed from their positions, and there was no new work for them. But Mrs. Ewing, admittedly soft-hearted certainly to a fault and possibly to a peril, kept her black laundress on. More than ever Big Lannie had reason to call her blessed.

All winter, Raymond stayed indoors. He sat at his spool and worsted, with Big Lannie's old sweater about his shoulders and, when his tattered knickerbockers would no longer hold together, a calico skirt of hers lapped around his waist. He lived, at his age, in the past; in the days when he had walked, proud and glad, in the street, with laughter in his ears. Always, when he talked of it, he must laugh back at that laughter.

Since he could remember, he had not been allowed to go out when Big Lannie thought the weather unfit. This he had accepted without question, and so he accepted his incarceration through the mean weeks of the winter. But then one day it was spring, so surely that he could tell it even in the smoky, stinking rooms of the house, and he cried out with joy because now he might walk in the street again. Big Lannie had to explain to him that his rags were too thin to shield him, and that there were no odd jobs for her, and so no clothes and shoes for him.

Raymond did not talk about the street any more, and his fingers were slow at his spool.

Big Lannie did something she had never done before; she begged of her employer. She asked Mrs. Ewing to give her some of Mr. Ewing's old clothes for Raymond. She looked at the floor and mumbled so that Mrs. Ewing requested her to talk *up*. When Mrs. Ewing understood, she was, she said, surprised. She had, she said, a great, great many demands on her charity, and she would have supposed that Big Lannie, of all people, might have known that she did everything she could, and, in fact, a good deal more. She spoke of inches and ells. She said that if she found she could spare anything, Big Lannie was kindly to remember it was to be just for this once.

When Big Lannie was leaving at the end of her day's work, Mrs. Ewing brought her a package with her own hands. There, she said, was a suit and a pair of shoes; beautiful, grand things that people would think she was just a crazy to go giving away like that. She simply didn't know, she said, what Mr. Ewing would say to her for being such a crazy. She explained that that was the way she was when anyone got around her, all the while Big Lannie was trying to thank her.

Big Lannie had never before seen Raymond behave as he did when she brought him home the package. He jumped and danced and clapped his hands, he tried to squeak and squealed instead, he tore off the paper himself, and ran his fingers over the close-woven cloth and held it to his face and kissed it. He put on the shoes and clattered about in them, digging with his toes and heels to keep them on; he made Big Lannie pin the trousers around his waist and roll them up over his shins. He babbled of the morrow when he would walk in the street, and could not say his words for laughing.

Big Lannie must work for Mrs. Ewing the next day, and she had thought to bid Raymond wait until she could stay at home and dress him herself in his new garments. But she heard him laugh again; she could not tell him he must wait. He might go out at noon next day, she said, when the sun was so warm that he would not take cold at his first outing; one of the neighbors across the hall would help him with the clothes. Raymond chuckled and sang his little songs until he went to sleep.

After Big Lannie left in the morning, the neighbor came in to Raymond, bringing a pan of cold pork and corn bread for his lunch. She had a call for a half-day's work, and she could not stay to see him start out for his walk. She helped him put on the trousers and pinned and rolled them for him, and she laced the shoes as snug as they would go on his feet. Then she told him not to go out till the noon whistles blew, and kissed him, and left.

Raymond was too happy to be impatient. He sat and thought of the street and smiled and sang. Not until he heard the whistles did he go to the drawer where Big Lannie had laid the coat, and take it out and put it on. He felt it soft on his bare back, he twisted his shoulders to let it fall warm and loose from them. As he folded the sleeves back over his thin arms, his heart beat so that the cloth above it fluttered.

The stairs were difficult for him to manage, in the big shoes, but the very slowness of the descent was delicious to him. His anticipation was like honey in his mouth.

Then he came out into the yard, and turned his face in the gentle air. It was all good again; it was all given back again. As quickly as he could, he gained the walk and set forth, guiding himself by the fence. He could not wait; he called out, so that he would hear gay calls in return, he laughed so that laughter would answer him.

He heard it. He was so glad that he took his hand from the fence and turned and stretched out his arms and held up his smiling face to welcome it. He stood there, and his smile died on his face, and his welcoming arms stiffened and shook.

It was not the laughter he had known; it was not the laughter he had lived on. It was like great flails beating him flat, great prongs tearing his flesh from his bones. It was coming at him, to kill him. It drew slyly back, and then it smashed against him. It swirled around and over him, and he could not breathe. He screamed and tried to run through it, and fell, and it licked over him, howling higher. His clothes unrolled, and his shoes flapped on his feet. Each time he could rise, he fell again. It was as if the street were perpendicular before him, and the laughter leaping at his back. He could not find the fence, he did not know which way he was turned. He lay screaming, in blood and dust and darkness.

When Big Lannie came home, she found him on the floor in a corner of the room, moaning and whimpering. He still wore his new clothes, cut and torn and dusty, and there was dried blood on his mouth and his palms. Her heart had leapt in alarm when he had not opened the door at her footstep, and she cried out so frantically to ask what had happened that she frightened him into wild weeping. She could not understand what he said; it was something about the street, and laughing at him, and make them go away, and don't let him go in the street no more. She did not try to make him explain. She took him in her arms and rocked him, and told him, over and over, never mind, don't care, everything's all right. Neither he nor she believed her words.

But her voice was soft and her arms warm. Raymond's sobs softened, and trembled away. She held him, rocking silently and rhythmically, a long time. Then gently she set him on his feet, and took from his shoulders Mr. Ewing's old full-dress coat.

THE CALENDAR

Barbara Ann Porte

Barbara Ann Porte is a versatile writer of I Can Read *titles, humor novels for the middle grades and* I Only Made Up the Roses, *a young adult novel. Her short story, "The Calendar" (found in* Jesse's Ghost and Other Stories) *is perfect to tell to your students who are impatient with doing their chores, including their homework. I like to tell just a portion of it.*

There was a girl one time who never would do any of her chores, at least not well, and never in the proper order. It wasn't that she didn't try. She just couldn't seem to get things straight. She wasn't dumb, not by a long shot. She simply was not organized. Not a crime, of course, but inconvenient.

"You've got to get organized," that girl's mother told her over and over and over. Her mother, you see, was organized. Oh, she kept after her all right. After her and after her until she'd hear her own self shouting. "Hush," she would say then, glad they lived in the country with no neighbors to hear. There was just the girl's dad, and he was busy milking cows and shutting up his ears against the woman's sound, for it was high-pitched anytime that she was cranky, and having that girl for a daughter, she was very often cranky.

Well, such bickering and such reminding and such forgetting went on day in and day out, month in and month out, year after year until the girl was maybe twelve, perhaps thirteen, almost older than a girl.

Then when it was almost the New Year and snow was on the ground, the mother came home from town one day, lugging a heavy package wrapped up in bright paper. It was a gift, a calendar. It was a century calendar, and it was for the girl. For a hundred years she wouldn't need a new one.

"Here, have it," said the woman to her daughter. "Have and keep it. I will show you how." One thing about the girl's mother, you see, she was always willing to show how. She always knew the right and only way. The girl believed her. It was the only thing she had to go by.

So the girl's mother showed her how to write down her list of chores and other things to do neatly in the squares for the days she meant to do them and how to cross each one off in order when she'd done it. "List everything," her mother said, so she did.

On Monday she might write: "dusting, churning, clean the cobwebs from the barn, shell the beans for soup," and so on. She would cross off each chore when it was finished until she got to "brush my teeth" and "go to bed." Then she'd go to bed. Only sometimes, before she fell asleep, she'd look ahead to see what Tuesday held. Or, if she'd finished early on a Monday, she might do a Tuesday chore, then cross it off, leaving Tuesday free for Wednesday work. Now that she was better organized, this happened more and more. There came days when she was weeks, then weeks when she was months, before herself. Oh, was that girl's mother ever pleased. Why wouldn't she be? This went on for a long, long time until one day, the day I'm telling you about—on that day the girl came into the kitchen where her mother stood cooking.

"It's done," said the girl. "I have done it." She said it loud, in a proud, not girlish way.

And when the woman looked up from the pot that she was stirring, she did not see her daughter standing there in front of her. No, she didn't. Instead, she saw an old, old woman, older than herself, her voice old-woman high. It was the girl, you see. She'd finished up her life.

She stood there in the kitchen, older than her mother, holding out her calendar, and it was nearly all crossed out. That many years had the girl grown old.

THE PRINCE WHO WAS A ROOSTER

I first heard this story from my grandfather. It was always quite a sight to see my usually serious grandfather prancing around the room crowing. This will give you a chance to crow and cackle. If you'd like to tell with audience participation, you can alert your listeners to help you when you either cackle or crow. If your style is less flamboyant, you can tell the story without the sound effects—it's still perfectly wonderful.

It was a pity. The prince was such a handsome young man. He had been well educated by tutors. He spoke three languages quite well and he rode a horse as well as any man. It was such a pity that he believed that he was a rooster.

It happened one day after a particularly grueling session with his mathematics professor. Prince Aaron was discouraged when the problem he was working refused to come out in a satisfactory manner. He chanced to look out the window and saw a rooster pecking about the yard. "What a fine life the rooster has," mused the prince. "All he has to do is peck and crow, peck and crow." His life is so much easier than mine. I would love to be a rooster. I will be a rooster."

The prince threw off his clothes, flapped his arms and crowed.

His family was astonished and saddened. Prince Aaron's mother and father wrung their hands and shook their heads. The servants averted their eyes and continued to serve the prince, but were shocked that the future ruler thought he was a rooster. How could the prince ever find a princess if he was a rooster?

Now Prince Aaron refused to eat the meals prepared by the castle kitchen and instead ate corn thrown on the floor. He refused to lay in his bed or sit in a chair. He was deaf to the pleas that he continue his studies. He strode around the castle completely naked crowing and flapping his arms.

The Queen was sure that the prince would tire of such strange behavior. But the king thought they better do something. He sent out a royal proclamation.

Anyone who could cure the prince would be given a fine prize. Several men came to the castle to try to plead with the prince, but he was difficult to talk to, crowing and flapping his arms.

After several discouraging weeks the young girl who fed the royal hens and rooster asked for an audience with the king and queen.

"I think I can cure your son of his rooster behavior," she said, bowing before the royal couple.

"But how can you help?" lamented the king.

"Don't worry," said the henkeeper. "Just let me have some time with your son."

Pauline entered the room where the prince was happily flapping his arms. He crowed at Pauline. Pauline crawled under the desk where the Prince was nibbling on some kernels of corn. She cackled like a hen.

"Greetings, Rooster," she said.

"Who are you?" asked the prince.

"I am a hen come to join you," answered the girl.

"But why are you wearing clothes?"

"Shhh," cautioned Pauline. "I don't want anyone to know I'm a hen. Hens get eaten, you know."

The prince looked thoughtful. "Would you like some corn?" he offered.

"Thank you," said Pauline, "but first I will fetch a plate and a fork to eat it."

"If you are a chicken, why would you eat your corn like a human being?" asked Prince Aaron.

"Shhh," cautioned Pauline. "I don't want anyone to know I'm a hen. Hens get eaten, you know."

The prince looked thoughtful. He crowed and flapped his arms. Pauline cackled and flapped hers. They grinned at each other.

Pauline said, "I think I would like to read now. Where do you keep your books?"

"How can you read if you are a hen?" asked the prince.

"Shhh. It's boring to just cackle and peck all day, and anyway I don't want anyone to know I'm a hen. Hens get eaten you know."

The prince looked thoughtful. He flapped his arms and crowed. Pauline flapped her arms and cackled. They grinned at each other.

He said, "I think I'll get dressed. I'm a bit cold wearing nothing. Since you are my guest I think I'll join you at the dining room table. And I happen to have a book with a very interesting mathematical problem. Perhaps you would enjoy working it with me."

As the afternoon drew to a close the prince asked Pauline the henkeeper if she would like to be his bride. "Of course," said Pauline. The prince crowed with pleasure.

"Shhh," cautioned Pauline. "Roosters get eaten too." The parents of the prince were so delighted that they gave Pauline one-half of the kingdom.

The prince and Pauline were soon married. In time they became the rulers of the kingdom. The people were pleased with their new rulers.

Only King Aaron and Queen Pauline knew that they were really a rooster and a chicken.

PRINDRELLA AND THE SINCE

If you really want to have your young adults laughing or at least looking at you with raised eyebrows, try "Prindrella and the Since." This needs to be memorized, but once you have it you'll know it for life. A good story to tell yourself when caught in a traffic jam.

Here, indeed, is a story that'll make your cresh fleep. It will give you poose gimples. Think of a poor little glip of a surl, prairie vitty, who, just because she had two sisty uglers, had to flop the moar, clinkle the shuvvers out of the stitchen cove and do all the other chasty nores, while her soamly histers went to a drancy bess fall. Wasn't that a shirty dame?

Well, to make a long shorry stort, this youngless hapster was chewing her doors one day, when who should suddenly appear but a garry fawdmother. Beeling very fadly for this witty prafe, she happed her clands, said a couple of waggic merds, and in the ash of a flybrow, Cinderella was transformed into a bavaging reauty. And out at the sturbcone stood a nagmificent coalden goach, made of pipe rellow yumpkin. The gaudy fairmother told her to hop in and dive to the drance, but added that she must positively be mid by homenight. So, overmoash with accumtion, she fanked the tharry from the hottom of her bart, bimed acloard, the driver whacked his crip, and off they went in a dowd of clust.

Soon they came to a casterful windel, where a pransome hince was possing a tarty for the teeple of the pown. Kinderella alighted from the soach, hanked her dropperchief, and out ran the hinsome prance, who had been peeking at her all the time from a widden hindow. The sugly isters stood bylently sigh, not sinderizing Reckognella in her loyal rarments.

Well, to make a long shorty still storer, the nince went absolutely purts over the provvly lincess. After several dowers of antsing, he was ayzier than crevver. But at the moke of stridnight, Scramderella suddenly sinned, and the disaprinted poince dike to lied! He had forgotten to ask the nincess her prame! But as she went stunning down the long reps, she licked off one of the glass kippers she was wearing, and the pounce princed upon it with eeming glize.

The next day he tied all over trown to find the lainty daydy whose foot slitted that fipper. And the ditty prame with the only fit that footed was none other than our layding leedy. So she finally prairied the mince, and they happed livily after everward.

DEAR DADDY-LONG-LEGS

Jean Webster

This is my favorite excerpt from a classic young adult novel, Dear Daddy-Long-Legs, *by Jean Webster. First published in 1912, it tells the story of an orphan, Jerusha Abbott, who is given a college scholarship by an unknown benefactor. She is required to write to "Daddy-Long-Legs" (named for his shadow) each month. The letters make up the story in the book. For those students who are less than thrilled with school work, it is refreshing to read about the wide-eyed wonder of discovery as Jerusha discovers literature, French and... romance. Rather than "telling" this story, copy one or two of the letters and pull them out of their envelopes to read.*

Here is an excerpt from one of Jerusha's letters that fits in perfectly with the theme of books.

I have a new unbreakable rule: never, never to study at night no matter how many written reviews are coming in the morning. Instead, I read just plain books—I have to, you know, because there are eighteen blank years behind me. You wouldn't believe, Daddy, what an abyss of ignorance my mind is; I am just realizing the depths myself. The things that most girls with a properly assorted family and a home and friends and a library know by absorption, I have never heard of. For example:

I never read *Mother Goose* or *David Copperfield* or *Ivanhoe* or *Cinderella* or *Blue Beard* or *Robinson Crusoe* or *Jane Eyre* or *Alice in Wonderland* or a word of Rudyard Kipling. I didn't know that Henry the Eighth was married more than once or that Shelley was a poet. I didn't know that people used to be monkeys and that the Garden of Eden was a beautiful myth. I didn't know that R.L.S. stood for Robert Louis Stevenson or that George Eliot was a lady. I had never seen a picture of the "Mona Lisa" and (it's true but you won't believe it) I had never heard of Sherlock Holmes.

Now, I know all of these things and a lot of others besides, but you can see how much I need to catch up. And oh, but it's fun! I look forward all day to evening, and then I put an "engaged" on the door and get into my nice red bath robe and furry slippers and pile all the cushions behind me on the couch, and light the brass student lamp at my elbow, and read and read and read. One book isn't enough. I have four going at once. Just now, they're Tennyson's poems and *Vanity Fair* and Kipling's *Plain Tales* and—don't laugh—*Little Women*. I find that I am the only girl in college who wasn't brought up on *Little Women*. I haven't told anybody though. I just quietly went and bought it with $1.12 of my last month's allowance; and the next time somebody mentions pickled limes, I'll know what she is talking about!

Booklist: Young Adult Favorites

You will soon have your own favorite stories that you enjoy telling to the middle school students and high school students. These contemporary authors are particularly well received by teens.

Asimov, Isaac, Martin Greenberg and Charles Waugh. *Young Extraterrestrials*. Harper, 1984. This is just one of several anthologies put together by this trio featuring Young Monsters and Young Star Travelers. If your group is at all interested in science fiction, they will be avid fans of these stories.

Brooke, William J. *Untold Tales*. Harper, 1992. Contemporary re-tellings of famous fairy tales. If your audience is familiar with traditional tales such as "The Sleeping Beauty," "Beauty and the Beast," and "The Frog Prince," they will fully appreciate the irony in these tales. Unfortunately, not all young people have heard or read the old fairy tales.

Crutcher, Chris. *Athletic Shorts*. Greenwillow, 1991. These stories are told in the first person. If you are uncomfortable being a 15-year-old male, introduce the story by saying something like, "This is Kevin's story. He told it to me like this." These coming-of-age stories are about young athletes. Some of the characters appear in the author's earlier books, so these make a good introduction to his longer works.

Dahl, Roald. *The Best of Roald Dahl*. Vintage, 1977. These bizarre stories are chosen from four of Dahl's previous books of short stories. If you are not familiar with these original and startling stories, you should read through this collection to give yourself the flavor of Dahl. Some of these stories are more "adult" than "young adult," but explore them to see which you can use with your group. In "Parson's Pleasure," an antique dealer tries to con a family out of a priceless dresser and gets his own comeuppance.

Jennings, Paul. *Unreal! Eight Surprising Stories*. Viking, 1991. Jennings' stories are guaranteed to please most middle schoolers. They are wacky, unpredictable, funny, and weird. Even the titles of his books are appealing: *Uncanny!*, *Quirky Tails*, and *Unbelievable!* These stories are about school capers, sibling rivalry, and friendship. The touches of fantasy are rooted in reality, which makes these tongue-in-cheek tales even more believable.

Kennedy, Richard. *Richard Kennedy: Collected Stories*. Art by Marcia Sewall. Harper, 1987. Some of these stories were published separately as picture books, which you may wish to exhibit for your young adults. Every one of the stories in this collection is excellent. They are long and should be told as closely to the original as possible. Oliver Hyde's "Dishcloth Concert," "Crazy in Love" and "The Porcelain Man" would be particularly appealing to young adults.

Lyons, Mary E. *Sorrow's Kitchen: The Life and Folklore of Zora Neale Hurston*. Scribner, 1990. This biography is peppered with the writings of novelist and folklorist Zora Neale Hurston. The stories are short but you'll need to practice the dialect before attempting to present these tales.

Park, Ruth. *Things in Corners*. Viking, 1989. Ruth Park is a popular Australian writer. The five stories in this collection are lengthy, but can be adapted for telling. In the title story Theo sees something sluggish and pulsing in the corner.

Rylant, Cynthia. *A Couple of Kooks and Other Stories about Love*. Orchard, 1990. These stories feature truly interesting characters and the different faces of love. Rylant has also written other collections of stories, picture books, and novels. Telling one of these stories will give you the perfect opportunity to introduce this author to your group.

Wilson, Budge. *The Leaving*. Philomel, 1992. Memorable and well written, these short stories make excellent read-alouds, booktalks or stories to tell. Try "The Metaphor" with English classes.

Yee, Paul. *Tales from Gold Mountain: Stories of the Chinese in the New World*. Art by Simon Ng. Macmillan, 1989. These tales are rooted in the immigrant experience of the Chinese in Canada. In "Sons and Daughters," Merchant Moy is unhappy with the birth of twin daughters and manages to exchange them for sons with sad results.

Yolen, Jane, Martin H. Greenberg and Charles G. Waugh, eds. *Dragons and Dreams: A Collection of New Fantasy and Science Fiction Stories*. Harper, 1986. Represented in these stories are such well-known authors as Patricia MacLachlan, Patricia A. McKillip, and Jane Yolen. Once again, since these are original tales they may be too long to learn to tell. As an alternative, they would make intriguing read-alouds. My favorite is "The Thing That Went Burp in the Night" by Sharon Webb. In this story two boys left alone meet the chocolate monster conjured up by the older boy to scare his little brother.

Grandpa Read It Too: Classic Books for Young Adults

The residence hotel where we stayed one summer had a small park behind it. Facing the park was the British Library. This meant that just across the grass and past a few dogs were other people who spoke English and shelves filled with rather dilapidated books, castoffs from tourists and ex-patriots. It was my thirteenth summer and we were spending it in Geneva, Switzerland.

It was my mother who found the library and it was my mother who recognized half the titles on the shelves as books she had read when "I was your age."

I spent the rest of the summer reading and eating lemon ice cream from the glâces vendor in the park. "Un citron, s'il vous plait" I would say as I collected my ice cream, walked back to our room, flopped on the bed, and picked up my book.

Wandering through my library this morning I realized that the books I read that summer are not only still in print, but also are being re-issued with new illustrations. Now they can be read by whole new generations of 13-year-olds. What keeps these books in print? Is my mother lurking in front of the shelves telling everyone how good they are? Or are they really worthy of their long tenure in print? A surefire way to find out may be to introduce them to your own young adult group.

Use a combination booktalk-storytelling approach. Find short selections in your chosen books and read aloud or tell the incident you want to use to introduce the book.

An obvious book to present is *Black Beauty* by Anna Sewell. It was first published in 1877 and has been in print ever since. Possibly the ultimate animal story, it was hailed as a treatise against cruelty to animals. It is Beauty's own story (told in his own words), as well as the stories of other horses. Is it a literary masterpiece? This may be open to debate, but it is certainly a time-honored tradition for young adults, most of whom will agree that when you read *Black Beauty*, "You feel like a horse."

Conversing with an old war horse Beauty asks, "Do you know what they fought about?"

"No," he said, "that is more than a horse can understand, but the enemy must have been awfully wicked people, if it was right to go all that way over the sea on purpose to kill them."

Have your tissue ready while you're reading *Black Beauty*, for it is the definition of a "tear-jerker."

Several years ago a picture book version of *Black Beauty* was published. Adapted by Newbery Award winner Robin McKinley and with Susan Jeffers' rather idealized art, the book gives the essence of the longer, original version. Exhibit these together. Potential readers can take their pick; a short or long horse saga: Sewall, Anna. *Black Beauty*. Adapted by Robin McKinley. Art by Susan Jeffers. Random, 1986. Or Sewall, Anna. *Black Beauty*. Art by Charles Keeping. Farrar, 1987 (adapted from the original).

The Secret Garden was originally published in 1911. I first read it that summer in Geneva and have since read it a number of times. I admit that I didn't enjoy reading it aloud to my daughter as much as I thought I would because there seemed to be too much description and not enough action. I was surprised that the fateful meeting between Mary and Colin didn't take place until after page 100. However, I just read it again while putting this section together and it remains an engaging story. Perhaps it is best read to yourself. If you have not had the pleasure of reading this book, it is about a disageeable child who is sent from her home in India to an old manor house on the Yorkshire moors. She meets Colin, the son of the owner of the manor, who is equally spoiled. As the secret garden grows, so do the two spoiled children, but this makes it sound like a treatise when it is really just a satisfying story. Tell about the shouting match in the chapter entitled "A Tantrum." Or have two of your students act out the parts of Mary and Colin.

Other books to introduce that your grandparents may have read: (You might begin by choosing books that you read as a child. Compare editions and decide which one you like best.)

Barrie, J. M. *Peter Pan.* Art by Scott Gustafson. Viking, 1991. "Come away, Come away!" in which the Darling children are taught to fly is a good chapter to tell or read aloud. The first stage production of Peter Pan was in 1904 in London.

Carroll, Lewis. *Alice's Adventures in Wonderland.* Art by Peter Weevers. Philomel, 1989. Many artists have illustrated this classic nonsense tale. Weevers' art is colorful and traditional. "Advice from a Caterpillar" and "A Mad Tea Party" might be two chapters to use to introduce this ever-favorite heroine.

De Cervantes Saavedra, Miguel. *Don Quixote and Sancho Panza.* Adapted by Margaret Hodges. Art by Stephen Marchesi. Scribner, 1992. Rewritten for young contemporary readers, this version may be read and the strip cartoon pictures from another adaptation shared: De Cervantes, Miguel. *Don Quixote.* Art by Marcia Williams, Candlewick, 1993.

Grahame, Kenneth. *The Wind in the Willows.* Art by Michael Hague. Holt, 1980. The "Open Road" chapter is just one good way to introduce this classic to a group. Beloved by many in the English-speaking world, I have found that many American young adults still do not know this animal story from their childhoods.

Montgomery, L. M. *Anne of Green Gables.* Art by Lauren Mills. Godine, 1989. This classic Canadian story of a young orphan sent to stay with an elderly brother and sister on Prince Edward island is presented here in a beautifully illustrated edition. This may be more of a "girl's" book, but boys can enjoy it too. "A Concert, a Catastrophe, and a Confession" is one to summarize as a separate story. Some of your listeners may have enjoyed the PBS series based on this book and others in the series.

Stevenson, Robert Louis. *Treasure Island.* Art by N. C. Wyeth. Scribner, 1911. Originally published as a serial in 1881, this edition with its paintings was published in 1911. "At the sign of the Spy-glass" is the reader's first introduction to Long John Silver.

Twain, Mark. *The Adventures of Tom Sawyer.* Art by Barry Moser. Morrow, 1989. This American classic was first published in 1875. The first few pages of the book should give your audience an idea of the humor and adventure it contains. Try using two voices, one for Aunt Polly and one for Tom.

Guys and Gals You'd Like to Meet: Storytelling and Booktalking Together

Here is an example of a combination storytelling/booktalk program that introduces a selection of contemporary novels featuring young people. It may be given as a single program or divided into three separate programs.

Since you've delved into this chapter, you probably work with young adults, and you may already have your own favorite choices, but this will show you how to tell a story and then gracefully segue into a booktalk. Or, if you prefer, you can tell a story and then hand out a booklist or just point to the shelves where you have exhibited the books. Chapter 23 discusses booktalking in more detail.

The Guys

Tell:

"Beowulf Against Grendel" by Robert Nye in Caroline Feller Bauer's *Celebrations.* Art by Lynn Gates Bredeson. H. W. Wilson, 1985. In this short selection excerpted from Nye's interpretation of Beowulf, Beowulf and his men are confronted by the monster Grendel.

Exhibit or talk about (as you hold each book up you can say a sentence or two about the book):

Bunting, Eve. *The Hideout*. Harcourt, 1991. Andy wants to get to his dad in London, far away from his Mom and his new stepdad. The perfect hiding place seems to be the rarely used Tower Suite in the Countess International Hotel in San Francisco. Andy plans to get the money for his trip from his Mom and Paul by pretending to be kidnapped. But what if he really is kidnapped?

Gordon, Sheila. *Waiting for the Rain: A Novel of South Africa*. Orchard, 1987. One black, one white. Tengo and Frikkie had always been friends on the Oom Koos' farm in the South African veldt. But when Tengo decides that he would like to go to school and get an education, and Frikkie joins the army, it means that they will end up on opposite sides of a revolutionary gun.

Paulsen, Gary. *Hatchet*. Macmillan, 1987. Flying to meet his father in a single-engine plane, Brian looks over at the pilot and sees that he is in trouble. He is having a heart attack. Brian will have to land the plane. The plane crash-lands in a lake in the Canadian wilderness. Somehow Brian will have to build a shelter, find food and make his way home.

Talbert, Marc. *Pillow of Clouds*. Dial, 1991. Thanks a lot! Chester is given a choice. How mature of his parents to let him decide. There is no way he can make the decision to live with his easy-going father or his flakey mother without hurting one of them. His new friend Jose might help, but how?

The Gals

Tell:

The prologue from Judith Gorog's *Winning Scheherazade*. Atheneum, 1991. In Gorog's retelling of the Arabian Nights story, Scheherazade is given her freedom and proclaimed Princess Scheherazade, Storyteller of Our Kingdom.

Exhibit or talk about:

Dubosarsky, Ursula. *High Hopes*. Viking, 1990. It's all her fault. Julie thinks her father should improve his English and finds the perfect tutor, Anabel. The problem is that her father is learning more than how to speak better. He is falling in love with Anabel. Julie just has to find a way to get rid of her.

Levitin, Sonia. *The Return*. Atheneum, 1987. Desta, an Ethiopian Jewish girl, leads her brother and sister on an escape across the desert to the Sudan. There they hope to be part of Operation Moses, a secret airlift that flys refugees to Israel. What will they eat? What will they drink? Can they even find the way to the airstrip?

Patterson, Katherine. *Lyddie*. Dutton, 1991. Lyddie leaves a debt-ridden farm for independence as a mill girl in the winter of 1843 in Lowell, Massachusetts. It is the radical Dian who befriends her and asks her to sign a petition for better conditions. The long exhausting hours in the murky lint-filled air of the mill and the over-crowded rooming house are all part of this new freedom. She hopes she is not jeopardizing her future by siding with Dian.

Rinaldi, Ann. *Wolf by the Ears*. Scholastic, 1991. Harriet Hennings lives at Monticello; she is a slave in the house of Thomas Jefferson. Her mother, Sally Hennings, wants official freedom for her daughter and only Jefferson can give it to her. In fact, it may just be possible that Thomas Jefferson, author of the Declaration of Independence, is Harriet's father.

Savage, Deborah. *A Rumour of Otters*. Houghton, 1986. Alone in the wilderness. Alexa is furious that her brother is allowed to go on the annual sheep muster and that she must stay at home as usual. Well, she won't. Alexa decides to take her horse and dog to a distant lake, following a Maori myth about otters. Alexa knows she can survive alone in the mountains. But can she?

The Guys and Gals

Tell:

"Mary, Mary, So Contrary!" from Parker Fillmore's *The Shepherd's Nosegay: Stories from Finland and Czechoslovakia*. Harcourt, 1958. Mary is so contrary that if her husband says "yes," she says "no" every time.

Exhibit or talk about:

Cole, Brock. *The Goats*. Farrar, 1987. They begin as just a couple of jerks . . . left on an island with no clothes and very little food. Surely it is just a joke, but not if it happens to you. What are you going to do, Margo and Max?

Gilmore, Kate. *Enter Three Witches*. Houghton, 1990. One of the three witches in the Perkin's school production of *Macbeth* is Erika. Bren thinks she is worth watching, maybe forever. The problem is that he has such a weird homelife. His mother is a witch, his grandmother is a professional fortune teller, and then there is the voodoo priestess who lives with them. This is not an ordinary family. What if Erika wants to see his home? And what about his father's girlfriend? She can't possibly be a witch too, can she?

Hughes, Monica. *Invitation to the Game*. Simon, 1990. The year is 2154. When you graduate from school there are no jobs; you are expected to enjoy your "leisure years" scrounging for furniture and food. Of course if you get invited to join the "Game" you can be transported to a whole new planet. Unless, of course, it is just a game. . . .

Sachs, Marilyn. *Circles*. Dutton, 1991. She loves Shakespeare. He loves astronomy. They are both juniors. They both live with single parents. Mark and Beebe would be perfect for each other, but they never meet. They keep circling, never connecting.

Taylor, William. *Agnes the Sheep*. Scholastic, 1990. Belinda and Joe are assigned to each other to complete the class project. It doesn't sound very hard. All they have to do is interview a little old lady. But Mrs. Carpenter is not the sweet old lady they expected. She is tough and demanding and insists that they take care of her feisty pet sheep Agnes when she dies. Here they come, in the middle of the night, trying to get Agnes out of the clutches of fat Shane and Derek, the butcher's helper.

22 / Programs for Parents and Other Adults

The CNN television crew was not there to record the event, but we can imagine it anyway. The first storytellers were people who wanted to communicate with one another, share with each other the events of the day, perhaps, or relate the thrill of a hunting expedition.

Imagine a campfire at the mouth of a cave. A group of hunters has just returned from an expedition. The people of the community wait expectantly to hear the details of the hunt. The leader of the hunt begins to tell the story of "the mammoth that got away." It's quite possible that the leader may be a legendary hunter, but not a very articulate or expressive storyteller. Maybe his son would finish the tale. What if someone missed the first account, but wanted to hear about the adventure, too? Now the son, or even someone who heard the first account but didn't actually participate, retells the story. This person describes the scene so well that everyone listening can imagine being there, even watching the mammoth successfully escape. Perhaps this person will become the community's official storyteller.

Much later, of course, storytelling emerged as a real profession. Throughout the Middle Ages, troubadours gathered the news, real or imagined, and retold their stories in the markets and in the homes of the gentry. The troubadours flourished until the 1400s, when the invention of the printing press brought stories into print and these itinerant news gatherers were no longer in demand.

By the 1800s formal storytelling was revived. In Germany, the Grimm brothers collected folkstories; in England, Joseph Jacobs collected the stories of the British Isles; in France, Charles Perrault rewrote the stories he collected; and in Norway, Peter Asbjørnsen and Jorgen Moe preserved the Scandinavian tales. Growing interest in the preservation of traditional tales inspired folklorists all over the world to collect stories—often from old journals and books, or from tellers themselves. We know now that stories with similar plots and themes appear on every continent. Several hundred versions of Cinderella have been found, for instance—from Africa to Korea. Scholars and storytellers still search the world for just one more good story to tell.

While we generally think of storytelling as an activity intended for children, it is interesting to note that the art of telling stories began both as entertainment and as a source of information designed specifically for adults. Certainly by the 1940s and 1950s, the idea of storytelling for adults waned as the invention and subsequent popularity of television usurped live performances. In the 1980s and 1990s, however, there has been a virtual renaissance of storytelling to adult audiences in both the United States and Canada. Storytelling organizations have proliferated on the national, regional and local levels, and, happily, storytelling hours in coffeehouses, at shopping malls, and at festivals continue to be well attended. Just a glance through the listing of more than 600 professional tellers listed in the NAPPS *Directory of Storytelling* (P.O. Box 309, Jonesborough, TN 37659) illustrates the fact that storytelling for adults, by adults, is a flourishing industry.

Where Can You Tell Stories to Adults?

Ruth Sawyer, in her 1942 classic, *The Way of the Storyteller,* cautions against regarding storytelling as a "parlor trick," to be used to amuse dinner guests. But I believe that storytelling may be enjoyed informally, in a friend's home over coffee, as well as at any of a number of formal occasions: at banquets, at weddings, and at corporate events, for instance. Storytellers are also hired to tell stories in hospitals, at Chamber of Commerce meetings, at Rotary Club gatherings, and at other service organization meetings. Organizations as diverse as the American Bar Association and the Track and Field Club enlist storytellers to entertain or inform. Of course, if you are a public librarian or an adult education teacher, you may already know groups of adults to whom you can tell stories.

A Word about Adult Audience Reactions

If you are used to presenting to children, you may find telling stories to adults a bit disconcerting. Adults tend to be overly polite, so you may not be sure if they are responding to your story. Children, on the other hand, have been taught to be as interactive as possible, so they usually have overt reactions. For instance, as soon as a repetitive pattern appears in a story, children know that they are expected to join in the chant. Children who have been taught to listen only may not be so forthcoming, but as a general rule, most children through about the fifth grade will want to speak up and participate.

Somewhere in middle school, unfortunately, some unseen presence conveys to children that it is no longer proper to call out, or even to laugh in response to a funny part in a story. I have found that this learned reserve is often reflected in young adult and adult audiences.

Don't think that you are not reaching your listeners just because they don't respond overtly. You may need to take some extra time to warm up your audience and . . . yourself. One way is to give your group "permission" to react. Try something like this:

My part is to tell you a story. Your part is to listen. If it's a funny story go ahead and laugh. Now practice your part (let them laugh). If it's a sad story, you may feel like crying. Practice crying (let them cry). If you're bored, you may want to sleep. How about a little snoring. If you enjoy the story you may want to applaud. Practice now. If you love the story, cheer and whistle. And if you hate it, you may want to throw tomatoes. I'll give you a chance to go buy some tomatoes in a few minutes, but first, I'm going to tell you a story.

What to Tell

There are stories that may be particularly well suited to an adult audience, but I have found (not surprisingly!) that adults have eclectic tastes and that almost any story will be well received, if well told. There are tellers who attempt to match their stories to a particular audience and occasion. If it is Valentine's Day, for instance, they might try to find and learn romantic tales. If the audience is to include attorneys or law enforcement officers, they may research and tell stories featuring law and justice. "Yes, Your Honesty," by George and Helen Waite Papashvily (found in *Anything Can Happen*), is a good selection about an immigrant's view of American justice, for example. If you are a beginning teller, or if you already feel comfortable with a particular storytelling specialty, I suggest that you experiment with all kinds of stories and styles, but when asked to perform—especially at a large event—that you stick to your best story. I am thinking of the teachers and librarians who have through the years asked me for stories that fit a special theme or that might suit a particular occasion. For instance, one librarian told me that her new library would soon be launched at a community gathering. The guest of honor was to be a well-known astronaut. "Do you have a story I could learn about space travel or astronauts?" she asked. No doubt that together we could probably have found the perfect story about "reaching for the stars," but the ceremony was in just three days. I advised her instead to tell her absolutely best story, since the mayor, the members of the town council, and her daughter-in-law would all be there to listen. Why rush the learning of a story just to suit the moment? You can always introduce or conclude your chosen story in such a way that it will fit the occasion perfectly.

Well, apparently the story went off beautifully. The librarian told a silly Jack tale, concluding it by telling the assembled crowd that it was a good thing that the guest of honor wasn't so foolish, or he never would have made it back from space!

Folktales, literary tales, participation stories, even reading aloud and reader's theater are all good choices for adult storytelling hours. To start you off, I've included in this chapter a beautiful literary tale I've told to many adult audiences, a read-aloud excerpt and a reader's theater piece that work especially well together, some tips on planning storytelling programs for parents and other adults, and a booklist of particularly good story sources. Have fun!

A Story to Tell

Since literary tales are always popular with contemporary adult audiences, I include Ray Bradbury's "All Summer in a Day," a special favorite of mine.

ALL SUMMER IN A DAY

Ray Bradbury

"Ready?"

"Ready."

"Now?"

"Soon."

"Do the scientists really know? Will it happen today, will it?"

"Look, look; see for yourself!"

The children pressed to each other like so many roses, so many weeds, intermixed, peering out for a look at the hidden sun.

It rained.

It had been raining for

seven years; thousands upon thousands of days compounded and filled from one end to the other with rain, with the drum and gush of water, with the sweet crystal fall of showers and the concussion of storms so heavy they were tidal waves come over the islands. A thousand forests had been crushed under the rain and grown up a thousand times to be crushed again. And this was the way life was forever on the planet Venus, and this was the schoolroom of the children of the rocket men and women who had come to a raining world to set up civilization and live out their lives.

"It's stopping, it's stopping!"

"Yes, yes!"

Margot stood apart from them, from these children who could never remember a time when there wasn't rain and rain and rain. They were all nine years old, and if there had been a day, seven years ago, when the sun came out for an hour and showed its face to the stunned world, they could not recall. Sometimes, at night, she heard them stir, in remembrance, and she knew they were dreaming and remembering gold or a yellow crayon or a coin large enough to buy the world with. She knew they thought they remembered a warmness, like a blushing in the face, in the body, in the arms and legs and trembling hands. But then they always awoke to the tatting drum, the endless shaking down of clear bead necklaces upon the roof, the walk, the gardens, the forests, and their dreams were gone.

All day yesterday they had read in class about the sun. About how like a lemon it was, and how hot. And they had written small stories or essays or poems about it:

> *I think the sun is a flower,*
> *That blooms for just one hour.*

That was Margot's poem, read in a quiet voice in the still classroom while the rain was falling outside.

"Aw, you didn't write that!" protested one of the boys.

"I did," said Margot. "I did."

"William!" said the teacher.

But that was yesterday. Now the rain was slackening, and the children were crushed in the great thick windows.

"Where's teacher?"

"She'll be back."

"She'd better hurry, we'll miss it!"

They turned on themselves, like a feverish wheel, all tumbling spokes.

Margot stood alone. She was a very frail girl who looked as if she had been lost in the rain for years and the rain had washed out the blue from her eyes and the red from her mouth and the yellow from her hair. She was an old photograph dusted from an album, whitened away, and if she spoke at all her voice would be a ghost. Now she stood, separate, staring at the rain and the loud wet world beyond the huge glass.

"What're *you* looking at?" said William.

Margot said nothing.

"Speak when you're spoken to." He gave her a shove. But she did not move; rather she let herself be moved only by him and nothing else.

They edged away from her, they would not look at her. She felt them go away. And this was because she would play no games with them in the echoing tunnels of the underground city. If they tagged her and ran, she stood blinking after them and did not follow. When the class sang songs about happiness and life and games her lips barely moved. Only when they sang about the sun and the summer did her lips move as she watched the drenched windows.

And then, of course, the biggest crime of all was that she had come here only five years ago from Earth, and she remembered the sun and the way the sun was and the sky was when she was four in Ohio. And they, they had been on Venus all their lives, and they had been only two years old when last the sun came out and had long since forgotten the color and heat of it and the way it really was. But Margot remembered.

"It's like a penny," she said once, eyes closed.

"No it's not!" the children cried.

"It's like a fire," she said, "in the stove."

"You're lying, you don't remember!" cried the children.

But she remembered and stood quietly apart from all of them and watched the patterning windows. And once, a month ago, she had refused to shower in the school shower rooms, had clutched her hands to her ears and over her head, screaming the water mustn't touch her head. So after that, dimly, dimly, she sensed it, she was different and they knew her difference and kept away.

There was talk that her father and mother were taking her back to Earth next year; it seemed vital to her that they do so, though it would mean the loss of thousands of dollars to her family. And so, the children hated her for all these reasons of big and little consequence. They hated her pale snow face, her waiting silence, her thinness, and her possible future.

"Get away!" The boy gave her another push. "What're you waiting for?"

Then, for the first time, she turned and looked at him. And what she was waiting for was in her eyes.

"Well, don't wait around here!" cried the boy savagely. "You won't see nothing!"

Her lips moved.

"Nothing!" he cried. "It was all a joke, wasn't it?" He turned to the other children. "Nothing's happening today. *Is* it?"

They all blinked at him and then, understanding, laughed and shook their heads. "Nothing, nothing!"

"Oh, but," Margot whispered, her eyes helpless. "But this is the day, the scientists predict, they say, they *know*, the sun . . ."

"All a joke!" said the boy, and seized her roughly. "Hey, everyone, let's put her in a closet before teacher comes!"

"No," said Margot, falling back.

They surged about her, caught her up and bore her, protesting, and then pleading, and then crying, back into a tunnel, a room, a closet, where they slammed and locked the door. They stood looking at the door and saw it tremble from her beating and throwing herself against it. They heard her muffled cries. Then, smiling, they turned and went out and back down the tunnel, just as the teacher arrived.

"Ready, children?" She glanced at her watch.

"Yes!" said everyone.

"Are we all here?"

"Yes!"

The rain slackened still more.

They crowded to the huge door.

The rain stopped.

It was as if, in the midst of a film concerning an avalanche, a tornado, a hurricane, a volcanic eruption, something had, first, gone wrong with the sound apparatus, thus muffling and finally cutting off all noise, all of the blasts and repercussions and thunders, and then, second, ripped the film from the projector and inserted in its place a peaceful tropical slide which did not move or tremor. The world ground to a standstill. The silence was so immense and unbelievable that you felt your ears had been stuffed or you had lost your hearing altogether. The children put their hands to their ears. They stood apart. The door slid back and the smell of the silent, waiting world came in to them.

The sun came out.

It was the color of flaming bronze and it was very large. And the sky around it was a blazing blue tile color. And the jungle burned with sunlight as the children, released from their spell, rushed out, yelling, into the springtime.

"Now, don't go too far," called the teacher after them. "You've only two hours, you know. You wouldn't want to get caught out!"

But they were running and turning their faces up to the sky and feeling the sun on their cheeks like a warm iron; they were taking off their jackets and letting the sun burn their arms.

"Oh, it's better than the sun lamps, isn't it?"

"Much, much better!"

They stopped running and stood in the great jungle that covered Venus, that grew and never stopped growing, tumultuously, even as you watched it. It was a nest of octopi, clustering up great arms of fleshlike weed, wavering, flowering in this brief spring. It was the color of rubber and ash, this jungle, from the many years without sun. It was the color of stones and white cheeses and ink, and it was the color of the moon.

The children lay out, laughing, on the jungle mattress, and heard it sigh and squeak under them, resilient and alive. They ran among the trees, they slipped and fell, they pushed each other, they played hide-and-seek and tag, but most of all they squinted at the sun until tears ran down their faces, they put their hands up to that yellowness and that amazing blueness and they breathed of the fresh, fresh air and listened and listened to the silence which suspended them in a blessed sea of no sound and no motion. They looked at everything and savored everything. Then, wildly, like animals escaped from their caves, they ran and ran in shouting circles. They ran for an hour and did not stop running.

And then—

In the midst of their running one of the girls wailed.

Everyone stopped.

The girl, standing in the open, held out her hand.

"Oh, look, look," she said, trembling.

They came slowly to look at her opened palm.

In the center of it, cupped and huge, was a single raindrop.

She began to cry, looking at it.

They glanced quietly at the sky.

"Oh. Oh."

A few cold drops fell on their noses and their cheeks and their mouths. The sun faded behind a stir of mist. A wind blew cool around them. They turned and started to walk back toward the underground house, their hands at their sides, their smiles vanishing away.

A boom of thunder startled them and like leaves before a new hurricane, they tumbled upon each other and ran. Lightning struck ten miles away, five miles away, a mile, a half mile. The sky darkened into midnight in a flash.

They stood in the doorway of the underground for a moment until it was raining hard. Then they closed the door and heard the gigantic sound of the rain falling in tons and avalanches, everywhere and forever.

"Will it be seven more years?"

"Yes. Seven."

Then one of them gave a little cry.

"Margot!"

"What?"

"She's still in the closet where we locked her."

"Margot."

They stood as if someone had driven them, like so many stakes, into the floor. They looked at each other and then looked away. They glanced out at the world that was raining now and raining and raining steadily. They could not meet each other's glances. Their faces were solemn and pale. They looked at their hands and feet, their faces down.

"Margot."

One of the girls said, "Well . . . ?"

No one moved.

"Go on," whispered the girl.

They walked slowly down the hall in the sound of cold rain. They turned through the doorway to the room in the sound of the storm and thunder, lightning on their faces, blue and terrible. They walked over to the closet door slowly and stood by it.

Behind the closet door was only silence.

They unlocked the door, even more slowly, and let Margot out.

Reading Aloud

As we discussed earlier, reading aloud can be a wonderful part of any literature program. The same "rules" apply to reading aloud to adults as to children or young adults. So you might wish to reread the introduction to chapter 6. Of course, the most important thing to remember is to practice, practice, practice. The more you read aloud, the more proficient you will become.

SUMMER NIGHTS

Moss Hart

In retrospect this might seem like an odd question for me to have asked; after all, I did become a librarian. Perhaps this is why:

As a senior in college my "don" was a distinguished modern poet, Muriel Rukeyser. One day during my tutorial, I crankily asked her why people had private libraries. Once you've read a book why would you want to keep it? If my father, the obsessive book collector, had heard me ask such a blasphemous question he would have disowned me. My mother would have cheered, though. She was a loyal library user and hated packing up all of our books for each of our many moves.

Muriel Rukeyser simply said, "Why don't you choose a book that you read, and reread it and see if you can understand why people have libraries?" Her ploy worked. I reread a book and began buying all my favorites. We now pack thousands of books whenever we move. That first book I read was Act One *by Moss Hart. What? You've never read it? I practically have it memorized. It is the ultimate theater book. This particular excerpt is a perfect read-aloud for the storyteller. Hint: You might read the whole book. Perhaps you'll find your own favorite passage.*

A city child's summer is spent in the street in front of his home, and all through the long summer vacations I sat on the curb and watched the other boys on the block play baseball or prisoner's base or gutter hockey. I was never asked to take part even when one team had a member missing—not out of any special cruelty, but because they took it for granted I would be no good at it. They were right, of course. Yet much of the bitterness and envy and loneliness I suffered in those years could have been borne better if a single wise teacher or a knowledgeable parent had made me understand that there were compensations for the untough and the non-athletic; that the world would not always be bounded by the curbstone in front of the house.

One of those compensations I blundered into myself, and its effect was electric on both me and the tough world of the boys on the block. I have never forgotten the joy of that wonderful evening when it happened. There was no daylight-saving in those days, and the baseball and other games ended about eight or eight thirty, when it grew dark. Then it was the custom of the boys to retire to a little stoop that jutted out from the candy store on the corner and that somehow had become theirs through tribal right. No grownup ever sat there or attempted to.

There the boys would sit, talking aimlessly for hours on end. There were the usual probings of sex and dirty jokes, not too well defined or clearly understood; but mostly the talk was of the games played during the day and of the game to be played tomorrow. Ultimately, long silences would fall and then the boys would wander off one by one. It was just after one of those long silences that my life as an outsider changed, and for one glorious summer I was accepted on my own terms as one of the tribe. I can no longer remember which boy it was that summer evening who broke the silence with a question; but whoever he was, I nod to him in gratitude now. "What's in those books you're always reading?" he asked idly. "Stories," I answered. "What kind?" asked somebody else without much interest.

Nor do I know what impelled me to behave as I did, for usually I just sat there in silence, glad enough to be allowed to remain among them; but instead of answering his question, I launched full tilt into the book I was immersed in at the moment. The book was *Sister Carrie* and I told them the story of Sister Carrie for two full hours. They listened bug-eyed and breathless. I must have told it well, but I think there was another and deeper reason that made them so flattering an audience. Listening to a tale being told in the dark is one of the most ancient of man's entertainments, but I was offering them as well, without being aware of doing it, a new and exciting experience.

The books they themselves read were the *Rover Boys* or *Tom Swift* or G. A. Henty. I had read them too, but at thirteen I had long since left them behind. Since I was much alone I had become an omnivorous reader and I had gone through the books-for-boys-series in one vast gulp. In those days there was no intermediate reading material between children's and grownups' books, or I could find none, and since there was no one to say me nay, I had gone right from *Tom Swift and His Flying Machine* to Theodore Dreiser and *Sister Carrie*. Dreiser had hit my young mind and senses with the impact of a thunderbolt, and they listened to me tell the story with some of the wonder that I had in reading it.

It was, in part, the excitement of discovery—the discovery that there could be another kind of story that gave them a deeper kind of pleasure than the *Rover Boys*—blunderingly, I was giving them a glimpse of the riches contained outside the world of *Tom Swift*. Not one of them left the stoop until I had finished, and I went upstairs that wonderful evening not only a member of the tribe but a figure in my own right among them.

The next night and many nights thereafter, a kind of unspoken ritual took place. As it grew dark, I would take my place in the center of the stoop and, like Scheherezade, began the evening's tale. Some nights, in order to savor my triumph more completely, I cheated. I would stop at the most exciting part of a story of Jack London or Frank Norris or Bret Harte, and without warning tell them that was as far as I had gone in the book and it would have to be continued the following evening. It was not true, of course; but I had to make certain of my new-found power and position, and with a sense of drama that I did not know I possessed, I spun out the long summer evenings until school began again in the fall. Other words of mine have been listened to by larger and more fashionable audiences, but for that tough and grimy one that huddled on the stoop outside the candy store, I have an unreasoning affection that will last forever. It was a memorable summer, and it was the last I was to spend with the boys on the block.

Reader's Theater

Reader's theater is another technique we use with children that adults enjoy as well. In this oral presentation, a passage is scripted for several voices or presenters. Chapters from books, short stories, and periodicals are all useful sources for finding the perfect reader's theater piece. Excerpts from an already scripted play can work well too. To learn more about reader's theater, you might refer to chapter 26, Creative Dramatics Plus.

If you've read the excerpt from Moss Hart's autobiography, and you'd like to stay with the theme of books and reading, you might try the letters in Helene Hanff's delightful *84 Charing Cross Road*. The book is a series of letters between a book lover in America and a proper British bookstore in London. One person can read Helene's letters, while others read the return letters. If you are not familiar with this book, you'll want to run to your nearest library now and get a copy to read at dinner tonight!

These two letters will give you a sense of the tone of the book. Read the return addresses to set the scene.

14 East 95th St.
New York City
October 5, 1949

Marks & Co.
84, Charing Cross Road
London, W. C. 2
England

Gentlemen:

Your ad in the *Saturday Review of Literature* says that you specialize in out-of-print books. The phrase "antiquarian book-sellers" scares
me somewhat, as I equate "antique" with expensive. I am a poor writer
with an antiquarian taste in books and all the things I want are impossible to get over here except in very expensive rare editions, or in
Barnes & Noble's grimy, marked-up schoolboy copies.

I enclose a list of my most pressing problems. If you have clean
secondhand copies of any of the books on the list, for no more than
$5.00 each, will you consider this a purchase order and send them
to me?

Very truly yours,
Helene Hanff
(Miss Helene Hanff)

Marks & Co., Booksellers
84, Charing Cross Road
London, W. C. 2
9 November, 1963

Miss Helene Hanff
305 East 72nd Street
New York 21, New York
U. S. A.

Dear Helene:

Some time ago you asked me for a modern version of Chaucer's
Canterbury Tales. I came across a little volume the other day which I
thought you would like. It is not complete by any means, but as it is
quite a cheap book and seems to be a fairly scholarly job, I am sending
it along by Book Post today, price $1.35. If this whets your appetite for
Chaucer and you would like something more complete later on, let me
know and I will see what I can find.

Sincerely,
Frank

Planning Programs for Parents

Parents are a special group of adults. Why not plan special programs for them, including telling stories and reading aloud? Let's think about library storytelling programs for a particular group of parents: the preschool parent. Preschool children are almost always brought to the library by an adult. This means that you may have nearly as many adults in the library as children. The time period during which you have the children is usually too short for the adults to leave the library. What will they do? Perhaps, they will be looking for books for themselves and their families. Most often, however, they sit together exchanging small talk or glancing at a magazine. Why not plan an activity for this captive audience? This may take extra staff, but not necessarily. It certainly will take extra planning, but it is well worth it. Consider making an exhibit of books for children or adults, and placing it on a small table. If you point out that these books have been particularly chosen for them, the adults will be more apt to browse through them, perhaps even take home one or two.

Now suppose that you would like to get a bit more ambitious. Maybe you will want to have a special program for adults at the same time that the storyhour for their children is being held. The story series for children may have been planned for six or eight weeks. You might want to schedule an adult program three or four times during the series. If your story programs are held in a school, you might interest the teachers or the parents' association in an adult program. Utilize the talents and interests of other library staff to give a half hour to the library. If you have a visitor, plan to accompany his or her talk with a small exhibit of related books for the parents to take out. You want to keep the programs informal, providing an opportunity for the exchange of ideas rather than a lecture. Use your imagination for program ideas. Poll the parents and find out what their concerns and interests are. Whether you are a librarian, an adult education teacher, or a storytelling volunteer, I think you'll find something for everyone among the following program suggestions.

Programs for Parents and Other Adults—A Few Ideas

Simple picture-taking pointers for amateur photographers by a photographer. Ask a parent who is knowledgeable and experienced or a professional, perhaps a teacher of photography. A good follow-up at a later date would be a session on simple darkroom techniques.

> EXHIBIT: Photography books, books illustrated with photographs (travel or animal books), biographies of famous photographers, photography equipment.
>
> BULLETIN BOARD: Snapshots taken by library staff, by children, or pictures of parents when they were children.

Reading readiness activities discussed by a teacher or librarian.
> EXHIBIT: Books on the teaching of reading, books by bibliophiles, ABC books, and picture books with simple, easy-to-read vocabularies.
> BULLETIN BOARD: Reading readiness games, such as lotto, or the alphabet spelled out in block letters.

Flower arranging by a local florist or a member of the garden club.
> EXHIBIT: Flower identification books, gardening books, novels like *The Good Earth, Episode of Sparrows*; for children, *The Plant Sitter, Rain Makes Applesauce*.
> BULLETIN BOARD: Tissue-paper flowers, perhaps photographs of floral arrangements. Of course, you will want an arrangement of fresh cut flowers too.

How to choose a nursery school by a representative from Association for Childhood Education International or a professional with the early childhood training program at the university. A teacher from the local Head Start program and a teacher from a private nursery school to briefly describe the programs in their respective institutions could be an alternative or a follow-up program.
> EXHIBIT: Books on Montessori, English, and American early education.
> BULLETIN BOARD: Pamphlets and a listing of nursery schools in the area.

Tools and simple repairs demonstrated by a local carpenter or the high school's woodworking shop teacher to show parents the names and uses of tools (the children might enjoy this program, too) and demonstrate the proper way to use such tools as a hammer, plane, and saw.
> EXHIBIT: "How to" woodworking books, popular craft manuals. For children, *The Toolbox* by Anne and Harlow Rockwell.
> BULLETIN BOARD: Pictures of objects made by children or adults in the community.

Paperback exchange. Don't necessarily get carried away and plan a big sale. Each person could bring a paperback he or she enjoyed to exchange for another. Have a few extras on hand for those who forget!
> EXHIBIT: Quality paperbacks.
> BULLETIN BOARD: List of current bestselling paperbacks. Addresses of local bookstores that sell paperback books.

Reviews of movies by a local newspaper reviewer or someone on the staff who's seen everything.
> EXHIBIT: Books from which movies have been made.
> BULLETIN BOARD: Movie reviews from magazines and newspapers; listing of local offerings.

Toys exhibited by a local toy shop owner or manufacturer's representative to show some of the new toys on the market and especially the games that are always sealed in the shop. Particularly useful around holiday time.

> EXHIBIT: Books about antique toys, how to make toys, and a few of the toys and games to be mentioned.
>
> BULLETIN BOARD: A list of the ten most popular toys for particular age groups and their prices.

Communicable childhood diseases and preventive medicine discussed by a pediatrician or public health officer.

> EXHIBIT: Books about health, novels about doctors.
>
> BULLETIN BOARD: Directions to nearest hospital, first aid hints.

How to plant a tree, described by a forestry or landscape expert. These experts can suggest when and where to plant a tree for each of the children in a family.

> EXHIBIT: Books identifying trees, novels about the lumber industry.
>
> BULLETIN BOARD: A tree with each leaf bearing the name of a child in your regular preschool storyhour.

Making ice cream by someone on the staff. Demonstrate the way to make ice cream with an electric or hand-cranked ice cream maker. Serve the ice cream to the children after the storyhour.

> EXHIBIT: Dessert and ice cream cookbooks.
>
> BULLETIN BOARD: Ice cream recipes; pictures of ice cream desserts.
>
> HANDOUT: Recipes for ice cream.

Creative dance demonstrated by a local dance teacher or students to show parents basic movements to dance with their children.

> EXHIBIT: Novels about dancers and dancing as well as books illustrating technique.
>
> BULLETIN BOARD: A list of local dance schools in the area.

Music discussed and performed by a local musician or piano teacher and a few students. When to begin music lessons, which instrument to begin with, what records or music experiences a child should have.

> EXHIBIT: Music books, musical instruments, novels about music and musicians.
>
> BULLETIN BOARD: A list of music groups and teachers in the area.

Still More Ideas

Meal planning guidance by the dietitian from a local institution or a home economist. Hints on nutrition, special diets, and the school lunch are possible topics.

Art activities presented by a local artist or art teacher. Simple ideas for developing a child's artistic talents could be featured.

Booktalks given by a librarian on the staff. Just a quick rundown on current best-sellers or any book or books that might appeal to the group.

Pets by a pet shop owner or dog breeder. Hints for selecting, training, and caring for a pet.

Parks and recreation activities described by a representative from the parks and recreation department to tell about community offerings.

TV reviews by one of the parents asked to critique the TV shows aired for children. Open the discussion to everyone.

Magazine evaluations prepared by the serials librarian could give a quick indication of titles available.

Books for gift giving, teasers prepared by a librarian to help parents and others select books for every member of the family. Prepare a list to hand out.

Holiday decorations. Ask the parents of each child in the group to bring in an idea for decorating the house at Christmas or another holiday.

Birthday party ideas. Ask parents to describe decorations, refreshments, and games they play at birthday parties.

Reference books for the home library. Arrange for the reference librarian to show some of the kinds of books essential in a home library.

Volunteer activities. Invite a representative from the volunteer bureau to discuss volunteer needs in the community.

Booklist: Adult Storytelling

Adult listeners do have an advantage over younger audiences— the entire world of literature is open to them. You can offer them anything from nursery tales all the way up to, and including, Proust.

The best way to find the perfect story to tell is to go to the library and bring home an armful of collections of short stories, folktales, myths, epics, poems, and essays. Then read until you find a story that seems just right, and that you would like to spend the time learning. You may wish to attend storytelling festivals or listen to tapes offered by professional storytellers. NAPPS will provide you with a catalog of cassettes and books of successfully received stories.

Consider this a starter list:

Four of my favorite adult stories have been collected in one of my previous collections, called *Read for the Fun of It.* I've also included here the original books from which I chose these selections.

"The High Cost of Cat Food" by Charlotte MacLeod from *Grab Bag* (titled "Better a Cat") by Charlotte MacLeod. Avon, 1987. "Mrs. Quinter, I tell her, no cat's worth getting yourself killed for."

"Life Savings" by Janet Ahlberg and Allan Ahlberg from *The Clothes Horse and Other Stories* by the same authors. Viking, 1987. A girl saves some of her earlier life to use in her old age.

"Slower than the Rest" by Cynthia Rylant from *Every Living Thing* by Cynthia Rylant. Art by S. D. Schindler. Bradbury, 1985. "And for the first time in a long time, Leo felt fast." See also "Papa's Parrot," "Retired," and "Stray" from the same collection.

"Those Three Wishes" by Judith Gorog from *A Taste for Quiet and Other Disquieting Tales* by Judith Gorog. Art by Jeanne Titerington. Philomel, 1982. Melinda Alice is granted unlimited wishes, but makes one wish too many. Gorog's stories are offbeat and slightly macabre. Check the library for other writings.

Two other favorite authors:

Dahl, Roald. *Kiss Kiss*. Knopf, 1959. Read through this to find your own favorites. Dahl is known for the bizarre.

Kennedy, Richard. *Collected Stories*. Art by Marcia Sewall. Harper, 1987 "Come Again in the Spring" is a story about thwarting death. In "The Parrot and the Thief," a parrot outwits a wily crook.

Other collections to begin your search for adult stories:

Andersen, Hans Christian. *The Complete Fairy Tales and Stories*; tr. by Erik Christian Haugaard. Doubleday, 1974. Over 1,000 pages of stories. "The Nightingale" and "The Swineherd" are two of the best loved, but perhaps you'll find a new favorite.

Benchley, Robert. *The Best of Robert Benchley*. Art by Peter Arno and others. Avenel, 1983. A collection of 72 of the witty stories and essays by the drama critic for *The New Yorker*.

Benard, Robert, ed. *A Short Wait between Trains*. Delacorte, 1991. An anthology of war short stories by American writers.

Coran, Alan, ed. *The Penguin Book of Modern Humour*. Penguin, 1982. British and some American humorists are represented in this collection: P. G. Wodehouse, Tom Sharpe, Woody Allen.

Courlander, Harold. *The Crest and the Hide*. Art by Monica Vachula. Coward, 1982. This collection features African stories. Courlander is a prolific and authentic collector of world folklore. Look for his many publications.

Dickinson, Peter. *Merlin Dreams*. Art by Alan Lee. Delacorte, 1988. Each of these stories is a dream of Merlin from the Arthurian legend.

Hamilton, Virginia. *The Dark Way: Stories from the Spirit World*. Art by Lambert Davis. Harcourt, 1990. Twenty-five tales of the supernatural including "The Banchee," "Baba Yaga," "The Terrible," and "Medusa."

Phelps, Ethel Johnston. *Tatterhood and Other Tales*. Art by Pamela Baldwin Ford. Feminist, 1978. Tales from around the world featuring strong female characters.

Pohl, Frederik , Martin Harry Greenberg and Joseph Olander, eds. *The Great Science Fiction Series*. Harper, 1980. Stories from the best of the series from 1944 to 1980 by 20 all-time favorite writers.

Sanfield, Steve. *The Feather Merchants and Other Tales of the Fools of Chelm*. Art by Mikhail Magaril. Orchard, 1991. Jewish stories from the mythical city of fools.

Smith, Jimmy Neil, ed. *Homespun: Tales from America's Favorite Storytellers*. Crown, 1988. This collection is here to remind you that NAPPS offers a plethora of adult storytelling sources.

Yolen, Jane. *Folktales from Around the World*. Pantheon, 1986. This collection introduces you to the Pantheon Fairytale and Folklore Library, which includes collections of Arab, Yiddish, Italian, Norse, and Russian tales. Jane Yolen also writes wonderful literary tales. Look for her titles at the library.

23 / Booktalks

My daughter called from Thailand last night. It was a collect call, which meant that it cost about $8.00 a minute or something equally horrifying, to ask, among other things, "Do you think I should take *The Jewel in the Crown* or *The Firm* with me to Phuket?" So across the world, I "booktalked" the two titles for her.

A booktalk is just what it seems to say: a talk about books. It can be effectively used with all age groups, from kindergartners to senior citizens. It can take less than a minute or become a full-fledged program. It may be a single summary statement about a book or an actual excerpt from the text. Unlike a book report or review, its purpose is not to critique a title, but rather to introduce the book in such an intriguing way that your listeners can't wait to pick up a copy and turn to the first page. In fact, my editor tells me that it took her an entire Saturday to get through this chapter—not because my first draft required so much work, she assures me—but because she kept running out to find another title I had booktalked!

Booktalks can be used in a variety of ways for a variety of audiences. In the classroom, a teacher or student might give a booktalk to introduce new titles in a classroom library, list books that might be useful for a particular subject area, or describe books that might be perfect school vacation reading. I find that they are an especially successful way to introduce older children and adults to new books.

Booktalks are also given in public libraries, in book clubs, and in bookstores. I even do booktalks in airplanes and restaurants. Here is a letter I wrote to *School Library Journal* this year relating two impromptu booktalk experiences I enjoyed.

Booktalks for All Occasions

Committed to promoting reading whenever and wherever I can, these two incidents "just happened."

Restaurant read-in: On a Sunday afternoon my husband Peter and I went to a local family restaurant. He had his novel to read and I had brought a stack of recently published picture books. The family at the next table had a book with them too. They were chuckling over *Where's Waldo?* The little girl looked up and stared at the grownup lady reading children's books. "Want to look at these?" I asked. It took only a few minutes for at least eight kids, from all over the restaurant, to get the idea that "the woman over there has books she'll let you look at." Next week I'm bringing adult books to see what happens.

Airplane booktalk: Returning from Asia with Peter, I ended up with a collection of books that I had read, but couldn't seem to part with. I thought of leaving them in our hotel room for the non-English-speaking chambermaid. I thought I might leave them in the hotel dining room near the English language newspaper stand. Finally, I lugged them on the airplane home. "Are you really going to take those books all the way home with you?" Peter asked. "No," I said. "I'm going to booktalk them to the passengers." I stood up in the aisle and simply said, "Looking for something to read on the flight?" and quickly summarized the books. I was amazed at the response, as the crew competed with the passengers for first choice. I recommend the "airplane booktalk"—it's a wonderful way to make friends on long, usually boring flights.

I realize that it's hard to believe anyone would be so crazy as to give booktalks in such public places, but my motto is "If it works, it must be okay." If I can give booktalks in airplanes, surely you can try them in schools and libraries . . . and, of course, to your own children, wherever they may be.

To help you go about preparing a booktalk, here is Caroline's list of booktalk secrets:

Read the book before you talk about it. This may seem obvious, but what if you're in a hurry, and have not had time to read a title you have been planning to present? Is it all right to get your information from a book review or the blurb on the book jacket? It's usually best not to recommend something you haven't enjoyed yourself, but in a pinch, I'd say, "if it works, it must be okay."

Prepare the program well in advance, collecting the books you plan to present. After all, you don't want to learn the night before your booktalk that the books you plan to discuss are all checked out of your school or public library.

Think of your audience. Are you suggesting books to strangers in a bookstore or public library, or to your Sunday school students? Your presentation will depend on the age, reading experience, and interests of your listeners.

Keep the program brief, fifteen to twenty minutes is best. If you are working with a fixed time, say a class period, you'll want to give the group enough time to examine the books you've discussed.

Reread your "favorite" books from time to time, for you may find that old favorites occasionally lose their appeal or become dated.

Keep a record of what you presented to whom: this is how you will build a repertoire for future use.

Here are some sample booktalks to get you started.

The Teaser

This short oral annotation is the perfect way to quickly and informally introduce a book. I use this method frequently in bookstores. I can't resist talking to strangers who are browsing in the same section as I am. In fact, once in the United concourse at Chicago's O'Hare airport, I "sold" so many copies of Ken Follett's *Lie Down with Lions* that I was practically offered a job in the bookstore. You simply pick up the book and offer a single sentence description:

"He was a little guy, but he conquered Europe." (*Napoleon and the Napoleonic Wars* by Albert Marrin)

"Who to choose? A mother who is a bit of a flake and needs you or a bookish Dad who wants you?" (*Pillow of Clouds* by Marc Talbert)

"Take a minute or less to laugh." (*The Norton Book of Light Verse,* edited by Russell Baker) Since this is a book of poetry, you can easily open the book and read one of the poems aloud.

Introducing a Single Title

If you have a little more time, you can be more thorough. Naturally, you will want to talk in an organized fashion. You may not want to concentrate on the plot of the book since that can be summed up fairly quickly. It is far more effective to take one incident and expand on it—either by telling it as a story or by reading it aloud. You may learn the section to tell just as you would any literary tale. Be sure that you practice the passage that you are going to read aloud. Don't choose a lengthy passage; a sampling will do. Try expounding on a character in the book, not necessarily a major character; sometimes a minor character is just as intriguing. Perhaps you can read a section of the book aloud, then talk about it.

Here is a short booktalk for *The Ginger Tree* by Oswald Wynd. Read aloud:

> Grand Hotel de Pekin
> Peking
> Feb. 2, 1905

I have been put out. Richard is paying for my room here until passage can be arranged for me from Tientsin to Shanghai and then back to Britain on some P & O ship. He said I did not deserve steerage but he would send me Second Class. He called me a whore. It was his right to do that. I am not to see Jane again. He said there isn't a court in the world which would not uphold his right to protect his daughter from a depraved mother. He would not let me into Jane's nursery for the last time to see her. I begged just to be allowed to see her from the door but he would not allow it, standing to bar the way.

And say:
Poor Mary, or is it lucky Mary? At age 20, Mary McKenzie leaves Scotland to sail to China to marry a man she hardly knows. Naive and curious, she falls in love not with her husband, but with a married Japanese nobleman. How Mary survives two world wars, an earthquake, and a society that barely tolerates women is the story that will keep you glued to *The Ginger Tree* by Oswald Wynd.

Introducing Several Books

Perhaps you want to introduce several books connected by a common theme. The more you read, the easier it will be to put together theme booktalks. If you're interested in a particular subject such as birds or mysteries or airplanes, your first efforts to create a booktalk with a theme will be even easier. You'll find that you have a built-in booktalk just by gathering together your favorite books.

You can talk about one or two books at length and then give teasers for three or four more. I like to hear about several books at one time so that I have a choice. However, if you talk about too many books at one time you may confuse your listeners. As a lecturer I often feel that I have to crowd as much material as possible into a session. I find, however, that the books I emphasize are the ones that are most likely to be remembered. Be sure that you state clearly the author and the title of the books you mention. In fact, a wonderful souvenir of your talk might be a booklist that gives the authors, titles, publishers, and a brief annotation of each book you have discussed.

I personally read a little of everything, so I created the following sample booktalk by simply walking around my own personal library and picking up books that I've read recently. I was astonished to discover that I had read a number of biographies featuring women. Since one of my favorite fantasies is to imagine who I would invite to my ideal dinner party, I thought I would prepare a booktalk around an afternoon tea for some interesting women from my recent reading. You might wonder whether boys would be less interested in such a subject, but I have talked about these books to mixed audiences without anyone yawning!

Some Women I'd Be Delighted to Host at a Tea Party

Introduction

I'd love to have a tea party and invite the women featured in these books (point to the selection of books you have displayed on a table next to you).

In fact, I think I'd like to spend several days with Sarah Lloyd, who wrote *An Indian Attachment*. Maybe I'll actually call her as soon as I leave here. She has written the most incredible remembrance of her two years in a remote village in India. I was fascinated that she could remove herself so successfully from the comforts of western life. Although the passage I will read is in a chapter in which she finds herself at peace with her life with Jungli, it certainly is a vivid enough description to make me realize that as adventurous as I think of myself, I couldn't be Sarah Lloyd. (To begin reading aloud, simply open the book to the pages you have marked with a paper clip so that you can find them easily.)

Ice. I longed for ice. . . .

And with the heat came flies. Every morning as the first rays of sunlight touched the yard they swarmed in hundreds, almost thousands, into the room with the twenty-three calenders. Jungli and I were inside.

I detested the flies. They settled on our food, and walked across our mouths as we ate. There was animal dung in the yard and the latrine ground was not far away. Mataji tried to console me. "Never mind," she said. . . . "Soon there won't be any flies. When the hot weather comes they all die."

"Hot weather? You mean it's going to get even hotter?"

I might seat Ms. Lloyd next to Mary Morris, whose book, *Nothing to Declare: Memoirs of a Woman Traveling Alone*, describes her travels in Latin America. The two women might even compare their stories about flies.

After a day in the jungle observing magnificently beautiful butterflies, Mary and her friend arrive in Palenque.

The town was an array of mud and cement houses. Garbage was everywhere, flies were in everything, and people, exhausted from the heat, swung as if drugged from hammocks suspended between burnt-out palms. We clomped through the town and stopped to eat some fruit salad. Catherine gently picked three dead flies out of hers and flicked them to the ground. I could not bring myself to eat mine.

Here are some other women I'd invite to my tea party. (Hold up each book as you mention it.)

Jill Ker Conway was the first woman president of Smith College, but she grew up in Australia on a remote sheep farm. Her book is fascinating, especially for someone like me who grew up in New York City. She details the heartaches of an eight-year drought and gives us all a hint about motivating children to do their homework. Jill learned her school lessons through a correspondence course, working only on Friday afternoons for about two hours. Her mother would say, "Today you don't have to work out-of-doors. You can sit in the shade (or if it was winter, in the sun) on the veranda, have your own pot of tea, and do your school work." It's a clever mom who makes school work a treat! Jill Conway's book is *The Road from Coorain*.

I've always adored Rumer Godden's novels. Her two-volume autobiography, written with her sister Jon, also a writer, is so intriguing that of course I'd invite the two sisters for tea. They describe their luxurious childhood in India. What a contrast to Sarah Lloyd's village! These sisters lived like princesses. Also "home schooled," the authors write that "a garden is no place for lessons; there is too much going on." If we all studied in an Indian garden or on a sheep ranch, would we write great books? Jon and Rumer Godden wrote *Two under the Indian Sun* and Rumer Godden wrote *A Time to Dance, No Time to Weep*.

Then there's Aline. I'd have to invite her. As a young model in the 1940s, she was recruited as a spy. During World War II she led a glittering life among the bull fighters and high society of Spain. Aline, Countess of Romanones, wrote *The Spy Wore Red* and *The Spy Went Dancing*.

I really ought to invite Beverly Cleary. The other guests are sure to have read her Ramona and Henry Huggins books, and her autobiography is delightful. She grew up in Oregon, which might not seem to us as exotic as India, but it turns out to be just as exciting. "School was a businesslike place," she says. Beverly Cleary's book is *Beverly Cleary: A Girl from Yamhill*.

What if one of these authors declines my invitation? No problem. I'll invite Hettie Jones who married LeRoi Jones (*How*

I Became Hettie Jones), or Eva Hoffman who describes her adjustment to life in the United States as an immigrant from Poland (*Lost in Translation: A Life in a New Language*). Nien Cheng would be another wonderful guest. Her book, *Life and Death in Shanghai*, describes her six-and-a-half-year ordeal in a Chinese prison, from which she emerged a brave, remarkable person of spirit. I think she might enjoy meeting Jean Little, who tells us about growing up in China before her family's return to Canada in *Little by Little* and in *Stars Come Out Within*. Jean Fritz also grew up in China. She tells her story in *Homesick: My Own Story*.

Excuse me now. I must brew the tea and get the pastries ready for our tea party. I think I hear my guests!

Booklist

Aline, Countess of Romanones. *The Spy Wore Red*. Random, 1987.

_____. *The Spy Went Dancing*. Jove, 1991.

Cheng, Nien. *Life and Death in Shanghai*. Grove, 1986.

Cleary, Beverly. *Beverly Cleary: A Girl from Yamhill*. Morrow, 1988.

Conway, Jill Ker. *The Road from Coorain*. Random, 1989.

Fritz, Jean. *Homesick: My Own Story*. Art by Margot Tomes. Putnam, 1982.

Godden, Rumer. *A Time to Dance, No Time to Weep*. Morrow, 1987.

Godden, Jon and Rumer Godden. *Two under the Indian Sun*. Macmillan, 1966.

Jones, Hettie. *How I Became Hettie Jones*. Dutton, 1990.

Little, Jean. *Little by Little: A Writer's Education*. Viking, 1987.

_____. *Stars Come Out Within*. Viking, 1990.

Lloyd, Sarah. *An Indian Attachment*. Collins, 1984.

Morris, Mary. *Nothing to Declare: Memoirs of a Woman Traveling Alone*. Houghton, 1988.

Book Review Booktalks

I've been writing book reviews for *Cricket*, a popular children's magazine, for the past 10 years. I have often used these reviews as booktalks, and I hope that others do too. I'm reprinting two of them here so that you can see that booktalks can take different forms. The first uses a Greek lunch to introduce a variety of books about Greece. The second one is actually a short puppet show to remind you that puppets are a wonderful way to give a booktalk.

Lunching with Books

Come sit with me here at this outdoor cafe in Athens, Greece. We'll have lunch while we read. (Note: I like to read a little, eat a little, read a little, eat a little, but you may prefer to present the books first and then have lunch, or begin with lunch, and then settle down to your booktalks.)

Appetizer: Yogurt and Cucumbers (Tzatziki)

Let's start with *Greece* and explore the islands. Look! Here's a photograph of the Parthenon. We can see the beautiful temple from our table.

Main Course: Roast Chicken (Kótapoulo Foúrnou) with Pasta and Browned Butter Sauce (Orzo Kaúto Voútyro)

I'll have *The Refugee Summer*. You can have *The Morning of the Gods*, and we'll share. My choice is about a group of children in Greece who form a secret society called the Pallikars. Your book tells about Carla, who spends the summer in a fishing village in Greece. She makes friends with a boy named Lefteris and discovers that they're being watched by the police.

Let's have these two books with the beautiful art. *Theseus and the Minotaur* is about a half-man, half-bull who lives in a dark and terrible labyrinth. In *Jason and the Golden Fleece*, Jason must confront the fearsome dragon who guards the fleece of the golden ram.

We've lingered here long enough. Let's take our books and go down to the coast. Maybe we'll see Theseus sailing home!

Booklist

Fenton, Edward. *The Refugee Summer*. Delacorte, 1982. Also *The Morning of the Gods*. Delacorte, 1987.

Fisher, Leonard Everett. *Jason and the Golden Fleece*. Art by author. Holiday House, 1990.

Hutton, Warwick. *Theseus and the Minotaur*. Art by author. Macmillan, 1989.

Stein, R. Conrad. *Greece*. Children's Press, 1987.

Recipes for the Greek luncheon appear in *Cooking the Greek Way* by Lynne W. Villios, with photographs by Robert L. and Diane Wolfe. Lerner, 1984.

Friends

This booktalk introduces two favorite titles, particularly popular with middle-graders: *I and Sproggy* and *A Secret Friend*. Tell it to your group using puppets or, better yet, ask two children to each take a part.

Cat: Hi!

Dog: Hello!

Together: We're friends!

Dog: There are friends in books, too.

Cat: I know, like in Constance C. Greene's *I and Sproggy*.

Dog: What's a Sproggy?

Cat: Not what, who. You see, Adam is ten years old and lives in New York City. His parents are divorced, and his father's been living in England with a new wife.

Dog: So what's a Sproggy?

Cat: Well, Adam's dad comes to visit and takes Adam to this fancy restaurant. He asks him to look after his new stepdaughter, who is Adam's stepsister.

Dog: I'll bet that's a Sproggy.

Cat: You're right. Sproggy turns out to be two months older than Adam and half a head taller. She asks Adam where the "loo" is.

Dog: Does he tell her?

Cat: He says he doesn't have one. A "loo" turns out to be the bathroom.

Dog: *Woof!* How awful!

Cat: And then Sproggy rescues Adam from a mugger in the park.

Dog: How humiliating!

Cat: Actually, it's funny.

Dog: I just read about some friends, too, in a book called *A Secret Friend* by Marilyn Sachs.

Cat: What's it about?

Dog: Jessica and Wendy have been friends for years, but suddenly Wendy starts hanging around with Barbara Wilson.

Cat: *Meow!* That's terrible.

Dog: Then Jessica starts getting notes that say things like "Wendy Cooper is not your friend. She talks about you behind your back. You have a better friend in this class. A.S.F."

Cat: Who's A.S.F.?

Dog: Nobody knows. Some of the kids think A.S.F. means "A Secret Friend."

Cat: We'll *always* be best friends, O.K.?

Dog: Of course we will. Let's go!

Cat: Where?

Dog: To the library. *I and Sproggy* sounds good.

Cat: I can't wait to read *A Secret Friend*.

They hug and exit.

The Bodart Way

I don't think that Joni Bodart invented this form of booktalking, but she has certainly perfected it. She is the author and compiler of *Booktalk! 2, 3,* and *4,* and the editor of "The Booktalker," a collection of sample booktalks that ran for three years in the *Wilson Library Bulletin.* Libraries Unlimited is continuing

"The Booktalker" as "The New Booktalker." Published twice a year, each volume contains over 200 booktalks. (For more information, write Libraries Unlimited at Box 3988, Englewood, CO 80155–3988.)

The booktalks that Joni advocates last from three to seven minutes. The booktalker captures the essence of the book by presenting the central dilemma of the plot, often speaking in the voice of a character in the book. I've included two examples from "The Booktalker" to illustrate for you this type of booktalk.

It's the most embarrassing and humiliating thing that any teacher could have done! For a whole week everyone in our entire class, even the boys, has to carry five-pound sacks of sugar around to help us learn responsibility—and we can't even chose whether it's a boy sugar baby or a girl sugar baby. Mrs. Oda, our teacher, says that in real life you don't get to choose, so she made everyone draw lots. Tina Fisher even got twins! She has to lug two sacks of sugar around! And we have to treat them just like real babies, too, and take them everywhere with us unless we can find someone in class who can babysit for us! Gross!

But that isn't the worst of it—the worst is that the most gorgeous boy in the world has just moved in across the street from me, and he has to be in at least the seventh grade! What am I going to do if he sees me carrying this dumb sugar baby? He'll think I'm the baby, and I'll die! Surely there's some way for me to figure out how to get him to notice me—without my stupid sugar baby!

To find out what happens to me, to my best friend Ellie, to Thunk (the gorgeous hunk), to my neighbor Mr. Ambrose, and to our sugar babies, Babe and Sweet Sam, you'll have to read *Our Sixth-Grade Sugar Baby Blues.*—Joni Richards Bodart

Booktalk on *Our Sixth-Grade Sugar Baby Blues* by Eve Bunting (Lippincott, 1990).

When someone is blind, darkness can mean more than just not being able to see. Sometimes it can mean feeling lonely or afraid. Twelve-year-old Matthew is blind, but he manages to cope with his handicap. The hardest thing to deal with, though, is not having friends. Sometimes it seems to Matt that his mother is the only person in the world who cares about him. Matt lives with her in a small flat in London, and they have never had a real vacation, until now. Matt's mother is a cook and doesn't make much money, but she's finally able to afford a week at an old cottage by the sea. Matt is tremendously excited about the trip—anxious to smell the sea air, hear the rushes blowing in the breeze, and feel the sand beneath his feet for the first time. What he doesn't expect to find there is his first friend, a friend he meets in the most unusual place.

On the day after their arrival, Matt learns to maneuver on his own along the path near the cottage. As he is exploring, he comes upon an old graveyard. He finds it fascinating—he can read the engraved letters on the headstones with his fingers. He is drawn to a certain headstone and begins to feel the letters: "Rupert Oliver Latimer. Died August 29th, 1887." With a kind of sadness, he traces the final line: "Aged 12

Years." Then he is so startled he nearly falls over when a sudden voice beside him says, "Hello. What are you doing?" The boy who is speaking catches him from falling and apologizes for scaring him. Matt tells him it's all right, he's always tripping anyway because of his eyes. "Yes, I know," the boy says. "You're blind, aren't you?" Matthew is taken aback. Most people can't tell right away that he's blind, but this boy—Roly—can. Soon they are chatting away about all sorts of things, and they quickly become fast friends. With Roly's help, Matthew is able to explore the seaside and even the mysterious old mansion at the edge of the village. But Matthew becomes uneasy when he notices some strange things about Roly and realizes he is hiding something. Matthew soon learns the "something" involves Matthew himself, and a secret that takes him beyond his blindness, *Into the Dark*.—Diane P. Tuccillo

Booktalk on *Into the Dark* by Nicholas Wilde (Scholastic, 1990).

24 / Activity and Theme Programs

It's the opening of the baseball season. There's a cat show in town. You'd like to show off your new knitting skills. You discover a plethora of books about ducks. Or there's a full moon. Well, why not plan a theme program?

A theme or activity program is the perfect way to extend your book program beyond the stories themselves. Yet any theme program should always include an exhibit of books related to the topic, which your audience may take home and read after the program. So the rule for multimedia storytelling holds true here too: while theme programs may go beyond the stories, they should never leave them too far behind.

Regularly scheduled group meetings, like library book clubs, summer reading clubs, and scouting meetings, all lend themselves well to an extended program. Of course classroom teachers are fortunate because they may be able to dedicate an entire week or even a month to a special theme—say "Farm Animal Week" or "Celebrate the Arts Month"—devoting a special hour each day or week to the chosen theme. Activities such as writing, word games, arts and crafts, or cooking can all be added to the program, so long as time, materials, and facilities permit.

You will find that theme programs can certainly be challenging to put together. Gathering all the materials that relate to a holiday, an animal, a season, or a subject can become a full-time scavenger hunt! Try not to get too carried away by including materials that may fit the theme, but that are mediocre and not worth the time and preparation they require. On the other hand, don't eliminate books or stories that you love, just because they never quite fit into your chosen themes. If you are locked into a Valentine's Day program, yet would dearly love to tell a story about an old grey wolf, you can always say something like, "I'd like to send a valentine to one of my favorite stories, 'The Old Grey Wolf'," and then go ahead and tell it. No one will mind if the story isn't about hearts and flowers.

When you are contemplating an activity make sure that you take into consideration the size of your group and the size of your facility. If you are going to teach a folk dance, you will need to remove any chairs that are in your hall. If you are teaching a cooking class, everyone may need to see what you are demonstrating on the stove. If you are putting together paper boxes, you will need to have enough table space, paper, and scissors. Think about the cost of the materials, and the time it may take to gather them together.

In this chapter, I've included three of my favorite, full-length theme programs (*The Moon and the Stars*, *Fashion*, and *Baseball*) that you can begin with immediately, simply by gathering the supplies called for and the books that are recommended. I've also included lots of less ambitious "mini-programs" that are so popular and easy to do, you'll wonder how you ever managed without them! Finally, I've included a special section on multi-cultural programming.

For more ideas, browse through the guides listed below. Some of these books may over emphasize the "curriculum," (thereby diminishing the idea that literature is fun!), but I think you'll find lots of useful activities, booklists, and story ideas here.

Booklist: Theme Program Resources

Bauer, Caroline Feller. *Celebrations: Read-Aloud Holiday and Theme Book Programs*. Art by Lynn Gates Bredeson. H. W. Wilson, 1985.

Drew, Ros. *Bears: Theme Unit*. Creative Teaching Press, 1990. (Creative Teaching Press, 10701 Holder St., Cypress, CA 90630, publishes a long list of thematic guides.)

Irving, Jan. *Fanfares: Programs for Classrooms and Libraries*. Art by Karen Myers. Libraries Unlimited, 1990.

Irving, Jan and Robin Currie. *Full Speed Ahead: Stories and Activities for Children on Transportation*. Art by Karen Wolf. Libraries Unlimited, 1988.

_____. *Raising the Roof: Children's Stories and Activities on Houses*. Art by Marijean Trew. Libraries Unlimited, 1991.

Jensen, Janice. *Literature-based Learning Activities Kit: Ready-to-use Whole Language Lessons and Worksheets for Grades 2–6.* Art by Susan Jerde. Center for Applied Research in Education, 1991.

Landes, Sonia. *A Curriculum Guide to the Tale of Peter Rabbit.* Book Wise (26 Arlington Street, Cambridge, MA 02140), 1987.

McElmeel, Sharron L. *My Bag of Book Tricks.* Art by Deborah L. McElmeel. Libraries Unlimited, 1989.

Parry, Caroline. *Let's Celebrate!* Kid Can, 1984.

The Moon and the Stars

One of my most popular programs for preschool, primary, and middle school children.

Tell

Many Moons by James Thurber. (Choose either the original, 1943 version with art by Louis Slobodkin, or the 1990 version with art by Marc Simont.) In this story Princess Lenore desperately wants the moon. The Lord High Chamberlain, The Royal Mathematician, and the Royal Wizard all find the task impossible. It is the Court Jester who finally gets the moon for the Princess. This story is long to learn, but it follows a logical sequence that should make your task easier. After you tell the story, you may want to share both the original and newer illustrations with your group. And . . . I promise not to tell if you would rather read the story than tell it!

Souvenir

Gold stars from stationery or craft stores or Full Moon Cookies from the recipe below.

Poetry

The moon in the water
Turned a somersault
And floated away.
—Ryata

How lovely,
Through the torn paper window
The Milky Way.
—Issa

The stars are too many to count.
The stars make sixes and sevens.
The stars tell nothing—and everything.
The stars look scattered.
Stars are so far away they never speak
     when spoken to.
                              —Carl Sandburg

IN A STARRY ORCHARD

Lean your ladder light
against a tree by night.

Climbing, examine how
stars hang on every bough.

Wearing a gossamer glove
on your right hand, remove

the ripest fruit of all:
that star about to fall.
                              —Norma Farber

STARS

It's very hard,
oh, very hard
to cut a paper star,

And so I blink
each time I think
how many stars there are.

I look up high
and think, "Oh, my,
the stars are bright and fine,

But who had time
to make them all
and get them all to shine?"
                              —Aileen Fisher

Activity

A Recipe for Full Moon Cookies
    People used to say that the moon was made of green cheese.
But what would the moon be like if it was made of peanut butter
and honey? Yummy. This recipe for Full Moon Cookies requires
no stove and no cooking.

You need: ½ cup wheat germ   3 cups dried milk
1½ cups peanut butter   ¾ cups graham cracker
1½ cups honey   crumbs
    Powdered sugar

How to: Mix ingredients thoroughly. Then form into balls and roll in powdered sugar. Makes about five dozen moons.

Books to Exhibit

Moon and star books—perfect before-bedtime reading.

Asch, Frank. *Happy Birthday Moon.* Art by author. Prentice, 1982. Bear finds the perfect present for the moon. Also *Mooncake* (Prentice, 1983).

Bradman, Tony. *It Came from Outer Space.* Art by Carol Wright. Dial, 1992. The surprise in this book is that the space person is from earth, the school children from another planet.

Greer, Gery and Bob Ruddick. *Let Me off This Spaceship!* Art by Blanche Sims. Harper, 1991. Tod and Billy are captured by space creatures in this wacky story.

Heckman, Philip. *The Moon Is Following Me.* Art by Mary O'Keefe Young. Atheneum, 1991. A child watches the full moon as her family drives home from a visit with her grandparents.

Hort, Lenny. *How Many Stars in the Sky?* Art by James E. Ransome. Tambourine, 1991. A young boy and his father drive into the country to count the stars.

Jones, Brian. *Space: A Three-Dimensional Journey.* Art by Richard Clifton-Day. Dial, 1991. A pop-up look at space.

Lewis, J. Patrick. *The Moonbow of Mr. B. Bones.* Art by Dirk Zimmer. Knopf, 1992. There really was a moonbow in the peddler's jar.

Osborne, Mary Pope. *Moonhorse.* Art by S. M. Saelig. Knopf, 1991. A winged horse takes a child on a ride through the night sky.

Oughton, Jerrie. *How the Stars Fell into the Sky: A Navajo Legend.* Art by Lisa Desimini. Houghton, 1992. A lovely narrative that explains the star patterns in the sky.

Ride, Sally with Susan Okie. *To Space and Back.* Lothrop, 1986. Color photos and an enthusiastic text give the reader an excellent view of space flight.

Ryder, Joanne. *The Bear on the Moon.* Art by Carol Lacey. Morrow, 1991. A polar bear plays on the "moon."

"The Sack of Diamonds" by Helen Kronberg Olson, in *Read for the Fun of It* by Caroline Feller Bauer. H. W. Wilson, 1992. An old woman uses her slingshot to put the stars in the sky.

Simon, Seymour. *Venus.* Illustrated with photographs. Morrow, 1992. This is just one of Simon's excellent photo essays on the stars and the planets.

Turner, Charles. *The Turtle and the Moon.* Art by Melissa Bay Mathis. Dutton, 1991. A lonely turtle makes friends with the moon.

Ungerer, Tomi. *Moon Man.* Art by author. Delacorte, 1966. Re-issued in 1991, this is a sophisticated story with art to match about the moonman who outwits the police by waxing and waning.

"Why the Sun and the Moon Live in the Sky" in *How Many Spots Does a Leopard Have?* by Julius Lester. Art by David Shannon. Scholastic, 1989.

"Finally the Sun and Moon were so high in the sky they weren't sure how to get down."

"The Wishing Star" in *Waiting-for-Spring Stories* by Bethany Roberts. Harper, 1984. Rabbit helps star get his wish.

Yolen, Jane. *Owl Moon*. Art by John Schoenherr. Philomel, 1987. Winner of the Caldecott award, this lovely book tells of a moonlit night and a search for owls.

Young, James. *Everyone Loves the Moon*. Art by author. Little, 1991. Cows, bears, and cats are among the animals that love the moon in this picture book poem.

Yorinks, Arthur. *Company's Coming*. Art by David Small. Crown, 1988. Moe and Shirley invite visitors from outer space to share a barbecue.

Fashion

This is an ever-popular program with middle school students and young adults.

Tell

"The Emperor's New Clothes" from *It's Perfectly True* by Hans Christian Andersen; translated by Paul Leyssac and illustrated by Vilhelm Pedersen. The Emperor is so vain he'll believe anything. This classic story can be found in most Andersen collections. Then go on to tell "Dinner with Halil" in *Once the Hodja* by Alice Geer Kelsey and illustrated by Frank Dobias. In this story, the Hodja thinks that a dinner invitation was issued to his clothes rather than to him.

Introduction

Have you ever wondered why we wear clothes? An obvious reason is for insulation against rain, wind, and cold. Protection against animals, insects, brambles, and plants might be another reason. Add to these the need for modesty, and we have many of the reasons for getting dressed in the morning! Clothing also serves to show others a certain social position. In order to be different, ladies and gentlemen of money and position adopt new clothing ideas. If enough people copy the new style, a fashion trend is born. Before 1900 only royalty could afford to play the game of fashion, but after the First World War, magazines, films, and "ready-to-wear" clothing brought the changes in fashion to millions of people. Today, designers invent new fashions for clothing manufacturers who, in cooperation with fashion magazines and textile manufacturers, promote new styles that influence current ideas about clothes.

Where do clothing designers get their ideas? The most talented use their own imaginations. The less experienced and less ingenious copy ideas from many different sources, including their competitors. Just standing on the street corner in what is considered the "fashionable part" of a large city might produce a few ideas. What are the trendsetters wearing?

Costume design in film and theater can constitute a source of ideas. Current fashion magazines that concentrate on "high fashion," or the most extreme fashions, can yield ideas for the trend-conscious. A look into the past will often yield ideas—what is "in" today may have been the height of fashion hundreds of years ago.

Can books be the source of fashion ideas? People wear clothes in books, of course. Let's look at some children's books for possible ideas.

Activities

Fashions in children's books. Choose books from your library's collection that show contemporary clothing as well as "fairy-tale" or imaginative clothing. Let your group browse through the books. If possible, your students should be seated around tables so that they can better share the books. They may come to the conclusion that artists aren't very imaginative when it comes to clothing, or they might find that fairy-tale people seem to be more creatively dressed than characters in contemporary stories. This is one way of getting young adults to take a close look at some of our better picture books, too.

Here are four brief fashion analyses:

Buck, Pearl S. *The Chinese Story Teller.* Art by Regina Shekerjian. John Day, 1971. The children are wearing colorful, simple summer clothes and the grandmother a classic long-sleeved dress of simple cut.

　The story then shifts to a much earlier era. The crowd is wearing traditional Chinese peasant costumes: cotton coats with frog closings and pants. Cloth slippers cover their feet.

　The next part of the book is a retelling of an old Chinese folktale. The people are wearing more formal classic Chinese dress. The artist has used a folk art of China: paper cutouts to dress his characters. The story ends with a return to the modern scene, but this time Grandma is drawn only in outline and her dress could almost be an old Chinese gown.

De Brunhoff, Jean. *The Story of Babar;* translated from the French by Merle Haas. Art by author. Random, 1937. This book was first published in France in 1933, but it is still enjoyed today by adults as well as children. Like many children's stories, this book is about an animal, in this instance an elephant, that dresses like a person.

　In the forest where he is born Babar wears no clothes but when he arrives in the city he buys "a shirt with a collar and tie, a suit of a becoming shade of green, then a handsome derby hat, and also shoes with spats";

then he has his picture taken. Although this book was written so long ago, and maybe men (or elephants) no longer wear hats, the artist gives the feel of Babar as a well-dressed gentleman. The old lady, his friend, wears a black dress throughout the book, and the reader feels she is properly attired for the gentle friend that she is. When Babar's cousins Arthur and Celeste arrive from the forest, they also arrive with no clothes and Babar buys them "some fine clothes"—for Arthur a red and white sailor suit and for Celeste a polka dot dress. The clothes seem to be ageless and clearly tell the story.

Goodall, John S. *Great Days of a Country House*. Art by author. Macmillan, 1992. This book shows the life and times of a country house in Britain from the Tudor period (1485) through the present day. Double spread art shows the fashions of the times from the perspectives of both the gentry and the working class. It is particularly interesting to note the very formal clothing worn throughout the book, until the present day when almost anything seems in fashion.

Zemach, Harve. *Duffy and the Devil: A Cornish Tale*. Art by Margot Zemach. Farrar, 1973. Margot Zemach won a Caldecott award for the illustrations in this book, mostly of people.

At the beginning of the story Duffy is described as a "lazy bufflehead" who "gallivants with the boys all day long and never stops at home to boil the porridge, nor knit the stockings, nor spin the yarn!" The artist shows this "gashly" girl with untidy braids, overweight, her stockings falling down, and her weskit unbuttoned.

When the girl marries and becomes Lady Duffy Lovel of Trove, she wears "satin gowns and the best of silks and laces and red-heeled shoes from France."

Despite her new riches, Duffy is still the same girl and the artist shows her overdressed and hair still straggling from under her bonnet.

As for the artist's interpretation of Squire Lovel's clothes, well, what could be funnier than the climax of the story when the Squire's "stockings dropped from his legs and the homespun from his back. He had to come home with nothing on but his hat and his shoes."

Up for discussion. Voice your opinions about clothing:

a. Do you wear what you feel comfortable in or what your friends are wearing, or what your parents choose for you?

b. Who are the "trendsetters" in your class? What gives them this distinction?

c. Do clothes seem to be more comfortable today than 100 years ago? What does this show about changing life-styles?

d. Do clothes give a person status? Can you tell by what a person is wearing which his or her profession is?

e. Does your school have a dress code? Do you think this should be enforced? Is it useful or necessary?

f. Do you think it is improper to wear a bikini to church or temple on a hot day? Why or why not?

g. What is the purpose of wearing a uniform?

h. Which would you rather have: one costly pair of pants or several less expensive ones?

i. Which would you rather have if you were a skier: good equipment or fashionable clothes? Why?

j. Is being one of the "Ten Best Dressed People in America" an enviable position?

k. Do hair styles, shoe styles, and skirt lengths reflect something about our society?

Fashion observation. Stand in a busy intersection or on your high school campus. Take notes on what most people seem to be wearing. Summarize the fashion of that particular group. The same thing can be done with those in a room. Include hair styles in your observations. Provide each observer with his or her own fashion notebook (see Favor).

Fashion design. Provide paper and felt tip pens, crayons, charcoal, pencils, scraps of fabric, a collection of buttons, beads, trim, and glue. Individually, in pairs, or as a group, solve one of the following fashion problems by drawing or making a collage:

Design shoes for the year 2500
Design a hat to wear to a coronation
Design a child's outfit for Christmas morning
Design a ball gown for Cinderella
Design an ornament for a man or woman
Design a fabric for a dress or tie
Design an outfit for your first trip to Venus.

If your group has designed individually, let each participant or pair of participants give a fashion show by describing the fabric, style, price, and function of the clothes they have designed.

Newspaper fashion show

Provide: A stack of newspapers
Several pairs of scissors
A roll of masking tape

How to: Divide the larger group into groups of five. Have each group design and make some sort of body covering in fifteen minutes to model before the class. Each small group should choose a fashion commentator to describe each model's costume.

Favor

Fashion notebook. Use the pages of a mail-order catalog or fashion magazine as the covers for a notebook. Staple sheets of blank paper to the cover for the fashion observers to use in taking notes on current fashions.

Note: This program should include both sexes. Some of us tend to believe that only girls are interested in clothes, yet the multi-billion dollar fashion industry is dominated by men.

Books to Exhibit

Boucher, François. *20,000 Years of Fashion: The History of Costume and Personal Adornment.* Expanded edition. Illustrated. Abrams, 1987.

Martin, Linda. *The Way We Were: Fashion Illustrations of Children's Wear 1870–1970.* Scribner, 1978.

Mulvagh, Jane. *Vogue Fashion: History of the 20th Century.* Illustrated. Viking, 1988.

O'Hara, Georgina. *The Encyclopedia of Fashion.* Illustrated. Abrams, 1986.

Peacock, John. *The Chronicle of Western Fashion.* Abrams, 1991.

Wilcox, Claire. *Modern Fashion in Detail.* Overlook, 1991.

Yarwood, Doreen. *Costume of the Western World: Pictorial Guide and Glossary.* Art by author. St. Martins, 1980.

Baseball

A perfect springtime program for anyone who likes baseball.

Tell or read aloud

"The Southpaw" by Judith Viorst in *Free to Be ... You and Me*, edited by Francine Klagsbrun. Two friends share barbs when Richard won't let Janet play on his team. (I like to read this story from torn scraps of paper, as if I'm actually reading from Richard and Janet's letters to each other.)

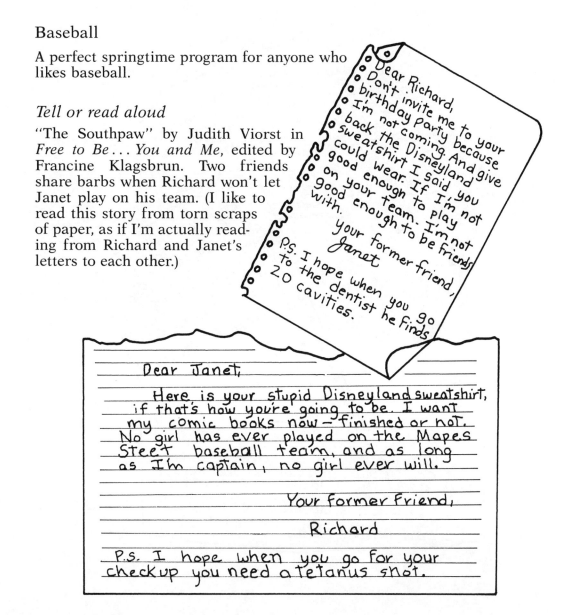

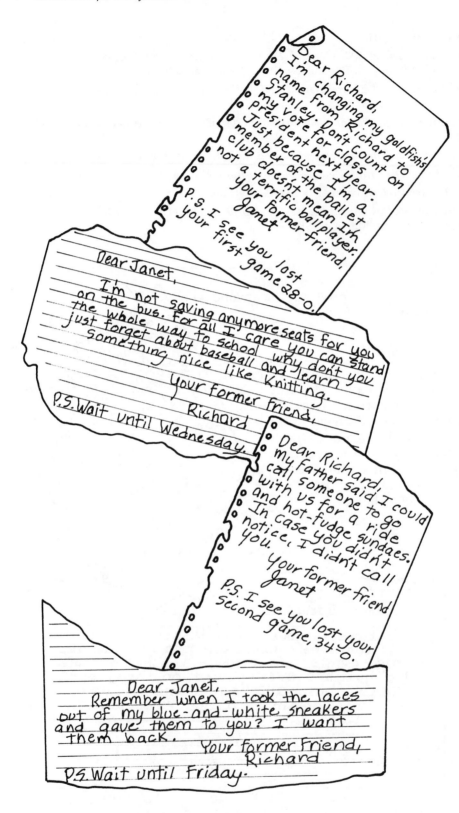

Dear Richard,
I'm changing my goldfish's name from Richard to Stanley. Don't count on my vote for class president next year. Just because I'm a member of the ballet club doesn't mean I'm not a terrific ballplayer.
Your former friend,
Janet
P.S. I see you lost your first game 28-0.

Dear Janet,
I'm not saving any more seats for you on the bus. For all I care you can stand the whole way to school. Why don't you just forget about baseball and learn something nice like knitting.
Your former friend,
Richard
P.S. Wait until Wednesday.

Dear Richard, I could my father said I call someone to go with us for a ride and hot-fudge sundaes. In case you didn't notice, I didn't call you.
Your former friend
Janet
P.S. I see you lost your second game, 34-0.

Dear Janet,
Remember when I took the laces out of my blue-and-white sneakers and gave them to you? I want them back.
Your former friend,
Richard
P.S. Wait until Friday.

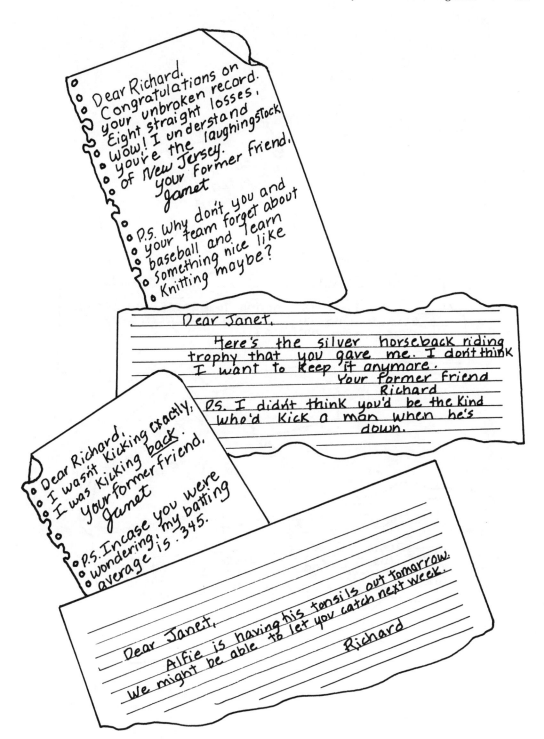

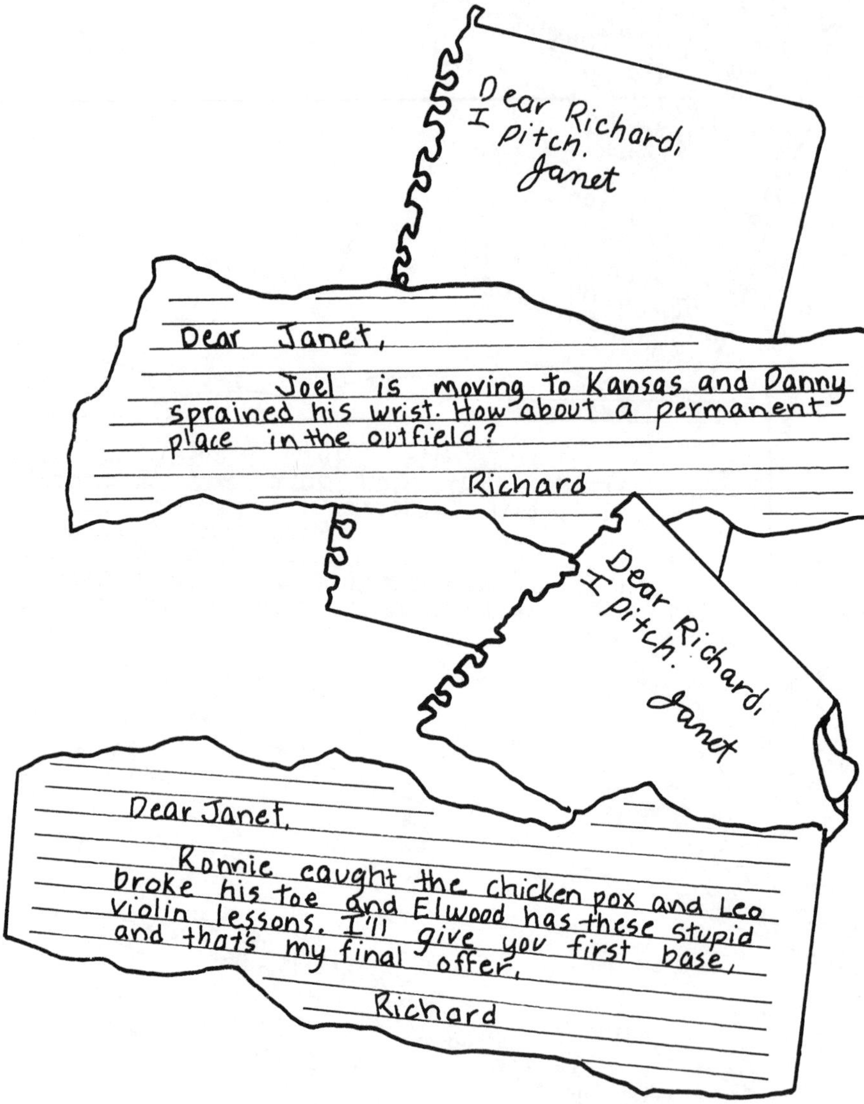

Dear Richard,
I pitch.
Janet

Dear Janet,

Joel is moving to Kansas and Danny sprained his wrist. How about a permanent place in the outfield?

Richard

Dear Richard,
I pitch.
Janet

Dear Janet,

Ronnie caught the chicken pox and Leo broke his toe and Elwood has these stupid violin lessons. I'll give you first base, and that's my final offer.

Richard

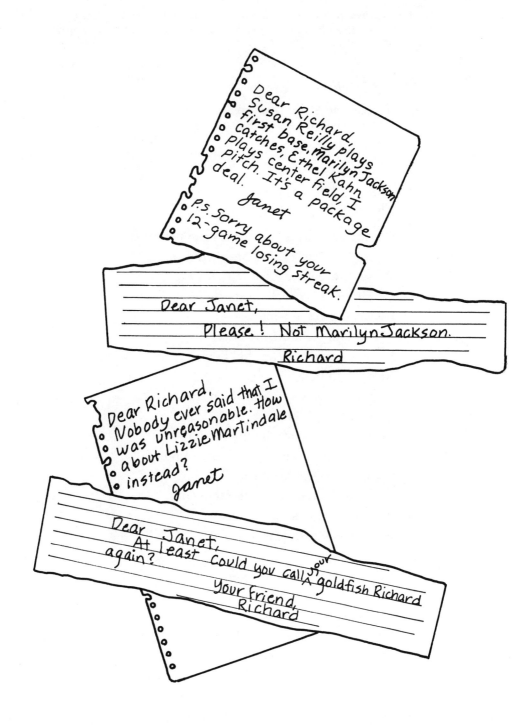

Baseball Program

More stories, poetry, riddles, booklist, and activities in "B Is for Baseball" in
  Celebrations by Caroline Feller Bauer. Art by Lynn Gates Bredeson. H. W.
  Wilson, 1985.

Magic Trick

Basch's Baseball Pitch. This magic trick is available with baseball cards and
  patter from Joyce Basch, Box 683, Cypress, CA 90630.

Baseball Terms

Post these on a bulletin board or read aloud to demonstrate the vagaries of the
  English language. (From *The Joy of Lex* by Gyles Brandreth, Quill, 1983)

He was born with two strikes against him.

He couldn't get to first base with that girl.

He sure threw me a curve that time.

I'll take a rain check on it.

He went to bat for me.

I liked him right off the bat.

He was way out in left field on that one.

He's a foul ball.

I think you're way off base on that.

It was a smash hit.

Let's take a seventh inning stretch.

I hope to touch all bases on this report.

Could you pinch-hit for me?

He doesn't even know who's on first.

I just call 'em as I see 'em.

He's only a bush leaguer.

Major league all the way.

We'll hit 'em where they ain't.

He was safe by a mile.

He has a lot on the ball.

He really dropped the ball that time.

We'll rally in the ninth.

No game's over until the last man's out.

Activity

A Recipe for Baseball Cookies

Make the Full Moon Cookies, given in *The Moon and the
Stars* program, but call them Baseball Cookies instead!

Books to Exhibit

Adler, David. A. *Jackie Robinson: He Was the First.* Art by Robert Casilla. Holiday, 1989. Ages 8–12. A short biography that spans this very famous baseball player's life from boyhood to major league.

Berkow, Ira. *Hank Greenberg: Hall of Fame Slugger.* Art by Mick Ellison. Jewish Publication Society, 1991. Ages 9–12. From the Bronx to the ballpark with a famous home-run hitter.

Christopher, Matt. *The Lucky Baseball Bat.* Art by Dee deRosa. Little, 1991. Ages 7–9. Martin loses his lucky bat. Will he regain his confidence? Look for other stories by this author.

Day, Alexandra. *Frank and Ernest Play Ball.* Scholastic, 1990. All ages. Learn baseball slang with a bear and an elephant.

Gollenbock, Peter. *Teammates.* Art by Paul Bacon. Harcourt, 1990. Ages 7–12. Pee Wee Reese publicly shows his friendship for Jackie Robinson, the first black major league player.

Herzig, Alison Cragin. *The Boonsville Bombers.* Art by Dan Andreasen. Viking, 1991. Ages 7–10. Emma wants to be on her brother's baseball team.

Hotze, Sollace. *Summer Endings.* Clarion, 1991. Ages 9–12. Christine sells tickets for fans to watch the Wrigley Field baseball games from her terrace at the end of World War II.

Hurwitz, Johanna. *Baseball Fever.* Art by Ray Cruz. Morrow, 1981. Ages 7–11. Ezra loves the Mets, but his father would rather play chess.

Kessler, Leonard. *Old Turtle's Baseball Stories.* Greenwillow, 1982. Ages 6–9. A team of animal players tell stories of the games of summer.

Latimer, Jim. *Fox under First Base.* Art by Lisa McCue. Scribner's, 1991. Ages 7–10. Detective Chief Inspector Porcupine investigates the disappearance of 100 baseballs. You'll meet Fox and Bear in this read-aloud choice.

Rosenbloom, Joseph. *Sports Riddles.* Art by Sam Q. Weissman. Harcourt, 1982. Ages 6–9. Baseball is featured in some of these silly riddles.

Rosenblum, Richard. *Brooklyn Dodger Day.* Art by author. Atheneum, 1991. Ages 6–9. In picture-book format, a 1946 Dodger game is described from a boy's point of view.

Thayer, Ernest Lawrence. *Casey at the Bat.* Art by Paul Frame. Prentice, 1964. All ages! The classic poem illustrated with photo-like drawings.

For Young Adults and Adults

Alexander, Charles C. *Our Game: An American Baseball History.* Holt, 1991. A narrative history of the game.

Cromartie, Warren with Robert Whiting. *Slugging It Out in Japan.* Kodansha International, 1991. An American ball player joins a Japanese team.

Dickson, Paul. *Baseball's Greatest Quotations.* Harper, 1991. A giant collection of quotes about baseball.

Dinhofer, Shelly Mehlman. *The Art of Baseball.* Harmony, 1990. Paintings, sculpture, and folk art all about baseball in a "coffee table" offering.

Einstein, Charles, ed. *The Fireside Book of Baseball.* 4th ed. Simon, 1987. Articles, fiction, and poetry

The Face of Baseball. Photos by John Weiss. Essay by Wilfrid Sheed. Thomasson Grant (Charlottesville, Va.), 1990.

Shaara, Michael. *For Love of the Game*. Carroll and Graf, 1991. A novel about a baseball legend's last game.

Thorn, John and Pete Palmer, eds. *Total Baseball*. 2nd ed. Warner, 1991. For the truly dedicated fan, 2,628 pages of baseball statistics.

Games

Grand Slam Baseball Board Game (Grand Slam Pastimes, Box 2049, Elizabethtown, KY 42701).

Sports Illustrated Superstar Baseball (Avalon Hill Game Co., Baltimore, MD 21214).

Strat-O-Matic Baseball. Strat-o-matic (46 Railroad Pl., Glenhead, NY 11545).

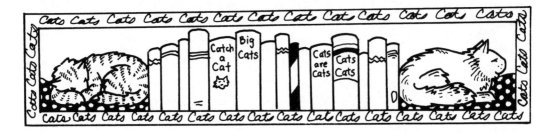

Mini-Theme Programs

Use the resources of your school or public library to try these short and easy storytelling programs.

Catch a Cat Idea

Share *Millions of Cats* by Wanda Gág (Coward, 1928). Tell this classic children's tale with your listeners wearing cat masks they can make themselves. Using paper or light poster board, enlarge the pattern shown here, or create your own. Finish the mask with yarn whiskers and yarn stapled to the mask for attaching to the head.

Activity

Cat Game

Play the "Minister's Cat" with your group.

How to: Players sit in a circle. The leader says, "The Minister's Cat is an able cat." The next player must add an attribute to the Minister's Cat that begins with B, like "The Minister's Cat is a beastly cat." The next player's description must begin with C, "The Minister's Cat is a clever cat," and so on around the circle. If a player can't think of a word, he or she is out. The next person in line begins at the point where the previous player missed, or, for variety, at any point in the alphabet.

Exhibit or share the following books:

Larrick, Nancy, ed. *Cats Are Cats.* Philomel, 1988. This is a selection of poems about cats with glorious art by Caldecott winner, Ed Young.

Simon, Seymour. *Big Cats.* Harper, 1991. This photo essay describes the characteristics of the tiger, the lion, and the jaguar.

Stevens, Janet. *How the Manx Cat Lost Its Tail.* Art by author. Harcourt, 1990. This is a Noah's ark variant with action-filled art to share.

Read a Duck

Share a book featuring ducks (there are many in the library); then wow your children with a string of ducks. Enlarge the template shown to 8½ inches in height. Accordian fold drawing paper or tissue paper to fit the template, then cut out the spaces and open the ducks.

Here are some duck book suggestions:

Dabcovich, Lydia. *Ducks Fly.* Art by author. Dutton, 1990. A little duck learns to fly when . . . he has to!

Ellis, Anne Leo. *Dabble Duck.* Art by Sue Truesdell. Harper, 1984. Jason and his duck Dabble adopt a hurt puppy.

Flack, Marjorie. *Angus and the Ducks.* Art by author. Doubleday, 1930. Angus, the scotty, is curious about the strange animals on the other side of the fence.

Gibson, Betty. *The Story of Little Quack.* Art by Kady MacDonald Denton. Little, Brown, 1991. A duck befriends a little boy.

Gordon, Gaelyn. *Duckat.* Art by Chris Gaskin. Scholastic, 1992. A duck acts like a cat.

McCloskey, Robert. *Make Way for Ducklings* Art by author. Viking, 1941. The classic story about a family of ducks in Boston.

Pinkwater, Daniel. *Ducks!* Art by author. Little, Brown, 1984. Only Pinkwater could write this rather bizarre story of a duck encountered in a candy store.

Moose versus Wolf

Tell, share aloud, or present with puppets:

Mucky Moose by Jonathan Allen (Macmillan, 1991). A yucky mucky moose is so dirty that a wolf can't manage to capture him. This selection is silly and very funny.

Accompany this telling with a moose puppet from Gund (Edison, N. J.) or use a soft, silky stuffed moose available from Furrywinkles (Carousel, P.O. Box 1328, Minneapolis, Minnesota 55440). Also, Dakin makes an expressive wolf puppet (1649 Adrian Rd., Burlingame, CA 94010).

Exhibit or share the following:

Latimer, Jim. *Going the Moose Way Home.* Art by Donald Carrick. Scribner, 1988. These short stories feature a warm-hearted moose. These tales are short enough to learn to tell and charming.

Lawrence, R.D. *Wolves.* Sierra Club/Little, 1990. This offers a non-fiction description of the lives of wolves, excellent color photos to share.

Locker, Thomas. *The Land of Gray Wolf.* Dial, 1991. Full-color paintings depict the story of land destroyed, land renewed, and the return of the wolf.

Murphy, Jim. *The Call of the Wolves.* Art by Mark A. Weatherby. Scholastic, 1989. Illegal hunters disturb the natural lives of a pack of wolves in this picture book.

Numeroff, Laura Joffe. *If You Give a Moose a Muffin.* Art by Felicia Bond. Harper, 1991. Amusing text and art describe what happens when you give a moose a muffin.

Wiseman, B. *Morris the Moose.* Harper, 1989. Morris mistakes a cow and a deer for a moose—an I Can Read title.

The Frog Prince Revisited

Tell your favorite version of "The Frog Prince," then share one or all of the following:

"Ali Baba and Princess Farrah" from *Ali Baba Bernstein* by Johanna Hurwitz (Morrow, 1985). Valerie and David Bernstein (aka Ali Baba Bernstein) dare each other to kiss a frog. A scripted version of this chapter appears in *Presenting Reader's Theater* by Caroline Feller Bauer (H. W. Wilson, 1989).

Grimm, Jacob. *The Frog Prince.* McGraw, 1974. This version of the traditional tale is illustrated with Paul Galdone's lively art.

Isele, Elizabeth. *The Frog Princess.* Art by Michael Hague. Crowell, 1984. Ivan must marry a frog.

Scieszka, Jon. *The Frog Prince Continued.* Art by Steve Johnson. Viking, 1991. And now that he is a prince and married, does he live happily ever after?

Vesey, A. *The Princess and the Frog.* Art by author. Little, 1985. Although the frog is kissed by a princess, he remains . . . a frog.

Activity

Teach your group to make the paper-folded frog in chapter 1.

Walk a Story

Take a walk and pretend you are an animal, an old woman, or a robot. Now share one or all of these:

Anholt, Catherine. *Tom's Rainbow Walk.* Art by author. Little, 1989. Grandma knits Tom a sweater with all the colors of the rainbow. Give each child a piece of rainbow yarn to take home as a souvenir.

Kasza, Keiko. *When the Elephant Walks.* Art by author. Putnam's, 1990. This is a circle story that can easily be acted out. Animals scare each other when the elephant takes a walk.

Turner, Ethel. *Walking to School.* Art by Peter Gouldthorpe. Orchard, 1989. A five-year-old bravely walks to school. Peter Gouldthorpe's art is reminiscent of old photographs.

Williams, Sue. *I Went Walking.* Art by Julie Vivas. Harcourt, 1989. The large format and clear simple drawings make this the perfect book to share with a group. Act this out too.

Celebrate the Inanimate

Ever wonder if a chair could fall in love?

Tell

Annette Penny's "Sunday Boots and Working Boots" in *The Read-to-Me Treasury*, ed. by Sally Grindley (Doubleday, 1989). A pair of working boots find that they are special after all.

Then share these with a group:

Pochocki, Ethel. *Rosebud and Red Flannel*. Holt, 1991. An uppity nightgown finally falls in love with a lowly but caring pair of longjohns. A delight to tell or share aloud. An original choice for Valentine's Day.

Tennyson, Noel. *The Lady's Chair and the Ottoman*. Art by author. Lothrop, 1987. An ottoman longs to be near his love—a lady's chair.

Woolf, Virginia. *Nurse Lugton's Curtain*. Art by Julie Vivas. Harcourt, 1991. The animals depicted on Nurse's curtain come alive when she naps. Vivas's art work is worth sharing.

Activity

Do you own an object that leads a secret life? Tell or write a story about it.

Knitting

Do you know how to knit? Most children these days have never seen anyone knitting. Show your children how to do it.

Tell

Little Things by Anne Laurin. Art by Marcia Sewall (Atheneum, 1978). Mrs. B knits and knits while Mr. B waits patiently for meals. When the blanket Mrs. B is knitting completely covers the house and the yard, Mr. B takes action. If you are a knitter, you could give each member of the audience a knitted square.

And share or exhibit:

Blackwood, Mary. *Derek the Knitting Dinosaur*. Art by Kerry Argent. Carolrhoda, 1990. Derek's talent saves his family from freezing.

Wild, Margaret. *Mr. Nick's Knitting*. Art by Dee Huxley. Harcourt, 1988. Mr. Nick and Mrs. Jolly knit together on the train every morning, but one day Mrs. Jolly isn't on the train. . . .

Potatoes

Yes, even the lowly potato can be the theme of your story session.

Tell

"The Potato Party" in *The Potato Party and Other Troll Tales* by Loreen Leedy. Art by author (Holiday, 1989). A troll family tries to solve their problem of eating too many potatoes.

And share or exhibit:

Lobel, Anita. *Potatoes, Potatoes*. Art by author. Harper, 1967. The theme of this book is that wars are never won.

McDonald, Megan. *The Potato Man*. Art by Ted Lewin, Orchard, 1991. A young boy teases a potato man on East Street.

Porter, Sue. *One Potato*. Art by author. Bradbury, 1989. Four farm animals argue over a single potato. The illustrations are big enough to share with a large group.

Activity

Decorate potato heads.

You need: Odd-shaped potatoes, one for each member in your group
A selection of vegetables such as olives, broccoli, carrots
Toothpicks

How to: Using the toothpicks, attach vegetables to potatoes to create interesting characters. Then let your group create a dialogue between the finished potatoes.

A Story in a Box

Wrap a box up as a present. Open it to reveal another box. And then another. Tell your children that inside *this* box is the magic of stories.

Tell

"The Box" by Bruce Colville in *Dragons and Dreams*, ed. by Jane Yolen, Martin H. Greenberg, and Charles G. Waugh (Harper, 1986). This is a rather puzzling story about a boy who carries around a box given to him by an angel.

After you have told the story, share one or more of these books to show your audience what other authors have done with the idea of "box."

Boyd, Lizi. *Willy and the Cardboard Boxes*. Art by author. Viking, 1991. Willy's dad gives him some boxes to play with when he visits the office.

Hale, Irina. *Boxman*. Art by author. Viking, 1992. Bob wears a box on his head all day long.

Lillegard, Dee. *Sitting in My Box*. Art by Jon Agee. Dutton, 1989. A little boy is visited by jungle animals as he sits in a cardboard box. Good to use with creative drama or stuffed animals.

Shannon, George. *The Box*. Art by Jose Aruego and Ariane Dewey. Greenwillow, 1983. Mom's present is a box within a box within a box that contains her son, Squirrel.

Weiss, Nicki. *Surprise Box*. Art by author. Putnam, 1991. Minimal text and colorful art show a little girl surprising her granny with a surprise box.

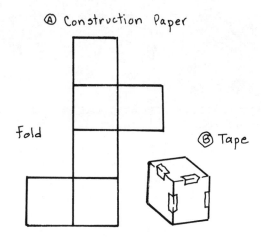

ⒶConstruction Paper

Fold

ⒷTape

Activity

Make a box. Put your thoughts in it.

Multicultural Programs

When I was a child there were very few books featuring children of African-American, Asian-American, Latino, or American Indian descent. Many of the books that were read then eventually fell into disrepute: *Little Black Sambo, Epaminondas,* and, until it was edited, *The Story of Doctor Dolittle.* Julius Lester and Van Dyke Park's new versions of the Joel Chandler Harris's Brer Rabbit stories have kept these tales alive despite racist overtones in the original versions.

In the 1960s a new awareness of our pluralistic society resulted in a rash of "multicultural" books. Many of these were poorly written and have long since disappeared. I still have some of them, though, because I was so thrilled that finally there were books that included everyone.

In the beginning, many of the publishers eager to fairly represent all cultures had their artists paint every third child black, every fourth child Asian, and so on. It was forced and it looked forced. By the 1970s and 1980s, we got better at representing children of various ethnic groups, but the exciting trend of multicultural books had waned.

Now in the 1990s there is an explosion of books that attempt to show children as they live in other countries and throughout the United States. However, as we see more and more new books for all ages, there is also increasing criticism that many of these books do not reflect the authentic experiences of many ethnic groups.

I think we need to approach this category of literature in two ways. The first way is not to isolate it in a category of its own at all—but to make sure that our everyday storytelling programs are as ethnically diverse as we are. In my baseball program above, for instance, I've included two very different books about Jackie Robinson, the first African American to play baseball in the major leagues. In my winter holiday programs, I like to

include books about Christmas, Hanukkah, Chinese New Year, and Kwanzaa—an African-American holiday festival. The objective here, of course, is to illustrate the richness of American culture in every storytelling program, rather than reserving "multicultural" books for special, isolated occasions.

The second way is to celebrate a special event—Martin Luther King, Jr.'s birthday or Cinco de Mayo, for instance—by developing a book program that explores a particular culture through folktales, contemporary stories, picture books, and so on. This may appear to contradict what I have just said above! But the important thing to remember is that such special programs shouldn't be a substitute for including multicultural literature in all of our programs. They simply provide an opportunity to introduce children, young adults, and adults to a wonderful variety of folklore, fiction, and informational books on very special occasions.

I wish you were here with me so that I could show you some of the books that surround me as I write. I'll show them to you anyway. Don't be sad if I don't talk about your particular favorite; unfortunately, we don't have time to look at them all here.

Here's one that I read as a child. I loved it then and still own it. I'm afraid to reread it, though, lest there are inaccuracies or racist overtones. I tell everyone that all I know about South America is in this book: *Donald Duck Sees South America*. You see, we moved many times when I was a child. And practically every time we moved, it seemed, the class had just finished a study of South America, or was just about to study the continent as my family prepared to leave. But one of the facts that stuck with me for 40 years was proven on a trip to Brazil. In the book, Donald is unhappy because he doesn't speak Spanish. He hires tutors who come in and teach him the language every night and every day and even in the shower-bath. As a child I found the picture of Donald taking his bath with a battery of tutors speaking to him very funny. It still gives me a chuckle. When Donald emerges from his hotel in Rio, he discovers that the Brazilians speak Portuguese and not Spanish!

Other people must have enjoyed this book as much as I did, because it is still occasionally available in secondhand bookstores.

A book I've been showing around the world is Peter Spier's *People*. The year that it was published I was chair of the Notable Books Committee for the Children's Division of the American

Library Association. I was disappointed that the book didn't make the notable list and lobbied for it shamelessly. To me it foreshadowed a whole new trend in the ways in which we depict people different from ourselves. Formerly, I think, we tried to illustrate that we were all the same. "Everyone has a nose. Everyone has two eyes," we would tell our children. But Peter Spier told it differently in numerous small drawings that show how people are different one from the other. He shows different eye shapes, different noses, different homes, different food, different clothing. He concludes by pointing out that it would be "dreadfully dull" if we all looked and acted the same. How wonderful it is that each and everyone of us is different. Celebrating the individuality of people is the theme of this book. Why didn't it make the list? Several members on the committee objected to several of the drawings. Showing that some people like noise, while others prefer quiet, Spier shows a librarian with a finger to her mouth, obviously saying "shh." I have a feeling that this tired symbol offended some of the librarians on the committee. And, I remember, some of the committee members objected to a picture of a jail illustrating that some people are good and others bad. "Who says that just because you're in jail you are 'bad?'" someone questioned.

Here are several collections to help acquaint you with the wonderful variety of multicultural literature available.

Coming to America

Leonard Everett Fisher's *Ellis Isand*, William Jay Jacobs's *Ellis Island*, and Russell Freedman's *Immigrant Kids* show through photographs the arrival of many immigrants in America at Ellis Island and their adjustment to life in America.

A New Home in America

Books showing a more recent immigrant experience are available for both children and young adults. *Children of the River* by Linda Crew is a thoughtful and revealing novel about a 15-year-old Cambodian girl who comes to a farming community in Oregon, and her reactions to her new life in America. *New Kids on the Block* is a series of interviews with teenagers newly arrived in the United States and their candid views on life here. Maxine Rosenberg follows four children from different countries in *Making a New Home in America*.

American Lives

Photo essays show children from different ethnic backgrounds as they go about growing up in America. *Eskimo Boy* is an honest portrayal that beautifully illustrates the experience of living in an Inupiaq Eskimo village, while it shows a father's drinking problem. *Hector Lives in the United States Now* is the story of a Mexican-American child; *Pueblo Boy: Growing Up in Two Worlds* depicts a Pueblo Indian boy's life in New Mexico; while *Hoang Anh: A Vietnamese-American Boy* tells the story of a boy who eats pizza and plays football while he continues to enjoy his Vietnamese heritage.

Learning about Children in Other Countries

Two photographers introduce Americans to children in other countries in two separate series. Jan Reynolds has captured the life and setting of people in a series titled "Vanishing Cultures." *Down Under* features the aborigines of Australia; *Far North* shows us the life of the Samis in Finmark or Lapland. The Tuareg of the Sahara are depicted in *Sahara,* and the Sherpa and Tibetan people are shown in *Himalaya.* Matti A. Pitkanen's series introduces the reader to the lives of children in China and Tibet, and to the grandchildren of the Incas in South America. Looking at these photos will give you a glimpse into a way of life that is fast disappearing and help illustrate to your children that not everyone's life experience is the same.

Picture Books Tell the Story

Beautifully illustrated picture books also give us an inside view of life in other countries and in the United States. In *The Day of Ahmed's Secret* we get a chance to follow a young boy and his donkey cart through the busy streets of Cairo. In *New Shoes for Silvia,* a little girl in Nicaragua grows into her new shoes. In *Somewhere in Africa,* we learn about a boy who lives in a city instead of our imagined Africa of wild animals, and in *Chicken Sunday* children in a multi-ethnic neighborhood find a way to earn the money to buy Eula Mae Walker a special Easter bonnet.

Biography

The Invisible Thread by Yoshiko Uchida is the autobiography of a Japanese-American children's author. In her fiction she has told about the Japanese internment during World War II. Here she writes about her own experiences in an internment camp.

Ragtime Tumpie is a picture book biography of the exotic dancer Josephine Baker. The book shows Josephine as a child and only in an author's note at the end does the author tell us that this child who was so interested in music and dance grew up to be a famous resistance fighter and dancer.

Booklist

Bode, Janet. *New Kids on the Block: Oral Histories of Immigrant Teens.* Watts, 1989.

Crew, Linda. *Children of the River.* Delacorte, 1989.

Fisher, Leonard Everett. *Ellis Island: Gateway to the New World.* Holiday, 1986.

Freedman, Russell. *Immigrant Kids*. Illustrated with photos. Dutton, 1980.

Heide, Florence Parry and Judith Heide Gilliland. *The Day of Ahmed's Secret*. Art by Ted Lewin. Lothrop, 1990.

Hewett, Joan. *Hector Lives in the United States Now: The Story of a Mexican-American Child*. Photos by Richard Hewett. Lippincott, 1990.

Hoyt-Goldsmith, Diane. *Hoang Anh: A Vietnamese-American Boy*. Photos by Lawrence Migdale. Holiday, 1992.

Hurwitz, Johanna. *New Shoes for Silvia*. Art by Amy Pickney. Morrow, 1993.

Jacobs, William Jay. *Ellis Island: New Hope in a New Land*. Scribner, 1990.

Keegan, Marcia. *Pueblo Boy: Growing Up in Two Worlds*. Cobblehill, 1991.

Kendall, Russ. *Eskimo Boy: Life in an Inupiaq Eskimo Village*. Illustrated with photos. Scholastic, 1992.

Mennen, Ingrid and Niki Daly. *Somewhere in Africa*. Art by Nicolaas Maritz. *Somewhere in Africa*. Dutton, 1990.

Pitkänen, Matti A. *The Children of Nepal*. Photos by author. Carolrhoda, 1990.

Polacco, Patricia. *Chicken Sunday*. Art by author. Philomel, 1992.

Reynolds, Jan. *Down Under: Vanishing Cultures*. Harcourt, 1992.

_____. *Far North: Vanishing Cultures*. Harcourt, 1992.

_____. *Himalaya: Vanishing Cultures*. Harcourt, 1991.

_____. *Sahara: Vanishing Cultures*. Harcourt, 1991.

Rosenberg, Maxine B. *Making a New Home in America*. Photos by George Ancona. Lothrop, 1986.

Schroeder, Alan. *Ragtime Tumpie*. Art by Bernie Fuchs. Joy Street/Little, 1989.

Uchida, Yoshiko. *The Invisible Thread*. Messner, 1991.

25 / Book Parties

If you agree with me that enjoying books and stories is as important as eating, you will probably understand that storytelling should not be confined to a particular time and place: between math and science, or between dinner and bed. In fact, why not combine your love of books with your love of food. At the next party you give, you can feature books and serve book-related goodies. Snack time can also be both book- and food-oriented. When you plan a special storyhour or book program serve a treat appropriate to the occasion. You might find that you can call on parents to lend their time and talents for this project. My friend Johanna, a school librarian, almost always serves a book treat along with stories. Wouldn't you like to go to her school?

Placecards and Placemats

In a more formal party situation, you can begin by setting the table with a book theme. Choose a book or subject to feature. Tell a story. When the story is finished, provide the guests with paper and crayons to design their own place cards and place mats. Suggest that they illustrate the story they just heard. Less creative, but still decorative, is to make outline drawings of the book and allow the children to color them. For a more permanent book place mat, use poster board and cover the drawing with clear contact paper or laminate. Felt cutouts can also be used to decorate colored poster board and covered with acetate.

Book Decorations to Look at or Eat

Make book-shaped ornaments to decorate a home, library, classroom, Christmas tree, or for a special party.

Baker's Clay Decorations

This dough is inedible, to be used for decorative purposes only! However, even though these "cookies" are not meant for eating, they are certainly not poisonous. My dog once ate an ornament in the shape of a "Wild Thing" with great relish and was still full of energy to beg for more.

Blueberries for Sal

You will need:
    4 cups unsifted all-purpose flour
    1 cup salt
    1½ cups water

How to: Combine ingredients and mix thoroughly with hands. More water can be added, a little at a time, if dough is too stiff. When dough is thoroughly mixed, remove it from the bowl and knead from four to six minutes. Shape as desired. Bake on a cookie sheet in a preheated 350° oven for an hour or more, depending on the size of the "cookies." Some larger pieces will take two hours, perhaps longer. Test with a toothpick for doneness. Use a spatula to remove forms to a cake rack to cool.

Make Way for Ducklings

When completely cooled, decorate with paint. Spray finished pieces with clear fixative to keep dough from breaking or softening. The cookies are attractive without paint too, but do cover them with fixative, shellac, or varnish to make them last. Decorations can be hung by piercing the dough shapes before baking.

Ethel's Book Cookies

These are edible ornaments to make in the shape of book characters. The recipe was created by a former student of mine. Yum yum!

Ingredients: ¾ cup shortening (part butter or margarine)
1 cup sugar
2 eggs
½ teaspoon lemon or vanilla flavoring
2½ cups flour
1 teaspoon salt
1 teaspoon baking powder

How to: Mix shortening, sugar, eggs, and flavoring thoroughly. Measure flour. Stir flour, baking powder, and salt together; blend in egg mixture. Chill at least one hour.

Heat oven to 400°. Roll dough 1/8″ thick on lightly floured board. Cut with cookie cutters or use cardboard patterns. Place

Little Red
Riding Hood

on ungreased baking sheets. Bake six to eight minutes, or until cookies are a delicate golden color. Decorate with egg yolk paint or icing. Yields about 4 dozen cookies.

Egg Yolk Paint: Blend well one egg yolk and ¼ teaspoon water. Divide mixture into cups. Add different food colorings. Paint on the cookies.

Icing: 1 cup sifted confectioners sugar
¼ teaspoon salt
½ teaspoon vanilla or other flavoring
1½ tablespoons cream or 1 tablespoon water

How to: Blend sugar, salt, and flavoring. Add cream to make it easy to spread. If desired, tint with food coloring. Spread on cookies with spatula. This makes enough icing for 3 to 5 dozen cookies.

Commercial cookie cutters in the shape of animals or other objects appropriate to a story or book often can be found at the hardware store or the housewares section of department stores. You can also make your own special cookie patterns.

How to: Draw a shape or trace an illustration, transfer it to stiff cardboard, then cut it out. Place the cardboard pattern on the cookie dough and cut around it with a sharp paring knife.

Book and Food Pairs

Book sharing is enhanced by food sharing. Following are a few of the treats, snacks, main dishes, and side dishes that are suggested by some favorite books. Add a treat to your programs. If it is not always possible for you to serve a treat in your classroom or library, don't forget your own family. Serve a story-oriented treat to them tonight.

Apples and Applesauce

Hogrogian, Nonny. *Apples*. Art by author. Macmillan, 1972.

Scheer, Julian. *Rain Makes Applesauce*. Art by Marvin Bileck. Holiday, 1964.

Bread

Joly-Berbesson, Fanny. *Marceau Bonappétit*. Art by Agnès Mathieu. Carol-rhoda, 1989.

Norris, Ann. *Bread Bread Bread*. Photos by Ken Heyman. Lothrop, 1989.

Bread and Jam

Hoban, Russell. *Bread and Jam for Frances*. Art by Lillian Hoban. Harper, 1964.

Lord, John Vernon. *The Giant Jam Sandwich*; verses by Janet Burroway; stories and pictures by author. Houghton, 1973.

Singer, Isaac Bashevis. "The First Shlemiel" in *Zlateh the Goat*; tr. by the author and Elizabeth Shub. Art by Maurice Sendak. Harper, 1966.

Cake

Murphy, Jill. *A Piece of Cake*. Art by author. Putnam, 1989.

"Roz's Birthday" in *Roz and Ozzie* by Johanna Hurwitz. Art by Eileen McKeating. Morrow, 1992.

Cheese and Toasted Cheese Sandwiches

Blaine, Marge. *The Terrible Thing That Happened at Our House*. Art by John C. Wallner. Parents, 1975.

Garrison, Christian. *Flim and Flam and the Big Cheese*. Art by Diane Goode. Bradbury, 1976.

Chocolate Turtles

Blume, Judy. "Dribble" in *Tales of a Fourth Grade Nothing*. Art by Roy Doty. Dutton, 1972.

Recipe for chocolate turtles

You need: 1½ cups flour 1 egg
 ¼ teaspoon baking soda 1 egg yolk (reserve white)
 ¼ teaspoon salt ½ teaspoon vanilla
 ½ cup butter pecan halves
 ½ cup packed brown sugar

How to: Sift flour, baking soda, and salt together. Cream butter and sugar and blend into flour. Add egg and egg yolk and vanilla. Make dough into balls. Arrange pecan halves in groups of three on greased baking sheet to resemble head and legs of a turtle. Dip bottom of each ball into egg white and press into nuts. Bake at 350° for 10 to 12 minutes. Frost with chocolate frosting.

Chocolate frosting: 6 oz. package semisweet chocolate chips
 pinch of salt
 ½ cup sour cream
 ½ teaspoon vanilla

How to: Melt chocolate in double boiler. Add salt and sour cream. Add vanilla.

Christmas Dinner

"The Cratchits' Christmas Dinner" excerpted in *Tell It Again: Great Tales from Around the World*, ed. by Margaret Hodges. Art by Joan Berg. Dial, 1963. Or in Dickens, Charles. *A Christmas Carol* (Harper, 1844).

Ungerer, Tomi. *Zeralda's Ogre*. Art by author. Harper, 1967.

Wilder, Laura Ingalls. "Christmas" in *Little House in the Big Woods*. Art by Garth Williams. Harper, 1953.

Cookies

Alexander, Sue. *World Famous Muriel and the Magic Mystery*. Art by Marla Frazee. Crowell, 1990.

Hoban, Lillian. *Arthur's Christmas Cookies*. Art by author. Harper, 1972.

Numeroff, Laura Joffe. *If You Give a Mouse a Cookie*. Art by Felicia Bond. Harper, 1985.

Doughnuts

McCloskey, Robert. "The Doughnuts" in *Homer Price*. Art by author. Viking, 1943.

Stamaty, Mark. *Who Needs Doughnuts?* Dial, 1973.

Fruit

Ehlert, Lois. *Eating the Alphabet*. Art by author. Harcourt, 1989.

Zolotow, Charlotte. *Mr. Rabbit and the Lovely Present*. Art by Maurice Sendak. Harper, 1962.

Fudge

Howe, James. *Harold and Chester in Hot Fudge*. Art by Leslie Morrill. Morrow, 1990.

Gingerbread

The Gingerbread Man. Retold by Eric A. Kimmel. Art by Megan Lloyd. Holiday House, 1993.

Van Woerkom, Dorothy. *The Queen Who Couldn't Bake Gingerbread*. Art by Paul Galdone. Knopf, 1975.

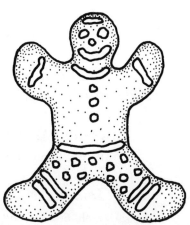

Recipe for gingerbread people
You need: ¼ cup butter
           ½ cup sugar (white or brown)
           ½ cup dark molasses
           3½ cups flour, sifted
           1 teaspoon baking soda
           ½ teaspoon cinnamon
           1 teaspoon ginger
           ½ teaspoon salt
           5 tablespoons water (about)
           raisins

How to: Cream butter and sugar together. Add the molasses. Sift the flour, baking soda, and spices together and add to the creamed mixture, a little at a time. Water may be added as mixture gets too thick to handle. Use your hands to mix the dough. Chill dough about half an hour for easier handling. Roll dough to any desired thickness on buttered baking pan and cut out two gingerbread people with patterns you've made or bought. Decorate with raisins. Bake at 350° for 8 to 10 minutes, depending on thickness. Cool. Decorate with icing. (There are also commercial gingerbread cookie mixes on the market for quicker cookie making!)

Icing: Combine ¼ cup confectioners (powdered) sugar with a few drops of water. Stir to make a paste. A drop or two of food coloring can be added. Use a pastry tube or toothpick to decorate your gingerbread people.

Gourmet Cooking

"The Most Magnificent Cook of All" in *It's Time for Storyhour*, ed. by Elizabeth Hough Sechrist and Janette Woolsey. Art by Elsie Jane McCorkell. Macrae Smith, 1964.

Home Canned Fruit

Keller, Gottfried. "Hungry Hans" in *Best Book of Read Aloud Stories*, ed. by Pauline Rush Evans. Art by Adolph Le Moult and George Wilde. Doubleday, 1966.

Homemade Jelly

Newell, Hope. "How She Kept Herself Cheerful" in *The Little Old Woman Who Used Her Head and Other Stories*. Art by Margaret Ruse and Anne Merriman Peck. Nelson, 1973.

Honey

Milne, A. A. *Winnie the Pooh*. Art by E. H. Shepard. Dutton, 1926.

Hot Dogs

Kessler, Ethel and Leonard Kessler. *Stan the Hot Dog Man*. Art by Leonard Kessler. Harper, 1990.

Jelly Beans

 Hoban, Lillian. *The Sugar Snow Spring*. Art by author. Harper, 1973.

Lemon Meringue Pie

Parish, Peggy. *Amelia Bedelia*. Art by Fritz Siebel. Harper, 1963.

Lemonade

Asch, Frank. *Good Lemonade*. Art by Marie Zimmerman. Watts, 1976.

Lima Beans

Viorst, Judith. *Alexander and the Terrible, Horrible, No Good, Very Bad Day.* Art by Ray Cruz. Atheneum, 1972.

Muffins

Numeroff, Laura Joffe. *If You Give a Moose a Muffin.* Art by Felicia Bond. Harper, 1991.

Oranges

Cohen, Barbara. *Gooseberries to Oranges.* Art by Beverly Brodsky. Lothrop, 1982.

Rogow, Zack. *Oranges.* Art by Mary Szilagyi. Orchard, 1988.

Peanut Butter Sandwiches

Cleary, Beverly. *The Mouse and the Motorcycle.* Art by Louis Darling. Morrow, 1965.

Popcorn

Greene, Ellin. "Princess Rosetta and the Popcorn Man" from *The Pot of Gold* by Mary E. Wilkins. Art by Trina Schart Hyman. Lothrop, 1971.

Preston, Edna. *Pop Corn and Ma Goodness.* Art by Robert A. Parker. Viking, 1969.

Sandburg, Carl. "Huckabuck Family and How They Raised Popcorn in Nebraska" in *The Sandburg Treasury.* Art by Paul Bacon. Harcourt, 1970.

Wilder, Laura Ingalls. "Happy Winter Days" in *By the Shores of Silver Lake.* Art by Garth Williams. Harper, 1953.

Pudding

Kunhardt, Dorothy. *Pudding Is Nice.* Art by author. The Bookstore Press (Patterson's Wheeltrack, Freeport, ME 04032), 1975.

Pumpkin Pie

"The Pumpkin Giant" in *The Lost Half-Hour*, ed. by Eulalie Steinmetz Ross. Art by Enrico Arno. Harcourt, 1963.

Wilder, Laura Ingalls. "Wonderful Machine" in *Little House in the Big Woods.* Art by Garth Williams, Harper, 1953.

Raspberry Tarts

Thurber, James. *Many Moons.* Art by Marc Simont. Harcourt, 1990.

Rice

Dooley, Norah. *Everybody Cooks Rice.* Art by Peter J. Thompson. Carolrhoda, 1991.

Towle, Faith M. *The Magic Cooking Pot: A Folktale of India.* Art by author. Houghton, 1975.

Sausage

Perrault, Charles. "The Ridiculous Wishes" in *Perrault's Fairy Tales*; tr. by Sasha Moorsom. Art by Landa Crommelynck. Doubleday, 1972.

Spaghetti

dePaola, Tomie. *Strega Nona*. Art by author. Prentice-Hall, 1975.

Joslin, Sesyle. *What Do You Say, Dear?* Art by Maurice Sendak. Young Scott, 1958.

Rey, H. A. *Curious George Takes a Job*. Art by author. Houghton, 1947.

Stone Candy

Brown, Marcia. *Stone Soup*. Art by author. Scribner, 1947.

Steig, William. *Sylvester and the Magic Pebble*. Art by author. Windmill, 1969.

At Teatime

Burningham, John. *Mr. Gumpy's Outing*. Art by author. Holt, 1970.

Carroll, Lewis (pseud. for Charles L. Dodgson). "The Mad Tea Party" in *Alice's Adventures in Wonderland*. Art by Arthur Rackham. Doubleday, 1907.

Travers, Pamela L. "Laughing Gas" from *Mary Poppins*. Art by Mary Shepard. Reynal & Hitchcock, 1934.

Tomato Sandwiches

Fitzhugh, Louise. *Harriet, the Spy*. Art by author. Harper, 1964.

Walnuts

Babbitt, Natalie. "Nuts" in *The Devil's Storybook*. Art by author. Farrar, 1974.

Fun Food Facts Bulletin Board

Put these fun food facts up on a chalkboard or bulletin board or use them as transitional material between stories in your book and food program.

In ancient Greece, it was so much trouble to start a fire that most people bought prepared food from stalls in the market and brought it home to eat. Fast-food stores have a longer history than we realize!

In France, snails (known as escargot) are considered a delicacy.

Chinese fortune cookies are an American invention.

A popular Japanese treat is sushi, cooled and vinegared rice garnished with a variety of raw seafood and seaweed.

Americans eat more than 245 million ice cream cones a year.

Peanut butter celebrated its 100th birthday in 1990.

Ancient Egyptians sometimes used bread as money.

Americans eat more than 100 pounds of sugar per capita each year.

Sandwiches were invented by the Fourth Earl of Sandwich, John Montague, who didn't want to leave the gambling table long enough to eat. He ordered two pieces of bread with the meat between them so that he would not have to interrupt his game.

There are between 14,000 and 17,000 different varieties of beans and peas (the official name for this family of plants is leguminosae).

Activities

Creative Drama

Read *Yummers!* by James Marshall to your group, then recreate some of the scenes in the story. You will remember that the story is about Eugene, a tortoise, and Emily, a pig. Eugene suggests that Emily take a walk with him, exercising to lose weight. But as they walk through town, Emily indulges in an eating feast! Children will enjoy taking the parts of the food salespeople as they act out the story.

The Restaurant Game

This can begin as a game, but you might decide to offer the real thing. One year I arrived at the Dhaka (Bangladesh) International School before Valentine's Day. The fourth grade class had prepared lunch (the students who were serving wore white gloves and the maitre d' was wearing a suit) for the elementary school staff. Your class might enjoy planning a meal for a special guest or for the administrators (see my book, *This Way to Books*, for a poetry meal complete with recipes).

> You need: Menus collected from the restaurants in your town
> Play money or real money
> Order pad and pencil
> Diners and a restaurant staff

> How to: Enact a meal in a restaurant. Customers order from the menu, servers take the order and serve the food. At the end of the meal, the diner pays the bill.

Note: This activity can be as simple as described above or your group can elaborate on it by writing your own menus (a creative writing project), preparing real food, and actually serving a meal.

Poetry Suggests Food Too

IF THE MOON WERE MADE OF CHEESE

If the moon were made of cheese
I would reach into the sky
for a late-night snacking sandwich
Of ham and moon on rye.

—Jeff Moss

I eat my gumdrops
one at a time.
Red, yellow,
orange, purple—
I have a rainbow
inside of me.
  —Freya Littledale

POTATO CHIPS

A potato chip is something
  never ceasing to amuse
I love its funny wrinkles
and the crunchy way it chews.
—Anthony E. Gallagher

BANANAS AND CREAM

Bananas and cream.
Bananas and cream,
All we could say was
Bananas and cream.

We couldn't say fruit,
We wouldn't say cow,
We didn't say sugar—
We don't say it now.

Bananas and cream,
Bananas and cream,
All we could shout was
Bananas and cream.

We didn't say why,
We didn't say how;
We forgot it was fruit,
We forgot the old cow;
We never said sugar,
We only said WOW!

Bananas and cream,
Bananas and cream;
All that we want is
Bananas and cream!

We didn't say dish,
We didn't say spoon;
We said not tomorrow,
But NOW and HOW SOON.

Bananas and cream,
Bananas and cream?
We yelled for bananas
Bananas and scream!
—David McCord

Make some banana spread

> You need: 1 banana
> 1 tablespoon honey
> 1 teaspoon lemon juice
> 2 teaspoons sugar

> How to: Mash banana and sugar. Add lemon juice and honey. Spread on a biscuit and enjoy.

EIGHTEEN FLAVORS

Eighteen luscious, scrumptious flavors—
Chocolate, lime and cherry,
Coffee, pumpkin, fudge-banana
Caramel cream and boysenberry.
Rocky road and toasted almond,
Butterscotch, vanilla dip,
Butter brickle, apple ripple,
Coconut and mocha chip,
Brandy peach and lemon custard,
Each scoop lovely, smooth and round,
Tallest ice-cream cone in town,
Lying there (sniff) on the ground.

—Shel Silverstein

I LIKED GROWING

I liked growing.
That was nice.
The leaves were soft
The sun was hot.
I was warm and red and round
Then someone dropped me in a pot.
Being a strawberry isn't all pleasing.
This morning they put me in ice cream.
I'm freezing.

—Karla Kuskin

Make your own strawberry ice cream

> You need: 1 10-oz. pkg. of sliced frozen strawberries
> 1 cup sugar
> 1 pint commercial sour cream

> How to: Defrost berries. Add sugar and sour cream. Stir mixture well and put in refrigerator tray to freeze. To prevent ice crystals from forming, stir at 25-minute intervals three times. Now forget it until you need it at booktime.

PEANUT BUTTER

"Peanut butter, considered as a spread . . ."
"How else could you consider it, my friend?"
"Well, by the spoonful; or, if sick in bed,
By licking it from the index finger's end."
                                        —David McCord

Make some peanut butter

> Shell a cup of peanuts. Remove inner skin. Grind in a blender until desired consistency. Vegetable oil, preferably peanut oil, may be added for a smoother spread.

Booklist: Poetry Featuring Food

Adoff, Arnold. *Chocolate Dreams.* Art by Turi MacCombie. Lothrop, 1989. Poems about chocolate.

_____. *Eats.* Art by Susan Russo. Lothrop, 1979. Free verse featuring food.

Bennett, Jill, ed. *A Packet of Poems.* Art by Paddy Mounter. Oxford, 1982. Lots of poems about food from Eleanor Farjeon, Felice Holman, Shel Silverstein and others.

Cole, William. *Poem Stew.* Art by Karen Ann Ewihaus. Lippincott, 1981. Featuring poems about food and manners.

Goldstein, Bobbye S., ed. *What's on the Menu?* Art by Chris Demarest. Viking, 1992. Upbeat food poetry.

Hearn, Michael Patrick. *The Chocolate Book.* Art by Anthony Chen and others. Caedmon, 1983. Stories and poems about chocolate.

Hopkins, Lee Bennett. *Munching: Poems about Eating.* Art by Nelle Davis. Little, 1985. English and American poets and food.

A Story to Tell

JOHN WINS A BET

Steve Sanfield

Steve Sanfield, a professional storyteller, has collected tales about High John the Conqueror. These traditional trickster stories were told during the era of slavery in America. High John is always the winner in these earthy and amusing tales.

Watermelons are as much a part of summer in the South as long, lazy days, and there wasn't a farm or a plantation that didn't have its own watermelon patch. When the melons were ripe, some farmers would fill their wagons with the big, green fruit and take them to town to sell.

One of the most successful watermelon peddlers was a man named Dillon, who used all kinds of tricks to attract buyers to his wagon. Sometimes he hired a banjo player to gather a crowd. Other times he held weight-guessing contests. The person whose guess came closest to the exact weight of the melon won it as a prize. Each Saturday the town folks would pay a visit to Dillon's wagon to see what might be going on.

But one Saturday he made a mistake. That day he held up a forty-pounder and said, "I'll give five dollars to anyone who can eat this melon to the rind, but if he doesn't eat it all, he'll have to pay me a dollar for it."

John, who happened to be standing in the crowd, walked up to the wagon and asked, "Will you give me an hour to decide?"

Mr. Dillon thought it was a strange request, but he agreed, providing, of course, that no one else wanted to try. Well, a forty-pound watermelon is about as big as a small dog or a very large cat, and nobody else was in a mind to try eating it.

It was still there when John returned an hour later and announced he was ready. He cut the melon open and started eating. He went at it like a man who'd been made hungry by a three-day fever, stopping only to catch his breath and spit huge mouthfuls of seeds. Less than ten minutes after he started, all that was left of that forty-pound watermelon was a pile of white and green rind.

Everyone was amazed at this prodigious display of eating—no one more so that Mr. Dillon himself. He had never dreamed he would lose this bet.

"John," he announced, "you won fair and square, and I'm going to give you that five dollars, but before I do I'd like to know why you needed an hour to decide."

"Well," John replied, "it's like this. I knew I had a watermelon at home that was just about the same size, so I went home and ate it. And I figured if I could eat that one, I could eat this one too."

Booklist: Stories to Tell Featuring Food

"Johnny Appleseed" in *American Tall Tales* by Mary Pope Osborne. Art by Michael McCurdy. Knopf, 1991. John Chapman travels for 40 years sowing apple seeds.

Patron, Susan. *Burgoo Stew*. Art by Mike Shenon. Orchard, 1991. Upbeat version of *Stone Soup*.

"Paul Bunyan and the Popcorn Blizzard" in *Read for the Fun of It* by Caroline Feller Bauer. H. W. Wilson, 1992. Paul brings popcorn to the American desert.

"Smart Ice Cream" in *Unreal!* by Paul Jennings. Viking, 1985. A vendor gives away ice cream that removes pimples, shortens noses, and makes you smart.

"Strawberries" by Gayle Ross in *Homespun: Tales from America's Favorite Storytellers*, ed. by Jimmy Neil Smith. Crown, 1988. A Cherokee legend explains that the world's first strawberries brought peace between men and women.

"The Thing That Goes Burp in the Night" by Sharon Webb in *Dragons and Dreams*, ed. by Jane Yolen et al. Harper, 1986. A monster comes after John Thomas and his brother Billy in search of chocolate.

The Woman Who Flummoxed the Fairies. Art by Susan Gaber. Harcourt, 1990. A master baker outwits the fairies. Also in *Heather and Broom* by Sorche Nic Leodhas. Holt, 1960.

Food Books Good Enough to Read

Picture Books

Alexander, Sue. *World Famous Muriel*. Art by Chris Demarest. Little, 1984. The famous tightrope walker loves peanut butter cookies.

Asch, Frank. *Popcorn*. Art by author. Parents, 1979. A bear and his friends indulge in popcorn—lots of it.

Brimmer, Larry Dave. *Country Bear's Good Neighbor*. Orchard, 1988. Bear bakes a pie for the little girl who lent him the ingredients.

Carle, Eric. *What's for Lunch?* Art by author. Philomel, 1982. What do animals eat?

Chorao, Kay. *The Cherry Pie Baby*. Dutton, 1989. Annie trades a cherry pie for Beau's baby brother.

Cocca-Leffler, Maryann. *Wednesday Is Spaghetti Day*. Art by author. Scholastic, 1990. A cat invites her friends for lunch.

Cohen, Barbara. *The Carp in the Bathtub*. Lothrop, 1972. Two children try to save Joe, a carp, who is destined for gefilte fish.

dePaola, Tomie. *Fin McCoul*. Art by author. Holiday, 1981. Oonagh and Fin outwit the giant Cucullin.

———. *Tony's Bread: An Italian Folktale*. Art by author. Putnam, 1989. How panettone, the sweet Italian bread, was first baked.

Esterl, Arnica. *The Fine Round Cake*; tr. by Pauline Heil. Art by Andre J. Dugin and Olga Dugin. Four Winds, 1991. Adapted from Joseph Jacobs's "Johnny-Cake."

Friedman, Ina R. *How My Parents Learned to Eat*. Art by Allen Say. Houghton, 1984. An American sailor and a Japanese girl trade cultures and marry.

Galdone, Paul. *The Gingerbread Boy*. Art by author. Seabury, 1975. A gingerbread boy is chased by animals and people until a fox eats him. The classic in picture-book form. For an American version of this tale, check Ruth Sawyer's *Journey Cake, Ho!* with art by Robert McCloskey (Viking, 1953).

Gibbons, Gail. *Margie's Diner*. Art by author. Crowell, 1989. All about running a diner.

Ginsburg, Mirra. *The Night It Rained Pancakes*. Art by Douglas Florian. Greenwillow, 1990. Stepan outwits the lord of the manor.

Greeson, Janet. *The Stingy Baker*. Art by David LaRochelle. Carolrhoda, 1990. Maybe this is the way a baker's dozen came to be.

Haddon, Mark. *Tony and the Tomato Soup*. Harcourt, 1989. A variant on "The Midas Touch."

Hayes, Sarah. *This Is the Bear and the Picnic Lunch*. Art by author. Little, 1989. Cumulative tale to read aloud.

Kelley, True. *Let's Eat!* Art by author. Dutton, 1989. A picture dictionary of places, utensils, times, and food with colorful, sprightly art.

Lobel, Arnold. "Ice Cream" in *Frog and Toad All Year.* Art by author. Harper, 1976. What do you do with melting ice cream? Another great piece in this series is "Cookies" from *Frog and Toad Together* (Harper, 1972).

McCully, Emily Arnold. *Picnic.* Art by author. Harper, 1984. A little mouse gets lost on his way to a family picnic. A wordless picture book.

Mosel, Arlene. *The Funny Little Woman.* Art by Blair Lent. Dutton, 1972. The funny little woman follows her dumpling to the world of the Oni.

Murphy, Jill. *A Piece of Cake.* Art by author. Putnam, 1989. An elephant family goes on a diet.

Novak, Matt. *Mr. Floop's Lunch.* Art by author. Orchard, 1990. Mr. Floop shares his lunch with birds, dogs, and squirrels.

Oxenbury, Helen. *Eating Out.* Art by author. Dial, 1983. At a restaurant with baby.

Polacco, Patricia. *Thunder Cake.* Art by author. Philomel, 1990. Grandma shows a little girl how to make a cake while a storm rages.

Porter, Sue. *One Potato.* Art by author. Bradbury, 1989. Farm animals argue over who will eat the last potato.

Pryor, Ainslie. *The Baby Blue Cat and the Whole Batch of Cookies.* Puffin, 1989. Baby Blue Cat eats all the cookies baked by Mama Cat for her four kittens.

Roffey, Maureen. *Mealtime.* Art by author. Four Winds, 1988. Questions and answers for the youngest about food and eating.

Taylor, Judy. *Dudley and the Strawberry Shake.* Art by Peter Cross. Putnam, 1987. Dudley picks the biggest strawberry and finds himself on a dog.

Watanabe, Shigeo. *What a Good Lunch.* Art by Yasuo Ohtomo. Collins, 1980. "Eating is harder than I thought." A bear eats spaghetti and strawberry jam.

Yee, Paul. *Roses Sing on New Snow.* Art by Harvey Chan. Macmillan, 1992. The magic is in the cook, not the recipe.

Longer Books

Cone, Molly. *Mishmash and the Big Fat Problem.* Houghton, 1982. Pete's dog Mishmash has a weight problem.

Conford, Ellen. *What's Cooking, Jenny Archer?* Little, 1990. Jenny tries to make money by making school lunches for her friends.

Davis, Edward E. *Bruno the Pretzel Man.* Art by Marc Simont. Harper, 1984. A pretzel man finds out that he is as important as his customers.

Greenberg, Jan. *The Pig-Out Blues.* Farrar, 1982. Jodie goes on a crash diet.

Heide, Florence Parry. *Banana Twist*. Holiday, 1978. Two boys meet in a city elevator—reluctant friends who enjoy strange food combinations.

Hermes, Patricia. *Kevin Corbett Eats Flies*. Art by Carol Newsom. Harcourt, 1986. "The way to impress somebody is to make them a turkey dinner."

Hurwitz, Johanna. *Aldo Applesauce*. Art by John Wallner. Morrow, 1981. Aldo becomes a vegetarian in this funny book.

_____. *Tough-Luck Karen*. Art by Diane DeGroat. Morrow, 1982. Karen wants to be a famous chef, but now there is school . . . and problems.

Juster, Norton. "The Royal Banquet" in *The Phantom Tollbooth*. Art by Jules Feiffer. Random, 1961. Be careful what you say—or you may have to eat your words.

Lindsay, Norman. *The Magic Pudding: The Adventures of Paul Bunyip Bluegum*. Argus & Robertson, 1918. The Australian classic. Lots of nonsense verse and narrative—including a bandicoot stealing a watermelon, and "none of the ordinary breakfast rules."

Lipsyte, Robert. *One Fat Summer*. Harper, 1977. Bobby Marx slims down with hard work.

MacDonald, Betty. "The Slow-Eater Tiny-Bite-Taker" in *Mrs. Piggle Wiggle*. Lippincott, 1957. Mrs. Piggle Wiggle can cure anything.

Milne, A. A. *Winnie the Pooh*. Art by Ernest H. Shepard. Dutton, 1961. And we all know Pooh loves honey.

Nelson, Theresa. *The 25¢ Miracle*. Bradbury, 1986. Elvira invites her teacher to dinner to meet her father.

Paulsen, Gary. *Hatchet*. Bradbury, 1987. The lone survivor after a plane crash, Brian must learn to find food.

Rockwell, Thomas. *How to Eat Fried Worms and Other Plays*. Art by Joel Schick. Delacorte, 1980. Billy bets that he can eat 15 worms in 15 days in the title play.

Ruby, Lois. *Pig-Out Inn*. Houghton, 1987. Some interesting characters visit this truck stop.

Shyer, Marlene Fanta. *Grandpa Ritz and the Luscious Lovelies*. Scribner, 1985. Grandpa and Philip are treated to delicacies by Grandpa's women friends.

Sunderlin, Sylvia. *Antrim's Orange*. Art by Diane deGroat. Scribner, 1976. Excellent read-aloud story about the sharing of a precious orange.

Non-fiction Books about Food

Boynton, Sandra. *Chocolate: The Consuming Passion*. Art by author. Workman, 1982. Humor for the chocoholic.

Burns, Marilyn. *Good for Me! All about Food in Thirty-two Bites.* Art by Sandy Clifford. Little, 1978. Explores many aspects of food. Enjoy browsing through these facts and fictions.

dePaola, Tomie. *The Popcorn Book.* Art by author. Holiday, 1978. The history of popcorn, recipes, and a snowstorm of popped corn.

Ehlert, Lois. *Eating the Alphabet: Fruits and Vegetables from A to Z.* Harcourt, 1989. Bold and bright food good enough to eat.

Gibbons, Gail. *The Milk Makers.* Art by author. Macmillan, 1985. The story of milk in picture-essay form—from cow to you.

Giblin, James Cross. *From Hand to Mouth or How We Invented Knives, Forks, Spoons, Chopsticks, and the Table Manners to Go with Them.* Crowell, 1987. Fascinating facts about eating utensils and their roles in society.

Krensky, Stephen. *Scoop after Scoop: A History of Ice Cream.* Art by Richard Rosenblum. Atheneum, 1986. The title tells the story: the complete history of ice cream.

Morris, Ann. *Bread, Bread, Bread.* Photos by Ken Heyman. Lothrop, 1989. Good-enough-to-eat-photographs show bread around the world.

Parnall, Peter. *Apple Tree.* Art by author. Macmillan, 1987. A year in the life of an apple tree.

Pillar, Marjorie. *Pizza Man.* Photos by author. Crowell, 1990. Photo essay that shows how a pizza-maker works.

Rylant, Cynthia. "At the Supper Table" in *A Blue-Eyed Daisy.* Bradbury, 1985. A dog brings a family back together at the supper table.

Walker, Barbara M. *The Little House Cookbook: Frontier Foods from Laura Ingalls Wilder.* Art by Garth Williams. Harper, 1979. Pioneer recipes.

Adult Resources Featuring Food

"Eat a Poem" Program in *This Way to Books* by Caroline Feller Bauer. H. W. Wilson, 1983.

Irving, Jan and Robin Currie. *Mudluscious: Stories and Activities Featuring Food for Preschool Children.* Art by Robert B. Phillips. Libraries Unlimited, 1986.

26 / Creative Dramatics Plus

Are children as imaginative as they used to be? I have no scientific proof, but it seems to me as a 30-year veteran in the storytelling field that young people are not able to visualize characters and scenes in their minds as they did when I first entered the library profession.

Television may be the major culprit, for if children are always shown the action they may have less practice in using their own imaginations. Creative drama can help spark a child's imagination.

The most active and in some ways the most satisfying type of participation program can be a series involving creative dramatics. In this activity the audience spontaneously acts out the stories they have heard. A creative dramatics series is not to be confused with a class in drama since it is not expected to result in a polished performance. Rather it explores the methods and emotions of self-expression.

Plan to spend at least five sessions on this activity so that both you, the leader, and your group can fully benefit from these explorations into informal drama. If you are a classroom teacher, you may wish to schedule creative drama during your usual storytelling hour—perhaps every afternoon at one o'clock for a week. If you are a public or school librarian you can assure the same continuity by announcing your creative drama program on a colorful flyer and posting a sign-up sheet for participants. For the most part you will be telling stories and reciting poems as inspiration for pantomime and improvisation. If you are interested in formal theater as an art form and you think your group might be too, you could plan to spend some time discussing the history and forms of drama. This might be a good time to plan a field trip to a play in your community.

Many professionals consider creative dramatics merely an exercise in learning to think logically, understand feelings and emotions, carry out directions, and work with others. It seems to me, however, that such a series could accomplish much more. Learning to use your imagination, to express yourself in language and movement, and just learning to play creatively are worthwhile activities in themselves.

Starting at the End

Everyone has their own idea of how best to introduce children to creative dramatics. In my reading I've found that most experts would agree that the method I recommend, although it has always worked well for me, is starting backwards. My only word of caution is that this seems to work better with children, who are naturally more spontaneous and creative, than with adults who seem afraid to express themselves for fear of ridicule. It also works better if the individuals know each other. My plan of programming for creative dramatics is to skip the preliminaries and plunge directly into playmaking. When the children have fully explored the creation and acting out of a story then we go back to the beginning and more slowly experiment with the component parts of characterization and acting.

Acting Out a Story

In this first phase, let your group take as much responsibility as possible for the making and implementing of decisions. If your group is made up of those who have been listening to stories you can simply say "Choose one of the stories that we've heard this term and put on a play." If the group is young, or doesn't know any stories or needs more direction, begin by telling a story. Next let the children discuss the following.

The characters in the story:

> How many
> Physical characteristics
> Personality: kind, gentle, evil, mean
> Emotional changes: e.g., the prince desires the princess, is afraid to fight the dragon, is brave, is happy to win the princess.

The settings of the story: time and place

How much time elapses
How many scene changes are there
What would each of the settings look like, e.g., the prince's home, the dragon's cave, the princess's room, the castle hall?

The action of the story: think through the story to find out what actually takes place.

Keep this preliminary discussion to a minimum at your first session. The play's the thing and you will want to get on with it. Next cast the play. In this first session I always try to let the children decide who will play which role. If this does not work, assign parts. It is true that everyone should get a chance to be a player, but not necessarily at the same session. Those who had lead parts one week can have walk-on parts the next time. Don't forget that people can play inanimate objects as well as animals or humans. After all, the stones in *Stone Soup* are leading characters. Don't feel that everyone in the group must have a part, either. The players will need stage hands and a director. Those who are not acting will become the audience, as important a role as those performing the story.

Reread or retell the story one more time to refresh your group's memory, and if people seem unsure of the order of events you may jot them down on the chalkboard. Adults I've worked with always assure me that they are familiar with *Little Red Riding Hood* until they find themselves in the middle of the forest; then they can never remember what happens next!

Now let the players decide how they will put on the story. Set a time limit for preparation, and then on with the show. I don't discuss anything after the "play." Usually everyone has had a wonderful time, feeling the first triumph of self-expression and I don't want to dampen their enthusiasm with criticism, no matter how constructive.

Continue at the Beginning

The Senses

The next several sessions should involve a more serious and methodical consideration of the senses and emotions. An awareness of the way in which our five senses work helps to establish a clear

basis from which to project these senses to an audience. Most of the information that we receive comes through our eyes and secondarily through our ears. The senses of touch, taste, and smell can be developed further to make children more aware of themselves and the world around them. Prepare several experiments to demonstrate the operation of the five senses, but don't try to cover too much ground in a single session. A good basic reference is Neil Ardley's *The Science Book of the Senses*.

Taste

Taste test. Bring a variety of tastables to the group. Let each child taste each individual thing and record on a piece of paper what he or she was eating. It is important that the children don't get a visual clue or even a textural clue before tasting. You'll need help to administer this test. Use the children who have already taken the test to help with the others. Put a blindfold on each child and place a dab of each of the foods in turn on each tongue. Find foods that give a variety of tastes. Here are a few that are easy to handle and usually readily available:

Catsup	Toothpaste
Butter	Honey
Peanut butter	Shredded coconut
Brown sugar	Molasses
Canned fruit	Syrup
Salt	
White sugar	} Same consistency—opposite taste

Discuss, that is try to orally describe, the taste of each food substance and others you remember. Explore as many adjectives that relate to sensations and taste as you can: sweet, sour, crunchy, slippery, bitter, mild, sticky, salty, curdled, tangy, spicy, hot.

As a group prepare and eat invisible foods: mashed potatoes, an artichoke, a carrot, an ice cream cone, a steak, spaghetti. Try it once with no observation, then a second time asking questions such as: Do you eat that with your fingers? Will you need a fork and knife? What does it taste like? Show us how it tastes. Participants often overreact to get the taste across. Point out that in actual everyday eating a mild reaction to taste is more acceptable.

Now plan a pretend menu and, as a group, enjoy an imaginary dinner party, combining silent actions with conversations reacting to the food served. Try to make your menus varied with different tastes. Make it a potluck supper. Each child brings something to the party and in pantomime tastes his or her offering and describes to the group the way the food tastes. Is feeling or touching a part of taste?

Books featuring taste:

Babbitt, Natalie. *The Search for Delicious.* Art by author. Farrar, 1985. Which food fits the dictionary definition of "delicious"?

Boujon, Claude. *Bon Appétit, Mr. Rabbit!* Art by author. Macmillan, 1987. Could you eat almost anything?

Demarest, Chris L. *No Peas for Nellie.* Art by Arnold Lobel. Macmillan, 1988. Nellie lists the food she would rather eat: a furry spider, a slimy salamander, and a hairy warthog.

Smell

The sense of smell is the least developed of our senses, yet in many animals it is the most highly developed. Discuss with your group the need for a sense of smell in humans and animals.

Smell test. Choose a variety of smells for the group to identify. Each item should be in its own container. Empty, small plastic containers are available at the drugstore, or an egg carton with slots cut in the top will work. You may need an assistant for this activity, since you do not want to give the group any visual clues to the ingredients. These will make a good start and are readily available:

Vinegar	Spices: curry, mustard, cinnamon, and
Calamine lotion	cloves
Talcum powder	Cocoa
Coffee	A carnation or some other flower
Mouthwash	Turpentine

Often a particular smell will bring back memories of a forgotten occasion. Discuss some of these odors: burning leaves might remind you of fall, baking bread of Thanksgiving dinner, the smell of coffee of Sunday breakfast, the smell of ether of the time you had your tonsils removed. Caramel corn might remind you of the circus.

Books featuring smell:

Machotka, Hana. *Breathtaking Noses.* Photos by author. Morrow, 1992.

Moncure, Jane Belk. *What Your Nose Knows!* Art by Lois Axeman. Children's Press, 1982.

Saunder, Susan. *A Sniff in Time.* Art by Michael Mariano. Macmillan, 1982.

Silverstein, Robert, and Alvin Silverstein and Virginia Silverstein. *Smell: The Subtle Sense.* Art by Ann Neumann. Morrow, 1992. How and what we smell.

Touch

Most people relate touch to hands, and yet we actually use our whole bodies to touch. The development of this tactile sense varies greatly within a group.

Touch test. Put various objects into a bag and let the children feel the objects, naming and describing each. Use a:

Flashlight battery	Marble
Paper clip	Penny
Toy car	Sandpaper
Lipstick case	
Cardboard shapes (circle, square, diamond, rectangle, hexagon)	

Fabric board. Collect different samples of fabrics and attach them to a board. Let your group feel the difference in texture and discuss the adjectives that describe each example: soft, rough, smooth, stiff, pliable, spongy, silky, rigid, patterned. Use:

Fur	Grosgrain	Lace	Wool
Velvet	Vinyl	Plastic	Polyester
Silk	Corduroy	Satin	Fleece

Feel and show. Collect a number of objects. Actually run your hands over and around each one. Choose some members of your audience to do this too. What determines the feel of an object? Its texture? An object's size and shape are also important. Put the object out of sight, then examine the same object through touch in your imagination. Then have each participant describe what he or she has handled.

Books about touch:

Allington, Richard L. and Kathleen Cowles. *Touching.* Art by Yoshi Miyake. Random, 1981.

Baer, Edith. *The Wonder of Hands.* Photos by Tana Hoban. Parents, 1970.

Kunhardt, Dorothy. *Pat the Bunny.* Art by author. Simon and Schuster, 1940.

Newberry, Clare Turley. *The Kitten's ABC.* Art by author. Harper, 1965.

Oxenbury, Helen. *I Touch.* Art by author. Random, 1985.

Witte, Patricia, and Eva K. Evans. *Touch Me Book.* Art by Harlow Rockwell. Capitol, 1961.

Sound

Once when my daughter was younger, she and I were driving together through a rain storm when she observed that it was raining but she couldn't hear the rain. We stopped by the side of the road and I turned off the motor. Now we could hear the rain and some birds. We listened for other sounds and heard a boy shouting, a dog barking. When the car was restarted we noticed that the windshield wipers, the motor, and the radio all helped to drown out the sound of the rain. Both of us learned that the world is full of sounds that we often ignore.

Sound test. In this exercise everyone in the group shuts their eyes and listens while you make a variety of sounds. Include:

> Shake beads in a bottle
> Shuffle a deck of cards
> Click a ball point pen
> Open and close a zipper
> Tear transparent or masking tape from a dispenser
> Cut with scissors
> Shift coins from hand to hand
> Wrinkle paper
> Rattle seeds in a package

Ask your listeners to guess what is making each sound and have them describe it.

Sound vs. speech. The use of gibberish in an exercise is usually considered to be of more benefit to the advanced student, but I find that beginning students enjoy and are capable of experimenting with sounds. The idea is to use sounds but not words to get a point across. These may be singing rhythms or gibberish. The rhythm and intonation of speech should tell the audience what the character is trying to get across. Try these individually:

Give an enthusiastic speech supporting a favorite cause
Speak on the telephone angrily, sweetly, or questioningly

Select two people and ask them to use only sounds, no words to:

Have an argument
Teach a concept

Sound observation. Have your group sit quietly on the floor. Close your eyes. Consciously listen to the sounds outside the room. Now listen to the sounds in the room. Now eliminate from your consciousness all external sounds and listen to the sounds of your own body. As I write this, if I concentrate I can hear my husband faxing a memo in the next room, and a bird making occasional remarks outside the window. In the room where I'm working I can now hear the buzz of the fluorescent light and the drip of the sink behind me. I'll probably have to switch working areas now that I realize how noisy it is in here!

Books exploring sound:

Brown, Margaret Wise. *The Noisy Book*. Harper, 1939. See others in this series also.

Dunbar, Joyce. *Four Fierce Kittens*. Art by Jakki Wood. Scholastic, 1991.

Fife, Dale H. *The Empty Lot*. Art by Jim Arnosky. Little, 1991.

Fox, Mem. *Night Noises*. Art by Terry Denton. Harcourt, 1989.

Lemieux, Michéle. *What's That Noise?* Morrow, 1984.

Martin, Bill Jr. *Polar Bear, Polar Bear What Do You Hear?* Art by Eric Carle. Holt, 1991.

Ryder, Joanne. *When the Woods Hum?* Art by Catherine Stock. Morrow, 1991.

Showers, Paul. *The Listening Walk*. Art by Aliki. Harper, 1991.

Wynne-Jones, Tim. *The Hour of the Frog*. Art by Catharine O'Neil. Little, 1989.

Sight

Although sight is the most developed of the senses some people "see" better than others, in an artistic sense. Try to develop the art of seeing. Looking through a pinhole can help you do this.

Imagine what you would see if you were an ant in a cornfield. What would you see? If you were a giant in the same cornfield how would you see things differently? Take a piece of cardboard. Make a tiny hole in it with a fine pin. Now walk around indoors or outdoors and look at the world through the tiny pinhole. Do you see things differently? How?

Object test. Place a number of objects on a tray:

Fork	Toy truck
Whistle	Feather
Penny	Banana
Sock	Cup
Pliers	Watch

Pass the tray around. Let each person look at it for 30 seconds. Cover the tray. How many objects on the tray can each list? The same exercise can be conducted with a collection of photographs or pictures cut from magazines.

Observation test. Select someone to leave the room. Have the other participants list what the absent person is wearing. Next, choose something that everyone in the group has passed so many times they no longer really see it: the statue in front of the school, the motto above the library door, or the like. Have all the participants write down its description. Read some of these to the group and discuss the need to develop the habit of observing.

Books featuring seeing:

Hoban, Tana. *Look Again!* Photos by author. Macmillan, 1971.

Isadora, Rachel. *I See.* Art by author. Greenwillow, 1985.

Macdonald, Maryann. *Little Hippo Gets Glasses.* Art by Anna King. Dial, 1991.

Martin, Bill Jr. and John Archambault. *Knots on a Counting Rope.* Art by Ted Rand. Holt, 1987.

Young, Ed. *Seven Blind Mice.* Art by author. Philomel, 1992.

Books featuring visual games:

Dunbar, Fiona. *You'll Never Guess!* Art by author. Dial, 1991.

Handford, Martin. *Where's Waldo?* Little, 1987.

Jonas, Ann. *Round Trip.* Art by author. Greenwillow, 1983.

MacDonald, Suse. *Alphabatics.* Art by author. Bradbury, 1986.

Marzolla, Jean. *I Spy: A Book of Picture Riddles.* Photos by Walter Wick. Scholastic, 1992.

Pomerantz, Charlotte. *Where's the Bear?* Art by Byron Barton. Greenwillow, 1984.

Shaw, Charles. *It Looked like Spilt Milk.* Art by author. Harper, 1947.

Wilson, April. *Look Again! The Second Ultimate Spot-the-Difference Book.* Art by author. Dial, 1992.

Yektai, Niki. *What's Missing?* Art by Susannah Ryan. Clarion, 1987.

Pantomime

The next exercises you can attempt with your group are pantomime. In these exercises use body movements and facial expressions without words to express actions and emotions.

Pass an object. Sit in a circle. Pass a "hot potato" or a "precious wine glass." Then pick someone to decide on an imaginary object to pass. The last person tells what it was that was being passed. Let the children enjoy themselves, but caution them to pay attention. Don't be too critical until they've had some experience.

Action pantomimes

Fly a kite	Walk a tightrope
Catch a fish	Row a boat
Pick a delicate blossom	Play the piano
Pull a stubborn weed	Push a stalled car
Pick a flower with thorns	Lift a heavy tray
Walk a dog	Make a snowman

Action exercises. Now stand in a semicircle with room for each child to move around. Try some of these exercises as a group, individually or with a partner.

Grow from a seed to a flower
Melt slowly like an iceberg in the sun
Wave goodbye to your best friend
Wave goodbye to someone you dislike but are polite to
A wooden soldier picks a flower
A small child picks a flower
Open an imaginary door
Take a shower
Look in a mirror (your partner mirrors your actions)
Read a sad book
Climb a ladder
Blow up a balloon
Ride a horse
Explore a cave
Play a game of tennis

Longer pantomime exercises

Watch a sports event on television
Watch a sports event in a crowded stadium
Wait in a dentist's office with a painful tooth
Eat spaghetti at a formal dinner party
Ride a carousel
Be a fish enjoying a frolic in the ocean
Be a snowflake falling on a flower
Be the wind blowing over a tree
Be a cat stalking a bird

Write the following ideas on cards. Let each child pick a card and act out the activity described while the group guesses what the performer is doing.

Open a:

Package of seeds	Umbrella	Sewing kit
Can of paint	Letter	Jar of glue
Safe	Chinese fortune	Box of stationery
Bottle of catsup	cookie	

You are:

Happy	Tired	Excited
Sad	Cold	Sleepy
Hungry	Hot	
Worried	Thirsty	

You are a:

Rabbit	Squirrel	Chicken
Cat	Bird	Elephant
Tiger	Fish	
Monkey	Horse	

You are a:

Hairdresser	Teacher
Musician	Painter
Cook	Dancer
Librarian	Shoemaker

Doing these exercises to music adds another dimension to pantomime. Try using a tape deck or compact disc player, or, if you are lucky enough to have a piano and a talented pianist to accompany you, all the better. Do the exercises both with and without music.

Animal Bag

Assemble a variety of wooden animals, or cut an assortment of animal shapes from poster board, or use animal crackers for this activity. Place the animals in a bag or box. Each child picks an animal from the bag and acts out in pantomime the animal's movements. To add books to this activity, let each child search in the library for a story or poem that represents his or her animal.

Charades

My father worked for the United Nations, and my parents were constantly entertaining government officials from foreign countries. Occasionally after a dinner party they would play charades, and this was my first introduction to the brilliance of nonverbal theater. Divide your group into two teams. Each group separately makes a list of short phrases: enough for each player on the opposite team. Decide in advance if you will use movies, book, song or play titles, proverbs, or historical events. (Of course I always suggest using book titles!) Write each charade on a slip of paper. Each player in turn is given a phrase his or her teammates must figure out as the charade is acted. He or she may work on the whole phrase, single words, or even syllables. The way the game was played in my home was that each person on both teams was given a chance: no winners, no losers. If you wish, however, you may time each team, the one with the lowest total time winning. The game involves everyone: guessing a teammate's charade and acting one out.

Of course it's more fun for the members of each group to work out their own hand signals to indicate common words and phrases, but there are some obvious symbols such as:

> Sounds like: pull earlobe or cup ear
> Longer word: pull two hands apart
> Shorter word: chop one hand against opposite palm
> Small word: (and, on, a, the, to) show thumb and forefinger close together
> The whole phrase: show a circle with your arms
> Antonyms: hold hands together and turn hands over
> Synonyms: make circle motion towards you
> He: point to boy
> She: point to girl
> I: point to eye
> Start over: motion with hands like umpire calling baseball "safe"

Improvisation

Improvisation adds speech to creative drama, but it is not scripted speech. Suggest a topic and let the children act it out. Try not to direct the play too much, and if possible let the children choose their parts and set up the action.

Try these exercises in expressing one's thoughts orally. Give the children a chance to collect their thoughts before they begin and don't let them talk for too long. Have them describe what it feels like:

> To be an ant in a department store
> Not to be asked to a birthday party
> To win a championship auto race
> To fail the spelling test

Next, without using their hands or body, have the children describe how to:

Make a bed
Ride a bicycle
Play pin the tail on the donkey
Jump rope
Get into a sleeping bag

Then try more advanced problems in expressing oral thought. Have each:

Describe a member of his or her family, good points and bad
Impress someone with the need for a stoplight across from the school
Argue in front of the United Nations for funds for one's favorite cause
Confess to mother that he or she broke her favorite vase.

The following are useful as group activities:

Scene: Living room
  Characters: Two friends
  Situation: The friend has come to visit. The hostess is newly engaged, with a new ring; she wants her friend to notice the ring without actually telling her about it.

Scene: Living room
  Characters: Father, mother, children
  Situation: Family conference to discuss summer vacation.

Scene: Veterinarian's office
  Characters: Various people and their pets (eccentric old lady, young boy, etc.)
  Situation: Each person describes his or her pet's problem to an attendant.

Scene: A meeting hall
  Characters: Principal, teachers, trustees, parents, students, reporters
  Situation: Choose a problem and have a meeting.

Stories to Dramatize

Many stories lend themselves to dramatization. After you have experimented with some of the creative dramatics exercises given here, you might try a story. To begin, read the story aloud to your group. Then, list the various parts on a chalkboard and let people volunteer for parts they would like to play. Now read the story again. You may also want to outline the order of action if your audience has never played "let's pretend" before. The important thing to remember, however, is that it's not necessary for the children to memorize their lines. Instead the idea is to follow the general outline of the plot and act out the story. These two stories are perfect starters for beginning creative drama groups. Both are extended jokes and easy to retell in play form.

THE PEPPER SOUP

This story is easy to dramatize. There is lots of action to mime, and children can make up their own dialogue to embellish the story.

Elizabeth and Eric were in charge of the younger children while Mom and Dad were working. "What shall we make for dinner?" asked Eric. It was a special day because it was their parents' wedding anniversary.

"Dad loves beef stew. Let's try making it."

"I'll get the pot."

"I'll cut up the beef."

"I'll slice the carrots."

"I'll slice the celery."

"I'll tear the bay leaves into small pieces."

"I'll peel the potatoes."

"I'll slice the onions. I'm crying."

Put the beef in the pot. Put the carrots in the pot. Put the celery in the pot. Put the bay leaves in the pot. Put the potatoes in the pot. Put the onions in the pot. Now, stir the stew and put in a pinch of salt.

Let's go finish our chores while it simmers.

Eric went into the garden. Elizabeth went into the laundry room. Kim went to the bedroom. Randy went into the living room. Lou went to the barn.

Then Eric suddenly remembered the stew. He called to the other children:

"We forgot to put pepper in the stew. I'm busy weeding the garden. I can't do it."

"I haven't got the time," said Elizabeth. "I'm just doing the wash."

"I'm upstairs," said Kim, "making my bed."

"Sorry," said Randy. "I'm washing the windows."

"I'm milking the cow," called Lou.

Eric stopped working. "I'd better put the pepper in the stew." Eric went into the kitchen and put some pepper in the pot and returned to the garden.

Elizabeth dried her hands. "I better put some pepper in the stew." Elizabeth went into the kitchen and put some pepper in the pot and returned to the laundry room.

Kim smoothed the bed. "I better put some pepper in the stew." Kim went into the kitchen and put some pepper in the pot and returned to the bedroom.

Randy wrung out the window cloth. "I better put some pepper in the pot." Randy went into the kitchen and put some pepper in the pot and returned to the living room.

Lou stopped milking the cow. "I better put some pepper in the pot." Lou went into the kitchen and put some pepper in the pot and returned to the barn.

"The stew is ready. Let's set the table." The children came into the dining room and set the table.

"Just in time. Here come Mom and Dad."

"Surprise! We've made your favorite stew for your anniversary."

Eric carried the stew to the table and served it to the family.

Mom tasted the stew and coughed. Dad tasted the stew and sputtered. Eric tasted the stew and laughed. Elizabeth, Kim, Randy and Lou all tasted the stew. "Yuck." "Fire!" "Hot." "Wow!" "Help!" they said while fanning themselves.

"I think we all found the time to put pepper in the stew," said Eric. "It's no longer beef stew. It's pepper stew!"

"Thank you for all your effort," said Mom.

"Yes, thanks," said Dad. "Let's go out to dinner. After all, it's our anniversary."

"Hurray for pepper stew!" cheered Lou.

THE SILLY FARMER

Pleasant DeSpain

Pleasant DeSpain is a professional storyteller from the Seattle, Washington area. His two-volume collection of stories is particularly useful for the teller in search of short humorous stories. "The Silly Farmer" is an Ethiopian tale from Twenty-Two Splendid Tales to Tell. *Read aloud or tell the story, then have your group act it out as a creative drama exercise.*

Once there was a silly farmer named Zaheed. One day his wife told him that she was going to have a baby. Zaheed asked her what kind of baby it would be, but she didn't know.

"Then," said Zaheed, "I will visit the wise old woman who lives at the base of the mountains. She has magic, both black and white, and she will be able to tell me."

He took a gold piece that he had hidden deep in his mattress and walked all morning until he reached the old witch's hut.

"I've come to ask you a difficult question," said Zaheed. "And if you can give me a satisfactory answer, I'll pay you with this piece of gold."

The old woman stared at him with dark eyes and nodded her agreement.

"My wife is going to have a child, but she doesn't know what kind it will be. Can you tell me!"

The old woman opened a small wooden chest and removed three ancient bones. She tossed them on the ground and studied the pattern they made. She shook her head and said, "Ehh."

Zaheed shook his head and said, "Ehh."

She tossed them again and studied the pattern. "Ahh!"

"Ahh!" repeated Zaheed.

Once more she tossed the bones and studied the pattern. "Of course!" she exclaimed.

"Of course!" shouted Zaheed.

"Your wife's child will be either a boy or a girl."

"How wonderful!" said Zaheed. He gave the witch the gold piece and ran home to tell his wife the good news.

Several months later his wife had a fat baby girl. "You see," Zaheed told all of his neighbors, "the old woman was right!"

Soon it was time to baptise the girl, but Zaheed and his wife couldn't think of a proper name for her.

"I'll go ask the old woman," said Zaheed. "She is wise and will tell me our daughter's name."

He took another piece of gold from the mattress and walked back to the witch's hut. After Zaheed explained the problem, the old woman took the bones from the chest and tossed them onto the floor. "Ahh!" said she.

"Ahh!" said Zaheed.

Again she tossed the bones. "Of course!"

"Of course!" repeated Zaheed.

"Give me the gold," said the witch, "and I will whisper the child's name into your hands."

Zaheed did as she said and extended his hands. She quickly whispered into them and said, "Now close your hands tight so that you won't lose it on the way home."

The farmer ran toward home with his hands clasped together. When he came to his neighbor's farm he saw several of the men pitching hay into tall stacks. "I have it! I have it!" he cried. "The name of my daughter is here in my hands!"

Just then he slipped on some loose hay and fell to the ground. His hands came apart, and he yelled, "Now I've lost it! Quickly, help me find it again!"

Several of the men ran up and helped Zaheed search through the haystack with their pitchforks.

Soon after, a woman from the village walked by and asked what they were looking for. Zaheed explained how the witch had given him the name and how he had lost it.

"It is nonsense!" she declared. "Simply nonsense!"

"Oh, thank you!" said Zaheed. "I thought I had lost it forever."

When he got home the silly farmer explained everything to his wife. "The witch whispered the name into my hands, but I lost it on the way home. The neighbor woman found it and told it to me. Our daughter's name is Nonsense! Simply Nonsense!"

And they call her Simply Nonsense, to this very day.

Storytelling with Masks

Masks have been used to tell stories in many cultures. Native North Americans, the native people of Sri Lanka, and the tribes of Africa are particularly noted for their use of masks in storytelling.

As a storyteller, you may want to experiment with the use of masks when telling a story. Audience participation in creative drama is also easily encouraged when players can instantly become another character by putting on a mask.

Masks are both intriguing to make and amusing to use while telling a story. Use a mask to introduce a story or show it at the end of the story as an illustration or exhibit. You can even wear a mask while telling a story, but if you do use this method, be sure that you can be heard through the mask. The two stories that follow work especially well with masks.

DIRT FOR SALE: A STORY FROM MEXICO

Consider wearing Ortega's mask at the end of the story when he revisits the ditchdiggers. It is also very funny to wear it as he frightens the robbers. You might try it both ways to see which method works best for your style of telling.

Ortega was not very clever. It was hard for him to make a living. The young men of the village sneered when he came into town to look for work. They teased him whenever they had the time to think up a good prank.

"What are you doing?" asked Ortega as he watched the men dig a hole for the pipeline near the sea.

The foreman was hot and tired. He didn't have time for Ortega's silly questions. Surely anyone else could see that the men were digging a hole for a pipe.

"What does it look like?" snapped the foreman. "We are digging up dirt to sell. You can get a great deal of money for this fine dirt. If you'd like you can dig here and take away any dirt that you dig up."

"How wonderful," thought Ortega. "Now I will be rich." He took the foreman's shovel and the foreman and his men sat under a shade tree and joked and laughed while Ortega worked in the hot sun. By the end of the day the hole was dug. Ortega put the dirt in a big sack and hoisted it onto his shoulders. It was heavy to carry, but he felt good, for soon he would be rich. He thanked the men who congratulated him for being so clever. The workmen were delighted that they had tricked Ortega into doing their work. They laughed that anyone could be such a simpleton.

Ortega went to the town market to try to sell his dirt. "Dirt for sale," he called. People stopped and stared. Some actually laughed. "Surely it is some kind of joke. He can't really be trying to sell dirt," a woman said to her husband.

Ortega was disappoined but not discouraged. He hefted the heavy bag on his shoulders and walked up and down the narrow aisles of the market between stalls hawking his dirt. "Dirt for sale. Dirt for sale."

Most people ignored him, though some giggled or laughed out loud. A mask seller was carrying bark masks on a stick. He watched Ortega as he lugged the heavy sack of dirt through the crowded market. He approached Ortega and said, "Silly man. No one will buy dirt."

Ortega explained how he had dug in the ground all day in exchange for the valuable dirt.

"You've been tricked," the mask seller said. "You're so silly you should wear a mask and sell yourself as a clown."

Ortega was so upset that he looked as though he would cry. The mask seller took pity on him and, thinking to make him feel better, took one of his masks off the stick and gave it to Ortega. "Here," he said, "this will make you feel better." Ortega took the mask and thanked the man. It was a colorful mask painted with bright colors. Ortega dumped the dirt out of the sack and put the mask in the sack to take home.

It was so late in the afternoon that Ortega thought he would spend the night near the marketplace and not take the long walk to his little hut on the other side of town. He lay down and lay the brown sack over himself. It was cold with the wind blowing, so Ortega took the bark mask and put it on his face for added warmth. Soon he was fast asleep. He dreamt about warm glowing gold.

Later that night a band of robbers decided to camp just a few feet from where Ortega was sleeping. They had several bags of gold with them. They talked about the gold and what they would buy with it in the market the next day. The leader of the band was pacing as he talked and chanced to look down at the sleeping Ortega. By the glow of their fire Ortega was a frightening sight with his garish mask and brown sack body.

The robber screamed, "A demon! It's a demon! Run everyone!" The shouting woke Ortega. He was hungry and thirsty. Perhaps these men had some food to give him. He stood up with the brown burlap sack swinging from his neck and the mask with its open mouth leering. "I'm hungry," wailed Ortega. The robbers became even more frightened. "The demon is going to eat us! Run!" "I'm hungry," wailed Ortega. Now the robbers ran as fast as they could. Ortega tried to run after them but he got tangled in the sack. He couldn't see well with the mask covering his head and he tripped over the sack of gold.

When he picked himself up and took the mask off his head he found the bags of gold. "What's this?" he said. "This is just like my dream. I'm rich."

The next morning Ortega walked into the market and bought himself some new clothes. He would decide later how to spend the rest of the money. There was a lot of gold. He would be rich for many years.

Ortega bought a new leather sack for his new belongings and the bark mask. "When I build a new house I will put a mound of dirt in front of the house with the mask on top of it," he decided.

He hired a carriage drawn by four horses to take him home. When he passed the men working on the ditch he had the coachman stop. The ditchdiggers were astonished. Could this be that silly Ortega who had believed their ridiculous story about selling dirt?

Ortega stepped down from the carriage. He walked slowly toward the men, giving them enough time to look with envy at his new clothes.

"Just thought I'd stop and say 'thank you.' I loved your suggestion to sell dirt. Let me know when you have another good idea."

LAZY AS AN OX: A KOREAN TALE

This is a morality tale, leavened by Wan Le's antics as an ox. If you tell this story to children they will be amused at the storyteller holding a mask to her or his face and bellowing, "Moo!" Adults are never sure whether they should laugh or not. Perhaps they have thought once or twice that life might be easier as an ox.

Wan Le was an apprentice to a mask-maker. But no one was very confident that Wan Le would actually learn enough to fashion masks himself since he was quite lazy. The Master often discovered him taking a nap in the courtyard using a half-finished mask as a sunshade.

There was some talk in the village that Wan Le would actually lose his apprenticeship and have no job at all. In such an industrious nation it was almost unheard of to be chronically lazy.

Wan Le's mother was even more upset than the mask-maker. She worried about what would happen to her son if he continued to be so lethargic.

"You don't seem happy in your work. You are always avoiding it," she said one night when Wan Le returned home after another non-productive day. "Is there some other profession that would please you more?"

Wan Le was almost too lazy to answer. In fact, he felt ready for his nap, the third of the day. How to end his mother's nightly tongue-lashing? He chanced to look outside and saw their ox lying by the door, switching flies with his tail. "I'd like to be an ox," answered Wan Le.

"They seem to have the perfect life, lying about in the pastures and on the roadways."

Wan Le's mother was angry. What a foolish boy she had raised. "Go then and be an ox," she said.

The next morning Wan Le walked slowly to the mask-maker's shop. He would be late as usual. He thought, but not very hard, as he shuffled along. "It would be nice to be an ox," he thought. "They have someone to feed them and a place to live." Arriving at the shop he found that today's task was to finish painting an oxen mask for the spring festival. Wan Le sighed. He would have to work fast and furiously all day. There might not even be time for a nap. "I'd better take my nap now," mused Wan Le. Even though Wan Le had just arrived for work, he lay down on his workbench and laid the unfinished ox mask on his face. Soon he was fast asleep, dreaming of sleeping, no doubt.

When Wan Le awoke he walked outside for a breath of fresh air. The mask still covered his face.

A herd of oxen being driven to market were coming down the road. The ox master saw Wan Le in the doorway. "Here ox. Get a move on." Wan Le laughed to be mistaken for an ox, but the mask muffled his voice, so it sounded like "Moo."

Soon he found himself being herded along with the oxen. He tried to remove his mask, but it was stuck fast to his face. "Moo," called Wan Le. Driven with the rest of the herd to the holding pen, Wan Le found that he had gotten his wish. He was treated just like an ox. For supper there was a meager supply of hay, which he had to share with the other oxen. "Moo, Moo," bellowed Wan Le. It wasn't so wonderful to be an ox after all. In the next few days, he had to haul heavy wagons loaded with goods for the market. There was no time to rest, and it was hard, monotonous work throughout the day. At night he worked pulling a wagon with travelers from one town to the other. "Moo, Moo," complained Wan Le, but no one listened.

Wan Le was so exhausted from his work as an ox that he hardly remembered what it was like to be a man. One day he found himself driven back to his home town and chanced to see his old master carrying a load of bark, materials for a new line of handcrafted masks. At the time Wan Le was hauling a load of grain to market. He was tired and thirsty. His ox brain began to work and he found himself thinking that he should volunteer to help carry the mask-maker's materials. "Moo, Moo," bellowed Wan Le as he strained against the wagon load. The ox mask fell to the ground. Wan Le found himself a man again.

"There you are," said the master. "I was wondering where you've been."

"Let me help you carry that bark," volunteered Wan Le.

Wan Le became a respected mask-maker. His work was bought by scholars and peasants alike. His specialty was the carving of life-like representations of the faces of tired oxen.

His mother always wondered why he always kept an early unfinished mask hanging on the wall. But it served as a reminder to Wan Le that an oxen's life is not a lazy one.

"Moo."

Reader's Theater

Unlike creative drama exercises and plays, where a group acts out a story without worrying too much about getting each line right, in reader's theater the focus is on *reading:* the idea is for each character to hold a copy of the script and actually read his or her lines aloud. I couldn't read very well in second and third grade, but I loved to show off by being in plays. Reader's theater was perfect for me; practice in reading and a chance to be a star, sort of. I've written a whole book of stories and poems that I've scripted in memory of my own schooldays. It's called *Presenting Reader's Theater: Plays and Poems to Read Aloud.* If you'd like to start today, however, here are three poems to begin with: two I've scripted myself, the other ("A Boy and His Dog") was originally written in script form.

voice one: Broom Balancing
voice two: by Kathleen Fraser

voice one: Millicent can play the flute
voice two: and Francine can dance a jig.
voice three: but I can balance a broom.

voice one: Susanna knows how to bake cookies
voice two: and Harold can stand on one foot
voice three: but I can balance a broom

voice one: Jeffrey can climb a ladder backwards
voice two: and Andrew can count to five thousand and two,
voice three: but I can balance a broom.
Do you think a circus might discover me?

A BOY AND HIS DOG

Zaro Weil

Boy: Here dog
Dog: Woof
Boy: Good dog
Dog: Woof woof
Boy: Now sit
Dog: Woof woof woof
Boy: Now stand
Dog: Woof woof woof woof

Boy: Roll over
Dog: Woof woof woof woof woof
Boy: Now speak
Dog: Here boy

voice one: To catch a fish
voice two: by Eloise Greenfield

voice one: It takes more than a wish
              to catch a fish
voice two: you take the hook
              you add the bait
              you concentrate
voice one: and then you wait
              you wait you wait
voice two: but not a bite
              the fish don't have
              an appetite
voice one: so tell them what
              good bait you've got
              and how your bait
              can hit the spot
voice two: this works a whole
              lot better than
              a wish
voice one: if you really want to catch
              a fish.

Audience

I'd like to add a word about being a good member of the audience. Impress upon your listeners that this role is every bit as important as the players. A performer relies totally on the response of the audience and they have an obligation to show their emotions, to laugh when it's funny, and cry when it's sad. My husband and I attended a formal dance at which there was entertainment that we particularly enjoyed. The performers were having a difficult time acting over the general social buzz in the back of the room. When they were finished they thanked "the table over there" for their attention. The table they indicated was ours. We felt like we were very special. All we had done was show our enjoyment outwardly, and the performers had reacted favorably.

Evaluation

In creative dramatics, it is traditional to learn by "talking about it." The members of the group evaluate each other. This makes for a different kind of growth: thinking about what you see; articulating your thoughts; and being constructive in your comments rather than destructive. As a leader you have a responsibility to see that comments really contribute to the group's understanding. I do caution you, however, not to let the critique diminish the pleasure of the activity!

Prop Box and Costume Box

It is not necessary to have costumes and props, but it is fun to dress up. Collecting props and making scenery are sometimes even more intriguing than acting. Collect old clothes for your costume box. Accessories such as hats, costume jewelry, and shoes are particularly useful. Props can be almost anything. Containers such as baskets (Little Red Riding Hood) and pails (Jack and Jill) always come in handy. If you are going to act out fairy tales you'll probably enjoy a crown or two, a magic wand, and maybe a jeweled box. Household objects—brooms, dishes and silverware—are often needed. Building blocks can be made to represent almost anything if you just will them to be something. Four large boxes 3 feet by 4 feet, painted in bright colors, can be used for large pieces: a bed, table, chairs or even a mountain. Depending on the amount of time that you have to spend with creative dramatics, you might want to plan one session making props for the prop box or designing costumes, for these are creative pursuits in their own right.

Booklist: Creative Dramatics Plus

Many stories translate well to creative dramatics. Here are some favorites. I've chosen mostly picture books because they can be read in one sitting. Experiment with showing the pictures as you read the story or not showing them at all. Most of the stories cover a wide age grouping, and even young adults will enjoy acting out these simple tales.

Many of the stories in the bibliographies at the end of chapter 5 and in chapter 19 will be useful in creative dramatics as well.

Aardema, Verna. *Traveling to Tondo: A Tale of the Nkundo of Zaire.* Art by Will Hillenbrand. Knopf, 1991. "If a thing is not wise to do, it is best to say N-YEH!"

Aragon, Jane Chelsea. *Salt Hands.* Art by Ted Rand. Dutton, 1989. In the quiet and dark of the night a little girl gentles a deer.

Baylor, Byrd. *Everybody Needs a Rock*. Art by Peter Parnall. Scribner, 1974. How to find and cherish a friend. The rock has a good part.

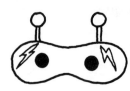

Bradman, Tony. *It Came from Outer Space*. Art by Carol Wright. Dial, 1992. School children think a spaceman from outer space is strange. It turns out that the visitor is from earth, the children from another planet. Good opportunity to use masks.

Brown, Marcia. *Once a Mouse*. Art by author. Scribner, 1947. This story is based on a fable. The cast to dramatize this consists mostly of animals.

Burns, Marilyn. *The Book of Think (or How to Solve a Problem Twice Your Size)*. Art by Martha Weston. Little, 1976. Good book to begin discussions about understanding one's self. Discusses logic, tunnel vision, and general problem-solving.

Calmenson, Stephanie. *The Children's Aesop*. Art by Robert Byrd. Boyd's Mill, 1988. "The Hare and the Tortoise" and "The Milkmaid and Her Pail" are included in this collection of 28 fables.

_____. *The Principal's New Clothes*. Art by Denise Brunkus. Scholastic, 1989. A school setting for Hans Christian Andersen's "The Emperor's New Clothes."

Carew, Jan. *The Third Gift*. Art by Leo and Diane Dillon. Little, 1974. This beautiful African tale might be performed best with a combination narrator and actors.

Carrick, Carol. *Left Behind*. Art by Donald Carrick. Clarion, 1988. On a school field trip, a little boy gets lost on the New York subway.

Daugherty, James. *Andy and the Lion*. Art by author. Viking, 1938. Two major characters, but lots of minor ones and plenty of action make this story a good choice for dramatics.

Elkin, Benjamin. *How the Tsar Drinks Tea*. Art by Anita Lobel. Parents, 1971. A peasant and the Tsar turn out to do things the same way. The people in the Tsar's court give an opportunity for young players to act many types.

Great Children's Stories: The Classic Volland Edition. Art by Frederick Richardson. Hubbard/Rand, 1972. Classic tales include "The Old Woman and Her Pig" and "Chicken Licken."

Hill, Donna. *Ms. Glee Was Waiting*. Art by Diane Dawson. Atheneum, 1978. Laura has many excuses for being late to her piano lesson.

Hughes, Shirley. *Alfie Gets in First*. Art by author. Lothrop, 1981. Alfie locks himself in the house and the neighborhood tries to set him free.

Lee, Allison. *A Handbook of Creative Dance and Drama: Ideas for Teachers*. Heinemann, 1992. Ideas for using drama exercises with elementary school children.

Lionni, Leo. *Frederick*. Art by author. Pantheon, 1967. A mouse teaches his friends the worth of words. All the players are mice. The action of working is good exercise. This is best done with a narrator.

Marzolla, Jean. *Pretend You're a Cat*. Art by Jerry Pinkney. Dial, 1990. Young players can imitate these animals while reciting poetry.

McCloskey, Robert. *Blueberries for Sal*. Art by author. Viking, 1966. A mother bear and her cub, a human mother and her child in a good mix-up.

McCully, Emily Arnold. *The Evil Spell*. Art by author. Harper, 1990. Edwin Bear learns to overcome his stage fright in a charming story to share.

McKissack, Patricia C. *Flossie and the Fox*. Art by Rachel Isadora. Dial, 1986. Flossie outwits a fox on the way to Miz Violas.

Mooser, Stephen. *The Ghost with the Halloween Hiccups*. Art by Tomie de Paola. Watts, 1977. Mr. Penny tries to stop his hiccups before the play.

Morgan, Pierr. *The Turnip: An Old Russian Folktale*. Art by author. Philomel, 1990. The whole family tries to pull an enormous turnip from the ground.

Mueller, Virginia. *Monster's Birthday Hiccups*. Art by Lynn Munsinger. Whitman, 1991. Everyone tries to help monster get rid of his hiccups.

Myers, Bernice. *Not This Bear!* Art by author. Four Winds, 1968. Bears mistake a little boy for their cousin. Lot of good action.

Noble, Trinka. *The King's Tea*. Art by author. Dial, 1979. Who ruined the King's tea?

Oxenbury, Helen. *Pig Tale*. Art by author. Morrow, 1973. Two pigs learn that their life is the good life after all.

Polacco, Patricia. *Meteor!* Art by author. Dodd, 1987. Townspeople celebrate the arrival of a meteor.

Pulver, Robin. *Mrs. Toggle's Zipper*. Art by R. W. Alley. Four Winds, 1990. Everyone in school tries to fix Mrs. Toggle's broken zipper.

Raskin, Ellen. *Nothing Ever Happens on My Block*. Art by author. Atheneum, 1966. A young boy complains of boredom while fascinating events occur all around him.

"Rats on the Roof" in *Rats on the Roof* by James Marshall. Art by author. Dial, 1991. Otis and Sophie dog attempt to hire a cat to rid their roof of rats.

Root, Phyllis. *Soup for Supper*. Art by Sue Truesdell. Harper, 1986. The wee small woman prepares soup with her new friend, Giant Rumbleton.

Sawicki, Norma Jean. *Something for Mom*. Lothrop, 1987. Mom is urging her daughter to breakfast, but Matilda is busy preparing a surprise.

Schick, Eleanor. *I Have Another Language: The Language Is Dance*. Macmillan, 1992. A young girl thinks about her joy in dancing.

Sendak, Maurice. *Where the Wild Things Are*. Art by author. Harper, 1963. Children enjoy cavorting in "the wild rumpus" as wild things.

Seuss, Dr. (pseud. for Theodor Seuss Geisel). *The 500 Hats of Bartholomew Cubbins*. Art by author. Vanguard, 1938. Bartholomew has a dreadful time removing his hat to honor the king.

Shapiro, Arnold. *"Could I Keep Him?"* Art by Pat Harris. Barrons, 1990. Finally a little boy and his Mom come to an agreement about a pet.

Stewart, Sarah. *The Money Tree*. Art by David Small. Farrar, 1991. Miss McGillicuddy is a bit surprised when money starts to grow on her tree.

Turkle, Brinton. *Deep in the Forest*. Art by author. Dutton, 1976. One of many wordless picture books being published. Look, then act out in pantomime or with dialogue. This one is a variant of "The Three Bears."

Viorst, Judith. *Alexander and the Terrible, Horrible, No Good, Very Bad Day*. Art by Ray Cruz. Atheneum, 1972. Everything goes wrong in just one day.

Williams, Sue. *I Went Walking*. Art by Julie Vivas. Harcourt, 1989. "What did you see?" when a little boy goes walking.

Zemach, Harve. *Duffy and the Devil: A Cornish Tale*. Art by Margot Zemach. Farrar, 1973.

_____. *A Penny a Look*. Art by Margot Zemach. Farrar, 1971. Just two of the funny books by the Zemachs that are filled with interesting characters to imitate.

And don't forget Grimm's fairy tales, Russian fairy tales, and such fantasy as *The Peterkin Papers* by Lucretia P. Hale (Osgood, 1880).

Booklist: Picture Books about Young Players

Bauer, Caroline Feller. *Putting on a Play*. Art by Cyd Moore. Scott, Foresman, 1992. A script to produce is included along with descriptions of props, settings, and costumes.

Hoffman, Mary. *Amazing Grace*. Art by Caroline Binch. Dial, 1991. Grace, who pretends to be characters from books, ends up as the lead in "Peter Pan," despite the doubts of her classmates.

Johnson, Dolores. *The Best Bug to Be*. Art by author. Macmillan, 1992. Kelly would have liked a more exciting part in the play, but resolves to be the "best bumblebee."

Krementz, Jill. *A Very Young Actress*. Photos. Knopf, 1991. Photo essay shows a 10-year-old girl as she auditions for, rehearses, and stars in a production of *Annie 2*.

McCully, Emily Arnold. *Speak Up, Blanche!* Art by author. Harper, 1991. Blanche, a lamb, would like a part in the play, but finds that she is a scene designer with real talent.

Tryon, Leslie. *Albert's Play*. Art by author. Atheneum, 1992. Albert the duck puts on a production of "The Owl and the Pussycat."

Booklist: Novels Featuring Child Performers

Avi. *Romeo and Juliet Together (and alive!) at Last*. Orchard, 1987. The 8th grade puts on a hilarious production of *Romeo and Juliet*. Guaranteed laughs.

Booth, Coleen E. *Going Live*. Scribner's, 1992. The youngest member of a children's television show tells about the ups and downs of a professional life.

Cresswell, Helen. *Absolute Zero*. Macmillan, 1978. Jack's dog becomes a television star.

Gilmore, Kate. *Enter Three Witches*. Houghton, 1990. New York City and a production of *Macbeth* are featured in this romance between two high school students.

Harris, Mark Jonathan. *Confessions of a Prime Time Kid*. Lothrop, 1985. "Somebody's got to tell the truth about what it's like for kid actors."

Miles, Betty. *The Secret Life of the Underwear Champ*. Art by Dan Jones. Knopf, 1981. Larry is excited about his job on television until he discovers that his part is in an underwear commercial.

Myers, Walter Dean. *The Mouse Rap*. Harper, 1990. Sheri tries to persuade Mouse and his friends to join the dance contest.

Shyer, Marlene Fanta. *Adorable Sunday*. Scribner, 1983. Follow Sunday in her career as a television model.

Booklist: Not for Children Only

The books that follow are for children but should also give adults good ideas for creative dramatics:

Baylor, Byrd. *Sometimes I Dance Mountains*. Photos by Bill Sears; art by Ken Longtemps. Scribner, 1973. Photographs of a young girl dancing her feelings.

Carr, Rachel. *Be a Frog, a Bird, or a Tree*. Photos by Edward Kimball, Jr.; art by Don Hedin. Doubleday, 1973. Creative yoga exercises for children. Photographs of children in action make this an excellent guide to creative movement.

Marceau, Marcel. *The Story of Bip*. Art by author. Harper, 1976. The famous French mime writes and illustrates a fantasy featuring his best-known character. A look into the whimsical mind of an artist.

Mendoza, George. *The Marcel Marceau Alphabet Book*. Photos by Milton H. Greene. Doubleday, 1970. A famous mime acts out the letters of the alphabet in black-and-white photographs.

Booklist: Adult References

DeMille, Richard. *Put Your Mother on the Ceiling: Children's Imagination Games*. Viking, 1973. Ways to stimulate children's creativity through "imagination games."

Ehrlich, Harriet, ed. *Creative Dramatics Handbook*. Photos. Office of Curriculum and Instruction, School District of Philadelphia, 1971. Distributed by NCTE, 1111 Kenyon Road, Urbana, IL 61801. #08970. A how-to-do-it handbook.

Elkind, Samuel. *Improvisation Handbook*. Scott, Foresman, 1976. Theater games and scenes to perform.

MacDonald, Margaret Read. *The Skit Book: 101 Skits from Kids*. Art by Marie-Louise Scull. Shoe String, 1990. Short skits that are perfect to introduce children to creative dramatics.

Sierra, Judy and Robert Kaminski. *Multi-Cultural Folktales: Stories to Tell Young Children*. Oryx, 1991. These stories include suggestions for telling using feltboard figures and puppets, and can be adapted for creative drama.

Thistle, Louise. *Dramatizing Aesop's Fables: Creative Scripts for the Elementary Classroom*. Dale Seymour (Box 10888, Palo Alto, CA 94303), 1992.

General Index

In addition to general subjects, this index includes titles excluded from the Title Index: those of literary selections reproduced in this book (poems, fingerplays, story jokes, stories) as well as titles of individual games, tricks, and songs.

ABC and counting picture books, 348, 349, 350, 386
"The Accident" (story joke), 381
Acting. *See* Creative dramatics
Acting out, a story, 58, 487–88
Action rhymes, 360–65
Active games, 194–95
Activities
  for book parties, 477
  reading-readiness, 426
  See also Games
Activity programs, 11–12, 442–67
  animals, 458–60
  baseball, 451–58
  boxes, 462
  celebrating the inanimate, 461
  fashion, 447–51
  knitting, 461
  moon and stars, 444–47
  multicultural, 464–67
  walk-a-story, 460
Adolescents. *See* Young adults
Adults
  audience reactions of, 415
  creative dramatics references for, 511
  food books for (bibliography), 485
  magic books for, 294
  picture books for, 104
  reader's theater for, 423–24
  reading aloud to, 421–23
Adults, sample programs for, 413–30
  children's health, 427
  creative dance, 428
  flower arranging, 426
  ice cream making, 427
  movie reviews, 426
  music, 428

nursery school selection, 426
paperback exchange, 426
photography, 425
tools and simple repairs, 426
toys, 427
tree planting, 427
Adventure stories, 114
Advertisements. *See also* Promotion
  paid, 38
Aesop's fables, 130, 132
Africa
  folktales of, 120
  stories about, 66, 467
African-Americans, books about, 72, 99, 100, 101
Age levels, programs for, 6–9
  See also Adults, sample programs for; Intermediate grades; Preschool and primary programs
"All Summer in a Day" (story, Bradbury), 416–20
Alphabet picture books, 348, 386
"Alphabet Salesperson" (game), 187
American Indians. *See* Native Americans
Anansi, stories about, 67, 70, 82, 385
Andersen, Hans Christian, 112–13
  stories of, 122, 127, 430
Animal bag (pantomine exercise), 495
Animal head puppets, 274–75
"Animal Salad" (song, Birkenhead-Couture), 316–17
Animals
  folktales about, 113–14
  live, use in storyhour introductions, 44–45
  picture books about, 347–48

in puppetry, 261, 262, 272–76
read-aloud books about, 98–99
sign language representations of, 190
stuffed, stories about, 79
stuffed, use in storyhours, 46
See also specific animals
"The Ant Hill" (fingerplay), 360
Anthologies
poetry, 164–65
short stories, 406–8
as story sources, 144
Antique advertising cards, 21
Antique books, 43
Antonyms, 188
Apples and applesauce, bibliography, 340, 471
Apron
storytelling, 45–46
Velcro, 223
"Archimedes' Puzzle" (game), 192
"Arithmetic" (poem, Sandburg), 161–62
Art and artists, stories about, 67
Artifacts, for introducing storyhour, 42–49
Association for Library Service to Children, 339
Audience, 6–9
adult, 415
eye contact with, 62
Audiotapes, 45
storytelling, 145
Authors, stories about, 67
Autograph rhymes and mottoes, 183

Badges, promotional, 34
Baker's clay decorations, 469–70
Balloons
bibliography, 340–41
as program souvenirs, 50
promotional, 34
Banana spread (recipe), 479
"Bananas and Cream" (poem, McCord), 478
Baron Munchausen, 115
Basch's Baseball Pitch (magic trick), 456
Baseball
activity program, 451–58
bibliography, 457–58
games, 458
Baseball cookies, 456
Baths, picture books about, 341
Beads, as program souvenirs, 50
Bears
picture books about, 341
sign language representations of, 190
"Beautiful Dream" (story joke), 379

Bible
proverbs of, 185
stories based on, 141–43
Bibliographies
adult storytelling, 429–30
animal books, 347–48, 459–60
autograph rhymes, 183
baseball, 457–58
biographies, 288–89
booktalk programs, 437, 438–39
boxes, 462–63
chalkboards, 219–20
classic books, 408–9
color, 212
creative dramatics, 507–11
dog books, 69, 287, 343
duck books, 343, 459
epics, 138–39
ethnic groups, 466–67
fables, 132–33
family storytelling, 149–50
fans, 192
fashion, 448–49, 451
film and video reviews, 248
fingerplays, 365
folk games, 195–96
folk toys, 197
folklore references, 150–51
folktales, 120–21
food, 481–85
forests, 291
ghost stories, 393
hieroglyphs, 191
illustrated single tales, 78–85
intermediate grade-level books, 383–88
Johanna Hurwitz program, 383
jokes, 180
jump stories, 394–95
legends, 139–40
literary sources, 145–46
literary tales, 126–29
magic, 294–96
magic tricks, 287
moon and star books, 446–47
multicultural, 466–67
music, 323–29
myths, 135–36
object stories, 213–14
for overhead projector use, 241
paper stories, 199–200
papercraft ideas, 198, 369
participation stories, 359–60
picture books (intermediate grade-level), 386–88
picture books for preschool and primary programs, 340–51
picture books for puppetry, 277
poetry, 162–72
potatoes, 462
proverbs, 185

puppetry, 262, 264, 277–79
read-aloud books, 98–104
religious sources, 142–43
riddle books, 176–77, 290
senses, 489–90, 491, 492, 493
short story collections, 85–89
sign language, 190
stories with rhythmic phrases, 304
string games, 194
taste, 490
television production, 254
tongue twisters, 178
video production, 248
walking, 460
word games, 189–90
young adult books, 406–8
Big books, 206–7
Biographies
  bibliography, 288–89
  ethnic, 466
  for reading aloud, 99–100
  as story sources, 144
"Biography Prediction" (magic trick), 287–88
Birds, stories about, 67
Birthdays, picture books about, 341
Black History Month, stories for, 72, 99, 100, 101
Blocks, handmade, 48
Board stories, 215–33
  chalk, 217–20
  flannel or felt, 220–21
  hook 'n' loop, 222–23
  magnetic, 221–22
  paperbacks for, 223–24
  Velcro, 221, 222–23, 232–33
Bodart, Joni, 439–40
Body puppets, 263
Book bracelets, 46
Book characters, as story symbols, 17
Book cookies, recipe, 470–71
Book parties, 428, 468–85
  decorations for, 469–71
  food and, 470–85
  introducing one book, 434
  introducing several books, 434–47
  placecards and placemats for, 468–69
"Book Telepathy" (magic trick), 289–90
Bookmarks, 14, 32–33
Books
  antique, 43
  big, 206–7
  classic, 408–10
  coloring, 21, 43
  discarded, 19
  garage sale, 20
  giant, 47
  miniature, 48

paperbacks, 223–24, 426
  picture books about, 341
  sale, 20
Bookstores, 13–14
Booktalk programs, 428, 431–41
  for all occasions, 432–33
  bibliographies, 437, 438–39
  Bodart method of, 439–41
  sample, 434
  storytelling with, 410–12
"Botania" (magic trick), 289
Boxes
  bibliography, 462–63
  for introducing storyhours, 43
  stack, 45
"A Boy and His Dog" (poem, Weil), 505–6
Bread and jam, bibliography, 472
"Broom Balancing" (poem, Fraser), 505
Bulletin boards, 18–19
  fun food facts for, 476–77
  lettering aids for, 21
Bumper stickers, promotional, 34
"A Bunny" (fingerplay), 362
Burton, LeVar, 250
Buttons
  as program souvenirs, 50
  promotional, 34

"The Calendar" (story, Porte), 402–3
Camcorders, for film-making, 244–45
Camels, stories about, 67–68
Candy, chocolate turtles (recipe), 472–73
"A Canner" (tongue twister), 177
Cards
  antique advertising, 21
  flip, 205–6
  greeting, 20, 33, 45
Caring, picture books about, 341
Caroline's Corner (television program), 251
Catalogs, publisher, 19
Cats
  activity program about, 458–59
  stories about, 68, 113, 120, 154, 171, 172, 459
"Cat's cradle" (game), 193–94
Chairs, picture books about, 341
Chalkboard, 33, 215, 217–20
Chalkwalk, 33–34
"The Change Bag" (magic trick), 289
Characters
  book, 17
  folk, 115
  in puppetry, 267
Charades, 495–96
Chase, Richard, 174
Cheese and toasted cheese sandwiches, bibliography, 472

"Cheese, Peas and Chocolate Pudding" (story), 75, 353–55
Chickens, picture books about, 341–42
Child performers, novels about, 510
Children
as poets, 157–58, 163
See also Intermediate grades; Preschool and primary programs; Toddlers; Young adults
Children's health, as adult program topic, 427
"The China Spaniel" (story, Hughes), 298–99
Chinese hat puppet theater, 265
"The Chocolate Cake" (fingerplay), 363
Chocolate turtles candy (recipe), 472–73
Choral speaking, in poetry, 158
Christmas
picture books about, 342
stories about, 72, 171, 472
Christmas dinner, bibliography, 472
Cinderella, 69, 83, 87, 114
Circuses, picture books about, 342
Cleverness, stories about, 68
Closing, of storyhours, 49–52
"Clothe the Naked" (story, Parker), 395–401
Clothes, stories about, 68
Clothespin dolls, 47
Coats, picture books about, 342
Collections
short story, 85–89
See also Bibliographies
Color
picture books about, 342
stories about, 211–12
Coloring books, 21, 43
Conference pick-ups, 19
Conjuring, 281. See also Magic tricks
types of, 282–83
Containers, 44. See also Boxes
"Continuous Story" (game), 186–87
Conundrum, 175
Cookies
baseball, 456
bibliography, 473
Ethel's book, 470–71
moon, 445–46
as program souvenirs, 50
Cooks, stories about, 68–69
Copy machine, 208
Copying, of slides, 235
Costume box, 507
Counting, picture books about, 349, 350
Cowboys, picture books about, 342
"The Cows" (board story), 231–32

"Cows and Horses Walk on Four Feet" (song, Bates), 313
Cows, picture books about, 342
Crafts, for introducing storyhours, 42–43, 46–49
Creation
of blocks, 48
of films, 244–48
of puppet theaters, 265
of puppets, 259–64, 271, 274–75, 277–79
of slides, 235–36
of songs, 301
of tee-shirt art, 43–44
Creative dance, as adult program topic, 428
Creative dramatics, 486–511
acting out a story, 58, 487–88
bibliography, 507–11
for book parties, 477
charades, 495–96
costumes for, 507
exploring the senses with, 488–93
improvisation, 496–97
introducing children to, 487
pantomime, 494–95
props for, 507
reader's theater, 383, 423–24, 505–7
stories to dramatize, 497–504
Cricket (magazine), 145
Cumulative tales, 113

Dance and dancing, 301–2
as adult program topic, 428
picture books about, 342–43
stories about, 69
"David Game" (game), 382
"Dear Daddy-Long-Legs" (story, Webster), 405–6
Decorations, 15–21
baker's clay, 469–70
for book parties, 469–71
for holidays, 44
for special storyhours, 18
Dial-a-story, 10–11
Dialects, storyteller's use of, 58
"The Dinner" (story joke), 381
Dinosaurs, picture books about, 343
"Dirt for Sale: A Story from Mexico" 501–2
Discipline, during storyhours, 51–52
Divorce, picture books about, 343
"The Dog and Cat Go to Market" (puppet play), 272–73
"Dog to Cat" (game), 187
Dogs
picture books about, 343
stories about, 69, 287
Doll-house furniture, 43
Dolls
clothespin, 47

nesting, 45
  stories about, 69
  as storytelling symbols, 17
  use in storyhour, 46
Doorknob hangers, 36–37
Doughnuts, bibliography, 473
"The Dove Pan" (magic trick), 294
"Down with President Stomach"
    (play), 376–78
Dragons
  books about, 42
  stories about, 70
Dramatics. *See* Creative dramatics
Drawing stories, 218
Drawings, as exhibit picture source,
    20
Droll stories, 114–15. *See also*
    Humorous stories
Ducks
  activity programs about, 459
  picture books about, 343
"The Ducks" (fingerplay), 362
"Dunderbeck's Machine" (song,
    Soule), 311

Earth Day, fold-and-cut story for,
    367
Eisenhower, Dwight D., on stage
    fright, 60
"The Elephant" (fingerplay), 362
Elephant jokes, 276
Elephants, books about, 81, 94, 128,
    130, 387
England
  epics of, 136–37
  folktales of, 117–18
Epics, 136–39
  bibliography, 138–39
Equipment, 14
  overhead projector, 238–41
  photocopy transparency machine,
    240
  screens, 237
  for slides, 235, 237
Ethel's book cookies, recipe, 470–71
Exhibits, 15–21
  bulletin board, 18–19
  for introducing storyhour, 42–49
  lettering aids for, 21
  picture sources for, 19–21
  table, 16
Eye contact, with audience, 62

Fables, 129–33
  Aesop's, 130, 132
  bibliography, 132–33
  of India, 131–32
  Krylov's, 131
  La Fontaine's, 131
Fabric board, 491
Fairies, books about, 42

Fairy tales
  picture books about, 343
  See also specific fairy tales
"The Fall" (story joke), 379
Families, stories about, 70, 146–50
Family storyhours, 8–9
Fan, rosette, 210
Fan language, 191–92
Fantasy, for reading aloud, 100–101
Farjeon, Eleanor, 113, 123
"The Farm" (fingerplay), 365
Fashion activity program, 447–51
  activities, 448–50
  favor for, 450
  references to exhibit at, 451
Fathers, picture books about, 343, 344
Fax machine, use in publicity, 7
Feelings, picture books about, 344
Felt boards, 220–21
  books for, 232–33
Festival
  poetry, 157–58
  storytelling, 11
Fiction
  historical (for reading aloud),
    101–2
  about magic, 296
"Fiddle-de-dee" (film), 245
Field trips, musical, 302
Figurines, 44
Films, 242–48
  commercial, 242–43
  creating, 244–48
  hand-drawn, 246–47
  of poetry, 159
  scratch, 159, 246
  selection of, 243
  showing of, 243–44
"Finding a Friend" (puppet play),
    268–69
Finger puppets, 44, 260
"Fingerplay" (fingerplay), 361
Fingerplays, 360–65
  "The Ant Hill," 360
  bibliography, 365
  "A Bunny," 362
  "The Chocolate Cake," 363
  "The Ducks," 362
  "The Elephant," 362
  "The Farm," 365
  "Fingerplay," 361
  "The Frogs," 361
  "Grandma and Grandpa," 363
  "Japanese Rhyme," 360
  "The Lady," 362
  "Lion Hunt," 364–65
  "The Mouse," 362
  "Ten Little Gypsies," 363
  "Touch Your Nose," 361
Flannel boards, 220–21. *See also* Felt
    boards

Flip cards, 205–6
Flower arranging program, for
    adults, 426
"A Fly" (tongue twister), 177
Foam-ball puppets, 271
Fold-and-cut stories, 365–69
Folk characters, 115
Folk games, 192–96
    active games, 194–95
    bibliography, 195–96
    string games, 193–94
Folk songs, 306–7
    for chalkboard use, 219
Folk toys, 196–97
Folklore, 173–214
    jokes as, 173, 178–83
    non-narrative sources of, 173–214
    for reading aloud, 101
    references about, 150–51
    riddles as, 173, 175–78
    tongue twisters as, 173
Folktales, 111–21
    adventure, 114
    animal tales, 113–14
    bibliography, 120–21
    cumulative, 113
    folk characters, 115
    how-and-why, 114
    humorous, 114–15
    illustrated, 78–85
    literary, 112–13
    regional, 115–20
    repetitive, 113
    romantic, 114
Food
    and book parties, 469–85
    books about, 471–76, 480, 482–85
    picture books about, 482–83
    poetry about, 478–80
    as program souvenirs, 50
    stories about, 481
    for storytelling programs, 15
    taste and, 489
    See also Recipes; names of specific
        foods
Foolishness, stories about, 70
Forests, bibliography, 291
Forgetfulness, stories about, 70
"The Four Thieves" (magic trick),
    292
Foxes, stories about, 70, 133, 154,
    172, 305, 457
France, folktales of, 116
Friends
    booktalk about, 438–39
    picture books about, 344
"The Frog" (poem), 160–61
"The Frog on the Log" (poem,
    Orleans), 158
Frog Prince activity program, 460

Frogs
    picture books about, 344, 348
    stories about, 83, 154, 172, 220
"The Frogs" (fingerplay), 361
Fruit, bibliography, 473
Fudge, bibliography, 473
Full Moon cookies, recipe, 445–46
Furniture, for doll houses, 43

Games
    active, 194–95
    "Alphabet Salesperson," 187
    antique, 43
    "Archimedes' Puzzle," 192
    baseball, 458
    "Continuous Story," 186–87
    "Dog to Cat," 187
    folk, 192–96
    "Ghost," 186
    "Hangman," 186
    "I Packed My Trunk," 186
    "Kick the Can," 195
    "Minister's Cat," 458
    "The Newspaper Game," 187
    "Picto Puzzle," 187
    "Pump Pump Pull Away," 195
    "The Restaurant Game," 477
    string, 193–94
    tangrams, 192–93
    "Telegram," 187
    visual, bibliography, 493
Garage sale books, 20
Gardens, picture books about, 344
Gardner, John, 126
Germany, folktales, of, 116–17
Gestures, in storytelling, 62
Getchell, Myra, 25
"Ghost" (game), 186
Ghost stories, 391–93
Giant books, 47
Gifts, 14–15
    stories about, 71
Gingerbread, bibliography, 473
Gingerbread people, recipe, 473–74
Glove puppets, 259–60
"Go Fish" (game), 47
"The Goat Well" (story, Courlander),
    320–22
Goats, stories about, 71, 412
"The Golden Arm" (story), 394
Gorog, Judith, 126
Gourmet cooking, story about, 474
Grand Slam Baseball Board Game
    (game), 458
"Grandma and the Birds" (family
    story), 146–48
"Grandpa and Grandma"
    (fingerplay), 363
Grandparents, favorite books of,
    408–10

"Grass Is Always Greener" (story joke), 378
Greece
  epics of, 137
  myths of, 134
Greed, stories about, 71
Greeting cards, 20
  as bookmarks, 33
  as exhibits, 45
Grimm, Jacob and Wilhelm Grimm, 116–17, 120
Guest storytellers, 22–24
Guests, unwanted, stories about, 78

Halloween
  stories about, 72
  stories for, 391–93
"Hangman" (game), 186
"Henry and Mary" (fold-and-cut story), 367
Heroes
  national, 136–38
  tall-tale, 119–20
Heroines, stories about, 71
"Hickety, pickety, my black hen . . ." (fold-and-cut story), 366
Hieroglyphs, 191
High John the Conquerer, story about, 480–81
"Hilary's Chant" (jump-rope rhyme), 181
Historical fiction, for reading aloud, 101–2
Holidays
  decorations and exhibits for, 18
  decorations for, 44
  favors and treats for, 14–15
  stories about, 72–73
  See also specific holidays
Home canned fruit, story about, 474
Homemade jelly, story about, 474
Homographs, 188
Homonyms, 188
Honey, bibliography, 474
Hoop 'n' loop board, 222–23. *See also* Velcro board
Horses, stories about, 73
Hot dogs, book about, 474
"House for Sale" (story joke), 380
Houses, picture books about, 344
Housman, Laurence, 113, 125
How and why stories, 114
"How to Make a Small House into a Large One" (story), 351–53
Humorous stories
  folktales, 114–15
  for reading aloud, 102
  See also Jokes; Riddles; Tongue twisters

Hurwitz, Johanna, reading-aloud program about, 381–82
"Hush, Little Children" (song, Soule), 307

"I Liked Growing" (poem, Kuskin), 479
"I Love a Rainy Day" (song, Birkenhead-Couture), 314–15
"I Packed My Trunk" (game), 186
Ice cream making, as adult program topic, 427
Ice cream, recipe, 479
Iceland, myths of, 134–35
"If the Moon Were Made of Cheese" (poem, Moss), 478
"If You're Happy" (song), 303
Illustrated single tales, bibliography, 78–85
Illustrations
  of poetry, 159
  of poetry (bibliography), 165–67
  See also Picture sources
Immigrants, books about, 465, 466–67
Improvisation, 496–97
"In a Starry Orchard" (poem, Farber), 445
Inanimate objects
  as activity program theme, 461
  picture books about, 387
India
  epics of, 137–38
  fables of, 131–32
Instruments, homemade rhythm, 302–3
  songs to use with, 303–4
Intermediate grades
  classic book list for, 383–85
  multimedia for, 383
  participation programs for, 376–81
  picture books for (bibliography), 386–88
  programs for, 7–8, 370–88
  storytelling for, 370–76
  See also Young adults
Introduction
  of booktalks, 434–37
  of poetry, 155–56
  of preschool and primary programs, 338
  of storyhour, 40–49
Invitations, for storyhour, 35

Jamaican stories, 66–67
"Japanese Rhyme" (fingerplay), 360
Jelly beans, book about, 474
Jewish celebrations, stories about, 72–73, 143

Jewish proverbs, 184–85
"John and Mary" (story joke), 380
"John Wins a Bet" (story, Sanfield), 480–81
Jokes, 178–80
    elephant, 276
    story, 378–81
Jump stories, 394–95
"Jump-rope rhyme" (Payne), 182
Junk mail, as exhibit picture source, 19

Kennedy, Richard, 126
"Kick the Can" (game), 195
Kipling, Rudyard, 113, 124
Knitting activity program, 461
Krylov, Ivan Andreevich, 131
Kwanzaa, books about, 73

La Fontaine, Jean de, 131
"The Lady" (fingerplay), 362
Ladybug (magazine), 145
Language, non-verbal, 104, 190
"Large Boots" (song, Soule), 308–9
Laziness, stories about, 73
"Lazy as an Ox: A Korean Tale" (story to dramatize), 503–4
Leach, Maria, 174
Learning to tell
    poetry, 155
    stories, 54–58
Legends, 139–40
Lemon meringue pie, book about, 474
Lemonade, book about, 474
"The Letter" (story joke), 379
Lettering aids
    for exhibits, 21
    for posters, 31
Lifestories (game), 149
Light show, for overhead projection, 239–40
Lima beans, book about, 475
"Lines and Squares" (poem, Milne), 160
"Lion Hunt" (fingerplay), 364–65
Lions, picture books about, 347
Literary sources, 143–46
Literary tales, 121–29
    bibliography, 126–29
    Carl Sandburg, 124–25, 161–62
    Eleanor Farjeon, 113, 123
    Hans Christian Andersen, 112–13, 122
    Howard Pyle, 123–24
    John Gardner, 126
    Laurence Housman, 113, 125
    Rudyard Kipling, 113, 124
    Ruth Sawyer, 122–23
"The Little Bird's Ball" (song, Soule), 312

"Little Bo-Peep" (fold-and-cut story), 368
"Little Brother" (jump-rope rhyme), 182
"Little Miss Muffet" (fold-and-cut story), 366
"Little Red Riding Hood," exhibits for, 18
Location, of storytelling programs, 12–14
    for adult storytelling, 414
"The Lost Ring" (story joke), 379

Magazines
    children's, 145
    as exhibit picture source, 20
Magic, 280–96
    books about, 283–84
    mechanical, 283
    patter and presentation, 285
    using, 284–85
    videos about, 296
Magic tricks, 282–83, 285–94
    baseball, 456
    "Biography Prediction," 287–89
    "Book Telepathy," 289–90
    "Botania," 289
    "The Change Bag," 289
    "The Dove Pan," 294
    "The Four Thieves," 292
    "Mixing Colors," 285–86
    "Prediction Pencil," 291
    "A Proverb Trick," 291–92
    "Read to Your Dog," 286–87
    "Riddle Trick," 290
    "Spring Flowers," 289
    "Television versus Books," 293
Magicians, organizations of, 284
Magnetic board, 221–22
    books for, 232–33
    paperbacks for, 223–24
Magnetic puppets, 264
Mailers, 36
Maps, story, 49
Marionettes, 260
"Marlo" (story), 322–23
Marriage, stories about, 73–74
Martin, Ron, 191
"Mary, Mary, quite contrary . . ." (fold-and-cut story), 366
Masks, 263
    storytelling with, 501–2
Memorable people, read-aloud stories about, 103–4
Metaphors, 188–89
Mice, picture books about, 347, 348
Middle grades. See Intermediate grades
Milne, A. A., 160
Miniature books, 48
Minisigns, 32

Minispeeches, 36
"Minister's Cat" (game), 458
Mini-theme programs, 458–63
"Mixing Colors" (magic trick), 285–86
Mood-setting, for storyhours, 41
  with music, 45
Moon and Stars theme program,
  444–47
Moon, bibliography, 446–47
Moon cookies, recipe, 445–46
Moose versus Wolf activity program,
  459–60
Mosquitoes, stories about, 74
Mother Goose books, 153
Mothers, picture books about, 344
"The Mouse" (fingerplay), 362
Movie review program, for adults, 426
Muffins, book about, 475
Multicultural programs, 463–67
Multimedia storytelling, 201–329
  magic, 280–96
  music, 297–329
  overhead projectors for, 238–41
  pictures and objects for, 205–14
  for preschool and primary
    children, 360
  puppetry, 256–79
  slides, 234–37
  television and radio, 249–54
Multimedia techniques
  light show magic, 239–40
  overlays, 240–41
  transparencies, 238–39, 240
Multiplication, stories about, 74
Music, 297–329
  as adult program topic, 428
  for board story presentations, 217
  dance, 301–2
  field trips, 302
  homemade rhythm instruments,
    302–3
  for mood-setting, 45
  in multimedia presentations,
    299–303
  picture books about (bibliography),
    326–28
  singing, 300–301
  stories about, 74–75, 320–23
  stories with rhythmic phrases,
    303–4
  use of recordings, 45
Music box, 45
Myths, 133–36
  bibliography, 135–36
  Greek and Roman, 134
  Norse, 134–35

Names, stories about, 75
Narrative sources, for storytelling,
  109–51
  epics, 136–39

fables, 129–33
folktales, 111–21
legends, 139–40
literary sources, 143–46
literary tales, 121–29
myths, 133–36
religious, 140–43
National Association for the
  Preservation and Perpetuation of
  Storytelling (NAPPS),
  storytelling festival, 11
National Directory of Storytelling, 28
National Story League, 26, 28
Native Americans
  books about, 135, 136, 139, 140,
    385, 465, 466
  sign language of, 190
"New Booktalker," 439
New York Public Library
  storyhour, 13
  storytelling festival, 11
"The Newspaper Game" (game), 187
Newspapers
  use in magic, 199
  use in publicity, 37
"Night of 1,000 Stars" reading-aloud
  program, 381–83
Night, stories about, 75
Night workers, picture books about,
  344
Non-fiction
  about food, 484–85
  for reading aloud, 102–3
Non-narrative sources, for
  storytelling, 173–99
  antonyms, 188
  autograph rhymes and mottoes,
    183
  fan language, 191–92
  folk games, 192–96
  folk toys, 196–97
  hieroglyphs, 191
  homographs, 188
  homonyms, 188
  jokes, 178–80
  paper stories, 197–200
  proverbs, 184–85
  riddles, 175–77
  sign language, 190
  skip-rope rhymes, 180–83
  tongue twisters, 177–78
  word games, 186–89
Nonsense verse, 153
Nonsense words, stories about, 75
Norway, folktales of, 118–19
Novels, as literary sources, 144
Nursery school selection program,
  for adults, 426

Object stories, 208–14
Observation test, 493

"Old Betty Blue . . ." (fold-and-cut story), 367
"Old Joe Finly" (song, Soule), 310
Older children. See Intermediate grades; Young adults
Opposites, picture books about, 344–45
Oral literature, 145
Oranges, bibliography, 475
Organizations
  Association for Library Service to Children, 339
  of magicians, 284
  National Association for the Preservation and Perpetuation of Storytelling, 11
  National Story League, 26, 28
  Storytelling Guild of Medford, Oregon, 25–26
Origami, 15, 196–99
"The Ossopit Tree" (board story), 224–27
Overlays, 240–41

Painted rocks, 48
Pantomime, 494–95
Paper lantern, 210–11
Paper stories, 197–200
Paperback cut-ups, 207
Paperback exchange program, 426
Paperbacks, in board stories, 223–24
Papercraft
  fold-and-cut stories, 196–99, 365–69
  for object stories, 209–11
Parents, programs for, 425–29
Participation stories and programs
  for intermediate grades, 376–81
  for preschool and primary children, 355–60
Patter and presentation, in magic, 285
"Peanut butter" (poem, McCord), 480
Peanut butter, recipe, 480
Peanut butter sandwiches, book about, 475
Pebbles, as program souvenirs, 50
"Pedro Courts Maria" (puppet play), 269–70, 272
"The Pepper Soup" (story to dramatize), 498–99
"Peter, Peter Pumpkin Eater" (fold-and-cut story), 366
"The Photo" (story joke), 381
Photocopied pictures, 21, 208
Photocopy transparency machines, 240
Photographic slides, 236–37
Photographs, for exhibits, 20
Photography program, for adults, 425

"Picto Puzzle" (game), 187
Picture books
  about acting, 510
  bibliography, 347–51
  classic (bibliography), 347–48
  about dogs, 287
  of family reminiscences, 150
  about food, 482–83
  for intermediate grades (bibliography), 386–88
  about magic, 295
  multicultural, 466, 467
  about music (bibliography), 326–28
  for older children and adults, 104
  about puppetry, 277
  of songs, 304–6
  for toddlers, 348–50
  See also under specific subjects, e.g., Fathers, picture books about
Picture puzzlers, picture books about, 345
Picture sources, 19–21, 205–8
  for slides, 235–36
Placecards, 468–69
Placemats, 468–69
Planning, of programs, 5–21
  preschool and primary programs, 337–38
Plays
  "A Boy and His Dog", 505–7
  "Down with President Stomach", 376–78
  for puppets, 267–70
  See also Creative dramatics; Fingerplays
"Pockets" (poem, Merriam), 213
Poetry, 152–72
  adult references, 163
  anthologies (bibliography), 164–65
  bibliography, 162–72
  choral work, 58
  festival, 157–58
  about food, 478–80
  illustrations of, 154, 159, 165–67
  introducing, 155–156
  learning, 155
  Mother Goose, 153
  program, 157
  to read aloud, 154, 155, 162–65
  selection of, 152–55
  with themes, 154–55, 170–72
  as tradition in storyhour, 159–60
  visual, 156–57
  for young children, 153–54
  for young children (bibliography), 163–64
  See also titles of individual poems
Poetry break, 156
Poets, of the past (bibliography), 167–70

Popcorn, book about, 475
Portable doorway puppet theater, 265
Postcards, 20, 45
Posters, promotional, 30–32
"Potato Chips" (poem, Gallagher), 478
Potatoes
    as activity program theme, 461–62
    books about, 461, 462–63
Practice story, 62–66
"Prediction Pencil" (magic trick), 291
Preparation, of stories, 53–58
Preplanning, of storyhours, 12–21
    decorations and exhibits, 15–21
    equipment checklist, 14
    favors and treats, 14–15
    physical location, 12–14
    storytelling symbol, 17
Preschool and primary programs, 7,
        335–69
    content of, 338
    fingerplays for, 360–65
    fold-and-cut stories for, 365–69
    follow-up activities for, 338
    introducing of, 338
    multimedia storytelling in, 360
    participation stories for, 355–60
    picture books for, 339–51
    picture books for (bibliography),
        340–51
    planning and production, 337–38
    stories for, 351–59
"The Prince Who Was a Rooster"
        (story), 403–4
Princes and princesses, books about,
        76, 129, 460, 475
"Prindrella and the Since" (story),
        405
Production
    magic, 282
    of television shows, 251–54
Programs, 331–511. *See also*
        Storyhours
    activity, 11–12
    for adults, 413–30
    book parties, 428, 468–85
    booktalks, 431–41
    closing of, 49–52
    creative dramatics, 486–511
    dial-a-story, 10–11
    for the intermediate grades,
        370–88
    introduction of, 40–49
    mini-theme, 458–63
    mood-setting for, 41, 45
    multicultural, 463–67
    for parents, 425–29
    poetry, 157
    preplanning of, 12–21
    for preschool and primary grades,
        335–69
    series, 9–10

single, 9
special events, 10
storytelling festival, 11
techniques, 9–12
for young adults, 389–412
Projector
    opaque, 206
    overhead, 238–41
    slide, 234, 235, 237
Promotion, 29–39
Prop box, 507
"A Proverb Trick" (magic trick),
        291–92
Proverbs, 184–85
Publicity. *See* Promotion
Publishers' catalogs, as exhibit
        picture source, 19
Pudding, book about, 475
"Pump Pump Pull Away" (game), 195
Puppetry, 256–79
    bibliography, 277–79
    music for, 329
    plays for, 267–70
    in poetry programs, 157
    stages for, 264–65
    tradition of, 258
Puppets
    body, 263
    commercial hand, 259
    exchangable animal head, 274–75
    finger, 44, 260, 269, 276
    foam ball, 271
    glove, 259–60
    hand, 258–60, 269
    as hosts, 266
    magnetic, 264
    marionettes, 260
    shadow, 257, 258, 263–64
    stick, 260–62
    for storyhour introduction, 45
    types, 258–64
    uses for, 265–67
Puss in Boots, books about, 81, 83,
        345
Puzzles, 48
Pyle, Howard, 123–24

Radio, 254–55
    use in publicity, 38
"Rain on the green grass . . ."
        (fold-and-cut story), 366
Rain, stories about, 76
Rainy days, books about, 144, 170,
        172, 278, 295
Raspberry tart, book about, 475
"Read to Your Dog" (magic trick),
        286–87
Reader's theater, 383, 505–7
    for adults, 423–24
Reading aloud, 90–104
    to adult audiences, 421–23

choosing materials for, 91–93
how-to's of, 93–94
programs for, 381–83
stories for, 104
Reading, picture books about, 341
Reading-readiness program, for
adults, 426
Recipes
banana spread, 479
chocolate turtles, 472–73
Ethel's book cookies, 470–71
full moon cookies, 445–46
gingerbread people, 473–74
peanut butter, 480
strawberry ice cream, 479
Recordings, 45
Relatives, picture books about, 345
See also Fathers; Mothers;
Grandparents
Religion, as story source, 140–43
Repetitive tales, 113
Rhymes
action, 360–65
autograph, 183
for chalkboards, 219
skip-rope, 180–83
Rhythm instruments, homemade,
302–3
songs for, 303–4
Rice, bibliography, 475
"Riddle Trick" (magic trick), 290
Riddles, 175–77
picture books about, 345
in puppetry, 276
stories about, 76
word-game, 188
"Ring Around the Rosie"
(fold-and-cut story), 368–69
"Ring in the String" (game), 193–94
Robin Hood, books about, 136–37
"Rocking Horse" (song, Borba), 313
Rocks, painted, 48
Roll stories, 207–8
Romantic stories, 114
Rome, myths of, 134
"Ropes" (song, Birkenhead-Couture),
318–19
"Roses are red . . ." (fold-and-cut
story), 368
Rosette fan, 210
Rumpelstiltskin, stories about, 84
"Running the Gauntlet" (poem,
Fraser), 161

Sale books, 20
"Salt, Mustard" (jump-rope rhyme),
182
Sandburg, Carl, 124–25
Sandwich boards, 477
Sandwiches, books about, 475, 476
Sausages, book about, 476

Sawyer, Ruth, 122–23
Scandinavia, myths of, 134–35
Scary stories, 390–95
School assemblies, as storytelling
setting, 13
Scratch films, 159, 246
Sea, books about, 345
"Seashells" (tongue twister), 178
Seeds, as program souvenirs, 49–50
Senses, 488–93
sight, 492–93
sound, 491–92
taste, 489
touch, 490–91
Sesame Street (television program),
250, 258
Shadow puppets, 257, 263–64
Shoes, stories about, 76
Shops, picture books about, 345
Short stories
short, short, 76
for young adults, 395–408
Sight, 492–93
Sign language, 104, 190
Skip-rope rhymes, 180–83
Slides, 234–37
copying of, 235
equipment for, 235
handmade, 236
photographic, 236–37
screens, 237
Smell, sense of, 490
Sneezes, stories about, 77
Snow
picture books about, 345–46
stories about, 77
"Some Favorite Words" (poem,
Edwards), 162
Songs
"Animal Salad" (Birkenhead-
Couture), 316–17
"Cows and Horses Walk on Four
Feet" (Bates), 313
"Dunderbeck's Machine" (Soule),
311
"I Love a Rainy Day"
(Birkenhead-Couture), 314–15
"If You're Happy," 303
"Large Boots" (Soule), 308–9
"Little Bird's Ball" (Soule), 312
"Old Joe Finly" (Soule), 310
picture books of, 304–6
for rhythmic instruments, 303–4
"Rocking Horse" (Birkenhead-
Couture), 313
"Ropes" (Birkenhead-Couture),
318–19
to sing, 306–19
"Thanksgiving Song" (Givier), 314
"Tin Ford" (Rubenstein), 304
Sound, 491–92

Sources, for storytelling, 107–99
  narrative, 107–51
  non-narrative, 173–99
"Southpaw," (story, Viorst), 451–56
Souvenirs, 14–15, 49–51
  promotional, 32–33
Spaghetti, bibliography, 476
Spiders, stories about, 66–67. *See
  also* Anansi, stories about
Sports Illustrated Superstar
  Baseball (game), 458
"Spring Flowers" (magic trick), 289
Stage fright, 61
Stages, for puppets, 264–65
Stamps, 19
"Stars" (poem, Fisher; Sandburg),
  445
Stars, bibliography, 446–47
Stick puppets, 260–62
Stickers, as exhibit picture source,
  20
Stories
  acting out of, 58, 487–88
  adventure, 114
  board, 215–33
  to dramatize, 497–504
  droll and humorous, 114–15
  fold-and-cut, 365–69
  how-and-why, 114
  Jamaican, 67
  learning, 54–58
  object, 208–14
  participation, 355–60
  practice, 62–66
  preparation of, 53–58
  romantic, 114
  short, short, 76–77
Story bag, 48–49
Story jokes, 378–81
Story map, 49
Storyhours
  audience, 6–9, 62, 415
  discipline in, 51–52
  family, 8–9
  locations, 12–14, 414
  planning for, 5–21, 337–38
Storytelling Guild of Medford,
  Oregon, 25–26
"Strange Events in the Life of the
  Delmonico Family" (story,
  Mahy), 228–31
Strat-O-Matic baseball (game), 458
Strawberry ice cream recipe, 479
String games, 193–94
String puppets, 260
Student storytellers, 26–38
"Summer Nights" (story, Hart),
  421–23
Supernatural characters, in
  folktales, 115
Supernatural stories, 390–94

Sweden, folktales of, 118–19
Symbols, storytelling, 17, 41

Table exhibits, 16
Tall-tales, 119–20
Tangrams, 192–93
Taste, 490
Teachers, as storytellers, 30
Teaser, booktalk, 433
Teatime, bibliography, 476
Tee shirts, art work for, 43–44
Teeth, picture books about, 346
"Telegram" (game), 187
Telephone, use in publicity, 36
Television, 249–54
  personnel, 253–54
  production of shows, 251–54
  use in publicity, 38
"Television versus Books" (magic
  trick), 293
"Ten Little Gypsies" (fingerplay),
  363
"Thanksgiving Song" (song, Givier),
  314
Theaters
  for puppets, 264–65
  reader's, 383, 423–24, 505–7
Tickets, for storyhours, 35
Tikki Tikki Tembo (Mosel), 57
"Time for School" (story joke), 379
Time, picture books about, 346
"Tin Ford" (song, Rubenstein), 304
"To Catch a Fish" (poem, Greenfield),
  506
Toddlers
  picture books for, 348–51
  as storytelling audience, 6–7
Tomato sandwiches, book about, 476
Tongue twisters, 173, 177–78
Touch, 490–91
"Touch Your Nose" (fingerplay), 361
Toys
  as adult program topic, 427
  folk, 196–97
  paper, 197–200
Transparencies, 238–39. *See also*
  Projector, overhead
  tracings, 240
Treasure trunk, 46
Tree planting, as adult program
  topic, 427
Trees, picture books about, 346
Tricks, magic. *See* Magic tricks
Tricksters, stories about, 77, 115
Trucks, picture books about, 346
Turtles, stories about, 77, 98, 167,
  446
"Two of Everything" (story, Ritchie),
  74, 372–78

United States, folktales of, 119–20

Valentine's Day, 73
"Vancouver" (poem, Heidbreder), 212
Velcro apron and vest, 223
Velcro board, 220, 221, 222–23
    books for, 232–33
Videos, 242–48
    about magic, 296
    making of, 244–48
    selection of, 243
    showing of, 243–44
Visual aids, for poetry, 156–57
Visual games, bibliography, 493
Visual poetry, 156–57
Volunteers
    for publicity campaigns, 38
    as storytellers, 25–28

Waking up, picture books about, 346
Walk-a-story activity program, 460
Wallpaper sample, as exhibit picture source, 20
Walnuts, book about, 476
Weddings, picture books about, 346
"Wee Willie Winkie" (fold-and-cut story), 368

"Where's the Fish?" (story joke), 380
"Wind and Fire" (object story), 209–10
Wind, stories about, 78
"The Winter Hiker" (story joke), 380
Wishes, stories about, 78
"A Word from Smokey the Bear" (magic trick), 291
Word games, 186–87
Word play, picture books about, 346
Word-game riddles, 188
Wrapping paper, as exhibit picture source, 20
Writers, stories about, 67

Yolen, Jane, 125
Young adults
    baseball books for, 457–58
    bibliographies, 393, 394–95, 406–8, 409–12
    classic books for, 408–10
    programs for, 8, 389–412
    short stories for, 395–406
    storytelling/booktalk programs for, 410–12

Title Index

ABC Exhibit (Fisher), 387

Abiyoyo (Seeger), 327

Aboriginal Fables and Legendary Tales (Reed), 133

Absolute Zero (Cresswell), 287, 510

Across Town (Sara), 104

Adam and the Wolf (Gunthorp), 232

Adorable Sunday (Shyer), 510

Adventures of High John the Conqueror (Sanfield), 88, 101

Adventures of Nanabush (Coatsworth and Coatsworth), 85

Adventures of Rama (Gaer), 138

Adventures of Tom Sawyer (Twain), 410

Aesop (McKendry, comp.), 130, 132

Aesop's Fables (Jones), 130, 132

Agnes the Sheep (Taylor), 99, 412

"Ah Tcha the Sleeper" (Chrisman), 73

Aha! Gotcha (Gardner), 189

Aida (Price), 327

Aladdin and the Wonderful Lamp (Carrick), 79

Albert's Play (Tryon), 510

Aldo Applesauce (Hurwitz), 484

Aldo Ice Cream (Hurwitz), 382

Alex Is My Friend (Russo), 344

Alexander and the Terrible, Horrible, No Good, Very Bad Day (Viorst), 475, 509

Alfie Gets in First (Hughes), 508

"Ali and the Camels" (Gilstrap), 67

"Ali Baba and Princess Farrah" (Bauer), 383, 460

"Ali Baba and Princess Farrah" (Hurwitz), 460

Ali Baba Bernstein (Hurwitz), 102

Alice's Adventures in Wonderland (Carroll), 100, 409

Alison's Zinnia (Lobel), 344

All Jahdu Storybook (Hamilton), 128

All the Colors of the Race (Adoff), 170

All the Small Poems (Worth), 170

Alligator Pie (Lee), 168

Alphabetics (MacDonald), 493

ALSC Notable Films/Videos, Filmstrips, Recordings, and Software 1992 and YALSA Selected Films for Young Adults (American Library Association), 248

Always Wondering (Fisher), 168

Amazing Grace (Hoffman), 510

Amelia Bedelia (Parish), 474

American Children's Folklore (Bronner), 150

American Folk Toys and How to Make Them (Schnacke), 197

American Folklore (Dorson), 150

American Indian Myths and Legends (Erdoes and Ortiz), 139

American Sports Poems (Knudson and Swenson), 171

American Tall Tales (Osborne), 101

Amos (Seligson and Schneider), 99, 287, 343

Amy the Dancing Bear (Simon), 327

Anancy and Mr. Dry-Bone (French), 80

"Anansi and His Visitor, Turtle" (Kaula), 77

Anansi the Spider (McDermott), 70, 82

Anastasia Again! (Lowry), 385

Anastasia at This Address (Lowry), 102

And Still the Turtle Watched (MacGill-Callahan), 82

And the Green Grass Grew All Around (Schwartz), 165

And to Think That I Saw It on Mulberry Street (Suess), 159, 169, 233, 348

Androcles and the Lion (Paxton), 130, 133

Androcles and the Lion (Stevens), 83

Andy and the Lion (Daugherty), 130, 132, 347, 508

Andy Toots His Horn (Ziefert), 327

Angus and the Cat (Flack), 349

Angus and the Ducks (Flack), 347, 459

Anna Banana (Cole), 182

Anne Frank (Hurwitz), 100

Anne of Green Gables (Montgomery), 410

Anno's Aesop (Anno), 132

Answered Prayer and Other Yemenite Folktales (Gold and Caspi), 86

Antarctica (Cowcher), 386

Anteater Named Arthur (Waber), 277

Antics (Hepworth), 387

Antrim's Orange (Sunderlin), 484

"Apple of Contentment" (Pyle), 124

Apple Tree (Parnall), 340, 485

Apples (Hogrogian), 471

Appointment (Maugham), 387

April Fool's Magic (Baker), 295

Are You There God? It's Me, Margaret (Blume), 384

Arrow to the Sun (McDermott), 82

Arroz Con Leche (Delacre, ed.), 324

Art of Baseball (Dinhofer), 457

Art of the Puppet (Baird), 278

Art of the Storyteller (Shedlock), 111

Arthur Meets the President (Brown), 386

Arthur's Birthday (Brown), 341

Arthur's Christmas Cookies (Hoban), 473

Ask Mr. Bear (Flack), 232

Aska's Animals (Day), 170

At Daddy's on Saturday (Girard), 343

"At the Supper Table" (Rylant), 485

Athletic Shorts (Crutcher), 407

Aunt Flossie's Hats (and Crab Cakes Later) (Howard), 72

Aunt Lulu (Pinkwater), 341

Auntie's Knitting a Baby (Simmie), 169

AV Marketplace, 248

"B Is for Baseball" (Bauer), 456

Babe, the Gallant Pig (King-Smith), 99, 287, 385

Baby Beebee Bird (Massie), 359

Baby Blue Cat and the Whole Batch of Cookies (Pryor), 483

Baby Sister for Frances (Hoban), 50

Baby's Song Book (Poston, comp.), 324

Baby's World, 350

Back in the Beforetime (Curry), 86

Back to Class (Glenn), 168

Backstage at Bunraku (Adachi), 277

Badger and the Magic Fan (Johnson), 192, 295

Bag of Moonshine (Garner), 86

"Baker's Daughter" (Bianco), 68

Baldur and the Mistletoe (Hodges), 135

Ballet Shoes (Streatfield), 328, 386

Balloon Video (video, Flora), 296

Balloons (Zubrowski), 50

Balloons and Other Poems (Chandra), 167

Banana Twist (Heide), 484

"Bandalee" (Sherlock), 66

Banner in the Sky (Ullman), 386

"Barber's Clever Wife" (Steel), 71

Barn Dance! (Martin and Archambault), 327, 343

Barnyard Tracks (Duffy), 219

Bartholomew Fair (Stoltz), 102

Baseball Fever (Hurwitz), 382, 457

Baseball in April and Other Stories (Soto), 129, 386

Baseball's Greatest Quotations (Dickson), 457

Be a Frog, a Bird, or a Tree (Carr), 511

Be a Magician (video), 296

Bear in Mind (Goldstein), 171

Bear on the Moon (Ryder), 446

Bearhead (Kimmel), 81

Bears (Drew), 443

Bear's Picture (Pinkwater), 220

"Beautiful Birch" (Ginsburg), 71

Beauty and the Beast (De Beaumont), 80

Behind the King's Kitchen (Smith and Ra), 177

Ben and Me (Lawson), 101, 385

Beneath a Blue Umbrella (Prelutsky), 167

Benjamin Franklin (Adler), 288

Benjamin's Balloon (Baker), 340

Bently and Egg (Joyce), 326

Beowulf (Nye), 137, 138

"Beowulf Against Grendel" (Nye), 410

Berlioz the Bear (Brett), 326

Best Bug to Be (Johnson), 510

Best Christmas Pageant Ever (Robinson), 386

Best of Aesop's Fables (Clark), 132

Best of Roald Dahl (Dahl), 407

Best of Robert Benchley (Benchley), 430

Best Town in the World (Baylor), 166

Best Videos for Children and Young Adults (Gallant), 248

Best Wishes, Amen (Morrison), 183
Best Witches (Yolen), 172
Best-Loved Stories Told at the
    National Storytelling Festival
    (National Association for the
    Preservation and Perpetuation of
    Storytelling), 85
Betsy Byars (Byars), 288
Beverly Cleary (Cleary), 436, 437
Beware of the Aunts! (Thomson), 345
Beyond the Myth (Brooks), 288
Bible Stories (Kossoff), 143
Bicycle Rider (Scioscia), 72
Big Bear's Treasury, 347
Big Book of Tongue Twisters and
    Double Talk (Arnold), 178
Big Cats (Simon), 459
Big Laughs for Little People (Smith),
    294
Big Red Barn (Brown), 349
"Big Toe " (Schwartz), 394
Biggest Pumpkin Ever (Kroll), 233
Bill Peet (Peet), 289
Bionic Bunny Show (Brown), 254
Birches (Frost), 166
Bird Book (Shaw, ed.), 154, 172
"Bird's Wisdom," 67
Birthday Magic (Baker), 295
Black Americans: A History in Their
    Own Words, 72
Blackberry Ink (Merriam), 213
Blaze and the Forest Fire (Anderson),
    291
Blitzcat (Westhall), 102
Blue Balloon (Inkpen), 341
"Bluebeard" (Lang), 73
Blueberries for Sal (McCloskey), 349,
    508
Bon Appetit, Mr. Rabbit! (Boujon),
    489
Boo! Stories to Make You Jump
    (Cecil), 393
Book of Greek Myths (d'Aulaire and
    d'Aulaire), 134, 135
Book of Solo Games (Brandreth),
    193, 195
Book of Think (Burns), 508
Books Children Will Sit Still For
    (Freeman), 97
Booktalk!, 439
Boonsville Bombers (Herzig), 457
Boots and His Brothers (Kimmel), 81
Boots and the Glass Mountain
    (Martin), 82
Borreguita and the Coyote
    (Aardema), 79
"Box" (Colville), 462
Box (Shannon), 463
Boxman (Hale), 462
Boy Scout Songbook (Boy Scouts of
    America), 325

Boy Who Could Do Anything and
    Other Mexican Folk Tales
    (Brenner), 85, 290
"Boy Who Drew Cats" (Hearn), 67
Boy Who Loved Music (Lasker), 327
Boy's King Arthur (Lanier), 138
Brats (Kennedy), 171
Bravo, Tanya (Gauch), 326, 342
Bread and Honey (Asch), 219
Bread and Jam for Frances (Hoban),
    472
Bread Bread Bread (Norris), 472, 485
Breathtaking Noses (Machotka), 490
Bremen Town Musicians (Wilhelm),
    74, 262, 327
Brian Wildsmith's Bible Stories
    (Turner), 143
Brian Wildsmith's Circus
    (Wildsmith), 342
Bridge to Terabithia (Paterson), 385
Brocaded Slipper and Other
    Vietnamese Tales (Vuong), 88
Brooklyn Dodger Day (Rosenblum),
    457
"Brother Rabbit and the
    Mosquitoes" (Bleecker), 74
Brown Bear, Brown Bear, What Do
    You See? (Martin), 348
Bruno the Pretzel Man (Davis), 102,
    483
Bubba and Babba (Polushkin), 341
Buffalo Girls, 305
Buffalo Hunt (Freedman), 103
Building a House (Barton), 344
Bunnicula (Howe and Howe), 98
Burgoo Stew (Patron), 50, 101, 213,
    481
Buried Treasure (Ross), 123
Butterfly Jar (Moss), 169
Button Box (Reid), 50
By the Sea (Koch), 345

Cakes and Miracles (Diamond), 142
Cakes and Miracles (Goldin), 72
Call of the Wild (London), 92
Call of the Wolves (Murphy), 460
Canadian Childhoods, 103
Canadian Children's Treasury, 144,
    145
Canary Prince (Nones), 67
"Cap O'Rushes" (Jacobs), 69, 118, 121
Caps for Sale (Slobodkina), 233, 350
Careers in Television (Blumenthal),
    254
Carp in the Bathtub (Cohen), 482
Carrot Seed (Krauss), 51, 347
Carrot/Parrot (Martin), 345
Carry Go Bring Come (Samuels), 346
Casey at the Bat (Thayer), 457
"Cat and the Mouse" (Jacobs), 113,
    121

Cat Book (Shaw, ed.), 154, 172
Cat in the Hat (Seuss), 46
Catlore (Zaum), 89
Cats Are Cats (Larrick), 171, 459
"Celebration" (Sanfield), 72
Celebration of American Family
    Folklore (Zeitlin), 149
Celebrations (Bauer), 144, 145, 443
Chair for My Mother (William), 341,
    388
Chalk Box Story (Freeman), 219
Chanticleer and the Fox (Chaucer),
    130, 132
Chanukah Guest (Kimmel), 73
Charlotte's Web (White), 92, 386
Cherry Pie Baby (Chorao), 482
Chester and Uncle Willoughby
    (Edwards), 387
Chicken Man (Edwards), 341
Chicken Sunday (Polacco), 466, 467
Children of Egypt (Pitkanen and
    Harkonen), 103
Children of Nepal (Pitkanen), 467
Children of the River (Crew), 103,
    465, 466
Children Tell Stories (Hamilton and
    Weiss), 111
Children's Aesop (Calmenson), 508
Children's Almanac of Words at Play
    (Espy), 189
Children's Folklore Review, 150
Children's Homer (Colum), 135, 137,
    138
Child's Book of Things (Strickland),
    351
Child's Christmas in Wales
    (Thomas), 72
Child's Garden of Verses (Stevenson),
    153, 169
Child's Prayer (Titherington), 143
Child's Treasury of Seaside Verse
    (Daniel), 159, 164, 170
Chimney Sweeps (Giblin), 103
"China Spaniel" (Hughes), 75
"Chinese Fairy Tale" (Housman), 67
Chinese Mirror (Ginsburg), 277
Chinese Story Teller (Buck), 448
Chocolate (Boynton), 169
Chocolate Book (Hearn), 480
Chocolate Dreams (Adoff), 170, 480
Chocolate Moose for Dinner
    (Gwynne), 188, 189
Chortles (Merriam), 169
"Christmas" (Wilder), 473
"Christmas Apple" (Sawyer), 72
Christmas in the Stable (Duncan),
    170
"Christmas Roast" (Rettich), 72
Christmas Tree Memories (Aliki), 342
Christopher Columbus (Levinson),
    289

Chronicle of Western Fashion
    (Peacock), 451
"Chunk o' Meat" (Chase), 395
"Cinderella" (Lang), 69
Cinderella (Perrault), 83, 87
Cinderella and Other Tales from
    Perrault (Perrault), 87
Circle of Giving (Howard), 104
Circles (Sachs), 412
Circus (De Regniers), 342
Circus! (Spier), 342
City of Gold and Other Stories from
    the Old Testament (Dickinson),
    143
Clancey's Coat (Bunting), 342
Class Clown (Hurwitz), 382, 385
Classic Animal Stories (O'Mara), 87
"Clever Elsie" (Grimm Brothers), 68
"Clever Grethel" (Bleecker), 68
"Clever Manka" (Fillmore), 68
Climb into the Bell Tower
    (Livingston), 163
Climbing Jacob's Ladder (Langstaff),
    143
Clothes Horse and Other Stories
    (Ahlberg and Ahlberg), 126
Coal Mine Peaches (Dionetti), 150
Cock-a-Doodle-Doo (Brandenberg),
    262
Cock-a-Doodle-Doo! (Runcie), 262
Cock-a-Doodle-Doo! (Shone), 262
Cock-a-Doodle-Dudley (Peet), 262, 345
Coconut Kind of Day (Joseph), 168
Collected Stories (Kennedy), 430
Color Box (Dodds), 212, 285–86, 342
Color Dance (Jonas), 212
Color Farm (Ehlert), 285, 349
Color Zoo (Ehlert), 285, 342
Colors (Goennel), 212
Come a Tide (Lyon), 387
Come Again in the Spring (Kennedy),
    77
Comedy Magic Textbook (Roper), 294
Comedy Warmups (Ginn), 294
Commodore Perry in the Land of the
    Shogun (Blumberg), 144, 145,
    288
Company's Coming (Yorinks), 447
Complete Book of Games (Wood and
    Goddard), 196
Complete Book of Poetry (Currell),
    278
Complete Fairy Tales and Stories
    (Andersen), 122, 127, 430
Complete Guide to Home Video
    Production (Levine), 248
"Conceited Elephant and the Very
    Lively Mosquito" (Lobagola), 74
Confessions of a Prime Time Kid
    (Harris), 510
Conjuring (Hawkesworth), 294

Consider the Lemming (Steig), 172
Contest (Hogrogian), 81
Cooking the Greek Way (Villios), 438
Corduroy (Freeman), 347
Costume of the Western World
    (Yarwood), 451
"Could I Keep Him?" (Shapiro), 509
Counting Book (Sis), 350
Country Bear's Good Neighbor
    (Brimmer), 482
Country Bunny and the Little Gold
    Shoes (Heyward), 347
Country Far Away (Gray), 387
Couple of Kooks and Other Stories
    about Love (Rylant), 128, 407
Cow That Went Oink (Most), 262, 345
Cow Who Fell in the Canal
    (Krasilovsky), 342
Cowboy and the Black-eyed Pea
    (Johnston), 128
Cowboys (Rounds), 342
Cows Are Going to Paris (Kirby), 102,
    387
"Crab and the Jaguar" (Karrick), 75
"Cratchits' Christmas Dinner"
    (Hodges), 473
Creative Dramatics Handbook
    (Ehrlich), 511
Creative Fingerplays and Action
    Rhymes (Defty), 365
Creative Storytelling (Maguire), 111
Crest and the Hide (Courlander), 430
Cricket Boy (Ziner), 85
Crickets and Frogs (Mistral), 130, 132
Cup of Sunshine (Bennett), 163
Curious George Takes a Job (Rey), 476
Curriculum Guide to the Tale of
    Peter Rabbit (Landes), 444
Custard and Company (Nash), 169

Dabble Duck (Ellis), 343, 459
Daddies (Greenspun), 343
Daddies Boat (Monfried), 344
Daddy (Caines), 343
Dads Are Such Fun (Wood), 343
Dancing Camel (Byars), 67
Dancing Kettle and Other Japanese
    Folk Tales (Uchida), 120, 121
Dancing Skeleton (DeFelice), 104
Dancing Teepees (Sneve), 172
Dancing with the Indians (Medearis),
    327
Dark Way (Hamilton), 86, 430
David's Psalms (Eisler), 143
Day Jimmy's Boa Ate the Wash
    (Noble), 348
Day of Ahmed's Secret (Heide), 466,
    467
Day of the Blizzard (Moskin), 101
Daydreamers (Greenfield), 166
Deep in the Forest (Turkle), 509

Derek the Knitting Dinosaur
    (Blackwood), 461
Devil's Bridge (Scribner), 140
Devil's Donkey (Brittain), 100
Dial-A-Croc (Dumbleton), 344
Diamond Tree (Schwartz and Rush),
    88
Diaries of Lewis Carroll (Dodgson),
    219
Dibble and Dabble in Showtime
    (Saunders and Saunders), 343
Dick Whittington and His Cat
    (Brown), 118
"Did the Tailor Have a Nightmare?"
    (Serwer), 78
Dinosaurs (Hopkins), 155
Directing Puppet Theater (Fijan and
    Ballard), 278
Discontented Dervishes and Other
    Persian Tales from Sa'di
    (Scholey), 88
Djugurba, 133, 135
"Doctor and Detective Too" (Hatch),
    69–70
Doctor Coyote (Bierhorst), 130, 132
"Doctor Know It All" (Grimm
    Brothers), 70
Does God Have a Big Toe? (Gellman),
    143
Don Quixote (De Cervantes), 410
Don Quixote and Sancho Panza (De
    Cervantes Saavedra), 410
Donna O'Neeshuck Was Chased by
    Some Cows (Grossman), 342
Don't Count Your Chicks (d'Aulaire
    and d'Aulaire), 292
Don't Forget the Bacon! (Hutchins),
    359
The Doorbell Rang (Hutchins), 219
Dora's Book (Edwards), 341
Dos and Taboos of Body Language
    around the World (Axtell), 190
"Doughnuts" (McCloskey), 74, 473
Down Under (Reynolds), 466, 467
Dragon, Dragon and Other Tales
    (Gardner), 126, 127
Dragons and Dreams (Yolen,
    Greenberg and Waugh), 129, 408
Dragon's Fat Cat (Pilkey), 277
Dragon's Milk (Fletcher), 100
Dramatizing Aesop's Fables (Thistle),
    511
Draw Me a Star (Carle), 241
Dream Weaver (Yolen), 129
Dream Wolf (Goble), 80
"Dribble" (Blume), 472
Duckat (Gordon), 343, 459
Ducks! (Pinkwater), 459
Ducks Fly (Dabcovich), 349, 459
Dudley and the Strawberry Shake
    (Taylor), 483

Duffy and the Devil (Zemach), 85, 449, 509
Dwarf Giant (Lobel), 81

East O' the Sun and West O' the Moon (Asbjørnsen and Moe), 118–19
"Eat a Poem" Program (Bauer), 485
Eating Out (Oxenbury), 483
Eating the Alphabet (Ehlert), 473, 485
Eats (Adoff), 480
"Ebenezer-Never-Could-Sneezer" (Patillo), 77
Educational Film and Video Locator, 248
Eentsy, Weentsy Spider (Cole and Calmenson), 164
Egg! (Wood), 233
Egyptian Hieroglyphs for Everyone (Scott and Scott), 191
"El Enamo" (Finger), 70
Elephant and His Secret (Mistral), 130
Elephant's Child (Kipling), 81, 94, 128
"Ellie's Valentine" (Rylant), 73
Ellis Island: Gateway to the New World (Fisher), 465, 466
Ellis Island: New Hope in a New Land (Jacobs), 465, 467
"Elsie Piddock Skips in Her Sleep" (Farjeon), 71, 123, 127, 182–83
Emma's Snowball (Miller), 346
Emperor's New Clothes (Andersen), 68, 79
Empty Lot (Fife), 492
Enchanted Flute (McAllister), 327
Encyclopaedia of Children's Magic (Adair), 294
Encyclopedia of Fashion (O'Hara), 451
Endless Party (Delessert and Schmid), 143
Endless Steppe (Hautzig), 94, 99, 385
English Fables and Fairy Stories (Reeves), 118, 121
Enter Three Witches (Gilmore), 412, 510
Eric Carle's Animals Animals (Whipple), 167
Eric Carle's Dragons and Other Creatures That Never Were (Whipple), 172
Erie Canal, 305
Ernest and Celestine at the Circus (Vincent), 342
Eskimo Boy (Kendall), 103, 465
Esteban and the Ghost (Hancock), 80
Even the Devil Is Afraid of a Shrew (Stadler), 73, 83

Every Living Thing (Rylant), 99, 386
Everybody Cooks Rice (Dooley), 475
Everybody Needs a Rock (Baylor), 213, 508
Everyone Loves the Moon (Young), 447
Evil Spell (McCully), 508
Exactly the Opposite (Hoban), 345
Exploding Frog and Other Fables (MacFarland), 132
Eye of the Needle (Sloat), 83
Eye Winker, Tom Tinker, Chin Chopper (Glazer), 365

Faber Book of Modern Fairy Tales (Corrin and Corrin), 127
Fables (Lobel), 132
Fables of Aesop (Kent), 130
Face of Baseball (Weiss), 457
Facts and Fictions of Minna Pratt (McLachlan), 328
Fairy Tales of Ireland (Yeats), 89
Faithful Elephants (Tsuchiya), 388
Family Read-Aloud Holiday Treasury (Low), 87
Family Storytelling Handbook (Pellowski), 149
Family Tales, Family Wisdom (Akeret), 149
Fanciful Finger Friends from Sea and Shore (Pittman), 278
Fanfares (Irving), 443
Fantastic Theater (Sierra), 278
Far North (Reynolds), 467
Farm Day (Henley), 349
Fat Cat (Kent), 81, 113, 121
Fat Fanny, Beanpole Bertha, and the Boys (Porte), 102, 328, 386
Fathers, Mothers, Sisters, Brothers (Hoberman), 171
Favorite Folktales from Around the World (Yolen), 89
Favorite Scary Stories of American Children (Young and Dockrey), 393
Favorite Tales from Many Lands (Retan), 87
Feather Merchants and Other Tales of the Fools of Chelm (Sanfield), 88, 430
Feathers and Tails (Kherdian), 132
Fiddle-I-Fee, 305
Fifteen Fables of Krylov (Krylov), 131, 132
Fifty Stories for 8 year olds (Greenwood), 86
Film and Video (Staples), 248
Fin McCoul (dePaola), 80, 482
Fine Round Cake (Esterl), 482
Finger Plays for Nursery and Kindergarten (Poulsson), 365

Finger Rhymes (Brown), 365
Fingerplay Friends (Leighton), 365
Fire Bringer (Hodges), 80, 81, 139, 140
Fire on the Mountain and Other Ethiopian Stories (Courlander), 120
Fireside Book of Baseball (Einstein, ed.), 457
Fireside Book of Children's Songs (Winn, ed.), 325
Fireside Book of Folk Songs (Boni, ed.), 323
Fireside Book of Fun and Game Songs (Winn, ed.), 325
First Morning (Bernstein and Kobrin), 79, 133, 135
First Poetry Book (Foster), 165
"First Shlemiel" (Singer), 59, 74, 472
First Things First (Fraser), 185
"Fisherman and His Wife" (Grimm Brothers), 71, 114
Five Chinese Brothers (Bishop), 70
500 Hats of Bartholomew Cubbins (Seuss), 509
Five Little Monkeys Jumping on the Bed (Christelow), 349
"Flea" (Ross), 76, 123
"Flea" (Sawyer), 129
Flight (Burleigh), 99, 289, 290, 386
Flim and Flam and the Big Cheese (Garrison), 472
Flossie and the Fox (McKissack), 82, 509
Fly Away Home (Bunting), 386
Folding Stories (Kallevig), 200
Folk Tales for Puppets (Mahlmann and Jones), 278
Folk Toys around the World (Joseph), 197
Folklore: An Annotated Bibliography and Index to Single Editions (Ziegler, comp.), 111
Folklore of Canada (Fowke), 86
The Folktale (Thompson), 151
Folktales from Around the World (Yolen), 430
Follow Me! (Gerstein), 343
The Fool and the Fish (Afanasyev), 79
"Fool's Paradise" (Singer), 73
For Laughing Out Loud (Prelutsky), 165
For Love of the Game (Shaara), 458
For Reading Out Loud (Kimmel), 98
For Strawberry Jam or Fireflies (Hartman), 346
Forgotten Forest (Anholt), 291
Four and Twenty Dinosaurs (Most), 164
Four Fierce Kittens (Dunbar), 492

Four Questions (Sherman), 143
Fourth Question (Wang), 70
"Fox and the Bear" (Uchida), 70
Fox Book (Shaw, ed.), 154, 172
Fox under First Base (Latimer), 457
Fox Went Out on a Chilly Night, 305
Foxfire Book (Wigginton), 149, 150
Foxy Fables (Ross), 133
Frank and Ernest Play Ball (Day), 457
Franklin Delano Roosevelt (Friedman), 144, 145
Frederick (Lionni), 347, 508
Frederick Ferdinand Fox (Miller), 387
Frederick's Fables (Lionni), 132
Free to Be . . . You and Me (Viorst), 325, 451
Freedom Songs (Moore), 101
Freight Train (Crew), 349
Frog and the Birdsong (Velthuijs), 344
Frog and Toad Are Friends (Lobel), 348
Frog Book (Shaw, ed.), 154, 172
Frog Prince (Grimm Brothers), 460
Frog Prince (Ormerod), 83
Frog Prince Continued (Scieszka), 460
Frog Princess (Isele), 460
Frog's Riddle (Thompson), 220
From Hand to Mouth or How We Invented Knives, Forks, Spoons, Chopsticks, and the Table Manners to Go with Them (Giblin), 485
Full Speed Ahead (Irving), 443
Fun with Hieroglyphs (Roehrig), 191
Funk and Wagnalls Standard Dictionary of Folklore, Mythology and Legend, 151
Funny Little Woman (Mosel), 69, 82, 483

Galileo (Fisher), 288
Galimoto (Williams), 388
Games and Songs of American Children (Newell), 196
Games for the Very Young (Matterson), 365
Gassire's Lute (Jablow), 138
General Stores (Field), 345
George and Martha (Marshall), 50, 348
Georgia Music (Griffith), 104, 326
Georgia O'Keefe (Turner), 289
Gestures (Axtell), 190
"Get Up and Bar the Door" (Johnson), 78
Ghost with the Halloween Hiccups (Mooser), 509

Ghoul at Your Fingertips, 393
Giant Apple (Scheffler), 340
Giant Jam Sandwich (Lord), 472
Gift of the Girl Who Couldn't Hear
    (Shreve), 104
Gift of the Magi (O. Henry), 72
Ginger Tree (Wynd), 434
Gingerbread Boy (Galdone), 80, 482
Gingerbread Man (Kimmel), 473
Girl Who Cried Flowers and Other
    Tales (Yolen), 125, 129
Girl Who Loved the Wind (Yolen), 84,
    125, 129
Girl with the Silver Eyes (Roberts),
    100
Give Yourself a Fright (Aiken), 393
Glass Slipper (Farjeon), 123, 127
"Go Close the Door" (Simon), 78
Go in and out the Window: An
    Illustrated Songbook for Young
    People, 324
Go Tell Aunt Rhody, 305
"Goat Well" (Courlander), 71
Goats (Cole), 412
God on Every Mountain Top (Baylor),
    142
Going Live (Booth), 510
Going the Moose Way Home
    (Latimer), 459
Going to Sleep on the Farm
    (Lewison), 262
Gold and Silver, Silver and Gold
    (Schwartz), 88
"Gold Bug" (Poe), 128
"Golden Fish" (Ransome), 71
"Golden Shoes," 76
Goldilocks and the Three Bears
    (Marshall), 343
Gold's Gloom (Ryder, tr.), 131, 132
Golem (McDermott), 82, 141, 143
Gone Is Gone (Gág), 74, 80, 119, 120
Gonna Sing My Head Off! (Krull),
    324
Good Books, Good Times! (Hopkins),
    155
Good Days Bad Days (Anholt), 344
Good for Me! (Burns), 485
Good Lemonade (Asch), 474
Good Night, Mr. Tom (Magorian), 104
Good Queen Bess (Stanley and
    Vennema), 100, 289
Goodnight Moon (Brown), 213, 351
Goodnight Moon (Wise), 208–9
Good-Night, Owl! (Hutchins), 233,
    347, 349
Gooseberries to Oranges (Cohen),
    475
Grandfather Tales (Chase), 120
Grandfather Tang's Story (Tompert),
    193
Grandpa Bud (Godds), 232

Grandpa Ritz and the Luscious
    Lovelies (Shyer), 484
Grandparents' Houses (Streich), 172
Grass Green Gallup (Hubbell), 171
Great American Gold Rush
    (Blumberg), 102
Great Ancestor Hunt (Perl), 149
Great Big Enormous Turnip (Tolstoi),
    359
Great Brain (Fitzgerald), 101
Great Bullocky Race (Page), 102
Great Children's Stories: The Classic
    Volland Edition, 508
Great Composers (Ventura), 289, 327
Great Days of a Country House
    (Goodall), 449
Great Little Madison (Fritz), 288
Great Science Fiction Series (Pohl,
    Greenberg and Olander), 430
Great Song Book (John), 324
Great Swedish Fairy Tales (Olenius),
    121
Great Wall of China (Fisher), 387
Greece (Stein), 438
Greek Gods and Heroes (Graves),
    134, 135
Greek Myths (Coolidge), 135
Green Queen (Sharratt), 233
Grimm's Fairy Tales (Grimm
    Brothers), 120
Growing Colors (McMillan), 212, 342
"Gudbrand-on-the-Hillside"
    (Asbjørnsen), 74, 119, 120
Gudgekin the Thistle Girl and Other
    Tales (Gardner), 126, 127
"Guest for Halil" (Kelsey), 68
Gunniwolf (Harper), 76, 80, 359
Guy Who Was Five Minutes Late
    (Grossman), 346

Hailstones amd Halibut Bones
    (O'Neill), 172
Halloween (Bauer), 170
Halloween ABC (Merriam), 172
Halloween Mask for Monster
    (Mueller), 277
Handbook of Creative Dance and
    Drama (Lee), 508
Handmade Alphabet (Rankin), 104,
    190
Handtalk Zoo (Ancona and Miller),
    190
Hank Greenberg (Berkow), 457
Hanky-Panky (Burns), 197
Happy Birthday Moon (Asch), 446
Happy Origami (Miyawaki), 369
Hare and the Tortoise (Wildsmith), 84
Harold and Chester in Hot Fudge
    (Howe), 50, 473
Harold and the Purple Crayon
    (Johnson, pseud.), 219

Harriet, the Spy (Fitzhugh), 476
Harry the Dirty Dog (Zion), 348
Harry's Dog (Porte), 144, 145
Harry's Mom (Porte), 144, 146
Hatchet (Paulsen), 385, 411, 484
Hat-Shaking Dance and Other Ashanti Tales from Ghana (Courlander and Prempeh), 66–67, 120
Hattie and the Fox (Fox), 207, 349
Hauntings (Hodges), 393
Have You Seen My Duckling? (Tafuri), 350
Hawaiian Legends of Ghosts and Ghost-Gods (Westervelt), 139, 140
He Wakes Me (James), 346
Hector Lives in the United States Now (Hewett), 465–66, 467
Hello, Tree! (Ryder), 346
Henny Penny (Butler), 79
Henry and the Red Stripes (Christelow), 219
Hercules (Evslin), 138
Herds of Thunder, Manes of Gold (Coville), 127
Herds of Words (MacCarthy), 387
Here's to Ewe (Walton and Walton), 177
The Hero (Raglan), 151
The Heroes (Kingsley), 136
Hershel of Ostropol (Kimmel), 101
Hey, Hay? (Terban), 177
Hey Riddle Riddle! (Pirotta and Hellen), 241
Hey World, Here I Am! (Little), 168
Hi Ho! The Rattlin' Bog, and Other Folk Songs for Group Singing (Langstaff, comp.), 324
Hidden Stories in Plants (Pellowski), 214
Hide and Shriek (Walton and Walton), 177
Hideout (Bunting), 411
Hieroglyphs (Katan and Mintz), 191
"High Cost of Cat Food" (MacLeod), 429
High Hopes (Dubosarsky), 411
Hildilid's Night (Ryan), 75
Himalaya (Reynolds), 466, 467
Hist Whist and Other Poems for Children (Cummings), 168
Ho Ho Ho! Riddles about Santa Claus (Walton and Walton), 177
Hoang Anh (Hoyt-Goldsmith), 289, 466, 467
Hobyahs (Stern), 359
Hodgepodge Book (Emrich), 189
Holiday Puppets (Ross), 278
Homemade Band (Palmer), 328
Homer Price (McCloskey), 50, 74
Homesick (Fritz), 99, 437

Homespun (Smith), 88, 430
Homonyms (Hanson), 189
Honey, I Love and Other Poems (Greenfield), 168
Hoot Howl Hiss (Koch), 345
Hopeful Trout and Other Limericks (Ciardi), 168
Hopscotch around the World (Langford), 195
Hopscotch, Hangman, Hot Potato, and Ha, Ha, Ha (Maguire), 196
"Horned Goat" (Borski), 71
Host of Surprises (Hooper), 294
Hour of the Frog (Wynne-Jones), 344, 492
How a Horse Grew Hoarse on the Site Where He Sighted a Bare Bear (Hanlon), 189
How a House Is Built (Gibbons), 344
"How Boots Befooled the King" (Pyle), 70
"How Bozo the Button Buster Busted All His Buttons When a Mouse Came" (Sandburg), 75, 128
How Do Apples Grow? (Maestro), 50, 340
How Do I Put It On? (Watanabe), 360
How Does It Feel to Be Old? (Farber), 166
How I Became Hettie Jones (Jones), 436–37
How I Captured a Dinosaur (Schwartz), 343
How I Hunted the Little Fellows (Zhitkov), 388
How Many Spots Does a Leopard Have? (Lester), 87
How Many Stars in the Sky? (Hort), 446
How My Parents Learned to Eat (Friedman), 482
"How She Kept Herself Cheerful" (Newell), 474
How the Animals Got Their Colors (Rosen), 286
"How the Camel Got His Hump" (Kipling), 67, 128
"How the Camel Got His Proud Look" (Ross), 67, 114, 121
"How the Clever Doctor Tricked Death" (Andrade), 77
How the First Rainbow Was Made (Robbins), 83
How the Forest Grew (Jaspersohn), 291
"How the Good Gifts Were Used by Two" (Pyle), 71, 124
How the Guinea Fowl Got Her Spots (Knutson), 81
How the Manx Cat Lost Its Tail (Stevens), 459

How the Ox Star Fell from Heaven (Hong), 387

How the People Sang the Mountains Up (Leach), 114, 121

How the Stars Fell into the Sky (Oughton), 446

How the Tsar Drinks Tea (Elkin), 508

"How to Become a Witch" (Leach), 76

How to Eat Fried Worms and Other Plays (Rockwell), 484

How to Make Super Pop-ups (Irvine), 369

How to Make Your Own Videos (Schwartz), 248

Howling Dog (Pearson), 343

"Huckabuck Family and How They Raised Popcorn in Nebraska" (Sandburg), 475

"Hug Me" (Stern), 359

"Hungry Hans" (Keller), 474

Hunky Dory Ate It (Evans), 343

Hunting of Chas McGill and Other Stories (Westall), 393

"Husband Who Was to Mind the House" (Asbjørnsen and Moe), 119, 120

Hush Little Baby, 305

Hush, Little Children, 307

I Feel Like Dancing (Barboza), 326

I Have Another Language (Schick), 509

I Know an Old Lady Who Swallowed a Fly, 305

I Know an Old Lady Who Swallowed a Fly (Westcott), 233

I Never Saw a Purple Cow and Other Nonsense Verse (Clark), 170

I Saw Esau (Opie and Opie), 151

I See (Isadora), 493

I See Something You Don't See (Koontz), 177, 219

I Spy (Marzolla), 493

I Touch (Oxenbury), 491

I Went Walking (Williams), 350, 460, 509

I Will Tell You of Peach Stone (Zimelman), 50

"Icarus and Daedalus" (Peabody), 70

"Ice Cream" (Lobel), 483

Ice Cream Store (Lee), 168

If I Had a Paka (Pomerantz), 167

If I Were in Charge of the World and Other Worries (Viorst), 169

If You Give a Moose a Muffin (Numeroff), 50, 460, 475

If You Give a Mouse a Cookie (Numeroff), 348, 473

"If You Had a Wish" (Association for Childhood Education International), 78

If You Made a Million (Schwartz), 50, 103

If You're Happy and You Know It, 324

Iliad and Odyssey of Homer (Picard), 138

Iliad and the Odyssey (Werner), 137, 138

Illustrated Treasury of Songs, 324

I'm Going to Pet a Worm Today and Other Poems (Levy), 168

I'm Going to Sing (Bryan), 323

Imaginary Gardens (Sullivan, ed.), 159, 165, 167

Immigrant Kids (Freedman), 467

Improvisation Handbook (Elkind), 511

In a Dark, Dark, Dark Wood (Carter), 395

In a Dark, Dark Room (Schwartz), 144, 145

In a Messy, Messy Room and Other Strange Stories (Gorog), 126, 127

In a Spring Garden (Lewis), 166, 233

In a Word (Ernst), 189

In the Beginning (Hamilton), 135

In the Eyes of the Cat (Demi), 170

In the Middle of the Night (Henderson), 344

In the Tall, Tall Grass (Fleming), 359

In the Year of the Boar and Jackie Robinson (Lord), 104

Inch Boy (Morimoto), 82

Incident at Hawk's Hill (Eckert), 98

Incredible Indoor Games Book (Gregson), 195

Index to Fairy Tales 1949–1972 (Ireland, comp.), 111

Indian Attachment (Lloyd), 435, 437

Indian in the Cupboard (Banks), 100

Indian Mythology (Ions), 135

Ingri and Edgar Parin d'Aulaire's Book of Greek Myths (d'Aulaire and d'Aulaire), 134, 135

Invisible Thread (Uchida), 466, 467

Invitation to the Game (Hughes), 412

Is It Magic? (Lagercrantz and Lagercrantz), 295

Is It Red? Is It Yellow? Is It Blue? (Hoban), 342

Is Your Mama a Llama? (Guarino), 349

Island of the Blue Dolphin (O'Dell), 385

It Came from Outer Space (Bradman), 446, 508

It Does Not Say Meow! (De Regniers), 345

It Looked like Spilt Milk (Shaw), 233, 493

"It's a Good Honest Name" (King-Smith), 75

It's About Time (video, Ginn), 296
It's Christmas (Prelutsky), 172
It's Halloween (Prelutsky), 172
It's Perfectly True (Andersen), 122, 127, 447
It's Raining Cats and Dogs and Other Beastly Expressions (Ammer), 189
It's Thanksgiving (Prelutsky), 172
It's Too Noisy! (Cole), 345
It's Valentine's Day (Prelutsky), 172

Jabberwocky (Carroll), 166
"Jack and Old Ragedy Bones" (Haley), 304
Jack Kent's Fables of Aesop (Kent), 132
Jack Tales (Chase), 120
Jackie Robinson (Adler), 457
Jacks and Jack Games (Weigle), 196
Jamberry (Degan), 166, 349
Jane Yolen's Mother Goose Songbook (Yolen), 326
Jane Yolen's Songs of Summer (Yolen), 325
Japanese Tales (Tyler), 88
Jason and the Golden Fleece (Fisher), 135, 438
Jataka Tales (Babbitt), 132
Jataka Tales: Fables from the Buddha (DeRoin), 132
"Jean Labadie's Big Black Dog" (Carlson), 69
Jennie's Hat (Keats), 208, 213
Jesse Builds a Road (Pringle), 346
Jesse's Ghost and Other Stories (Porte), 128
Jewish Stories One Generation Tells Another (Schram), 88
"Jigsaw Puzzle" (Stamper), 72
Jimmy's Boa and the Big Birthday Bash (Noble), 341
Jingle Bells, 305
John and the Fiddler (Foley), 328
John Burningham's Colors (Burningham), 212
John Henry (Keats), 81
"Johnny Appleseed" (Osborne), 481
Johnny Crow's Garden (Brooke), 153, 163
Join the Band! (Pillar), 328
"Jolly Tailor" (Borski and Miller), 76
"Jolly Tailor Who Became King" (Bleecker), 142
Jorinda and Joringel (Grimm Brothers), 67
Journey of Meng (Rappaport), 83
Joyful Noise (Fleischman), 171
"Juan Bobo" (Ramírez de Arellano), 75
Juggling Book (Carlo, pseud.), 195

Julie of the Wolves (George), 385
Julius (Kligsheim), 103
Jump Rope! (Skolnik), 183
Jumping Jack (audiocassette, Torrance), 395
Jungle Book (Kipling), 124, 128
Just beyond Reach and Other Riddle Poems (Nims), 290
Just like Daddy (Asch), 359
Just Plain Fancy (Polacco), 388
Just So Stories (Kipling), 128

Kenji and the Magic Geese (Johnson), 241
Kevin Corbett Eats Flies (Hermes), 484
Kickle Snifters and Other Fearsome Critters (Schwartz), 190
Kid Next Door and Other Headaches (Smith), 102
Kidbiz (Ginn), 294
Kid's Book of Questions (Stock), 149
Kids' Games (Wiswell), 196
Kids' World Almanac Rhyming Dictionary (Israel and Streep), 163
King and the Tortoise (Mollel), 233
King Arthur (Talbot), 138
King Bidgood's in the Bathtub (Wood), 341, 360
"King Clothes" (Jagendorf), 68
"King of the Cats" (Galdone), 68
King Stork (Pyle), 124, 128
King Who Rained (Gwynne), 188, 189
Kingfisher Book of Children's Poetry (Rosen), 165
King's Day (Aliki), 99
King's Tea (Noble), 509
"Kisander" (Sherlock), 67
Kiss, Kiss (Dahl), 430
Kitchen Knight (Hodges), 137, 138
Kitten's ABC (Newberry), 491
Knee-High Man and Other Stories (Lester), 385
Knick Knack Paddywack, 305
Knock at a Star (Kennedy and Kennedy), 165
Knots on a Counting Rope (Martin and Archambault), 493
Kwanzaa (Porter), 73

Ladder to the Sky (Esbensen), 139
"Lady Who Put Salt in Her Coffee" (Hale), 69
Lady's Chair and the Ottoman" (Tennyson), 341, 461
"Lady's Room" (Farjeon), 123, 127
LaLa Salama (Bozylinsky), 232
Land of Gray Wolf (Locker), 460
Land of the Long White Cloud (Kawana), 87

Language of the Puppet (Kominz and Levenson, eds.), 278

Lap-Time Song and Play Book (Yolen, ed.), 325

Larger than Life (San Souci), 140

Las Navidades (Delacre, ed.), 324

Last Dinosaur (Murphy), 388

Last Slices of Rainbow and Other Stories (Aiken), 127

Last Time I Saw Harris (Remkiewicz), 212

Lateral Thinking Puzzlers (Sloane), 196

Laugh a Minute Joke Book (Perret), 180

"Laughing Gas" (Travers), 476

Laura Ingalls Wilder Songbook (Garson, comp.), 325

Law of Gravity (Hurwitz), 382

"Lazy Heinz" (Grimm Brothers), 73

Lazy Lion (Hadithi and Kennaway), 80

"Leave Well Enough Alone" (Dobbs), 78

Leaving (Wilson), 407

Left Behind (Carrick), 508

Legend of King Arthur (Lister), 101, 138

Legend of the Milky Way (Lee), 140

"Legend of the Royal Palm" (Belpré), 120

Legends of the Hawaiian Forest (Lee), 140

Lentil (McCloskey), 327

Leo the Late Bloomer (Krauss), 289, 347

Let Freedom Ring (Livingston), 72

Let Me Off This Spaceship! (Greer and Ruddick), 446

Let's Celebrate! (Parry), 444

Let's Celebrate: Festival Poems (Foster), 171

Let's Do a Poem (Larrick), 163

Let's Eat! (Kelley), 483

Let's Make Rabbits (Lionni), 213

Life and Death in Shanghai (Cheng), 437

Life and Times of the Apple (Micucci), 50, 95, 340

"Life Savings" (Ahlberg and Ahlberg), 429

Light and Shadow (Livingston), 166

Lightning inside You and Other Native American Riddles (Bierhorst), 176, 290

Lights! Camera! Action! How a Movie Is Made (Gibbons), 254

Lili at Ballet (Isadora), 326

Lion (Du Bois), 219

Lion and the Ostrich Chicks and Other African Folk Tales (Bryan), 85

Lion and the Rat (Wildsmith), 84

Lion Sneezed (Leach), 136

Listening for the Crack of Dawn (Davis), 149

Listening Walk (Showers), 492

Literature-based Learning Activities Kit (Jensen), 444

Little Band (Sage), 327

Little Blue and Little Yellow (Lionni), 220, 284

Little by Little (Little), 100, 385, 437

Little Chalk Man (Ctvrtek), 219

Little Dog Laughed and Other Nursery Rhymes (Cousins), 164, 166

Little Fear (Wrightson), 101

Little Hippo Gets Glasses (Macdonald), 493

Little House (Burton), 347

Little House Cookbook (Walker), 485

Little House in the Big Woods (Wilder), 386

Little Mouse's Painting (Wolkstein), 84

Little Old Lady Who Was Not Afraid of Anything (Williams), 233

Little Peep (Kent), 262

"Little Pieces of the West Wind" (Garrison), 78

Little Pig's Puppet Book (Watson), 277

Little Polar Bear (de Beer), 341

Little Red Hen (Zemach), 343

Little Red Hen/La Pequeña Gallina Roja (Williams), 233

Little Red House (Sawicki), 214

Little Things (Laurin), 461

Loathsome Dragon (Wiesner and Kahng), 70

Lon Po Po (Young), 84

London Bridge Is Falling Down!, 306

"Long, Broad and Sharpsight" (Manning-Saunders), 70

Long Red Scarf (Hilton), 213

Look Again! (Hoban), 493

Look Again! The Second Ultimate Spot-the-Difference Book (Wilson), 493

Look Back and See (MacDonald), 87

Look! Look! Look! (Hoban), 241

Lore and Language of School Children (Opie and Opie), 151

"Lost Half Hour" (Beston), 70

Lost in Translation (Hoffman), 437

Louis the Fish (Yorinks), 388

Lucky Baseball Bat (Christopher), 457

Ludwig von Beethoven (Thompson), 328

Lullabies and Night Songs (Engvick, ed.), 325

Lyddie (Paterson), 102, 411

MA nDA LA (Adoff), 153, 166
Macmillan Book of Greek Gods and Heroes (Low), 136
"Mad Tea Party" (Carroll), 476
Madeline (Bemelmans), 154, 159, 166, 347
Maebelle's Suitcase (Tusa), 214
Magic across the Table (Severn), 294
Magic Book (Roberts), 296
Magic City Library of Magic (Behnke), 294
Magic Comedy (Severn), 294
Magic Cooking Pot (Towle), 84, 475
Magic Dog (Edmunds), 296
Magic Fan (Baker), 192, 295
"Magic Glass" (Hughes), 69
Magic Handbook (Eldin), 294
Magic in Your Pockets (Severn), 294
Magic Leaf (Morris), 82
Magic of Marionettes (Masson), 278
Magic of Reading (video, Hickman), 296
Magic Orange Tree and Other Haitian Folktales (Wolkstein, ed.), 89
Magic Pudding (Lindsay), 484
Magic Pumpkin (Skurzynski), 50
Magic Secrets (Wyler and Amers), 295
Magic with Paper (Severn), 200, 294
"Magical Horse" (Yep), 73
Magician (Shulevitz), 141, 143
Magician's Apprentice (McGowan), 296
Mail-Order Wings (Gormley), 100
Make Better Videos with Your Camcorder (Thomas), 248
Make Way for Ducklings (McCloskey), 348, 459
Make Your Own Musical Instruments (McLean), 328
Make Your Own . . . Videos, Commercials, Radio Shows, Special Effects and More (Fun Group), 248
Making a New Home in America (Rosenberg), 465, 467
Mama Don't Allow (Hurd), 326
Mammoth Book of Word Games (Manchester), 190
Man Who Tried to Save Time (Krasilvosky), 346
Many Kinds of Magic (Scott), 88
Many Luscious Lollipops (Heller), 15, 387
Many Moons (Thurber), 475
Many Stars and More String Games (Gryski), 194
Marceau Bonappétit (Joly-Berbesson), 472
Marcel Marceau Alphabet Book (Mendoza), 511

Margie's Diner (Gibbons), 482
Marionettes (Beaton and Beaton), 278
Martin Luther King, Jr. (Adler), 72, 99
"Mary, Mary, So Contrary!" (Fillmore), 74, 412
"Master of All Masters" (Jacobs), 75
Master of All Masters, 118, 121
Matepo (McAllister), 82
Math-a-Magic (White and Broekel), 295
Matilda (Dahl), 385
Maurice Sendak's Really Rosie (Sendak), 325
Max, the Bad-Talking Parrot (Demuth), 277
Max, the Music-Maker (Stecher), 329
McBroom Tells a Lie (Fleischman), 80
Me and My Shadows (Joyce), 264
Mealtime (Roffey), 483
Mean Soup (Everitt), 344
Meet the Orchestra (Hayes), 326
Merlin Dreams (Dickinson), 127, 430
Merry Adventures of Robin Hood (Pyle), 136, 138
Merry-Go-Round Poetry Book (Larrick, ed.), 164
Meteor! (Polacco), 509
Mexican-American Folklore (West, ed.), 89
Mice Are Nice (Larrick), 171
Michael Foreman's Mother Goose (Foreman), 164
Michael Hague's Favorite Hans Christian Andersen Fairy Tales (Andersen), 127
Midnight Fox (Byars), 98, 384
Midnight Snowman (Bauer), 345
"Mighty Mikko" (Fillmore), 70, 114
Mighty Ones (DeJong), 141, 142
Mighty Tree (Gackenbach), 291, 346
Milk Makers (Gibbons), 485
"Milky Way" (Lin), 75
Millions of Cats (Gág), 74, 347, 458
Millionth Egg (Myers), 342
Ming Lo Moves the Mountain (Lobel), 81
Mirandy and Brother Wind (McKissack), 327
Miriam's Well (Bach and Exum), 141, 142
Mishmash and the Big Fat Problem (Cone), 483
Miss Mary Mack and Other Children's Street Rhymes (Cole and Calmenson), 170
Miss Penny and Mr. Grubbs (Ernst), 344

Missing Piece (Silverstein), 220
Mrs. Frisby and the Rats of NIMH (O'Brien), 385
Mrs. Goose's Baby (Voake), 342
Mrs. Toggle's Zipper (Pulver), 509
Ms. Gee Was Waiting (Hill), 508
Mr. Bear's Chair (Graham), 341
"Mr. Benjamin Ram and His Wonderful Fiddle" (Lester), 74
Mr. Floop's Lunch (Novak), 483
Mr. Gumpy's Outing (Burningham), 476
Mr. Mistoffelees with Mungojerrie and Rumpelteazer (Eliot), 295
Mr. Mysterious and Company (Fleischman), 296
Mr. Nick's Knitting (Wild), 461
Mr. Popper's Penguins (Atwater), 384
Mr. Rabbit and the Lovely Present (Zolotow), 214, 350, 473
"Mr. Samson Cat" (Karrick), 68
The Mitten (Brett), 79
The Mixed-Up Chameleon (Carle), 219
Modern Fashion in Detail (Wilcox), 451
Molly McCullough and Tom the Rogue (Stevens), 83
"Molly Whuppie" (Jacob), 71
Mommy, Buy Me a China Doll (Zemach), 306
Mommy's Office (Hazen), 344
Momotaro the Peach Boy (Shute), 83
Money Tree (Stewart), 50, 509
Monkey and the Crocodile (Galdone), 80
Monkey's Haircut and Other Stories Told by the Maya (Bierhorst), 85
Monster Book of Sounds (Snow), 345
Monster Soup and Other Spooky Poems (Evans), 72
Monsters (Epstein), 150
Monster's Birthday Hiccups (Mueller), 509
Month-Brothers (Marshak), 82
Monument (Paulsen), 104
Moon Is Following Me (Heckman), 446
Moon Man (Ungerer), 446
Moon Ribbon and Other Tales (Yolen), 125, 129
Moonbow of Mr. B. Bones (Lewis), 446
Moonhorse (Osborne), 446
Moonsong Lullaby (Highwater), 166
Morning Milking (Morris), 346
Morris the Moose (Wiseman), 460
Moses' Ark (Bach), 142
"Most Magnificent Cook of All" (Sechrist and Woolsey), 474
Mother Crocodile (Guy), 80

Mother for Choco (Kasza), 344
Mother, Mother, I Want Another (Polushkin), 350, 359
Mother Tongue (Bryson), 189
Mouse and the Motorcycle (Cleary), 100, 475
Mouse Book (Shaw, ed.), 172
Mouse in My Roof (Edwards), 168
Mouse Rap (Myers), 510
Mozart Season (Wolff), 328
Mozart Tonight (Downing), 288, 326
Mucky Moose (Allen), 277, 459
Mudluscious (Irving), 485
Mufaro's Beautiful Daughters (Steptoe), 133
Multi-Cultural Folktales (Sierra and Kaminski), 511
Multimedia Approach to Children's Literature (Hunt), 248
Munching (Hopkins), 480
"Murdoch's Rath" (Ewing), 69
Music Lessons for Alex (Arnold), 328
Music Mouse (Lionni), 327
Music, Music for Everyone (Williams), 327
Music of What Happens Stories (Janeczko, ed.), 171
Musical Instruments You Can Make (Hayes), 328
Musical Story Hours (Painter), 111, 278, 329
My Backyard History Book (Weitzman), 149
My Bag of Book Tricks (McElmeel), 444
My Barn (Brown), 262
My Dog (Goennel), 287, 349
My Father (Collins), 343
My First Animals (Paterson), 350
My First Kwanzaa Book (Newton-Chocolate), 73
My Grandmother's Journey (Cech), 103, 150
My Grandmother's Stories (Geras), 86, 149
My Great-Aunt Arizona (Houston), 150, 288
My House Mi Casa (Emberley), 344
My Little Red Car (Demarest), 241
My Mother's Getting Married (Drescher), 346
My Mother's House (Christiansen), 343
My Red Umbrella (Bright), 232
My Sister Looks like a Pear (Anderson), 163
Mythology (Hamilton), 134
Mythology of Mexico and Central America (Bierhorst), 133, 135
Mythology of South America (Bierhorst), 133, 135

Nadia the Willful (Alexander), 79
Nail Soup (Zemach), 78
Naked Bear (Bierhorst), 85
Napping House (Wood), 350
Nathan's Balloon Adventure
  (Deacre), 340
Near the Window Tree (Kuskin), 168
"Nella's Dancing Shoes" (Farjeon), 69
New Coat for Anna (Ziefert), 342
New Complete Hoyle (Frey,
  Mott-Smith and Moorhead), 195
New Creatures (Gerstein), 387
New Golden Bough (Frazer), 150
New Kid on the Block (Prelutsky),
  169
New Kids on the Block (Bode), 465,
  466
New Patches for Old (Walker and
  Vysal), 68, 84
New Read-Aloud Handbook
  (Trelease), 97–98
New Shoes for Silvia (Hurwitz), 466,
  467
"New Year's Hats for Statues"
  (Uchida), 77
New Year's Magic (Baker), 295
Newspaper Magic (Anderson and
  Marshall), 199
Night before Christmas (Moore), 72
Night It Rained Pancakes (Ginsburg),
  482
Night Noises (Fox), 345, 492
Night Ones (Grossman), 344
Night Tree (Bunting), 342
Nightingale (Andersen), 74, 326
Nightwaves Scary Tales for After
  Dark (McDonald), 393
Nijinsky (Brighton), 342
Nine O'Clock Lullaby (Singer), 346
No Bath for Boris (White), 341
No More Baths (Cole), 341
No Peas for Nellie (Demarest), 489
No Stars Tonight (Smucker), 150
No Swimming in Dark Pond and
  Other Chilling Tales (Gorog), 127,
  393
Noah and the Rainbow (Bollinger),
  142
Noah's Ark, 143
Noah's Cats and the Devil's Fire
  (Olson), 388
Noisy Book (Brown), 492
Nonstop Nonsense (Mahy), 145
Norse Gods and Giants (d'Aulaire
  and d'Aulaire), 135
North American Indian Sign
  Language (Liptak), 190
North Wind and the Sun
  (Wildsmith), 84
Norton Book of Light Verse (Baker,
  ed.), 433

Norwegian Folk Tales (Asbjørnsen
  and Moe), 119, 120
Nose Tree (Hutton), 81
Not This Bear! (Myers), 509
Nothing But the Truth (Avi), 103
Nothing Ever Happens on My Block
  (Raskin), 509
Nothing to Declare (Morris), 436, 437
Nothing's Impossible! (Sheridan),
  295
Not-Just-Anybody Family (Byars),
  144, 145
Now We Are Six (Milne), 159
Now You See It (Broekel and White),
  295
Number the Stars (Lowry), 101
"Nuremberg Stove" (de la Ramee), 67
Nurse Lugton's Curtain (Woolf), 461
"Nuts" (Babbitt), 77, 476
Nutshell Library (Sendak), 348

"Obsession with Clothes" (Peretz), 68
Odyssey of Homer (Picard), 137
Of Pelicans and Pussycats (Lear), 168
Of Quarks, Quasars and Other
  Quirks (Brewton), 170
Of Swans, Sugarplums, and Satin
  Slippers (Verdy), 327
"Ogre Who Built a Bridge" (Uchida),
  75
Oh, A-Hunting We Will Go
  (Langstaff), 219, 306
Oh Lord, I Wish I Was a Buzzard
  (Goldberg), 216
Oh Snow (Mayper), 346
Oh, What Nonsense! (Cole), 290
Old Coot (Christian), 127
Old MacDonald Had a Farm, 241,
  306, 350
Old Rocking Chair (Root), 341
Old Turtle's Baseball Stories
  (Kessler), 457
Old Turtle's 90 Knock-Knocks, Jokes,
  and Riddles (Kessler), 180
"Old Woman and the Tramp"
  (Djurkla), 78
Old Woman and the Willy Nilly Man
  (Wright), 76
On City Streets (Larrick), 165
On Granddaddy's Farm (Allen), 150
On Monday When It Rained
  (Kachenmeister), 344
On Mother's Lap (Scott), 344
On My Honor (Bauer), 103, 384
On the Air (Hautzig), 254
On the Banks of Plum Creek
  (Wilder), 220
On the Pampas (Brusca), 150
On Top of the World (Fraser), 103
Once a Mouse (Brown), 71, 79, 131,
  132, 508

Once in Puerto Rico (Belpre), 114
Once the Hodja (Kelsey), 447
Once under the Cherry Blossom
    (Say), 83
Once upon a Memory (Alessi), 149
One at a Time (McCord), 169
One Big Wish (Williams), 84
One Fat Summer (Lipsyte), 484
One Fine Day (Hogrogian), 113, 121
101 Rock 'n Roll Jokes and Riddles
    (Hall and Eisenberg), 180
One Potato (Porter), 462, 483
One Potato, Two Potato, Three Potato,
    Four (Colgin), 324
One Red Rooster (Caroll), 262
One Small Blue Bead (Baylor), 50
One Summer at Grandmother's
    House (Montaufier), 150
One Sun (Mcmillan), 172
1,000 Crazy Jokes for Kids
    (Johnstone), 180
One Wide River to Cross (Emberly),
    143
One Zillion Valentines (Modell), 73
One-Person Puppet Plays (Wright),
    279
Oonga Boonga (Wishinsky), 350
Oranges (Rogow), 475
Ordinary Jack (Cresswell), 102, 385
"Origin of the Balsam Tree"
    (Courlander), 120
Ornery Morning (Demuth), 262
Orphan Boy (Mollel), 82
"Orpheus" (Colum), 75
Oscar Wilde (Wilde), 129
Oté (Belpré), 79
Other World (Hodges), 135
Our Game (Alexander), 457
Our Sixth-Grade Sugar Baby Blues
    (Bunting), 440
Out on a Limb (Walton and Walton),
    177
Over in the Meadow (Keats), 305
Over in the Meadow: An Old Nursery
    Counting Rhyme (Galdone), 249
Over the River and Through the
    Woods, 305
Owl Book (Shaw, ed.), 154, 172
Owl Moon (Yolen), 447
Oxford Treasury of Children's Poems
    (Harrison and Stuart-Clark), 165

Packet of Poems (Bennett), 480
Paddington's Colors (Bond), 212
Paddington's Opposites (Bond), 344
Painting the Moon (Withers), 84
Palace of the Moon and Other Tales
    from Czechoslovakia (Wood), 89
"Palace on the Rock" (Hughes), 74
Paper Boats (Tagore), 50
Paper Cutting (Hawkesworth), 200

Paper Magic (McGill), 200
Paper Masks and Puppets for
    Stories, Songs and Plays (Feller
    and Feller), 199, 278
Paper Stories (Stangl), 369
Paperfolding Fun (Aytüre-Scheele),
    369
Parade (Crews), 241
Parent's Choice Magazine Guide to
    Video Cassettes for Children
    (Green, ed.), 248
Parrot and the Thief (Kennedy), 77,
    81
Party Games for All (Mason and
    Mitchell), 185
Pass the Poetry, Please! (Hopkins),
    163
Pat the Bunny (Kunhardt), 351, 491
Patrick's Dinosaurs (Carrick), 343
"Paul Bunyan and the Popcorn
    Blizzard" (Bauer), 481
Paul Revere's Ride (Longfellow), 167
Peace at Last (Murphy), 350, 359
Peacock Pie (de la Mare), 168
Pencil and Paper Games (Koch), 195
Penguin Book of Modern Humour
    (Coran, ed.), 430
Penny a Look (Zemach), 510
Pentagames, 196
People (Spier), 464–65
People Could Fly (Hamilton), 86
Pepper and Salt (Pyle), 123–24, 128
Perez and Martina (Belpré), 79
Persephone and the Springtime
    (Hodges), 135
Peter and the Wolf (Prokofieff), 306
Peter Pan (Barrie), 409
"Peterkins' Christmas Tree" (Hale),
    72
"Peterkins Try to Become Wise"
    (Hale), 67
Pets in Trumpets and Other
    Word-play Riddles (Most), 290
Phantom Animals (Cohen), 393
Phantom Tollbooth (Juster), 385
Phil the Ventriloquist (Kraus), 277,
    295
Philharmonic Gets Dressed (Kuskin),
    327
Pianist's Debut (Beirne), 328
Picnic (McCully), 483
Pie-Biter (McCunn), 82
Piece of Cake (Murphy), 472, 483
Piece of String Is a Wonderful Thing
    (Hindley), 194
Pig Tale (Oxenbury), 509
Piggybook (Browne), 104
Pig-Out Blues (Greenberg), 483
Pig-Out Inn (Ruby), 484
Pig's Picnic (Kaska), 359
Pillow of Clouds (Talbert), 411, 433

Pippi Longstocking (Lindgren), 385
"Pit and the Pendulum" (Poe), 128
Pizza for Breakfast (Kovalski), 15
Pizza Man (Pillar), 50, 485
Place My Words Are Looking For (Janeczko), 168
Planting a Rainbow (Ehlert), 212
Play of Words (Lederer), 190
Playtime Treasury (Corbett), 164
Please Mrs. Butler (Ahlberg), 167
Pleated Paper Folding (Hawkesworth), 200
Pocketful of Puppets: Activities for the Special Child (Sullivan), 279
Pocketful of Puppets: Mother Goose Rhymes (Hunt), 278
Poem Stew (Cole), 164, 480
Poem-Making (Livingston), 163
Poems for Brothers and Poems for Sisters (Livingston), 171
Poems Please! (Booth and Moore), 163
Poetry and the Child (Arnstein), 163
Poetry Is (Hughes), 163
"Pog Painted" (Haswell), 211, 212
Polar Bear, Polar Bear What Do You Hear? (Martin), 492
Pooh Song Book (Fraser-Simson), 325
"Poor Mr. Fingle" (Bianco), 70
"Poor Old Dog" (Lobel), 69
Pop Corn and Ma Goodness (Preston), 475
Popcorn (Asch), 482
Popcorn Book (dePaola), 485
Porker Finds a Chair (Nordquist), 341
"Pot of Gold" (Margolis), 75
Potato Man (McDonald), 462
"Potato Party and Other Troll Tales" (Leedy), 461
Potatoes, Potatoes (Lobel), 462
Practical Lessons in Magic (Hawkesworth), 294
Prescription for Better Home Video Movies (Fuller), 248
Pretend You're a Cat (Marzollo), 172, 508
Pretty Good Magic (Dubowski), 295
"Priceless Cats" (Johnson), 68
"Prince Sneeze" (Beston), 77
"Princess and Jose" (Brenner), 76
Princess and the Frog (Vesey), 460
"Princess and the Vagabond" (Sandburg), 129
"Princess on the Pea" (Andersen), 76
"Princess Rosetta and the Popcorn Man" (Greene), 475
Principal's New Clothes (Calmenson), 508
Professional Magic for Children (Ginn), 294

Proud Knight, Fair Lady (Lewis, tr.), 138
Proverbs (Hall), 185
Proverbs of Many Nations (Kelen), 185
Pudding Is Nice (Kundhart), 233, 475
Pueblo Boy (Keegan), 465, 466
Pumpernickel Tickle and Mean Green Cheese (Patz), 359
"Pumpkin Giant" (Ross), 475
"Pumpkin Giant" (Wilkins), 72
Pumpkins (Ray), 241
Puppet Show to Make (Hawkesworth), 278
Puppetry and Creative Dramatics (Champlin), 278
Puppets and Puppet Making (Marks and Burton), 278
Purple Coat (Hest), 342
Puss in Boots (Goodall), 345
Puss in Boots (Kirstein), 81, 345
Puss in Boots (Perrault), 83, 345
Put Your Mother on the Ceiling (DeMille), 511
Putting on a Play (Bauer), 510

Quack-Quack! (Whybrow), 345
Queen Who Couldn't Bake Gingerbread (Van Woerkom), 473
Quick and Easy Origami (Takahama), 369

Rabbit Magic (York), 296
"Rabbits" (Hurwitz), 383
Rachel Fister's Blister (MacDonald), 387
Raffi Singable Songbook (Raffi), 324
Ragtime Tumpie (Schroeder), 100, 466, 467
Rain Forest (Goodman), 291
Rain Makes Applesauce (Scheer), 471
Rain Player (Wisniewski), 84
Rain Rain, Go Away! (Langley), 164
Rainbow Crow (Van Laan), 140
Rainy Day (Bauer), 144, 170
Rainy Day Card Tricks (Bailey), 295
Rainy Day Puppets (Robson and Bailey), 278
Rainy Day Rhymes (Radley), 172
Raising the Roof (Irving), 443
Ramayana (Lal), 138
Ramayana (Seeger), 138
Ramona: Behind the Scenes of a Television Show (Scott), 254
Ramona Forever (Cleary), 384
Random Book of Poetry for Children (Prelutsky), 165
Random House Book of Ghost Stories (Hill), 393
Random House Book of Mother Goose (Lobel), 165

Rapunzel (Gág), 117
"Rapunzel" (Grimm Brothers), 120, 121
Rat-a-Tat, Pitter Pat (Benjamin), 349
"Rat-Catcher's Daughter" (Housman), 71, 125, 128
Rats on the Roof and Other Stories (Marshall), 99, 509
Rat's Tale (Seidler), 99
Raven's Light (Shetterly), 136
Raw Head, Bloody Bones (Lyon), 87, 393
Razzle-Dazzle Riddles (Maestro), 177
Read for the Fun of It (Bauer), 178
Read-Aloud Rhymes for the Very Young (Prelutsky, ed.), 165, 348
Real Mother Goose (Wright), 348
Real Nice Clambake (Hammerstein), 305
Real Tooth Fairy (Kaye), 346
Recording Your Family History (Fletcher), 149
Red Bear (Rikys), 233, 350
Red Dog, Blue Fly (Mathis), 172
Red Is Best (Stinson), 350
Red Leaf, Yellow Leaf (Ehlert), 346
Red Light, Stop: Green Light Go (Kulman), 233
Red Rover, Red Rover (Fowler), 195
Reflections on a Gift of Watermelon Pickle . . . and Other Modern Verse (Dunning), 164
Refugee Summer (Fenton), 438
Relatives Came (Rylant), 345
Remember Me When This You See! (Morrison), 183
Return (Levitin), 101, 411
Reynard the Fox (Hastings), 138
Rhyme Stew (Dahl), 170
Rhymes about Us (Chute), 153–54, 164
Rhymes around the Day (Thompson), 167
"Rhyming Ink" (Baker), 67
Rich Man and the Shoemaker (Wildsmith), 84
Richard Kennedy: Collected Stories (Kennedy), 128, 407
"Riddle in the Dark" (Tolkien), 76
"Riddlemaster" (Storr), 76
"Riddling Youngster" (Thompson), 76
Ride with the Sun (Courlander), 114
"Ridiculous Wishes" (Perrault), 476
Ring Out, Wild Bells (Hopkins), 171
Ring-a-Round-a-Rosy (Lamont), 164
Road from Coorain (Conway), 436, 437
Rocking-Horse Land (Housman), 73
Rod, Shadow, and Glove (Wright), 279

Romeo and Juliet Together (and alive) at Last! (Avi), 102, 384, 510
Rondo in C (Fleischman), 326
Roomrimes (Cassedy), 167
Rootabaga Stories (Sandburg), 124–25, 129
Root-a-Toot-Toot (Rockwell), 262
Rose, Where Did You Get That Red? (Koch), 163
Rosebud and Red Flannel (Pochocki), 388, 461
Rosemary's Witch (Turner), 101
Roses Sing on New Snow (Yee), 483
Rosie and the Rustlers (Gerrard), 342
Rosie's Baby Tooth (Macdonald), 346
Round Trip (Jonas), 493
Roundabout Turn (Charles), 154, 166
"Royal Banquet" (Juster), 484
"Roz's Birthday" (Hurwitz), 472
Rumour of Otters (Savage), 412
Rumpelstiltskin (Zelinsky), 84
Runaway Jonah and Other Tales (Wahl), 141, 143

"Sack of Diamonds" (Olson), 75, 446
Sahara (Reynolds), 466, 467
Sally and the Limpet (James), 341
Salt Hands (Aragon), 507
Sandburg Treasury (Sandburg), 128
Santa Cows (Edens), 342
Sarah Bear and Sweet Sidney (Patz), 341
Sarah, Plain and Tall (MacLachlan), 385
Scandinavian Folk and Fairy Tales (Booss), 85
Scary Book (Cole and Calmenson), 393
Scary Stories 3 (Schwartz), 88, 393
Science Book of the Senses (Ardley), 488
Science of Folklore (Krappe), 151
Science of Music (Berger), 328
Scoop after Scoop (Krensky), 485
"Scrap of Paper" (Dickinson), 67
Sea of Shining Gold and Other Tales from Japan (Uchida), 120, 121
Sea Songs (Livingston), 167
Seabrooke's Book (Seabrooke), 294
Search for Delicious (Babbitt), 489
Seasons of Splendour (Jaffrey), 86
Secret Birthday Message (Carle), 341
Secret Life of the Underwear Champ (Miles), 510
"Selfish Giant" (Wilde), 143
Self-working Paper Magic (Fulves), 294
Sesame Street Sign Language Fun with Linda Bove, 190
Seven Blind Mice (Young), 345, 493

Seven Chinese Brothers (Mahy), 82
Seven Good Years and Other Stories of I. L. Peretz (Peretz), 128
"Seven Lazy Sisters" (Olson), 67
Seven Ravens (Grimm Brothers), 121
Shadow Pictures Children Love to Make, 264
Shadow Puppets for Children (Zimmerman), 264
Shake My Sillies Out (Raffi), 306
Sharon, Lois and Bram's Mother Goose, 324
Shazam! Simple Science Magic (White and Broekel), 295
Sheep in a Jeep (Shaw), 167
Sheep in a Shop (Shaw), 346
Shepherd's Nosegay (Fillmore), 154
Shiloh (Naylor), 99
Shimmy Shake Earthquake (Jabar), 326
Shining Princess and Other Japanese Legends (Quale), 140
Short Wait between Trains (Benard, ed.), 430
"Shrewd Todie and Lyzer the Miser" (Singer), 71
Sideways Stories from Wayside School (Sacher), 102
Sign Language Talk (Greene and Dicker), 190
Silver Curlew (Farjeon), 123, 127
"Silver Hen" (Wilkins), 77
Silver Touch and Other Family Christmas Stories (Rettich), 128
Simon Boom Gives a Wedding (Suhl), 72, 84
Sing a Song of People (Lenski), 166
Sing a Song of Popcorn (de Regniers), 166
Sing a Song of Sixpence, 167
Sing Me a Window, 306
Singing Bee! (Hart), 324
Singing Games and Play-party Games (Chase), 325
Singing Tales of Africa (Robinson), 325
"Singing Tortoise" (Courlander and Herzog), 77
"Singing Turtle" (McDonald), 77
Sir Gawain and the Loathly Lady (Hastings), 101, 138
Sitting in My Box (Lillegard), 462
Sitting on the Farm, 305
Sixth Sense and Other Stories (Haas), 127
Skip to My Lou, 167, 306
Skit Book (MacDonald), 511
Sky Songs (Livingston), 167
Sleeping on the Wing (Koch and Farrell), 163

"Slow-Eater Tiny-Bite-Taker" (MacDonald), 484
"Slower than the Rest" (Rylant), 429
Slugging It Out in Japan (Cromartie), 457
Slugs (Greenberg), 171
Small TV Studio (Bermingham), 254
"Smart Ice Cream" (Jennings), 481
Smedge (Sharmat), 277
Smell (Silverstein, Silverstein and Silverstein), 490
"Smelly Sneakers" (Gorog), 76, 126
Sniff in Time (Saunders), 83, 490
"Snooks Family" (Tashjian), 76
Snowy Day (Bauer), 144, 170
Snowy Day (Keats), 349
Soap! Soap! Don't Forget the Soap! (Birdseye), 304
"Soap, Soap, Soap!" (Chase), 70, 304
Somebody and the Three Blairs (Tolhurst), 84
Someday Rider (Scott), 342
Someone Is Flying Balloons (Heylen), 165
Someone Saw a Spider (Climo), 85
Something for Mom (Sawicki), 509
Something on My Mind (Grimes), 166
Sometimes I Dance Mountains (Baylor), 326, 511
Sometimes I Feel like a Mouse (Modesitt), 344
Somewhere in Africa (Mennen), 466, 467
Song and Dance Man (Ackerman), 326
Songs of Peter Rabbit (Glass), 325
Sons of the Volsungs (Hosford), 135
"Sorcerer's Apprentice" (Green), 74
Sorrow's Kitchen (Lyons), 407
Sounder (Armstrong), 92
Soup Bone (Johnston), 81
Soup for Supper (Root), 509
Space (Jones), 446
Space Songs (Livingston), 167
Spacey Riddles (Hall and Eisenberg), 177
Speak to the Winds (Opoku), 185
Speak Up, Blanche! (McCully), 510
Spells of Enchantment (Zipes), 129
Spooky Poems (Bennett), 170
Sports Pages (Adoff), 170
Sports Riddles (Rosenbloom), 457
Spring Green (Selkowe), 211, 212
Spring of Butterflies and Other Folktales of China's Minority Peoples (Philip), 87
Spy Went Dancing (Aline, Countess of Romanones), 436, 437
Spy Wore Red (Aline, Countess of Romanones), 436, 437
Squire's Bride (Asbjørnsen), 83

Staging the Puppet Show (Magon), 278

Stamp Your Feet (Hays), 365

Stan the Hot Dog Man (Kessler and Kessler), 145, 474

Starring the Universal Nut Bev Bergeron (video), 296

Stars (Simon), 103

Stars Come Out Within (Little), 437

Star-Spangled Banana and Other Revolutionary Riddles (Keller), 290

"Steadfast Tin Soldier" (Andersen), 69

Stephen Hawking (Simon), 289

Stilts, Somersaults, and Headstands (Frazer), 159, 171

Stingy Baker (Greeson), 482

Stolen Fire (Baumann), 139

"Stolen Turnips, the Magic Tablecloth, the Sneezing Goat, and the Wooden Whistle" (Ransome), 77

Stone Soup (Brown), 78, 209, 213, 476

Stone Soup (Ross), 277

Stop Your Crowing Kasimir! (Scheffler), 104, 388

Stories (Iarusso), 111

Stories from the Arabian Nights (Housman), 129

Story, a Story (Haley), 80

Story Hour—Starring Megan! (Brillhart), 341

Story Hours with Puppets and Other Props (Painter), 111, 278

Story of Babar the Little Elephant (de Brunhoff), 347, 448

Story of Bip (Marceau), 511

Story of Doctor Dolittle (Lofting), 100, 385

Story of Ferdinand (Leaf), 347

Story of King Arthur and His Knights (Pyle), 137, 138

Story of Little Quack (Gibson), 343, 459

Story Vine (Pellowski), 214

"Storyteller" (Courlander), 76

Storyteller in Religious Education (Brown), 57

Storytelling (Colwell), 111

Storytelling: A Guide for Teachers (Farrell), 111, 292

Storytelling: Art and Technique (Baker), 110

Storytelling: Process and Practice (Livo and Rietz), 111

Storytelling for Young Adults (de Vos), 111

"Strawberries" (Ross), 481

Street Dancers (Hill), 328

Street Rhymes around the World (Yolen), 196

Street Talk (Turner), 172

Strega Nona (dePaola), 347, 476

Strider (Cleary), 287

String (Adkins), 194

String Figures and How to Make Them (Jayne), 194

Study of American Folklore (Brunvand), 150

Study of Folklore (Dundes), 150

Stuffer (Parnall), 388

Stupid Tiger and Other Tales (Raychaudhuri), 87

Sugar Snow Spring (Hoban), 474

Summer Endings (Hotze), 457

Sun Up (Tresselt), 346

"Sunday Boots and Working Boots" (Penny), 76, 461

Super String Games (Gryski), 194

Supergrandpa (Schwartz), 104, 388

Surprise (Shannon), 350

Surprise Box (Weiss), 463

Surprises (Hopkins), 165

Swan Lake (Helprin), 326

Swapping Song Book, (Ritchie), 325

Swineherd (Andersen), 71

Sylvester and the Magic Pebble (Steig), 50, 348, 476

"Tail" (Jacobs), 77

"Tail Who Wagged the Dog" (Krauss), 214

"Tailybone" (Holt), 395

Tailypo! (Wahl), 84, 395

Tailypo, a Ghost Story (Galdone), 395

Tale of a Black Cat (Withers), 220

Tale of Peter Rabbit (Potter), 348

Tale of the Mandarin Ducks (Paterson), 83

Tales for the . . . Perfect . . . Child (Heide), 102

Tales from Ancient Greece (Oldfield), 134, 136

Tales from Gold Mountain (Yee), 89, 407

Tales from the Mabinogion (Bowen), 138

Tales from the Roof of the World (Timpanelli), 88

Tales of Edgar Allan Poe (Poe), 128

Tales of the Early World (Hughes), 128

Tales of the Far North (Martin), 87

Tales of Trickery from the Land of Spoof (Schwartz), 88, 296

Tales of Uncle Remus (Lester), 101

Talk That Talk (Goss), 86

Talking Cat and Other Stories of French Canada (Carlson), 286

Talking like the Rain (Kennedy and Kennedy), 165
Talking Pot (Haviland), 101
Talking to the Sun (Koch), 159, 166
Tam Lin (Cooper), 80
Tam Lin (Yolen), 84
Tamarind Puppy and Other Poems (Pomerantz), 169
"Taming of Bucephalus" (Coville), 73
Tangram (Elffers), 193
Tar Beach (Ringgold), 290
Tatterhood and Other Tales (Phelps), 430
Teacher on Roller Skates and Other School Riddles (Adler), 290
Teachers and Writers Handbook of Poetic Forms (Padgett), 163
Teacher's Pet (Hurwitz), 383
Teammates (Golenbock), 99, 457
Technique of Television Production (Millerson), 254
Teddy Bear, Teddy Bear (Lawson), 349
"Teeny-Tiny" (Jacobs), 121, 395
Television Lighting Handbook (Sheriffs), 254
Television Production Handbook (Zettl), 254
Television Program (Stasheff et al.), 254
Tell and Draw Stories (Olsen), 220
"Tell-Tale Heart" (Poe), 128
Terrible Thing That Happened at Our House (Blaine), 472
Thank You, Jackie Robinson (Cohen), 385
Thanks Be to God (Baynes), 170
That's Good! That's Bad! (Cuyler), 345
Theodor and Mr. Balbini (Mathers), 277
There Was a Place and Other Poems (Livingston), 169
There's a Hole in the Bucket, 306
Theseus and the Minotaur (Hutton), 135, 438
They Dance in the Sky (Monroe), 136
"Thing That Goes Burp in the Night" (Webb), 481
Things in Corners (Park), 407
Think of Shadows (Moore), 169
Third Gift (Carew), 71, 508
Thirteen Moons on Turtle's Back (Bruchac), 166
This Is Not a Book about Dodos (Lehan), 220
This Is the Bear and the Picnic Lunch (Hayes), 482
This Little Pig Went to Market (Montgomerie), 365
This Old Man, 306

This Quiet Lady (Zolotow), 344
"Those Three Wishes" (Gorog), 429
Three Ancient Kings (Picard), 138
"Three Bears" (Jacobs), 121
Three Bears Rhyme Book (Yolen), 341
Three Billy Goats Gruff (Asbjørnsen and Moe), 71, 79, 119, 120
Three Blind Mice, 306
Three Brothers (Croll), 80
"Three Brothers and the Giant" (de Regniers), 70
"Three Fridays" (Kelsey), 77
Three Good Blankets (Luttrell), 82
Three in a Balloon (Wilson), 341
"Three Little Pigs" (Jacobs), 118, 121
"Three Sneezes" (Duvoisin), 77
Three Strong Women (Stamm), 83
"Three Wishes" (Jacobs), 78
"Three Wishes" (Picard), 78
Thump, Thump, Rat-a-Tat-Tat (Baer), 326, 348
Thunder Cake (Polacco), 483
Thunder of the Gods (Hosford), 135
Thunderbolt and Rainbow (Billout), 135
"Ticki, Ticki, Tembo" (Brown), 304
"Ticky-Picky Boom-Boom" (Sherlock), 71, 75
Tiger-Skin Rug (Rose), 277
Tikki Tikki Tembo (Mosel), 57, 82
Til All the Stars Have Fallen (Booth), 164
Time Out (Cresswell), 100, 296
Time to Dance, No Time to Weep (Godden), 436, 437
"Tinderbox" (Andersen), 69
To Space and Back (Ride and Okie), 103, 446
Toddler Time (Brown), 351
Tom Glazer's Treasury of Songs for Children (Glazer), 324
Tom Tichenor's Puppets (Tichenor), 279
"Tom Tit Tot" (Jacobs), 58, 75
Tom Tit Tot, 84, 118
Tom Tit Tot (Singer), 121
Tomfoolery (Schwartz), 190
Tomie dePaola's Book of Bible Stories (dePaola), 141, 143
Tomie dePaola's Book of Poems (dePaola), 164
Tomie dePaola's Favorite Nursery Tales (dePaola), 86
Tommy at the Grocery Store (Grossman), 345
Tom's Rainbow Walk (Anholt), 460
"Tongue Twister" (Wiseman), 178
Tongue-cut Sparrow (Ishii), 81
Tony and the Tomato Soup (Haddon), 482

Tony's Bread (dePaola), 482
Too Many Books! (Bauer), 341
Too Many Chickens! (Bourgeois), 341
Tool Book (Gibbons), 232
Tools (Robbins), 214
Torment of Mr. Gully (Clarke), 393
Total Baseball (Thorn and Palmer), 458
Touch Me Book (Witte and Evans), 491
Touching (Allington and Cowles), 491
Tough-Luck Karen (Hurwitz), 144, 145, 382, 484
Tower to Heaven (Dee), 80
Town Mouse and the Country Mouse (Craig), 343
Transfigured Hart (Yolen), 125, 129
Traveling Musicians of Bremen (Page), 327
Traveling to Tondo (Aardema), 507
Travels of Atunga (Clymer), 139
Treasure Island (Stevenson), 410
Treasury of Turkish Folktales for Children (Walker), 88
Tree in the Wood (Manson), 306
Tree of Cranes (Say), 342
Treeful of Pigs (Lobel), 277
Trees (Behn), 346
Tricks and Stunts to Fool Your Friends (Barry), 295
Truck (Crews), 346
True Story of the 3 Little Pigs (Scieszka), 104, 388
Tub People (Conrad), 341
Tuck Everlasting (Babbitt), 70, 100, 384
Tuesday (Weisner), 344
"Tuning" (Paulsen), 96–97
Turn About, Think About, Look About Book (Gardner), 241
Turnip (Morgan), 509
Turtle (Cummings), 98
Turtle and the Moon (Turner), 446
Turtle in July (Singer), 167
Twelve Dancing Princesses (Lang), 69
25¢ Miracle (Nelson), 484
Twenty Tellable Tales (MacDonald), 87
Twenty-Two Splendid Tales to Tell (De Spain), 86
Twister of Twists, A Tangler of Tongues (Schwartz), 178
Two Greedy Bears (Ginsburg), 80
263 Brain Busters (Phillips), 190
"Two Painters" (Untermeyer), 67
Two Pairs of Shoes (Travers), 84
Two Terrible Frights (Aylesworth), 277
2,000 Years of Fashion (Boucher), 451
Two under the Indian Sun (Godden), 436, 437

Two Weeks with the Queen (Gleitzman), 104
Two-Legged, Four-Legged, No-Legged Rhymes (Lewis), 168
Ty's One-Man Band (Walter), 327

Uncanny! Even More Surprising Stories (Jennings), 128
"Uncle Bouqui Rents a Horse" (Courlander), 74
Uncle Magic (Gauch), 295
Under All Silences (Gordon), 171
Under the Sunday Tree (Greenfield), 166
Unicorn Treasury (Coville), 127
Unreal! Eight Surprising Stories (Jennings), 407
Unreluctant Years (Smith), 134, 136
Untold Tales (Brooke), 406
Usborne Children's Songbook, 325
Uses of Enchantment (Bettelheim), 110

Vacation Time (Giovanni), 168
Valentine Magic/Presidents' Day Magic (Baker), 295
Valentine's Day (Gibbons), 73
Valentine's Day: Stories and Poems (Bauer), 85, 170
Vanishing Act (Morrison), 296
Vasilissa the Beautiful (Winthrop), 84
Velveteen Rabbit (Bianco), 46, 69, 79
Venus (Simon), 446
Very Hungry Caterpillar (Carle), 232, 347
Very Young Actress (Kremetz), 510
Viking Bedtime Treasury (Price and McVitty), 87
Violin Man (Hooper), 328
Visit to William Blake's Inn (Willard), 167
Vogue Fashion (Mulvagh), 451
Voices of the Wind (Booth), 170

Wackysaurus (Phillips), 180
Waiting for the Rain (Gordon), 411
Waiting to Waltz (Rylant), 169
Waiting-for-Spring Stories (Roberts), 277
Wake Up, Farm! (Tresselt), 346
Walking Catfish (Day), 387
Walking through the Jungle (Lacome), 233
Walking to School (Turner), 460
Wall (Bunting), 386
Walter's Magic Wand (Houghton), 295
Walter's Tail (Ernst), 343
Waltzing Matilda, 306
Wanted . . . Mud Blossom (Byars), 287

Warrior and the Wise Man
(Wisniewski), 104, 388

Watch the Stars Come Out
(Levinson), 150

Water Pennies and Other Poems
(Bodecker), 167

Watership Down (Adams), 98

Wave in Her Pocket (Joseph), 86

Way I Feel . . . Sometimes (de
Regniers), 168

Way of the Storyteller (Sawyer), 111,
122–23, 414

Way We Were (Martin), 451

We Keep a Store (Shelby), 345

We Play (Hoffman), 349

We'll Ride Elephants through
Brooklyn (Roth), 350

Wedding Procession of the Rag Doll
and the Broom Handle and Who
Was in It (Sandburg), 125, 129

Wednesday Is Spaghetti Day (Cocca-
Leffler), 482

Wednesday Surprise (Bunting), 341

"Wee Meg Barnileg and the Fairies"
(Sawyer), 69, 129

Westward Ho Ho Ho! (Hartman), 180

What a Good Lunch (Watanabe), 483

What Am I? (Calmenson), 345

What Are Street Games? (Ravielli),
196

What Can Rabbit Hear? (Cousins),
349

What Can Rabbit See? (Cousins), 349

What Do You Say, Dear? (Joslin), 476

What Does the Rain Play?
(Carlstrom), 304

What to Do After You Turn Off the
TV? (Lappe), 196

What Your Nose Knows! (Moncure),
490

What-a-Mess the Good (Muir), 287

What's Cooking, Jenny Archer?
(Conford), 483

What's for Lunch? (Carle), 482

What's Missing? (Yektai), 493

What's on the Menu? (Goldstein), 480

What's That Noise? (Lemieux), 349,
492

What's That Noise? (Roennfeldt), 345

Wheels on the Bus (Kovalski), 349

Wheels on the Bus, 306

When Bluebell Sang (Ernst), 326

When I Was Nine (Stevenson), 150

When I Was Young in the Mountains
(Rylant), 150

When Shlemiel Went to Warsaw and
Other Stories (Singer), 120, 121

When the Elephant Walks (Kasza),
460

When the Lights Go Out
(MacDonald), 87

"When the Rain Came Up from
China" (McCormick), 76

When the Rooster Crowed (Lillie),
262

"When the Wind Changed" (Park), 78

When the Woods Hum (Ryder), 291,
492

When We Were Very Young (Milne),
159, 169

Where Angels Glide at Dawn
(Ventura and Carlson), 127

Where the Sidewalk Ends
(Silverstein), 169

Where the Wild Things Are (Sendak),
46, 509

Where's Gomer? (Farber), 142, 143

Where's the Bear? (Pomerantz), 493

Where's Waldo? (Handford), 46, 493

Which Is the Best Place? (Ginsburg),
232

"Whickety Whack, Get into My
Sack!" (Haley), 304

Whistle for Willie (Keats), 347

Whistling Skeleton (Grinnell), 86

"White Cat," 116

Who Needs Doughnuts? (Stamaty),
473

Who Put the Butter in the Butterfly?
(Feldman), 189

Who Said Red? (Serfozo), 350

Who Sank the Boat? (Allen), 348

Who Shrank My Grandmother's
House? (Esbensen), 168, 171

Who Uses This? (Miller), 350

Who's Been Stepping in My
Porridge? (McNaughton), 169

Why Mosquitoes Buzz in People's
Ears (Aardema), 74

Why Noah Chose the Dove (Singer),
142, 143

"Why the Bear Is Stumpy-tailed"
(Asbjørnsen and Moe), 119, 120

"Why the Sea Is Salt" (Asbjørnsen
and Moe), 120

"Why the Sea Is Salt," 114

Why the Sun and the Moon Live in
the Sky (Dayrell), 114, 120

"Why the Sun and the Moon Live in
the Sky" (Lester), 446

Wider than the Sky (Elledge), 165

Wild Critters (Jones), 171

Wild Ducks and the Goose (Withers),
220

Wild Pill Hickok and Other Riddles
of the Old West (Adler), 176

Wilfrid Gordon McDonald Partridge
(Fox), 387

Will I Go to Heaven? (Mayle), 142,
143

Willy and the Cardboard Boxes
(Boyd), 462

Wind in the Willows (Grahame), 410
Windy Day (Bauer), 144, 145, 170
Winnie the Pooh (Milne), 50, 100, 474, 484
"Winnie the Pooh Goes Visiting" (Milne), 78
Winning Scheherazade (Gorog), 126, 127, 411
Wise Men of Helm and Their Merry Tales (Simon), 115, 121
Wise Women (Barchers), 85
"Wishes" (Babbitt), 78
Wishes, Lies and Dreams (Koch), 163
"Wishing Star" (Roberts), 447
Wolf and the Seven Little Kids (Grimm Brothers), 71
Wolf by the Ears (Rinaldi), 411
Wolf Plays Alone (Catalano), 326
Wolves (Lawrence), 460
"Woman Who Flummoxed the Fairies" (Alger), 69
Woman Who Flummoxed the Fairies (Gaber), 481
Woman with the Eggs (Andersen), 292
Wonder Clock (Pyle), 123–24, 128
Wonder of Hands (Baer), 491
Wonderful Machine (Wilder), 475
Wonderful Pumpkin (Hellsin), 50
Wonderful Shrinking Shirt (Anderson), 68, 359
Woody's 20 Grow Big Songs (Guthrie), 324
Words with Wrinkled Knees (Esbensen), 171
Working Frog (Parker), 344
World Book of Children's Games (Arnold), 195

World Famous Muriel and the Magic Mystery (Alexander), 50, 295, 473, 482
World of Storytelling (Pellowski), 111
World Tales (Shah), 88
World's Birthday: A Rosh Hashanah Story (Dickinson), 143
World's Birthday: A Rosh Hashanah Story (Goldin), 73
World's Great Stories (Untermeyer), 139, 140
World's Toughest Tongue Twisters (Rosenbloom), 178
Wretched Stone (Van Allsburg), 104
Writing Books for Children (Yolen), 125

Yankee Doodle (Bangs), 305
Yeh-shen (Louie), 82
Yellow Blue Jay (Hurwitz), 383
You Can Speak Up in Class (Gilbert), 103
You Don't Need Words! (Gross), 190, 359
You'll Never Guess! (Dunbar), 493
Young Extraterrestrials (Asimov, Greenberg and Waugh), 406
Yours 'til the Ice Cracks (Geringer), 183
Yours till Niagara Falls (Morrison), 183
Yummers! (Marshall), 213
"Yung-Kyung-Pyung" (Sherlock), 75

Zap! A Brief History of Television (Calabro), 254
Zeralda's Ogre (Ungerer), 84, 473
Zlateh the Goat (Singer), 115, 120, 121